JOHN WAYNE

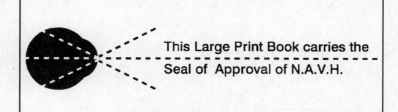

This Large Print Book carries the
Seal of Approval of N.A.V.H.

John Wayne

THE LIFE AND LEGEND

Scott Eyman

THORNDIKE PRESS
A part of Gale, Cengage Learning

GALE
CENGAGE Learning·

Farmington Hills, Mich • San Francisco • New York • Waterville, Maine
Meriden, Conn • Mason, Ohio • Chicago

Copyright © 2014 by Scott Eyman.
Source notes for *John Wayne* can be found in the original Simon & Schuster, Inc. edition.
All photographs are from the author's collection unless otherwise indicated.
Thorndike Press, a part of Gale, Cengage Learning.

ALL RIGHTS RESERVED
Thorndike Press® Large Print Biography.
The text of this Large Print edition is unabridged.
Other aspects of the book may vary from the original edition.
Set in 16 pt. Plantin.

LIBRARY OF CONGRESS CATALOGING-IN-PUBLICATION DATA

Eyman, Scott, 1951–
   John Wayne : the life and legend / by Scott Eyman. — Large print edition.
      pages ; cm. — (Thorndike Press large print biography)
   Includes bibliographical references.
   ISBN 978-1-4104-7108-6 (hardcover) — ISBN 1-4104-7108-X (hardcover)
   1. Wayne, John, 1907–1979. 2. Motion picture actors and actresses—United
States—Biography. 3. Large type books. I. Title.
PN2287.W454E96 2014b
791.4302'8092—dc23
[B]   2014012591

Published in 2014 by arrangement with Simon & Schuster, Inc.

Printed in the United States of America
1 2 3 4 5 6 7 18 17 16 15 14

*For Jeff Heise
And for Harry Carey Jr.,
Who said,
"Just put on my tombstone,
'He rode with the Duke.' "
Ride away . . .*

"That guy you see on the screen isn't really me. I'm Duke Morrison, and I never was and never will be a film personality like John Wayne. I know him well. I'm one of his closest students. I have to be. I make a living out of him."
— DUKE MORRISON, AKA JOHN WAYNE, 1957

"Other people, so I have read, treasure memorable moments in their lives: the time one climbed the Parthenon at sunrise, the summer night one met a lonely girl in Central Park and achieved with her a sweet and natural relationship, as they say in books. I too once met a girl in Central Park, but it is not much to remember. What I remember is the time John Wayne killed three men with a carbine as he was falling to the dusty street in *Stagecoach*."
THE MOVIEGOER, WALKER PERCY

CONTENTS

PROLOGUE 11

PART ONE: 1907–1939 29

PART TWO: 1939–1952 171

PART THREE: 1952–1961 357

PART FOUR: 1961–1979 573

EPILOGUE 896
ACKNOWLEDGMENTS 911
NOTES 917
BIBLIOGRAPHY 919

John Wayne, with the customized, sawed-off Winchester he twirls in his introductory shot in Stagecoach.

PROLOGUE

The scene had a problem, and the problem was the gun.

Dudley Nichols's script was specific: "There is the sharp report of a rifle and Curly jerks up his gun as Buck saws wildly at the ribbons.

"The stagecoach comes to a lurching stop before a young man who stands in the road beside his unsaddled horse. He has a saddle over one arm and a rifle carelessly swung in the other hand . . . It is Ringo . . .

"RINGO. You might need me and this Winchester. I saw a coupla ranches burnin' last night.
"CURLY. I guess you don't understand, kid. You're under arrest.
"RINGO (with charm). I ain't arguing about that, Curly. I just hate to part with a gun like this.

"Holding it by the lever, he gives it a jerk and it cocks with a click . . ."

John Ford loved the dialogue, which was in and of itself unusual, but the introduction of the Ringo Kid needed to be emphasized. Ford decided that the shot would begin with the actor doing something with the gun, then the camera would rapidly

11

track in from a full-length shot to an extreme close-up — an unusually emphatic camera movement for the period, and an extremely unusual one for Ford, who had grown to prefer a stable camera.

Since the actor was already coping with two large props, Ford decided to lose the horse. He told his young star what he was planning to do: "Work out something with the rifle," Ford said. "Or maybe just a pistol." He wasn't sure.

And just like that the problem was dropped in the lap of his star, a young — but not all that young — actor named John Wayne, better known to Ford and everybody else as Duke.

Wayne ran through the possibilities. Every actor in westerns could twirl a pistol, so that was out. Besides, the script specified a rifle cocked quickly with one hand, but later in the scene than what Ford was planning. In addition, Ford wanted him to do something flashy, but it couldn't happen too quickly for the audience to take it in. All the possibilities seemed to cancel each other out.

And then Yakima Canutt, Wayne's friend and the stunt coordinator on the film, offered an idea. When Canutt was a boy he had seen *Buffalo Bill's Wild West* show. As the overland stage raced around the arena, a messenger trailing behind the stagecoach had carried a rifle with a large ring loop which allowed him to spin the rifle in the air, cocking it with one hand. The crowd went wild. Canutt said that it had been thirty years ago and he still remembered the moment. More to the point, he had never seen anybody else do it.

Wayne sparked to the idea, as did Ford, but first they had to make it work. Ford instructed the prop department to manufacture a ring loop and install it on a standard-issue 1892 Winchester carbine. After the rifle was modified, Wayne began experimenting with the twirl move as Canutt remembered it, but there was a problem — the barrel of the rifle was too long — it wouldn't pass cleanly beneath Wayne's arm.

The Winchester went back to the prop department, where they sawed an inch or so off the end, then soldered the sight back on the shortened barrel.*

With that minor adjustment, the move was suddenly effortless. Wayne began rehearsing the twirling movement that would mark his entrance in the movie he had been waiting more than ten years to make — a film for John Ford, his friend, his mentor, his idol, the man he called "Coach" or, alternately — and more tellingly — "Pappy."

With any luck at all, he'd never have to go back to B westerns as long as he lived.

It's the late spring of 1939, and you're sitting in a theater watching *Stagecoach.* It's a western, not the most admired genre, and the cast is made up mostly of reliable character actors. But the reviews have been more than good, and John Ford has already achieved a measure of fame among critics

* One Winchester with a ring loop used by Wayne — he also did the move in *Circus World* and *True Grit* — does survive and the barrel has indeed been slightly sawed off. I'm grateful to Yakima Canutt for telling me about all this, to Jeff Morey and Joe Musso for explaining how it was done, and especially to Musso for showing me one of Wayne's customized rifles.

13

and moviegoers.

The first couple of minutes have already told you this is a movie made by filmmakers at the top of their game — precise, emphatic compositions, perfect editing that never leaves a shot on-screen for less time than it needs to be understood, unforced exposition that expertly delineates seven major characters inside of twelve minutes.

The story is basic. Seven strangers are crowded into a stagecoach, leaving a town called Tonto, heading through Indian territory to a town called Lordsburg. The seven people are traveling for seven different reasons, and the characters are deliberately contrasted in a way that goes beyond local color. A whore has a counterpart in a mousy, pregnant military bride; a pompous banker is balanced by a shady, dangerous gambler who can accurately gauge everybody's bad character, especially his own. Likewise, there is a meek little whiskey salesman who has to fend off a raucous alcoholic doctor.

There is also a sheriff, a bluff, hearty man who seems to believe in appearances. And there is one other character we are told about but don't immediately meet: an outlaw lurking somewhere out there, beyond Tonto, beyond civilization. He has escaped from jail, and he too needs to get to Lordsburg, for a private mission of revenge, a mission that the sheriff has pledged to prevent.

This collection of balanced opposites, the "respectable" confronted with the "disreputable," populate the stagecoach, the vehicle through which John Ford will assert the moral equality of the outcast and restate his claim for the western as the seminal American film genre.

The picture is eighteen minutes old when we

finally meet the Ringo Kid. There is a gunshot off-camera, there is a location shot of the stagecoach quickly pulling up. Cut to a tall, lean man standing against a process background of Monument Valley with a saddle draped over one arm and a rifle in his other hand. The camera rushes in as he twirl-cocks the rifle with one hand.

If you look at the rifle, it seems to be a tiny bit short, but nobody has ever looked at anything but the actor's face. Midway through the camera's rapid track-in, it loses focus for a half a second, then comes to rest in a huge, sharp close-up.

It is a good face — handsome but not pretty, assertive but not bullying. There are two beads of sweat coursing down his cheek, although whether that is a detail of character that Ford wanted or a result of the pressure of synchonizing a complicated physical movement with a complicated camera movement is lost to time.

The camera gazes for a few long seconds on the face, letting us examine the blue eyes that photograph gray on black and white film, the shadow on the right side, the suggestion of sweat on the brow, the strength of the features. As the camera lingers, the intimidating aura of the Ringo Kid as outlined by the other characters dissolves. What we see is not a dangerous outlaw but a boyish young man in bold relief — a gentle but resolute character.

The actor leaps off the screen in a way the character doesn't in the script, and in a way the actor hadn't in his previous movies. This is an actor you have probably seen before, in one movie or another, but never like this, never showcased with such elemental force. John Wayne has been around the movies for more than ten years, first

15

as a prop man, occasionally as an extra, then fronting a great widescreen spectacle of early sound that lost a great deal of money.

Cast into oblivion by that film's failure, he made his way through the Depression with large parts in tiny films and tiny parts in large films. Before *Stagecoach,* he has appeared in more than eighty movies — some good, most bad or indifferent.

But with this scene — no, with this moment — looks, temperament, talent, part, and presentation collide and unite. The audience sees, truly sees John Wayne for the first time.

"We are not a culture that readily associates 'beauty' with 'manly,' " wrote the critic Michael Ventura about this moment, "but this face has that combination and something more: . . . an awareness of wilderness, a sense that here is a man meant to move in great spaces. That's vague, but that's the best I can do. Whitman has a line in 'Song of the Open Road': 'Here a great personal deed has room.' "

To put it more bluntly: this is less an expertly choreographed entrance for an actor than it is the annunciation of a star. John Ford is telling us that this man warrants our attention in a way that transcends the immediate narrative of the movie.

For the next forty years, John Wayne continually proved Ford's point. The literary theorist Roland Barthes wrote that "Mass culture is a machine for showing desire," and successive generations desired John Wayne in a way shared by no other star of his generation.

This was . . . curious. Wayne was thirty-two years old when he made *Stagecoach,* and still possessed a youthful aura, but that was replaced by other things as he aged and expanded — from remind-

16

ing people of their brother or son, he gradually assumed a role as everyone's father, then, inevitably, as age and weight congealed, everyone's grandfather.

None of that made much difference to his audience. For twenty-five out of twenty-six years — 1949 to 1974 — Wayne was in the list of top ten box-office stars. In nineteen of those years, he was in the top four. Thirty-five years after his death, he was still listed as one of America's five favorite movie stars. (The others on the list, Denzel Washington and Tom Cruise among them, had the considerable advantage of being alive.)

Clark Gable, Tyrone Power, and Gary Cooper were all much bigger stars when Wayne began his ascent, but they have largely receded into the past. Wayne became more than a movie star for his time; rather, he became indivisibly associated with America itself, even if it was an America that was dead by the time he was born, and he was personifying a folklore easier to locate in the nineteenth century than the twentieth.

Stagecoach was a picture that could and in fact did fall apart several times before it finally got made, and it got made only because of the determination of John Ford, who believed in John Wayne more than John Wayne believed in himself. Ford was born John Martin Feeney in Maine in 1894, and by the time he met Duke Morrison in 1926, Ford — he took the screen name of his brother, the actor Francis Ford — had been directing movies for ten years and had already made his first great film: *The Iron Horse.*

In the succeeding years, Ford was drawn by the young man's inexhaustible energy, his willingness to do anything asked of him. For Duke Morrison

17

enthusiastically adopted the perpetual challenge of a big man with ambition — to do everything better, harder, longer than anyone else.

"On every picture, there is at least one day when nothing seems to go right," Ford said. "When things are going wrong, Duke is a mighty fine man to have around. He will run half the length of the valley to tell the second unit that we are planning to shoot another take. He rarely asks a man to do a job he can do himself."

Other co-workers concurred, and valued Wayne for his willingness to extend himself far beyond the limited portfolio of an actor. "I've seen him put his shoulder to a location wagon that was stuck," said the cameraman Bert Glennon, "or hold a pair of shears and a comb for a hairdresser when she had to make a hurried change on one of the characters."

This never changed. Thirty-six years after *Stagecoach,* he made *The Shootist,* his last movie. The scene: a dying gunfighter named J. B. Books goes to a barbershop.

As Wayne settled himself into the barber chair for the scene, a prop man began to cut thin strands of fake hair and arrange them around the perimeter of the chair. Wayne and Alfred Dennis, the actor playing the barber, began to run their lines. Wayne stopped and watched what the prop man was doing.

"That won't work," said the star.

"Sir?"

"You're not cutting off enough hair. The camera is ten feet away. It won't read the little hairs that you're cutting off. Give it to me."

Wayne grabbed the prop hair and scissors and began chopping off giant hunks of hair, four and five inches long, throwing them around the barber chair. Rationally, these chunks would come from a man with shoulder-length hair, but Wayne knew that when it comes to movies, the eye is irrelevant. The only thing that matters is what the lens sees.

The young prop man didn't know that Wayne began his career as a prop man, and wasn't about to lower his standards. In all the reviews and analyses of the picture then and later, the huge hunks of hair at the bottom of the barber chair always go unnoticed.

John Wayne always knew what the camera would see; he always knew what the audience would believe.

John Ford was profoundly Irish in every possible way, and his character was accompanied by an assortment of more or less symptomatic demons. He was defensive, in total control of his art, if not his life, and he was some sort of genius. "He was talented, and he was intolerable," was the succinct opinion of Maureen O'Hara.

Andre de Toth, a director whom Ford promoted, said, "He was not a social person. He kept to his boat, to the studio, and to his Jack Daniel's. There wasn't a lot of dialogue in his life, and there wasn't a lot of dialogue in his movies.

"*He was making motion pictures.* He was sure of the art he wanted to make, but not much else. People put up with Jack Ford for one reason: he always told you what he thought was the truth. That's what you see in a Ford film: honesty."

In contrast to the largely impenetrable and essentially solitary Ford, Wayne had few obvious demons. He drank — but never allowed it to control his life or interfere with his work. He smoked incessantly, ate what he wanted, enjoyed the company of women, adored the company of men. He was like his mentor in one way only: he invariably said what he thought.

Ford had bought Ernest Haycox's original story for *Stagecoach* in 1936 and circled the idea of making his former prop man the star of a western. After flirtations with a couple of other actors, he made up his mind: Duke would be the Ringo Kid.

"It isn't enough for an actor to look the part and say his lines well," said Ford. "Something else has to come across to audiences — something which no director can instill or create — the quality of being a real man."

Wayne embodied one other quality Ford needed: "He was the only person I could think of at the time who could personify great strength and determination without talking much. That sounds easy, perhaps. But it's not. Either you have it or you don't."

Like all excellent directors only more so, Ford was a manipulator, a man capable of thinking on three or four levels at once, and he enjoyed Wayne because the actor was completely different than he was. Wayne was a creature of spontaneity, with a bubbling enthusiasm for every new project and for life itself, and little interest in the contemplation of mistakes, of roads not taken. The most important movie of Wayne's life was always the next one.

"Duke has always been able to enjoy life . . . to swallow and digest it in big, unchewed pieces. Depending upon the circumstances, he can be a roughneck, or a perfect gentleman. He's my boy, always has been; always will be."

Just before they began production on *Stage-*

coach, John Ford took the young man aside and told him that he had a great future ahead of him.

He had no idea just how right he was.

The decade of B westerns had been Wayne's movie prep school, the learning equivalent of years in repertory theater. In 1939, Wayne was relatively unknown only to the critics in the big cities. As far as they were concerned, he had the stink of dozens of disposable B movies about him.

But as far as the audience was concerned, Wayne had paid his dues. They had watched the big man for nearly ten years; they had seen him mature as a man and as an actor. They had always liked him, and they had grown to respect him as well. Wayne may not have been a star in New York, but he was assuredly a star in Waco and Rockville and Atlanta.

Wayne hadn't played a variety of parts, but he had carefully observed actors who did. He had seen how even a bad movie was impossible without teamwork on the part of the cast and crew.

"Doing those B westerns he learned how to be resilient," said the actor William Bakewell, who did time with him in some of these films. "He learned what to lean on and how to bring his best foot forward. You had to get up on your lines. You had to be a quick study because they didn't want to waste any time or film. . . . Doing those quickie westerns, he learned how to be John Wayne."

Aesthetically, Wayne walked right into an American archetype. The part of the Ringo Kid — the way Ford presented the actor, the way the actor played the part — served as the template for about half of his career: dignity, intent, competence, and, if necessary, skill in combat, all added to a foundation of innate likability.

Wayne had spent ten years in limbo after *The Big Trail,* working for some of the worst directors in the business. Now, after a single turn working for one of the best, his life would never be the same again, but he never seemed entirely convinced that there was anything inevitable about it, or even that he had done it on his own recognizance.

"The reason Ford made a star of me," he grumbled to John Ford's grandson late in his life, "was that I played cards with him."

In his early years, Wayne's acting was tinged with a tentative self-consciousness; it was acting that didn't seem to be acting, that had a way of intimately involving his audience rather than keeping them at an admiring distance.

Soon enough, he would play the tired, benevolent Nathan Brittles in *She Wore a Yellow Ribbon,* the fierce, my-way-or-die Tom Dunson in *Red River,* the hesitant retired boxer Sean Thornton in *The Quiet Man,* the lonely isolate Ethan Edwards in *The Searchers,* as well as ten other varied characterizations fully deserving the overused adjective "great."

The watchful, shy young actor of the 1930s became a man burdened by responsibility and pain too terrible to fully share, gradually segueing into a feisty old guy who could still uncork a jug . . . or twirl a Winchester. Alone among the great movie stars, Wayne dared to show us the most perilous as well as the most moving of the seven ages of man.

As Randy Roberts and James Olson pointed out, "He was *so* American, *so* like his country — big, bold, confident, powerful, loud, violent and occasionally overbearing, but simultaneously forgiving, gentle, innocent, and naive. . . . John Wayne was his country's alter ego."

I first met John Wayne in August 1972. He was not merely big, he was huge, with hands that could span home plate — the largest hands I have ever seen on a human being. It was not so much his height — six feet three and three quarters inches, as he attested in a military application during World War II — it was his bulk: very broad shoulders and a large chest that, in his youth, spiraled down to a slim waist. By the time I met him, a good-sized man could stand behind him and never be seen.

At the same time, there was an unexpected delicacy about him. He had small feet for a man his size — size 10 or so, as opposed to the 14 or 16 that might be expected. This accounted for his carefully balanced walk, the arms slightly bent at the elbows for balance.

And there was also a surprising graciousness of manner and a quiet way of speaking. He was shooting a TV show at CBS at the time, and regarded himself impassively in the makeup mirror in between sips of a scotch and water. Every once in a while, he would contentedly puff on a slim cigar, even though he had lost a lung to cancer eight years earlier. He answered my questions calmly, getting enthusiastic mainly when talking about directors.

My hair was undoubtedly longer than he liked, but he didn't seem to mind. I loved John Ford and so did he. At the end of a long day on the set, he walked over, shook my hand, and said, "I hope you got what you wanted. I'm not such a terrible right-wing monster, am I?"

His general attitude, on that day and on several

days thereafter, was a perceptible relief that he could have a conversation about something besides cancer or politics.

Most actors are disappointing when you meet them — often smaller than life, they need writers and cameramen to give them their aura of command. Not John Wayne. He liked to talk about chess, Indian lore, and western art, but above all he liked to talk about movies. It was the movies that had converted the son of a reliably unsuccessful drugstore clerk, a young man who managed to win a football scholarship to USC only to lose it, into a rich man with a kind of immortality. In no other actor was the apparent line between the private man and the public image so narrow.

In the movies, he played searchers, warriors, men who settled the West or fought for democracy in the Pacific. His characters' taste for the fulfillment of an American imperative was usually based on patriotic conviction, rarely for economic opportunity. He came to embody a sort of race memory of Manifest Destiny, the nineteenth century as it should have been.

For decades, his image was in fashion and then it went out of fashion. His strength was seen as authoritarian, his overwhelming sense of the past held up as proof of his archaic nature. A man of complex ideals was nudged aside in a time of expedient desires.

But eventually, the wheel comes around again.

These are the movies of John Wayne. Not all of them — by actual count there are 169, give or take, depending on whether you allow guest appearances or not — just the best, in no particular order:

24

The Searchers
The Man Who Shot Liberty Valance
Red River
She Wore a Yellow Ribbon
The Shootist
Stagecoach
They Were Expendable
Fort Apache
Hondo
Sands of Iwo Jima
Rio Grande
The Quiet Man
Island in the Sky
Rio Bravo
True Grit

It can be seen that, while Wayne would make important films in many genres, it was the western that made him a star, and it was the western that kept him a star. As Charles Silver of the Museum of Modern Art wittily observed, "Wayne made westerns for twice as long as it took to fight the Indian wars. He made westerns for about as long as it actually took to settle the continent west of the Missouri."

It was the western that defined John Wayne for audiences the world over, that made him the symbol of America to the world at large. In many ways, it still does.

Audiences traditionally assume that movie stars are just playing themselves, a gross oversimplification that ignores the massive adjustments that changed Duke Morrison from Winterset, Iowa, into John Wayne.

As the briefest glance at any of Wayne's early B westerns shows, the easy, likable personality was there from the beginning, but so was a lumbering gaucheness not far removed from a high school play. The accoutrements that spelled John Wayne were added incrementally, painstakingly, intentionally. The John Wayne of 1932 has little to offer except his looks and personality; the Wayne of 1938 is a greatly improved actor of authority and concision. Duke Morrison built John Wayne the actor, John Wayne the businessman, John Wayne the icon, brick by brick. "He worked hard to be a graceful big man," said Harry Carey Jr. "It didn't just happen."

As a man, Wayne could be demanding and impatient, as everybody from prop men to directors found out, but he had an innate gregariousness, an interest in other people, that was unexpected and charming. "What was different than the roles he played," said his oldest son, Michael, "was that he would listen to people. He wanted to hear what they thought. He was a listener as well as a talker."

His daughter Toni said, "He was an expert in western Indian tribes. He was a history buff who knew all about the Civil War. He knew what battle was where, and how many men died at this place. He knew an awful lot about Oriental art, about Native American art. He knew an awful lot about a lot of things."

He was also a demon chess player. Although he wasn't quite tournament caliber, he would make up for technical flaws with controlled aggression and by psyching out opponents. "Is *that* the move you're gonna make?" he would say with an air of deep regret. "You're sure? Well, okay." The opponent was soon convinced that he had blown the game. He did the same thing playing bridge.

But when it came to making movies, there was no guile involved. He relished the process. He almost never went off to his trailer during the lengthy period when shots were being set up, but hung around the set, preparing, playing chess, joshing with the crew. For Wayne, a movie set was home, and he loved being home.

Forged by years of working for little money and less acclaim, Wayne became the compleat professional. "I never saw him miss a word," said Harry Carey Jr. "I never saw him late. I never saw him with a hangover. Oh, all right, I saw him with a hangover, but he was really a good man to work with."

The years of laboring in thankless vineyards produced an actor who could effortlessly command a scene simply by entering it, who could communicate complex emotions without words. His own strength of character was easily lent to the men he played, but that strength often derived from an isolation that came at a terrible cost. Wayne's power as an actor, and his greatest triumph, was that he never shied away from the ultimate implications of his screen image.

All this earned him his place as America's idea of itself, a man big enough, expansive enough to serve as a metaphoric battlefield for America's conflicting desires. He wasn't born that way. As a boy he was insecure, bedeviled by poverty and nightmares. Until he accreted the security of a screen character, whose certainties he gradually made his own, he regularly berated himself for his clumsiness in the craft he pursued with such passion.

So the story of John Wayne is simultaneously the story of Duke Morrison — an awkward boy who transformed himself into the symbol of American self-confidence.

There have been several biographies of John Wayne over the years, mostly written by two disparate breeds: rapt fans, or scholars — alternating currents of hero worship and a quizzical wonder mixed with covert — or not so covert — disdain.

I knew Wayne slightly, but until I invested four years in research I couldn't claim any special insights into the man other than witnessing his good humor, his courtesy, his surprising sensitivity.

"Had you read the O'Neill plays?" I bumptiously asked him once, regarding John Ford's film of *The Long Voyage Home.*

He could have blown me right out of the water, and probably should have. Instead, he eyed me wearily, sighed, and quietly said, "I'd been to college; I'd read O'Neill."

Point taken.

John Wayne's story is about many things — it's about the construction of an image, the forging of a monumental career that itself became a kind of monument. It's about a terribly shy, tentative boy reinventing himself as a man with a command personality, of a man who loved family but who couldn't sustain a marriage, and of a great friendship that resulted in great films.

And it's also about a twentieth-century conservatism considered dangerously extreme that became mainstream in the twenty-first century.

It is, in short, a life that could only have been lived by one man.

■ ■ ■ ■

Part One:
1907–1939

■ ■ ■ ■

"The son of a bitch looked like a man."
— RAOUL WALSH

CHAPTER ONE

The man the world would come to know as John Wayne was not born Marion Michael Morrison — as tradition would have it — nor was he born Marion Mitchell Morrison — as revisionist tradition would have it. His name at birth was actually Marion Robert Morrison. What is definitive is the date — May 26, 1907 — and the place: a house the Morrisons were renting from Mr. M. E. Smith, a pharmacist who owned the Smith Drug Store. The house was and is at the corner of Second and South Streets in Winterset, Iowa, populated at the time by 2,956 people. The room was and is a small back corner that spans about eight feet by fifteen feet in a house of 860 square feet.

The birth announcement ran in the May 30, 1907, edition of the Winterset *Madisonian* complete with a typo: "A 13 pound son arrived at the home Mr. and Mrs. Clyde Morrison, Monday morning." Sometime after Marion became famous his birth certificate disappeared from the courthouse, although conspiracy theorists should know that an entry in the Madison County Record of Births (Book 2, page 329) attests to the town, name, date, and parents.

Gazing down at young Morrison, Dr. Jessie Smith undoubtedly realized that he was going to be a big boy. Dr. Smith was one of the rare turn-of-the-century women doctors, universally remembered as "a faithful physician and a steadfast friend," according to Father Paul Barrus, who was born in Winterset five years before the town's most famous citizen.

Winterset, Iowa, is thirty-five miles southwest of Des Moines, 350 miles west of Chicago. It's a pleasant small town, the seat of Madison County, as in *The Bridges of . . .* In the hundred-odd years since, the population has incrementally increased to 4,800. Before the birth of Marion Morrison, Winterset's only distinction was the residency of George Washington Carver in the 1880s.

This is the world Marion Morrison was born into:

At the Candy Kitchen on the east side of the public square, ice cream sodas cost 15 cents. If a housewife telephoned for groceries, they would be delivered within the hour. On Wednesday evenings, the Methodist church and the Baptist church would both call the faithful to worship in the evening by ringing their bells. The Methodist bell was light and silvery, the Baptist bell much deeper. The Catholic church would toll its bell on Sundays, or when a parishioner died. Every year in the Winterset High School, a Civil War veteran named Cooper would give an eyewitness account of Pickett's Charge. In the event of an outbreak of diphtheria or smallpox, individual houses that were affected would have large QUARANTINE signs (yellow, with black letters) displayed in the front yards.

Winterset had two black citizens. One was Char-

32

lie Moore, and the other his son, Main, who graduated from Winterset High in 1896. There was also a man known only as "Nigger John," who lived in a shack south of the southwest corner of the square, but he wasn't counted in the official census. (There was a pre–Civil War stone house on Summit Street leading toward Council Bluffs that was said to have been a station on the Underground Railroad.)

Every year, a production of *Uncle Tom's Cabin* would play Winterset, and the actress who played Little Eva would drive her ponies in a parade around the square. Funerals took place at home, and sitting up with the dead the night before burial was a part of mourning. Every day at 4:40 P.M., people would attentively gather at the railroad station to see who came in from Des Moines.

In short, it was the sort of place that needed the presence of Professor Harold Hill to stir things up. There might have been trouble in River City, but there was never any trouble in Winterset.

Much has been made of the admittedly odd discrepancy of the birth name and the official name he carried until he entered show business, but there wasn't really much to it. As Wayne would explain on his application for the OSS during World War II, "Name supposedly changed to Marion Michael Morrison when brother born and named Robert. There is no legal record of this change. Registered in school as Marion Mitchell Morrison, my grandfather's name — never corrected same."

All of this sloppy switching happened in Earlham, where the family moved in 1910, and where Marion's younger brother, Robert, was born in

33

December 1911. Using a child's name as the pea in a now-you-see-it-now-you-don't shell game was only the beginning of Marion's ragged childhood.

What probably happened is that his mother, a formidably strong-willed — read borderline unpleasant — woman born Mary Brown in 1885 in Lincoln, Nebraska, simply appropriated the older boy's middle name for the preferred new arrival.

Both of Marion's parents were born into the nervous middle class; Mary's father had been a proofreader for a Des Moines newspaper, while Clyde Morrison's father had been a real estate agent. Clyde was born in 1884 in Monmouth, Illinois, but grew up in Iowa and attended Simpson College on a football scholarship. He started in his freshman year, but was relegated to the second string midway through the season.

"Morrison did well [in an early game] but does not get into condition for proper work," reported a local newspaper. In his second year, Clyde Morrison rode the bench. He left school before graduation and served an internship as a pharmacist in Waterloo, Iowa, where he met his future wife. Clyde Leonard Morrison and Mary Brown were married in Knoxville, Iowa, on September 29, 1905, and shortly afterward settled down to a war of marital attrition in which Clyde was always failing and Mary was always judging.

The Morrisons had moved to Winterset in 1906, where Clyde worked as a pharmacist's clerk at Smith's Drug Store on the town square. According to the memories of Father Barrus, Mrs. Morrison was considered "different" from other Winterset women, most of whom had grown up together. She was an outsider, and content with that status. Her best friend was Hazel Benge, who also kept a certain distance from most people. Alice Miller, a neighbor of the Morrisons, remembered seeing Mary, whom family and friends called "Molly," pushing the carriage with her newborn boy around the town square and home again. Sometimes a neighbor would take over young Marion's daily constitutional down South Second Street.

Then and later, Clyde was always liked — the standard line about him was that if he "only had four bits left in his pocket, he'd give one quarter to a friend, buy a beer for himself, and sit down and talk." The standard line about Molly was that she was a grievance collector with a long memory and a good person to stay away from. "Molly Morrison was a stern woman," said Alice Miller. "You had to be real careful around her. She could fly off the handle when you least expected it."

The house where Marion Morrison was born, at 224 South Second Street, was built around 1880 and contains four rooms. It remained in private hands until 1981, when it was purchased by the chamber of commerce and restored to look like it did in the first decade of the twentieth century, with period furniture donated by residents, but with some of the original grace notes remaining — generous amounts of woodwork throughout the house, as well as stained glass in the parlor windows and the front door.

"Just about all I remember about Winterset is riding horses, playing football, and the time I thought I discovered electricity," said John Wayne years later. "It was when my brother Robert was born. I went in to see him, rubbed my shoes on the rug, and accidentally touched the metal foot of the bed. Sparks shot off. I thought I had found one of the wonders of the universe. I didn't know that Benjamin Franklin had beaten me to the discovery by about 150 years."

None of this happened in Winterset, because Marion was only about two years old when the family left for nearby Brooklyn, 105 miles east of Davenport. Within another year, the Morrisons moved to Earlham, where Clyde bought a Rexall pharmacy at 328 Ohio Street.

Clyde's business ventures had a way of going belly-up, and in December 1911, Clyde declared bankruptcy and lost the pharmacy. He then got a clerk's job in Keokuk, while Molly tended young Marion in Earlham. But the boy always preferred his father, and Molly didn't have the temperament to jolly him along. She told Clyde to come get his son. He took him back to Keokuk and on September 3 enrolled him in the first grade at the George Washington Elementary School.

Neither Winterset, Brooklyn, Earlham, or Keokuk was ever visited by John Wayne in later years — he was always far more interested in the future than the past. Besides, chronic instability isn't attractive to a child, either at the time or retrospectively.

By 1913, they were in Des Moines, living off of Molly's family. Late in 1914, Clyde's father wrote to his son that some land he had bought in California needed someone to work it. Would Clyde be interested? Since there were no other offers pending, he would.

By that time, Marion probably wanted to drop his brother on his head, for Molly Morrison openly doted on Robert, as she would all her life. Marion sensed the favoritism and continued preferring his father.

The older boy's resentment of his mother would always be between the lines, if for no other reason than it would have been bad manners for a midwestern gentleman born in the first decade of the twentieth century to criticize a parent. He would speak of her strength of character, her strong sense of right and wrong, and her temper — all of which he inherited. But there was never much affection in his reminiscences of her, unlike his memories of Clyde Morrison: "My father was the kindest, most patient man I ever knew." Further complicating his life was his name. Children made fun of him, asked him why he had a girl's name and why his mother didn't dress him in skirts. Not surprisingly, in later years he didn't particularly like to talk about his childhood; his last wife said that the stories came out only in fragments during their twenty years together. Mainly, he felt unloved by his mother and was quietly distressed by his father's ineffectuality.

In 1914 the Morrison family moved to Palmdale, on the edge of the Mojave desert. Clyde's father had spent $3,000 for eighty acres, and according to the homestead rules then in effect, if they could develop the property they could leverage their eighty acres into the surrounding 560 acres. Within the family, it would be claimed that Clyde had developed tuberculosis and needed a dry climate.

He sure got one.

Clyde Morrison took over a farmhouse, "a glorified shack," according to his son. There was no gas, electricity, or running water. Nearby was a small barn, twelve feet by sixteen feet. When they were finished unpacking, they looked around and saw . . . nothing. Wayne remembered it as "barren, deserted country. . . . Palmdale was in the middle of nowhere." In addition, Clyde Morrison didn't know anything about farming. Other than that, it was a great move.

That same year, young Morrison saw the first newspaper headline to make an impression: "WAR DECLARED." The nearest town was Lancaster, eight miles away, which had been settled by Mexican railroad workers. Lancaster got electricity the same year the Morrisons moved to Palmdale, a town with two paved streets, five saloons, two hotels, two banks, and a dry goods store. There was also a two-hundred-foot watering trough for the horses and an annual rabbit hunt. All it lacked was Frederic Remington to paint it. Molly Morrison was appalled, and when Molly Morrison was appalled, somebody was going to suffer.

Marion began attending the Lancaster Grammar School, eight long miles from Palmdale, riding a horse named Jenny back and forth every day. Twice a week, he would stop at the general store to pick up groceries. One time the general store had a good buy on several cases of tunafish, which provided a dietary staple for the Morrisons for months on end. In later years, he would always try to avoid tunafish.

Sometimes he'd pretend there were outlaws lurking on the deserted country roads, but there weren't any outlaws and barely anybody else. "All I ran across were a few scrubby palms, some mesquite, a pack of jack rabbits and a few lazy rattlesnakes."

Once, the boy let a younger friend ride Jenny

the full length of the town, which he remembered was about the distance between two telephone poles. The friend fell off the horse. "[She] was no thoroughbred, but I couldn't have loved [her] more if she had been. I was really crazy about that horse!"

Unfortunately, Jenny had a congenital stomach ailment that caused emaciation. Jenny was young Morrison's responsibility as well as his transportation to and from school. Some nosy women decided that the horse was being abused, and reported the family to the local Humane Society. Marion stoutly insisted he was always feeding his horse, that he carried oats for the horse even on their daily commute to and from school.

His teacher and his parents stood up for him. The county vet examined the horse and diagnosed the wasting disease, but a sense of outrage over being falsely accused never left him. "I learned you can't always judge a person or a situation by the way it appears on the surface," he remembered. "You have to look deeply into things before you're in a position to make a proper decision." Jenny never got healthier and eventually had to be put down.

Clyde Morrison tried planting corn and wheat, because they were more valuable crops than hay or alfalfa, but corn and wheat needed more water than he had. With a lot of work, the plants might sprout, but the jackrabbits ate everything. Then there was the heat — 118 degrees in the summer, 90 degrees in the house. Further complicating the literal hothouse atmosphere was the fact that Molly's parents were living with them, making sure no harm befell their little girl. Finally, they bailed out for Los Angeles, after strongly advising their daughter and son-in-law to do the same.

For a couple of years, the Morrisons barely got by. "Mostly we ate potatoes or beans in one form or another," he remembered. "One Halloween, Mom gave us a big treat — frankfurters."

The Morrisons couldn't afford a replacement for Jenny, so Marion began to walk to school, or hitch a ride on another family's wagon. In any case, he had to get up at five in the morning in order to finish his chores before he could go to school, where once again he was taunted because of his name. Nevertheless, he was well behaved and a good student — he would always be a good student.

He learned lessons that weren't taught in school, mainly admonitions from his father about self-reliance. "Never expect anything from anybody," his father told him. "Don't take things for granted. The world doesn't owe you a living. You have to work for everything you get; nobody's coming around with plums on a silver platter." The lessons took, and in later years formed the core of his conservative political philosophy.

In later years, he asserted that the two years the family spent in the desert were too much for his mother and too much for the marriage. Clyde Morrison had one decent corn harvest before the market plunged. He had failed yet again, and Mary Morrison wouldn't let him forget it. She berated him in front of his sons, branding him a failure and enumerating the myriad ways in which he had disappointed his children. Increasingly, she doted on her younger son. Wayne's daughter Aissa believed that her father first resented his mother, then became bitter about her.

The boy was frankly miserable, and had to

content himself with reading the Sears Roebuck catalogues every farming family lived with. He read them cover to cover, over and over again, and would circle all the things he wanted but couldn't afford. "I used to dream that someday I'd have enough dollars to order everything in that damn catalogue. Catalogues became an obsession with me."

Catalogues would stay an obsession with him, and when he was rich and famous he would do a great deal of his shopping from mail-order catalogues, which always signified the height of luxury.

The fights between Mary and Clyde became ugly, and the marriage, never solid to begin with, became irreparable. A generalized anxiety began to beset the boy; in one of his few admissions of fear, young Morrison remembered patrolling their land with a rifle while his father worked the corn. His job was to shoot any rattlesnakes that appeared.

On the upside, it taught him to be a good rifle shot. On the downside, if he missed, his father could die. "Shooting those snakes also gave me many sleepless nights — visions of thousands of slithering snakes coming after me. I used to wake up in a cold sweat in the middle of the night, but my dad, or my family, never knew it. I kept my fears to myself."

Clyde's father began suffering from the onset of dementia, as well as tuberculosis. Clyde had to commit him to a sanitarium in Glendale for a few weeks, after which he was transferred to a veterans hospital. Clyde and his family visited his father a couple of times in Glendale, and Molly began agitating for a move.

Young Morrison remembered that the last straw

41

came in the unprepossessing form of black-eyed peas. "We had five acres of greenery going, beautiful tender young shoots," he remembered. "We went away for a weekend, and when we came back, they'd been completely eaten by rabbits. . . . That broke them. They never made that adjustment where they could get together again."

Clyde Morrison finally agreed that he wasn't cut out for agriculture and the family moved to Glendale, about ten miles from Los Angeles, at the juncture of the San Fernando and San Gabriel valleys. Clyde got a job in a drugstore and began saving money to open his own place.

A year after the Morrisons arrived, Forest Lawn cemetery opened in Glendale, whose population was about eight thousand. The town had five schools, five banks, fifteen churches, two newspapers, a City Hall at 613 Broadway, a couple of markets and general stores, and three drugstores. Fred Stofft, who would become a neighborhood pal of Marion's in Glendale, remembered that "there was no industry there. All the men that lived there worked in Los Angeles. It was a very nice town, about a 20 minute ride into Los Angeles on the Red Car."

All of that would change, and soon, as the population and opportunities of Southern California exploded. (By 1930, Glendale's population would be 62,736.) The Morrisons lived at 421 South Isabel, Clyde worked at the Glendale Pharmacy on West Broadway, and they joined the First Methodist Church. It was certainly an improvement over Palmdale.

Young Marion was about nine years old when he picked up his lifelong nickname. Big Duke was the name of the family Airedale, a dog that Wayne

42

always remembered as "very good. . . . He chased the fire engines and I chased Duke."

The Airedale's name was no accident, for Duke was also the name of the great cowboy star Tom Mix's large, indeterminate hound, as the boy would surely have known — Tom Mix was one of his favorite movie stars. Duke — Morrison's Duke — would occasionally sleep at the fire station until his boy came back from school to pick him up. The firemen christened young Morrison "Little Duke," which was gradually shortened to "Duke."

These would seem to have been hard years for the young boy, although there was a temporary financial respite when Clyde's father died, leaving him a small inheritance. But that didn't last long and Clyde resumed his habit of downward mobility. The family moved every year or two.

"[Clyde] was lucky if he cleared $100 a month," said his son. He remembered that the firemen gave him milk, telling him to take it home to his cat. But the Morrisons didn't have a cat — the milk was really for Duke and his brother. He was also bullied by older, larger boys. One day he walked by the firehouse with a black eye, and one of the firemen started giving him lessons in self-defense.

By 1917, the ten-year-old Duke Morrison was attending Intermediate School at Wilson and Kenwood and getting good grades. The family was living in a small house in the heart of downtown Glendale at 136 North Geneva, behind City Hall. Duke's neighborhood hangouts included the Litchfield Lumberyard and Sawmill a block or two down the street on Geneva, Lund's Blacksmith Shop on Wilson, and Malscher's Livery Stables on North Glendale, where he occasionally went horseback riding.

One neighbor was named McCalveny, who supplied some much needed raffish charm for the boy. Wayne remembered that Mr. McCalveny ran guns for Pancho Villa. "They went from rags to riches every other month," said Wayne. "If they were eating beans, the gun-running business was bad, and if the neighbors were invited in, business was good."

From the time he was in the seventh grade, Duke had to supply his own spending money and clothes. A girl in the neighborhood remembered him as "quiet, withdrawn." Delivering the *Los Angeles Examiner* put enough money in his pocket to pay for the movies that he loved.

While young Morrison was not growing up in the heart of the movie business, he wasn't exiled from it either. Glendale had a couple of working movie studios — Sierra Photoplays, which opened for business in 1917, and Kalem — or Astra — Studios, which opened in 1913 and was in operation until 1924 on North Verdugo Road. Wayne occasionally spoke of watching Kalem star Helen Holmes working on the streets of Glendale. Production crews and actors were frequent sights around town, where young Duke, along with other neighborhood kids, watched with open mouth and beating heart.

Duke Morrison's learning experiences were not always pleasant, but deeply imprinted on his ethical compass. He remembered catching a bee, and tying a thread around the creature so all it could do was fly in circles. A boy who was about three years older and had recently arrived from Poland walked by and said, "Don't do that." Morrison ignored him and kept tormenting the bee, at which point, he remembered, "The roof fell in."

He found himself lying on the ground with the Polish boy standing over him. With a heavy accent, the boy said, "I've just come from a war, from Poland. Don't ever be cruel to animals. Or people."

"It was quite a lesson," Duke said. "I'll never forget it."

The *Examiner* was a morning paper, so Duke had to get up at four in the morning for his deliveries. He had begun playing football, and after school there was practice, and then he would make deliveries for the drugstore on his bicycle.

While Duke was growing up, his parents continued to fight. Sometimes Molly — "a very beautiful red head," according to Fred Stofft — would come sailing into the pharmacy in high dudgeon to berate Clyde for some perceived or actual failure. Clyde's drinking had picked up and Molly's anger hadn't abated. She insisted that Duke drag his little brother along wherever he happened to be going.

In 1919, Duke joined the Boy Scouts and stayed active in the troop until high school graduation, although he never made Eagle Scout. He also joined the YMCA, which put the boys on boats, inspiring a love for the sea that lasted the rest of his life.

In 1921, Clyde and Mary Morrison separated. Bob went with his mother to Long Beach, Duke stayed with his father in Glendale. Each of the boys developed a personality that was the antithesis of the parent they lived with — Duke became ambitious and driven like his mother, while Bob was compliant and easygoing like his father. Not that Mary Morrison cared, for Bob would always be her favorite child, which provoked no end of

45

quizzical confusion from outsiders observing the family dynamic over the years.

From the public record, Duke's years in Glendale could be drawn from Booth Tarkington's *Penrod* stories: in March of 1920, Duke made the pages of the local paper for the first time: "Clyde Morrison's eldest son Marion M. got the thumb of his left hand caught between the chain and sprocket wheel of his bicycle last Saturday while tuning it up for practice on the boy's speedway at the corner of Hawthorne and Central Avenue, in hope of entering some of the races. The flesh was badly lacerated and the joint spread somewhat, necessitating the care of a surgeon, but the boy is getting along very favorably."

It seems that Duke had problems with two-wheel vehicles; another time he was riding a motorcycle down Brand Boulevard on the trolley tracks. It was raining, he lost control of the bike and laid it down. The motorcycle slid and wedged itself under a mailbox. Duke just walked away and left it — motorcycles were too dangerous.

That same month, Clyde bought a six-room house at 313 West Garfield Avenue in Glendale. The year before, they had sold a house at 404 North Isabel and had bided their time living in an apartment over the Glendale Pharmacy.

The boy was still on the quiet side, and between his job delivering papers in the morning, making deliveries for the pharmacy, attending Boy Scout meetings and DeMolay, he couldn't have been spending much time at home — which was probably the general idea. In whatever spare time he had, he would haunt the Glendale library, reading the romantic novels of Sir Walter Scott, James Fenimore Cooper, and Arthur Conan Doyle. "He was well-dressed and intelligent, but very shy and retiring," remembered a classmate.

Clyde had been forced to learn the piano as a young boy, so he told Duke that he could choose any musical instrument he wanted to play. Duke chose the banjo. His teacher was a boy named Fat Stockbridge, who was a year or two older. But all of Duke's extracurricular activities meant that he didn't have any time for practice. When he and Stockbridge would get together, Duke would have made no progress, so Stockbridge would amuse himself by playing dirty songs on the banjo. A few years later, Morrison pawned his banjo to pay for a fraternity weekend at Lake Arrowhead. "That was the end of my musical career," he would observe.

Money was tight — money would be tight for decades. Recreation had to be grabbed in an impromptu fashion. He learned to swim in the legendarily shallow Los Angeles River and recalled raucous weekends on the waterfront.

"Me and a bunch of kids would come down to the Balboa Peninsula to do some 'poor boy sailing' in these round bottom boats. I remember we all used to go over to this big mud flat over there and do surf dives in the mud."

A surf dive?

A surf dive, he would explain, was accomplished by following a wave back to the ocean and then diving, belly down, into a long slide on the slippery mud. "It was a lot of fun. And then we'd go over to the flat by the pier and do the same thing there until we were just covered with this mud. And then we'd run over to the pier and run all the girls off while yelling and jumping around in this dried mud."

It was a simpler time. But the purity of these pastimes, which had probably been practiced since the Civil War, never left him. Nor would the scalding humiliation implied by the term "poor boy sailing."

One of his father's failed pharmacies was in the Jensen Building in Glendale, which also housed a movie theater. The man who ran the theater was a friend of Clyde's, so he let his movie-struck son go to the movies as often as possible. Duke remembered seeing *The Four Horsemen of the Apocalypse* twice a day for the entire week it played in Glendale, although, in common with most of young America, his favorite actor was not Rudolph Valentino but Douglas Fairbanks. "I admired his dueling, his stunts, his fearlessness in the face of danger, and his impish grin when he was about to kiss his lady-love."

After Fairbanks, Duke's favorite actor was Harry Carey, because, he remembered, "he looked real." In time, Duke would replace Harry Carey as John Ford's equally real man of the West, and Carey would become an important influence on Wayne's sense of acting, although the two had very different backgrounds.★

The neighborhood kids played cowboys and Indians, but they also played "movies"; that is, the kids would pretend to be actors, or a director, or even a cameraman — the camera was made out

★ Carey was born in the Bronx in 1878, the son of a judge. He initially studied to be a lawyer, then gave it up to write and act. Carey wrote a successful play called *Montana,* and used his own horse onstage every night, while the critics noted his walk — a "swagger" said one.

of a cigar box. When it was young Morrison's turn to be the hero, he would usually mimic Fairbanks, and once he remembered leaping out of a second-story window while holding on to some grape vines. "I ruined a beautiful grape arbor," he said.

The *Glendale Evening News* reported in the summer of 1922 that young Morrison was part of a large delegation of boys from the local YMCA to attend a camp on Catalina Island. As 1923 got under way, Clyde Morrison rated a small article in the local paper: "To C. L. Morrison falls the honor and responsibility of the management of the Jensen's Palace Grand drug store. Mr. Morrison is a well known drug store man to Glendalians . . . he has conducted a business of his own and has also been connected with the Roberts and Echols drug stores."

Early in 1923, Duke took another YMCA cruise, this time to the Santa Cruz Islands. By 1923, young Morrison was a fledgling football star, playing at 155 pounds for an excellent Glendale High team. In November, Glendale High came from behind to beat archrival San Bernardino 15–10 in the semifinal for the state championship. Duke played left guard on both offense and defense, and the local paper's breathless reportage left no doubt that Notre Dame's Four Horsemen were going to have some competition: "The whole line played well . . . Dotson, Morrison, Brucker and Phillipps showed up well both on offensive and defensive."

"Morrison was supposed to be opposite *the* prep guard in Southern California," reported the *Glendale Evening News'* high school football reporter. "If he was, Morrison has established his right to that title, for he made that jackrabbit look like a fuzzy bunny. He also uncorked some good points when [teammate Howard] Elliott was taken out."

At this point, Duke's interests focused mostly on athletics, but he was also developing an interest in performing. That said, athletics definitely had the edge. He played everything and he played it well. A neighborhood girl named Mildred Power remembered that she used to stand outside a fence on East Broadway where the local boys erected a makeshift basketball court. The most prominent of them, by dint of his size, curly hair, and overall good looks, was young Morrison. "Duke was the tallest and the most handsome thing you ever saw. I was in awe."

Throughout these years, the Morrison family was moving constantly. The Glendale public library doesn't have a complete run of city directories, but the ones they do have show different addresses for the family nearly every year between 1915 and 1925. They first show up in Glendale in 1915 living at 421 South Isabel; a year later they're at 315 South Geneva. By 1919 they're at 443 West Colorado; two years after that they're at 815 South Central; and in 1922 they're at 129 South Kenwood.

What makes all this intriguing is that Clyde Morrison bought a six-room house in 1920. The address was 313 Garfield Avenue. Either he rented the house out, or, more likely, lost it soon after buying it — rental income would have made a yearly move unnecessary. Wayne's attitude toward his father gradually became one of affectionate forbearance. He evinced sympathy for him and the values he taught him, which included football. "I was very envious of Duke," said a Glendale friend named Frank Hoyt. "His father would use

50

every spare moment to teach him how to pass the ball and tackle. They were very close."

Morrison was regarded as a top athlete, but with a slight problem: "He could have been a great football player, but he never wanted to hurt anybody," said one teammate. The family always needed money, so Duke learned the value of constant effort. Eugene Clarke, a friend in the Glendale period who followed Duke to USC, remembered that they worked on ice wagons, ran errands, mowed lawns, and filled in the times they weren't working by playing baseball and football.

There are people who always look like themselves, even as children, and Duke Morrison was one of them. As a boy, his face was round, but his eyes already had their familiar oriental shape. By the time he entered high school, he had definitely begun to assume the form the world would know. He was lean and very tall, over six feet, with dark, curly brown hair. He had another growth spurt in high school and by graduation weighed 170 and had assumed his full height of six feet and three and three quarter inches. His face lengthened, which made his cheekbones more prominent, and his blue eyes peered out from behind almond-shaped lids. He was gorgeous.

"I don't think it's possible to realize from watching his movies how absolutely stunningly handsome he was then," remembered a classmate named Dorothy Hacker. "His looks alone could stop traffic. He was about the handsomest young man that ever walked on two legs."

Dorothy Hacker sounds as if she was carrying a blazing torch for Duke Morrison, but she wasn't the only one. "My girlfriend and I used to go into the drugstore," said Ruth Conrad. "I had a crush

51

on him, but I don't know whether he ever realized."

Duke's only problem with women was shyness.
"He was very bashful with girls in high school,"
said Dorothy Hacker. "He was very popular, but
as far as I know he didn't date in those days."

The record, in the form of the 1924–1925 Glendale Union High School yearbook, *The Stylus,*
reports that Duke Morrison was in serious training to be a big man on campus. He was on the
sports staff of the school paper, one of the student
assistants in the cafeteria, received a bronze pin
for scholastic honors, was in the Boy's G club. He
also studied journalism, and that bore fruit in
some breathless sports stories bylined "M.M.M."
in the *Explosion* — the Glendale High School
newspaper:

> By winning today's game from the Covina "Colts,"
> Glendale can cinch the league title. The fracas
> this afternoon will be the hardest league game
> because there is so much at stake and because
> the teams are so evenly matched.
>
> Both teams have nine lettermen back; both
> teams have about the same amount of avoirdu-
> pois to back up against. Glendale is noted for its
> end around play as ground gainers, likewise
> Covina has the same style plays.

Other sports stories Duke Morrison wrote
embodied much the same enthusiasm, not to
mention a flamboyant vocabulary:

> Facing Alhambra today in the third league game
> of the season, Glendale will have much different

52

opposition than she had last week, when she trounced the "Wildcats" 25–0. As in the case of the Citrus-Glendale game, the two opposing teams have never been beaten by a high school team; this alone insures a hard fight for honors in this afternoon's tussle.

Glendale's varsity has more than the Alhambra team to fight when it enters the field today; it must also conquer overconfidence.

The young man liked his semicolons, and apparently never turned down an extracurricular activity — he was also in charge of advertising for the school paper.

In all of Duke's reminiscences of his time in high school, he never pointed out his early interest in performing, because that would have run counter to his preferred narrative of falling into show business by accident. But he appeared in the school play — Marc Connelly's *Dulcy* — in the role of Mr. Forbes; he appeared in the senior play as well — *The First Lady of the Land,* a historical drama about James and Dolley Madison and Aaron Burr.

When he wasn't in front of the footlights, he was behind the scenes, working on the stage crew. Wayne loved his drama teacher, so when she suggested that he give Cardinal Wolsey's farewell speech with two days' notice, he decided to go for it.

"I studied like a son of a bitch," he told me. He traveled to the Pasadena Playhouse, where the competition was taking place, to find a group of young actors who, as he put it, "were all so fucking Shakespearean. I felt like a goddamned fool up there." He froze up.

There was a similar contest for best essay, and young Duke won the contest for a piece he wrote on World War I. The award was the opportunity to recite the essay at the graduation ceremonies.

There was a line in his essay that went, "The worst things the Germans had done . . ." but as Duke rehearsed, he kept forgetting the word "had." His teacher was helping him rehearse, and she insisted over and over again that if he left out the word "had" he'd sound like an oaf, so he focused hard on that single word.

Came the day when the essay was to be recited, Duke looked right at his teacher and said, "The worst thing the Germans HAD done . . ." and promptly went completely blank. After a few seconds of struggle, he simply bowed and walked off the stage.

By this time Duke Morrison was a serious overachiever, more than comfortable academically, with a demonstrable bent for the public arena. There were also unconfirmed rumors that the parents of the attractive girls at Glendale High didn't want their daughters to date him because they thought he ran with a fast crowd. Members of that crowd stoutly denied the charge.

"He was just a good, clean-cut guy," remembered his best friend, Ralf Eckles. "We were raised that way." But rambunctious exuberance was beginning to be a prominent feature of Morrison's personality. One day the pranks got a little out of hand. Eckles and Morrison spread asafetida, a gum resin used as an antispasmodic, around the halls and classrooms of Glendale High. It was a fairly vile chemical and everybody within smelling distance got nauseated.

A chemistry professor found the bottle and took

it to Clyde Morrison, who asked his son to spell asafetida. Duke spelled it out exactly as it was on the label of the bottle, which misspelled the word. Clyde turned his son in, and both Eckles and Duke had to apologize in front of the entire school.

The yearbook had a fanciful preview of what the various students would be doing in the year 1940. The crystal ball for Duke Morrison involved him being president of the Glendale Ice Cream Company and authoring a book entitled *The Most Famous Men Have Humble Beginnings.*

His peers regarded him as a leader. "He was mature and conservative," said Bob Hatch, who was vice president to Morrison's president for the graduating class of 1925. "He had confidence and maturity that most of us didn't have . . . he was a good leader." Even his teachers liked him; Park Turrell, who taught chemistry, remembered Morrison as a "fine student who got an A in [the] course."

As nearly as Ralf Eckles could recall, the boys met in fifth grade. Eckles remembered his friend as always in control of himself, "never in trouble and not looking for it." The closest the two boys came to juvenile delinquency was trying to sneak into the Palace Grand movie theater. On the other hand, Saturday nights could get a little dull in Glendale.

"Our Saturday night pastime," remembered Eckles, "was to get a case of rotten eggs or old tomatoes, and take my father's car, which had a rumble seat. The old streetcars used to have an open section at the rear that people would stand on during the summer. We had lots of fun peppering them with eggs and tomatoes."

The boys' other casual pastimes involved greasing the tracks of the Eagle Rock–Glendale streetcar and watching it slide backward downhill. One time a classmate took his father's Reo automobile, which came with balloon tires. Morrison and Eckles deflated the tires and crossed a train trestle with the car. "There were five or six of us in that car and the trestle was a little narrow, but we made it."

The same group rented a cabin in Big Bear and got stuck in a snowstorm. "Duke and I were outside the car, trying to find the road. Some rangers came by and started yelling at us. They told us we were on the lake. We could have gone right through the ice!"

Another close friend was a diminutive young man named Bob Bradbury, whose father was a film director who would make a dozen or so films with young Morrison. Bob Bradbury would change his name to Bob Steele and become a western star, not to mention nearly a lifelong presence around his high school buddy.

By the time Duke graduated from high school in 1925, he was president of the senior class, president of the Latin Society, president of the Lettermen's Club, on the staff of the school newspaper, chairman of the Senior Dance, chairman of the Ring Committee, and a member of the debate team. He remembered that he graduated with a 94 average.

This man who would excel at playing outsiders was as a boy a consummate insider, popular with his classmates, obviously destined for great things. In the years to come, he would be amused by the gap between his image — which, it must be pointed out, he strenuously cultivated — and the

56

man he started out to be. "This so-called last of the cowboys," he would say with an amused smile. "I could say 'isn't' as well as 'ain't.' "

Duke gave some thought to a career in the Navy, or said he did. He would tell his oldest son, Michael, that he took the test for admittance to Annapolis and came in third in the state. Unfortunately, each state got to place two people per year, and Morrison was odd man out. "A pimply-faced kid like you beat me out," he told his son, then considered tactics not taken. "If they'd have known I could have played football, I'd have been in Annapolis. . . . You've gotta remember that Glendale was a small town, and we weren't on to sophisticated things like buying athletes. I never even spoke to my high school coach about what I wanted to do."

If Annapolis was out, Los Angeles was in. Between his academics and his football expertise, the boy was more than good enough for the University of Southern California. "One thing [USC] insisted [on] was that he have good grades," remembered Vic Francy, who was attending USC while working as an assistant coach at Glendale High. "I checked his record and he had 19 A's." Beginning in September 1925, Duke Morrison began attending the University of Southern California on a football scholarship.

CHAPTER TWO

A USC athletic scholarship was not generous; it covered tuition, which was $280 a year, and one meal a day on weekdays — if you were on the varsity. "The training table was a five-day-a-week thing," said Eugene Clarke, who lettered in football for Coach Howard Jones in 1930 and '31. "We sort of had to scratch around for our other meals and for all of our meals on weekends. We were always pretty hungry by Monday mornings."

When Duke Morrison reported for his first workout, Howard Jones liked what he saw. Morrison was taller than anybody else on the squad and was soon moved from guard, where he'd played in high school, to tackle.

The USC freshman team did spectacularly well, and so did Morrison; the team won all seven of their games, scoring 261 points to their opponents' 20. Only three opponents managed to score at all, and the team's first victim was the Glendale High team, who got creamed 47–0. Morrison must have had some conflicted loyalties, but not enough to stop him from earning a freshman letter and being singled out in the USC yearbook along with the rest of the line for his "work on the forward wall."

Morrison was taking the standard pre-law curriculum, and soon became a leader of the freshman debate team. He joined Sigma Chi fraternity and was again well liked by everybody, although he lacked the aggression that is a necessary part of frat life. One time he got out of a hazing by putting some ketchup in his mouth and letting it dribble down his chin. The other boys thought he was bleeding and let him go, but then Morrison started laughing, and gave his own game away.

Except for the constant worry about money, everything seemed to be coming together. In later years, Duke would talk about the embarrassment of being in the fraternity and having to cover the holes in his shoes with cardboard. He remembered bartering washing dishes and busing tables at the fraternity house in exchange for his meals, and working with the phone company as a map plotter, figuring out where old telephone lines ran, for 60 cents an hour.

Otherwise, he was in good standing. He was developing a gregarious personality, and since he was happy to see most people, most people were happy to see him. He wore the traditional freshman beanie, got paddled when he forgot to address upperclassmen as "sir," walked around with his pants legs rolled up as part of his initiation. For a boy who had always felt like an outsider, to be accepted, to be liked, was crucial.

The first eighteen years of Duke Morrison's life gave birth to a political philosophy centered on self-sufficiency. Surreptitiously, he was also engaged in a comprehensive search for parental substitutes, which was ironic because the second half of his life would largely revolve around

59

portrayals of parental substitutes — an actor seeking self-definition in his work, then imposing that definition on his life.

The first of the men that Morrison idolized was Howard Jones, the football coach at USC, who recruited him for the team known as the Thundering Herd. Jones was born in Ohio in 1885 and won seven Pacific Coast Conference championships, five Division One national championships, and five Rose Bowls before his early death in 1941. He was an aloof autocrat who couldn't delegate, lived and breathed his job and was completely intimidating. "If you'd just made a good play and were coming off the field, [Jones] wasn't the type to pat you on the back," said a player named Ray George. "He just gave you that look, just a hint of a smile, and you'd know if he was happy."

In short, Jones was everything Clyde Morrison wasn't.

The same year he entered USC, Duke Morrison moved out of his father's house and got a place of his own at 207 West Windsor in Glendale. The city directory listed him as "Morrison, Marion M., student." Duke was always independent, and from the time he entered college he began making his own way in life. But it was immediately clear that Duke, along with several other kids on the team, were in dire need of money.

Luckily, Howard Jones had friends.

In the spring of 1926, at the end of Morrison's freshman year, Jones sent Duke and a couple of other boys over to the Fox studio. "Last year," he explained, "I got Tom Mix a good box for the [football] games. He said if there was ever anything he could do for me, he would do it." Jones wanted Mix to get the boys summer jobs. This was standard practice for local colleges at the time, and a lot of the Southern California football players of Morrison's time became movie professionals: Cotton Warburton became a film editor, and Aaron Rosenberg became a producer, as did Howard Christie and Mike Frankovich.

The Fox lot was on Western Avenue, and Morrison and his friends found the Mix company shooting on the set of a western town, with the star resplendent in a startlingly white ten gallon hat. They showed him a letter of introduction from Jones, and Mix responded by showing them books of clippings and photographs about Tom Mix in Europe, Tom Mix in Africa, Tom Mix in Catalina. He announced that "a star owes it to his public to keep in fine physical condition. I want you to be my trainers." In the meantime, Morrison and Don Williams, a quarterback, could work in the prop department. Mix called someone and told him to put the boys on the payroll.

This was on a Friday. On Monday, Morrison and Williams reported for work. Wearing his white Stetson, Mix drove onto the lot in a black Locomobile trimmed in red. Williams and Morrison said, "Good morning, Mr. Mix." The star responded with a blank look. Mix had forgotten about them and didn't seem interested in being reminded. "That was the last encounter I ever had with Tom Mix," said Wayne. But the boys were given jobs on the swing gang at $35 a week, lugging furniture and props around the various sets.

As far as Morrison was concerned, Tom Mix was a blowhard who broke a promise. "Duke

61

never really got over that," said an employee in later years. "Duke [always] had a hard-on for this guy. Fifty years later he still didn't like the man." Long after Duke Morrison had become John Wayne, Tom Mix's last wife came to Wayne's office. She wondered if Wayne would be interested in buying Tom Mix's personal phone. It was made of mother-of-pearl, had Mix's initials on it, and was a thing of beauty.

"What am I going to do with it?" asked Wayne coldly.

Mix's wife kept spinning. "You might know somebody that's interested to have Tom Mix's telephone. Maybe you could just leave it out at your house and people would see it."

Wayne could never resist a sob story, so he gave her some money, but never used the phone. It was found in storage after he died.

Duke Morrison's life in the movies had actually begun before he showed up on the Fox lot. His entrée was apparently doubling for Francis X. Bushman Jr. in an MGM football movie called *Brown of Harvard*, released in April 1926.

Bushman eventually left the movies, changed his name to Ralph Bushman, and became an air conditioning repairman. A quarter century later, he remembered what happened. "I had been running up and down the field until I was exhausted. Finally I had to make the long run down the field and be tackled on the one yard line. Since my back was to be to the camera I asked for a double. The man they sent in to double for me was . . . named Marion Michael Morrison, now known as John Wayne."

"I got seven and a half dollars for it," remembered Wayne. As Bushman indicated, the young Duke is not visible in the picture, so we have to take everybody's word for his participation.

Wayne also remembered working as an extra in "a Norman Kerry picture at MGM in which I was dressed in a Scotsman outfit, but for the life of me, I could not tell you the name." The picture was the excellent *Annie Laurie,* starring Lillian Gish, shot in the summer of 1926 and released in May of 1927. (Fun Fact: the director of *Annie Laurie* was John S. Robertson, who years later was the subject of the Byrds song "Old John Robertson.")

A blue-collar boy who loved football could publicly acknowledge a fairly limited list of enthusiasms. Loving the movies was okay — who doesn't love the movies? But wanting to be an actor? Not likely. Then, and for the rest of his life, Wayne would claim that he had backed into the movie business simply by being eager and young, that acting was the furthest thing from his mind.

But it's obvious that Duke Morrison had already set his sights on his future profession. Sam White, the brother of the comedy producers Jack and Jules White, remembered that a bunch of boys from the USC football team were hired to work in a comedy two-reeler centering on football that was being directed by Norman Taurog. Sam White used to go to the barbershop at the corner of Western and Sunset as did Morrison, who continually pestered White for work.

"Why don't you get your brother Jack to give me an acting job?"

"Have you any experience as an actor?"

"No, but hell, I can do it. There's nothing to it."

"I'll see if I can, but I doubt it very much."

63

The main problem was that White didn't see exactly where Morrison could fit in silent comedies. "Maybe you could play a mean heavy or something because of your size, or a henchman, but I don't see how you could play a lead because he doesn't use guys of your type."

"Well, ask him anyhow," said Morrison.

Jack White wasn't interested in football players who wanted to act, but Morrison was determined, as he would be all his life. And in fact, Duke did get at least some work in silent comedies, as the historian Richard Roberts discovered nearly ninety years later, when he uncovered stills proving that Duke worked as an extra in a now lost two-reel comedy for Educational Studios entitled *Seeing Stars.* He's a head taller than everybody else, wearing what was undoubtedly his own suit, and earned $5 a day. The film was released in October of 1927, and would probably have been shot in the early summer of that year. It also fits with his recollections of having bit parts at the Educational Studio after he met a certain famous director at Fox in late 1926.

Bit parts weren't what he had in mind, and Duke Morrison's ambitions had a way of being fulfilled. He decided to bide his time and keep playing football. He was young; he'd get his shot.

In September 1926, Morrison was assigned to work on a picture unpromisingly called *Mother Machree.* Duke's job was to herd geese that were being used for rural atmosphere. When they weren't waddling down the street, the geese liked to rest under the sets, and it was Morrison's job to herd them into a chicken-wire enclosure and keep them in one place so they could be quickly found when needed.

As he told the story to Peter Bogdanovich, one day, Morrison heard a loud, sarcastic voice yelling, "Hey, gooseherder!"

It was the director.

"You're one of Howard Jones' bright boys?"

"Yes."

"And you call yourself a football player?"

"I don't — mean — well . . ."

"You're a guard, eh? Let's see you get down in position."

Morrison assumed the three-point stance, whereupon the director quickly kicked the boy's hand out from under him. Morrison collapsed on his face. "And you call yourself a guard. I'll bet you couldn't even take me out."

"I'd like to try."

The director trotted about twenty yards away, then came at Morrison. Instead of trying to tackle him, Morrison stuck out a leg and hit the director in the chest, knocking him down.

"He sat there," remembered Wayne, "and for a minute it was a case of whether or not I had a future in the motion picture business — I didn't realize how important it was then. But he took it humorously and laughed like hell — and the crew laughed. When he laughed, they laughed — they waited their turn. But that started our association."

There it was, a nearly fifty-year relationship in microcosm — goading and torment, followed by release and friendship.

The director's name was John Ford. He was thirty-two years old and had been a football star in high school in Portland, Maine, where he was known as "Bull" Feeney (his real name) for the

65

way he crashed into the line. His team had won the Maine state championship, but all Duke Morrison knew was that Ford was tall, rangy, tough, sarcastic — in total command of a movie set, and, apparently, life.

At this point, John Ford was a craftsman on his way to becoming an artist, not that he would ever admit to yearnings for the latter. He had been working at Fox since 1920, and had directed *The Iron Horse,* his first huge hit, in 1924. He had a wife named Mary, two children, a drinking problem, an unmatched gift for visual narrative.

Duke Morrison had found his enduring father substitute.

Money continued to be an issue for the boy. He resorted to selling the football tickets each of the players received. Sophomores got one ticket for each home game, juniors two, seniors four, and the captain of the team got six. Most of these tickets were sold for extra income, and Wayne began buying tickets off the other players for $7.50 or $10 apiece, selling them for $15. One time he sold two tickets for $50 and it felt like his ship had come in. He always saved one ticket for his father, and a half century later he would say "Wish I still could."

But shortly after beginning his junior year, Duke Morrison got hurt. Various stories were told over the years, but Eugene Clarke had the advantage of being an eyewitness:

One day we went to Balboa and there were a lot of pretty USC sorority girls down there that day and we decided to do a little showing off. We jumped in the water — it was Duke's idea — and

66

started to do what the kids nowadays call body surfing. The waves were pretty high, real rough, and one of them caught the Duke and tossed him ashore with a badly wrenched right shoulder.

We had to report for the start of football practice a few days later and when the first scrimmages started, Duke's shoulder was still in bad shape. Now, Duke was a tackle, you understand, and Howard Jones always insisted that when you blocked the opposing lineman, you hit him with your right shoulder, hit him real hard.

If the Duke tried to do that with his injured shoulder it would have killed him. So what he tried to do was twist his body around so he could block with his left shoulder. Well, Jones saw him do that and that was all he needed. All hell broke loose. Jones accused the Duke of being yellow, of being afraid to block and demoted him to the scrubs.

It was an event that would prove a huge boon in the long term, but at the time it must have been devastating. It meant that Morrison wasn't on the 1927 team that lost only one game — 7–6 to Notre Dame — or on the 1928 team that went undefeated and won the national championship, with the minor assistance of a young backbench tackle named Wardell Bond, "Ward" for short.

Woody Strode, who became part of the John Ford stock company in its last years, was an all-around athlete who once played for the Los Angeles Rams. He didn't buy the story about the damaged shoulder. "It's unlikely," he said, "almost unthinkable, that a good coach would drop a promising [player] because of one injury. Duke just was not good enough to stay on the team."

Strode believed Wayne was too slow. Maybe, but Strode was seven years younger than Wayne and never played football with him. In the absence of any other contrary testimony, Eugene Clarke's story has to be regarded as the best available version of the truth.

Duke Morrison was informed that his football scholarship was not being renewed. If he wanted to stay in school, he'd have to pay his own way. The core problem went beyond his shoulder, or, for that matter, his foot speed, and involved the perennial bête noire of the Morrisons — money.

"I had borrowed money to go to school the year before," Wayne explained. "The scholarship only took care of your entrance fees. I had other expenses. As a consequence, when I paid them all back, I didn't have any money to go back to school, and my shoulder was hurting so I figured, what the hell, I'll lay out this one year so I won't lose my eligibility for that year and I'll catch up on some money."

Losing the scholarship was no joke. It meant that Duke couldn't get his one meal a day at the training table, which meant that he couldn't eat. The actual tuition was far beyond Clyde Morrison's ability to pay. (Duke's brother, Bob, had better luck in football, if nowhere else; he earned a letter as a USC fullback in 1932.)

"He had to go to work," says Ralf Eckles. "He had no place to go and he knew my folks, so I brought him home and he lived upstairs over our garage for a while."

"Duke was in bad shape financially," said Eugene Clarke. "He owed money to the fraternity for his dues, room and board, and he didn't have a dime. The fraternity was urging him to pay up;

he felt his football playing days were over because of his bad shoulder. So he did what he felt he had to do; he quit school and went to work at the studios."

The fact that young Morrison was staying at a friend's house rather than home with his father might indicate either a breach or stubborn self-determination, probably the latter — if there was a disagreement between the boy and his father, Duke never spoke of it.

Either way, Duke had already fallen in love with the woman he would marry. Lindsley Parsons, whose life would intersect with Morrison's in the movie business, was a Kappa Alpha from UCLA, while Morrison was a Sigma Chi from USC. The two young men got to know each other at the beach at Balboa.

"[Duke] was down there particularly because Duke Kahanamoku was there," remembered Parsons. "Duke had bought one of those ten-ton mahogany surfboards, and the only place he could use it was down at the Newport jetty. There'd been a wreck of a big sailing schooner down there that one of the picture companies had used, and the wreck had caused some sandbars that made some beautiful waves to ride. He and some of the big swimmers used to swim around the jetty and I would try to do it myself and they'd generally go clear around and be on land again by the time I got about halfway out."

One of Duke's fraternity brothers set him up on a blind date with a girl named Carmen Saenz. They went to the Rendezvous Ballroom in Balboa, then back to the girl's house, where he first set eyes on Carmen's sister, Josephine. And that, as they say, was that.

The Rendezvous became the place for Duke and Josie, as well as for a lot of other young couples. It was, remembered Lindsley Parsons, "a little thing right on Front Street there. . . . Josephine and her sister Carmen were the most beautiful girls in Balboa that summer, in fact I think any summer we went down there."

The kids were all broke, which posed a problem because you had to buy a ticket for every dance. Morrison and Parsons grew skilled at scrounging discarded or lost tickets off the dance floor. If they found one, they would separate the pasteboard into two halves and get two dances for the price of none.

The actor William Bakewell had been dating Loretta Young and became close to her family and her sisters, who were all devout Catholics. "Josephine Saenz had gone to convent with Loretta, Polly Ann and Sally, and she became like a member of the family. She was over there all the time. And she started to go with this guy named Duke Morrison."

Josephine Saenz was totally unlike any woman Duke had ever met. Specifically, she was totally unlike Mary Morrison. Josephine embodied class, breeding, intelligence, and composure. Her father, Dr. José Saenz, had a medical degree but had made his living operating a string of pharmacies. In 1921, Haiti, Panama, the Dominican Republic, and El Salvador retained Saenz as their consul for the city of Los Angeles.

Duke seems to have committed to Josephine quickly, but Josephine . . . Josephine wasn't too sure, and the Saenz family was definitely on the fence. The more they learned about the boy, the less sure they were. A football player from a

70

broken marriage, who had lost his scholarship, who lived in Glendale, was in love with their ardently Catholic, aspiring socialite daughter from Hancock Park?

Working in Duke's favor with the Saenz family was his total lack of pretense and his honesty. Working in Duke's favor with Josephine were his looks. Despite the Saenz family's discontent, Duke and Josie found ways to keep the relationship alive for the next several years, although Josie's family forbade marriage until such time as Duke proved he could support his prospective wife and children in a suitable manner.

"Their friends told me they were great fun," said Gretchen Wayne, the wife of Michael Wayne, and Josie's daughter-in-law. "They loved games, loved jokes, loved to laugh. Her education didn't encompass more than a year or two of college, but she was properly reared. And she was very smart, very good with math. She was a Roman Catholic, who seriously lived her religion. A great person."

Duke never held a grudge about his misfortune at the USC football program; certainly, he became the most famous dropout USC ever had, and he followed the football program carefully. As Gretchen Wayne would observe, "You didn't want to be around him if the Trojans lost."

"I think the lesson you learn on the football field is basic," he would say in later years. "If the player on the other side of the scrimmage line is as good or better than you, you don't care what color, religion or nationality he is, you respect him. I've tried to live by that all my life."

And so Duke Morrison went back to lugging props at the Fox studio in the summer of 1927, more or less planning on working there for a year, saving his money, and going back to USC in the fall of 1928.

In that summer of 1927, Wayne was working on another picture for John Ford. *Four Sons,* an epic in the style, if not the equivalent emotional impact, of Murnau's *Sunrise. Four Sons* called for Morrison to wait for a door to open on the set, after which he would throw some maple leaves in front of a fan to blow past the doorway. After the take, Morrison would sweep up the leaves and wait for the next take.

After several takes, Duke's concentration wandered and he lost track of the order of his duties. He started to sweep up the leaves, then looked up and saw two cameras staring right at him. The cameras were turning. "And looking at me are the cameraman, and John Ford, and the wife of the man who was head of the studio then. Shit, there I was! I just threw down my goddamn broom and started to walk off."

Once again, Ford was amused by the young man's earnestness, his boyishness. The studio musicians played some martial music and marched Morrison over to the heir of the Archduke Leopold, who was working on the picture, and who pinned a medal on him. Then they marched him back to Ford. Morrison bent over and received a kick in the ass from the director.

That would have been the end of it, but he eventually had to leave the set because Margaret Mann — the actress playing the mother of the four sons — kept breaking up every time she saw him. "I was never so goddamn embarrassed in my life," said Wayne.

Ford decided that the boy's handsome face and eager, gauche quality might make him screen material, and he gave him a nice bit in his picture *Hangman's House,* a moody, beautiful film about the Irish Troubles that started production in January 1928. The scene is a steeplechase, and young Duke Morrison is unbilled but clearly visible as a spectator who eventually stomps down a picket fence — not the last time Ford would seize on the young man's enthusiasm.

Morrison was in another scene that didn't make it out of the cutting room. He was playing a poor Irish boy brought before a hanging judge, who pronounced sentence upon him. The judge was played by the splendid old ham Hobart Bosworth, and he intoned his lines: "You shall hang by the neck until you are dead, dead, dead." Morrison thought it was a pretty corny line reading, even if it was a silent film. He blurted out "AAAAMEN!"

"There had been a lot of noise," he remembered. "Suddenly there was silence." Ford made a loud, emphatic pronouncement: "Get that son of a bitch out of the prisoner's box! Get him off the stage! Get him off the goddamned lot! I don't *ever* want to see him again."

For neither the first nor the last time, Duke thought his movie career was over, but propman Lefty Hough came up and told him to just get out of sight, that Ford only wanted him out of the way in case he had angered Bosworth. Morrison's banishment lasted no more than a couple of days.

Since he had joined the circus, Morrison decided to check out the other tents. Warner Bros. was making a picture called *Noah's Ark* that, naturally enough, featured a spectacular flood sequence. The call went out for extras over six feet tall willing to work for $15 a day. The job entailed risking their lives while rivers of water and, just for good measure, a temple, washed over them.

Duke Morrison was one of the extras, as was a young man named Andy Devine, even though he was under six feet. "Another fella and I were standing together," Wayne remembered in later years, "and Andy came up beside me and he says, 'Hey, give me a hand, will you?' And he put a hand on my shoulder and a hand on this other guy's shoulder, and . . . he's the first one they picked, you know."

Devine was also standing on a couple of bricks that he'd brought in order to make himself look taller.

After two summers of working at Fox, Duke Morrison had saved $500 — a fortune as far as the Morrison family was concerned. Besides propping, he was a general dogsbody around the Fox lot; one of his more demeaning jobs involved pasting labels for premium booze on bottles that actually contained cheap bootleg hooch for Fox executives who wanted to impress their girlfriends.

One night, Wayne and Josie were chaperoning Polly Ann Young, Loretta's sister, who had a date with a Fox executive. On the way to the Ambassador Hotel, the executive said, "I just happen to have a bottle of really good Scotch . . ." Morrison recognized the fake label. The executive wondered why he looked so unhappy.

Wayne was becoming acclimated to the movie business — its perpetual excitement, its neuroses, its personalities: the roughnecks, the wranglers, the stuntmen, and the far more sophisticated Ford, who enjoyed playing the part of a roughneck. "He was a labored learned man," Wayne

74

would say of his mentor, who "absorbed everything — mood, wine, lines, everything."

The sojourns at MGM and Warners were for extra pocket money; Fox was for living expenses, and Morrison was beginning to rethink his plan to head back to USC. "Everybody that I was in school with had an uncle or father in the law, and I started to realize that I was going to end up writing briefs for about ten years for these fellows who I thought I was smarter than. And I was kind of losing my feeling for that.

"But at the same time I was getting such enthusiasm out of working with Jack Ford and with the people that were in the movie business in those days — the prop men, the grips, the cameramen. The attitude was that it was our picture, everybody was working for the picture, there were no departmental heads and union bosses telling us what we could and couldn't do. And luckily for me Jack Ford needed a prop man."

Wayne's obvious worship of Ford led him to initially think of becoming a director, or at least work in the production side of the business. "I just looked up to this man Ford — he was a big hero to me. He was intelligent and quick-thinking. Had great initiative. It was just wonderful to be around him. He kept you alive and on your toes. Of course, I started watching what he was doing, how he was working on people."

Morrison had grown up in a poverty further afflicted by Mary Morrison's shanty-Irish pretensions. In comparison, Duke liked the rough-and-tumble honesty of a comfortably blue-collar environment.

"There were a lot of tough guys around in those days, working in the picture business," he would

75

reminisce to a friend years later.

Some of them were really tough. Their idea of a Saturday night was to go over to Pickwick Stables and look for a fight. They wanted a fight and if they couldn't find one they'd start one. That was a big thing for them, to knock somebody around.

Probably the toughest of all those guys was a guy by the name of Art Acord, who was also a leading man in cheap westerns. Acord was really tough. He bit a guy's ear off in a fight once — that's the kind of tough he was. With that kind of tough you're going to make some enemies along the line. He made a lot of them. And some of them tried to do him in. Hell, they shot him, they stabbed him, finally killed him. The only way they could kill him was to poison him. They finally did it, they poisoned him. He was the toughest son of a bitch I ever saw.

Acord died in Mexico under mysterious circumstances in 1931, and Duke's version of his demise is widely believed to be accurate. He also casually mentioned knowing Wyatt Earp, as well as Stuart Lake, Earp's first biographer. There's no independent confirmation, but it's certain that Tom Mix was a pallbearer at Earp's 1930 funeral, and Earp was also an acquaintance of Ford's. It's possible that Ford could have introduced the young prop man to the fabled lawman.

The stuntman Yakima Canutt believed that Wayne's behind-the-scenes exposure to such authentically hard men played a major part in his screen character. Wayne, says Canutt, "thrived on working with the cowboys. He never pretended he was a real cowboy, just a screen cowboy, but he picked up on what those men were like, and he'd find ways of bringing those things out in his pictures. That's partly why Wayne was so realistic as a cowboy."

In January and February of 1929, Ford was shooting *The Black Watch,* and Duke Morrison was propping, but he was already part of Ford's social circle; Myrna Loy, who was playing a femme fatale in *The Black Watch,* was invited to a party at Ford's house where Morrison was lurking around the edges of the room, "young and handsome . . . and as shy as I was." Loy understood what was happening: "Jack was grooming him."

In the late spring of 1929, Morrison was still propping for $35 a week when Ford asked for his help. He had been assigned a picture called *Salute,* which called for locations at the Naval Academy, and he wanted to use some of the USC football players in small parts. The studio's liaison to USC wasn't having any luck, so he asked Morrison if he wanted the job.

Morrison set up a lunch for Howard Jones and Ford, which went well. The salaries on offer were from $50 to $75 a week, but the clincher for Jones seems to have been Morrison's claim that the boys would have plenty of time to visit Washington, D.C., for on-site civics lessons. With that, a group of athletes and ex-athletes were freed up for six weeks of location shooting. One of the players — "a big ugly bastard" according to Morrison — was Ward Bond. Bond already had established a reputation as a drinker, so Morrison thought it best to keep him off the set, but the casting director liked him. Bond was hired.

In *Salute,* Ford's first, requisitely awkward talkie,

Duke Morrison plays a naval cadet named Bill who razzes new recruits. Fox's in-house paperwork bills him twelfth, six spots behind Ward Bond and right below Stepin Fetchit. Duke Morrison's first line of spoken movie dialogue was only innocuous at the time: "He doesn't mean the audience. What do the actors do, Mister?"

As relentless weather molds obstinate stone, so John Ford began molding Duke Morrison. "Duke . . . was just a stick of wood when he came away from USC," said the director Allan Dwan. "Jack gave him character."

A pattern was already forming: everything Ford gave Wayne to do, he did with alacrity. Ford again encountered Morrison's game heart on the set of a submarine picture called *Men Without Women,* shot off Catalina Island. The scene called for some actors to disappear under the water, grab some air from a hose beneath the water, then come up gasping as if they were shipwrecked sailors.

But the day was gray and unpleasant, the water was cold, the waves were high, and the actors were far from enthusiastic about their appointed task. Years later, Ford told his version of the story: "Our two blankety-blank stunt men who were supposed to come up in bubbles, like they'd been shot out of an escape hatch, said it was too rough to work. The blanks.

"Well, Duke was standing up on the top deck of this boat we were on. He wasn't supposed to go in the water at all, but I asked him if he'd try this stunt. He never said a word, except 'Sure.' Dove right into the water from that deck.

"I knew right then that boy had the stuff and was going places."

"I could see," said Ford, "that here was a boy

who was working for something — not like most of the other guys, just hanging around to pick up a few fast bucks. Duke was really ambitious and willing to work."

Duke would always remember the years when the movies first beckoned, then receded, with nostalgia. This was in contrast to just a few years later, when he'd be starring in B westerns, a regimen he always regarded as demeaning. "You could operate in every department of pictures," he reminisced in 1968. "You didn't need a union card. I was a carpenter. I was a juicer. I rigged lights. I helped build sets. Carried props. Hauled furniture. I got to know the nuts and bolts of making pictures." He concluded this reverie with the most crucial criterion of all: "More importantly, I was made to feel like I belonged."

The lonely boy was becoming less lonely. He even got a union card. In 1929, Duke Morrison became member number 34854 of Local 37 of the International Alliance of Theatrical Stage Employees and Moving Picture Machine Operators, affiliated with the AFL. He kept his membership card for the rest of his life.

And he was still nibbling around the edges of acting. His first screen credit — as "Duke Morrison" — actually came in a Fox campus musical called *Words and Music* that was barely released in September 1929 (it had a New York run of one day!). He also became friendly with George O'Brien, John Ford's favorite leading man of the period. O'Brien got him another small part in a movie called *Rough Romance,* which came out in June 1930. But by that time, Duke Morrison was no longer Duke Morrison. He had a new name and a new career — the very one he had been

79

hoping, dreaming, and planning for most of his young life.

CHAPTER THREE

The story of the christening of John Wayne varied only slightly in the telling. Raoul Walsh had approached Fox production head Winfield Sheehan regarding a western about the pioneers' trek west. The film was to be based on a *Saturday Evening Post* serial by Hal G. Evarts entitled "The Shaggy Legion" that ran from November 30, 1929, to January 4, 1930, and was later published as a novel. The serial's title referred to the last great herd of buffalo, but Walsh's imagination converted it into a vast saga of western expansion, a sound version of *The Covered Wagon* or *The Iron Horse* — two of the greatest hits of the silent era. Fox signed Evarts to a screenwriting contract in February 1930 that paid $1,000 a week.

That was easy; the hard part was the casting. As Evarts would write, "the male lead must be a true replica of the pioneer type — somewhat diffident with women, being unused to them, but a bear-cat among the men of the plains. Walsh was afraid that the sophistication of an experienced actor would creep through and be apparent to the audience. As against that was the probability that a man chosen from the ranks of the inexperienced would be unable to carry the part in so big a picture."

When people at the studio grumbled about Walsh's plans to use an unknown, he told them, "I don't want an actor. I want someone to get out there and act natural — be himself. . . . I'll make an actor out of him if need be."

As Walsh said at the time, "If there was one thing I did not want, it was an established star for the role of Breck Coleman . . . I wanted . . . a personality, not an actor."

Walsh remembered that the critical moment came when he saw Duke Morrison lugging some furniture across the soundstage for John Ford's *Born Reckless,* which was being shot early in 1930. "He was in his early 20s — laughing and the expression on his face was so warm and wholesome that I stopped and watched. I noticed the fine physique of the boy, his careless strength, the grace of his movement."

Walsh walked over and asked the boy his name. The gangling youngster looked him over and said, "I know you. You directed *What Price Glory.* The name's Morrison." He explained that he wanted to be in pictures but "this is as far as I've come."

"What else can you do besides handle props?" Walsh asked.

"I can play football."

"I believe you. Let's see how much you want to be an actor. Let your hair grow. Come and see me in two weeks."

Duke believed that Walsh had first noticed him at a Fox company picnic a week or so earlier. Morrison was hungover, having a beer, wearing a Harris tweed suit, and eventually competed in a walking contest, which he narrowly won against a "little grip that's just right on my ass."

A few days later, Walsh saw Wayne crossing the lot with a table on his head and "it must have reminded him of the picnic. Actually, I was goin' to a Ford set, and Walsh asked [producer] Edmund Grainger who I was, and Eddie yelled to me. I came over, we were introduced, and then Walsh came over to the set. I guess he talked to Ford then. That night, as I was leaving, Eddie came around: 'Jesus, don't cut your hair — Walsh wants to take a test of you for this picture.' "

The clock was ticking — the picture had to start shooting in the spring — and Walsh needed a leading man right away. "The part wasn't too exacting," remembered Walsh. "What I needed was a feeling of honesty, of sincerity, and Wayne had it."

In the future, Duke would claim that he was thunderstruck by the invitation to act, that "it was the furthest thing from my mind." But in 1946, he confided to the gossip columnist Louella Parsons that John Ford thought he had the makings of an actor rather than a technician, and "I was ashamed to admit I was hipped on the idea of acting. That's why I started in with the props."

There was a screen test of course — million-dollar movies weren't hung on people who might not photograph. Before that, Morrison was sent to a drama coach, who he recalled as one of many "phonies" who washed up in Hollywood after the coming of sound to teach elocution. "All day long, this drama coach had me declaiming in deep, stentorian tones. Over and over again, I had to roar, 'Tell that great white mountain hello for me.' After a few weeks of that, I quit. A Shakespearian delivery wasn't for me."

Morrison reported back to Raoul Walsh, who set up a different test. There was no script, no

83

lines to memorize. Instead, Walsh had Ian Keith and Marguerite Churchill, both experienced actors, ask him questions in character, with Duke responding in character.

How long was the trip? Will we see buffalo? Any danger of Indian attack? Wayne felt self-conscious with the camera on him, a feeling that would plague him for years, so he combatively turned the tables. "Where you from, Mister?" he asked Keith. "Why do you want to go west? Can you handle a rifle?"

Walsh called "Cut!" A week later John Ford told the boy he had the job. He was no longer making $35 a week; Fox generously gave their new star a whopping $75 a week.

And since Marion "Duke" Morrison was not a name that carried much synchronicity for the part of a fearless young scout, studio head Winfield Sheehan decided to change his name. Raoul Walsh claimed that he came up with the name "Wayne," and that Sheehan added the "John," but Duke said that the whole thing was Sheehan's idea. Sheehan was a fan of Mad Anthony Wayne, the Revolutionary War general, because "he had been tough and a non-conformist." The "John" seems to have been an afterthought, but it worked — gave the two halves of the name the equivalence of two blocks of granite that miraculously fit together.

As far as the newly christened star was concerned, the name was irrelevant. "I was known as Marion Morrison to my family and older friends, and I had become Duke Morrison to my generation — neither of which is a good theatrical name. Duke Morrison would sound too much like a stuntman or something, and Marion Morrison

84

would have probably got me in more fights than I'd normally get in." In Fox's eyes, "Marion" was a problem even retrospectively; they decided to tell the press, in the person of Louella Parsons, that the boy's name had actually been Wayne Morrison before they changed his name.

The emotional reality was that he would always think of himself as Duke Morrison, not the fictional construct known as John Wayne. In fact, he never legally changed his name; on his death certificate, he's listed as "Marion Morrison (John Wayne)" and for the sake of psychological clarity he always asked people to refer to him as "Duke," not John. "It took me a long time," he reminisced in 1975. "I never have really become accustomed to the John. Nobody ever really calls me John . . . I've always been Duke, or Marion or John Wayne. It's a name that goes well together and it's like one word — John Wayne. But if they say John, Christ, I don't look around today. And when they say Jack, boy, you know they don't know me."

Duke Morrison knew all too well the deprivations of fear and loneliness, the humiliation of poverty, the pain of powerlessness and not a little psychological neglect. He was learning self-reliance (which was very much to his taste), the virtue of hard work (ditto), as well as what he always regarded as the dubious nature of solitude. "John Wayne" would be the vehicle through which Duke Morrison acquired power — as an actor and as a man.

With the casting complete, production of the picture Fox was calling *The Big Trail* began to move forward. According to Hal Evarts, Raoul Walsh wanted to emphasize authenticity of setting, costume, and props as much as possible. Complicating Walsh's desire was the fact that the Missouri River near Kansas City, the actual embarkation point for many wagon trains, was now dotted with smokestacks and railroads.

Walsh decided that he and Evarts would go on a location recce, and that they would customize the story and dialogue to the locations. Whereupon they set off east across the Teton Pass by sled, bound for Jackson Hole. "After a 30 mile sled trip across the range, we landed in Jackson a few hours after nightfall," wrote Evarts. "We cruised the valley for two days by sled, then headed out over the pass. A blizzard was in progress; not a cold one, but a wet, sloppy one, the snow falling in wet chunks. . . .

"Through it all, we plugged and plugged on the story — adding here, cutting there, while we were preparing to leave for other locations within a few days time."

While Walsh and Evarts were constructing their story, the studio began buying and building thousands of props — yokes, wagon covers, a host of other articles. An old cowhand named Jack Padjan was sent to Wyoming to select Indians from the Arapaho tribe, and a batch of them set up headquarters across the street from the Fox administration building.

Fox issued a press release about their new star, and the process was so hurried that most of it was actually true: "John Wayne was born in Winterset, Iowa, on May 26, 1907. The son of Clyde Leonard Morrison and Mary Brown. Educated in the George Washington Grammar School of Keokuk, Iowa and later at the Lancaster Grammar School in Lancaster, California, to which place his parents moved when he was at an early age. Graduating from the Lancaster School, he entered Glendale High School in Glendale, California, and from there he entered University of Southern California in Los Angeles . . ."

The press release asserted that he broke his ankle in his junior year which cost him the season, and that he left college and "decided to learn to make motion pictures. Secured a position as prop boy and propped on *Mother Machree, Speakeasy, Strong Boy, The Black Watch* and *Louis Beretti* [the production title of *Born Reckless*]. . . .

"Wayne brought to the part of Breck Coleman absolutely no stage or screen experience other than appearing while at the University of Southern California in a couple of college dramas."

All in all, pretty close to the truth, although no mention was made of his parents' divorce, which was finalized on February 20, 1930. By that time, Clyde was spending time with Florence Buck, a twenty-nine-year-old divorcée with a daughter. A few weeks after the divorce was final, Clyde and Florence got married. The marriage would prove to be a success, and Clyde's drinking moderated, although his difficulties with steady employment remained. A few years later, his situation stabilized, and he eventually became president of the Beverly Hills Lions Club.

It was now the spring of 1930. The studio quickly took some stills of their young star examining guns in the studio prop room along with Dan Clark, who had photographed Tom Mix for years, and Louis Witte, who was in charge of the equipment.

They also began papering the country with the story of his discovery, and characterized him as "a youth who bids fair to prove the screen sensation of 1930 . . . a smile that is one in a million, a marvelous speaking voice, a fearless rider, a fine natural actor and he has everything the femmes want in their leading man. Less than two years ago Wayne was playing football at USC. Watch this boy go."

Not everybody thought Wayne was a good bet. One trade paper columnist said, "I can't see how anybody could stretch their imagination so far as to gamble $2 million on a novice to make good in a picture that cries for an actor with years and years of experience."

To which Raoul Walsh replied, with considerable insight into his new leading man's essential character, "I selected Morrison, whose name, by the way, will be John Wayne from now on . . . primarily because he is a real pioneer type . . . but most of all because he can start over any trail and finish."

As the script was finalized, Walsh told the newly christened John Wayne to keep letting his hair grow — pioneers weren't neatly trimmed. And one other thing: learn how to throw a knife without camera trickery. Wayne went to an expert knife man named Steve Clemente, who worked with the young man for several weeks. Clemente explained that in theory it was simple: throw the knife so it makes one revolution in twelve feet, or two revolutions in twenty-four feet. More revolutions or fewer increase the likelihood that the knife will land handle-in and fall with a clatter rather than pierce the wood target with an impressive *thunk!*

In practice, it was not so simple, but he learned. A few weeks later, hair shaggy, armed with a knife he knew how to throw, John Wayne was off to make his first western.

William Fox was the lone wolf among the founding generation of movie moguls, one who was always reaching for authentic innovation. Other studios brought over great European filmmakers, but they tended to hobble them by forcing them into the Hollywood mold. Fox brought over F. W. Murnau from Germany and gave him carte blanche to make *Sunrise,* thereby creating one of cinema's great glories, and one with a synchronized musical score on the soundtrack — also one of Fox's imported innovations.

Along with a soundtrack, Fox wanted an image of equivalent grandeur, which is why he called his new 70mm widescreen process Grandeur — the impetus for *The Big Trail* was visual, not narrative. Fox had been personally financing development of the process since 1927 along with partner Harley Clarke, who was involved in the manufacture of 85 percent of the country's projection equipment.

In essence, Grandeur was 70mm film shot by a specially designed Mitchell camera and projected onto a larger than normal panoramic screen. 70mm film had been around since cinema's infancy, but had always been a novelty because of its unwieldy nature. *The Big Trail* would be Fox's third and final attempt at promoting 70mm widescreen production, a mini-boomlet that encompassed more than ten features made by six different movie companies (Fox, Warners, RKO, Paramount, Universal, and United Artists all experimented with 70mm films released between late 1929 and the end of 1930).

Grandeur was just one component of Fox's attempt to corner the American film industry. He owned Grandeur personally, also personally owned the cameras and film perforators that made the 70mm projection possible. While he was developing Grandeur, Fox was also buying the controlling shares in Metro-Goldwyn-Mayer and Loew's theaters from Marcus Loew's widow. The purchase was made mostly on credit, and was slowly unraveled by the 1929 stock market crash that led Fox into the financial abyss, but until then William Fox came closer than any single person ever has to financial and creative hegemony over an art form.

The studio's first release in Grandeur, *Happy Days,* had been favorably reviewed by the critics and made a profit of $132,000 on a budget of $584,000 — not really much more than the average Fox budget. In the spring of 1930, just as production of *The Big Trail* was getting under way, Fox ordered forty additional Grandeur cameras.

In most respects, Fox kept the possibilities for disaster to a minimum. The Grandeur cameras were reliable Mitchells, the film inside them was reliable Eastman Type Two Panchromatic. The main difficulties were in finding lenses that could do justice to the increased range — cameraman Arthur Edeson did tests of at least ten identical lenses before he found one that met the increased optical standards of the format — and a slight tendency of the 70mm stock to buckle. The latter was a serious problem — a jam of 70mm film not only damaged the camera but burned out the motor, and the middle of the Grand Tetons is no place to wait for a shipment of motors from the studio.

Walsh's crew encompassed two hundred people, with 185 wagons and ninety-three speaking parts. There were thirty-eight men in the camera crew alone. The roster was swelled by the fact that the studio was shooting Spanish, German, French, and Italian versions of the dialogue scenes, replacing the American actors with native casts. (The same long shots would be used in all the versions; the future director Fred Zinnemann wrote the dialogue for the German version.) All this resulted in an enormous production, with a five-month shooting schedule and a premiere that was scheduled to follow right on the heels of the last shot.

Raoul Walsh began shooting *The Big Trail* on April 20, 1930, and finished on August 20.* The first shot was of two hundred wagons, 1,700 head of cattle, and forty people breaking camp just before making their trek across the plains and the mountains. It had been precisely two days since Walsh showed up on location, and the shot was completed by 10:30 in the morning. Day after day, the cast and crew were up at 5 A.M., while the stockmen were up a half hour before that. Dinner was generally held off till about 8 P.M.

Almost the entire picture was shot on location, with the only movie artifice being some studio close-ups of Wayne riding, and a few matte shots. Initially, Wayne was afflicted with the *turistas* — diarrhea. For a few days, he was flat on his back and unable to work, but he was eventually moti-

* That August, the trade papers added up Fox's indebtedness and figured out that the company had $45 million in debt payments due within the next six months, not counting $7 million in creditor judgments. Receivership, not prosperity, was just around the corner.

vated by the suggestion that some other $75 a week actor could be enlisted to play the part.

Despite the loss of eighteen pounds, Wayne struggled to his feet and began working. "My first scene was carrying an actor named Tully Marshall, who was known to booze it up quite a bit," remembered Wayne. "He had a big jug in his hand in this scene, and I set him down and we have a drink with another guy. They passed the jug to me first, and I dug back into it. It was straight rotgut bootleg whiskey. I'd been puking and crapping blood for a week and now I just poured that raw stuff right down my throat. After the scene, you can bet I called him every kind of an old bastard." (In the film, Wayne never drinks from the jug; he must have been referring to an earlier take.)

Marguerite Churchill, the film's leading lady, didn't much like acting, and didn't like the movies at all; she retired soon after she married George O'Brien. In later years, their son Darcy O'Brien always noticed a strange undertone in his mother's behavior whenever she was around Wayne — the normally severe woman became slightly awkward and girlish. Darcy came to believe the two had had an affair during production of *The Big Trail*.

Besides the stars, there was the usual amount of pairing off between the crew and the locals, and a little bit more. Co-star Ian Keith was spending a great deal of time with Raoul Walsh's wife. One night there was a fight between Cheyenne Flynn, a cowboy, and Charlie Stevens, who was Geronimo's grandson. Flynn accused Stevens of cheating at cards, and Robert Parrish, a fourteen-year-old who was working as an extra, heard Flynn say, "I'm going to bite your ear off, you goddamn half-breed." There was the sound of a scuffle, and a diminishing whine as Stevens beat his retreat. The next morning, Parrish found a bite-sized piece of Stevens's ear covered with ants. Parrish put a piece of rawhide through the hunk and hung it as a decoration on his cabin door.

The Big Trail was one of those movies whose production replicates the experiences it depicts. When Walsh and company showed up in Yuma, Hal Evarts was amazed to find that an entire frontier town had been built and was ready to be photographed, complete with costumes and props for five hundred actors, bit players, and extras.

Walsh had audaciously cast a movie with leading actors who were all basically inexperienced. Tyrone Power Sr., who was playing the heavy, had been on the stage for decades and had appeared in silent movies but had never made a talkie. In June 1930, while on location, he wrote his son, the future matinee idol, that "The picture is coming along, and I do believe is even now considered by the experts in the studio to be a marvel. I am fortunate to be associated with such a fine type of screenplay. I find that the work has but very little to do with stage acting, as I know it. The scenes are strikingly brief, and take hours to *shoot.* The episodes do not follow each other, and sometimes I do not comprehend where we are. . . . Well, one day you will see it, and see what an infernal blackguard your father is, and hear him growl and roar over the plains and mountains." (Power collapsed and died in his son's arms soon after the film was completed.)

There were twenty-six days of shooting around Yuma, eight weeks around Jackson Hole, as well as Yellowstone and Sequoia national parks. For a riverboat scene, the crew moved to Sacramento. They traveled by rail: eight Pullman cars full of actors and crew, fed by two dining cars, preceded by twenty-one cars of baggage, props, wardrobe, wagons, horses, oxen — the paraphernalia needed to outfit a wagon train.

The movie carried an unusual sense of physical authenticity, a stark, semidocumentary flavor. A reporter who visited the set noted an even dozen cameras being used for the long shots, three of them Grandeur cameras. A mudhole sequence, with the wagons stuck amidst thunder, lightning, and torrential rains, was possible only because hydraulic pumps drew a million and a half gallons out of the Colorado River every day for seven days.

Hal Evarts was a trapper, guide, and surveyor of the Indian territory who knew the reality of the people and the times. Besides *The Big Trail,* Evarts also wrote William S. Hart's valedictory film, *Tumbleweeds.* He would die young in 1934 at the age of forty-seven, but he left behind a manuscript entitled "Log of The Big Trail" that is more or less a diary of the film's gestation and production.

Evarts was very much under the sway of Frederick Jackson Turner's doctrine of Manifest Destiny; just as our ancestors weren't afraid of Indians, Evarts wasn't afraid of overwriting: "A sturdy race of pioneers, they were not to be daunted by hardship or privations. Devastated by cholera, parched by the blazing sun, numbed by shrieking mountain blizzards, assailed by savages, tortured by thirst or soaked by flood, gaunt from hunger, the land-hungry horde marched doggedly down the path of the setting sun — no more to be deterred than swarming locusts."

Walsh and Arthur Edeson weren't able to see

94

rushes until they got back to Hollywood — they were shooting 500,000 feet of 70mm film flying blind. The filmmakers found that most of the difficulties of the new system fell on the director, because he had to pay more attention to the background action — "the depth of focus demanded by Grandeur makes the background an important part of the picture," noted Edeson.

Walsh compensated for his thin story by filling his movie with epic scenes: a buffalo stampede, an Indian attack on the wagon train, thunderstorms, blizzards, and, especially, the transport of cattle and wagons over the mountains, done just as the pioneers had done it sixty and seventy years before. At times, the film is less like a Hollywood movie than a beautifully composed newsreel circa 1870.

For that awe-inspiring sequence of getting over the mountains, Walsh and company decided on a cliff on Spread Creek. "Expert packers were up hours before daylight and lashed heavy camera equipment on horses and mules and packed them up the steep backbone of the ridge behind the cliff," wrote Hal Evarts. "Heavy sound trucks were windlassed up grades that no car could have made under its own power. Everything was ready. Then a storm blew in over the Tetons."

After several days of rain, Walsh finally got his scene. "Lowering wagons and stock down that cliff by log booms and pulleys was a tough job," wrote Evarts. "Once lowered, it required an hour or more to get a wagon from the bottoms to the top of the cliff again. Stock hands worked tirelessly. Hollywood extra women went down ropes hand over hand, risking their lives again and again. Later, certain of them were delighted to find that an extra five dollars a day had been added to their pay checks for the period they had put in on the cliff location."

By the time the cast and crew were done with the eight weeks of locations in and around Jackson Hole, they had been away from home for nearly four months — Walsh, Evarts, and a few others for a lot longer than that. After the last shot was taken in August, Walsh ordered the company bugler to play "Taps," and much of the company was dispersed, although a small second unit went up to Montana to shoot the buffalo sequence for two days. For the final sequence, Walsh took Wayne and a small crew to Sequoia National Park to shoot the conclusion, and with that the saga of the making of *The Big Trail* came to an end.

Wayne emerged from his trial by fire with reservations about Walsh — not as a director, but as a human being. On one of the last days of production, Walsh volunteered to stand in for Wayne in a scene that called for a close-up of Ian Keith getting punched. It was Keith's last shot of the film, and Walsh told Keith he'd feint with his left but would throw his right. During the take, Walsh feinted with his right and threw his left, sucker punching the actor because of his attentions to Walsh's wife.

On the train ride back to Hollywood, Wayne was playing cards when somebody came and told him he was needed in an adjacent car to break up a fight. Some of the stuntmen were beating an actor named Frederick Burton half to death.

It seems that Walsh believed that Burton was fooling around with either his wife — it would seem Mrs. Walsh got around — or his mistress.

Wayne was fuzzy on which woman was involved, but he remembered Burton's name, and he also remembered that Walsh had told the stuntmen to take care of his business. Wayne broke up the fight, but he never regained respect for a man who delegated his dirty work.

As the picture went into postproduction, everything seemed to be coming together for its young star. Fox executives forecast a gross of $4 million for *The Big Trail,* and they believed that John Wayne was going to become another Tom Mix; they lined up two more westerns for him: *Wyoming Wonder* and *No Favors Asked.*

The Big Trail opened in Hollywood at Grauman's Chinese on October 2, 1930. Grauman's forecourt was turned into a frontier encampment, and the short preceding the feature was a Movietone interview with George Bernard Shaw. In attendance for the premiere was an interesting conglomeration of notables from a variety of studios: Alexander Korda, Henry King, Victor McLaglen, Frank Borzage, Irving Thalberg, Marie Dressler, Louis B. Mayer, Stan Laurel and Oliver Hardy, Walter Huston, George Bancroft, Gary Cooper, Buddy Rogers, Lupe Velez, and Nancy Carroll. Also attending were Clyde Morrison, his new wife, and his son the movie star. Wayne's Sigma Chi fraternity from USC gathered to pay homage to their former brother at the premiere.

Fox flooded papers all over the country with publicity and photographs, and a lot of papers played along: "Sweeping Across 7 States . . . The story of a Love Enduring Untold Hardships . . . Fighting merciless savages . . . Imperiled by stampeded buffalo . . . Driving battered wagon trains across searing deserts . . . Starving . . . Thirsting . . . Lovers Fighting side by side . . . In the most glorious and thrilling adventure you ever witnessed." Mainly, the thrust of the ads was Manifest Destiny: "Thrills! Adventure! Romance! In 1001 gripping patterns woven from the bone and sinew of the heroic souls who bartered comfort, security and life itself for a share in the vision of the West."

Some of the ads were devoted to building up the new star, with a dramatic charcoal drawing of the young man and introductory copy: "John Wayne — Acclaimed by critics — hailed by the public."

Fox also decided to give its new star what might be called backdoor publicity. An article in *Motion Picture* magazine devoted most of its length to the dreary workaholic nature of young stars, who worked, studied, apprenticed, and lacked the colorful theatrical flourish of silent stars such as John Gilbert.

At the very end of the article, in a postscript, John Wayne brings up the rear as a prop man spotted by Raoul Walsh. "And — in a twinkling — the young man was under contract and was announced as the lead for the picture. Meet Mr. John Wayne, new motion picture celeb!"

Oddly, the ads and publicity didn't mention Grandeur, because the 70mm equipment was apparently installed only at Grauman's and New York's Roxy. Most of the country saw the film in the conventional 35mm version that was advertised as "All Talking Fox . . . The Most Important Picture Ever Produced."

Many critics rhapsodized: *Film Daily* said that the "impressive epic of the west has the romance, colorful background, action and thrills for universal appeal . . . John Wayne, as a frontier scout, [scores] big." "Photography soars to new and unscaled heights in Raoul Walsh's great epic of the west," wrote Elizabeth Yeaman in the Hollywood *Daily Citizen.* "John Wayne, a newcomer to the screen, is most prepossessing in appearance. In his buckskin suit, his long, lean physique presents a picturesque character. He was not an actor when Walsh selected him for this picture and did not become an actor in this picture. As a consequence, his every word and deed is outstanding for its naturalness and naïve force." *The New York Times* thought that the movie was as stimulating as John Ford's *The Iron Horse,* which it termed "that old silent film classic." (*The Iron Horse* was all of six years old at the time.)

Others weren't so sure about the picture or its star. Sime Silverman in *Variety* thought that the film "will do a certain business because of its magnitude, but it is not a holdover picture." Silverman also said that the filmmakers had erred by refusing to cast stars in the picture. "Young Wayne, wholly inexperienced, shows it but also suggests he can be built up."

Wayne traveled east to do some publicity for the picture dressed in his buckskin costume and holding his rifle. The photographers shot him as he posed in the doorway of his train compartment, holding a rifle in one hand and tipping his white hat in the other (in the film he wears a black hat). Nobody bothered to remind Wayne that he was wearing a wristwatch.

The Big Trail is a film of diametric opposites: awe-inspiring visuals and stilted acting. Wayne, twenty-two years old at the time the film began shooting, is a stunning physical specimen — tall, rangy, extremely handsome. The historian Jane Tompkins was struck by the difference between the Wayne of *The Big Trail* and the later, leathery Wayne: "The expression of the young John Wayne . . . is tender, and more than a little wistful; it is delicate and incredibly sensitive. Pure and sweet; shy, really and demure." The difference is that the young man was the authentic Duke Morrison; the older man was the hardened construct called John Wayne.

The young version is sometimes awkward in his line readings, and his reactions are occasionally over the top, as they often were in the first phase of his career. Nevertheless, for a kid who was lugging props a few months before, a kid with aptitude but little training or experience, he's not bad, and his star quality is fully present.

Most importantly, the film presents Wayne's screen character in rough sketch form. Despite his youth, Breck Coleman is tough and in charge, with a natural air of command that's accepted by the other characters. "You fight, that's life," he asserts at one point. "You stop fighting, that's death." It's a line that could have been dropped into *Red River, The Searchers, The Alamo,* or any major Wayne movie from the coming decades. If the western is the foundational myth of America in movie form, then Breck Coleman is the rough, occasionally halting foundation myth of John Wayne.

The young star's combination of physical strength and grace is already apparent. In his otherwise surly book about Wayne, Garry Wills was amazed by a throwaway shot in which Wayne comes up behind a woman, lifts her by her elbows,

100

flips her around so she's facing him, and hugs her. "He does not *throw* her, even slightly, and catch her after turning her; he just handles her as if she were an empty cardboard box, weightless and unresisting." Wayne's physical and emotional strength were always matched by an equivalent control and sense of purpose; at the beginning of his career or at its end, he never made a clumsy gesture.

Marguerite Churchill is attractive and professional but not distinguished, and Tyrone Power Sr. gives a roaring performance of pure ham — he makes Wallace Beery look subtle — that seems to have been the model for the Wolf in Disney's *The Three Little Pigs.* Ward Bond shows up on the periphery sporting a beard.

A passion for performance was clearly present in Wayne very early, but so was an uneasiness with his choice, the same uneasiness that would be present in the lives of other actors: Barrymore, Flynn, Holden, etc. Perhaps acting was an unsuitable job for a man? Wayne would spend the rest of his life insisting that he wasn't an actor, he was a reactor, which was really just a backdoor way of asserting his masculinity.

In truth, Wayne instinctively grasped something very close to the modern American concept of acting, which emphasizes behavior over the dialogue-based English tradition. Behavior works for all sorts of parts, but is insufficient when confronted with, say, Shakespeare, which has to be spoken. But Wayne's characters would always be defined as much by movement and attitude as by words.

Raoul Walsh's shots are much more carefully composed than most of his work; the dimensions of the 70mm frame mandate a lot of extras and background action, and the lenses don't let Walsh get any closer than a chest close-up. The lack of intimacy is compensated for by the majestic long shots. Generally, Walsh frames his shots so as to leave a third to a half of the frame open to landscape or background action.

Walsh's images made *The Big Trail* an authentic epic, but they weren't able to prevent it from being an authentic epic flop. It ran for eight weeks at the Chinese Theatre — a good run — but only two weeks at the Roxy. More importantly, *The Big Trail* underperformed in conventional 35mm showings in the rest of the country. Theater chains, having just expensively retooled for sound, weren't interested in expensively retooling yet again. Absent any widespread public demand for 70mm, it was easier to just let it wither away.

Unfortunately, the 35mm version of the film didn't fully show off the film's primary virtues — its physical re-creation of the pioneer experience. The mini-widescreen boom of 1929–1930 died quickly, and went underground until revived in the early 1950s as a means of luring audiences back to the movies after the erosion wrought by television. (More people have seen the widescreen version of *The Big Trail* since its rediscovery in 1986 than ever saw it in 1930.)

Winterset, Iowa, finally got to see the movie in January 1931. The *Madisonian* featured the story with the headline: "John Wayne, a Winterset Boy, in Talkies at the Iowa." The story continued, "John Wayne is the stage name of Marion Michael Morrison, as he was known to all his friends."

With a negative cost of $1.7 million, *The Big Trail* amassed only $945,000 in domestic rentals, another $242,000 in foreign rentals. The foreign language versions added $200,234 to the budget, and returned a tiny profit of $9,264. When the accountants had completed their grim task, it was clear that *The Big Trail* was a financial bloodbath — the loss topped $1 million.

As the film scholar William K. Everson noted, it's strange that Fox hadn't handed *The Big Trail* to John Ford, who had already demonstrated great expertise with westerns; it might not have been a better picture, but it assuredly would have been better organized, hence less expensive, hence more commercial. The failure of *The Big Trail* affected Raoul Walsh's career to the extent that Fox never again gave him that kind of budget. But the bulk of the movie's failure fell on its young star. *The Big Trail* was the last A picture John Wayne would make for nearly ten years, as Fox quickly canceled his prospective starring vehicles.

Wayne next showed up in a Fox programmer called *Girls Demand Excitement,* directed by the choreographer Seymour Felix, which began shooting in November 1930 after the failure of *The Big Trail* was apparent. Wayne's co-star was Virginia Cherrill, the leading lady of Chaplin's *City Lights.*

Wayne always regarded *Girls Demand Excitement* as the nadir of his professional life. "I was the fellow who was sour grapes, who played basketball to try to get the girls out of school. Well, I want to tell you something, I never tried to get a girl out of school in my life. I'd want them right there. . . . [Felix] had girls and boys sitting in trees and sticking their heads out of class windows and hugging each other. It was just so goddamn ridiculous that I was hanging my head."

Actually, *Girls Demand Excitement,* while innocuous, is not really as bad as Wayne thought; as Richard Roberts noted, had it been made a year earlier, or two years later, it would have made a good musical in the vein of *Good News.* Wayne plays a gardener who works for the family of the charisma-free Cherrill, a spoiled rich girl. In college, she and Wayne find themselves in a fraternity/sorority war. Wayne's performance is relaxed and without mannerisms.

Variety noted that "John Wayne is the same young man who was in *The Big Trail* and also is here spotted in a farce that does little to set him off." Wayne's next appearance for Fox came in May 1931, when he showed up in a small part in something called *Three Girls Lost.*

Wayne was slinking around Fox, embarrassed about the failure of *The Big Trail,* utterly demoralized by *Girls Demand Excitement,* when he ran into Will Rogers, the biggest star on the lot. Rogers saw that Wayne was down and asked what the trouble was. Wayne explained his situation, and the sensible Rogers told him, "You're working, aren't you? Just keep working."

Wayne always remembered that moment as "the best advice I ever got — just keep working and learning, however bad the picture . . . and boy, I made some lousy pictures." For the rest of his life Wayne always put more stock in being a working actor than in biding his time waiting for just the right part in just the right movie.

Three Girls Lost completed filming in mid-January of 1931, at which point Fox released the young actor. That made it official: John Wayne had been a white-hot new star at twenty-two, and he was washed up at twenty-three.

His time in the wilderness was just beginning,

but that time would give him an image, a personality, and a technique. That time would prove his salvation.

CHAPTER FOUR

After Fox dumped him, Wayne landed a six-month contract at Columbia. *Men Are Like That,* his first picture for the studio, was an adaptation of the Augustus Thomas play *Arizona,* which sounds like a western but isn't. Wayne's co-star was Laura La Plante, a charming leading lady of silent pictures who was equally charming in talkies. The script was by Robert Riskin, soon to start working with Frank Capra, the director the capable George B. Seitz.

Wayne plays a young football star/officer who loves the ladies then leaves them. The jilted La Plante marries Wayne's commanding officer, whereupon Wayne starts up with La Plante's sister. There are all sorts of racy possibilities, few of which are realized.

It's a mediocre movie, but it captures Wayne in the chrysalis stage of his career, without an outdoor background to accommodate his rough performance. The mannerisms that would become familiar — the wrinkling of the forehead, the pauses in the middle of his lines — are absent, although he does clench his jaw to indicate anger. His inexperience is mainly demonstrated by the fact that he doesn't really listen to the other actors, just waits for his cue.

The critics were harsher than they needed to be — the stink of *The Big Trail* was all over Wayne, and the dogs barked their condescension for a decade and more. *The New York Times* said that "[It is] hardly a film that can be characterized as good entertainment. . . . Miss La Plante is not convincing any more than John Wayne is in the part of Denton."

Columbia boss Harry Cohn must have been unimpressed, because for the rest of the contract Wayne was given roles that were little more than insults — a corpse in *The Deceiver,* billing beneath Buck Jones and Tim McCoy in a couple of westerns. Complicating Wayne's stay at Columbia was Cohn's belief that Wayne was having an affair with a young actress whom Cohn regarded as his personal property.

"It was a goddamned lie," Wayne told me, still furious more than forty years later. "I'd been brought up to respect older people, and he talked to me like I was a sewer rat." At one point, Cohn screamed at Wayne, "You keep your goddamned fly buttoned at my studio!" Wayne reacted to the unjust accusation with a lifelong slow burn. Cohn began a process of harassment calculated to provoke Wayne to break his contract — unless he was scheduled to work on a given day, he was barred from the studio.

But the cowboy star Buck Jones decided to use Wayne in spite of Cohn. Jones would invite the younger man to go boating around Catalina whenever Jones was on the outs with his wife. Jones and Wayne had something in common — they had both worked for John Ford. Wayne never forgot the gesture that came at a time when he was increasingly desperate and thinking about trying boxing, because the movie business just seemed too tough. Buck Jones spent the rest of his life in B westerns, and Wayne always remembered him with affection: "Buck Jones was one of the real heroes of our business. He went back into that [Cocoanut Grove nightclub fire in] Boston three times after people and the fourth time he didn't come back out. But there's no memorial to him, there's no thought [for him]. Ours is the business of what did you do for me today . . . they certainly forgot old Buck."

Within a single year, Fox had washed its hands of Wayne and he was let go at Columbia. If he wanted to keep working, if he wanted to maintain any standing at all in the eyes of Josie's parents, he had little choice except to become one of the all-purpose jobbing actors haunting Poverty Row, the area around Sunset Boulevard and Gower Street. Toward the end of 1931, Wayne signed to do three serials for Mascot, a small company run by a man named Nat Levine.

The salary on offer was $2,000 — not $2,000 apiece, but $2,000 for all three serials, $2,000 for six-day weeks, twelve- to sixteen-hour days for the eighteen to twenty-one days it usually took to make one of Levine's serials. To get the films made on time, two directors worked simultaneously, one on interiors, one on exteriors. Working for Mascot meant that you weren't paid for acting, you were paid for endurance and for the willingness to work cheap.

The money was terrible, but it was the pit of the Depression, and Wayne was damaged goods twice over. There was only one catch: it was Levine's

108

intention to start shooting a serial called *Shadow of the Eagle* the very next day. Was Wayne willing to start shooting tomorrow, for that money and not a dime more?

The next day at four in the morning, Levine picked up Wayne in his chauffeur-driven Packard. He had thoughtfully brought breakfast so they could save some time. While Wayne ate his danish, Levine outlined the story of the serial Wayne was about to start shooting as soon as the sun came up.

"We were asked to be on location *before* sunup, so that shooting could start as soon as the first rays of the sun broke over the horizon," remembered one Mascot veteran. "We would sit there, poised — the cameras ready, performers on their horses. When the earliest rays broke across the valley, the director would jump up and yell 'Roll 'Em,' and away we'd go." When the sun went down, flares would be lit and held by crew members so close-ups could be shot.

Mascot had been formed by Levine in 1927, when he was only twenty-eight years old. He had been the personal secretary for theater magnate Marcus Loew, then went to work for the distributor of the Felix the Cat cartoons. Levine operated on the states-rights fringe of the movie business and specialized in making features for $30,000, serials for $40,000. As with everybody on Poverty Row, Mascot was thinly capitalized. Much of Levine's running debt was absorbed by Herbert Yates, who ran Consolidated Film Industries, the company that did the lab work for Mascot as well as most other Poverty Row outfits.

Mascot's headquarters were above a contractor's warehouse on Santa Monica Boulevard, just down

109

the street from Hollywood Memorial (now Hollywood Forever) Cemetery. To keep costs down, the only generators used were for cameras; Levine didn't use lights for exteriors, only reflectors. In fact, he didn't even have a studio of his own until 1933, when he leased the bankrupt Mack Sennett lot in North Hollywood (today it's CBS Television City). Levine rented everything, including his sound equipment, which he got for so much per day from Walt Disney.

Shadow of the Eagle, Wayne's first Mascot serial, began shooting in December 1931, with Wayne playing a stunt pilot working for a small carnival who tries to clear the name of the owner, who has been a father figure. Wayne had gained some assurance since *The Big Trail,* although considering the caliber of the filmmaking around him it wasn't really necessary.

Except for the credits, there's no music — too expensive — and a lot of the exteriors have no sound at all, which saved the company money because they only rented the sound equipment for interiors. There were very few second or third takes.

In the serial's final chapter, Wayne trips and nearly falls, but director Ford Beebe keeps the footage. Wayne remembered one day when they didn't finish until midnight, after Beebe had made 114 shots. They had to be ready to go just eight hours later, so most of the company slept in their cars rather than drive back home.

The cast of *Shadow of the Eagle* is notable only for the presence of Yakima Canutt, who would become Hollywood's greatest stuntman, not to mention a close friend and working companion of Wayne's, and Billy West, the leading Chaplin imitator of silent films, here playing the small part of a clown.

Canutt had been hired to double Wayne in addition to playing a henchman. Canutt called a friend who had already worked with the star to find out what kind of man he was. "You'll like him," said the friend. "He's really great. And when it comes to ribbing, he'll hold his own — even with you."

The practical jokes began early. An actor named Bud Osborne told Wayne that Canutt was a spy for Nat Levine — everything that went on would be reported back to the producer. For a few days, Canutt pretended to be writing in a little black book, and Wayne reacted by giving him dirty looks and keeping his distance.

Then Osborne took Wayne behind the set for a quick drink, and Canutt came around the opposite corner. Canutt checked the time and wrote in his little black book. Wayne lost his temper and went for him, but Osborne and a few others grabbed him and let him in on the joke. Wayne thought it was hilarious, and the picture proceeded as smoothly as it could considering the endless hours necessary to get the picture shot on schedule.

Wayne remembered that it was the shared pain of the Mascot experience that sealed his friendship with Canutt. One terrible day, the company worked till midnight shooting dialogue scenes at the studio, then had a 5 A.M. call at a rock quarry in the San Fernando Valley. Wayne had no car and the buses didn't run that early, so he asked Levine for help. Levine let him have a Chevy convertible to drive home for a few hours sleep in order to guarantee that he'd be on location on schedule.

When he got to the rock quarry, it was still dark,

but one man had beat him to the location and had built a fire. Wayne went over and knelt down by the fire to get warm. "It doesn't take very long to spend all night out here," said Yakima Canutt. Canutt pegged their friendship from those minutes of mutually shared weariness.

Making these serials was the movie equivalent of a forced march, and Wayne was always slightly embarrassed about them. They were more humiliation than he preferred to remember, and more exhaustion than he expected to endure. On one of the Mascot serials, he worked for twenty-six straight hours — not abnormal for a low-end production in the pre-union days.

Wayne's other two Mascot serials — *The Three Musketeers* (shot in April 1932, released April 1933) and *The Hurricane Express* (shot in July 1932, released August 1932) — represent a slight upgrade from *Shadow of the Eagle.* Among the actors in *The Three Musketeers* are silent stars Jack Mulhall, William Desmond, Raymond Hatton, and future star Lon Chaney Jr., working under his real name of Creighton Chaney. Wayne's leading lady was Ruth Hall, who would later marry the cinematographer Lee Garmes.

The Hurricane Express, while crude in terms of production, has considerable charm, as it divides its time between the air, the railroads, and the dusty roads of Depression-era America — it's a movie without a lot of pavement. Wayne slugs his way through a small army, usually by the simple expedient of picking someone up over his head like a sack of grain and heaving him in the general direction of his adversaries. He performs the twelve chapters of the serial dressed in one rather well-cut gray business suit — his entire wardrobe.

One of the primary locations was a railroad station in Saugus, north of Los Angeles, where a hobo was cooking stew by the side of the tracks. It smelled good, so Wayne went over and had breakfast with him. Canutt remembered that the company "got the biggest kick out of it." At one point, the action moves to Bronson Canyon, a mile or so from Hollywood, where, twenty-five years later Wayne would perform a scene with considerably more emotional and spiritual impact than anything in *The Hurricane Express:* the climax of *The Searchers.*

Independent serials of the 1930s are generally a sluggish lot, but Mascot's serials run, jump, leap, and fight more than they talk. The miniatures are good too. Levine seems to have been instrumental in instituting the practice of cheater episodes, that is, a recap episode that would be made up largely of footage from earlier chapters, or, failing that, simply recycling footage — Chapter 11 of *The Hurricane Express* uses some footage for at least the second or third time. As for the star, Wayne's look of surprise rivals Jimmy Finlayson's double take in Laurel and Hardy comedies.

Wayne remembered Nat Levine as entertaining but incredibly cheap. "We had a party one day, lots of guests and everything," Wayne reminisced. "Levine had a diamond ring on, and, as a gag, [stuntmen] tried to take it off him. Well, the son of a bitch put up one hell of a fight and ended the whole party. He wasn't going to give up that diamond ring. And I knew he was close with a buck; if they'd come to me first, I could have told them not to bother."

In the midst of fulfilling his Mascot deal, Wayne continued to pick up whatever work he could. In

113

April and May of 1932, he worked ten days at Paramount on a B picture called *Lady and Gent.* Wayne was billed fifth, behind George Bancroft, Wynne Gibson, Charles Starrett, and James Gleason. His salary was $150 a week — Bancroft got $6,600.

In the middle of 1932, Wayne signed a contract with Leon Schlesinger, who had an in at Warner Bros. Schlesinger had been the principal of Pacific Title and Art, which made titles for silent movies. When sound came in, the market for titles shrank in a hurry, and Schlesinger began exploring ways to make money from talkies. By 1930 he was buying cartoons from Hugh Harman and Rudolf Ising for $4,500 apiece and selling them to Warners for $5,000 to $6,000 apiece. He proposed to do the same thing with westerns starring John Wayne.

Schlesinger produced six Wayne westerns, made in as few as three days apiece, which was possible only because the action sequences were built around silent footage originally shot for Ken Maynard's silent westerns at First National, which Warner Bros. now owned.

Again, Harry Cohn tried to blackball Wayne, calling Warners' Sid Rogell and telling him that Wayne was an unreliable drunk. Wayne suggested to Rogell that Cohn say that in front of him so he could "bust his face wide open." Rogell called Wayne back to say that they could make a deal. "What happened?" asked Wayne. "He wouldn't say it in front of you," said Rogell.

Wayne's understandable grudge against Cohn grew till it enveloped all of Columbia Pictures. It was Wayne's first experience with arbitrary cruelty. "I had only dealt with nice people all my life," he told me. In later years, Wayne took great satisfaction in never making another movie for Columbia. "There were plenty of opportunities," he said. "Harry would come and say, 'Duke, you'd be just great in this — what do you want?' I'd say, 'Gosh, Harry, I just haven't got the time.' That's the only delight I ever had with that guy."

Using the big action scenes from the Maynard films — among the best series westerns of the silent era — and combining them with Warners' well-appointed and detailed interior sets, which were far beyond the budgetary reach of most B western producers, meant that the Schlesinger pictures had an unusual production gloss, even if the directors were run-of-the-mill B movie talents.

The six Schlesinger pictures paid Wayne $850 each, more money for less work than he was getting from Nat Levine. They have more stock footage than the norm, but they also have tighter scripts and better casts. In *Ride Him Cowboy,* the first of the series to be released (shot in July 1932, released a month later), the comic relief is in the capable hands of Mack Sennett veteran Harry Gribbon, while the great Henry B. Walthall, D. W. Griffith's Little Colonel from *The Birth of a Nation,* plays the heroine's father. (He also shows up in another Schlesinger quickie, *Somewhere in Sonora,* as does Paul Fix, who would figure importantly in Wayne's career.)

There are welcome touches of lunatic humor — a jury walks in one door to deliberate and immediately files right back out another door. The slaphappy overtones happen too consistently to be accidental; in *The Telegraph Trail,* Yakima Canutt plays an Indian named High Wolf.

Any action footage outside of a basic fistfight derives from the Maynard silents, but the filmmakers working on the Warners films were always trying, and the films are full of little grace notes unusual for the product and the period. In *Haunted Gold,* the 274th variation on *The Cat and the Canary,* there are animated bats in the credits that foretell Schlesinger's lengthy career as the executive producer of Warners' cartoon department.

Despite the presence of some medium-appalling darky humor in *Haunted Gold,* the Schlesinger pictures are always at least passable, and they're very well shot by Ted McCord and Nick Musuraca. (Theory: the cameraman was more important to B westerns than the director.) Mainly, they avoid that unmistakable overtone of dead air that permeates so much Poverty Row product, because they have the trademarked Warner Bros. zip and charm, which was also a feature of the ads.

"Here he is again," announced one ad, over a big, smiling face of Wayne. "ACTION gallops across the screen," said another. "The most daring of the cowboy stars and the world's brainiest horse give you more thrills, scares, surprises in five minutes than you usually see in a whole picture." Throughout the six Schlesinger productions, in all of which "Duke" the white stallion gets second billing, Wayne was costumed in clothes similar to Ken Maynard's to make the matching of shots easier. And yes, Duke the horse was named after his rider.

The internal evidence of the films suggests that Wayne was continuing to work on his craft. He's far less stiff in front of the camera than he was only two years before. The boyishness is still there — he would never really lose that — and so is a gentleness that was a primary component of his personality in these years, and the quality that appealed to John Ford. His delivery of dialogue is more natural, and he's far more comfortable in scenes with actresses than he had been before.

That said, while Wayne can hold his own with the other younger actors in these pictures, he's unable to compete with Henry B. Walthall, although the frenetic pace of production would probably have defeated anybody but the most seasoned old pros.

For Wayne, these pictures would always be a trial by fire, something he had to do, and he took little pride in them. "I made $250 a week," he said one day while looking at stills from this period. (Actually, $850 per picture.) "I was the star of these damn pictures. John Wayne this and that. $250 a week. No makeup man. I'd bring my car out there and put on the headlights at 4:30 in the morning and get a mirror and put on my own makeup. That was it.

"I'd change my clothes, read the lines, change my clothes, read some more lines. We'd start before dawn, using flares to light close-ups. When the sun came up, we'd do some medium-range shots. In full daylight, we'd do the distance shots, following the sun up one side of the hill and down the other side. It didn't matter who was the director. They had no chance and I had no chance. They could sell five reels of film with me riding a horse."

The mainly juvenile audiences of B westerns mandated dialogue that wasn't much more complicated than "Indians! Circle the wagons! Get the women and children under cover!!" (actual dialogue), but within those limitations Wayne was gaining ground in terms of his skills, even if he was losing ground in terms of his collaborators.

On the other hand, the environment was to his liking. "Nothing is so discouraging to an actor than to have to work for long hours upon hours in brightly lighted interior sets," he would write in a guest column around this time. "On western locations, which are generally three or four hundred miles from Los Angeles up in the mountains, we arise at five in the morning, then [spend] practically the entire day in the saddle — running, riding, chasing and jumping."

His enthusiasm for a lifestyle he regarded as intrinsically healthy derived at least partially from John Ford, who grew to love making westerns for many reasons, among them the fact that they got him away from a town he was ambivalent about, and from people in that town whom he wasn't at all ambivalent about: those who tried to tell him how to make pictures.

While Wayne was grinding out the westerns, his contract with Schlesinger got him a few bits at Warners. (He had eleven features and one serial released in 1933 alone.) The Busby Berkeley musical *Footlight Parade* uses a quick shot of Wayne in a film within the film before the musical numbers start. And he played a couple of tiny parts for a tough young director named William Wellman, with whom he would collaborate far more rewardingly twenty years later. In Wellman's *Central Airport,* Wayne has no billing and no lines, but he does get a chance to dive into the studio tank and drown. In *College Coach,* Wayne walks up to Dick Powell and wishes him luck.

Also at Warners, there was another brief bit supporting Douglas Fairbanks Jr. in *The Life of Jimmy Dolan,* and a better part in the rough-and-ready

Baby Face as one of the men Barbara Stanwyck beds and discards on her way to the penthouse.

The trajectory was unmistakable: Wayne could headline B westerns made for undiscerning audiences of kids or rural roughnecks, but for A or even A minus pictures, he was fit only for throwaways or bits.

Near the tail end of his westerns for Leon Schlesinger, Wayne played the lead in a picture called *His Private Secretary,* which was made by a company called Screencraft Productions somewhere in the darkest reaches of Poverty Row. The production manager was the young Sam Katzman, in the early stages of a forty-year career that would never be even tangentially involved with a good movie.

The plot of *His Private Secretary* is pretty strong for a five-day wonder — girl-crazy rich boy goes to work for his dad, gets fired, meets and marries a smart young girl, who goes to work for the father and earns his trust. Father and son are reconciled through the young wife. With a bit more polish it could have worked for an A picture at MGM, with an upmarket cast: Robert Montgomery, Joan Crawford, Lewis Stone.

What's surprising is that for the first time, Wayne is *good:* charming, naturalistic, and believable, even though he's working far out of his comfort zone. If anybody in the industry had seen *His Private Secretary,* it might have provided a different path for a young actor already being typecast in action films. But the problem with Poverty Row was that nobody gave you points for effort. The *Motion Picture Herald* sniffed, "There are no outstanding names with which to decorate the marquee, the two leading players being Evalyn

Knapp and John Wayne, familiar names but that is all." The romantic drama was a brief respite between stints at Mascot.

But before that, there was marriage.

When Josie and Duke finally announced their engagement in December 1932, there were twelve lines about the upcoming nuptials in *The New York Times.* Wayne got second billing.

They were married on June 24, 1933, at the Bel Air home of Loretta Young. The ceremony was performed by a priest from the Church of the Immaculate Conception, and Wayne signed the certificate as "Marion Mitchell Morrison." A couple of new friends named Henry Fonda and Grant Withers also attended. The best man and the ushers were all drawn from Wayne's Sigma Chi fraternity brothers.

Josie was, of course, a serious Catholic, but Loretta Young never let her religion get in the way of a location affair. Years later, Wayne was at the Beverly Wilshire Hotel. He looked around and noted that he hadn't been there in a long time, since soon after his marriage, when he and Josie had accompanied Young to a lunch/dance. They were the beards for Spencer Tracy, who was having a torrid fling with Young despite his status as a married man.

As was his wont in this period, Tracy got drunk, which meant he got belligerent. Neither Wayne nor Josie was interested in going dancing with him. They got a room and Wayne dragged Tracy upstairs and slung him on the bed. Wayne was bending over, taking Tracy's shoes off, when Tracy reared up and sucker punched Wayne in the mouth.

"Split my lip and, needless to say, it hurt," remembered Wayne. "Jesus Christ, my lip's all puffed up, my nose is bleeding, the drunken bastard gives me a Sunday punch while I'm taking his shoes off.

"What followed was a reflex action on my part, but I'm not sorry about it. I really busted him one. I put him to sleep for good. He probably woke up about two days later. I didn't know and I didn't give a damn. All I knew is that he was out. I closed the door and went to the dance."

Wayne and his new wife moved to a three-room apartment in Hancock Park that was close to her parents' house, so they could be within her social circle. As Wayne and Josie set up housekeeping, he told her in no uncertain terms that "I don't do light bulbs. I make enough money to call professionals." He associated being handy around the house with the poverty that had enveloped him as a child, something he had neither the desire nor the intention to replicate. He was done with plumbing and yardwork, and always would be.

Children soon followed: Michael in 1934, Antonia (Toni) in 1936, Patrick in 1939, and Melinda in 1940. Although he loved his wife, Wayne was not immune to the temptations endemic to the movie business. His friend Paul Fix would say that Wayne was never a "mainstream womanizer. . . . Duke would occasionally stray, but he always felt so guilty about cheating on Josephine, he usually broke it off as quick as he could. He just wasn't immoral enough to, let's say, 'put it about,' the way a lot of Hollywood leading men did."

Wayne came from an insecure blue-collar background, and he was clearly marrying up. At the

121

same time, Josie was marrying down, which would prove to be a critical problem for the marriage. Yakima Canutt would come to believe that the marriage was problematic from the beginning because Josie "didn't respect John's profession."

Wayne was beginning to assemble the core group of cronies that would surround him for the rest of his life — Ford, Canutt, Paul Fix, a dozen others. Besides Ford's yacht, their most frequent meeting place was the Hollywood Athletic Club, which also attracted such hard drinkers as Frank Borzage and Johnny Weissmuller.

The producer Paul Malvern promoted a western series starring Wayne at Monogram. It was a long way down from Warners, and even a distance from Columbia. Monogram was usually a place where actors ended up, not started out, but work was work.

This time, twelve pictures were planned (there were eventually sixteen), and they came to be known as the Lone Star westerns. The Lone Stars, while not as entertaining as the six Warner Bros. westerns, have had a far wider audience because of their public domain status and their narrative lunacy — they've probably been in continual circulation longer than anything outside of the twelve two-reel comedies Charlie Chaplin made at Mutual in 1916–1917.

None of the Lone Stars is really good, except by the bizarre standards of 1930s B westerns. The sets consist of sparsely populated dusty towns for the locations and stage flats for the interiors. But there's little or no stock footage, and making an hour of action footage in five or six stringently budgeted days means that you're not shooting a movie so much as you're shooting a schedule.

The supporting casts are mostly has-beens and never-wases — Reed Howes, who backs up Wayne in *The Dawn Rider,* was a busted Arrow collar man from the 1920s. Most of the pictures were directed by Robert N. Bradbury, whose son Bob had been a pal of Duke's in Glendale. Bradbury had an eye for good locations and liked flashy little camera accents such as whip pans.

Bradbury also wrote a lot of the scripts, and he had a vivid, if shopworn imagination — the Lone Star westerns offer mad killers in florid disguises, secret passages, and a plethora of mistaken identities — anybody found kneeling by a dead body is automatically assumed to be the killer.

Malvern's great gift was in spotting talent that was willing to work cheap. His cameraman was a young man named Archie Stout, who had been working at Paramount shooting remakes of old Jack Holt silents for Henry Hathaway. (Stout would go on to shoot the first several years of the Hopalong Cassidy series, and was eventually hired by John Ford and William Wellman.)

Malvern, who would go on to a career at Universal, where he produced horror pictures and some of the lucrative Maria Montez/Jon Hall Arabian nights movies, also had an eye for good character actors such as George "Gabby" Hayes. Yakima Canutt is in most of the pictures, usually as the dog heavy★ and to double Wayne.

★ B westerns had a rigorous pecking order. The heavy was usually the saloon owner or the banker, a slick operator, often with a mustache, who could operate behind a veil of assumed decency. The dog heavy was the lead henchman, and was called the dog heavy

In many of the films, Canutt doubles Wayne chasing Canutt, i.e., Canutt chases himself. (Canutt's bald spot gives away his presence when he's doubling Wayne in fight scenes; so does his square body.) During one picture Malvern forgot to hire a second stuntman for an action sequence that involved Canutt, doubling Wayne, leaping from a running horse onto a railroad handcar. If Canutt doubled Wayne, there was nobody to double Canutt as the bad guy on the handcar.

Wayne looked at Canutt, and Canutt looked at Wayne. They exchanged clothes, and Canutt doubled Wayne while Wayne doubled Canutt — Canutt made the transfer from the horse to the handcar with Wayne catching him, and they started fighting in a long shot. The long shot completed, they changed clothes and went back to playing themselves.

It was typical of the can-do spirit that animated B picture production of the era. "It was good experience," Wayne would say with the benefit of hindsight. "In westerns, you meet a hardy bunch of characters. There is no jealousy on such pictures. You can't steal a scene in a quickie — there just isn't enough time. Everybody is pulling for the picture. . . . [It was] get the scene on film and get on to the next scene. They were rotten pictures, most of them. But they taught me three things: How to work. How to take orders, and how to get on with the action."

As far as Wayne was concerned, Canutt's only

---

because he was a crude, unshaven lout who would kick a dog or, alternately, hurt a horse in the beginning of the picture, firmly establishing his bad guy bona fides.

drawback was that he wasn't a good actor, although the stuntman ended up influencing the young actor through reverse example. Canutt also seems to have served as a sort of unwitting mentor for Wayne's screen character. Just before he died, Wayne recalled how Canutt would react when one of the wranglers or stuntmen got rambunctious off-screen.

"I saw a couple of them chivvi and challenge him and watched his reactions. When in real trouble he had a half humorous glint in his eye and talked very straight and very direct to his opponent. You had a feeling that there was a steel spring waiting to be released; but when he played a heavy in my pictures he made grimaces and raised his voice and snarled. I tried to explain to him that his *real* attitude was better than his *reel* attitude for motion pictures. He didn't react to it, but I did; and I copied his *real* attitude when I face odds before the magic box."

Canutt was a godsend in all sorts of ways — a fiend for work, a good man to have on a film set, and big enough to effectively double the star. But the influence went only so far. Over the years there were various intimations that Wayne had also copied Canutt's walk, which anyone who knew Canutt, let alone watched him in the movies, knew was ridiculous. As Wayne pointed out, "We don't have anywhere near similar strides."

A young man named Paul Fix was around too, playing shiftless heavies or weaklings. Fix had been in the movies since the silent days, and over nearly a sixty-year career proved he could play just about anything. Wayne was only too conscious of his own shortcomings — he was a star before he was an actor — and asked Fix to work with him as an acting coach. Late in his life, Wayne said that "Paul Fix is the first actor who gave me any confidence."

Fix said that Wayne's problem was a pervasive feeling of awkwardness. "His main trouble," remembered Fix in 1969, "was with those big hands of his. He didn't know what to do with them. And he had some bad mannerisms, like always wrinkling his brow.

"My job, other than playing the role I was signed for, was to watch Wayne. We worked out a set of hand signals so I could tell him what he was doing wrong without the director knowing. . . . Duke was not what you would call a natural actor, but he learned. And when he learned, he mastered one of the hardest things of all — to act natural. And he does it so well that a lot of people still don't know he's acting."

Wayne had grown up on the films of Tom Mix and Buck Jones, so he knew the western genre and its conventions, and he wasn't crazy about some of them. "I felt many of the Western stars of the twenties and thirties were too goddamn perfect. They never drank nor smoked. They never wanted to go to bed with a beautiful girl. They never had a fight. A heavy might throw a chair at them, and they just looked surprised and didn't fight back in this spirit. They were too goddamn sweet and pure to be dirty fighters.

"Well, I wanted to be a dirty fighter if that was the only way to fight back. If somebody throws a chair at you, hell, you pick up a chair and belt him right back. I was trying to play a man who gets dirty, who sweats sometimes, who enjoys really kissing a gal he likes, who gets angry, who fights clean whenever possible but will fight dirty if he has to. You could say I made the Western hero a roughneck."

Wayne was exaggerating, but not by much. William S. Hart in particular played a character who embodied the title of one of his early films: *The Knight of the Trail.* The next generation of cowboys presented by the major studios — Tom Mix and Buck Jones at Fox, Tim McCoy at MGM — provided less behavioral gloss to go with the increased production gloss. The films from the B studios were even scruffier.

There isn't room for much acting in the Lone Stars, so Wayne has to rely on his physicality. In *The Lawless Frontier,* Wayne flips off a surfboard he's riding through a sluice run, hops up, grabs a railroad tie passing overhead, raises his legs, and crawls through. The action is slightly under-cranked to make it seem faster than it really was, but Douglas Fairbanks couldn't have executed the move any more gracefully. (Wayne also rode a sluice run in *The Lucky Texan* — B movies didn't let a good visual gimmick lie fallow for long.)

The Lone Stars were released every six weeks or so over a year and a half, from December 1933 (*Sagebrush Trail*) to July 1935 (*Paradise Canyon*). Their budgets were starvation level: $8,000 to $12,000, with the star getting $1,000 to $1,500 a picture — a major upgrade from the $2,000 he got from Mascot for three months' work making three serials. The Lone Stars have energy and they showcase the unassuming clarity of their star; dramatically, they have a ratty charm deriving from eccentric narrative asides.

The first reel of *The Lucky Texan* is exactly like a play — a dark and stormy night, with nervous honeymooners at a lonely hotel. In the same movie, Yakima Canutt tries to bulldog a burro and is momentarily overmatched. You can hear the crew laughing at the result. George "Gabby" Hayes plays an old actor who used to star in *Charley's Aunt,* which means he has to dress up in drag. He turns out to be rather fetching, and even shows some leg.

The Lone Stars that weren't written by Robert Bradbury were written by Lindsley Parsons, Duke Morrison's old surfing buddy. The intervening years had seen Parsons become, first, a newspaper reporter, then an unemployed newspaper reporter. He was driving down Sunset Boulevard when he saw a sign announcing "Trem Carr Productions." Parsons knew Carr as a friend of his mother-in-law and decided it couldn't hurt to make a pitch.

He introduced himself to Carr and asked if he needed a publicity man. Carr said that he had just started Monogram Pictures, and they could indeed use a publicity man, especially one who could draw the ads. "Are you an artist?" he asked Parsons.

Parsons said he was. He promptly went home to get some sketches done by his uncle, who actually was an artist. Parsons got the job, figuring Monogram would do until something better opened up. Nothing better opened up, so he spent his life in the movie business.

One day Parsons went into Paul Malvern's office where a screenwriter was complaining he had completely run out of ideas. Parsons rushed back to his office and batted out a four-page synopsis. "Later on sometimes I'd have to dictate these Waynes," Parsons told Leonard Maltin, "so [my wife would] say, 'Well, you sound just like John

Wayne.' And I said, 'Well, that's [who] I'm writing for. . . . One of the reasons we got along so well was 'cause I could write dialogue he could talk."

Parsons found that screenwriting paid better than publicity — Malvern paid him between $100 and $200 per script. It was the Depression, Parsons had a wife and child, so an extra hundred dollars for a week's work was a godsend.

Parsons concurred with Paul Fix's judgment about Wayne's lack of self-confidence. "We'd be out on location, he'd do a dialogue sequence and he'd just cuss himself out terribly. He'd go off behind a rock and talk about how lousy he was."

Many of these early B westerns were shot at Kernville, a little western town that eventually ended up at the bottom of a man-made lake. Failing that, they were made at Newhall, and the cast and crew would arrive before sunrise to build a bonfire to warm up the cameras so that the crew could start shooting the minute the sun came up over the hill — you couldn't run cold cameras.

Lindsley Parsons remembered Robert Bradbury as "good enough to get by," but if you were still middle-aged on Poverty Row, you were going to grow old there as well. The money was from hunger, but Parsons and everybody else tried to make the pictures as good as they could be, given the exigencies.

"Certainly I tried to get something different in the scripts," said Parsons.

I would walk around the lot and try to find something distinctive. In one case, they had an old 1914 Ford touring car and I said, "I got to write this into a John Wayne picture." I went in to see Paulie [Malvern] and I told him the opening I had in mind — John Wayne's riding along on a desert trail someplace and then this old prospector stumbles and just looks like he's at the bitter end and he says "Look, my Sally is over the hill and I've gotta have some water."

So John Wayne says sure, takes his canteen to go over the hill and Sally is the Ford. . . .

You had to think of something different. Sometimes it was a novel beginning. John Wayne stopping by a creek and taking a drink of water out of the creek and somebody sticks a gun in his back. Where do you go from there? Another one, where he drives up in front of a small town saloon, there's practically nobody on the street, he hears the sound of a mechanical piano in there, and he goes in — everybody's dead. . . . You cut to the wall and there are two eyes watching him. Good opening. All you needed was a good opening to get those things started off.

Wayne was bruised by failure and insecurity, but Parsons remembered him as soldiering on despite feeling "pretty low." At that point, Wayne's primary goal was to keep working — he too was a married man, and his son, Michael, was the first of what would become a large brood. "I was tall, curly haired, shy and a clod-kicker," Wayne remembered from the vantage point of 1952. "I could say, 'Reach for the sky, mister!' pretty well, but beyond that I was the leading character in the nightmares of [acting teacher and character actress] Madame Ouspenskaya."

"He wasn't trying to perfect his acting," said Lindsley Parsons. "He had no confidence in his acting, but he was coming across as a personality. . . . He had a steady home at Monogram and

130

Lone Star and we became very well acquainted. I attended the christening of his first son, and we both got very drunk together. . . . We got loaded quite a few times; if you could get hold of whiskey you drank it. In fact, we had our own bootlegger and I still remember his phone number: Gladstone 8000."

Parsons remembered that Wayne would be very formal at times, even with his peer group. He always called Parsons "Mr. Parsons" when there were other people around, and "Lin" when they were alone. They only quarreled "when we were drinking, which was quite often. I used to delight in teasing him and arguing with him. He had adopted this very strict, Republican, conservative attitude even in those days and I would fight with him. I know that he wanted to hit me but he couldn't because I was so small. I can remember one time we were coming back on the bus with a bunch of the [Monogram] exchange men and he got so mad at me he picked me up and put me up on the luggage rack on the bus."

Wayne wasn't the worst actor among the B movie cowboys, but he wasn't the best either. He was taller than Bob Steele — everybody was — but at this stage in their careers, Steele was a better actor. Wayne was sexier than Hoot Gibson, but Gibson was a better rider. What Wayne had was charm, great good looks, a wonderful smile, and the beginnings of technical and physical assurance to go with the assertiveness that was written into the characters, if not always the performances.

Throughout these pictures, Wayne is always at least adequate, and sometimes more than that. The very real physicality is there — in *West of the*

Divide, he does a backward somersault — and so is a strength of personality fascinating to watch in embryo form. He's occasionally gauche but always sincere and winning; he's not a natural actor by any means, but he is a natural star, and you can watch him working at both polishing and transcending his innate gifts. He's incrementally assembling the pieces, working on presentation, working on movement, working on dialogue, and always being a good co-worker.

"He was pretty tall and skinny," remembered Cecilia Parker, who was the leading lady in one of the Lone Stars for $125 a few years before she became part of the Andy Hardy ensemble at MGM. "I liked him. He was a real nice young man. He was tall and slender and he was on his honeymoon — he had just gotten married. He was late to work many mornings — he drove a little Ford convertible. But he was a real nice young man.

"He was a natural, a typical western gentleman. Very easy to work with. And yet he had enough — I don't know how to put it — moxie to make you believe that he could take care of a situation."

The picture Parker worked on was called *Riders of Destiny* — the picture where Wayne plays "Singin' Sandy" Saunders, who is, a bystander informs us, "the most notorious gunman since Billy the Kid." Aside from the narrative incongruity of a singing gunfighter, there was a technical problem: Wayne couldn't sing. Nevertheless, Singin' Sandy strides down the street while Wayne mouths a song whose lyrics proclaim, "There'll be blood a-running in town before night . . ." Unfortunately, the singing voice doesn't sound anything like Wayne's speaking voice.

132

"That was Paul Malvern's idea," said Lindsley Parsons. "The reason he thought he could get away with it was that [Bob Bradbury's] other son . . . was a doctor or a dentist but a beautiful singer. So we figured that John Wayne would be fiddling with this guitar and singing but back in the brush there we've actually got Bradbury's other son doing the singing."

Wayne's acute discomfort is palpable. It was one more humiliation for a man who was becoming all too accustomed to them — Singin' Sandy is the clip that's always dragged out to illustrate the ignominious beginnings of Wayne's career. It was awful and he knew it, but he also knew he couldn't refuse to do it. As he would tell a co-star forty years later, "I was one step up from being a stuntman. It was a big step. I didn't want to go back."

The working conditions of the Lone Stars were not appreciably better than the working conditions on the Warners or Mascot pictures. "It wasn't glamorous," said Cecilia Parker. "It was dirty work. I mean you got dusty dirty. And you were tired, you worked from sunup to sundown. And we had a production manager who said, 'Let's go boys, the light is getting yellow.' And that meant hurry up. No mistakes because there were hardly any retakes. You did it, and if it wasn't done right . . . you just cut it out, eliminated it."

The tackiness didn't affect Wayne's mood. Sammy McKim, a child actor who worked with Wayne in three westerns in the mid-1930s, said that he "was pleasant, always had a smile and a 'good morning' for you when you met on the set. He kept to himself pretty much at that time, he wasn't flamboyant. . . . He was a quality person."

On Saturday nights, when the picture had to be finished even if they had to work till sunrise on Sunday, the pick-me-up was something called "graveyard stew," which was a bowl of hot milk with chopped-up bread. It doesn't sound like much, but Cecilia Parker remembered that "at midnight, it tastes good." Of course, some of the actors spiked their graveyard stew with something besides milk.

Not even child actors were exempt from the push to complete films on time. Children were supposed to work only five hours of an eight-hour day, with three hours held over for schooling, but Sammy McKim remembered that on the last day of one of the Lone Stars, the production manager told McKim's grandfather that they had about two more hours of work and needed Sammy.

McKim's grandfather was instructed to take Sammy out of the studio, say good night to the schoolteacher and get in their car, then wait for the schoolteacher to leave the premises. At that point, they were to drive around to an alley, and knock on a metal door in the back of the western street set. "I worked 'til ten or 11 o'clock that night — and I enjoyed it. It was part of the picture and these were my friends I worked with."

McKim touched on a major point that made the circumstances bearable — a camaraderie that came as a natural by-product of a small unit pulling together. McKim spoke of "a closeness . . . that came about. And it was genuine, and I don't care if it was one of the smaller players, or a stunt-man. . . . He was accepted just as much as the assistant cameraman and somebody working in the prop wagon. It had a family feel about it."

It was on one of the Lone Star pictures that

Wayne ran into Pardner Jones, one of Hollywood's legendary characters. Jones was the best sharpshooter in the business, a man John Ford had used as far back as *The Iron Horse.* The scene called for Wayne to be tied up with a shelf full of clay pots around him that were to be shot off.

Wayne had initially felt quite secure about the scene because he had heard all about Pardner Jones, but when he came on the set he was startled to find that Jones was a bald-headed old man reading a newspaper with the help of a magnifying glass the size of a shaving mirror.

After Wayne was tied up, the director called out "Pardner?" and the old man grabbed a 30/30. The director explained the shot and Jones said, "Turn 'em over." He quickly blew away three of the clay pots, with the shards falling all over Wayne. Jones went back to reading his newspaper.

"I was about ready to call wardrobe," said Wayne.

For the rest of his life, Wayne sought to replicate this kind of congenial team atmosphere on his sets. Actors reappeared for decades, sometimes from the John Ford stock company, sometimes from Wayne's own group. Then there were the behind-the-camera personnel — makeup men, stuntmen, wranglers, second unit directors.

Because a film company takes its emotional temperature from the star and the director — and in B westerns the star was usually more powerful than the director — Wayne would usually be right in the middle of the joshing and the camaraderie. The atmosphere was family, and there was no question who the big brother was.

Most of the people who worked with Wayne in these days never dreamed that he would eventually become an airport, a postage stamp, and a congressional medal. Cecilia Parker was the exception. "He had something about him. He had a certain aura about him. You knew he was going to go somewhere."

But Louella Parsons spoke for the majority when she wrote that whenever Wayne was spotted at a Hollywood party he looked bored, unhappy, and sleepy. "Well, I *was* sleepy," he retorted. "Nobody realized that I was making six day epics then, one right after the other, and riding and doing what I hoped was acting in every minute of them."

These were blue-collar movies, made by blue-collar personalities. In *The Trail Beyond,* Noah Beery Sr. and Jr. shared screen time with Wayne. Beery Sr. got into a disagreement with Paul Malvern, and Malvern asked Yakima Canutt if, as a personal favor, he would beat the hell out of Beery in an upcoming fight scene.

"I'd be glad to," replied Canutt, "if you'll make him say to me the things he said to you."

On another of these one-week wonders, Wayne's co-star was a precocious fifteen-year-old named Ann Rutherford. "I thought he was a very nice man," she remembered seventy-five years later.

He was off with the guys all the time, while I was trying to figure out which side of the horse to get on.

We worked twenty-four hours a day, six days a week. The locations were usually Victorville or Lone Pine, or someplace else where there was no noise at all, just the noise we made making the picture. They could work you till midnight and then you'd have a 6 A.M. call. They told you not to look at the klieg lights, but you always did and

136

you'd get klieg eyes and they'd put cool sliced potatoes on your face. The potatoes would help, although you looked like an idiot.

The cowboys rode over the hills very fast aiming and shooting, and after the director yelled "Print!" everybody got off the horses, went to makeup, and became an Indian. So you could easily spend the day shooting at yourself. That was the way they shot westerns. I was making $150 a week.

Rutherford's memories of Wayne were of a man happy to be working.

He'd had a brief flurry, then nothing. He looked on this as another shot. He did anything they asked of him; he was gung ho. But he was already married and had a kid or two. The crew all loved him. And what was not to like? You've got to like anybody who walks around like they're clutching a diamond in their rear end and makes it pay.

He was absolutely a man's man. They all stood around with their knives whittling on a piece of wood. They made themselves very happy in their own peculiar way. The directors were fresh from being someone's second assistant. I don't think they timed lunch. If we were on location, a food wagon came around with stuff whenever there was a break. I made about fourteen of these in seven months, so I don't remember the names.

Although it would have made economic sense to make the pictures in groups of two or three — David Selznick did it at MGM with Tim McCoy in the late 1920s, and some of the later Hopalong Cassidy pictures were also shot two at a time —

Rutherford remembered that the Wayne westerns were made one at a time.

> The only time I felt I was in a factory operation was when they made serials. On serials, you wouldn't even rehearse. I made one [for Mascot!] called *Fighting Marines,* with Grant Withers. They told me to drive past the camera, and I had to tell them I couldn't drive. "No problem," they said. "We'll have a guy on the floor and if you get in trouble, just call him."
>
> I got in and happily drove past the camera and hit a bump and the guy on the floor bounced into the picture. "Print it!" they said. That's the way they made serials.

Although these pictures got no respect, and didn't earn any, there was a good amount of money to be made. To take just one group as an example: the six westerns Wayne made for Leon Schlesinger at Warner Bros. were carried on the books as costing $28,000 apiece, which undoubtedly meant at least $10,000 of studio overhead was being tacked on to each picture, or Warners was paying Schlesinger $28,000 for each completed picture. None grossed more than $224,000, but none grossed less than $193,000. Cumulatively, the six pictures were carried on the books as having cost $168,000 and earning a total of $1.25 million, for a net profit that must have been in the vicinity of $850,000.

The Lone Star westerns wouldn't have grossed anywhere near as much as the Schlesinger productions — Monogram's distribution system was a wheezy old Locomobile compared to Warners' streamlined Chevrolet — but even if they only grossed half as much, they cost a lot less than $28,000 apiece.

B westerns weren't prestigious or well paid, but they were building John Wayne's career.

In 1935, Herbert Yates proposed a deal to Nat Levine at Mascot and Trem Carr at Monogram: Merge both studios with Yates's Consolidated Film Industries to form something called Republic Productions. This new entity would buy out a bunch of other Poverty Row players — Liberty Pictures, Majestic Pictures, Chesterfield Pictures. In essence, Poverty Row production would be centralized under one umbrella organization. Levine would run production, Carr would supervise, Yates would run the business.

It sounded like a good deal for all concerned — Levine thought that it was going to get harder and harder for independents to compete with the major studios, who had their own distribution chains and theaters. Levine and Carr took the deal. No more Monogram pictures were released until 1937, when the company was reorganized and picked up more or less where it left off until after World War II, when it was reorganized yet again as a more upscale entity called Allied Artists.

John Wayne's career was now in the hands of Republic and Herbert Yates. Yates had been born in Brooklyn in 1880 and had spent his youth in the tobacco business, first working for the legendarily unpleasant George Washington Hill of the American Tobacco Company, later with Liggett & Myers. Yates got into the laboratory business during World War I, and in 1922 he created Consolidated Film Industries. By the early 1930s, Yates was extending as much as $500,000 in credit per year to Levine to process Mascot's negatives, work prints, and release prints.

In retrospect, Herbert Yates would be nearly as important to Wayne's career as John Ford although far less famous, not to mention far less talented. Yates was what Wayne termed "a shrewd business-man" — a nice way of saying that he didn't have a creative bone in his pear-shaped body. For Yates, movies were a business, no more and no less. There was a lot of money to be made from the efficient manufacture of low-end goods, and Yates's operation would quickly become expert.

Over the years, Yates would run dozens of handsome young men who could ride a horse through his B western mill. Only one of them would raise himself out of Republic's corral. In time, Wayne would become to Republic what Clark Gable was to MGM — their biggest star, their symbol of masculinity, their annuity.

For several years after *The Big Trail,* John Ford cut Wayne dead. Wayne never even pretended to understand what was going through Ford's mind, although resentment at a protégé making a lunge for success with another A list director might come pretty close. Ford was always probing for signs of premature abandonment, and always prepared to abandon someone else for years at a time.

But by the mid-1930s, Wayne was once more a part of Ford's social circle; he, Ward Bond, and a few others were regular guests on Ford's yacht, or over at his house for all-night poker sessions.

The unspoken question was when, if ever, Ford would offer Wayne a part in a John Ford production. "I never expected anything from Jack," Wayne would say. "He knew mine was a friendship. Very few people considered what a private man he was, but I was private, too." Wayne would complain about the pictures he was making, and Ford would listen, then say, "Get all the experience you can, in anything you can get."

He knew what he was talking about; Ford had spent nearly ten years directing cheap westerns and programmers before he got his big-budget break with *The Iron Horse,* and he was unwilling to promote his young friend beyond his level of competence. Besides that, Ford wasn't making westerns in the mid-1930s, because westerns in that period were mostly relegated to the bottom half of double features — the movies Duke was making.

Working for Monogram and Republic was a long way down from working for Raoul Walsh at Fox, but Wayne was quickly learning the difference between A pictures and B pictures. Wayne would say that the important things he learned in these years involved the ability to deliver exposition, and the ability to do nothing. Most actors, he would say, can deliver extreme emotions — anger, fear, and so forth. What's difficult is to convincingly deliver straight lines: "The cattle train is due at four."

B movies embodied a different theory of storytelling than A movies, because they were often made for rural audiences or kids, where the narrative had to be broader than a picture made for relatively sophisticated adults. These movies taught Wayne how to attract attention without resorting to scene-stealing mannerisms.

As Wayne would later explain it to Peter

141

Bogdanovich, "The quickie [pictures] . . . are those kinds of pictures in which you tell the audience what you're going to do, then you go do it, and then you tell them what you've done, then you tell them what you're going to do next."

Watching Wayne in these pictures from the mid-1930s proves that he was watching and learning. The reactions that had once been far too large were increasingly unobtrusive. Wayne is listening, then reacting — he's becoming a thinking actor.

In so many respects, Wayne was part of his own audience: a product of small-town Middle America, traditionally known as flyover country as far as New York and Hollywood are concerned. But it was in Middle America that Wayne found his audience, and it was for Middle America that he would still be making pictures forty years later.

In February 1937, Yates bought out Nat Levine for a reported $2 million. After a few unsuccessful stints as a producer at MGM and Grand National, Levine's gambling careened out of control. He blew all of his money and in his old age managed a movie theater.

As for Herbert Yates, aside from being an effective corporate warrior, he would prove to have the inestimable attribute of reliably bad taste. He would have only one apparent vulnerability: his hopeless love for an ice skater named Vera Hruba Ralston, whom he spent fifteen years trying to turn into a motion picture star at a terrible cost to Republic stockholders, not to mention her leading men — including John Wayne. For years, Yates took the back page of *Variety* and *The Hollywood Reporter* and ran a picture of her captioned "The World's Most Beautiful Woman."

"That old fool," said Ann Rutherford. "We were all so sorry for her. They'd call lunch and she'd have to skip her meal and help him put his mittens on and help him skate in circles around the ice rink on the Republic lot." It was some kind of great love affair.

But as far as Wayne was concerned, he could just as easily work for Herb Yates as Trem Carr or Nat Levine. He buckled down to the new combine. For the next several years, Wayne would make between four and seven B pictures per year. The last of his first batch of westerns at Republic was called *Winds of the Wasteland,* shot in eleven days in May 1936. It cost $16,700, and Wayne earned $1,750 for his labors. The director was Mack V. Wright, who had last worked with Wayne on the considerably better series at Warners in 1932. Except for a nice point-of-view tracking shot of an abandoned town as Wayne and Lane Chandler ride in, and a decent stagecoach race, it's a film of minor interest.

But Wayne continued to work, and to learn. As he would note in a different context years later, Republic had a particularly nice ring to it.

CHAPTER FIVE

In 1936–1937, Wayne made a batch of six pictures at Universal. None of them was a western — one was an adaptation of Jack London's "The Abysmal Brute." The series was an obvious attempt to broaden his appeal and see if he had any commercial traction outside the genre he had already made his own. The subject matter varied from sports to adventure, the running times were all around sixty minutes, and the films were released between September 1936 and December 1937. All of them (*Sea Spoilers, Conflict, California Straight Ahead!, I Cover the War, Idol of the Crowds,* and *Adventure's End*) are heavier on plot than on action. In other words, the films are a halfway house between the Lone Star westerns and the bigger things that were down the road.

None of this was accidental; as the *Motion Picture Herald* noted of *Adventure's End,* "This production is another of the series of John Wayne starring vehicles which are presenting him as a strong, action type of hero, yet subtly over the course of time are investing in him as material for higher budgeted productions."

At the time, Universal was mostly subsisting on B movies — the only big star the company had

144

was Deanna Durbin. The Wayne vehicles were made by old friends Trem Carr and Paul Malvern, who had quickly sensed that Herb Yates didn't want anybody running Republic except Herb Yates.

Trem Carr paid Wayne better money — Wayne got $6,000 a picture — and also made better pictures. The Universal pictures took between ten and fourteen days to make and cost between $60,000 and $75,000, with Universal absorbing about 90 percent of the cost and Carr paying the rest. The films were strong enough to play on either half of a double feature, and they were extremely ambitious from a production point of view, as is attested by a series of memos from Universal.

On *I Cover the War,* scheduled for eleven days of production, with five of them on location at Lone Pine and Red Rock, one M. F. Murphy wrote, "Considering the number of sets, both interior and exterior this story requires, I feel quite certain in stating that we could not turn out this show for $70,000, considering our overhead, if produced as written." A month later, the script had been trimmed slightly and Murphy was still impressed. "We feel it should make a good buy for us at the $65,000 mark. Beyond question, this subject is really a more ambitious undertaking than the usual run of stories made at this price." (In fact, Universal paid only $60,000 for the picture.)

Similarly, *Adventure's End,* the last of the Universal pictures, scheduled for thirteen days of shooting, was characterized by the studio as an "exceptionally difficult one to produce. The attached budget, amounting to $82,120.50 which we have checked over, is most conservative. The physical problems connected with the making of a subject like this on our own back lot . . . will be numerous and unable to foresee. It fact, it is quite a gamble and we will watch with great interest the final results."

Most of these films have effective locations — *Sea Spoilers* was shot around Catalina, *I Cover the War* at Lone Pine — and they're ably photographed by Archie Stout, although the young Stanley Cortez does duty on the latter picture, in which Wayne plays an intrepid newsreel cameraman. And they're a definite step up in that the exposition is delegated to supporting actors, not the star.

There are occasional fluffs that remind you that a ten-day picture is still a ten-day picture; in *I Cover the War,* Wayne begins some dialogue before his cue, backs off, then picks it up a moment later at the right time. In an A picture, this would have meant a retake, but Universal elected to keep it in, undoubtedly because of time — director Arthur Lubin rammed through as many as fifty-one shots per day on *I Cover the War.*

During *Sea Spoilers,* Wayne roomed with co-star William Bakewell, who had first met him when he was beginning to date Josie. "We had 4:30 calls in the morning," remembered Bakewell. "We'd go out on the Coast Guard cutters to shoot, but rather than go to sleep early, he'd say, 'Come on, let's go down . . . and get a nightcap.' " After a week of getting to bed at two and getting up at 4:30, Bakewell was exhausted. "I thought, 'My God, if this keeps up, I'll look like the advance man for a famine.' "

A couple of the Universals are quite entertaining, notably *I Cover the War* and *California Straight*

146

Ahead!, a trucking movie that predates Warners' *They Drive by Night,* not to mention *The Wages of Fear.* In all of these pictures, Wayne's innate honesty makes you buy some pretty outlandish premises, not to mention a lot of stock footage. (At its best, acting, like fiction, is the lie that tells the truth, and Wayne was developing the knack of telling his lies with absolute sincerity.)

Director Arthur Lubin remembered that Universal decided to make *Adventure's End* simply because the story matched up with a schooner on the Universal back lot. "That's the way pictures were made," remembered Lubin. "They said, 'Well, what sets are up these days that we can make pictures on that won't cost us much money?' "

The only real stiff in the bunch is *Idol of the Crowds,* in which Wayne plays a hockey star. The problem was, as Wayne remembered, "I'm from Southern California. I've never been on a pair of goddamn skates in my life." He always remembered the experience with a sense of burning humiliation.

An ice skating rink had been rented for twenty-four hours, during which all the hockey scenes would be shot. Wayne's memory was that he could not skate at all. "My ankles are rubbing on the ice, and I can't even stand up, but they pushed me around. . . . I was in the hospital for two fucking days after that."

Wayne did it, because "This was the Depression. If you wanted to work, you did what they told you to do."

Actually, Wayne could skate a little, as long as it was in a straight line. If you've always wanted to see John Wayne on skates, *Idol of the Crowds* is the

147

movie for you. But Wayne was a natural athlete, which is to say innately graceful, so he could perform almost any kind of physical activity.

But the retrospective anger is interesting — the Universals are much better pictures than the westerns at Monogram or Republic and he was making decent money in the bargain. But Wayne remembered only the embarrassment, probably because of the yawning chasm between the movies he wanted to make and the movies he actually was making. The fact that he was once again a member of John Ford's extended family would only have made his frustration worse.

Some of Wayne's frustrations could have been absorbed by a focus on family, but weren't. Duke had maintained his close relationship with his father. Clyde Morrison and his second wife had been present when Wayne married Josie, and Duke and Josie often brought their kids to their grandfather's house for dinner. Nancy Morrison, Clyde's stepdaughter, said that Wayne and his father always hugged when getting together, and Wayne would often kiss his father, whom she called "the most honest of men." Clyde never talked about his first marriage.

On March 4, 1937, Clyde Morrison drove his stepdaughter to school, said he didn't feel well and went home to lie down. A few minutes later he died of a heart attack. Wayne, his stepmother, and Josie went to the school to tell Nancy Morrison that her stepfather had died. "Duke was heartbroken, sobbing in the car as I was. He hugged me and we cried some more." Clyde Morrison was buried at Forest Lawn.

Whatever grief he felt about his father's death, Wayne had already developed that ability to compartmentalize familiar in high achievers. Decades later, he went to the funeral of an employee at the same cemetery. He looked around and said, "My dad's buried up here someplace. I've never been back since the funeral."

As far as the industry was concerned, the pictures Wayne made at Universal were B movies, but looked at with the benefit of hindsight they're B plus movies, with a fair amount of wit. In *I Cover the War,* Wayne and a friend are sent to a country called Samari, to which Wayne brightly replies, "Ah, an appointment in Samari!" Trem Carr was not about to leave any commercial stone unturned — *Conflict* combines a boxing movie with a logging movie, and ends with Wayne adopting an orphan!

The critics were a little kinder to these programmers than they had been to Wayne's past efforts. *Variety* wrote about the despised *Idol of the Crowds* that "A new John Wayne is revealed. He has a breezy role that definitely suits his personality and appearance. He carries off the part in an appreciable style, making the character thoroughly likeable and believable." *Variety* also liked *Adventure's End* and its star ("John Wayne gives another of his likeable heroic performances. However, the Wayne torso is given more display and is shown to better advantage."), but the *Motion Picture Herald* noted of *Sea Spoilers* that it was "reviewed at Loew's Ziegfeld Theater, New York, where a matinee audience gave no audible manifestation of reaction."

Despite the increasing budgets and salary, according to Lindsley Parsons, Wayne was miserable at Universal: "Poor John is wandering around dolefully and just wondering whatever is going to become of him." The studio seemed to regard him as little more than cannon fodder. "Universal had a kid by the name of John Wayne under contract," remembered Joseph H. Lewis, who began directing at Universal in 1937. "They thought he was horrible."

Wayne would come to feel that the Universal movies were a strategic mistake: "I had lost my stature as a western star — and got nothing in return," he told one reporter.

As the Universal deal drew to its end, Lindsley Parsons called Wayne and told him, " 'If you're not working, I think I can make another deal with Monogram that'll do us both some good.' He said, 'Oh, my God, I can't think of anything better,' " but then told Parsons that he had just signed another deal with Republic.

But before he went back to Republic, Wayne did a quickie for Paramount: *Born to the West,* shot in late August of 1937, a remake of a Zane Grey novel of the same title that had been made as a silent in 1926. It was a cheap picture, but a cheap picture at a major studio had a budget a cheap picture at a cheap studio could only dream of — Paramount spent a whopping $157,958 on the picture, or about ten times the budgets of the westerns Wayne had been making at Republic. Wayne's co-stars were Johnny Mack Brown and a great deal of stock footage; director Charles Barton had a better feel for the slam-bang Abbott and Costello comedies he would begin directing in a few years.

Johnny Mack Brown had a brief vogue in the late silent/early sound period — he'd been Mary Pickford's leading man in *Coquette* — but would spend the rest of his career in B westerns. Lurking in the nether regions of the cast was another star of the future: Alan Ladd.

"It was a few weeks over seventy years ago," remembered Marsha Hunt, Wayne's leading lady in *Born to the West.* Hunt was twenty years old at the time and recalled Wayne as "a pleasant man, awfully good with a horse, and he moved well, as an athlete does.

"I had no sense of difference between him and Johnny Mack Brown, who was a bigger name at the time, even though Wayne won the girl at the end of the story. Johnny had been an All-American at Alabama. The auditorium at Birmingham has his name engraved on a plaque. He's revered."

Hunt said that the film was given "time and attention. There was no sense that we were working on a poor relation vehicle. Wayne didn't treat what we did as anything special. It was a job, it was pleasant, it went well.

"We had games we played at night. We'd sit around dinner for an hour or two and call out a number. Everyone's seat had a number. If you were in the number four seat, you had to instantly yell out another number if four was called. Otherwise, you went to the end of the line, or we all shifted. It was just a matter of presence of mind and reflex, but we played it and played it and played it. It was a compatible company. Wayne was not flirtatious in the slightest; he was very respectful, but he didn't take any special interest in me."

Born to the West was just another western for two people who were both on their way to bigger and better things. Their paths would cross again in twenty years, when they would be at diametrically opposite stages in their careers, and in their politics.

While all this was going on, RKO was mulling over a replacement for its cowboy star George O'Brien. Wayne's name came up in the conversation, which prompted Ned Depinet, the company's head of distribution, to send frantic stop signs to the company president: "[We] believe would be mistake to distribute John Wayne westerns. He is in same category as dozen others with disadvantage having been sold cheaply and our opinion little prospect of gaining popularity. . . . He is one of poorest of so called western stars, seems miscast and his pictures [are] doing little at Universal. We believe we would be better to go ahead with George Smalley who has not been identified with cheap western pictures and with whom we would have chance building worthwhile singing western star like Autry."

RKO passed on Wayne, as well as the hopelessly obscure George Smalley; they replaced O'Brien with a younger, cheaper contract actor named Tim Holt. With the advantage of hindsight, it's easy to snicker at Depinet, but a survey of the western stars of 1937 shows that he was only betting probabilities. From the top, the most popular western stars of 1937 were Buck Jones, George O'Brien, Gene Autry, William Boyd, Ken Maynard, Dick Foran, John Wayne, Tim McCoy, Hoot Gibson, and Buster Crabbe.

Only Wayne would get out of B pictures, which were usually like the Mafia — once you were in, you were in for life.

In 1938, John Wayne climbed back in the saddle at Republic. His new contract, signed on May 7, specified eight pictures for the first year, all westerns, but no serials. His salary was $3,000 per picture, each one to have a maximum shooting schedule of ten days. Wayne was being paid $24,000 for about eighty working days a year — not a bad deal for 1938, if you could overlook the fact that he was making half of what he had been making with Trem Carr and Universal.

The standard contract mandated only forty weeks of salary a year, but Wayne's increasing domestic overhead forced him to ask for a check fifty-two weeks a year — $461.54 a week. There were four additional one-year options that would eventually raise his salary to $961.54 a week. Republic would supply costumes, but if Wayne were to be cast in a nonwestern — in which case the number of films he was required to make totaled only five — he had to supply his own wardrobe.

To sweeten the deal, Herbert Yates made a noncontractual promise that Wayne could star in a film about Sam Houston. But Yates lied — a motif at Republic. When the picture was made a year later, the star was Richard Dix. "You're not strong enough," Yates told Wayne.

Wayne embarked on a western series called "The Three Mesquiteers," which had been in production for about a year. The stars had been Robert Livingston and Ray "Crash" Corrigan, with Syd Saylor as the alleged comic relief. Yates promoted Livingston out of the B westerns so he could be groomed for potential stardom, and Wayne replaced Livingston.

Republic was still Republic, and always would be — the studio got the cowboys to go all-out in their chases by offering a bottle of bourbon to the

153

fastest rider. But Republic had its compensations, mainly an unpretentious air that was attractive to many who were put off by the impersonality of the major studios. Lorna Gray, who would later change her name to Adrian Booth, spent fifteen years at Republic and found it eminently preferable to Columbia, where she began her career.

"It was absolutely wonderful," she remembered at the age of ninety-four. "I was very happy for all the years I worked there. The boss [Herbert Yates] would send me a bouquet of flowers whenever I started another picture. It was a delightful studio. Nobody was ever rude."

The actress Peggy Stewart said that one of the main attractions of Republic was its hominess. "If you were shooting over on Stage One, you could see straight down the street, and you knew exactly who was working there. You'd yell down to some prop man and visit friends between scenes. There was so much kidding on that lot, because you were with those people six days a week."

The downside of the family atmosphere was that the head of the family was terribly cheap. "They would paint the wall of a set to the height of the leading man," said screenwriter Edmund Hartmann. "The top remained unpainted because they would only photograph to the height of the leading man. They didn't waste a thing!"

Adrian Booth recalled:

We did have to work very hard. On the serials, sometimes we had a two- or three- or even four-way call, which meant that you had to be up on your dialogue for as many as four different scenes from four different chapters that would be shot on the same set on the same day. Not everybody liked it. You had to be on time and you had to know your lines. Republic was very disciplined.

I made a serial called *Perils of Nyoka* with dear Kay Aldridge. I played Vultura, and I was always doing terrible things to Nyoka. One day Kay was standing on a ladder for a shot that involved her hanging by her wrists in front of some flaming thing. And the director said, "Now, honey, we're going to take the ladder away for just a second."

And Kay said, "Oh, Lord, send me a millionaire and make it soon." And she ended up marrying three of them!

The second of Wayne's Three Mesquiteers pictures was called *Overland Stage Raiders,* shot between August 6 and 15, 1938, and released late in September. It's a fairly standard Mesquiteers picture, except for the fact that the leading lady was Louise Brooks, the luminous erotic icon of G. W. Pabst's *Pandora's Box,* who drank and talked her way out of a potentially great career. Brooks received $300 for her performance in *Overland Stage Raiders.* She was a prodigiously self-destructive woman who knew a B movie when she saw it, but she also appreciated a beautiful young man.

"At sunrise one August morning I was driven in a company car to location on the ranch where Republic shot all its Westerns. Where was I supposed to go, I wondered, after I got out of the car and stood alone in a cloud of dust kicked up by a passing string of horses. . . . Up the road a bunch of cowboys were talking and laughing with two men who stood slightly apart from them. When the company car honked for them to get off the

155

road, the two men looked around, saw me and came to greet me. One was a cherub, five feet tall, carrying a bound script; the other was a cowboy, six feet four inches tall, wearing a lovely smile. The cherub, who was the director, George Sherman, introduced me to the cowboy, who was John Wayne. . . . Looking up at him, I thought, this is no actor but the hero of all mythology miraculously brought to life. . . . John was, in fact, that which Henry James defined as the greatest of all works of art — a purely beautiful being."

Brooks clearly adored Wayne, and they seem to be enjoying each other on-screen, but the cast-iron mediocrity of Republic's scripts forestalled interesting byplay between actors. Louise Brooks never made another movie.

Wayne made two more Mesquiteers pictures at Republic on equivalent schedules and budgets before his ship finally came in. *Santa Fe Stampede,* the first of them, was a vigorous little western co-starring William Farnum, a great roaring hero of the silent days. Republic is slowly becoming aware of what they have; Wayne is clearly The Star — the other two Mesquiteers are given virtually nothing to do.

Otherwise, the film is noticeable for the blood-curdling prevalence of the Running W, a trip wire used to bring horses down in a tumbling heap that killed more animals than hoof-and-mouth disease. Lorna Gray/Adrian Booth was paired up with Wayne and the Mesquiteers for a film called *Red River Range,* which was shot in October 1938 and released in December. She had told the studio that she knew how to ride, which was a baldfaced lie. The day before shooting started she rented a horse and spent the day in Griffith Park. The result was that on the day the picture started she was so sore she could barely move.

"Duke could see I didn't know what I was doing. But he was terribly, terribly nice to me anyway. He was a man who was interested in his career. He didn't play around. And I was scared to death; I was just hoping my shaking wouldn't show on camera. But he helped me get through it, and on the strength of *Red River Range* I did a lot more pictures for Republic."

Late one afternoon, Wayne and his leading lady were about to shoot a scene that called for them to walk across a porch and down a couple of steps. Before the director called "Action," Wayne leaned over to Gray and said, "I'm going to stumble over a nail. Then I'm going to do it a couple more times. Pay no attention."

"He stumbled over the nail, and Georgie Sherman reset the camera and he tripped a couple of more times, and I wondered why he was doing this — it was a simple scene. And then I realized he was stalling to kill the five minutes it would take for the extras to go into overtime. That's the kind of man he was — a wonderful man."

The Mesquiteers films aren't bad; they usually match Wayne with Ray Corrigan, a good all-around-hero type, and Raymond Hatton, a veteran of the early silent days with Cecil B. DeMille, playing the grizzled old-timer/comic relief. But they were still cheap westerns, and Wayne had taken a pay cut in exchange for long-term security. By this time, he must have been wondering if he'd ever get out of the B picture swamp.

For Wayne, these were grim years. Not in terms of income — he was making a decent living — but in terms of thwarted ambition. Month after month, year after year, Wayne was imprisoned in cheap westerns, with titles that all ran together — then and now. The budgets may have risen from $10,000 to $30,000 or $40,000, the lighting and supporting actors may have improved, but the schedules were still short and the dialogue was still from hunger. The frustration must have been enormous, and it began boiling over on the set.

George Sherman directed the last batch of B westerns that Wayne made at Republic, after which their careers diverged. Wayne would bring him back near the end of both their careers to direct *Big Jake,* or more precisely, to stand there while Wayne directed *Big Jake.* By that time, Wayne was famously peremptory on the set, and somebody asked Sherman if he had always been this way.

"Absolutely," said Sherman. "Just the same as he is now. The only difference is that nobody listened to him. He always knew everything. 'Oh, no, no, put it over there! Get a white horse!' Exactly the same. Right out of USC but nobody paid a goddamn bit of attention. But now he's John Wayne and they've gotta pay attention."

Wayne had incrementally risen from three-day pictures to six-day pictures to ten-day pictures, with corresponding increases in salary but very little increase in prestige. "I kept nagging at Ford," remembered Wayne. " 'When is it my turn?' He'd say, 'Just wait. I'll let you know when I get the right script.' And he did."

Right after Wayne finished shooting *Red River Range,* Ford found the script for Wayne. It was *Stagecoach.*

John Ford and his partner Merian C. Cooper

first presented their western to David Selznick in June 1937, but Selznick was not enthusiastic about the genre and bridled at featuring down-market talents like John Wayne and Claire Trevor in a Selznick production. He insisted on Gary Cooper and Marlene Dietrich. Ford and Cooper took their project and went home.

Ford nurtured *Stagecocach* while directing *The Hurricane* for Sam Goldwyn, and *Four Men and a Prayer* and *Submarine Patrol* for Fox. Finally, in the summer of 1938, *Stagecoach* found a home with producer Walter Wanger, who believed in John Ford and in the recurring nature of film cycles. Large-budget westerns had been out of style since the early 1930s and the simultaneous failures of *The Big Trail* and King Vidor's *Billy the Kid,* but Cecil B. DeMille's *The Plainsman* had been a big hit in 1936, and Frank Lloyd had made the similarly successful *Wells Fargo* in 1937.

"It was Ford who worked with Dudley Nichols in creating a fine script; and John Wayne as the Ringo Kid was also Ford's idea," said Wanger. On October 31, 1938, Ford started shooting his movie.

In the years to come, *Stagecoach* would become known almost as much for its locations as for its star. Unless you'd seen every western since Broncho Billy, you'd never seen locations like this before — a Garden of the Gods called Monument Valley.

There's not a lot of footage of the valley in *Stagecoach* — the crew spent no more than four days there — but each shot is majestically composed and emphatically placed, with swelling music behind it. In years to come, the question of who stumbled upon Monument Valley would become a hot if irrelevant topic, proving only that in the movie business, success has a thousand fathers, while failure is the proverbial redheaded stepchild.

Harry Goulding, who had lived in Monument Valley since 1921, said that he traveled to Los Angeles with a batch of professional photographs of the valley, and it was those photos that sold Wanger and Ford on doing the location work there. But Ford told his grandson, Dan, that George O'Brien had seen the valley first and came back raving about it. "Harry Goulding had given him a lot of pictures and I was entranced," said Ford.

And John Wayne would stoutly insist that Monument Valley was his idea. "I was hired as an assistant for a George O'Brien western, called, I believe, *Riders of the Purple Sage*. . . . One of my jobs was to get 400 head of cattle into Blue Canyon which was 150 miles from any paved road. A preacher who had a little church on the Hopi reservation agreed to help me gather them. In gathering those cattle, we horse-backed into Monument Valley."

Wayne's story is possible, although Monument Valley isn't featured in the 1930 version of *Riders of the Purple Sage* — it was shot in Sedona. (Wayne claimed only that the cattle were rounded up in the vicinity.)

Wayne said that he had held back the location for ten years until Ford cast him as the lead in *Stagecoach* and rhetorically wished he could find a fresh, picturesque area to represent the West. Wayne promptly suggested Monument Valley, to which Ford retorted that Wayne had been hired as an actor, not a director.

"Upon [Ford's] return from location hunting, I was standing with some of the crew when he approached and said, 'I have found the most colorful location that can ever be used for a picture.' Then he looked directly at me and said, 'Monument Valley.' And I assure you from that moment on, Jack Ford discovered Monument Valley."

John Wayne was not a slam dunk for the part of the Ringo Kid — Ford may have shot a test of Bruce Cabot as well as Wayne. Claire Trevor remembered that Wayne's test involved their long scene after the birth of the baby — the primary scene between the two characters. "The idea was that he was very respectful of me. He didn't know I was a hooker. Ford had us play the scene standing against a fence. At one point, Ford took Duke and shook him.

" 'What are you doing with your mouth?' Ford asked. 'Why are you moving your mouth so much? Don't you know that you don't act with your mouth in pictures? You act with your eyes!' "

Ford and Walter Wanger had to cut a deal for Wayne's loan-out from Republic. Ford called Republic, but they weren't overly interested in accommodating him. "They didn't want to bust up their schedule," was the way Wayne remembered it.

Ford asked Walter Wanger to go rattle Herb Yates's cage. Wanger came back to Ford and said, "I can't deal with these people. They're stupid." After much finagling, Republic let Wanger have Wayne for his pro-rated salary — a little more than $6,000 for six weeks' work. "They were so stupid that they didn't realize that they could've got $50,000–$60,000 for me [on loan-out]," said Wayne.

Ford wouldn't have been Ford if he hadn't indulged in some tormenting of his rookie once he started shooting, even if he'd known the rookie for more than ten years, even if the rookie was a seasoned pro. It was not unlike a fraternity hazing. "Don't you know how to walk?" Ford yelled. "You're as clumsy as a hippo. And stop slurring your dialogue and show some expression. You look like a poached egg."

Wayne had been making movies for a decade, but, as Yakima Canutt said, "He was new to the Big Leagues." Ford rode him mercilessly, made him completely self-conscious. "I said hold your position before you turn," Ford growled at Wayne on the set. "Chrissakes, can't you even walk? Not skip, just walk. Goddamn fairy. Put your feet down like you were a man."

Behind Wayne's back, Ford's attitude was 180 degrees away from the persistently brutal hiding he gave him to his face. "He'll be the biggest star ever," he told Wayne's co-star Louise Platt, "because he is the perfect Everyman."

Wayne nervously asked Yakima Canutt to run lines with him as he tried to come up with readings that Ford wouldn't decimate. But no matter what Wayne did, it was wrong. During a scene at a way station, Wayne had to wash his face, and Ford even seized on that for faulty technique. "Cut!" yelled Ford. "For Chrissakes, wash your face! Don't you ever wash it at home? You're daubing your face, you're *daubing* it!" Ford made Wayne do the shot over and over, until his face was nearly raw from the towel.

Wayne had a volatile temper, but with his Coach, his self-control was absolute. "Shit, I was so fucking mad I wanted to kill him," remembered

162

Wayne. "And he got the whole cast hating him for doin' that — until finally even Tim Holt, the young kid, was saying, 'Goddammit, quit picking on Duke like that.' "

Usually, Ford would bring the hammer down when Wayne was peripheral in a scene; if he had an important moment, Ford left him alone. Wayne would always believe that Ford was doing this to get the other actors — who were all more experienced and far more successful than Wayne — on the young man's side.

But he was also using shock therapy to snap Wayne out of the easy, uninflected display of masculine charm that had been his stock-in-trade. Ford knew that Wayne would always have that as part of his personality, but if the movie was going to succeed, if Wayne was going to act on a higher level, he was going to have to be able to communicate complexities beyond anything he had ever shown before, and Ford didn't believe he could do it unless he was spurred.

As for the rest of the cast, Thomas Mitchell was working on staying sober — two years and counting — while John Carradine mostly provoked conversations in which he could lay out the case for Edward de Vere as the true author of Shakespeare's plays.

After they had been on the picture a few weeks, Ford told Wayne to go look at some of the footage that Otho Lovering had been cutting together. Wayne noticed that Andy Devine, playing the stagecoach driver, had not had his reins outfitted with rubber exercisers — it looked like there was no tension on them. Wayne, an experienced prop man, had told Ford's prop man to get the rubber bands, but it hadn't been done and Wayne was irritated.

Wayne came back to the set and Ford asked him what he thought.

"Well, it's just magnificent, coach. I've never seen anything like it in my life."

"How do you like [Thomas] Mitchell?"

"Oh, he's great!"

"How do you like Claire Trevor?"

"Great!"

Well, how do you like yourself?"

"Well, hell, I'm playing you, so you know what I'm doing."

"Well, Jesus, Duke, you've looked at the whole goddamn thing, isn't there one criticism, one constructive criticism, that you can give me? You're acting like a schoolboy!"

Thus drawn in, Wayne complained about the slack reins, whereupon Ford halted production, brought the electricians down off the light grid, gathered the actors and crew and everybody around the center of the soundstage and said, "Well, I just sent our young star in to see his first effort. And he's very well satisfied with himself, and with the rest of the cast, but he thinks Andy Devine stinks!"

In varying degrees, Ford would indulge in these hazing rituals with unwary or inexperienced actors for the rest of his life. It wasn't personal; it was the way he told you he liked you. (If he didn't like you, he completely ignored you.) Beyond that, Ford's technique of handling actors was to keep them off balance, the better to be able to maintain unquestioned control of the production. For the next quarter century, Ford never really altered his method of handling Wayne: impatience and occasional abuse on the set, open affection off the set.

Dudley Nichols's screenplay is a model of concision and screen storytelling, and it works off the deeply Fordian premise that Americans reveal their true and, mostly, their best selves under pressure. The characters are all types, but they're deep, original types — at least for 1939. Each of them is written and played as a layered human being; only the banker Gatewood is no more than the sum of his selfishness, with dialogue that could be transposed directly to Fox News: "Government must not interfere with business. Reduce taxes! The national debt is something terrible!"

For all of Ford's professed exasperation toward his supposedly feckless protégé, he takes impeccable care of him. The Ringo Kid is sincere, without cant or hypocrisy, the moral center of the film as well as of the little community on the stagecoach. Much of Ford's artistry consists of his measured, carefully composed handling of the scenes within the cramped confines of the stagecoach, with predominantly triangular compositions that always make Ringo's silent reactions a cue for our own.

Wayne is far less reactive in *Stagecoach* than he was in most of his B westerns; Ford's scripts didn't require semaphoric acting, because he could communicate plot and dramatic tension visually, without undue emphases from his players. Ford knew that if the script and direction are finely tuned, an actor rarely has to act that much — the audience will project their own emotions into the space left by the filmmakers.

It's a film full of big, theatrical actors — Thomas Mitchell, John Carradine — who tamp it down,

165

and not even Barbara Stanwyck could give a better performance than Claire Trevor. Ford shoots the exteriors rapturously, the better to contrast with the tightly focused interiors in the stagecoach.

With Ford and Nichols both functioning at the top of their respective games, *Stagecoach* becomes more than a piece of movie history; it becomes American history. It's very nearly a perfect piece of construction and execution; the only obvious dramatic flaw is the extraneous song during the scene of the birth, although Ford even manages to work that into the plot, as listening vaqueros end up stealing the spare horses.

After *Stagecoach* finished shooting on December 22, 1938, four days over a tight thirty-three-day schedule, Wayne had six weeks off before trooping back to Republic and shooting the last four of his Three Mesquiteer westerns: *The Night Riders, Three Texas Steers, Wyoming Outlaw,* and *New Frontier.* The last was shot in seven days from June 26 to July 3, 1939, and buttressed by stock footage from sources as varied as *The Birth of a Nation* and *The Big Trail.*

When *Stagecoach* was released in February 1939, even the critics knew that something special had happened with its star. After noting that the cast lacked "strong marquee names," *Variety* relented by saying, "John Wayne, as the outlaw, displays talent hitherto only partially used — a forthright, restrained delivery and an appealing personality which here gets a new impetus." Kate Cameron in the New York *Daily News* wrote, "Every part is admirably acted . . . and John Wayne is so good in the role of the outlaw that one wonders why he has had to wait all this time since *The Big Trail* for another such opportunity."

Wayne responded with a full-page ad in the trades to let the movie community know that he was aware his participation in the movie was something special. It featured a smiling, full-face close-up of him in character. "My sincere thanks to Mr. Wanger and Mr. John Ford for the opportunity of playing the Ringo Kid in *Stagecoach.*"

Critical response hasn't varied much over the decades; Pauline Kael would write admiringly of Ford's "simple, clear, epic vision. . . . *Stagecoach* had a mixture of reverie and reverence about the American past that made the picture seem almost folk art."

On his first day back at Republic after *Stagecoach* opened, Wayne walked into the secretarial pool to get a letter typed. Several of the secretaries stood up and began applauding, and soon all the secretaries were clapping for their friend Duke. Wayne was startled and slightly embarrassed — and just kept repeating, "Thanks. Thanks so much."

Commercially, *Stagecoach* was only a modest success, but within the industry, Wayne was suddenly recognized as a viable leading man. Wayne would remember with pleasure a compliment from Robert Montgomery when they were making *They Were Expendable* six years later.

"Duke," he said, "when I saw *Stagecoach,* with all those wonderful actors, I thought of what a horrible shame it was to put a plain, straight guy like you in it. Three years later, when I saw *Stagecoach* again, I realized you were the best actor in the goddamn picture."

The Republic pictures Wayne made after *Stagecoach* are pretty much the mixture as before, although *Three Texas Steers* does have its outlandish charms, involving as it does Carole Landis, the great stuntman David Sharpe working as an actor, and an escaped, semi-tame circus gorilla who's much more amusing than Max Terhune, a ventriloquist whose dummy talks when he's not sitting on anybody's lap.

Ray Corrigan, for the only time in his career, anticipates Bette Davis when he looks around a room and exclaims "What a dump!" And George Sherman stages one priceless shot involving Wayne, Corrigan, Terhune, and a horse, all behind bars.

New Frontier was shot in the last week of June and the first week of July in 1939 and was released in August. Wayne's co-star was a young girl named Phyllis Isley, whose father, Phil Isley, was a major exhibitor in Texas and Oklahoma — a man that Republic had a vested interest in keeping happy. When Isley mentioned that his daughter seemed to have a knack for acting, Herb Yates offered to give her a shot, said shot including a serial entitled *Dick Tracy's G Men* and *New Frontier.* The latter is a good little movie, with a script that's overly ambitious for the short shooting schedule that George Sherman had to work with.★

Phyllis Isley is charming and projects her

★ *New Frontier* is an anti–New Deal movie at a time when that was unusual. Residents of a town called New Hope are informed that they're about to be flooded so their land can serve as a reservoir for a nearby city. The ranchers refuse to sell their land, defy the authorities and the construction team, and eventually win the right to stay.

personality, and the film has a sense of community unusual for B westerns. As always, Wayne sits tall in the saddle at ninety degrees, a posture he adopted from Tom Mix. As with his other Mesquiteer films, Sherman works mostly with pans, medium shots, and lateral tracking shots — tracking shots in or out took too much time to set up for the short schedules of B westerns.

Sherman couldn't quite transcend the limitations of B western scripts, as Joseph Lewis and William Witney would, although he does frame more locations in the background than was common for westerns in this budget range, getting a sense of the landscape as a character.

New Frontier would be the last of thirty-eight B westerns that Wayne had made since the debacle of *The Big Trail*. With *Stagecoach* grabbing reviews and earning money, Herb Yates realized that he had a star who had been hiding in plain sight for years. Actually, Yates had been wasting two stars — Phyllis Isley would soon change her name to Jennifer Jones and become one of the major leading ladies of the 1940s and 1950s, although not at Republic.

Herb Yates decided to promote Wayne to Republic's version of A pictures. They called Robert Livingston back to work on the Three Mesquiteer pictures, while Crash Corrigan also took off, to be replaced by Duncan Renaldo. (There would eventually be fifty-one Three Mesquiteer pictures.)

Stagecoach marked the smooth meshing of two monumental constructs. In the 96,000 acres of Monument Valley, John Ford found the ultimate frame for his pictures — sandstone buttes like fists punching through the earth's crust, as well as delicate architectural spires rising toward the sky

169

— a place of majesty and repose. Monument Valley gave the impression that it is as it has always been — permanent, implacable, sacred. At night, clouds descend and settle over the buttes and pillars like gods visiting their creation.

Ford had found the land he was born to put on the screen, as well as his mature style — meditative, with a symmetrical balance between character and theme.

And in his old pal Duke he had found a man to match the land.

■ ■ ■ ■

PART TWO:
1939–1952

■ ■ ■ ■

"Republic. I like the sound of the word . . ."
— *THE ALAMO*

CHAPTER SIX

Herbert Yates now set about building a two-pronged release strategy — the cheap westerns and serials would provide the foundational basis for the studio, while the more expensive pictures fronted by his new star would lift Republic to a higher level. The problem was that Yates had developed an effective system for the manufacture of low-cost movies that were reliably profitable, but he could never figure out an equivalent method for A pictures because he had only one star: John Wayne. As a result, most of Republic's A pictures that starred somebody besides Wayne lost money.

For Bs, Republic had the popular Gene Autry, a pretty fair country singer who couldn't act or perform a convincing fight. They also had a young wannabe named Roy Rogers, who could sing, ride, and be reasonably physical as well. Autry and Wayne shared similar tastes in scotch and spent years exchanging a standing joke: "Just think, Gene, if I hadn't quit singing, you wouldn't have happened," Wayne would say, to which Autry would reply, "Well, Duke, it wasn't my singing that made me a star. It was my acting!"

Republic's first big post-*Stagecoach* vehicle for

their new star was called *Dark Command,* about Quantrill's Raiders. To show that Republic was serious about upgrading, Yates borrowed Walter Pidgeon from MGM and director Raoul Walsh from Warners. But before that, Republic loaned out Wayne to RKO for *Allegheny Uprising,* which began shooting precisely two days after he finished the eight-day-wonder *New Frontier.*

Instead of one week, *Allegheny Uprising* shot for a full eight weeks. *Dark Command* was a massive upgrade as well — it took over forty days. Critics as well as audiences had been alerted to the possibility of Wayne's ascending star, and reacted accordingly. "John Wayne more than fulfills all previous promise," wrote *The Hollywood Reporter* of *Dark Command.*

Raoul Walsh, who made *Dark Command* ten years after *The Big Trail,* said of Wayne, "He underacts, and it's mighty effective. Not because he tries to underact — it's a hard thing to do, if you try — but because he can't overact. The trouble with most competent but ungifted actors, and that's what the Duke is, is that they think they're just wonderful. Wayne does not. . . . He'd read a script and shake his head. 'I can't do the part that way,' he'd say. 'It's too hard. I'm not good enough for it.' . . . You let Wayne alone, let him do the thing the way he feels he can, and he's fine."

So far so good. But as Wayne would learn, Republic would always be Republic — very good at their specialty, not very good at anything else. The character actor I. Stanford Jolley pointed out that serials and cheap westerns were primarily a training ground. "The high professionalism and teamwork at a small studio like Republic, with limited finances, could result in up to 100 [shots] a day. While over at MGM, say, if they got 10 [shots] a day, it was a small miracle."

John Ford knew that Wayne had delivered for him, and on some level always would. Ford next cast Wayne in Dudley Nichols's adaptation of Eugene O'Neill's *The Long Voyage Home.* Wayne read the script and always remembered the resulting fear. As he explained to me, "I was still under contract to Republic at the time. *The Long Voyage Home* was right after *Stagecoach,* but I was still doing six-day westerns. I'd finished one western at twelve o'clock at night and the next morning I had to start a picture where I was a Swedish sailor, presumably with an accent, with no chance for any coaching. I had to play a straight part as a Swede, and my accent couldn't clash with John Qualen's, who was playing a comic Swede. I want to tell you, that was quite a switch from the night before, knocking people around and jumping on a horse."

Wayne's memory was pardonably conflating Republic with cheap westerns. The picture he finished two days before starting *The Long Voyage Home* was not a six-day western but, rather, *Three Faces West,* a rather good Republic picture that cast Wayne as a young farmer trying to bring a doctor to his small town, and it had a shooting schedule of twenty days, not six.

But he was correct in that he was going from a stock part to something far out of his comfort zone: a sweet, unworldly sailor — with an accent. "I got to thinking of that long scene I was going to have to play with that woman [Mildred Natwick] — that he'd cut to her and she'd be do-

175

ing everything, and I'd just have to sit there and read these [lines.]"

Wayne went to Ford and said he needed help. "Well, Jesus, all right if you want to be a goddamn actor," said Ford. "You don't need it." But as far as Wayne was concerned, he did need it. Ford enlisted Osa Massen — she was actually Danish, but close enough — to give Wayne some coaching on the dialect.

"I took about two hours a day and went over the things that I was going to have to do. . . . [Ford] never heard it or anything until the day we were going to shoot and he said, 'Well, sit down here and read the lines.' I read the lines. He said, 'All right, put the camera here.' And he shot the scene. But that was the only really truly hard scene to do."

Playing a sensitive character part at this stage of his career was potentially disconcerting because Wayne had already decided on a public strategy of pretending to be an awkward lug who never particularly wanted to be an actor. The kid who had been movie-struck since childhood, who was involved in theatricals since high school, who had pestered Jack White for acting jobs in two-reel comedies, was now bashfully insistent that "I just can't act, that's all," and telling reporters that until Raoul Walsh had spotted him hauling a table across the Fox lot, he had never been the least bit interested in acting. Just an average boy from Glendale who played an average game of football, wanted to go to the Naval Academy and got waylaid. Life sure is strange.

A reporter visited the set of *The Long Voyage Home* on location at San Pedro harbor and noted the seriousness that permeated the set. There was none of the joshing typical of movie sets; Ford spoke very little, and when he did it was to the point. He sculpted the performances as surely as the setups, instructing Barry Fitzgerald to nod his head in a specific way, then demonstrating it. Ford and cameraman Gregg Toland consulted by taking turns looking through viewfinders and nodding agreement. Ford didn't mind taking more time rehearsing if it meant less time shooting; as a result, most scenes were knocked off in one or two takes.

Wayne has what amounts to a supporting part behind Thomas Mitchell's Driscoll, but Ford gives the younger actor top billing — a mark of his rapidly accreting commercial cachet after *Stagecoach*. Besides that, Wayne's Ole is the focus of all the other sailors, who are determined to get him back to Sweden.

Ford sets up the atmosphere of frustration and yearning with his audaciously dialogue-free first scene, as the SS *Glencairn* anchors off a tropical island. While sultry music plays, native women on shore caress themselves in overtly sexual gestures. On the boat the sailors move restlessly about, unable to relax without release.

Ford makes *The Long Voyage Home* a tone poem, gets rid of as many medium shots — God's most useless invention — as possible. Every composition is a knockout. But unlike, say, his film *The Fugitive,* also a nonstop progression of images suitable for framing, Ford never loses control of the story, or, rather, stories, as Dudley Nichols's excellent adaptation stitches together four of Eugene O'Neill's one-act plays.

Wayne's Ole is a lot like his Ringo Kid — a raw-boned farm boy with suspenders, but without a

177

grudge that has to be settled. Most of the sailors are alcoholics — Ian Hunter in particular captures the drunk's subterranean self-loathing. (The film reveals Ford's true feelings about alcoholism, without the blowsy comedy he often utilized as a diversion.) When the men engage in a recreational brawl, Ole acts as the peacemaker. He's the innocent younger brother, and the other men respect, love, and try to shelter him. He's also the only man with a pet — a parrot.

Ford gives Ward Bond a good part, and an affecting death scene, redolent of fear, pain, and guilt. Wayne's big scene comes near the end, in a run-down bar with some exhausted whores, in which Ole talks about his desire to go home. Wayne fights the accent to a draw, but effortlessly captures the character's sweetness.

In the end, Driscoll is shanghaied while saving Ole, and dies when he goes down on the "devil ship *Amindra.*" The survivors load Ole on the ship bound for home and troop back to the *Glencairn,* a grim line of professionals who hate the sea, even as they're continually drawn back into its grasp.

Like most of O'Neill, the movie is about lost souls and, beyond that, death. Besides Driscoll Yank (Ward Bond) dies, and the mysterious Smith (Ian Hunter) dies as well. Only Ole manages to be saved for a better life. Death shadows every moment of the film and whether a man lives or dies is mostly a matter of good or bad luck.

Ford and Nichols wisely strip out O'Neill's long speeches; Ford communicates the Irish fatalism poetically, with his camera. And Ford understands sailors, so the film always feels emotionally true. (The main set is the tramp steamer, which was reused a few years later for the Val Lewton film

The Ghost Ship.)

However potentially unsettling Wayne's part felt, he's utterly winning. Mildred Natwick, who played opposite Wayne, said, "I thought John Wayne was awfully good. . . . I liked him terribly much; he was helpful and good and easy to work with."

With *Stagecoach* and *The Long Voyage Home,* Ford unlocked the romanticism in Wayne, a gentleness behind the rugged externals. To paraphrase the film historian Jeanine Basinger, in the same way that Michelangelo looked at a block of Carrera marble and saw the figure that needed to be released, so Ford looked at Duke Morrison and saw John Wayne — a capacity for strength and violence that coexisted with a dangerous beauty.

Walter Wanger knew he had an art movie. He decided to double down, spending $50,000 to commission nine artists to paint scenes from the picture. Thomas Hart Benton chose a group scene of the *Glencairn* seamen; Grant Wood chose another group scene; James Chapin painted the death of Yank; Raphael Soyer painted the Limehouse sequence; Ernest Fiene did a portrait of Wayne. It didn't help; *The Long Voyage Home* lost over $224,000.

Years later at Catalina, a young man walked up to Wayne and asked him when he was going to make another picture like *The Long Voyage Home.* "I'd like to make one tomorrow," he replied.

"I was in the Merchant Marine when I saw it," said the young man, "and you played that guy like you were one of us." In 1949, Wayne cited it as the role he liked the best, although in later years he seldom mentioned it. When asked, he usually responded with the tale of his agony over the Swedish accent.

Within a year and a half after *Stagecoach,* Wayne made *The Long Voyage Home* for Ford, *Dark Command* for Raoul Walsh, *The Shepherd of the Hills* for Henry Hathaway, and *Seven Sinners* for Tay Garnett — completely different types of pictures for equally different but respected directors, in all of which he held the screen. And there were other opportunities, good ones, that he turned down.

In June of 1940, Hal Wallis and Warner Bros. pursued Wayne to play George Custer in *Santa Fe Trail.* Eighteen months earlier, Wayne would have lunged at a major part in a major picture from a major studio, but in mid-1940 he was uninterested.

"John Wayne was in this morning," wrote Jack Warner's assistant Steve Trilling to Wallis on June 24, "and . . . he was not keen about the part — did not feel it gave him enough opportunity to characterize it — that it was merely a straight part that just carried thru as a foil for J. E. B. Stuart [Errol Flynn]."

Ronald Reagan played Custer and spent the rest of his life complaining about how playing second lead to Errol Flynn was a recipe for professional oblivion.

Wayne's co-star in *Seven Sinners* was Marlene Dietrich, who was also coming off a career-changing hit: *Destry Rides Again.* The first time Dietrich saw Wayne was in the commissary at Universal. She leaned over to director Tay Garnett and said, "Daddy, buy me that."

Wayne had been trying to be a better husband, but he made an exception for Dietrich, as many did. It seems that Dietrich made the first move by inviting him into her dressing room. Wayne nervously looked around and said, "I wonder what time it is?" Dietrich lifted her skirt to reveal a garter with a watch attached. She looked at the watch, then moved toward Wayne, saying, "It's very early, darling. We have plenty of time."

Neither Wayne nor Dietrich attempted to conceal the affair. William Bakewell was acting in *Seven Sinners,* and he remembered that Wayne's arrival on the set would be met by Dietrich leaping into his arms and wrapping her legs around him. "He'd stand there grinning sheepishly, you know?"

On particularly hot days, Dietrich would have ice-cold champagne brought to the set for the cast and crew, and to pass the time while the lights were being shifted she would play the musical saw. "She would open her legs," remembered Bakewell, "put a regular saw in it and with a violin bow, play 'Annie Doesn't Live Here Anymore' with a wow in it. She was an interesting woman."

Wayne rarely spoke of what transpired behind closed doors with Dietrich, or with anybody else, but he retained fond memories of her. "She was great, just a German *hausfrau.* She used to cook pressurized beef to make beef bouillon for everybody. It may have been an act, but it brought her a great deal of enjoyment. 'Course, maybe one reason she enjoyed it so much was she didn't have to do it all the time."

As she grew older, it suited Dietrich's ego to deny that she and Wayne had had an affair, probably because he didn't fit in comfortably with her elite roster of European intellectual lovers — Josef von Sternberg, Erich Maria Remarque, Jean Ga-

181

bin, etc. "My mother thought all [Hollywood] people were vulgar," said her daughter, Maria Riva. "She thought *Lubitsch* was extremely vulgar." Dietrich also cast aspersions on Wayne's mind, although that had not been her main area of interest: "Wayne was not a bright or exciting type, [not] exactly brilliant, but neither was he bad."

But Wayne's co-workers knew they were having an affair, as did his friends, as did the FBI. Spurred by some barely literate letters claiming that Dietrich was a Nazi sympathizer — the truth was quite the reverse — the bureau began opening her letters and monitoring her bank accounts as well as her sex life. Besides Wayne, the FBI reported overlapping affairs with Gabin, Remarque, and Kay Francis.

Seven Sinners was shot from July to September 14, 1940. Of the film's budget of $739,000, $150,000 was going to Dietrich. When the picture was finished, Wayne wanted to contribute to the cost of the traditional cast party that the producer and stars front for the cast and crew, but Garnett and Dietrich refused because he was only making his Republic salary.

Dietrich is billed over the title, while Wayne gets "With . . ." billing. It's a pleasantly ramshackle affair bereft of plot but with a passel of great character actors (Mischa Auer, Oscar Homolka, Billy Gilbert, and the silent star Antonio Moreno). Dietrich sings "I Can't Give You Anything but Love, Baby."

What Steven Bach referred to as Wayne's "leatherneck masculinity" provided just as effective a seasoning for Dietrich's languid eroticism as Jimmy Stewart's hesitant willfulness had in *Destry Rides Again.* The material is vaguely Sternbergian,

182

but Tay Garnett directs it to imitate the rhythms of the hugely successful *Destry*.

The Shepherd of the Hills had already begun shooting in and around Big Bear Lake while *Seven Sinners* was wrapping up. Wayne went right from one set to another, a pattern that would become close to normal during World War II, when he would become one of the most popular, as well as most bankable, of Hollywood stars.

The Shepherd of the Hills was a remake of a successful silent film about moonshiners and prodigal fathers, this time in stunning pastoral Technicolor. It's essentially a Christian parable of forgiveness and by 1940 the material was verging on the archaic, but it had one advantage — the 1907 novel by Harold Bell Wright had sold more than a million copies. The director was a temperamental wild man named Henry Hathaway, who would play a major part in Wayne's career. Hathaway had directed *The Trail of the Lonesome Pine,* a similarly groundbreaking Technicolor picture, a few years earlier, so the assignment was logical.

"A funny thing about Wayne," said Hathaway. "Wayne is more particular about the pants he wears than anything in the world. . . . Unless he gets the thinnest kind of material, it drives him crazy. And I [told him], 'You've got to wear homespun. You can't wear cotton gabardine, for Chrissakes, or poplin or something. You've got to wear homespun.' "

Nearly twenty-five years later, Wayne walked into Hathaway's office at Paramount to discuss *The Sons of Katie Elder.* On Hathaway's wall was a still from *The Shepherd of the Hills* — Betty Field clothed in the homespun Hathaway had insisted on. Wayne stopped dead and stared at the picture.

"Do you remember those damn pants?" Wayne asked.

Trailing Wayne to the location at Big Bear was Dietrich, who stayed at Arrowhead, about twenty miles away. One morning a panicked Ward Bond sought out Harry Carey's wife, Ollie. Duke was missing, said Bond, and he didn't want to even think about what Hathaway would do to a star who failed to show up.

Ollie Carey knew very well where Wayne was. She got in her car and headed for Arrowhead. Snow had fallen the night before, and she was driving slowly when she came around a bend and saw a man walking toward her, "a tall, lanky figure, and of course, it was Duke." He quickly got in the car and she asked what happened.

Wayne explained that he'd started back from an evening with Dietrich, but his station wagon had hit a slick spot in the road and gone over an embankment. Wayne had jumped out before the crash, and had set out for Big Bear on foot. They got back to the location just as Hathaway was setting up his first shot. "I don't think he ever knew what was going on between Duke and Marlene," said Ollie Carey.

But Hathaway knew. "They had quite a thing going," he remembered in 1980. "I don't think he realized that I knew the extent of their relationship, but I was aware of what was going on."

In later years, Hathaway tended to push past images to story, which accounts for an impression of brusqueness and lack of personal style. But in the first decade of his career, Hathaway was a visually graceful director — he had been an assistant to von Sternberg and it showed. In *Shepherd of the Hills,* he pulls off some stunning shots

— Marc Lawrence trying to catch dust motes in a ray of sun, or a powerful scene of Beulah Bondi lighting her dead child on fire in a backwoods Viking funeral.

The picture provided Wayne's first opportunity to work with a boyhood idol, and unlike Tom Mix, Harry Carey wasn't a disappointment. If John Ford was the tough, demanding coach whose approval Wayne craved, Carey and his wife, Ollie, were surrogate parents who offered something approaching unconditional love. Their temperaments were well matched: Harry Carey was calm and good-humored, Ollie Carey was salty and plain-spoken. (It's no wonder that Ford cast her as a succession of flinty pioneer women.)

It was Ollie Carey who gave Wayne a piece of advice that became crucial in his career.

"Harry Carey always wore a good hat, a good pair of boots, and what he wore in between didn't matter too much," remembered Wayne.

He had a style of acting that has now become the way of acting in our business. He tried to play it down a little and be kind of natural. You have to keep things going and try and get your personality through, which is what Harry could do. I loved him, because I'd known him for years, and I was a young man and he was an older man.

Anyway, he and his wife were around . . . and I was talking about how I wanted to play every kind of part. The big hero that did everything, the heavies, everything. I wanted to play it all.

And Ollie Carey said, "Well, you big dumb son of a bitch."

I said, "What's the matter?"

185

She said, "Do you really mean what you said? That you'd like to play every kind of part? You think you're Sydney Carton?"

And I said, "Yes, I'd like to get the chance to play all those things."

And Harry was just standing there, and she said, "Do you want Harry Carey to be any different than he is in the movies?"

And I said, "No, of course not."

And she said, "The American public [have] decided to take you into their homes and their hearts. They like the man they see. Forget all this other junk. Be like Harry."

That was something I never forgot.

Duke Morrison had incrementally put together the pieces of a screen character over ten long years — a voice, a name, a walk that would grow more pronounced in the future, an overall attitude. He would continually analyze himself, as well as other actors, but Ollie Carey's advice served as a defining shot to the chops from a woman he loved and respected.

Maybe he needed to rethink his hunger for character parts; maybe he should concentrate on developing and playing John Wayne.

The relationship with Dietrich continued for another year and a half. Early in 1942, Wayne and Dietrich were reunited on a remake of *The Spoilers*. Dietrich's agent, Charles Feldman, had bought the remake rights to the Rex Beach novel for $17,500 in July 1941, packaged it, and turned around and sold it to Universal five months later for $50,000 and 25 percent of the profits.

Ollie Carey was amused by the affair. "You can

tell — the way they look, the way they talk to each other, the way they flirt. Of course, Marlene was double-gated, you know. She had a very masculine-looking young woman that hung around the place a lot. But even so, Duke was quite taken with her and I could tell that Marlene was taken with him as well."

The Spoilers was another hit, grossing nearly three times its cost.

Six months later, Wayne began his third and final film with Dietrich. *Pittsburgh* was again produced by Feldman, who sold Universal the script for a cheap $13,500, although the deal also involved the studio paying Feldman 12.5 percent of the first $240,000 in gross profits. (Feldman would eventually realize $147,843 as his share, a lot more than Wayne's flat $50,000 salary, which was also outpaced by Dietrich's $100,000 and Randolph Scott's $65,000.)

It's a very watchable picture, written by a mélange of mostly uncredited Feldman clients (Tom Reed, John Twist, Winston Miller, Robert Fellows) and directed for speed by the B movie veteran Lew Seiler, who took over when Arthur Lubin backed out.

The picture begins as capital and labor unite for the war effort, then flashes back to Wayne as "Pittsburgh" Markham, a coal miner who has no intention of working for anybody but himself. He's a self-confident master of men, and his charm barely covers his ruthlessness — he even two-times Dietrich, who, unbelievably, plays a woman called Josie.

Pittsburgh grows arrogant and corrupt, eventually marrying a ritzy society dame with whom he's uncomfortable. He's a ruthless boor who loses everything, then redeems himself by diving into war work. Dietrich's Josie ends up bringing the two warring men together in a deeply unlikely but commercially effective ending.

By this time, Wayne and Dietrich had, as you might expect, an easy rapport together. While the film could have been played as a heavy drama, Seiler paces it like a screwball comedy. *Pittsburgh* cost $630,782, and had world rentals of $1.9 million — a considerable success.

Wayne and Dietrich never worked together again, although there were occasional meetings. Wayne always broke into a fond smile when the subject of Dietrich came up, and his précis description of his experience both on- and off-screen was enthusiasm itself: "FANTASTIC!"

Throughout this period, Wayne's Josie was relegated to the part of the suffering wife. "Josephine was a wonderful gal, a very nice person, a real lady," remembered Carolyn Roos Olsen, the daughter of the man who would become Wayne's business manager. "It was a shame they couldn't have stayed together. But everybody's assumption was that her religion was strict; she had four children and didn't want any more, which meant that Duke's access to her was heavily restricted. And he started playing around."

Josie endured much, and she tried to keep the marriage together. It seems that she asked a Father McCoy to come to the house and counsel her husband about his extramarital adventures. Wayne could not have been thrilled about his wife's reliance on priests for domestic advice, but he was suitably contrite and promised to stop seeing Dietrich if Josie would let the matter drop and never bring it up again.

Moments after the priest left, Josie was talking about the affair. "That's when I knew the marriage was over," Wayne said. Wayne had been indulging himself with actresses for years, but Dietrich was very near the last straw. Sally Blane, Loretta Young's sister, said that she overheard Wayne telling a priest, "Father, you just don't know what it means to really *screw* a woman!"

Wayne halfheartedly attempted to justify his behavior by emphasizing the disparity in their social standing. "We'd go to the fancy social night spots," Wayne remembered near the end of his life. "Josephine was really into that. Hell, I was even in the Blue Book. I enjoyed some of these people, but a lot of them, I didn't. Josie's society crowd didn't look down on actors and movies. I was accepted by them. But my work threw me with people they didn't accept. When I had to tell Josie I was going out with this guy who spits tobacco, she just couldn't deal with it. So I just went out by myself and finally it got so I couldn't handle both worlds and Josie and I just sort of drifted apart."

"Josie was the greatest," said her daughter-in-law Gretchen Wayne.

But she had a temper. They each had tempers. Michael's dad always said, "I wish I had waited; I wish your mother could have been more patient with me. I was a young man; I thought [infidelity] was part of the contract."

Bob Hope's wife was patient; Ray Milland's wife was patient. When Grace Kelly went to work on a picture with Ray, Mal Milland knew the affair would be over when the film was over. Many Hollywood wives know that.

But Granny wouldn't put up with it. She just didn't have the patience for philandering. It put her in a terrible position. In those days you had to go downtown to the cardinal for a divorce. A marriage meant something.

The two lovers now enacted a sex-reversed "Pygmalion," as Dietrich introduced Wayne to Bö (pronounced "Boo") Roos, her business manager. Roos ran the Beverly Management Corporation, which had a roster of thirty clients that included Dietrich, Joan Crawford, Merle Oberon, Red Skelton, Johnny Weissmuller, Ray Milland, the Andrews Sisters, and Fred MacMurray.

Roos was a man's man, a ladies' man. He was born in 1903, made a fortune in the California real estate boom of the 1920s, and segued into money management. He sported a fedora, good suits, had a beautiful smile and blue eyes that women regarded as sexy. His standard fee was 3.5 percent of net return, and he usually invested his own money alongside his clients'. There was no written contract, because, said Roos's daughter, Carolyn Roos Olsen, "Movie stars are a different breed of cat. They're emotional, and the lack of a contract made them feel that they could come and go as they pleased. And it formed more of a friendship than a strictly legal arrangement."

Roos's wife was the daughter of a Beverly Hills builder, and Roos believed devoutly in real estate, partially because it was the easiest entity on which to get tax deductions. Roos and Fred MacMurray built several apartment buildings that still exist, one on Olympic, one on Spaulding. They also purchased the California Country Club in West Los Angeles, which did very well — Roos's (mostly correct) instincts were that golf would always be more popular than tennis, because tennis was too much like work.

Wayne was comfortable in business relationships that were also personal friendships — a quirk that would cost him a great deal of money over the years. He and Roos soon became buddies, with equivalent passions for the Republican Party and Mexico. "They should have had dual citizenships," said Olsen. They traveled together, bought a boat together — the *Nor'wester,* a big, wooden seventy-six-foot ship — drank together, played poker together.

But Roos still had to struggle with his most famous client, simply because once Wayne made up his mind, no further discussion was necessary. Even if Wayne got good advice, he was perfectly capable of ignoring it. Saying no to Wayne was not only not easy, it could be counterproductive.

"Duke was a man's man all the way," remembered Olsen. "He loved being with the guys, playing cards, drinking and smoking. That was the Duke. He talked that way too, and was forever apologizing to my mother for his language."

One story indicates the level of trust Wayne had in Roos; it also indicates his level of generosity. Roos had opened a place called the Cabana Club, a swimming pool/bar/getaway, but the timing was wrong — when it opened, the backyard swimming pool was common in Hollywood. One night, Roos glumly observed that the Cabana Club was in trouble. Wayne took out his checkbook and handed it to Roos. "Write in any amount you need to keep this place going and I'll sign the check."

As a friend, admirable; as a businessman, disastrous.

191

"I always thought Duke was an intelligent man," said Olsen, "but vulnerable when it came to the really nice guy con man type." Wayne was, with good reason, becoming optimistic about money — any temporary financial shortfall could be solved by doing another movie.

But other disasters wouldn't be so easily fixed. The woman who became Wayne's second wife was Bö Roos's fault. In August 1941, Roos took a group of clients to Mexico to see about an investment in a movie studio. Wayne, MacMurray, Milland, and Ward Bond were staying at the Hotel Reforma when Milland introduced Wayne to a young woman named Esperanza Baur Díaz Ceballos, known as "Chata," or "pug-nose." Wayne was immediately taken, despite the fact that Milland had been taken some time before, and she was generally regarded as Milland's private port of call.

Chata began flirting, Wayne responded and soon he was telling Roos that the great thing about Latin women was that they liked the simple things — marriage, family, children, a home. Roos was appalled. For one thing, Chata was quite obviously the woman you took to bed, not the woman you married, and he didn't believe that Chata — or her omnipresent mother — were remotely capable of being Hollywood wives.

"Dad's response to Chata was that Duke couldn't afford her," said Olsen. "How can I put this? She was a Mexican woman trained to be a friend to men. Oh, hell, she was a courtesan. I never thought she was attractive because she had blotchy skin; I couldn't understand what Duke saw in her. Dad knew her history, and Duke knew her history, but Duke fell in love."

Roos had several come-to-Jesus meetings with his client. In one room he was yelling at Wayne that he couldn't possibly afford another financial burden. In the next room, Carolyn Roos was talking to Chata, saying it was a bad idea to marry a man with so many family obligations. Then there was the fourteen-year age difference. All of their combined arguments failed to make a dent.

There was always a great deal of on/off, back/forth with Chata. The affair was tempestuous, and it was a preview of coming attractions. "We kept trying to talk him out of marrying her," said Olsen. "One time after a meeting at our house, he walked me out to my car and got in with me. He turned to me with tears in his eyes and said, 'Would you please call Chata and tell her I love her?'"

"Chata made a certain kind of sense," said Gretchen Wayne. "Her mother was a madam, and she came out of the brothels of Mexico." A man who had only recently been introduced to the further reaches of sensuality by Marlene Dietrich was now head over heels with his very own Mexican spitfire. Within a few months, Chata was in Hollywood, where she was put under contract by Herbert Yates. Chata became an accepted part of Wayne's life. Victor McLaglen's son Andrew remembered a night at John Ford's house on Odin Street when Wayne got down on his knees and told Chata how much he loved her.

In a background document probably written by Bev Barnett, Wayne's publicity man, the standard line for Wayne's rapidly approaching divorce was devised. It was not inaccurate so much as deeply self-serving: "Josie . . . was a Pasadena society girl. Duke's pals were Ward Bond and John Ford, both of whom she loathed. Duke liked to drink and raise hell; Josie liked to go to society parties in Pasadena. Wayne is not a tuxedo man. Duke always has said if he could make as much money propping, he would rather do that than act. Because a prop man can do as he pleases; a star can't. Duke is a passionate guy; Josie was cold. When that was brought up in court, she pointed to her four children. Wayne said . . . 'Yeah, four times in ten years.' On the surface they lived happily for ten years; the fact is they should never have been married in the first place."

Variations on this story appeared for years in newspapers and magazines.* Wayne seemed oblivious to the fact that he was tossing aside a loyal woman — and the mother of his children — in order to justify his atrocious taste in mistresses. Typically, Josie said nothing, then or later.

The emphasis on Wayne's discomfort with Josie's religion is illuminating. "Michael's dad always said he could be a Catholic intellectually," said Gretchen Wayne, "and in fact he converted on his deathbed. He loved to talk to priests, liked to play cards with them and loved discussing religion with them." But the urge toward Catholi-

---

* One version appeared in *Motion Picture* magazine in December 1952: "Josephine is a very devout Catholic, a woman wrapped up in church work and more charities than she is really able to find time for or afford. John is not a Catholic, and while many of his wife's projects were dear to him, and he admired her staunch religious fervor, he became an outsider in his own family and, like any man will, he drifted."

cism stalled when it came to actions rather than words.

Josie had kept quiet through Wayne's various flirtations and relationships with his co-stars, but the twin hits of Marlene Dietrich and Chata were more than she could bear. "The cause of the split was Chata," said Gretchen. "What happened was that Chata called him at home. *At night.* And he came home to find that Josie had piled all of his clothes out on the front lawn. That was it."

On June 20, 1942, Wayne and his wife separated. Mary Ford was appalled and wrote to her husband, who was heading up a reconnaissance outfit for the Navy during World War II called the Field Photo Service. "Can't you write and try to beat something into Duke's head. . . . He has gone completely berserk over that Esperanza Bauer [sic] and cares for no one. Thinks he is the hottest bet in pictures and says he is madly in love and nothing else matters. It's a damn shame that with a war going on he has to think about his lousy stinking tail. I only think of those gorgeous kids. It's really tragic."

Ford made a mild feint in Wayne's direction, making a slighting remark in a letter about "Mexican jumping beans," but Wayne wasn't having any, writing Ford back that he didn't "give a four letter word, if I can see my kids" and had had enough of "the local board of busy bodies" — obviously including Mary Ford.

While the terms of the divorce were negotiated, Wayne had to find someplace to live, and that place turned out to be the house of his friend and acting coach Paul Fix. At one point, Wayne and Fix were shooting *In Old Oklahoma,* so Wayne and Chata moved into Fix's den, which had a pull-out sofa bed. Fix's daughter Marilyn, who would later marry Harry Carey Jr., remembered that the guests stayed for months, with Wayne and her father regularly going off to work together.

"My mother got conned into packing their lunch every single day since they hated the commissary food. She made this huge lunch for them, and everybody on the set loved it, so it got bigger and bigger to the point where she was complaining, 'You know, I have to get up at the crack of dawn and make all these sandwiches and put in fruit and cookies and all that.' But she did it anyway. . . . Eventually, Duke and Chata moved to the Chateau Marmont." Harry Carey Jr. nodded in agreement, then added, "A famous shack-up place."

The negotiations over the divorce went on for a few years until it was finally granted in November 1944. It was final on December 26, 1945.

Wayne was hyperconscious of his image, and he knew that divorcing a universally respected woman like Josie was bound to make him the heavy. "Everyone in Hollywood considered me a heel for leaving four kids," he grumbled. "They didn't consider the fact that I gave her all I had and will continue to give it." Wayne forked over the house and car, $100,000 in securities and insurance, 20 percent of his gross income, and $200 a month for a trust fund for their children. It was a stiff settlement, but Wayne didn't complain. "She damned well deserves it. She's done a wonderful job with the kids."

For years after the divorce, Wayne would get up before dawn on the morning of December 25, drive to Josie's house and wait outside so he could be there when the kids woke up. For a time, he was bitter, but eventually the bitterness wore off, and he always paid tribute to Josie's aura of class and skills as a mother.

Wayne felt guilty about the divorce for the rest of his life. In later years he would admit to his children that he had made a terrible mistake: "I destroyed my first marriage. . . . I was a different man back then. I was much more selfish."

Among other things, Wayne told friends that he believed his son Michael never completely forgave him. Yet, in some respects, things didn't change that much. "I didn't spend a great deal of time with [my father] while I grew up," recalled Patrick Wayne. "My parents were divorced when I was four years old. I didn't live with him. I probably spent as much time with him as I would have anyway [without the divorce] because he was always away working."

Wayne's agent had been Leo Morrison since his days at Mascot. Morrison's best deal for Wayne had been $3,000 a picture at Republic. After making *Stagecoach* for John Ford on loan-out, for which he earned only his Republic salary, Wayne went right back to Republic and $3,000 a picture. He was furious, because he knew that opportunity had just knocked and, to all intents and purposes, nobody was home.

The most influential of Wayne's co-stars was not Claire Trevor, not Maureen O'Hara, but Marlene Dietrich, simply because it was Dietrich who introduced Wayne to the man who would impeccably manage his career for the next quarter century: Charles Feldman.

Generally known as the Jewish Clark Gable — he combed his hair the same way and affected the same rakish mustache — Feldman was one of the crucial figures in Hollywood history, although the moguls of 1941 would have laughed at the description. Feldman was one of the first agents to package his clients: that is, he would take a couple of acting clients, a writing client, a directing client and sell them as a package to a studio to make a specific picture. Myron Selznick did the same thing, but Feldman took it a step further than Selznick by occasionally producing the pictures himself. Over the years, Feldman, credited or uncredited, would produce pictures as varied as *Red River,* Orson Welles's *Macbeth, A Streetcar Named Desire,* and *The Seven Year Itch.*

Born in New York in 1904, Feldman was orphaned, then adopted. After attending the University of Michigan and USC, in 1928 he set up a law practice in Los Angeles. By 1932, he was a rising young agent, the head of the company he called Famous Artists. Personally, he was charming, sophisticated, extremely smart, and made it a point never to tell any single person everything that was going on — an archetypal big-picture man, Vito Corleone *and* Tom Hagen.

Feldman correctly understood that for an independent, power could derive only from product; for that product to stand out in a crowded marketplace it had to have the imprimatur of quality. As a result, he dealt almost exclusively in high-end representation. "Charlie was very stylish," remembered the actor-producer Norman Lloyd, "always immaculately dressed. He had an outstanding list of clients. . . . Charlie Feldman had the clout to pick up the phone and call a studio head on a first-name basis. He led a cosmopolitan life."

In the mid-1930s, Feldman snatched the young

actress Jean Howard away from Louis B. Mayer, then married her, which caused Mayer to temporarily ban him from MGM. In later years, Howard became one of Hollywood's premier lesbians, but the two continued to live together even after they divorced. Nobody quite understood the relationship, but they certainly understood Feldman's taste for exotic mistresses and an ever-growing client list.

In late July 1941, Wayne stopped paying commissions to Leo Morrison, who didn't take it lying down. Morrison filed a complaint with the Artists and Managers Guild against Feldman, charging that Feldman's discussions with Wayne, whom Morrison had represented since 1932 and whose contract had another year to run, was a clear violation of industry rules, not to mention etiquette.

In September, Morrison sued Feldman and Dietrich for inducing Wayne to break his contract, charging that Dietrich "used undue influence to weaken and undermine the mental capacity of actor John Wayne." This got into the newspapers, clearly implying Dietrich's relationship with Wayne. An internecine trade dispute had expanded to embarrass Wayne.

In response, Wayne said that he had been dissatisfied with Morrison for more than a year, that he had been negotiating on his own behalf for some time, and that "such negotiations, on at least two occasions, resulted in my obtaining offers in excess of the offers obtained by Leo Morrison." Furthermore, Wayne asserted that he had discussed representation with a number of other agents, and that he had been willing to compromise with Leo Morrison, who was always "arbitrary."

Wayne gave a deposition, as did Dietrich. Leo Morrison asked $150,000 for damages (after giving it some thought, he upped the damages to $225,000). On December 15, Morrison dropped both Feldman and Dietrich from the lawsuit in exchange for a token settlement of $2 apiece. That same day, Wayne signed — as both "Duke Morrison" and "John Wayne" — an agreement stating that he would continue to pay Morrison commissions through June of 1942.

Behind the entire affair was the realization that, after *Stagecoach,* Wayne was moving up to the big leagues and needed an agent who could negotiate on equal terms with the Mayers and Warners. Of the five or six agents qualified to do so, Feldman was first among equals, and Wayne never had cause to regret his decision.

On January 23, 1942, Wayne notified Republic that he had changed his representation to Charles Feldman. On May 3, Feldman completed negotiations with Republic on a new deal for Wayne. The contract called for five pictures over three years, with the first two pictures earning Wayne $25,000 apiece, and the last three bringing $35,000 apiece. Wayne was guaranteed star billing and the services of Paul Fix as dialogue director at $200 a week. There were no budget minimums on the first two pictures, but the negative costs on the last three were pegged at a minimum of $450,000 each. Finally, Republic could loan out Wayne to other studios, but not without his approval, and the studio agreed to give Wayne half of any salary overages they received.

It was a very good deal, not quite a great deal;

Feldman's influence was mainly felt in factors such as budgetary minimums — no small thing at a B picture studio like Republic. Clearly, Feldman saw Wayne as a franchise in the making, and his upgrading of Wayne's status had the desired effect. By 1944, Wayne was number twenty-four in the top twenty-five box office stars in the movie business; by the end of the decade he was number one. Simultaneously, Feldman began nudging Wayne toward producing, and by 1947, *Angel and the Badman* was billed as "A John Wayne Production."

Next to John Ford, Charles Feldman was the most crucial professional relationship of John Wayne's life.

These were busy years for Wayne. When he wasn't running from picture to picture, there were weekends on John Ford's yacht *Araner,* which provoked either envy or dismay, depending on how people felt about clannish Irishmen.

"Ford liked Duke," said Lindsley Parsons, "he liked Ward Bond and there were quite a few of them that would go out in that rotten boat of his, the *Araner,* that everybody thought the bottom was gonna fall out of. We'd see him over at the Isthmus. The whole group would go up and build a big pit and somebody would go out and shoot a wild pig and they'd barbeque it. Ward Bond professed to be the cook."

Around town, Wayne became known for his conviviality and willingness to stand a round for the house. One of his favorite places was a restaurant on the Sunset Strip called Eugene's. During the war, with curfews imposed, it was a bottle club, run more or less like a speakeasy during Prohibition — you had to knock on the door and be recognized.

Wayne told a story about a time when he was having a drink at Eugene's and there was a loud banging on the door. The maître d', a man named Al Murphy, who later went to work for Wayne, went to check it out and came back to Wayne.

"It's Bogart."

"Well, let him in."

"No. He owes us six hundred bucks. He won't pay us."

"Let him in, I'll take care of it."

Bogart came in, slightly the worse for wear, and took the stool next to Wayne. At the time, Bogart was married to the actress Mayo Methot; they formed a pair of violent alcoholics known as the Battling Bogarts. Wayne looked over and saw something sticking out of Bogart's back — an apple corer, stuck in up to the hilt.

Wayne said, "Oh, my God," and tried to pull it out, but it was stuck. He couldn't get it out until he put his foot on Bogart's back for leverage. After that, they took the actor to the hospital to get stitched up.

During the war years, Wayne developed a sideline in romantic comedies, largely because actors with a more native proficiency were unavailable by dint of service in the military. Whether working with Dietrich in *Seven Sinners, The Spoilers,* or *Pittsburgh* — the dynamic was similar: masculine forth-rightness tamed European decadence. Working with Jean Arthur in *A Lady Takes a Chance,* Claudette Colbert in *Without Reservations,* or even Joan Crawford in *Reunion in France,* Wayne tended to play an innocent American in over his head with this love business.

In Jeanine Basinger's words, Wayne as a romantic object was "embarrassed but effective. His style was to lean down toward the woman and offer her a straight deal. No love talk, just action. . . . Good or bad, he wanted a woman who was his equal. . . . When Wayne got serious, there was to be no fooling around, no coyness. He lunged toward his love and attacked her, not meaning to be brutal, but to make his intentions clear." Wayne's basic stance in a romantic comedy was not unlike the brusque transaction offered by Clark Gable, although Wayne was shyer and projected less tomcat.

Wayne's career was now going from strength to strength, medium to medium. Tay Garnett created an NBC radio show for Wayne called *Three Sheets to the Wind* which starred Wayne as an alcoholic detective — "My good man, bring me a scotch and soda," says Wayne's character on the first episode. "And not too much soda." The character was written to Wayne's already established specifications — at one point someone refers to him as "that all-American Gargantua."

The radio show was supposedly a stalking horse for a movie version, but that never happened. It had an interesting group of behind-the-scenes people; leading lady Helga Moray was Garnett's disputatious wife, and among the writers were Jerome Lawrence and Robert Lee, later to become rich and famous as the co-authors of *Auntie Mame* and *Inherit the Wind.*

The show lasted for only twenty-six weeks, beginning in February 1942, and the network seems to have blown it off — they ran it at the ungodly hour of 8:30 P.M. on Sunday nights on the East Coast, 11:30 P.M. on the West Coast.

203

It's possible that either Garnett or Feldman supplied Wayne with an introduction to Robert Fellows, who was born in 1903 to a shipbuilding family in California but was more interested in the movies. He always claimed that he got his start in the business by acting as one of Cecil B. DeMille's chair boys, who were delegated the task of following the director around on the set, and making sure that his director's chair was beneath him when he finally deigned to sit down.

Fellows climbed the ladder and became an assistant to Garnett, and later a successful producer at Paramount and RKO, supervising pictures with major stars such as Alan Ladd, Bing Crosby . . . and John Wayne. In a few years, Fellows would partner with Wayne in Wayne-Fellows Productions.

What clearly attracted Wayne to Fellows was their similar backgrounds as movie journeymen. "What Bob doesn't know about the business isn't worth knowing," Wayne would say. "He's been a stage manager, actor, assistant cutter, prop man, writer and director. Just name it." As always, Wayne had an innate distrust of the artiste — always excepting John Ford — and was attracted to the all-arounder, the pro.

DeMille's original choice for the second lead in *Reap the Wild Wind* was Joel McCrea, but he had committed to a Preston Sturges picture. DeMille began pursuing the newly hot John Wayne to play against Ray Milland. DeMille and Wayne had a history, although DeMille may have preferred not to acknowledge it. During the preparations for DeMille's 1936 epic *The Plainsman,* Leo Morrison got his client an interview for the part of

Wild Bill Hickok. Wayne was on time, but DeMille was running late. When he finally emerged from his office he told Wayne he was going to lunch. Reminded of the interview, he asked the actor to come into his office.

"He said to me, 'You were in *The Big Trail,* weren't you?' " remembered Wayne. " 'I saw it and you did just fine. But a lot of water has gone under the bridge since then.' " Wayne explained that he had been doing quickie pictures and that he had learned to read bad lines as well as anyone in the business, but he wanted a crack at better pictures. "I'll get back to you," said DeMille. That, said Wayne, "was DeMille's way of turning me down. To him I was now just a minor star of mere B westerns."

A few years later, right after *Stagecoach,* DeMille sent Wayne the script for *North West Mounted Police;* he was interested in Wayne for the part eventually played by Preston Foster. Wayne sent the script back with a note: "A lot of water's gone under the bridge."

Now DeMille sent him the script for *Reap the Wild Wind.* The actor stayed up all night reading it, then dictated his typically articulate reaction before he left on a trip the next morning. "I was disappointed in the lack of color and character in Jack Martin," Wayne wrote.

However, I recalled the picture of Martin that Mr. DeMille painted for us in his office, so I disregarded the play of the character as painted by the writers. . . . At the entrance of Steve [Milland] into the story Jack becomes negative in all scenes that include the three principals. I think there is a possibility of developing him into a

great character . . . [that] will add color to the
script as a whole. . . . This can be done simply
by making him an individualist played boldly and
impulsively instead of being played as a plod-
ding dullard. . . .

Jack should be brusque and sure of himself in
all physical situations because of the station of
life that he has reached at a youthful age. He
doesn't need to be a mental giant — maybe a
little short on logic, but must not be dull — must
possess a definite sense of humor to help him
through two or three melodramatic situations that
arise.

DeMille walked into the conference room where
screenwriters Jesse Lasky Jr., Alan Le May, and
Charles Bennett were working and read Wayne's
letter out loud. Wayne's analysis of the script was
focused, intelligent, and, given DeMille's distaste
for assertive actors, outrageous.

The writers waited for DeMille to explode and
vow never to hire that young pup as long as he
lived. Instead he looked at his writers and said, "If
an actor can see what's wrong and work it out,
why couldn't you?" It was the beginning of a close
relationship between two alpha males.

The script encored the central dynamic that
DeMille had used on *Union Pacific* and *North West
Mounted Police:* a stalwart hero (in *Reap the Wild
Wind* he does origami), and a lusty, semiheroic
figure who, through a single weakness of character,
turns bad but atones by dying nobly (Robert Pres-
ton in the earlier films, Wayne in the new one).
Nobody lovingly mounted dramatic clichés like
DeMille . . . and in Technicolor! At the end of the
picture, a giant squid is staked through the eye,

206

and the explosion of ink envelops the divers. Simultaneously, on the surface of the ocean, a tsunami hits.

For DeMille, too much was never enough.

DeMille even allowed Wayne to select his own costume, including a show-stopping orange scarf. The Technicolor consultant decreed the orange scarf off-limits, but DeMille stepped in and said if Wayne wanted to wear an orange scarf, then by God he would wear an orange scarf.

"Wayne was one of the few actors DeMille never yelled at," remembered Jesse Lasky Jr. "DeMille liked Wayne so much that he invited him to join him for lunch every day, which was an honor for any actor." When a group of exhibitors was touring the set the day a shipboard donnybrook was to be filmed, DeMille interrupted the rehearsal. "John, I want you to show them how to play this scene," he announced over the microphone.

Wayne demonstrated for the visitors how actors threw and took punches, then placed the actors and stuntmen and choreographed the fight scene. DeMille liked what he saw. "Action!" he called.

In Old California shows Republic trying to class up the Wayne franchise. He plays a dude druggist from Boston in a top hat and cane who says "Excuse me, pardon me" as he moves through the crowd. But he's not a man to be messed with. When he orders a glass of milk, he says, "Plain. No rum. And no comments," as he bends a coin between his fingers. Albert Dekker, as the boorish heavy, pushes him around not just once, but twice. Already the slow-to-anger Wayne persona is in place; we sit back comfortably, knowing that payback is coming.

207

The film functions as a sort of gentle parody of the image that was already beginning to coalesce. The script is unusually good for Republic, and most studios would have been happy to make it. Movies like *In Old California* show that while Republic didn't do Wayne any favors, they didn't do anything to hurt him either, mostly because his personality was unkillable.

Case in point: *Reunion in France,* for which Wayne was lent to MGM the same year as *In Old California,* in and of itself a hell of a note. As was normal for MGM, the script went through half a dozen hands, including Jan Lustig, Marvin Borowsky, Marc Connelly, and Charles Hoffman. One of the scripts ends with Wayne's character skywriting "COURAGE" in the air over Occupied Paris. Despite direction by Jules Dassin and an uncredited guest bit by Charles Laughton, it's a grievously awful film in which Joan Crawford plays a society butterfly in Paris ("Darling, my train leaves in less than an hour. Come with me to Biarritz!") just before the Germans march in and spoil the social season. Because of the Germans, Crawford quickly converts to the cause of selflessness and French nationalism.

Wayne, playing a downed American flier, doesn't make his entrance until the movie is forty-three minutes old. He seems to be enjoying himself, as well he might be — he's at MGM, and a crummy movie at MGM was worth more than the unlikely possibility of an excellent movie at Republic.

In the crucial year of 1942, Wayne made a picture for Cecil B. DeMille, two pictures with Marlene Dietrich (*The Spoilers* and *Pittsburgh*), a picture at MGM, and two at his home studio of Republic: *In Old California* and *Flying Tigers,* a patchwork script about Claire Chennault's air group that featured some of the best miniature work Hollywood could produce. They all made money, in some cases a great deal of it. It was in 1942 that Hollywood and the public came to the simultaneous realization that John Wayne was more than John Ford's protégé; he was a genuine leading man.

CHAPTER SEVEN

Hugh Krampe was seventeen when he enlisted in the Marines in 1943. He was in boot camp in San Diego when he began participating in the Friday night fights called "smokers" — tobacco companies handed out two and three packs of cigarettes to each soldier attending the fights. Platoons would put sixty-four pieces of paper in a hat, with one marked "boxer." The man that drew the fatal slip would square off against another guy in another platoon who drew the same slip.

Krampe was six foot one and 155 pounds, lean and mean, so he felt pretty confident when he drew the slip marked "boxer." Then he climbed into the ring that had been erected on an outdoor stage and saw his competition: "He was about six-five, 255 pounds, black, a former tackle on the Texas A&M football team. A giant." Krampe quickly began to calculate his rapidly increasing risk of mortality.

The announcer proclaimed that the assembled Marines had a special treat; that there would be a guest referee for this first round only, the well-known movie star John Wayne.

"John Wayne climbed into the ring and got between us. He looked at me, then he looked at the other guy and took it all in. 'Do you want to fight Queensbury rules, or John Wayne rules?' he asked us. Well, what choice did we have? We said 'John Wayne rules.' And he said 'Good.' And then he gave me a little wink, got out of the ring and sat down and hit the gong to start the round. In other words, there was no referee.

"He knew what I knew — that my only hope of surviving was not to fight but to outrun that big son of a bitch, which is what I proceeded to do. And he wouldn't let the timekeeper hit the gong to end the round. The round just kept going on and on."

Krampe was never sure if the fight — such as it was — lasted eight minutes or twenty minutes. All he knew was that after chasing him and fruitlessly swinging for a long, long time, the man from Texas A&M collapsed from exhaustion and an equally exhausted Krampe fell on top of him. He was the winner, sort of, and received a copper bracelet for his troubles.

Krampe remembered the experience all his long life. Shortly thereafter, he became one of the youngest drill instructors in Marine Corps history. Under the name Hugh O'Brian, he became a TV star in the 1950s and, more than thirty years after the match in San Diego, would be part of John Wayne's last movie.

Just before he began work on *Reap the Wild Wind,* Wayne filled out his Selective Service questionnaire. He gave his name as "Marion Mitchell Morrison (John Wayne)." On June 24, 1941, the draft board classified him 3-A (registrant with dependents).

That's how it stayed until December 3, 1943,

when he was reclassified 2-A, after a deferment claim was filed by a third party — undoubtedly Herbert Yates and Republic. The 2-A classification meant that the registrant had a talent or skill not replaceable by another person, a corollary to the government's rating of the film business as an essential industry for reasons of propaganda and morale.

Wayne's 2-A classification was good for six months, but another third-party request for a deferment was filed a couple of weeks later. Yet another third-party deferment request was filed on April 16, 1944, but the December 1943 deferment had run out before the board could classify the request, so Wayne was classified 1-A on May 3, 1944. On June 12, the April deferment request was acted upon, and Wayne was again downgraded to 2-A. Third-party deferments continued to be filed until May 1945, just as the war was ending, at which time Wayne was classified 4-A: deferred by reason of age. At this point, Wayne was thirty-eight years old.

In practice, the government's preference toward the movie industry meant that almost any actor or studio employee deemed important could receive an occupational deferment. Stars who served in combat usually enlisted. But many actors didn't want to claim deferments.

Like Wayne, Gene Autry was under contract to Republic. Autry was thirty-five at the time of Pearl Harbor, married with no children, albeit with three dependents (two sisters and a brother). Autry related how Herbert Yates tried to talk him out of enlisting: "This is an essential industry. We can go to Washington and get you a deferment. You won't be touched." But Autry told Yates, "I can't stay out. It would make me look bad and the movie business look bad."

Describing his thought processes, Autry wrote "There was nothing noble about it. I would have much rather kept counting my money and firing blanks. But there didn't seem to me to be any choice. If you were healthy, and able, you either served or you learned how to shave in the dark."

Autry went into the Army Air Corps in 1942, which only made Yates more determined to keep Wayne at Republic. Truthfully, every studio head was panicked about having their prime corporate assets disappear for a couple of years (at best). Mickey Rooney remembered that "L. B. Mayer didn't want me going into the service; he didn't want *anybody* going into the service." MGM had withheld a telegram from General Hap Arnold, the Air Force chief of staff, offering Clark Gable "a highly important commission." Even though he was over forty, Gable enlisted in the Air Force in August 1942 — Gable's friend Robert Stack believed he was suicidal over the death of his wife, Carole Lombard. Gable went through a grueling basic training in Miami with men half his age and flew a number of bombing missions as an aerial gunner.

Many actors refused the deferments they could have had for the asking — Henry Fonda was thirty-seven years old with three children when he enlisted in the Air Corps in 1942. Robert Montgomery enlisted in the Navy, as did Douglas Fairbanks Jr. Tyrone Power enlisted in the Marines, William Holden went into the Army. Stars that didn't go — Gary Cooper, Bing Crosby, James Cagney, among others — were over forty.

Over the years, a fairly extensive list of reasons

would be offered by Wayne and family members regarding his rigorously maintained noncombatant status, ranging from old football injuries to extensive dependents. It's certainly true that in the early days of the war, Selective Service made an effort not to disrupt families, but as the war ground on, and local draft boards had to meet increased quotas, it became normal for fathers to be inducted. By 1944, manpower needs were so extensive that distinctions between men who were fathers and men who weren't had ceased to exist as far as Selective Service was concerned.

Amidst the profusion of reasons for Wayne not going into the service, the one that appears to be the most medically valid was the presence of a recurring ear infection. "He had an ear infection actually caused from . . . that film he made called *Reap the Wild Wind*," said Michael Wayne. "It never left and every time he'd get in the water it would come back. So he was actually 4F."

As studio archives attest, Wayne did indeed have a recurring ear infection, but then he didn't have to go into the Navy.

Yet, contrary to those who feel it convenient to regard Wayne as a classic case of war wimp, it is clear that he did make some effort to get into the service. On August 2, 1943, he filled out an application for the OSS, under the name "Marion Robert Morrison (John Wayne)." The application stated that his nickname was Duke, that he was six feet three and three quarters inches tall, that he weighed 212 pounds, and that he used intoxicants "moderately."

His memberships were listed as Sigma Chi fraternity, the Screen Actors Guild, the American Federation of Radio Artists, and the Hollywood

Athletic Club. His foreign language was Latin, with a "slight" proficiency in speaking and a "fair" proficiency in reading. Sports and hobbies were listed as "swimming, above average; small boat sailing, average; football, played college ball at University of Southern California; squash and tennis, fair; deep-sea fishing, 7 marlin in two years; hunting, good field shot; horseback riding, have done falls and posse riding in pictures, not as easy as it sounds."

His character references were impeccable and calculated to appeal to Wild Bill Donovan, the founder of the OSS: Commander John Ford, and Commander Frank Wead. Also used as references were Bö Roos, MGM producer and screenwriter James Kevin McGuinness, and Robert Smith, managing editor of the Los Angeles *Daily News.*

Wayne's current Selective Service classification was left blank, and under particular qualifications he noted "Having a natural inclination and being suited physically and mentally to outdoor activity and having the ability to get along with any class of people might have a particular bearing on the position in which I might be of value to the Service."

Wayne followed up, going to Washington to interview with Donovan personally. Irene Nelson was one of Donovan's secretaries and remembered that "I couldn't believe [Wayne] was sitting there, right next to me at my desk."

What happened next is less a matter of record, more a matter of inference. According to Wayne, Ford introduced him to Donovan after first telling Donovan that Wayne would be good for something like the small boat work Sterling Hayden was doing in Cairo and Yugoslavia (Hayden was a superb sailor and organized a splinter fleet of schooners and caïques to run the German blockade). Wayne said that he had three pictures to make first and then wanted to "get in." Donovan introduced him to a major whose name Wayne couldn't remember.

Fade out.

Fade in.

Wayne has finished the three pictures and his marriage is on the rocks. He calls the major but has difficulty finding him. When he finally makes connections, the major is a colonel and asks why Wayne didn't answer the letter.

"A letter?" asked Wayne.

"I sent you a letter," said the colonel, "and said we were getting too many lieutenants and if you wanted to get in, you better get back here."

In this telling, it was Josie's fault for not forwarding the letter. But Irene Nelson, Donovan's secretary, said that Donovan didn't take Wayne because he didn't think he had any of the outside interests that might qualify him for undercover work.

Between the documents and an anecdotal mélange of excuses including recurring ailments or missed communications, it's possible to figure out a likely scenario.

In Wayne's letters to John Ford during the first two years of the war, he speaks often of his desire to finish just a few more pictures before he enlists, and in a handwritten, undated letter that's been provisionally ascribed to May 1942, he comes right out and asks for help: "Dear Pappy, Have you any suggestions on how I should get in? Can I get assigned to your outfit and if I could would you want me? How about the Marines? You have Army and Navy men under you — have you any

Marines or how about a Seabee or what would you suggest? . . . I just hate to ask favors, but for Christ sake you can suggest can't you!!!"

There is no response from Ford in either his or Wayne's papers.

Wayne made thirteen pictures during World War II at four different studios, and his hard work during the war years, not to mention the attendant lack of competition from stars who were in the service, meant that his career was given a huge boost simply by his presence. The poor boy from Glendale was either deeply embarrassed by Donovan's indifference to the offer of his services, or, alternatively, couldn't tear himself away from his ascending success.

This could have been overlooked if Wayne had hurled himself into war work, as, for instance, John Garfield did in starting the Hollywood Canteen, or as Bob Hope did in ceaselessly entertaining the troops. But according to Mary Ford, who was at the Canteen all the time — she ran the kitchen — Wayne's attendance was spotty. Besides making movies, he was divorcing his first wife, courting his second, and spending a lot of time with Ward Bond and other assorted cronies.

It's probable that Wayne was emotionally committed to working under Ford's command, was embarrassed about Donovan shying away from him at the height of the war, and simply wasn't willing to enlist and take his chances. Certainly, he had an image of himself as an officer under Ford. But, as he would say, "I would have had to go in as a private. I took a dim view of that."

Right after Christmas in 1943, Wayne embarked on a major USO tour to the southwest Pacific, from Brisbane, Australia, to New Guinea to New

Britain, playing several shows a day and visiting hospitals. The tour lasted for several months, in a tough theater — New Guinea consisted of hard rock, soft mud, and natives who thought nothing of dining on human flesh if the supply of wild pigs ran low. As Keith Honaker, a soldier in New Britain, said, "Going into battle was a diversion for us. We had absolutely nothing to do from the standpoint of recreation — we didn't even get newspapers, very seldom got any letters."

Wayne would claim that the only time he was ever truly frightened in his life came in a very rough flight over the Coral Sea. "I thought it was pretty stormy, and when it became more than uncomfortable, I looked back at a bunch of fighter pilots that were being shipped to Nadzab, and I saw that their faces were paler than the moon." Since the professionals were scared, Wayne felt he had leave to be terrified.

One of the men backing up Wayne in his show was Benjamin DeLoache, who later became a professor of voice at Yale. DeLoache was born in 1906 and made his debut in 1928 with Stokowski and the Philadelphia Orchestra. After that, he'd sung the American premiere of Alban Berg's *Wozzeck.* During the war, he'd been entertaining troops in Alaska, then Australia. After he hooked up with Wayne's unit, the star told him, "You know, Ben, I'd look like a fool if I put on that cowboy thing of mine. So there's nothing I can do, really, but I can introduce you, and I'll get you the biggest audiences that you ever sang for in your life."

Some days they'd do seven and eight shows, with DeLoache singing songs from *Oklahoma!*, and Wayne closing things out with a stirring rendition of "Minnie the Moocher." Then they'd go through the hospitals and talk to the men. "We were together a great, great deal," remembered DeLoache, "and I got to know him very well. John was a man of remarkable humility. He never took any credit for anything that God had to do with. What I mean by that is, he knew what he had done about his career, but he also knew the things about his career that he had nothing to do with. He had a wonderful humility along with that very, very strong personality."

Keith Honaker was a battalion adjutant on New Britain when he noticed a big man walking up a dusty road full of blown-up palm trees and bomb craters. The man was wearing a big hat and a Flying Tigers jacket. Honaker's first thought was that it was a smart-ass GI, but it turned out to be John Wayne, whose first words were, "Partner, where is Fred Stofft?"

Fred Stofft, Duke's pal from Glendale, was now a colonel commanding a battalion fighting in New Britain in an area called Arawe. Stofft had told people that Wayne and he had been childhood pals, but nobody believed him. Stofft came back from the front to be told there was somebody who wanted to see him in the shower, which consisted of a five-gallon can hanging from a canvas sling in a palm tree, with another hunk of canvas for a shower curtain.

Stofft approached the shower and heard a man singing in a voice that sounded familiar. He pulled back the canvas curtain and found Duke. He had jumped on a PT boat and brought his USO troupe with him.

After Wayne got out of the shower, Stofft took him to quarters, where Wayne reached down into his kit bag and handed his old friend a quart of whiskey. "I carried this all over the South Pacific until I could find you," he said.

"I'll bet there was a case when you started," said Stofft.

The troupe went on to another base, but Wayne stayed in New Britain for a couple of days. He went up in an artillery spotting plane and dropped some mortar shells on the Japanese position. "We like to went crazy when we found out what happened," said Honaker. "A man of that stature doing a thing like that."

A day or two later, Fred Stofft and his men had to clean out a nest of Japanese who were lobbing artillery into the American area. "I was up in the head of one of the landing craft," remembered Stofft. "I looked around and here alongside of me, here's Duke. And I said, 'What the devil are you doing here?' And he said, 'I want to go and see what's going on.'

"Well, if he'd have been hurt, we'd have been in trouble, because he had no business being up in that area anyway. . . . There was actual fighting and he was part of that."

Keith Honaker said that "He became one of us. He was just like everyone else. He showed us that he really was a down-to-earth guy. . . . He didn't ask for any protection. . . . He actually did off the screen what he did on the screen."

"We have developed a show that the men like," Wayne wrote Charles Feldman on January 26, 1944. "Someone should explain to our industry that these men deserve the best shows possible. When you look out and up into a natural bowl that only recently was jungle and see 5,000 and

6,000 men sitting in the rain and mud, you wish you had the best show on earth. These are wonderful guys when the going gets tough. They get back to fundamentals out here. It's the greatest thrill and privilege anyone can ever have to see them yell and relax in front of a show."

More than twenty years after the war, a soldier wrote his memories of Wayne. "This I will say for John 'The Duke' Wayne. He was what is known as a regular feller. There was none of this high-falutin' stuff about him. What we ate, he ate. Served medicated, warm water — which was all we had — he didn't holler that he wanted someone to fly down to Australia for ice. He drank his booze warm too — without a clamor.

"He showed no fear of Japanese soldiers, or mosquitoes or snakes or rats and other such unfriendly creatures which infested New Guinea."

Wayne said he'd like to see Mount Hagen, so a C-47 was ordered up for some sightseeing. "We had a good time with the natives, who were really from Nativesville," reported the soldier. "They wore bones in their noses; bones in their ears. Their attire consisted of a leaf here and one there. The women were naked except for a loin cloth. And all of them were painted up like the Fourth of July."

Wayne was gone for three months, and when he returned at the end of March he gave a press conference in Hollywood.

What the guys down there need are letters and cigars, more snapshots, phonograph needles and radios. Their GI bands need reeds, strings and orchestrations. And if you have any cigarette lighters, send 'em along.

221

The boys are starved for news from home and . . . the biggest day in their lives over there is when the mailman hands them an envelope postmarked "United States."

Those guys are in a war that's not only fighting, but work and sweat. They're where 130 degrees is a cool day, where they scrape flies off, where matches melt in their pockets and Jap daisy cutter bombs take legs off at the hips. They'll build stages out of old crates, then sit in mud and rain for three hours waiting for someone like me to say, "Hello, Joe."

Wayne's months on the USO tour were something, but even he realized they weren't enough. Wayne's stance along the sidelines during the war was something he didn't like to talk about in later years, which is indicative by itself. His secretary, Mary St. John, remembered that he suffered "terrible guilt and embarrassment" over his lack of any war service beyond a Hollywood sound stage. Both his last wife and his daughter Aissa believed that the guilt he felt over staying out of the service lasted for the rest of his life.

He never spoke about either his application or the interview with Donovan. What is certain is that in 1945, Donovan gave him a certificate that attested to Wayne's "Honorably Serv(ing) the United States of America as Member of The Office of Strategic Services" — the sort of boilerplate document handed out to secretaries. Wayne knew exactly what it was worth: "It was a copperhead," he told John Ford's grandson, Dan, "something Jack [Ford] had set up. It didn't mean anything."

For the rest of his life, Wayne would compensate

by being as much of a red, white, and blue patriot as the most ardent Marine, slaughtering freedom's enemies on the screen and leading by example — moral, if not practical.

In later years, the political left would come to view him as a hypocrite for never getting any closer to combat than fifty feet — besides the skirmish he attended in New Britain, some Vietcong bullets landed nearby during a 1966 tour of Vietnam. As for the right, and the military, they were never bothered overmuch by his lack of service. As General David Shoup, a Marine commandant and winner of the Medal of Honor, would say, Wayne would symbolize the Corps' "hell for leather, go and get-em attitude," a role that was far more important than any actor's actual service would have been. That was good enough for them.

Thirty years after World War II, late one night on location in Durango, Mexico, for a western, Wayne began reminiscing to a small group, thinking out loud as much as telling a story:

It was the Long Island North Shore somewhere. I was one of three well-known actors who were to help the Vanderbilts and Lodges put together a package to help the war. The affair was huge, maybe a thousand or more. We were introduced around, but the center of attention was the party itself. There were two orchestras, in adjoining ballrooms so big they couldn't hear each other.

Conversation was difficult, but I didn't realize why until a beautiful young debutante was introduced. She asked how tall I was, and laughed when she said, "And I thought I was tall at five feet eight." We laughed and she said,

"Have we met? What family are you a part of, Mr. Wayne?" I said I was just there to help with the fund-raising for a film to help the war. She wasn't the least condescending when she said, "Films? Motion Pictures?" I laughed and said yes. "Oh, how exciting that must be . . . I must see one someday." She meant it. She was beaming. She had never seen a movie. We chatted a bit more, and then she moved on. I don't think I ever felt more unimportant in my life.

And so John Wayne was reminded that underneath it all, he was still Duke Morrison.

Shortly after the USO tour was concluded, Chata was in Mexico and encountering visa trouble. Al Murphy, who had become Wayne's driver, believed that Josie was pulling strings to keep her out of the country. (It could just as easily have been Bö Roos or Charlie Feldman.) Murphy and his boss drove down to Tucson, Wayne crossed over the border and somehow brought Chata back with him. Murphy believed that if someone had been able to get between Wayne and Chata, he would have moved on — the relationship had the status of a sexual fever.

"I think Duke would have forgotten her quick enough," said Murphy. "But the problem was, he never did like anyone telling him what to do, pushing him around. . . . Somebody tried to keep that girl out of his life and it just didn't work."

Josie stayed angry for a long time. Ben De-Loache came to Hollywood for a visit and stayed with Wayne for a week. Wayne wanted DeLoache to meet his son Michael, but when they showed up at the house Josie refused to let the men see

224

the boy. No visitation was scheduled, therefore there would be no visitation.

The war, and Wayne's omnipresence in wartime movies, lifted him to an entirely different level of success. By doing so many different kinds of pictures opposite so many different kinds of leading ladies at studios with entirely different strands of movie DNA, Wayne showed off his range and ability.

Dakota is a good example of the mid-range entertainments Republic was devising for their star. It's chock-full of cronies to keep Wayne happy — Paul Fix, Grant Withers, Ward Bond — but there's a wild card lurking in the credits. The story, about Polish refugees on the Great Plains, a vague predecessor of *Heaven's Gate,* is by Carl Foreman, a political liberal with whom Wayne would cross swords in the future. (The film features some darky humor that was presumably introduced by hands other than Foreman's.)

The leading lady was Herbert Yates's mistress, Vera Hruba Ralston — not attractive, not talented, but terribly earnest — and the director was Republic house director Joseph Kane, for whom the term "journeyman" was invented.

Foreman seems to be trying for a sprawling, Edna Ferber–style saga, but the script is botched; the film ends with Wayne jawing impotently at Ralston while his voice is drowned out by a riverboat whistle. About half the film is played in front of a process screen. Republic would always be Republic. One of Herbert Yates's mantras was "Some people make dollar cigars. We make nickel cigars. Remember that." Although he had a million-dollar property in Wayne, Yates still made him endure collaborators such as Ralston and Kane — a man who made more than one hundred movies without an interesting shot to be found in any of them.

Wayne must have taken some consolation in the fact that his star was rising, and so was his income. Charlie Feldman noted in a memo that Wayne's acting income was $128,000 in 1942, $116,169.46 in 1943, $167,291.66 in 1944, and $220,000 in 1945. The trajectory was clearly ascending, and so was the caliber of films he was making everywhere but Republic.

Dakota was the fourth picture in the five-picture deal that Wayne had signed with Republic in 1943. The four pictures — *In Old Oklahoma, The Fighting Seabees, Flame of the Barbary Coast,* and *Dakota* — did very well (*Dakota* cost $843,545 and earned domestic rentals of $1.44 million). The money was rolling in, so Yates and Feldman worked out a new deal before the fifth picture was made.

The new contract was signed on October 25, 1945, and called for seven pictures over the next six years beginning January 15, 1946. Wayne was to receive 10 percent of the gross on each picture, with a guarantee of at least $100,000 per film and no cap on the amount that Wayne could receive. Minimum cost on each picture was set at $800,000 and Wayne and Yates had mutual approval of story, cast, director, cameraman, and associate producer. Also, Wayne had the option of taking a producer credit on any of the seven pictures. There was no longer any loan-out clause — Wayne made his own deals and kept all the money from pictures at other studios, and he also had the option of canceling the contract if Yates sold out or lost control of Republic.

All in all, it was a deal of unheard-of richness for the little studio in the valley, and it didn't stop there. Republic took out a $250,000 life insurance policy on its prime asset, and it was during this time that Wayne began to amass a collection of his films on 16mm, for which Republic billed him $100 a print. Once he moved from Van Nuys to Encino, and his projection equipment changed from 16mm to 35mm, Wayne upgraded his collection at a much greater cost — his 35mm print of *The Quiet Man* would cost him $1,039.

People who worked with Wayne loved the Encino house. The property was on the corner of Rancho and Louise, covered five acres, and had a long, curving driveway framed by huge oak trees that set the stage for the entrance of someone special — a star. Besides the house itself, which contained twenty-two rooms, there were stables and a two-bedroom pool house for guests or anybody who might have had a few too many. Wayne built a high brick wall around the property for security and also added an electric gate.

At this point, Wayne's enthusiasm for Yates and Republic knew no bounds, and he began to serve as Republic's agent in an attempt to lure John Ford to the studio. While Ford was shooting *They Were Expendable* for MGM at the end of 1944, Wayne tried to get the director together with Yates, but Ford demurred. "He said that if you had tried to contact him at MGM there would have been a message to that effect," Wayne cabled Yates, who in turn insisted that he had indeed called Ford. "I want to get you two together before they talk him into getting tied up someplace else," wrote Wayne.

"He keeps saying there is plenty of time — that he is still in the Navy but I want to see you two get together."

Aside from the fact that he was indeed still in the Navy, Ford also owed Darryl Zanuck a picture on his old prewar contract at Fox before he would be free to form the independent company he was planning with Merian C. Cooper. When Ford and Cooper finally formed Argosy Productions, they allied themselves with RKO. But Wayne and Yates kept circling, and they were persistent.

As Lindsley Parsons had found in the early 1930s, Wayne's politics were set quite early. When he was shooting *Flying Tigers* at Republic in 1942, his co-star was Anna Lee, a beautiful blonde newly arrived from England. As they were filming a dancing scene, Wayne asked her, "Are you a Republican?" But Lee thought Wayne had said, "Are you a publican?" that is, the operator of an English pub.

"No," she replied, "but I'm very fond of beer."

Wayne thought the non sequitur was hilarious, and he and Lee became friends. She would soon be a member of the John Ford stock company.

Wayne's conservatism became part of the larger Hollywood scene with the formation of the Motion Picture Alliance for the Preservation of American Ideals. The stimulus for the Alliance seems to have been a conference held at UCLA in early October of 1943. Mostly, it was attended by writers from South America, but among the attendees were Thomas Mann and Theodore Dreiser. Walt Disney was appalled at what he took to be the Red tint of the gathering, as was James Kevin McGuinness, a conservative Irish screenwriter and producer at MGM who had attempted to undermine the Screen Writers Guild in the mid-1930s by forming a company union called the Screen Playwrights. Shortly after the UCLA conference, McGuinness hosted a dinner for like-minded friends upset at what they saw as the leading edge of Communist infiltration in Hollywood, right behind unions. McGuinness's dinner led to a meeting at Chasen's for thirty others of similar political persuasion.

On February 4, 1944, two hundred people attended a meeting at the Beverly Wilshire, where Sam Wood was elected president of the newly christened Alliance, and Cedric Gibbons, Norman Taurog, and Walt Disney were elected vice presidents. Aside from the board, there were seventy-two other people listed as founding members of the organization, among them Clarence Brown, King Vidor, Hedda Hopper, Robert Taylor, Ginger Rogers, Barbara Stanwyck, Clark Gable, Gary Cooper, Adolphe Menjou, Ward Bond, and Richard Arlen.

With the formation of the Alliance, the uneasy cooperation between left and right that had formed after Pearl Harbor, much as a flimsy marriage might be held together for the children, collapsed.

The Alliance was immediately hailed by the Hearst press — no surprise there. Also chiming in with loud support was the *Los Angeles Examiner,* which said that "the subversive minority in the industry has connived and contrived to produce a long succession of insidious and evil motion pictures to the discredit of the industry and to the detriment of the country. . . . It has made pictures glorifying Communistic Russia, ignoring the oppressive and tyrannical character of Bolshevism and inventing virtues for it that have never existed."★

The Alliance, said Sam Wood, was "for everyone in the motion picture industry, regardless of position . . . none of us are 'joiners.' None of us are professional organizers or 'go to meeting' types."

Wood was a successful commercial director who was fond of employing the great production designer William Cameron Menzies to gussy up his utilitarian visual sense. Wood's most recent hit had been *For Whom the Bell Tolls,* which had been carefully denuded of Hemingway's political foundation — James Agee wrote that the movie gave the impression "that Gary Cooper is simply fighting for the Republican Party in a place where the New Deal has got particularly out of hand."

Wood went on to say that the Alliance wanted only to calm troubled waters. "Those highly indoctrinated shock units of the totalitarian wrecking crew have shrewdly led the people of the United States to believe that Hollywood is a hotbed of sedition and subversion, and that our industry is a battleground over which Communism is locked in death grips with Fascism. . . . We intend to correct that erroneous impression

★ Actually, there wasn't "a long succession of insidious and evil motion pictures" espousing the Communist line. There were two: Warners' *Mission to Moscow* and Goldwyn's *The North Star,* both of which were made at President Franklin Roosevelt's urging to sway the public to the side of our new Russian allies, but which went out of their way to portray Stalin's Russia as a cozy place radiant with benign social welfare.

immediately, and to assure the people of the United States that . . . Hollywood is a reservoir of Americanism."

Variety welcomed the Alliance with an enthusiastically illiterate editorial with the unintentionally humorous headline "Heading Right Way":

In times like these, the formation of the Motion Picture Alliance for the Preservation of American Ideals is most essential and necessary, as well as highly commendable . . . they are people of intelligence who can smell subversive propaganda as easily as limburger cheese, but not as tasty, and devise means to eradicate it from screen messages in any and every form. Also, they must see to it that regardless of religious belief, creed or color, there is no discrimination, and that hatred in this direction becomes extinct. . . .

It is time for films to return to their original function — ENTERTAINMENT.

Immediately, the Alliance members began fanning out to enlist like-minded members of the community. King Vidor tried to recruit the screenwriter William Ludwig, who had just written *American Romance* for him. "I know what the Alliance is against," said Ludwig, "but what are they for? . . . What is your organization for, King?"

There was a long pause, and Vidor said, "I'll have to talk to Sam Wood about that." He got up and left the office.

The anticommunist labor leader Roy Brewer remembered that the dominant person in the early years of the Alliance was James Kevin McGuinness, whom Brewer called "the spiritual leader.

He made a statement once that I've never forgotten; it was that every person was a child of God, and could never be any man's slave."

For those on the left, the Alliance was the vanguard of a warped, paranoid obsession with nonexistent traitors; for those on the right, it was an overdue reaction to the Soviet Communism that was a direct and insidious threat to the United States. The latter were immeasurably aided by the quick-change Russian turnaround from enemy to ally. The Alliance also became a home for those with a reflexive opposition to the New Deal — some of the first hearings of the newly formed House Un-American Activities Committee in the late 1930s were designed to "expose" the communist influences behind the WPA, the Federal Theater Project, the Art Project, and Writers' Project.

The left gradually became alarmed. The liberal New York newspaper *PM* quoted an Alliance spokesman to the effect that "There is no intention to attempt to deprive any worker of employment by reason of his known leanings toward Communism, Fascism, or other un-American beliefs, although it is among the purposes of the group to notify the employer of any such worker regarding the worker's tendencies."

It soon became obvious that a blacklist was not inadvertent collateral damage; rather, it was a goal. In March 1944, the Alliance sent a letter to Senator Robert Reynolds (D-N.C.), a noted conservative who had once informed the Senate that "Dictators are doing what is best for their people. Hitler and Mussolini have a date with destiny: it's foolish to oppose them, so why not play ball with them?" The letter pointed out the allegedly "flagrant manner in which the motion picture industrialists of Hollywood have been coddling Communists" and how "totalitarian-minded groups" were working to disseminate un-American ideas within the film industry.

Congressman John Rankin (D-Miss.) added to the tumult by accusing Hollywood movies of sending coded messages about German air raids so Communist spies and sympathizers in Europe would be unharmed. In April 1944, representatives of the House Committee on Un-American Activities appeared in Hollywood to begin taking statements.

Besides *Mission to Moscow* and *The North Star,* among the pictures the Motion Picture Alliance would eventually indict for spreading left-wing propaganda were *The Best Years of Our Lives, The Strange Love of Martha Ivers, A Medal for Benny, The Searching Wind, Watch on the Rhine, Pride of the Marines,* and *Margie.*

Margie?

The Alliance was (intentionally?) overestimating both the possibilities for subversion in a highly industrialized system of production and the number of Communists in the movie business. One solid estimate toted up about three hundred Communists in the industry — fifty to sixty actors, fifteen to twenty producers, and around 150 writers — about 1 percent of the workforce.

Roy Brewer was the international representative of IATSE, the major Hollywood guild union. Brewer remembered that it was Ayn Rand, the original antigovernment libertarian, who wrote the Alliance's declaration of principles. Brewer enjoyed chafing Rand: "Well, what about the streets, Ayn? Is it all right for the government to make the streets?"

Brewer was joking, but Rand was not noted for her sense of humor and took the question seriously. A few weeks later, she told Brewer, "I've been giving that a lot of thought, and I kind of believe that maybe there is a place for the government to build streets."

Rand wrote a pamphlet for the Alliance, entitled *Screen Guide for Americans,* which featured chapter headings such as "Don't Smear the Free Enterprise System," "Don't Deify the Common Man," and "Don't Smear Industrialists." The pamphlet asserted that "All too often, industrialists, bankers and businessmen are presented on the screen as villains, crooks, chiselers and exploiters," then outlined the Alliance's modus operandi:

The purpose of the Communists in Hollywood is not the production of political movies openly advocating Communism. Their purpose is to corrupt our moral premises by corrupting non-political movies — by introducing small, casual bits of propaganda into innocent stories — thus making people absorb the basic principles of Collectivism by indirection and implication.

The principle of free speech requires that we do not use police force to forbid the Communists the expression of their ideas — which means that we do not pass laws forbidding them to speak. But the principle of free speech does not require that we furnish the Communists with the means to preach their ideas, and does not imply that we owe them jobs and support to advocate our own destruction at our own expense.

Within a few months, *Variety* was modifying its

initially positive reading of the Alliance.

Let the Alliance name these "totalitarian-minded groups" it states are working to the detriment of the picture business in Hollywood. Tomorrow, the next day, or next week the Alliance can have without charge as many "Variety" pages as is needed to name these individuals and groups it maintains are un-American and subversive. And every individual and group that the Alliance names will be offered an equal opportunity to answer whatever charges are made. . . . Never mind going outside. Come down to Hollywood and Vine.
Lay it on the line, or get off and stay off the line.

Other journalists began to throw whatever weight they had behind *Variety*'s point of view. "According to [an] MPA spokesman the film industry is being perverted by the infiltration of communist propaganda," wrote Virginia Wright of the Los Angeles *Daily News.* "By no amount of 'insidious purpose' could a writer get something on the screen that did not meet with the approval of the front office. . . . So what the MPA actually says is that communist propaganda is coming from the men who run the studios — Zanuck, the Warners, Goldwyn, Mayer, Cohn, DeSylva, Koerner and the rest . . . we can only assume the alliance thinks studio executives are merely puppets in the hands of writers."
In the years to come, the Alliance and its allies would make much of guilt by association, but few people applied the same tactics to them. The columnist Hedda Hopper, for instance, was a

235

founding member and committee member of the MPA, as well as a braying horror who had been an ardent isolationist in the years before Pearl Harbor. She expressed strong animosity toward FDR, unions, the Democratic Party, and civil rights long before she climbed aboard the anti-communist bandwagon.

Nor was Hopper shy about using her media access — at one point she had a syndicated readership of 32 million in a nation of 160 million people — to proselytize for her beliefs. A March 1945 column contained nine items, only three of which were about the entertainment world. She was one of those people far more alarmed by Communism than Fascism; when Leni Riefenstahl came to Hollywood in 1938, Hopper defended her in several columns: "Leni's only here to sell her picture!" she wrote.

Inside and outside the film industry, it was widely believed that the MPA was mostly anti-Semitic (one of the few Jewish members was the writer Morrie Ryskind). One FBI agent reported at the time of the group's formation that "There is every possibility that persons anti-Semitic will attempt to rally around the MPA, making that organization definitely an anti-Semitic group."

Increasing this perception was the presence of James Kevin McGuinness, who had been widely regarded as anti-Semitic since the mid-1930s, when he exploded in a racist diatribe about Irving Thalberg. In March 1944, David Selznick confronted Sam Wood about his organization's bias, calling McGuinness "the biggest anti-Semite in Hollywood," and accusing McGuinness of presiding over a group called the Hundred Haters at the

Lakeside Golf Club, where McGuinness was president.

So the outlines of the blacklist were forming while World War II was still being fought. Interestingly, throughout the first years of the Motion Picture Alliance, the name of John Wayne is nowhere to be found, while any statements by Wayne in support of anticommunism went unrecorded.

For the time being, nothing much happened. Congress was still controlled by largely liberal Democrats, so the Alliance's spadework promoting an investigation was stymied by political reality and FDR's enormous popularity, not to mention the pressing business of winning the war — with the help of the nation's Russian ally.

But Roosevelt would not live to see victory, and the Alliance was playing a long game.

It could afford to wait.

CHAPTER EIGHT

Republic filmed *The Fighting Seabees* with an unusual roster of talent. The credited director was Edward Ludwig, but the stylish Robert Florey took over for a week, while the screenwriter was Borden Chase, who would gain a measure of fame with his original story and script for *Red River.* Ludwig would work with Wayne several times in the future, among them the underrated *Wake of the Red Witch.*

Wayne's rising status in the industry as well as at Republic is made clear in a memo written to him by associate producer Albert Cohen. Cohen forwarded the first three quarters of the script for *The Fighting Seabees* along with an explanation for the problems that were apparent:

> Dear Duke, When you read the first 98 pages of the attached . . . script, please bear in mind the following changes that we are now making in the front part of the script. . . .
>
> Donovan [Wayne's character] being an intelligent construction engineer, listens attentively and remarks that what Yarrow says makes sense and that as soon as he gets back to the states he will take it up with Washington and put the

idea over in 24 hours.

Yarrow patiently explains to Donovan that the Navy doesn't function that way — that the entire setup will have to be worked out in detail then sent through the usual channels, which may take several months. This again prompts Donovan to shoot off his mouth about 'Navy red tape', etc. . . .

These changes, while they actually amount to only dialogue changes, will help strengthen the friction between our two leading men.

The point is not the actual alterations, but the deference that the production team is showing Wayne by running the changes past him. This attention to Wayne's character development, not to mention acknowledging his already evident preferences in presentation, hadn't been the case a couple of years earlier, when he had been grinding out Three Mesquiteers pictures in bulk, but it would become the norm at Republic, as well as at every other studio.

The Fighting Seabees was yet another in the series of gung ho war pictures Wayne was making, ending with a kamikaze mission in which Wayne's character is killed taking out a Japanese tank. Albert Cohen got a letter from a woman saying she had just read in the paper that the film would be shot at the Seabees base at Port Hueneme.

"I am glad," she wrote. "My husband is in the Seabees and is at Port Hueneme. John Wayne is his favorite actor. He told me once that [he] is a 'man's man.' I just want to tell you how much he would enjoy telling him, 'Thank you for playing that part, John.' I am thanking you for him and for me.' "

239

In mid-1944, Wayne went over to RKO to make a western entitled *Tall in the Saddle.* The script, co-written by Paul Fix, had a couple of good lines ("I like grumpy old cusses," says Wayne at one point. "Hope to live long enough to be one.") and some incidental pleasures — the presence of both Gabby Hayes and Raymond Hatton make the film a veritable Old Coot jamboree.

Wayne took some pride in the picture; as he remembered it, *Tall in the Saddle* "was the first picture in which I found the story and made a deal with a studio for its development. I worked at half price at RKO in order to have complete control, regardless of whose names appeared on the titles."

Wayne remembered that nobody at the studio thought much of the project except Robert Fellows, the producer assigned to shepherd the production. Nevertheless, it was an extremely successful, if slightly dull movie. It cost only $565,754 — Wayne's salary was a flat $50,000 — and returned rentals of $2 million for a profit of $730,000. RKO and Wayne were soon in partnership, and Fellows also produced *Back to Bataan* a year later.

Tall in the Saddle would become the matrix for a particular kind of Wayne picture — modestly budgeted, but with the money on the screen, with the star front and center as the public liked to see him — all told, a guarantee of big profits.

Besides making money for everybody, *Tall in the Saddle* did one other thing: it broke up Paul Fix's marriage. Although Fix was an unprepossessing figure, he was charming and was rumored to be extremely well endowed — his nickname was "Blackjack," and it didn't refer to skill with cards. Fix became involved with Wayne's co-star Ella Raines. When Fix's daughter Marilyn married Harry Carey Jr., Raines wanted to come to the wedding, but Fix said that was impossible, which led to an escalating argument that culminated in Raines throwing a martini in Fix's face.

As Fix was leading his daughter down the aisle, the crowd at the church heard the unmistakable sound of someone leaning on a car horn outside. Nobody could figure out who would be that rude — nobody except Paul Fix.

Wayne had relied on Fix for acting advice for years, and was now turning to him for script advice as well. Between the demands of his career and the demands of his friends, quiet time was increasingly hard to find. Fix told a story about Wayne asking him to go away for a weekend, just the two of them, so they could work their way through the pile of scripts that were on offer. "People keep bugging me," Wayne explained. "Ward Bond, Grant Withers, these guys keep coming around saying, 'Hey Duke, lets's go out and do this and do that . . .' I've got to get away. I've got to read some of these scripts. I've got to find something I want to do."

They went down to Fallbrook, got there about noon, and at 4 P.M. there was a banging on the door. Ward Bond had tracked them down and was already drunk. Fix was not a drinker, but Wayne could never resist knocking a few back with "Old Ward." Resolution gave way, and Wayne figured the only way to handle the situation was to pretend to be as drunk as Bond. Open a bottle, pretend to drink, let Bond actually drink and let him pass out. Some of the liquor did find its way to Wayne's stomach, however, and he began to feel excessively convivial.

Soon, Bond was passed out on the floor. They picked him up and put him on the bed. He didn't seem to be breathing. "Christ, maybe he's dying," said Wayne.

"He's not dying," replied Fix. "I'll unbutton his shirt."

After they unbuttoned his shirt, Wayne observed Bond's chest rising and falling, and finally said, "Look at the hairy-chested son of a bitch." He took out his cigarette lighter and set fire to Bond's chest. The hair smoldered a little, then went out. Bond didn't wake up.

"Let's go get something to eat," Wayne said. "Leave him there! He's fucking drunk!"

Another time, Wayne and Bond went quail hunting, for which Bond loaned Wayne his 20-gauge shotgun. Bond was walking in a gully and Wayne was on a ridge above him when a covey broke loose near Bond. Wayne fired and got a quail, but he also got Bond, who was hit in the neck and shoulders. Bond said he had to have about forty birdshot picked out of his back, but the doctors missed some.

Years later, Bond was in New York when he began getting pains in his neck and head. When he was X-rayed, the doctors told him he had some foreign objects lodged in there — did he have any idea what they might be?

"That must be more of Duke's buckshot!" said Bond. Bond said that he could forgive Wayne shooting him, but couldn't forgive him for doing it with his own gun. Experiences like these led

Wayne and his friends to the conclusion that Bond was unkillable. The shotgun and the wounding became part of Wayne's and Bond's personal mythology, a yarn told around endless card and commissary tables.

After *Flame of the Barbary Coast* at Republic — Joseph Kane again — Wayne began shooting *Back to Bataan* for RKO. It's a story of the Philippine resistance, led by an American (Wayne) and a Filipino (Anthony Quinn, Hollywood's all-purpose ethnic).

Even as it was being shot the picture was being written by Ben Barzman, a committed leftist who was eventually blacklisted. Writing just ahead of the camera is difficult not just because of the pressure but because of intensely practical concerns — there's no room for an error in story construction, and you have to write scenes that will work for the sets that have already been built.

Barzman left behind a memoir in which he accused Wayne of subtle digs that were calculated to shatter whatever thin veneer of composure the writer could sustain in such frantic circumstances. One day Barzman delivered three pages that had to be shot immediately, and Wayne loudly announced, "Now, let's see what kind of golden hero our boy genius has made me today."

Barzman ignored the possibility that the sarcasm was directed as much at Wayne as at Barzman and retorted, "You always play a goddamn big dumb golden hero anyway!"

Wayne responded with a menacing look and began advancing on Barzman, who was half Wayne's size. Grabbing a fire ax off a studio wall, the writer stood there trying to look like he knew what to do with it.

"Jesus Christ Almighty," said Wayne, "a fucking fire ax!"

"Come on you big bastard!" yelled Barzman. "I'd love to use it on you!"

"Why, I believe you would!" said Wayne.

There was an uneasy pause, then Barzman said, "Since I was smaller than most kids, I was taught in Canada to defend myself with anything I could lay my hands on."

"Hurray for the Canadians," said Wayne. Then he looked curious. "A fire ax? How could you have finished the goddamn film without me?"

Barzman threw the ax away and began laughing, as did Wayne.

Writers' memoirs are full of scenes like this, and historians believe them at their peril. As Nora Ephron observed of the book written by her father, screenwriter Henry Ephron, he was always the hero and always telling Darryl Zanuck to go fuck himself. In the real world, writers who threaten movie stars have pronounced tendencies toward alcoholism and lengthy periods of unemployment.

But Barzman's memoir does capture Wayne's wry sense of humor, as well as his particular brand of conservatism. "He was far right, anti-Roosevelt, anti-spending taxpayers' money for welfare, education, public health or practically anything," wrote Barzman. "And he was staunchly anti-women's rights when women were Wacs and Waves overseas and doing hard, often dangerous work in war factories."

Despite all this, Wayne and Barzman developed a decent rapport. "You know what each cigarette costs me on account of that man in the White

244

House," Wayne asked Barzman one day. "Two dollars."

"Hell, Duke, there's a war on, and we all pay taxes."

"Not two bucks for a smoke you don't."

Wayne was determined to do his own stunts. When Barzman suggested that Wayne and Quinn sink beneath a pond that had recently frozen over in a cold snap, Wayne refused to use a double. Wayne's lips eventually turned blue, but he and Quinn did the stunt.

Also on the left was director Edward Dmytryk. Dmytryk liked Wayne, liked the way he "threw his . . . body around like a lightweight gymnast. His acting was honest, which is a good deal better than clever; he lived life with gusto; and he was already beginning to think of himself as some kind of political pundit, but we all make mistakes."

Back to Bataan is a comparatively violent film for its period — children die — and it also has a surface realism. But despite the fact that it's beautifully photographed by Nick Musuraca, and makes a concerted effort to portray the diversity involved in the war in the Philippines, the script has a boilerplate feel to it. Verisimilitude is further reduced by the fact that the narrator is the same man who breathlessly introduces the parodic Columbia serials directed by James Horne.

At the end of the movie, Wayne tells a Filipino child, "You're the guy we're fighting this war for" — a sentiment, and a line, that would be repeated nearly verbatim in a far more controversial Wayne movie about a far more controversial war several decades later.

But as far as RKO was concerned, *Back to Bataan* was another raging Wayne success; it cost

245

$1.2 million and returned domestic rentals of $2.2 million, earning a profit of $160,000 in its first year of release. Not long after the film was made, Robert Fellows invited Ben Barzman to a New Year's party at his house. Wayne was there and threw his arm around Barzman. "You remember you once asked me what I thought was the reason for my success?" said Wayne. "And I told you I always wondered myself. I never kidded myself it was because I was a great actor."

"Yeah, I remember. And you said some woman once stopped you for an autograph and told you why she thought all the women were nuts about you. But you couldn't remember what she said."

"I remember now," said Wayne. "She whispered to me, 'You have such wicked thighs!' "

MGM's *They Were Expendable* wasn't released until November of 1945, which undoubtedly damaged its commercial prospects — the picture had been in preparation since July of 1942, but MGM was never fast off the dime. Frank Wead worked on the script, as did George Froeschel and Jan Lustig, in concert with producer Sidney Franklin. Wead completed a partial script by April of 1943, shortly after which Norman Corwin began wrestling with the material. He didn't quite grasp the possibilities.

"The story in none of its forms so far has much heart," Corwin wrote in some notes on the project. "It lacks conviction and nobody gives a goddamn what happens to anybody. . . . There is no reason why this picture should not have a clear line of continuity: the telling of the short and hectic history of a squadron of men who knew they were doomed; the expensing of the expendables."

Corwin was always interested in the macro, so he spent a lot of time pondering the characterization of the Filipino characters, even though they're only a backdrop to the story of the PT boats. Corwin proposed a round-robin of narrators: "Thus Ensign Chandler might begin the story and carry us to the point where he is shot in the ankles and hospitalized. He could then apologize for not being able to carry the narration further and yield, let us say, to Reynolds. . . . Reynolds might then conduct the story until the time he gets it in the neck. Then perhaps one of the surviving four . . . might carry it through the end."

It was an interesting theoretical idea, but narration as a baton being passed around was sure to keep the audience from focusing on the characters. Corwin was ambivalent about the material; at one point, he devised a document he called "Arguments for and Against Its Production." In another memo, he wrote, "It is on the one hand a great, sprawling documentary about the fall of the Philippines in a strictly Naval sense — full of giant-sized incidents — and, on the other hand, the interwoven biography of four men — the canvas much smaller, tighter and more easily manageable."

Corwin had stumbled on the approach that Frank Wead and John Ford would emphasize. They simply alluded to the larger situation via a few lines of dialogue, with Ford's magnificently gloomy images as the foundational underpinning of a tight dramatic focus. Corwin was off the picture by the end of 1943 and Frank Wead was back on, finishing the script by November of 1944.

Ford shot the picture in and around Miami beginning in February 1945. It was an efficient shoot, enlivened by some glorious tropical nights. A young soldier named Bill Harbach, the son of the famed lyricist Otto Harbach ("Smoke Gets in Your Eyes"), was at a party with the cast.

"It was the first time I met Wayne," said Harbach, who would come back into Wayne's life a quarter century later. "I had Levi's on, and he had his Six-Foot club around him — Ward Bond and the rest of his cronies were just about the same size as him. Anyway, he said, 'Fellas, look, Levi's!' And he reached out and put his hands on my waist and lifted me up and swung me around to show the guys what I was wearing. I'm six feet and weighed about 160, and he handled me as if I was a bag of groceries. Amazing strength!"

Ford wisely chose to deemphasize his stars, because they were playing characters continually buffeted by circumstances out of their control. The narrative consists almost exclusively of military disasters, beginning shortly before Pearl Harbor, when PT boats couldn't get any traction with the naval brass, continuing through Subic Bay, Corregidor, and Bataan. *They Were Expendable* begins Ford's preoccupation with the contradictions of human history — the difference between actual events and the invariably more comfortable official version constructed over time, a central dynamic that motivates movies as varied as *Fort Apache* and *The Man Who Shot Liberty Valance*. *They Were Expendable* is also the most mournful movie about World War II until *Saving Private Ryan*.

Ford had the great freelance cameraman Joe August shoot the film, probably because he didn't believe that any of the MGM cameramen — used to glossy high-key lighting that illuminated every corner of every set — could or would give him the kind of images he wanted: shots of long, dark corridors peopled by small groups of grieving men.

Robert Montgomery gives the most effective performance in his post-juvenile period, and Wayne is self-effacing in a performance keyed not to action or heroism but to loss — the dramatic high point is Wayne's recitation of Robert Louis Stevenson's "Requiem" over two coffins: "Home is the sailor, home from the sea . . ."

Wayne's Rusty Ryan is the second in command to Montgomery's Brickley. Ryan is an impatient man only tempered by duty and his love for Sandy, a nurse on Corregidor, played by Donna Reed in a pitch-perfect performance. Ford is at his best capturing the exquisite gallantry of the officers at a dinner party where Sandy is the only guest. But the relationship never takes flight; in the end Sandy is lost to the war. She might be hiding in the hills, she might be a prisoner of the Japanese, she might be dead. We never find out. Either way, the work of the war has to go on.

It's a beautiful, understated picture about coping with a war of attrition — men die, their boats are destroyed, and the sailors are faced with a succession of fiascoes, culminating in the officers getting airlifted out while their men are left stranded. The film's great strength derives from the fact that it was conceived and executed by Ford and Wead — filmmakers who had been soldiers and who knew that war is about loss.

This magnificent, melancholy film earned great reviews and mediocre box office; for the audience, it was an unwelcome reminder of the worst days of a war that had just been won. Nevertheless, Wayne was recognized as a major contribution to the film's artistic success: "John Wayne registers the greatest acting job of his career," wrote one reviewer. "If anything, he is the film's standout."

Christmas of 1945 was taken up by a series of welcome-home parties that Mary Ford staged at the Ford house on Odin Street. After that, Ford went upstairs and drank himself into oblivion. For some reason, he grew obsessed with a record of Mexican revolutionary songs, and played them over and over. His daughter, Barbara, took care of him during the day, and Wayne came over at night, in full makeup and costume from *Without Reservations* at RKO. "I'll take my turn," Wayne told Barbara as he trooped upstairs, where he found Ford wrapped in a bedsheet surrounded by empty bottles. The two men whiled away the hours talking, with the Mexican war songs grinding away; whenever the record ended, Ford would start it over again.

There was nothing to do but wait for the storm to run its course.

Without Reservations was an entertaining if over-long romantic comedy directed by Mervyn LeRoy that paired Wayne with Claudette Colbert. The premise is creative: an author (Colbert) writes a novel about a man named Mark Winston that becomes more of a movement than a book. (Ayn Rand, anyone?) The book is purchased for the movies, which leads to Cary Grant turning the part down in a funny guest appearance (Jack Benny also shows up unbilled). The studio starts looking for an unknown.

On the train to California, Colbert meets Wayne, who embodies all aspects of her fictional hero. (Wayne's character is a rugged individualist who doesn't believe in social engineering.) He's asked to test for the movie, and his face assumes an expression of unbounded disgust. "An actor??!!" he exclaims. Eventually, the stubborn, uncorruptible American gets corrupted, but on his terms.

Throughout the movie, Wayne underplays the comedy, and he expresses a winning appreciation for his co-star — he drinks her in. He's sexy, romantic, obtainable. On the other hand, although Colbert was an actress with something approaching perfect pitch, here she seems a little overly flustered for such a soigné creature, especially one outfitted by Adrian.

Without Reservations would be one of Wayne's few overt attempts at a romantic comedy, and he acquits himself well. The audience enjoyed it, as did the studio and producers Jesse Lasky and Mervyn LeRoy — the profit topped $700,000. Wayne and Colbert liked each other a great deal; at the time, she was thinking about directing a picture, but hesitated because the producers wanted her to act in it as well.

"I guess what it really comes down to is that I didn't have the guts," she remembered. But Wayne thought she could direct, and he offered to work for her. "I knew he meant it," Colbert said. "I really cherish that remark. I mean, from the he-man of all time."

After years of push-pull across the U.S.-Mexican border, Wayne and Chata were finally married on January 17, 1946, at the Unity Presbyterian

251

Church in Long Beach. Mary Ford and Olive Carey were matrons of honor, and Ward Bond was best man. Herbert Yates gave the bride away, and Wayne's mother hosted the reception at the California Country Club.

John Ford boycotted the wedding, and he didn't mince words with his surrogate son: "Why'd you have to marry that whore?" he asked Wayne. The subject had to be closed between them, but in time Wayne would realize the wisdom of Ford's question.

The couple honeymooned at Waikiki Beach, where the newspapers were full of stories about their presence on the island. One day as Wayne and Chata were sunning themselves in front of the Royal Hawaiian, four sailors from John Rogers Air Station were taking a day of liberty. They spotted "a tall, handsome guy lying on a blanket beneath a palm tree and wearing sunshades and swim trunks." Next to him was a good-looking brunette clad in a white one-piece bathing suit and wearing dark glasses. Two of the sailors were from Texas and South Carolina respectively, and weren't about to say anything, but one was from New Jersey and he piped up, "Mr. Wayne, can we look at your wife?"

Wayne sat up, removed his sunglasses, stared, then smiled. He reached over to Chata, removed her sunglasses and said, "Sure, fellows, help yourselves. I kinda like to look at her myself." He stood up, shook hands with the sailors and thanked them for their service.

For a time, the marriage seemed to be in rough equilibrium. As Bev Barnett's backgrounder said, "She likes to drink; she liked Wayne's friends; they were happy in bed."

Michael Wayne would say that Chata was cute. Nice shape, pretty legs, good with the kids. "She was like a kid herself," said Mike's wife, Gretchen. "She drank like a man and loved to play cards, so that would have worked for Michael's dad. But the problem would be that if he was out playing cards, Chata wanted to be out playing cards too. She wasn't going to stay home and make bouquets. They never had any children; Michael's dad said it was because she was too mean."

Besides her presumed virtuosity in bed, Chata could match Wayne drink for drink, which made for a household with a high degree of volatility; one writer noted, "No one has ever accused Wayne of being shy in going after the things he wants . . . but he displays an incongruous timidity when it comes to insisting that Chata comply with his wishes."

Aside from her alcohol intake, there were other warning signs. Wayne was always fastidious about his hygiene and clothing, but Chata cut her own hair, bought her own clothes, and applied her own makeup. "She sometimes looked a bit peculiar and out of it," commented Mary St. John, Wayne's longtime secretary. Not only that, but she didn't like to shave her legs, which bothered Wayne a great deal although he didn't harp on it until she showed up at Charles Feldman's house for a Sunday brunch wearing a white tennis skirt, which emphasized her hirsute lower half.

But the main problem was Chata's temper, which got worse when she drank, which was most of the time. In late 1946, Wayne came into his Republic office with an ugly gash on his cheek. He sheepishly explained to Mary St. John that Chata had objected when Wayne wanted to leave a party the previous night. Chata was drunk, and when he picked her up and carried her to their car, she gouged his face.

Things got worse. Chata's mother moved in, and she drank nearly as much as her daughter. The women had expected a life of glamour, but Wayne worked very hard; he was in a brutal tax bracket; and there wasn't all that much left over at the end of the year. Chata began complaining to anyone who would listen that Wayne was obsessed with "thee beezness," that he didn't love her or sleep with her, he loved and slept with the pictures.

The drinking stepped up. Not just after six, but during the day. The actor Mike Mazurki's wife, Jeannette, remembered drinking with Chata one night while their husbands played cards: "She didn't speak much English and I recall she was quite pretty. I was 25 and a new bride then. I didn't have any children, and it was still the honeymoon stage for me. She had some tequila. We talked, but you really had to listen because her English wasn't very good. So we got plastered."

Mazurki found Chata pleasant and well meaning while sober, "but when she'd get half-looped she'd get so jealous she'd start throwing tantrums. She was a real alcoholic, as was her mother."

Bö Roos was forced into the role of mediator and Wayne spent a lot of time at his house trying to decompress after the arguments with Chata. Roos arranged reconciliations, then a second honeymoon in Hawaii, but not a long one. Duke had pictures to make.

Wayne was highly conscious of his coalescing

screen image. He would occasionally compare himself to Robert Montgomery, who had carved out a pleasant, innocuous "tennis, anyone" career at MGM until he grew weary of it and decided to change his image by playing a psychopath in *Night Must Fall.*

"He won an Oscar, but he lost his audience," said Wayne. "He was wonderful in the film but he fooled the people who had been going to his movies because he was 'a nice, bright young kid.' Suddenly they said, 'No, he's a dirty, miserable killer, a maniac.' [Audiences] become accustomed to you as an actor as they would a friend, and . . . you can surprise them but you can't fool them."

There are several problems with Wayne's premise. Although he was nominated for *Night Must Fall,* Montgomery didn't win the Oscar — Spencer Tracy did, for *Captains Courageous.* And the public response was hardly catastrophic; Montgomery's starring career continued without interruption for another thirteen years, through World War II and beyond, including the aforementioned strong turn in *They Were Expendable.* At that point, Montgomery got the directing bug, which increasingly occupied his time.

Wayne was far more disturbed by Montgomery's decision to play a killer than the public was — it was the sort of stunt casting in which he always refused to indulge. It was around this point that he began to think of the audience as an extended family and would turn down any part that he felt might violate their expectations of him.

Wayne's next picture was critically important to him in every way, for reasons that become clear with the opening title: "A John Wayne Produc-

255

tion." *The Angel and the Badman* was an interesting choice of material — a largely nonviolent western. The plot — a gunslinger is reformed by the love of a Quaker girl — and much of the development harks back not to John Ford but to the chiseled biblical morality of William S. Hart.

Wayne plays Quirt Evans, a wounded gunfighter on the run who providentially falls into the healing hands of a Quaker homestead, personified by Gail Russell radiating serenity. After his fairly indiscriminate behavior as a young man, Wayne was cleaning up his act, but if he didn't have an affair with Russell, he seems to have had a crush on her. He would pay tribute to her as having "wonderful possibilities; her eyes are very expressive. But I think her home studio [Paramount] has let her down in not giving her proper grooming and teaching her to be at her best, that is, how to handle herself. If it weren't for that handicap, I'm sure she'd be one of our big stars."

Years later, after Russell died of alcoholism at the age of thirty-six, Wayne would get agitated at the very mention of her name. "Gail was just such a beautiful young girl that some of those fucking sons of bitches at the studios had taken advantage of her. You know about the old casting couch? She'd been there a number of times. Well, it didn't happen with me. I gave her the part on her own merits. She was one person I never shouted at because I knew she was insecure. She had an anxiety problem, which I understood because I'd had that when I was just a kid. I felt all she needed was someone to show her some kindness."

Wayne's secretary, Mary St. John, didn't think that Wayne and Russell had an affair, and neither did Mike or Gretchen Wayne. "In the family gossip, I never heard that they had an affair," said Gretchen. "What I did hear was that he felt sorry for her. She was really beautiful. I know that Michael swore that nothing happened, and Michael and Pat were on location when *Angel and the Badman* was shot in the summer."

Angel and the Badman revolves around its polar opposites in an effective way, although it's slightly hampered by Republic's habit of shooting many exteriors in the studio in front of a process screen. The mix of character and action is uneven, but the film has charm, takes the idea of nonviolence seriously, and, for a first film by director James Edward Grant, is fairly well made.*

"It sure changes you when you're the producer as well as the star," Wayne observed in an interview on the set. "I used to be a little vague about when I reported to the studio mornings, but now I'm ahead of time. I know all my lines. I love all the other actors in the troupe who don't blow lines. I think we've got a swell story — I found it myself. I even think it's got a message. Anyhow, it's one I wanted to do. James Edward Grant wrote it, and the only way he'd sell it to me was for me to give him the chance to direct it. So I did. As a producer, I want to give new people chances. If they click, I'll feel that it will be a sort of repayment for the brand of friendship and trust that Jack Ford has given me."

The reviews were, by and large, excellent. *Variety* said, "John Wayne gets off to a spectacularly

* Bruce Cabot, who played the heavy, asserted that "[Wayne] finally had to take over as director. He didn't take the credit, but he did the directing." Wayne would confirm Cabot's story, but never on the record.

successful stint in his producing-starring deal at Republic . . . classes as a western but could aptly be called romantic drama . . . under any tag it is top quality film . . . and is a sure BO hit anywhere." Philip K. Scheuer wrote that the film was "very probably Republic's sweetest western. . . . John Wayne, who stars in it with Gail Russell, also produced it and on both counts he has done himself proud . . . told with sentiment, spunk and a leavening humor as well as commendable insight." The film had been budgeted at $948,035, but ended up costing $1.3 million. Domestic rentals alone were almost $1.8 million, but Republic claimed it lost $249,784 on the picture.

Angel and the Badman was Wayne's first collaboration with Grant, a former Chicago newspaperman who had all the virtues and vices of that largely vanished breed. Born in 1902, Grant was slightly stocky, very articulate, highly gregarious, generally alcoholic. By the age of twenty-one he had a column called "It's a Racket" about organized crime. He began writing stories for *The Saturday Evening Post, Liberty, Redbook,* and the like, right on down the periodical food chain to *Detective Fiction Weekly,* where he wrote a gem called "Dames Are Such Suckers."

A couple of Grant's stories were adapted by Poverty Row studios, but he struck it big when MGM bought one of his stories and turned it into a Spencer Tracy–Myrna Loy vehicle entitled *Whipsaw.* Irving Thalberg suggested that Grant wander around the lot and pay particular attention to directors and editors at work. Thalberg was one of the few Hollywood people whom Grant liked: "He was the first man in Hollywood — in fact at that time he was probably the only one — who treated writers with respect."

By that time, Grant had already acquired the drinking habits that would mark most of his life. "All the offices had bars," he remembered of MGM in those days. "You started drinking when you got to the studio, and didn't stop until you went to bed. If you went to bed. One writer I knew had a desk with eight drawers. Seven of them had nothing in them but liquor."

After writing and directing *Angel and the Badman,* Jimmy Grant would, with occasional time out for alcohol-fueled explosions, shadow Wayne for the rest of his life as a house writer — an official or unofficial rewrite man, who could write dialogue that fit Wayne's screen character comfortably.

"In my dad's opinion, Jimmy was the best writer for him," said Patrick Wayne. "My dad could just say his dialogue. Jimmy was a great character — a great friend, a smoker, a drinker. Eventually he stopped smoking and drinking, but by then it was too late. It was a great social and professional relationship."

A sample of Grant's humor is found in a mock studio bio he composed for himself a few years after he met Wayne: "James Edward Grant was born in a log cabin. . . . Splitting logs by day, he studied by night by the light of a log fire; this left very few logs for sale, so they were very poor.

"While clerking in a village store, he walked seven miles one night to return a three-penny overcharge to a lady customer; the broad did not succumb to this gambit, so he walked back the seven miles, unbanged.

"During this period, he wrote Gibbon's 'Decline and Fall of the Roman Empire.' "

Shared political conservatism was yet another bond between the two. Grant and Wayne became not only best friends, but traveling companions; over the years, there would be trips to Mexico, South America, and Europe. "After my dad died, Duke said my old man was the best friend he ever had," said Grant's son Colin. "He was Irish, a storyteller. They thought alike politically, and my dad could write dialogue that sounded like Duke could say it and it sounded real."

Most movies are adaptations, but Grant preferred to write original scripts. His working methods were those of an old newspaperman. He wouldn't outline, wouldn't organize. When the story was complete in his head and not before, he would get up between five or six in the morning, sit down at his electric typewriter — Grant was always one of the first with any new gizmo — and bang out the script with two fingers in a couple of weeks.

Grant was a good golfer — around a ten handicap — and was always up for chess or skirt chasing. "He was always playing around with somebody," said Colin. "My mother was great, a real lady, but I can't remember her ever hassling the old man about it. Once in a great while they would fight, but not much. Of course, she knew. Somebody once asked Robert Mitchum how he had stayed married to one woman for forty years in Hollywood. 'A lack of imagination,' he said."

Grant knew how to write scenes that Wayne could play. Tom Kane, who would become Wayne's story editor, outlined a classic Wayne setup: Wayne is camped by a river, his horse beside him. He's making some coffee. His horse snorts and Wayne says, "I see him." A man on a horse rides into the scene and starts to cross the river.

"I wouldn't cross if I were you," says Wayne.

"Why not? Afraid it'll muddy up your coffee water?"

The man rides into the river, which turns out to be quicksand and both horse and rider struggle to get to the other side. Wayne never looks up, never offers help.

Fade out.

Wayne rides into town. The man on horseback is in the saloon playing cards. Wayne and he exchange glances, and Wayne smiles knowingly.

The essence of the emerging Wayne character was strength and a knowledge of the way the world works, communicated in as few words as possible. The trick was to do it without over-asserting the actor's natural dominance. Grant fit right in with Wayne's core group, as he was cut from the same cloth: hard-drinking, conservative, pugnacious, and — mostly — Irish.

Around the same time Grant and Wayne made *Angel and the Badman,* Wayne became fascinated by the story of the Alamo, which fell to the Mexican dictator General Santa Anna on March 6, 1836, after a siege of thirteen days. Santa Anna referred to the battle as "a small affair," but it had massive ramifications — Sam Houston defeated Santa Anna at San Jacinto as a direct consequence, which resulted in Texas's independence from Mexico and, eventually, its statehood.

Wayne saw the Alamo as more than another one of the presumably glorious martyrdoms that history throws up every so often — Thermopylae, Masada. He saw the Alamo as a moral tale about America's perennial struggle for freedom from authoritarian influence.

The movies had dabbled in Alamo stories several times in the silent days and in *Man of Conquest,* a 1939 Republic picture with Richard Dix as Sam Houston. But they had all used the battle the way westerns used the Gunfight at the O.K. Corral — as a convenient hook on which to hang melodramatic plot machinations. Wayne would conceive of an Alamo movie as more than a movie, more than folklore. It would be a rallying cry.

In 1936, Wayne had been just another western star at Republic, but by 1946 he was a certified movie star, with a production deal and control over his own movies. He believed he knew who was responsible. "I'd like to get up on housetops and shout out what I owe to [John Ford]," Wayne told Louella Parsons in 1946. "I simply owe to him every mouthful I eat, every dollar I've got, and practically every bit of happiness I know, that's all." This feeling of indebtedness never changed.

Michael Wayne would come to believe that his father would have made it anyway — he was so determined, so focused. But Wayne knew that luck matters as much as talent, as much as determination, as much as anything. Wayne had executed the part of the Ringo Kid beautifully, but it was a great part in a great film — the showcase had made all the difference.

Wayne's on-the-record references to Ford over the years are consistently adoring, although in conversation he could be considerably more objective. But Ford was always a grudging personality, a father figure who maintained authority by withholding overt displays of affection, at least as far as outsiders were concerned. Gene Autry enjoyed telling a story about running into Ford in the steam room of the Lakeside Golf Club.

"I went in and he happened to be sitting there. So I was in the next day and he was there again. So I said, 'You gonna make a picture, John?' 'Yeah,' he said, 'I'm gonna make a picture with ol' Meathead.' I said 'Who's that?' and he said, 'Wayne. I'm gonna make a picture with Wayne.' "

Despite the condescension, Wayne believed that Ford was the ultimate in savvy and artistry. "He's a man whose judgment you can trust implicitly. When I'm working under him all I ask is 'What kind of clothes do you want me to wear?' The rest I leave up to him. He directs instinctively, rather than sticking to a book of set rules. If a scene comes off in a different manner than he'd planned, he's liable to say 'Print it!' He knows quality when he sees it."

Wayne had been making movies for more than fifteen years and had developed theories of movie-making that would never really change, theories that in large part stemmed from ten years of making crummy pictures rather than five or six years of making quality pictures. He defined the difference between B pictures and A pictures as the difference between action and reaction, between a quick punch to the jaw and the expression on a face. Wayne preferred to emphasize the eyes over the fist.

"One man should serve as producer and director. Making a film is like painting a picture. If you were having your portrait painted, you wouldn't have one artist do your eyes, another your nose and still a third your mouth. That's why I think, as nearly as possible, production control should be centered in the talents of a single individual."

Because he had worked in both large and small parts, he believed in the ensemble rather than the relentless star close-up. "Give the scene to whom it belongs, even if it's an extra. If I call a guy a bad name the audience is not interested in my reaction, which is already known, but his. So give him the camera angle."

As for content, he wanted depth of character when he could find it. "You go to a good track meet and see some fine action; you're amused for the time being, but the effect doesn't stick with you. A conversation with George Bernard Shaw, on the other hand, will." What he looked for, he said, was "an unusual viewpoint on the familiar."

And there was one other thing: Wayne was beginning to say that if he ever washed out as an actor, "I wouldn't mind directing." He never washed out as an actor, but, as dozens of directors would find out, that didn't stop him from directing anyway.

When FDR died in April 1945, his aura of spiritual and political authority died with him, and in the 1946 elections the Republicans took control of Congress. That April the Motion Picture Alliance began publishing a monthly newsletter entitled *The Vigil.* The first issue featured informational questions and answers:

Q: Why not Fascism?
A: We haven't yet found any Fascist Front organizations in our sector of the American scene, which is motion pictures. We're watching for them. If any Fascist groups do appear, we'll be in there swinging at them. . . .
Q: Are [there any Communist Front organiza-

tions] presently active?

A: Active indeed.

Q: What do you propose to do about it?

A: Inform you. It's a long list, but in time, you'll have the name of every one of our local Communist Front organizations, what it is, what it is doing, where it came from, and where it is going to go.

The Motion Picture Alliance helped bring about the first wave of congressional investigations of the movie industry in 1947, facilitated by Eric Johnston, who had taken over the Motion Picture Association of America from Will Hays in 1945. Johnston declared, "We'll have no more *Grapes of Wrath,* we'll have no more *Tobacco Road*s. We'll have no more films that show the seamy side of American life."

In May 1947, J. Parnell Thomas (R-N.J.) the new chairman of the House Un-American Activities Committee, came to Los Angeles and set up shop at the Biltmore Hotel, where he conducted preliminary interviews with many witnesses who would later be categorized as "friendly." Thomas, a fierce enemy of the New Deal, asked for names from the FBI's lists of suspected subversives. "Expedite," J. Edgar Hoover wrote on Thomas's letter. "I want to extend *every* assistance to this committee."

Most of the witnesses who testified at the Biltmore were members of the Motion Picture Alliance: Robert Taylor, James Kevin McGuinness, Adolphe Menjou, Richard Arlen. Jack Warner also testified, naming every person on his payroll that he suspected of being a Communist.

Some of the testimony leaked — Rupert Hughes

reported that the Screen Writers Guild was "lousy with Communists" and Ginger Rogers's mother testified that her daughter had refused to speak one obviously Communistic line: "Share and share alike."★

The congressman returned to Washington and a nervous summer silence descended on Hollywood. At the end of the summer, it was announced that HUAC would open hearings on the "Hollywood situation" on September 23, 1947.

While all this was going on, Ward Bond was extremely busy; always in demand as a character actor, he now began to function as a self-appointed Inspector Javert, checking out the anticommunist bona fides of various actors, writers, and directors. Bond was capable of either clearing suspects or hurling them into the darkness. In 1947 Anthony Quinn had a part in a film fall through at the last minute. Quinn was a member of the Actor's Lab, an offshoot of the Group Theatre, where Morris Carnovsky moderated the classes. The Alliance considered the Actor's Lab a clubhouse for Communists, and someone told Quinn that he needed to be cleared of subversion. "See Ward Bond," he was told.

Quinn made an appointment and showed up at Bond's house, but there didn't seem to be anyone

★ Lela Rogers had been given a job in story development at RKO to make her daughter happy. When that job was taken away from her, she called Hoover to say that "RKO people who handle the reviewing of stories and the selecting of vehicles for their stars are either Communist or fellow travelers and are allied in a common group against Ginger."

home. Calling out, he heard a voice from the back of the house: "Yeah, Tony, I wanna talk to you. I'm in the john, come on in."

Quinn walked in to find Bond on the toilet. Bond pointed to the edge of the bathtub and said, "Sit there."

Bond didn't beat around the bush. "You a commie, Tony, a red?"

"Hell, no. Jesus be my judge, I never been even pink, much less red. Ward, I'm a loyal American, for Chrissakes, you gotta believe me."

Bond, grunted, finished his task, and said, "OK, Tony, you're all right. Go to work." The part that had disappeared just as suddenly reappeared. Anthony Quinn never went back to the Actor's Lab.

That fall, nineteen "unfriendly" witnesses were subpoenaed, as well as twenty-six "friendlies" (only twenty-four testified), with the nineteen eventually being winnowed down to the so-called Hollywood Ten, chosen because the committee already knew they had all been members of the Communist Party. The FBI had at least one informant within the Los Angeles branch of the Communist Party and Hoover had authorized break-ins at the offices of the party during 1944 and 1945, during which the membership rolls were photographed. Because of the break-ins, the FBI had a list of 287 members of the party within the movie industry.

It was this information that enabled HUAC to lead party members to perjure themselves; the fact that the information had been illegally obtained was irrelevant because the HUAC investigations were not, technically speaking, a court proceeding.

Suddenly, it seemed like there was an informer for every Communist, not to mention everyone who had voted for Roosevelt. Sometimes informers informed on each other. Ida Lupino told the FBI she thought Sterling Hayden was a Communist; George Murphy was naming names at MGM, as was Mervyn LeRoy. Ronald Reagan was giving up members of the Screen Actors Guild, even as he and Emmet Lavery, head of the Screen Writers Guild, protested against the kangaroo court aspect of the proceedings.

Not everybody ran for cover. Katharine Hepburn spoke at a Progressive rally, after which she was accosted by an investigator for HUAC who asked her if she wanted to explain her remarks. Hepburn, he wrote in a report, "drew herself up" and asked if the agent thought she didn't look like an adult. Then she told him she knew full well what she had said, was fully capable of writing her own speeches, and needed to make no defense of her position.

Once again, Wayne was absent from the struggle. He spent some of the summer of 1947 hanging around the stages at Republic, where Orson Welles was shooting *Macbeth.* For Wayne, personality always trumped politics; if he liked you, he was willing to overlook your ideology, no matter how rancid it would have been otherwise. Wayne and Welles could not have been further apart in matters of politics, but Charles Feldman was producing the Welles picture. Besides that, Welles was a die-hard fan of John Ford, which would have been enough to absolve him of all taint in Wayne's eyes.

Another bond between the two men was their size — Welles was six-two — which is probably how the subject of the dangers of small men came up. Welles remembered that Wayne told him, "Always be careful to be sitting down with them."

Wayne's absence from the roster of friendly witnesses is curious. The blacklisted screenwriter Howard Koch (*Casablanca, The Sea Hawk*) thought it was another case of Herbert Yates's bargaining.

In some cases, the heads of the studios made deals with the Committee not to put a certain individual on the stand publicly. That was true not only of so-called suspects or what they liked to call the unfriendly witnesses, but also of friendly witnesses that the studio didn't want to have "tainted" by political publicity of any kind . . . somebody like Wayne is a good example. How are you going to get people rushing in to see him shooting down the Apaches when they start thinking of him as a guy wearing a suit and tie and saying what a great job all these seventy year old politicians with their glasses and bow ties are doing in defending America? Mixed message.

In other cases, individuals ignored the studios and made their own private arrangements to meet with Committee members or their agents without telling anybody. You heard Cary Grant's name a lot in that connection.

By November, the House was debating contempt of Congress citations for the ten witnesses who had refused to answer the "Are you now or have you ever been" question. That same month, the studios issued the Waldorf Statement, which broadened the standard morals clause in Hollywood contracts that enabled studios to fire those employees who had "brought themselves into disrepute" by "defying the institutions of the United States government."

And so the blacklist era began. There would be more hearings in 1950. The result was that dozens were jailed; hundreds lost their jobs; hundreds more left the country. Some died. Every motion picture union, from the Screen Actors Guild to the Screen Directors Guild, ultimately capitulated to the blacklist.

All this would be called by one writer, echoing Daniel Defoe, "The Plague Years." Dalton Trumbo had another name for it: "The Time of the Toad." During this period, the right-wing press regularly ganged up on performers who had committed the terrible sin of not serving in the military during World War II; the Hearst columnist Westbrook Pegler accused Danny Kaye of not "giving exactly his all during the war," then added the seasoning of anti-Semitism by mentioning Kaye's real name — Kaminski.

Pegler neglected to mention that many conservatives hadn't served, John Wayne among them. Nor did he note that the Roosevelt administration had granted dispensation to Hollywood so that patriotic movies could continue to be manufactured without the interruptions that would have occurred with wholesale drafting of the movie workforce.

But Wayne's absence from the fray was not permanent: Robert Taylor served as the president of the Motion Picture Alliance in the immediate postwar years, but in 1949 he was succeeded by Wayne, who would be reelected several times. Officers of the Alliance at the time included Charles Coburn, Hedda Hopper, Morrie Ryskind,

Robert Arthur, Clarence Brown, and Roy Brewer. The executive committee included Ward Bond, Borden Chase, Gary Cooper, John Ford*, Mike Frankovich, Clark Gable, Cedric Gibbons, Louis Lighton, Cliff Lyons, John Lee Mahin, James Kevin McGuinness, Adolphe Menjou, Fred Niblo, Pat O'Brien, Lela Rogers, Robert Taylor, and Sam Wood. A few years later, Cecil B. DeMille, Irene Dunne, and Dimitri Tiomkin would be added to the roster of the executive committee. All in all, the Alliance included a goodly number of the people who were part and parcel of Wayne's extended filmmaking family.

Estimating the membership of the Alliance in these years is difficult; about a thousand people would attend the large meetings held at the American Legion clubhouse in Hollywood. The Alliance had sufficient dues-paying members to maintain offices at 159 South Beverly Drive in Beverly Hills, so presumably the membership included many more people who didn't attend meetings.

In other words, the communists were outnumbered.

So Wayne made the transition from a quiet

* Ford's name would appear and disappear from the roster of the Alliance's membership and management several times without apparent cause. So far as can be determined, he never spoke about his own political drift to the right from his mid- and late 1930s position as a New Deal Democrat. By 1950, he was regarded by both liberal and centrist peers in the Directors Guild as conservative, although nowhere near as extreme as DeMille and some others.

conservative who avoided testifying to a leader of the pack. It's possible that he came out in public only after the battle over the Hollywood Ten was over and it was safe to shoot the wounded. It's also possible that slow-burning guilt was a motivating factor.

"He regretted not serving" in World War II, said Mary St. John. "He was not the kind of man to dwell on it or talk about it, but you knew he did. You could see it in his face when anyone asked him about his war record. He would tell them that he had not served, and it made him feel like a hypocrite."

Certainly, Wayne's politics began to affect his judgment of potential projects. At the end of 1948, Charles Feldman sent him Robert Rossen's script for *All the King's Men,* based on Robert Penn Warren's roman à clef about Huey Long. Wayne responded with a blistering letter that requested Feldman ask his other clients if they wanted to make a film that "smears the machinery of government for no purpose of humor or enlightenment," that "degrades all relationships," and is made up of "drunken mothers; conniving fathers; double-crossing sweethearts; bad, bad rich people; and bad, bad poor people if they want to get ahead."

He concluded by telling Feldman to take the script and "shove it up Robert Rossen's derriere."

Feldman responded with a defensive letter saying, "You are entitled to your opinion. I am entitled to mine." He went on to enumerate the project's attributes — a Pulitzer Prize for the novel, for which Columbia paid $200,000, and Robert Rossen as the writer-director. "I consider Rossen one of the best talents in this business, comparable to John Huston, [Frank] Capra and

[William] Wyler. We do not represent him!" Feldman closed by saying that if he had failed to submit the script to Wayne he would have been derelict in his agent's duties. "I have never quarreled with your judgment, and I won't do so now. To my knowledge you have been right more times than wrong, and perhaps I may have been wrong more times than right. This is my side of the story and I submitted it to you for the foregoing reasons."

All the King's Men eventually won Oscars for Best Picture and Best Actor for Broderick Crawford. Willie Stark was a great part but playing him would have violated Wayne's own personal belief system, and this he was not willing to do. He intended to play only men that mirrored his own beliefs, his own values, either partially or completely.

If there was a breach between Wayne and Feldman over *All the King's Men,* it was brief; Wayne occasionally bought Feldman gifts — sweaters to counteract what Wayne thought was excessive formality at Feldman's office — and the Feldman agency represented Wayne as long as its founder was alive.

By 1950, liberals were in full flight. *The New York Times* reported on an exchange of letters between Wayne and Walter Wanger, who had produced both *Stagecoach* and *The Long Voyage Home.* In 1944, Wanger wrote a letter to the Alliance stating that the organization "had made unsupported charges of Communism in the motion picture industry — it has linked throughout the nation the word 'Hollywood' and 'Red' and without proof."

A few years later, Wayne replied with a letter implying that Wanger owed the Alliance an apology. Wanger wrote a cringing letter back: "If any words of mine hurt your group, or any member of it, I can only express my regret. . . . I recognize that time and history have proven the correctness of the judgment of the Motion Picture Alliance and its foresight in recognizing the Communist menace."

Dissenters were now outliers. The Alliance passed a resolution calling on the city of Los Angeles to register all Communists. There wasn't a single vote against the motion.

And then Wayne stepped in it by refusing to be as murderously ardent as others in the organization. When Larry Parks appeared before the House Un-American Activities Committee in 1951, he said he was willing to testify about his own life, but begged not to be forced to name names. Borden Chase got a call from William Wheeler, an investigator for HUAC, who said that the committee wanted someone from the Alliance to stand up and say a good word for Parks. Chase asked for a letter from Wheeler for cover, and then wrote a statement for Wayne saying that Parks deserved to be forgiven.

But when Wayne read the statement at an Alliance meeting, Parks was still equivocating about naming names. Hedda Hopper "grabbed the microphone and ate Duke out in public," according to Chase. "Duke looked at me as if to say, 'How could you do this to me?'"

As he had all his life, Wayne retreated before an angry woman and apologized to Hopper. Parks eventually caved, but his career was destroyed — the right hated him because he was a weak ex-

Commie, the left hated him because he had named names.

Technically, the blacklist lasted until 1959, although the power of the Alliance diminished greatly during the 1950s. Over the years, to counter the left's narrative of unwarranted persecution and tragic death, the right devised a counternarrative that was a mirror image of the left's. It was best articulated in a 1951 issue of the Alliance's magazine. "Three leaders of the MPA have died from heart attacks brought on by the strain of this bitter conflict, in which the MPA leaders have been repeatedly knifed in the back by people who should have been fighting on their side.

"The three stalwarts were Victor Fleming and Sam Wood, two famous directors, and last month, James Kevin McGuinness, one of the outstanding executives in the history of the industry."

These dueling narratives have persisted to the present day. As late as 1953, Paramount studio head Frank Freeman wrote a letter to William Wyler warning him about privately associating with people that HUAC had named as Communists, among them writer Leonardo Bercovici and director Bernard Vorhaus. "Of course," wrote Freeman, "the question of guilt by association always arises and if you continue to invite identified Communists to visit you or be part of any affair that you give, then you will have charges leveled at you."

Nunnally Johnson, who had written *The Grapes of Wrath* for John Ford, referred to the Alliance as "that Duke Wayne–Ward Bond outfit that passed on everybody. So many outrageous things went on that made me ashamed of the whole industry . . . think of John Huston having to go and debase himself to an oaf like Ward Bond and promise never to be a bad boy again." Johnson always referred to the Alliance as "this Ku Klux Klan."

Wayne would never apologize for the excesses of the period, for the hundreds of people who were blacklisted and exiled, many for unexceptional liberal sympathies. Nor did he think he had anything to apologize for.

According to his second wife, Chata, Wayne's favorite songs were "People Will Say We're in Love" and "Till the End of Time." He liked to read in bed. He liked Cary Grant's movies, and would watch anything with Victor McLaglen or Barry Fitzgerald.

For years, Wayne had a general assistant named J. Hampton Scott, an African American whom everybody called "Scotty" and who served as security guard, valet, and cook, although nobody but Wayne thought he was competent in the kitchen. "He'd give you a steak that looked like a big chunk of coal," said one employee, "really burned, yet red on the inside, just the way Duke liked it." Likewise, his services as a valet could result in Wayne wearing one red sock and one white sock. Wayne had come to the conclusion that Scotty was color-blind, but stuck with him because he liked him.

But Chata brought with her the servants she'd had in Mexico, as well as a general distrust of Wayne's own group, who might not have the loyalty to her that she thought appropriate. She singled out Scott.

Wayne had to accommodate his wife, but he

wasn't about to can his friend, so he bought Scott a car wash on Central Avenue that provided him with a solid living, and the two men exchanged Christmas cards for years.

Chata was regarded with distrust by most of the people who survived the purge, not just because she liquidated people, but because she was so exhausting for the man who was their meal ticket. She was not without her good points. She made a genuine effort to relate to people, and always tried to find out what they liked, their hobbies and so forth, and customized Christmas and birthday gifts accordingly.

But it soon became obvious that the marriage was affecting Wayne negatively. At one point, his weight dropped to 170 pounds because of the constant nervous tension. "I know he loved her," said one employee. "I know that. They used to fight, she'd go home to Mexico and he'd run and find her and bring her back and start the honeymoon over. She just could never figure out that he couldn't chase her the rest of his life. Sometimes you've got to get down to business. You can't do it forever. She didn't have to go to work, but he had to."

One of the possible reasons for Wayne's absence from the political fray in the immediate postwar years was that he was engaged in making some of the best movies of his life. *Red River* began as a story by Borden Chase, a member of the Motion Picture Alliance who had worked on several films for Wayne by this time (*The Fighting Seabees, Flame of the Barbary Coast*). The director Vincent Sherman worked with Chase and characterized him as "anti-democratic and anti-liberal. . . . He felt Roosevelt was a traitor and that Hollywood was infested with Communists. . . . What amused me about him was that he seriously considered himself to be an important American writer, when the truth was that he was nothing more than a hack.

"He plotted his projects mechanically: get two men who love the same girl in a conflict about a big issue, have a fight here, a chase there, and a final big confrontation when the two men are reconciled. He thought the best love story was about two strong macho men. Women were merely sex objects."

With a few minor variations, Sherman's take does indeed describe a lot of Chase's writing, up to and including *Red River,* but none of Chase's other scripts was developed by Charles Feldman and Howard Hawks. Hawks paid Chase $50,000 for his story in January 1946 — it wouldn't be published until December and January 1947 in *The Saturday Evening Post* — and hired him at $1,250 a week to write the screenplay. In June 1946, Feldman sent Wayne the first ninety-five pages of the script. "I think it's great," Feldman wrote, "though I know Howard is still re-writing."

Chase completed his script, at which point Hawks brought in a young man named Charles Schnee for a rewrite. Schnee would become a notable screenwriter in the next ten years, with credits that included *The Furies* and *The Bad and the Beautiful.* Schnee's rewrite introduced the woman Tom Dunson leaves behind at the beginning of the film, cut a Civil War episode involving Matthew, Dunson's adopted son, and also cut the death of Cherry Valance. Schnee added an Indian attack, and made the woman who comes between father and son a card sharp instead of a prostitute.

The scripted ending was hanging fire — Chase's script ended with Matthew and Tess loading a wounded Dunson in the back of a wagon and taking him across the river to Texas, so he can die on American soil. But Hawks refused to kill off his main character, so Schnee's rewrite had the three principals crossing the river with Dunson alive and kicking.

Hawks's first choice for the part of Dunson was Gary Cooper, who turned it down because he thought the character was too ruthless. It was Feldman who suggested Wayne as the lead. Wayne's salary was set at a fairly measly $50,000, half of what he was getting at Republic, although Feldman guaranteed him $10,000 extra per week past twelve weeks of shooting, and 10 percent of the profits, with a guaranteed $75,000.

The budget was set at $1.75 million, funded by a consortium of bank and private loans, with Hawks earning $125,000 and 57 percent of the profits and Feldman earning 24 percent of the profits. United Artists would take its distribution off the top, followed by the investors and the banks. Hawks's and Feldman's Monterey Productions was last in line.

A young actress named Coleen Gray was under contract to Fox and was interested in the crucial part of Fen, the woman who offers Tom Dunson her loyalty and her body but is rejected and dies offscreen, thereby sealing Dunson's isolation.

"I knew nothing about Hawks or *Red River* or anything else, except that he was a famous, respected director," remembered Gray. "He was a very nice man; soft-spoken and intelligent, which is a joy. Supposedly, they had tested three hundred

279

people for Fen, so I came in late in the game, but I didn't know about any of it. Hawks told me, 'If you can get your voice down a couple of octaves, we'll test you.' This was on a Thursday or Friday, and he told me to go out in the hills and scream until I broke my voice.

"I said, 'Yes sir,' but I thought, 'Over my dead body.' I was a singer, and singers don't do anything to ruin their voices. But Hawks liked Lauren Bacall and Joanne Dru, those girls with low growls. I left and did not go out and scream. But when I did the test, I lowered my voice the best that I could. And apparently that was good enough."

Hawks chose Gray for the part, but there was a problem — Fox hadn't cleared her to make the test. Rod Amateau, Gray's husband, said, "When in doubt, go to the top." So Gray made an appointment with Darryl Zanuck. "I had never met him, but I knew two things: he was from Nebraska and he was a womanizer. I was scared. I didn't know what to do if he made a move at me.

"I went to his office and he shook hands and took me to his desk. I said, 'I'm so glad to meet you. I'm from Nebraska — from Staplehurst, and you're from Wahoo.' And I think if he had any ideas, that set him back on his haunches. At any rate, he didn't approach me. I was relieved, but also a little disappointed because I thought that meant he didn't think I was sexy.

"I told Zanuck that Hawks's picture was a grand opportunity and Fox wasn't doing anything with me at the moment. And he said, 'If Howard will call and ask for you, we'll see.' "

Gray called Hawks, Hawks called Zanuck, Zanuck said yes. And, as Gray remembered it, "I earned the undying enmity of the lower echelon of Fox executives, because I'd gone over their heads."

By the first week of September 1946, Gray joined the company on location in Elgin, Arizona, where filming began on a seventy-six-day schedule. But it rained in Elgin. "We sat around in our tents drumming our fingers and being restless," remembered Gray, who ended up reshooting her scene back at the Goldwyn studio months later.

"Fox had sent me to the Actor's Lab in Los Angeles to study the Method, and I was thinking about the part. I sat in the rainy tent with paper and pencil and decided to write out what I thought Fen had been like in her life up to the point we meet her in the film. That occupied some time and thought. And then I marched through the rain with my umbrella to Mr. Hawks's tent, and he came to the door and I explained to him what I had done.

" 'Would you please read this?' I asked him. 'I want to know if I'm on the right track.' He took it very quietly and solemnly and closed the door. And that was that. The next day it was sunny and we hadn't shot the scene yet. I asked Hawks about the pages I'd given him and asked him if I was on the right track. 'Yes, you are,' he said and we never discussed it further. He must have gotten a chuckle out of it, but he always treated me with respect. His direction to me just before we shot the scene was 'Be a woman.' "

The company was on location into early November before heading back to Hollywood, while Arthur Rosson stayed behind in Arizona, directing a second unit that put together the stampede sequence.

Gray found Wayne to be "very quiet, very polite, rather shy. He knew his lines and he was professional. It was my first movie, so I was in no position to judge anybody else. I didn't say anything to him because I was terrified. I was a young girl from Nebraska, and in all my career in Hollywood I was never able to overcome a certain basic shyness about not speaking unless you're spoken to. So he didn't talk and I didn't talk. We'd stand there kicking our toes in the sand. He did not seem to be a social person."

Hawks didn't shoot a lot of takes, and on Gray's first close-up of her big scene, he called "Print!" whereupon she piped up with "I can do it better." Hawks said okay, and Gray did it again. Hawks again said "Print!" and that's the one in the film.

A young actor named William Self joined the company and noticed the improvisatory nature of Hawks's method. "Something would catch his eye on the first take, and he'd throw things out, make some dialogue changes, and Wayne would do it easily. He wouldn't always do that — it depended on his level of comfort with a director. But he and Hawks were remarkable together — they were nimble and confident of each other."

But not always. Wayne had become extremely sensitive about his image, and he would complain in later years that Hawks "wanted to make me a big, blustering coward. 'You'll win an Academy Award,' he said. 'Yeah, yeah,' I said. Instead I played it as a strong man who was scared. After all, as a man you can be scared, but you can't be a coward."

Which is as succinct a summation of the John Wayne character as there is.

Hawks had a knack for choosing relatively

inexperienced actors and matching them up with champions who forced the younger talents to raise the level of their game. He did it with Lauren Bacall on *To Have and Have Not,* with Dorothy Malone on *The Big Sleep,* and with Montgomery Clift on *Red River,* after first trying to get Jack Buetel, the young actor who had starred in *The Outlaw.* But Howard Hughes wouldn't loan out Buetel, so Hawks settled on the young actor he had seen on Broadway in *You Touched Me.*

Clift was interested but hesitant — he wasn't sure he could handle the brutal fight with Wayne at the end of the picture. "You're an actor, aren't you?" asked Hawks. Swayed by that argument — and the $60,000 salary — Clift took the job.

Wayne wasn't at all sure Clift was the right choice. When he and Clift met in Hawks's office, Clift avoided looking him in the eye, which put Wayne off. He was also alarmed about the physical disparity between them — Clift was about six inches shorter than Wayne.

"Howard, do you think we can get anything going between that kid and myself?" he asked Hawks with a perceptible concern.

"I think you can," said the phlegmatic Hawks. After shooting a couple of scenes with Clift, Wayne told Hawks, "You're right. He can hold his own, anyway, but I don't think we can make a fight."

A mutual doubt was about all that Wayne and Clift shared. While the company waited for the rain to stop in Arizona, Wayne took Clift and Hawks's son David on a bear-hunting trip. "We never saw any bear, but we did get lost," remembered David Hawks. "The guide admitted that he didn't know the way back. So John Wayne took charge, and he really and truly led us back. One

283

horse fell, lost its footing, and we had to shoot it." Clift seems to have been appalled by the entire adventure, writing a friend, "You see what happens when you turn a bunch of fascists loose in the hills?"

They were two very different kinds of actors from two different generations, and Hawks had to figure out a middle ground that would accommodate them. Clift was introspective, a Method actor, and Wayne was purely instinctive.

"Wayne never read a script that I had," said Hawks. "He'd say, 'What am I supposed to do in this?' and I'd say, 'You're supposed to give the impression of this and that.' And he'd say 'OK.' He'd never learn lines before I talked to him, because he said that threw him off. He could memorize two pages of dialogue in three or four minutes, and then he just goes and does it. He's the easiest person I ever worked with because he doesn't discuss it and try to fine-tune it; he just goes and does it without squawking."

Clift would tell a friend that Wayne and Hawks "laughed and drank and told dirty jokes and slapped each other on the back. They tried to draw me into their circle but I couldn't go along with them. The machismo thing repelled me because it seemed so forced and unnecessary."

Without knowing it, the actors were replicating the generational difference between Matthew Garth and Tom Dunson. Hawks's film was about the passing of a torch from autocratic authority to a more humanistic style — it's really Hawks's version of a theme Ford would make his own in *The Man Who Shot Liberty Valance.*

The script wasn't set, the budget kept rising, but Clift just kept getting better, matching Wayne scene for scene. "Mr. Hawks took [Clift] aside and pointed out [stuntman, later actor] Richard Farnsworth," remembered Danny Sands, another stuntman on the picture. " 'Montgomery, you walk along behind him and watch him carefully. If he scratches his butt, you scratch yours. He's a real cowboy.' And he did, by God. Farnsworth took him and tutored him and, damn, he made a cowboy out of a hell of an actor."

But Clift's Method affectations irritated Wayne, as did his awkwardness with guns. One day he barked at the young actor, "Christ, my goddamn kid can do it, for Christ's sake and he's 11 years old. You can't do it? Do it!"

The trick to achieving competence at quick draws and twirls is to practice while kneeling on a bed. You'll drop the gun three hundred times, but you won't have to bend over three hundred times, which makes all the difference. Clift got up to speed very quickly, and even Wayne was eventually impressed with his dexterity.

"Monty drove him nuts," remembered Harry Carey Jr., who worked on the picture for several weeks. "He didn't like Monty as an actor. Years later, I said that I thought Monty was very effective in *Red River,* and Duke said, 'He was a pain in the ass.' But he didn't deny that he was effective."

Hawks's gift for staging was never more evident than in the final fight. "Wayne was aware that there was a great physical disparity between him and Clift," said William Self. "Wayne was a giant brute and, believe me, he could have killed Clift with one punch. Clift was very modestly built. The fact that Hawks could make those two fighting look at all realistic was remarkable."

When Clift saw the completed picture, he hated it. He felt the script had been watered down, and like a great many people ever since, he hated the ending, "because Joanne Dru settles it and it makes the showdown between me and John Wayne a farce."

With the unmotivated "you boys quit fighting" ending, Hawks shyed away from the ultimate implications of Dunson's character, even though some ardent auteurists defend it — as if an Old Testament patriarch like Dunson is suddenly going to see the error of his ways and hand everything over to a New Testament character like Matt. "It's true that Howard got up to that point without being ready for it," admitted Wayne. "Maybe the fact that it was right at the end of the picture made it more obvious."

By the time *Red River* was finished, it was a month over schedule and far over budget. Monterey Productions had to borrow an additional $200,000, then another $111,000, then still more — a whopping $639,000 overage in all. The film ended up costing $2.8 million, and the overage wiped out the profits that Hawks and Charles Feldman were counting on.

But Hawks hadn't frittered away all that extra time and money. He used it to make an authentic epic — the size of the characters matches the size of their task: to drive a herd of longhorn cattle one thousand miles from Texas to Missouri. Hawks adopted an appropriately expansive, panoramic style that stops short of either the pompous or elegiac.

Ford had used Wayne as a sort of overgrown country boy — his characters in *Stagecoach, The Long Voyage Home,* and even *They Were Expend-*

able are manifestly decent men, almost submissive until they're pushed too far. When Hawks gave Wayne the part of Tom Dunson, he gave him the missing arrow in his acting quiver — the freedom to play a domineering, wrongheaded son of a bitch. For the rest of his career, Wayne would shift between these two characters and, in definitive performances, combine them.

From the beginning, Dunson is unyielding. Although the luscious Fen tells him in unmistakable terms that "The sun only shines half the time; the other half is night," Dunson refuses to take her with him. He promises to send for her, and she promises to come, despite the fact that "you're wrong."

When Dunson finds out that she has been killed, he barely flinches. It's typical of the single-minded nature of a man who doesn't need a backstory. As the critic Dave Kehr wrote, "Here was a man who could get you through the worst the world had to offer. Here was a man who could kill you without a second thought."

Like any great actor, Wayne communicates with his body. During the scene when he tells Matt that he's going to kill him, Dunson's posture contradicts his words — he's leaning against his horse; the relaxed slant of his body belying the rigor of the threat. Dunson is close to being played out, but not so much that Matt or the others can relax. Dunson means to do what he says, and, as ragged as he is, he just might be able to do it. Contrasting with Wayne's indomitable Dunson is the tensile strength of Clift's Matthew Garth — a wiry watcher.

For the first time, Wayne plays an implacable force, and he's completely believable. *Red River* begins the transition of John Wayne from man to mountain. That the movie is about the great stakes involved in the tide of empire makes the character's ruthlessness viable.

Tom Dunson is Wayne's first comprehensive portrayal of the deeply ambivalent core of American manhood. Dunson embodies the allure of the authoritarian — the possibility of violence, the shying away from women and home — what Jonathan Lethem called "the dark pleasure of soured romanticism — all those things that reside unspoken at the center of our sense of what it means to be a man in America."

Red River was more than two years old by the time it was released late in 1948, after a frantic legal tussle between Howard Hughes and Hawks over what Hughes felt were untoward similarities between *Red River* and Hughes's bizarre *The Outlaw.* Hughes's ire stemmed from the climax, in which Dunson takes a series of shots at Matt that are meant to goad him into fighting, with one bullet creasing his cheek.

Hughes felt the entire scene was stolen from the end of *The Outlaw,* where Doc Holliday tries to force Billy the Kid to draw by nicking his earlobes. (Hawks had started directing *The Outlaw* in 1943 before walking off/getting fired.) Hughes wanted the entire four-minute confrontation taken out, an absurd demand, but one that came only a week or two before September 1, 1948, when the film was scheduled to open in 350 theaters in Texas, Arizona, and Oklahoma, where Wayne was a particularly potent box office draw. Hughes was threatening an injunction that could tie up the film for months.

"He's serious, Eddie," said Hughes's attorney

Loyd Wright to Edward Small, who was a major investor in the film. "I tell you Howard's serious. He means it."

Under ordinary circumstances, this sort of problem could have been negotiated, but Small and the rest of the investors were loath to endure any more delay in getting their money back. Small had worked with Hughes before and knew that "from his viewpoint, procrastination was to be employed to gain his ends."

Small had a meeting with Hughes in a projection room as they ran and reran the sequence. Hughes refused to alter his demand to remove the sequence, which would have left the picture with an abrupt cut and Montgomery Clift with an unexplained wound on his face. Finally, Small, Hawks, and Hughes had a meeting at one of Hughes's aircraft plants near Inglewood.

The conversation began in rancor, then got worse. "Both men were tall and lean, and I felt like the referee between two animated redwood trees," remembered Small. Finally, Small suggested that Hughes edit the sequence to suggest what Hawks, Feldman, and Small should do. Hughes made a few cuts, eliminating about twenty-four seconds, including a shot where Dunson's bullet creases Matt's cheek. Also removed were nine words of Wayne's dialogue: "Draw. Go on, draw. Well, then, I'll make you." As Small realized, "If I had made the same infinitesimal alterations, he probably wouldn't have accepted them."

The prints for *Red River* had already been manufactured, so editors fanned out across the Southwest to insert the revised sequence in the prints that had already been shipped to the

289

exchanges. (Since the original negative remained untouched, the face-creasing shot has remained in the film as far as posterity is concerned.)

Critics thought that Wayne's performance was remarkable; the trades praised both the picture ("a milestone in western film production," said *The Hollywood Reporter*) and Wayne. Even Bosley Crowther in *The New York Times* said that "this consistently able portrayer of two-fisted, two-gunned men surpasses himself in this picture."

Wayne always believed the film was crucial in his career. As he put it, "*Stagecoach* established me as a star; *Red River* established me as an actor."

While *Red River* slowly wound its way toward release, in the summer of 1947 Wayne trooped off to Monument Valley to make John Ford's *Fort Apache.* The writer and artist Stephen Longstreet was on the location for a week and was startled to hear good jazz playing on the Monument Valley PA system. John Huston, a classmate of Longstreet's in the 1920s — "John was already a lanky oddball," Longstreet remembered — visited the set, and Huston and Ford fell into a conversation about Joyce's *Dubliners,* with Ford quoting lines from memory.

Longstreet found Ford "a surly bastard, but I think it began as an act to hide behind and it became a habit. Ford had a love/hate affair with the universe. Inside he was a mushy romantic. *Read* his films — the beauty of his camera setups. But the world didn't live up to [his] idea of what it was going to be. . . . Ford was *the* great director of his era, but sour about the lost hopes of the world."

Longstreet noted a trait that some writers have mistakenly chosen to define as repressed homo-eroticism: "He fell in love with his leading actors. So, I noted, did DeMille when I wrote the dialogue for *The Greatest Show on Earth.* Both Ford and DeMille would have been shocked if you called them gay, but they favored macho men, to near-adoring them." In both cases, the motivation was not sexual, but an idealized projection of their masculine selves — neither Ford nor DeMille had recessive egos.

Ford's target on the set of *Fort Apache* was the inexperienced John Agar, who he generally referred to as "Mr. Temple." (At the time, Agar was married to Shirley Temple.) Wayne had been there many times and tried to calm the young man. "I was petrified," remembered Agar, "and I was working with people who I had grown up watching and I didn't know what the heck I was doing. All those guys were so helpful to me. They kept patting me on the back, saying, 'You're doing great kid, you're doing great.' Duke did that with me in every movie I made with him. He was always saying, 'Right in there, kid, you're doing fine, you're doing fine.'

"And when you have somebody like John Wayne saying that to you, it takes you up, boy, makes you feel like you're worthwhile. I had lost my dad when I was a little boy and I kinda looked up to him as like a Dad."

Agar never got over his feeling of indebtedness, and for good reason. Wayne cast him as late as *Chisum* in 1970, long after Agar had stopped working in anything but Z-list science fiction films. Agar would call him every Christmas to wish him a happy holiday.

After production moved to the Selznick studio for interiors, Ford hosted lunches in his office. One day the group included Wayne, Robert Parrish — a member of Ford's unit during the war — Merian Cooper, and Robert Wise, a friend of both Ford's and Parrish's. Ford dominated the conversation with tales of his and Parrish's wartime exploits, which was a trifle embarrassing because neither Wayne nor Wise had served. It would not be the only time Ford would point out Wayne's absence from combat.

Fort Apache is the basic template for the cavalry western, mostly idealized until the end. It's a fine, measured film, with some of the same respect for duty and responsibility as *They Were Expendable,* but with the addition of a dense sense of the social weave necessary for survival on an isolated outpost.

The film has provided difficulties for various critics for various reasons. John Gregory Dunne wrote eloquently about the cavalry westerns: "Ford was Irish, as I am, and among the Irish, sentimentality is often what passes for feelings, especially carnal feelings. Sex is so absent in Ford's Monument Valley that his desert forts seem almost monastic, his troopers castrati without even a passing interest in autoeroticism. His was basically an army without women, an army without whores . . . an oxymoron."

Passing over the impossibility of suggesting autoeroticism in a movie made in 1947, this is the sort of thing that can happen when people whose primary orientation is literary fiction write about the movies. Dunne's point certainly isn't true of *Fort Apache* — the soldiers' wives are a part of the film's emotional current — or *She Wore a Yellow*

Ribbon, where Joanne Dru's presence inflames the passions of Harry Carey Jr. and John Agar. And the driving motivation of *Rio Grande* is the curdled love between John Wayne and his wife, played by Maureen O'Hara.

What Dunne seems to have meant is that in *Fort Apache* and *She Wore a Yellow Ribbon* there's no sexual charge that needs to be taken seriously; the women are either spayed by domesticity or provoke easily dismissable crushes from manifestly immature brats. Dunne thought that all this was because Ford had been an officer in the Navy and had an overly romantic officer's view of troops.

Dunne makes Ford sound much less complicated than he actually was. It was Ford's intuitive genius to realize that despite their friendship, Henry Fonda and John Wayne were complete opposites — not just politically, but as actors and human beings. Fonda knew his own emotional limitations; he once told a friend that he didn't understand stage fright at all. "I can't wait to get on stage. I can't wait to become somebody else."

Ford utilized Fonda's rigidity — which translated as integrity in *Young Mr. Lincoln,* as cold anger in *The Grapes of Wrath* — and made him a martinet in *Fort Apache.* And as was usually the case with Ford — always excepting *The Searchers* — he used Wayne's gregariousness to make him an expansive earth father, comfortable with himself and his role in life.

Fonda's Colonel Owen Thursday is an unthinking military ideologue, responding with predictable knee-jerk reaction to whatever stimuli present themselves. Wayne's Kirby York is an adult, with an adult mind attuned to moral shades of gray. The film's tensions — between duty and impulse, between knowledge and intuition, between peace and war, between fact and legend — are a function of men in a complex situation forced to make complex decisions. Black and white is the stuff of movies, not life, and *Fort Apache* is unusually true to life.

The climax of *Fort Apache* involves Thursday's arrogance leading to the slaughter of him and his command. The film ends with the legendary binary scene where Ford acknowledges that the Army's handling of the Indians was unjust, unfair, and dishonorable, while allowing Kirby York to assert that Thursday was a noble man, worthy of the tradition the cavalry embodies. The roots of glory may be tainted, but the celebration of Thursday's faulty character and the men that followed him is presented with absolute sincerity.

This is more ambiguity than audiences — or most writers — are used to in the movies.

Years later, a writer asked Wayne if Kirby York completely believed the things he says about Thursday. "No, I think the character was saying that because the newspapermen were asking him things. Now he has to say something pleasant about this guy. He can't say, 'Why, the stupid son of a bitch . . . got all those guys killed and made a liar out of me to the Indians.' He can't say that because it would be bad for morale. It wouldn't do anybody any good for me to belittle the guy. . . . It's about the least provocative thing that he could say about that man, one way or the other."

The dramatic and moral tension in *Fort Apache* works because of the equal but opposing poles of the film's leading men. "Henry Fonda could do anything you asked him to do as an actor, but he was a cold, removed man," said Mark Rydell, who directed both Fonda and Wayne. "He was not, for instance, a very good father. He had an access to his unconscious when he was acting that he didn't have in day-to-day life. He executed anything professional without problems, but socially he was difficult. He didn't want to reveal himself, didn't want to expose who he really was. He came out of Omaha, the ultimate white-bread place, but I always felt his talent was Jewish. His personality and his heritage were WASP, but his talent was Jewish."

Fonda's participation in the Ford-Wayne cabal from the mid-1930s on was as close as he ever got to being one of the boys. Jane Fonda remembered that as a little girl she would occasionally come down for breakfast in the morning to find Wayne having a cup of coffee with his friend Hank.

Fonda enjoyed recalling a vacation involving himself, Wayne, and a few others on the *Araner* where they all ended up in Mazatlán. They were drinking and spotted an American couple who turned out to be on their honeymoon. Wayne invited the couple to sit with them. "At this point, someone brought in a boa constrictor," Fonda said, seemingly introducing a 180 degree bend in the story, but not really. The snake, it seems, was a pet of the hotel.

Wayne's vocabulary was seldom leashed, and at that point he uttered the word "Fuck." He then realized what he'd said in front of the young woman and tried to recoup by saying, "Shit, I'm sorry." This struck Fonda as the funniest thing he'd ever heard, and he went into hysterics that led to him passing out.

At that point, Wayne paid someone to drape the

boa constrictor over Fonda, who promptly woke up and discovered a huge snake wrapped around him. What Wayne and company didn't know was that Fonda didn't share their fear of snakes. "Duke, look what I got," said Fonda as he stood up holding the snake out toward Wayne.

The last thing Fonda saw that night was Wayne disappearing across the lobby and into the street with amazing speed.

Fonda would edge away from Wayne over politics — Fonda was always an unreconstructed New Deal liberal — and he turned his back on Ford after a final collaboration on *Mister Roberts* that collapsed when Ford began drinking on the set. Fonda and Ford barely spoke for the rest of the director's life, but Fonda and Wayne always maintained a mutual affection.

Coming back into the fold for *Fort Apache* was George O'Brien, who had been a great friend of Ford's in the silent days at Fox. RKO dropped O'Brien before the war, and after the war his career stalled. Marguerite, O'Brien's wife and Wayne's leading lady in *The Big Trail,* called Ford as he was about to go into production on *Fort Apache.*

"Jack, you've got to do something for George."

"I wouldn't do anything for the son of a bitch," replied Ford, who was still nursing his anger at O'Brien for leaving a drunken Ford behind during a 1931 trip to Manila.

She then played her ace: "Jack, if you don't, it will be the ruination of a good Catholic family."

It was a mark of her desperation, because Marguerite Churchill O'Brien loathed Ford ("A son of a bitch. Drunk, hateful, vicious."). But then

296

her son Darcy believed that the only person in Hollywood she had liked was Will Rogers.

Ford came through and offered O'Brien a nice supporting part. The two immediately fell back into their old relationship, which suited both men. "I spent two weeks with Wayne and his family at Catalina," remembered Darcy. "Ford was there on his yacht, the *Araner.* Pedro Armendáriz and his kid were there. It may have been the happiest two weeks of my childhood. We dived for abalone, and the area was totally unspoiled. Wayne was great to me. It was idyllic. And the most idyllic evening was at our house in Brentwood, which had a six-foot-high fireplace. Wayne was there, Ford was there, Harry Carey Jr., Stan Jones, and a few others. Stan Jones sang 'Ghost Riders in the Sky.' I was eight or nine. It was my idea of heaven."

CHAPTER NINE

Although Wayne was riding high creatively as well as commercially, these were actually difficult years for him. Besides the nonstop turbulence of his marriage to Chata, he increasingly felt that Republic wasn't being honest with him. Wayne was determined to make *The Alamo* — a project Herbert Yates regarded with profound misgivings. For one thing, it would be expensive; for another, Wayne wanted to direct the picture himself.

"I was never sick in my life," Wayne remembered about this period. "But I had a six month bout with an ulcer. That was when I was a pawn in everybody's hands, working for Yates at Republic Studio, and they were loaning me out to any studio for almost any kind of picture, and I was doing it just because they'd promised if I did, they'd produce and I could direct and star in *The Alamo.* Then they stalled.

"It was awful. Actors aren't supposed to have a brain in their heads, but I had enough to know if I was going to stay in this business, I'd better start moving up the ladder. That's when I got the ulcer. The doctors said to do what I was told and I'd be over it in six months. So I did everything they said — drank cream, ate baby food, brown-bagged it to work and finally, on the last day of the six months, I bought a couple of bottles of tequila and drank them. Then I knew I was cured."

Wayne remembered the ulcer as taking place when he was in his early thirties, but the connection to *The Alamo* firmly places it in the late 1940s, when he was in his early forties.

The move into producing, the ambitions for directing, were all a conscious attempt to build a foundation that didn't rely on acting. "I think I may be getting past it to keep playing the romantic lead," he had told Anthony Quinn when they were making a terrible picture at RKO called *Tycoon.* "I'm losing my goddamned hair, and I'm the wrong side of 40 now."

His only alternative was to venture deeper into production — the creative end of filmmaking.

While *Red River* was being reconstructed, John Ford saw the picture and realized that his pal had the chops of a character actor; in 1948 he gave Wayne two parts that demonstrated his range.

In May and June of 1948, Ford shot his remake of *Three Godfathers.* Harry Carey Sr. had starred in the original in 1916, and Chester Morris had done the first sound version in 1936. Ford's *3 Godfathers* was shot in thirty-two days, mostly on the outskirts of Death Valley. This time, Ford concentrated his ire on Harry Carey Jr., who was getting his first big part. (The film is dedicated to Carey Sr., who had recently died.) Despite his own psychological pain, Carey noted how skilled Wayne was, often needing no more than one take to pull off complicated scenes.

Carey could never understand how Ford could

be so unyielding in his refusal to praise Wayne, but there were actors who thought they understood. Eddie Albert worked for Ford as well as William Wyler, and he compared the two. "Willy would never, or very rarely, give you directions. He would just keep shooting until it looked right to him. He was always correct, but he drove a lot of actors crazy, including Olivier.

"That was the opposite of The Boss [Ford]. He would tell you pretty clearly what he wanted, and you very clearly learned not to fool around too much. The Boss gave directions in externals — 'cross over on that line,' that sort of thing. He didn't talk about the feelings of the characters. And when he worked with Duke, I think that was very helpful; Duke didn't come from the stage, and it wasn't natural for him to be studying things like motivation. Willy was doing films that were more cerebral than the Boss, whose films were mainly about *picture.*"

Corresponding to Albert's memory, Harry Carey Jr. recounted how Ford instructed him to walk toward a big rock on his right, then veer toward a smaller rock on his left. Carey did as he was told, but Ford yelled "Cut," then began hollering about how Carey had ignored his instructions. He concluded the tirade by pantomiming masturbation.

Wayne had been on the receiving end of this sort of thing, and had had enough. "He went right where you told him to," he said loudly. Ford looked at him. "Ah-ha — I forgot. Mr. Wayne here once produced a picture. So now he's decided to direct this one." And then he let it go.

It was a tough shoot, from eight to eleven in the morning, a long lunch to avoid the hottest part of the day, then from three to six in the afternoon. In later years, Ward Bond enjoyed telling a story about how Ford had directed him to ride out on his horse and wait for a signal to come into camera range from a couple of hundred yards away. In Bond's telling, Ford left him out there for three hours.

But the result was worth it — a sweet-natured Fordian parable about the Magi, here transmuted into forgiveness and regeneration involving Wayne, Pedro Armendáriz — whom the other characters address as "Pete," his offscreen nickname — and Harry Carey Jr., all archetypal good-bad men. (Wayne treats Carey's character as a younger brother, protectively telling him to be sure not to use his gun during a bank robbery.)

Chased into the desert by a posse, they come across a wagon with a dying woman (Mildred Natwick) who's about to give birth. They deliver the baby, bury the woman, and resolve to take the baby back to the nearest town: New Jerusalem. The horses are lost in a sandstorm, Carey and Armendáriz die, but Wayne soldiers on, determined to keep his promise to a dying woman.

In the end, Wayne gets the baby to New Jerusalem. Because of the extenuating circumstances, he's only sentenced to a year in jail for the bank robbery, during which time Bond and his wife — D. W. Griffith's great star Mae Marsh — will raise the baby.

Now thoroughly absorbed into the community, Wayne wears the suspenders and turned-up jeans of *Stagecoach.* As he leaves on the train, he waves in impeccably composed farewell while the ladies of the town sing "Bringing in the Sheaves."

3 Godfathers is a studiously nonviolent picture:

at one point, Ward Bond's sheriff refuses to pursue the outlaws into the desert, saying "They ain't paying me to kill folks." It's a reminder — as if you needed it — that Catholicism was a major component of John Ford's life. The film is not really first-rate, but it has a benevolence that puts it near the top of the second-rate. It's also a visual masterpiece — you can see the heat rising from the ground in some shots — that carries considerable spiritual emotion. Wayne's performance seamlessly combines fortitude, determination, anger, grief, responsibility, and exhaustion.

She Wore a Yellow Ribbon began production in October 1948, just after *Red River* went into release. It's majestically photographed by Winton Hoch, who had first collaborated with Ford on *3 Godfathers,* where it became clear that the cameraman was, along with Jack Cardiff, one of a handful of masters of Technicolor photography.

John Agar confirmed the legend about Ford shooting in a real thunderstorm in Monument Valley. "There was lightning all around us, and there's metal on bridles and saddles. The cinematographer was concerned and said, 'That's a wrap.' The lightning was cracking. But Ford said, 'No, we shoot.' So we shot through the thing, and the cameraman won the Academy Award. It's a true story — I was in the scene."

Wayne brought his son Michael to the location, and the boy always remembered the otherworldly beauty of nights in Monument Valley. Occasionally the company assembled for a sing-along. Goulding's Lodge, where the company was headquartered, was and is situated directly in front of a huge rock wall, and overlooks the valley. "Right

302

down below us, like a quarter of a mile," said Ben Johnson, "a fire would start up, and the Indians would start singing and dancing. The sound bounced off this rock wall and out into the valley. It was the eeriest sound."

Then there were the primitive living conditions. Ford and Wayne had private cabins, but the rest of the cast had to double up and share toilets and showers. None of the units had bathrooms. As for the shower, Harry Carey Jr. said, "The shower was an old five-gallon oil tin with holes in the bottom. It hung from a wooden beam." Since there was no hot water, morning showers tended to be abrupt, pro forma affairs.

Wayne's feeling about locations with Ford were different than his crabby reminiscences of the harried productions of B westerns.

I don't think we ever went out to make a classic. You went out to make the best picture you could with what you had to work with. John Ford developed characters as he went along. You never started a picture by saying "I'm going to be such-and-such a character with John Ford." Your character changed with the mood of the players and the effect of the elements.

There were a great many days when it was fun, especially on the action shots, with the open air, the setting, the background. But the scenes were work, they were always work, because you couldn't just walk in and read the farewell speech of Cardinal Wolsey. Ford might decide not to kill you.

The feeling of the men who worked on westerns was altogether different from the feeling on straight pictures. We lived in a tent city and at night we played cards. . . . Sometimes the Sons of the Pioneers were there, and they sang too. It was kind of captured companionship and we made the most of it. And most of it was delightful because it was different from the way we lived at home.

We'd put on entertainments for the kids. Actors who loved histrionics would do recitations. Victor McLaglen and I worked up an act in which we managed boxers, who were stunt men. We'd meet in the center of the ring and start punching, showing the things that they weren't supposed to do. The thing became a free-for-all. I broke it up throwing a bucket of water on the fighters and another bucket, full of confetti, at the kids.

Locations with Ford in Monument Valley became the ideal motion picture experience for Wayne: a band of brothers and the occasional sister, a family — mostly happy, occasionally beset by tension provoked by the patriarch, but always, always productive.

Winton Hoch gave Ford color images that no other Hollywood cameraman could get near, but that didn't mean he was exempt from Fordian traps. "He was always testing," Hoch told the historian John Gallagher.

We came out one morning in Monument Valley and we were at Goulding's Trading Post, right against a black cliff in a shadow and the sun was low out there and the view was beautiful. Monument Valley was just gorgeous.

It was cold and you could see your breath in front of your face. We just finished breakfast and we went out there all ready to go to work, and

[Ford] turned around and said, "What direction you wanna shoot this morning?"

The answer's very simple. If you start telling a director which direction to shoot, you'd better start telling him how to stage his action. I said, "Any direction you wanna shoot, Jack, is OK with me." All I had to do was open my mouth and make a suggestion. I woulda been chewed up and spit out in little pieces.

Ford grounds the picture in the physical — the breath of horses in the chilly morning, the stiffness in the legs of a sixty-five-year-old man — which makes it easier to endure the stage Irishness, which dates the comic relief. Irving Pichel narrates, as he did for Ford's *How Green Was My Valley.*

The film documents the last few weeks in the professional career of Captain Nathan Brittles (Wayne), as well as the last three weeks in the career of Victor McLaglen's Sergeant Quincannon. It is 1876, and Brittles is retiring from the cavalry, and none too soon — he walks like a man whose hips are starting to go. His objectives for his last three weeks of service are to finish with honor and not get anybody killed. But he's also clearly worried about what comes next — there's nothing else he wants to do, and he foresees a drift westward to nothing much.

Brittles visits the grave of his wife and two children, all of whom died in 1867 of causes that Ford leaves unexplained. Brittles fills her in on the latest news. "We had sad news today, Mary. George Custer was killed with his entire command. Miles Keough — you remember Miles? . . ."

The character has reached that regrettable age when beautiful young women look at him as fatherly, and he embodies an ornery patience that comes from a lifetime of sorrows. His attitude directly contradicts his motto: "Never apologize, it's a sign of weakness."

It's one of Ford's loosely structured, balladlike films in which he sets up the plot and conflicts in the first reel, promptly drops them for three or four reels of pure character, then rounds back to the plot for the ending. Brittles navigates between the rocks of the Indian wars and the hard place of army politics and lovelorn troopers with the same ease that Wayne brings to the performance. It's a film suffused with longing and remembrance, and a few flaming orange sunsets. It also has a lovely sense of lived life — the dogs that are forever hanging around the regiment.

As a visual achievement, *She Wore a Yellow Ribbon* is unsurpassed, at least by anyone not named John Ford. But hidden in the loose structure is an unforgettable character study. By retiring, Brittles is letting go of the last thing he has left to love, and Ford can't bear it. It's as if he's projecting himself into the character, imagining himself as a movie director grown old and unemployable, so he brings Brittles back as chief of civilian scouts. Brittles has lived with the army and will happily die with the army.*

---

* Wayne's opposite number is played by Chief John Big Tree, a Seneca Indian who had worked for Ford in *The Iron Horse* and *Stagecoach,* as well as a couple of films for DeMille. Big Tree was reputedly one of the Indian models for James Fraser when he designed the buffalo nickel.

Brittles represents the best part of the man playing him — a playful personality deeply attached to the earth, delighted at simple sights such as a herd of buffalo — a man more interested in preserving life than taking it. The film takes advantage of one of Wayne's greatest gifts as an actor: his ability to suggest an essential nobility of character between the lines and beneath rough manners. In this case, it derives from moments such as Brittles's deep emotion at being presented with a silver watch by his men — or the way the depleted old man slumps by his horse, but draws himself up to his full height to return a salute.

Wayne knew it was a virtuoso performance. As he put it, "*She Wore a Yellow Ribbon* turned out to be, I think, the best acting job I've done. As a matter of fact, it's about the only picture I've been in where I could play a character that was a little apart from the image that has developed for me over the years on the screen. I played a 65 year old man when I was 35 [actually, 42]."

Brittles embodies abstract qualities like honor and loyalty and Wayne makes them concrete with a total mastery of effect. It's a film that could only have been made by two men who existed in a perfect state of silent communication, where words were basically unnecessary, as with the autographed picture of Ford that hung in Wayne's house for decades: "To Duke from the Coach," it said. "John Ford, Hollywood '47."

Red River was an immediate hit when it was released in September 1948. It returned domestic rentals to United Artists of $4.5 million, making it the third most popular film of the year, after the Hope-Crosby *Road to Rio* and the MGM musical

Easter Parade. Another $2 million came in from the rest of the world.

Wayne's guaranteed share of the profits was $75,000, but Hawks kept him, along with a long list of other creditors, waiting until 1952. Charles Feldman kept Wayne on the reservation by making interim loans to the actor. Over the years, Wayne ended up receiving about $375,000 in salary and profit sharing.

As for Coleen Gray, in the years to come she would occasionally see Wayne at events around town, and she always gently kicked him in the shins and said, "Duke, you should have taken me with you!"

"He'd throw back his head and laugh," she remembered.

She Wore a Yellow Ribbon was released eight months later, in the summer of 1949 and proved a critical and commercial success. Wayne's expert portrayals of three widely varied characters — an obstinate warrior, a good bad man, and the gentle Nathan Brittles — cemented his reputation as a skilled actor, at least for anybody who wasn't predisposed toward disliking him.

Stagecoach began Wayne's career as a star, but the twin smash hits of *Red River* and *She Wore a Yellow Ribbon* capped his ascension to the top of the movie firmament. As the decade ended, Wayne was on a comparable level with Clark Gable and Gary Cooper — but he was making better movies.

CHAPTER TEN

In early 1949, John Ford set up a theatrical production of *What Price Glory?* as a fundraiser for the Order of the Purple Heart. Ford put together a spectacular cast — Wayne, Maureen O'Hara, Gregory Peck, Ward Bond (as Captain Flagg), Pat O'Brien (as Sergeant Quirt), Forrest Tucker, Ed Begley, Wallace Ford, Robert Armstrong, Harry Carey Jr., Larry Blake, James Lydon. Everybody worked for free, the sets were designed and built for free, and Western Costume donated the show's clothes.

For the part of the innkeeper, Ford originally cast Luis Alberni, but he turned out to have a case of stage fright amplified by alcoholism, so he was replaced by Oliver Hardy, who responded with a performance that James Cagney said was "the funniest thing I think I have ever seen. Roland Winters and I had to hang onto each other, we were laughing so much."

Ford supervised, Ralph Murphy directed, and the rehearsals were held at the Masquers Club in Hollywood, which was also the site of the dress rehearsal on February 21, 1949. *Variety* was there, and paid tribute to the excellence of the two leading men, and the "provocative, sultry" performance of Maureen O'Hara as Charmaine. Wayne was lumped in with Gregory Peck and Harry Carey Jr. for the "well-handled" smaller parts.

The next night *What Price Glory?* began its six-city, six-night tour in Long Beach. "The audience would just applaud when Ward [Bond] and [Pat] O'Brien came on stage," remembered Harry Carey Jr. "When Wayne made an entrance, they'd just gasp. . . . With Greg Peck, it was like Frank Sinatra. He was such a heartthrob, the girls would just start squealing when he came on stage."

Wayne was playing Lieutenant Cunningham — a small part, but it was the first time he'd been onstage since high school so his nerves were unsettled. "Duke and I dressed with Oliver Hardy, and it was a ball," remembered James Lydon. "Wayne was a little nervous at first, because he was unaccustomed to the theater, but I was raised in it, and Babe Hardy had toured all over the world. Babe and I were in the first act, and Duke worked at the end of the second act, and then the three of us would sit around until curtain calls.

"Duke and I would sit there as total acolytes, listening to Babe's stories. He was a great raconteur, and Duke was very much in awe of the great Oliver Hardy. It showed a side of Duke that very few people knew: he was a student of show business. He was always echoing his master, John Ford, and saying things like, 'I'm not an actor, I'm a reactor,' and other things he wasn't really sure of. Anything Ford said was gospel. But Duke loved Babe Hardy."

By the second performance, Wayne's nervousness had subsided. Lydon remembered that some of the actors suggested that Wayne go out drinking with them, but he said, "No. If the Old Man smells booze, he'll kill me."

The troupe traveled to San Francisco by train, with Hardy sitting in the club car with four or five cast members gathered around him. Reliably, Wayne was always one of them, drinking in the stories — of Laurel and Hardy meeting Harry Lauder in Scotland and a very ahistorical account of how Laurel and Hardy formed their partnership.

The show's final performance was at Grauman's Chinese on March 2, 1949, after which the business manager absconded with $82,000 in profits. Ford made the money up out of his own pocket.

Although the blacklist had landed with a menacing crash, and the Motion Picture Alliance was at the height of their influence, Lydon never heard Wayne say anything about politics at all. "Duke was just a private citizen and he kept his beliefs private. Now, Ward Bond was a thickheaded loudmouth. He was a good friend of Duke's, and he was the one screaming all sorts of things that nobody else cared about. But in my presence, Duke never said a word about any of that."

Ford used Lydon in a movie he shot shortly after the run of *What Price Glory?* called *When Willie Comes Marching Home.* Even though Lydon was a cousin — Ford's mother was Lydon's grandmother's sister — he ran into the same buzzsaw as Wayne, as every other actor.

He had done a long shot of Dan Dailey's family waiting for the train to come in. Then we started work on a tracking shot that ran past the family while they waited. We're rehearsing and the camera is pulling past and Ford says, "Stop."

He gets off the dolly and says, "Jim, was your

311

hair like that? And the tie?"

"Yes, Mr. Ford."

"You look too damn comfortable." And then he ran his hand through my hair and yanked the tie down and said, "That's better."

He turned around to go back to the dolly and that's when I made a horrible mistake. I said, "It won't match, Mr. Ford." And there was dead silence. He stopped and turned around and glared at me for a full 30 seconds. Finally, he said, "Are you a cutter now?"

And he didn't speak to me for two weeks. Not "Good Morning," not anything.

Like everybody else, I was in awe of him.

Watching Oliver Hardy onstage made Wayne realize that there was no reason the great comedian couldn't be working, so he offered Hardy a part in a film he was about to start at Republic called *The Fighting Kentuckian* — the second John Wayne Production. Hardy hesitated out of loyalty to his longtime screen partner Stan Laurel, who was inactive due to diabetes. Laurel told him to go ahead and make the picture, and Hardy proved to be a charming sidekick, with his Georgia accent proving particularly appropriate for a story taking place in the South of 1819.

Another creative infatuation of this period was between Wayne and Rex Ingram, the great director of such silent classics as *The Four Horsemen of the Apocalypse* and *Scaramouche.* Ingram was one of the great pictorialists of the movies' early years, but he hadn't made a picture since 1931 and had little interest in talkies.

Ingram didn't need money, but he hovered around Wayne for a couple of years before his death in 1950. William Clothier, Wayne's favorite cameraman, happened to be Ingram's next-door neighbor and remembered that Wayne and Ingram spent a fair amount of time trying to find something to do together. This was part and parcel of Wayne's great respect for directors who had earned their spurs in silent pictures, when Wayne fell under their spell — he had been a movie fan long before he had been an athlete or an actor.

For *The Fighting Kentuckian,* Wayne wanted a French leading lady: Danielle Darrieux, Simone Simon, perhaps Corinne Calvet. But Yates insisted that Wayne use Vera Hruba Ralston. "I don't want to malign her," Wayne said with a palpable weariness. "She didn't have the experience. She talked with this heavy Czech accent [and] I was looking for a light Parisian type of speech. . . . It hurt the picture, because we now had to hire other Czech and Austrian actors to play French characters so her accent would be matched. . . . Yates was one of the smartest businessmen I ever met. But when it came to the woman he loved, his business brains just went flying out the window." The film cost $1.3 million, earned domestic rentals of $1.75 million, and again Republic claimed a loss, this time $365,808.

Perhaps the most important by-product of *The Fighting Kentuckian* was that it brought Chuck Roberson into Wayne's circle, then into Ford's circle. Roberson was a tall, handsome stuntman who would become Wayne's primary double. (Yakima Canutt had gotten too old and too wide.) Roberson was also a competent actor and did a lot of double-dipping over the years, playing small parts as well as doubling Wayne so expertly that it's hard to tell them apart at thirty feet — Roberson could faultlessly imitate Wayne's straight-backed style of riding, as well as his pigeon-toed run. Ford named Roberson "Bad Chuck," because of his way with women and to differentiate him from Chuck Hayward, another stuntman, who was known as "Good Chuck."

Sands of Iwo Jima originated with Republic producer Edmund Grainger, who saw the line in a newspaper, and correctly figured that recreating the backstory of Joe Rosenthal's famous photo of the flag raising at Iwo Jima would make an exciting war picture.

Grainger banged out a forty-page treatment about a tough drill instructor and the men he leads into combat, then hired Harry Brown, who had recently written the novel on which Lewis Milestone based his excellent *A Walk in the Sun*. Grainger was happy with Brown's script, but those rare occasions when a good script showed up at Republic were always fraught — Herbert Yates might want it for Vera Hruba Ralston. "They handed me the script of *Iwo Jima*," remembered Allan Dwan, "and I asked if there was a part in it for Yates' girlfriend . . . because if there was, I wasn't going to do the picture."

At this point, the picture was supposed to cost around $250,000, with Forrest Tucker slated for the lead. "He [Yates] never mentioned Duke, because he wanted him for something else with Vera," said Dwan, who thought Tucker was a terrible idea. "Tucker lacked that zing that Wayne had . . . it was like a bulldog underneath all that tranquility." Dwan thought Wayne was the only man to star, as did Edmund Grainger, who was Michael Wayne's godfather.

Finally, after a few calls from Washington, and from the Marine Corps, Yates agreed that Wayne should make the movie. It was a time of congressional committees looking hard at military appropriations; there was some thought being given to folding the Marines into the Army, and the Marines thought that a big gung ho movie would serve as good propaganda for maintaining a stand-alone Corps.

At Wayne's suggestion, Jimmy Grant was brought in to polish the script. That same year, Grant earned $12,500 plus 10 percent of the profits for the screenplay of Republic's *Rock Island Trail,* and still later that year Yates paid him $15,000 for a script for *California Passage.* By comparison, Harry Brown got only $5,000 for the story and treatment of *Sands of Iwo Jima.* (The lowly writers of Republic's Roy Rogers westerns were lucky to get $3,000 per script.)

There was a good deal of friction between Grant, Brown, director Allan Dwan, and Grainger, but without Wayne there really wasn't going to be a movie, at least not a movie the size of *Sands of Iwo Jima,* so the star got his way.

Sands of Iwo Jima was shot in July and August of 1949. Republic paid some money to Camp Pendleton for their trouble, and in return had the use of an entire battalion for as long as it took to make the movie. The Marines gave the production a technical advisor, Captain Leonard Fribourg, who taught the actors how to handle their weapons, and who also ran interference with the brass to make sure that Republic got whatever it needed.

The actors remembered that the Marines of Camp Pendleton blended in with the actors staying at the Carlsbad Hotel. "There wasn't a feeling that, you know, here's an actor, and here's a Marine," said Wally Cassell. Leonard Fribourg remembered that the actors were appropriately gung ho. "They wanted to do it, wanted to co-operate. They wanted to wear the uniform right, the emblems, wanted to know what the stripes meant, wanted to know the Marine Corps lingo, and put the right words in the right place."

Richard Jaeckel remembered that he got into the habit of setting his alarm clock earlier and earlier "cause I knew each day was gonna be better than the preceding one because we were having such a great time, all of us — it was more than a job."

Fribourg said there was only one outright invention. In a scene where Wayne's Sergeant Stryker is teaching his men bayonet fighting, he loses his patience and intentionally clobbers a man with a rifle. When Wayne rehearsed the scene, Fribourg said that he "almost fell off my chair." He charged off to Allan Dwan and said there was no way a sergeant would hit his own man with a rifle butt. Dwan pointed out that the script had been approved by the Corps, but Fribourg was adamant. The matter went all the way to Washington, where Fribourg was overruled.

Dwan believed that for the first time Wayne related the qualities and flaws of the character he was playing to himself. "We had long conversations about the interpretation of the character. Sergeant Stryker was a man who was divorced from his wife and he had a son, and he got letters from his son. And yet he felt somehow guilty that he wasn't with his family — that he was off doing this other thing and that he had neglected his child.

"As we talked about Sergeant Stryker's relationship with his own family and with his son late one night, I looked at Duke and tears were rolling down his cheeks, and he mentioned his own son and his wife and how he had made mistakes and how the whole family had suffered for his mistakes."

Wayne would tell the military historian Lawrence Suid that he became "a sort of Richelieu of Republic" during the struggle to make *Sands of Iwo Jima*. He peppered Fribourg with questions, as well as a warrant officer who typified the Marine spirit that Wayne wanted to put on the screen. Wayne came to realize that the Marines didn't train men to die for their country; they trained men to be such expert fighters that they could fight for their country over and over again. "It was survival training," said Wayne of the boot camp process. "We learned that you didn't get to the bottom of the barrel toward the end of the war. You got to the young fellow who was so damn good that the older fellows couldn't hardly keep up with him."

"Wayne was terrific with young actors," remembered William Self, who played one of three Marine recruits that make an entrance in the middle of the movie. "They'd been shooting for quite a while, and we were all nervous because we weren't part of the established group. He sat down, ran lines with us, played chess with us. I wasn't any good at chess, but there weren't a lot of other guys to play with. He tried to put young actors at their ease."

He also tried to give young actors tricks of the

317

trade. When Wally Cassell had to exit a scene, Wayne said, "Don't respond that quickly. Before you make an exit, make a move first, then go. That gives you an extra four or five feet of film."

Richard Jaeckel was only twenty-two at the time, and he said, "You're pretty feisty at 22, but you weren't feisty around this guy, really. He just set the tone for everything. And yet when it came time to zig and zag, he'd horse around with the best of them, but when he declared, 'This is the time,' you'd better decide along with him because otherwise, it'd be hard; it'd be tough."

Leonard Fribourg might have been expected to look askance at an actor who had never served playing a military hero, but he called Wayne "a great American and a hell of a good guy that took care of people and made sure that they were in good shape. . . . And he was very fine with children." Fribourg's three-year-old daughter had a birthday while the film was in production, and Wayne insisted on attending the party and wishing her a happy birthday.

In coming years, Wayne would slowly accrete a reputation as a director killer — a star who could undermine or even appropriate the director's function if he didn't like what the director was doing. A childhood, adolescence, and young adulthood of utter powerlessness had resulted in a man who was determined to be the master of his own fate, not to mention image.

But his attitude toward the veteran Allan Dwan, whose credits went back to the World War I era and wonderful movies with Douglas Fairbanks Sr., was respectful. "Wayne knew all about Dwan's career," said Self, "and he felt good about him. They had a good relationship."

Sands of Iwo Jima was a big picture for Republic, and went over budget by more than $400,000, which didn't make Herbert Yates happy. "A philanthropist he was not," said Richard Jaeckel.*

When it was released in 1949, *Sands of Iwo Jima* was a smash hit, earning rentals of $4.2 million. The picture also earned Wayne his first Oscar nomination for Best Actor, up against Gregory Peck (*Twelve O'Clock High*), Kirk Douglas (*Champion*), Richard Todd (*The Hasty Heart*), and Broderick Crawford (*All the King's Men*). Crawford won.

By the end of 1949, John Ford's Argosy Productions was in trouble. *Fort Apache* had amassed a world gross of $4.3 million against a cost of $2.14 million, and *She Wore a Yellow Ribbon* had done nearly as well, but the profits weren't enough to pay off the dead loss of *The Fugitive,* which had been the first Argosy production for RKO. Argosy owed nearly $700,000 on the picture, and it also owed the bank $320,000 on the recently completed *Wagon Master.* Then there was $235,000

* Republic, like all the B picture studios, was a thinly capitalized business, since B pictures were an economically marginal product — most of the money derived from flat-fee bookings. Throughout the 1940s, Republic's annual profits, with the exception of a single year, stayed in a narrow range of about $500,000, in spite of the fact that the studio's gross was steadily increasing. Republic would make money throughout the 1950s, but it took only two bad years, in 1957 and 1958, when the studio lost $1.3 million and $1.4 million respectively, to put it out of business.

owed to Ford and Merian C. Cooper for unpaid salaries and other incidentals. On top of all that, neither Wayne nor Fonda had gotten their profit percentages from *Fort Apache.* Argosy had little choice but to sell its pictures to RKO in return for a clean financial slate.

With no better offers on the table for Argosy, Wayne's propaganda campaign about the benefits of Republic finally bore fruit. In January 1950, Argosy signed a three-picture deal with Republic. The contract specified that the pictures were to be made within a two-year period beginning March 6, 1950, and that none of the pictures would cost more than $1.25 million. Republic would pay for production costs, but except for the salaries of a couple of secretaries, Argosy had to pay the rest of its expenses. No provisions were made for salaries for Ford or Cooper; they and Argosy had to survive on the 50 percent of the profits that Yates agreed to pay them. In return for the tight financial parameters, Yates gave Ford final cut.

Bringing Coach to the studio cost Wayne a great deal of money. On both *Rio Grande* and *The Quiet Man,* the pictures Ford made for Republic in which Wayne starred, Wayne gave up his 10 percent of the profits and worked for a straight $100,000 per picture in order to keep the economics feasible.

Rio Grande was devised as a make-good so that Herbert Yates would finance *The Quiet Man* — Ford's dream project. In order to facilitate production, Ford shot it in Moab rather than Monument Valley, which was harder to get in and out of, thus requiring more time and money.

"Moab was much better than Monument Valley," remembered Mike Wayne. "You had motels with air conditioning and things like that, and you had a great restaurant, The Red Door. You weren't quite as remote as you were when working [in Monument Valley]. Then, it was almost like being in the cavalry, you know."

Yates insisted that the Sons of the Pioneers appear in *Rio Grande,* which Ford found appalling, but he found a way to work them in as a sort of musical Greek chorus, cavalry style.

Rio Grande was shot from mid-June to mid-July 1950. Mike Wayne was on summer vacation, so came on the shoot and hung out with the wranglers, stuntmen, and the prop men — the latter because they had the guns and Mike was interested in firearms. Hanging out with them was also a way of avoiding Ford, whose preferred term for Mike was "Numbnuts," even as he doted on his godson Pat Wayne.

Claude Jarman Jr., who had won a special Oscar for his performance in *The Yearling,* was playing the son of *Rio Grande* co-stars Wayne and O'Hara. "No one could ever know what Ford was thinking," remembered Jarman. Actors often did scenes that weren't in the script, and someone told Jarman not to bother to learn his lines, because they would probably all be changed anyway.

For a scene with Harry Carey Jr., Jarman mastered the difficult and dangerous stunt of Roman riding — riding two horses while standing up, one foot on each horse. This endeared Jarman to Ford, so he could do no wrong.

As always with young actors, Wayne was approachable and kind. In contrast to Maureen O'Hara's retrospective claims of perpetual humiliation at Ford's hands, Jarman said that "Ford adored Maureen. He treated her as a queen."

Esprit de corps was not an option; it was enforced. The cast and crew stayed at the same hotel, were driven to and from the set as a group, and ate their meals together. At night, there were more impromptu theatricals — Maureen O'Hara sang Irish songs, Victor McLaglen did vaudeville sketches he had performed as a young man, and Wayne had to sing. Badly.

O'Hara was making her first picture for the director since *How Green Was My Valley.* Wayne and O'Hara had met at Ford's house in May 1941, and found that their friendship carried over into their working process, although O'Hara was appalled at Ford's cruelty toward Wayne, which she termed "vicious . . . extremely severe."

Wayne took it — Wayne almost always took it — but not everybody would. One night over dinner, Ford thought Ben Johnson was unhappy over the way Ford had handled a scene that day. Ford began belittling him, calling him "stupid" over and over again. Johnson got up and left, but not before telling Ford quietly what he could do with his picture. Ben Johnson didn't work for John Ford for fifteen years.

Back at the studio, Wayne was enraged when he found out that Herbert Yates was refusing to pay him his percentage from *Sands of Iwo Jima,* which led him to go on strike and refuse to show up for several days of shooting. Yates went down to the inactive set and ordered Ford to shoot around Wayne. Ford flatly refused and told Yates to "quit messing around with my hired help." Wayne got his money and went back to work.

Because of the quid pro quo nature of the production, and the fact that Ford shot it very quickly — five weeks — using mostly first takes, Mike Wayne thought at the time that it "didn't have the same oomph that the other Ford pictures had. I really thought it was one of the lesser films. But when you look at it today, you really realize how good it is."

True. Although there are too many songs, *Rio Grande* is distinguished by the delicacy of its emotion and the beauty of its photography, including some stunning day-for-night work. Ford kicks in with his heroic imagery from the beginning, as the exhausted cavalry comes back from a mission to be met by the women of the fort, who gather to see if their men have survived.

Ford is a master of the gesture that reveals subtext. After Kirby Yorke — nobody has ever figured out the extra "e" in the name of the character from *Fort Apache* — and his son have an angry confrontation, the son leaves. Yorke walks over to the side of the canvas tent and silently checks his own height against the boy's, revealing a father's pride that he's too proud to admit.

For Ford, words are for story, images are for emotion . . . or beauty.

In its central situation of an estranged husband and wife whose essential passion for each other is never compromised, the film is a dry run for the central narrative of *The Quiet Man.* Wayne's performance is equal parts steel and grace — the burden of responsibility leavened by the realization of what that responsibility has cost him.

There are three words that chill the blood of the most indiscriminate movie lover: "Howard Hughes Presents." It wasn't always that way; Hughes began his career with some effective genre pieces in the silent and early sound days: *The Racket, Scarface, The Front Page.* But as he got richer and more heavily medicated, his films became underwritten and overshot, full of mismatched shots and grainy opticals — remnants of shooting schedules that were simultaneously endless and haphazard.

In 1948, Hughes bought a controlling interest in RKO. Wayne already had a loose arrangement with the studio, where he had made *Tall in the Saddle, Back to Bataan, Tycoon,* and, for Ford, *Fort Apache* and *She Wore a Yellow Ribbon.* Wayne and Hughes were alike in some respects — anticommunists — and unlike in others — Hughes was a promiscuous isolate.

The pictures Hughes produced for Wayne are among the most bizarre in the annals of Hollywood. They include *Flying Leathernecks* — a gung ho World War II movie directed by Nicholas Ray, of all people; *Jet Pilot* — a movie shot between December 1949 and May 1950 that wasn't released until 1957, directed by Josef von Sternberg, of all people; and *The Conqueror,* the legendarily terrible movie in which Wayne plays Genghis Khan, directed by Dick Powell . . . of all people.

Flying Leathernecks — the title sounds like a Mel Brooks parody of a war movie — was designed by Hughes as a test of Nicholas Ray's political and professional loyalty. Ray and Robert Ryan were liberal and Wayne and most of the rest of the cast weren't, which made for some interesting lunchtime discussions.

"Wayne would close all political discussions with 'You're full of shit!' " remembered Rod Amateau, the dialogue director. Despite that, the company grew fond of its star. "Wayne was always a very prudent, careful man," said Amateau. "He was kind to everybody. And he felt sorry that Nick made a lot of enemies. The reason Nick made enemies wasn't because he was a bad person, he honestly wasn't, he was a good, decent person. But he was so intense about his work. If nothing matters but the work, you're going to make enemies."

Ray was an acolyte of Elia Kazan and lived and breathed emotional conflict. Like his mentor, he brought something new and authentic to Hollywood. He was fascinated by Wayne's clarity of character, and stimulated by what he believed were untapped dramatic reservoirs. "I thought the Broadway drugstore critics who hadn't yet been asked out to Hollywood were just terribly imperceptive about him," said Ray. "He was a much better actor than most people gave him credit for being, almost daily full of nice surprises. But he was not flexible about himself. He couldn't conceive that I would be serious in wanting him to do O'Neill's *A Touch of the Poet*."

Flying Leathernecks and *The Conqueror* fall into known genres. *Jet Pilot* is something eccentrically homemade, something . . . insane. The narrative is conventionally anticommunist: a female Russian jet pilot seeks asylum in America, but she's a double agent intent on discovering American secrets. Marriage to Wayne and an immersion in American consumer culture turn her around.

Story aside, it's actually a movie about airplanes, and a lot of it is played for laughs. Von Sternberg hadn't directed a film in nearly ten years — his icy, arrogant personality and a string of flops had undone the reputation established by his string of

325

gloriously photographed films with Marlene Dietrich. Before *Jet Pilot,* he had worked as an uncredited assistant to King Vidor on *Duel in the Sun.* Hughes seems to have hired him at the behest of producer-writer Jules Furthman, who had worked with the director in his salad days at Paramount twenty years earlier.

Wayne's ears pricked up when von Sternberg noted Wayne's chessboard and made a remark about the excellence of his own game. "I played him without looking at the board," said Wayne. "And I beat him. Pure luck. He was livid."

"*Jet Pilot* was the first time I ever used a four-letter word on a movie set," remembered Janet Leigh.

It wasn't the last time, but it was the first. Von Sternberg was a very frustrating man. It's not that he yelled; it was his attitude. He was used to working in the days when you could be Hitler, with Marlene in complete thrall. He was talented, no question, but his way had gone.

Von Sternberg was a little man, very short. Slight. Duke was a giant. And strong. And Sternberg directed him to act as if Duke was the size of von Sternberg. In one scene he had me knocking Duke out! Sternberg directed him as if he was a little man instead of the big man he was.

I asked Duke, "Why don't you say something?"

And he said, "I'm afraid if I open my mouth I'll kill the son of a bitch."

Von Sternberg was never abusive, just aggravating, and controlling. He didn't think the camera operator could operate the camera, he had to do that. He had to light the scene — no one could do anything but him. It was strictly a solo flight; he wasn't a group player.

In one sense, it was Hughes's picture, but on the set, Sternberg was in control. And Jules Furthman was Hughes's messenger guy, a dear, sweet man with a porkpie hat. And he and Hughes ended up playing with that picture for seven years, so what had been innovative and new in terms of equipment and technology in terms of aerospace was old-hat. But whatever you think of the script, photographically it was very good.

Some idea of this exceedingly strange Cold War artifact can be gauged by its production history. Principal photography was done between October 1949 and February 1950. Additional scenes were shot between January 21 and February 9, 1951, and March 17 to April 2 of that same year. Aerial photography was done between August 30 and September 1, 1951, with additional aerial sequences shot by William Clothier between October 1951 and March 1953.

Clothier spent more than two hundred hours in the air and logged over thirty thousand miles while shooting 100,000 feet of Technicolor film in such locations as Edwards, Kelly, Eglin, Fargo, Great Falls, and Lowry Field Air Force bases, as well as March Field, and Hamilton Field in San Francisco. None other than Chuck Yeager flew the X-1 plane shown in the movie, as well as another plane for the drop and aerobatic sequences.

And when the picture was finally finished, Hughes sat on it.

In the summer of 1952, RKO's distribution wing was desperately in need of something to distribute — Hughes had drastically cut back production — and announced the picture for September. But September came and went and there was still no *Jet Pilot*. *Variety* announced that the picture was being carried on the studio inventory at a cost of $3.9 million — a staggering amount for 1952.

By the time the picture was finally released in 1957 — not by RKO, which had just gone out of business, but by Universal — the original budget of $1.4 million had probably quadrupled. Critics commented on the remarkably youthful appearances of its stars. Even though the film opened in more than four hundred theaters in one of the biggest releases of that era, audiences paid almost no attention — the picture had the stink of death about it.

It's a strange picture, with strange billing: "Starring John Wayne, Janet Leigh, and the United States Air Force." It's played partially for comedy as a sort of airborne *Ninotchka* — at one point Wayne calls Leigh "a silly Siberian cupcake" — partially as an anticommunist tract, partially as a thriller. It's unsuccessful in all aspects, although Wayne is reliably amusing when he gets flustered, and there's a lot to be flustered about. At one point, Hughes dubs in the sound of jet whooshes every time Janet Leigh takes off a piece of clothing.

With all the overage required, Hughes paid Wayne $201,666.68 to make the picture. It was a typical piece of chaos theory on the part of the richest amateur filmmaker in history. During one break from the production, Hughes, his date Jean Peters — later his wife — and Wayne were in Las Vegas when Hughes refused to walk into the Desert Inn.

"Everybody will be looking at me!" he explained.

"You asshole!" said Wayne. "You're with the most beautiful woman in the world! And John Wayne! And they're gonna look at you?"

Despite the huge infusion of cash, which was going to come in handy very soon, Wayne doubted the part was worth it. During production, James Edward Grant cabled Wayne, "ACCORDING TO CHRISTIAN SCIENCE IF YOU JUST PAY NO ATTENTION IT WILL GO AWAY."

At one point in 1949, opening a newspaper to the movie ads in Los Angeles was like looking at a John Wayne Film Festival. *Red River* was playing in Westwood, *Wake of the Red Witch* was playing in Hollywood, *3 Godfathers* was in Beverly Hills, and *Fort Apache* was appearing elsewhere. *She Wore a Yellow Ribbon* was in previews in Pasadena and bringing up the rear were reissues of *Stagecoach* and *The Long Voyage Home.* At the same time, some of the old Monogram pictures were already showing on the new invention called television.

The profusion of reissues was a function of a decade-long recession that hit the movie business in 1947. Movie attendance would plummet by 50 percent, four thousand theaters would go out of business, and the huge profits of World War II vanished. Mostly, this was because of television, but there was also a sense that the generation that had come back from the battlefields of Europe and the Pacific were finding the movies made under the restrictive Production Code a ridiculous evasion of the life it had seen firsthand.

The major studios coped by first reducing, then eliminating B movie production, which proved a godsend to fringe companies like Allied Artists — formerly Monogram — or (in a few years) American International. The studios also cut back on cartoons and newsreels and concentrated on making bigger and more expensive A pictures. For low-end talents, it got harder to make a living, but high-end talents were sellers in a market where the rest of the world was buying.

What made it remarkable was the concentrated quality of Wayne's new pictures. Even Republic's *Wake of the Red Witch,* which begins as *The Sea Wolf* and ends as *Peter Ibbetson,* with a strong dose of *Reap the Wild Wind,* has its haunting moments, as Gail Russell once again brings her strange, ethereal quality to the picture. Other actresses had to ramp up their aggression to come out on an equivalent basis with Wayne, but when Wayne worked with Russell he downshifted into a watchful swain who treated the delicate actress as if she might shatter.

This audience immersion in John Wayne would not hurt him; in most ways, he was immune from overexposure. When asked about what seemed to be hyperactivity, at least compared to most star rationing of a picture a year, or two every eighteen months, Wayne would explain, "To me, making a picture a year is like coming out of retirement every year, and that's too hard on the nervous system. . . . For my money, nothing improves your work like work itself. I figure an actor, if he's got any kind of role, should try to get better with each picture. The more pictures he makes, the more chance he's got of achieving that."

Mainstream papers such as *The New York Times* and the *Chicago Tribune* began to pay attention to Wayne. The *Times* quoted John Ford as saying

Wayne's popularity was simple: "Duke is the best actor in Hollywood. That's all."

Hedda Hopper quoted Wayne as saying his incessant activity was because he had to work for a living. "I don't have a capital gains setup like some of these guys, and I've got two families to feed. My business manager tells me it costs me $2,600 a month. I don't know where the money goes, but it's an awful lot, and I've got to keep hopping from Republic to RKO to Argosy to make it."

At this point, he had a deal with RKO for one picture annually, a similar deal with Warner Bros., and his Republic contract was still in force. Then there was John Ford, who always had right of first refusal on Wayne's services. The *Motion Picture Herald,* which was doing a story on Wayne's amazing ability to draw audiences at a time when the movie industry was hemorrhaging customers, noted that "Wayne talks less like an actor is supposed to than as a business man does."

Wayne didn't mind the reissues of the old Ford pictures, but he was uncomfortable with the Monogram westerns being exposed, pointing out that the movies were atrocious by the standards of 1949. Despite all that, the market seemed perfectly able to absorb as much John Wayne as there was to be had. "I hope he doesn't kill himself with overwork," said Ward Bond. "He used to say, 'Let's stretch out on a boat in the sun, tell a few lies and fish.' He doesn't have time to do that any more."

After World War II, John Ford had taken the $300,000 he'd earned directing *They Were Expendable* and bought eight acres in Reseda he dubbed the Field Photo Farm. It served as a clubhouse/rehabilitation center for veterans of Ford's unit, as well as damaged veterans who weren't part of Ford's operation.

Syd Kronenthal had been the supervisor of rehabilitation for the Veterans Administration in Los Angeles when he was hired to help Marlon Brando play a paraplegic in *The Men.* Kronenthal thought that Brando's dedication was extreme and almost certainly excessive; he lived the part to such an extent that he defecated in his bed, just as paraplegics did.

Kronenthal spent months at the Field Photo Farm, working with damaged veterans and watching the complex sociology of Ford's extended family, which was often more benevolent than his actual family.

"When Ford's daughter, Barbara, announced that she was marrying Robert Walker, Ford went at her in front of everybody," remembered Kronenthal.

He thought Walker was a bum. While he was railing at her, she didn't say much of anything. He berated her, she took it, he finished, then she left.

Ford wouldn't get drunk at the Field Photo Farm, but the other guys got loaded. They were all very right-wing, and when they got loaded they'd start spewing anti-Semitic remarks. The worst of them was Victor McLaglen, and Ward Bond was anti-Semitic as hell. They either didn't know I was Jewish or they forgot. I was just Syd, the supervisor of rehabilitation.

Wayne never said anything like that, but then he was close with Aaron Rosenberg, a producer who'd been an All-American at USC. Ford didn't talk like that either. His pet at the Field Photo Farm was a guy named Herb Wolfe, a Jewish paraplegic.

Wayne, Bö Roos, and Red Skelton were partners in the Culver City Hotel, where the midgets had stayed when they were making *The Wizard of Oz*. The hotel was decrepit and Wayne thought it was a poor investment. "Krony," he would ask Kronenthal, "how would you like to own a hotel?" Kronenthal begged off, but Wayne always made the place available for free if Kronenthal needed it for a fundraising event. "Anything I wanted, he would do."

Kronenthal found that "Ford and Wayne were both very sensitive to veterans. I came to believe that Wayne had a little compulsion about not having gone into the service. It was the same with Joe DiMaggio, who I knew. Hank Greenberg, Bob Feller, and Ted Williams signed up and went to war, but not DiMaggio.

"Wayne would sit and talk to the guys; he was very compatible, and he had a conscience. He didn't shy away from anything. After talking to the guys, he would come over and ask me questions — did they have feelings below the chest, or below the waist? Could they have a normal relationship with a woman? I would usually have to say no, and he would say, 'Oh, Jesus Christ! Oh, Jesus Christ.' He was just appalled."

After a few years of working at the Field Photo Farm, Kronenthal became recreation director in Culver City. Eventually, he helped Wayne out with the Culver City Hotel by putting him in touch with the YMCA, which bought it to use as a senior center. It's still there.

In March 1950, Wayne was reelected president of the Motion Picture Alliance at the annual meeting at the American Legion building on Highland Avenue. Other officers serving with Wayne were Charles Coburn as first vice president, Hedda Hopper as second vice president, Morrie Ryskind as third vice president, and Clarence Brown as treasurer.

At the same time, he embarked on a series of movies that spun off the relentless persona of *Red River.* George Waggner, who wrote and directed a couple of minor Wayne vehicles (*The Fighting Kentuckian* and *Operation Pacific*) explained how screenwriters made Wayne a sympathetic heavy: "The trick is to make him seem ruthless in his pursuit of a mission, but at the same time fix it so his fans will sympathize with the urge that drives him. It's also up to his writer to stick in a plot gimmick that will show him the error of his ways before the house lights go on."

As Waggner well knew, these characters were comfortable for Wayne to play because he was himself a man of relentless focus, perfectly capable of achieving any objective he set, no matter how long it took. Like, for instance, the next John Wayne Production. Or *The Alamo.*

A few years after World War II, Wayne's hair began to thin out; by 1950 he was wearing a toupee. He wasn't vain about it and ignored the condition offscreen. There are hundreds of family snapshots and home movies of a balding Wayne lying around like a lazy bear, or even out in public, although at those times he often wore a hat or baseball cap.

Without the toupee, he looked older, and, somehow, less like John Wayne.

The toupee symbolized the transition he hoped to make in his career — to a position where he wouldn't have to bother wearing one at all. In 1950, he launched another production at Republic, this one for a promising young writer-director named Budd Boetticher, who had written a script that Republic was inauspiciously calling *The Bullfighter and the Lady.* As a very young man, Boetticher had been a bullfighter and he was enthralled with the drama of the *corrida.* He devised a script about an American who enlists the aid of Mexico's greatest matador to help him become a bullfighter. No movie had ever caught the world of bullfighting, he believed; indeed, no movie would ever catch it better than the one John Wayne was to produce.

But it wasn't easy.

"[Wayne] heard about the screenplay that I had written," remembered Boetticher. "I met James Edward Grant, who eventually became the head of Alcoholics Anonymous in Los Angeles, and you have to really be a drunk to get that far. Duke hired him to write, in seventy-eight pages, the story of my life. He might as well have written the story about tennis." Wayne put Grant to work on supervising a rewrite of Boetticher's script. Boetticher diplomatically cabled Grant on April 26, 1950, "DEAR JAMES HAVE JUST FINISHED SCRIPT EXCITED ABOUT SOME DISAPPOINTED ABOUT SOME ELSE. FEEL IT IMPERATIVE THAT YOU JOIN ME OLD BOY."

"IF YOU ARE DISAPPOINTED I AM DELIGHTED," replied Grant, who was irritated by

335

what he believed were Boetticher's affectations. On the back of another telegram from Boetticher, Grant typed out a scathing response: "DISAPPOINTED ARE YOU? DO YOU RECALL HEARING EACH SCENE READ? END QUESTIONS BEGIN ANALYSIS. YOU WROTE TELEGRAM WHEN SOMEBODY GUESS WHO WAS LOOKING OVER YOUR SHOULDER AND YOU WERE ANXIOUS TO ACT LIKE JOHN FORD WHOM THANK GOD YOU AIN'T. MEET ME ELEVENTH AT AIRPORT."

Boetticher resisted Grant's changes and shot his own script. "Duke and I disagreed about a lot of things," said Boetticher shortly before his death. "Everyone who really knows me knows that I truly love John Wayne. But if they know me well, they'll also realize I really hated his guts."

With Wayne hovering, with Jimmy Grant and John Ford circling, Boetticher somehow managed to shoot a good picture in Mexico, with excellent performances from Robert Stack and Gilbert Roland. For Republic, it was a medium-budget picture — about $400,000. Wayne threw in what he remembered as "close to $50,000 of my own money to insure it being made well."

Boetticher acknowledged that without Wayne the picture would never have been made, but Wayne also interfered, sometimes overtly, sometimes after the fact. According to Boetticher, on the first day of shooting Wayne walked right in front of Boetticher, called "Cut" and began redirecting the actors, grabbing Robert Stack by the lapels and telling him, "Jesus Christ, Bob, if you're going to say the line, say it with some balls."

Called on it by Boetticher, Wayne backed off

and stayed away until the last day of the shoot, when he showed up for the wrap party. "He consumed half a bottle of tequila and a full bottle, which he gave to me. We locked arms and began drinking. Duke was so drunk he fell off a veranda into a bush. Chata was with him, and we all went to a bullfight together. Then Jimmy Grant turned up with eleven whores. Chata turned to Duke and said, 'If you even smile at those girls, I'm going to hit you.'"

Wayne didn't like Boetticher's cut of the film, which ran 124 minutes. "Wayne didn't believe that we had a good picture," said Boetticher. "They [Wayne, Grant, and Herbert Yates] referred to it as 'That Mexican Hassle.'" Wayne showed the picture to John Ford, who thought that the relationship between Robert Stack and Gilbert Roland was "a lot of chi-chi shit," after which Ford and Wayne cut thirty-seven minutes out of the film.

At any length, it's a fine picture, although the longer version is better, but Republic was not the studio to handle a serious picture about bullfighting — or anything else. *The Bullfighter and the Lady* came out at the same time as a larger-budgeted picture by a higher-profile director (Robert Rossen) called *The Brave Bulls*. Wayne proudly remembered that *Time* magazine gave the Boetticher picture the better review, "although, naturally, they failed to give me any credit." Wayne was already developing the suspicion that nothing connected with him was going to be respected by the eastern journalistic establishment. Mostly, he was correct.

The Bullfighter and the Lady was the beginning of a difficult, mutually wary relationship between

Wayne and Boetticher that lasted for twenty-five years. Wayne respected Boetticher's talent, but the younger man was too much of an alpha male to be entirely accepted by Wayne, who certainly fell under that category himself and would have appreciated some deference from a director to whom he had given a break.

"Duke couldn't box," remembered Boetticher. "But . . . he was one of the strongest men I've ever seen in my life. And when we were drinking, he'd really hate my guts. He thought I was cocky and wasn't as good as I thought I was.

"One time we were standing in front of a big new Electrolux refrigerator which was as tall as Duke. And he reared back to hit me . . . and telegraphed his punch. I was a boxer and slipped to one side and he hit my refrigerator and sprung the door. I gave the refrigerator to [actor] Walter Reed and that was the great thing in Walter's house — [the imprint of] Duke's fist was implanted in the refrigerator."

Gail Russell remained a part of the extended Wayne filmmaking family. Colin Grant, James Edward Grant's son, remembered attending one of Wayne's parties at the Encino house in 1952. Russell was there, too drunk to drive home. Colin was delegated with the task and took her to her house off Ventura Boulevard.

Colin spent a lot of time around Wayne that year. He was at the Encino house shooting pool one day when they decided to go to lunch at the Beverly Hills Hotel. Wayne was sporting a big *Taft for President* button and told Colin he could drive his new Cadillac. It was a lot of car for a young boy, but Wayne told him to take the Cahuenga

Pass and gun it.

They arrived at the hotel in one piece. Once they were seated, Wayne called his office staff to come over for lunch as well. At that point, a stranger was attracted by the Taft button and introduced himself to Wayne. The stranger explained that he was a campaign manager who had elected the first Republican in thirty years in the state of Arizona, but he was going to support Eisenhower because "he can get elected and Taft can't." His name, he told Wayne, was Barry Goldwater. The two men shook hands. They parted as friends, and would become even friendlier in coming years.

By the time they drove back through the mountains, neither Wayne nor Colin Grant was feeling any pain. Wayne wasn't done drinking, and ordered Colin to stop at a ramshackle old building that looked like a bar. "The place looked closed," remembered Grant. "But Duke got out of the car, went over and kicked open the door. He looked in and there was nothing there but cobwebs. And then he turned to us in the car and said, 'The son of a bitch is closed!'

"All I could say was 'I told you.'

"He was very funny — a cool guy."

Despite Barry Goldwater's rational attitude toward Dwight Eisenhower, Wayne's heart and mind usually went toward the most conservative candidate, so in 1952 he stayed a Robert Taft supporter. During the primary season, he went to a party carrying a bag full of Taft buttons and began handing them out. One of his employees refused to put one on, and Wayne said, "You must have some reason."

"Yeah, I do," said the man. He explained that

Taft had voted against a bill that provided amputees from World War II with special equipment that would enable them to drive cars. "I couldn't vote for a man like that," said the man. "I couldn't vote for him if he was running for dogcatcher. Being a veteran myself, that stuff is still pretty close to me, and that's just the way I feel."

Wayne nodded, said he understood, and nothing else was said about the matter.

Wayne's standing deal with Warner Bros. guaranteed a budget of at least $900,000 — he was always on guard against sliding back into cheap pictures — while his compensation was set at $17,500 a week for ten weeks. In December 1949, the contract was extended for another year at the same terms, and in 1951 the contract was extended yet again, with a new feature: he would get a percentage if any of his Warners movies was re-released within four years of American and Canadian release, or five years of release overseas — Wayne and Charles Feldman's response to Republic's habit of quickly reissuing any picture that was even a marginal hit.

The first picture under the deal with Warners was *Operation Pacific,* a submarine picture co-starring Patricia Neal. Wayne's reputation as a genial working companion preceded him, so Neal was surprised to find him "abrupt and unfriendly," not just with her but with the entire company. Gradually, word got around that he was in the midst of a bad situation with Chata, and the company gave him a wide berth. Wayne's marriage was entering its terminal phase.

For the next ten years, Wayne would center his movie activities around Warner Bros., which was run by the uneasy partnership of Harry and Jack Warner. Jack ran the studio, Harry ran the company. Harry's granddaughter Cass Warner Sperling remembers him as "the man gathering the money and keeping the studio alive for over fifty years. Jack? Jack was like a mosquito on a hot night."

The standard line on the brothers was that Harry was brilliant and honorable — he was the first movie mogul to pull his company out of Nazi Germany — and that Jack was a devious clown, but Harry was not without his deceptive side as well; his granddaughter remembers him talking about the early years of the company, when he planned stockholder meetings in the middle of winter in Podunk towns so as to minimize the number of attendees, as well as their complaints.

Jack was the classic youngest child in a large family, continually playing the Look-At-Me card in order to get attention. Warner and Wayne would develop a jocular, teasing relationship, helped by the fact that it was hard for either of them to stay angry. Jack frequently threw William Wellman and Howard Hawks off the lot, but he would always bring them back for another picture. His benevolence toward talent ended with Judy Garland, whose behavior threw *A Star Is Born* far over budget and cost the studio any chance of financial success; years later, he adamantly refused to cast her as Mama Rose in *Gypsy*.

On the emotional level, Jack Warner has always been an enigma; the man who could cheat his brother out of the studio and disinherit his son also had, alone among the founding generation of moguls, the capacity to continually reinvent his studio. Mayer, Zukor, and the rest were slamming

341

into old age and irrelevance in the 1950s, while Jack was coming up with James Dean, Natalie Wood, James Garner, and Warren Beatty. They didn't like him any more than Errol Flynn or Bette Davis had, but Jack Warner had the knack of finding star personalities. Some he developed; some, like John Wayne, he rented.

The first few pictures Wayne made at Warners were programmers; for another classic, he was once again blessed by John Ford, who finally managed to get his long-dreamed-of production of *The Quiet Man* off the ground at Republic.

In 1944, Maureen O'Hara was making *The Spanish Main* at RKO when John Ford came to visit. He was wearing her father's old battered hat, a new pair of pants that Mary Ford had bought him and he had aged by burning cigarette holes in the material. ("She went out of her mind trying to get him respectable," remembered O'Hara.)

A new cop was working the studio gate and wouldn't let Ford in the studio. Ford was enraged and left. He called a man he knew at RKO named Joe Nolan, who told O'Hara that Ford was furious. She called Ford and told him to come to RKO the next day, that there would be a red carpet from the gate to the set. The idea of the red carpet was attractive, so Ford grudgingly consented.

The reason for the visit was an agreement that Ford wanted O'Hara, Wayne, Victor McLaglen, and Barry Fitzgerald to sign. It was for a film called *The Quiet Man.* O'Hara signed, Frank Borzage witnessed.

For the next six years, every major studio in Hollywood turned down *The Quiet Man.* Every time John Ford made an art movie, audiences stayed away. And this was an Irish movie, for God's sake, and in Technicolor. "For years," said O'Hara, "Duke and I would go to see him and say, 'C'mon Pappy, let's make it already, or Duke will be playing McLaglen's role and I'll be playing the widow woman.' "

Herbert Yates didn't like the script — "It's a silly little Irish story that won't make a dime," he said. The first budget Ford prepared for *The Quiet Man* came in at $1.75 million, which was more than Republic had ever spent on one picture — a lot more. Ford got the budget down to $1.4 million, although weather delays would boost the actual outlay to $1.6 million. Even though Yates had agreed to finance the picture if Ford first made a western (*Rio Grande*), he tried to kill it with a backdoor approach, telling Wayne that *The Quiet Man* was a mistake, that it would hurt his career. He also told Wayne that he wanted nothing to do with it — the responsibility was all Ford's.

Then Yates began working on Ford to cut the budget. While Wayne was enjoying a trip to South America courtesy of Howard Hughes, Ford wired him: "AFTER MUCH FUSS AND FEATHERS, MUCH WRANGLING, FIST-FIGHTS AND HARSH WORDS, THE BUDGET IS SET EXCEPTING, OF COURSE, FOR YOUR SALARY WHICH YOU WILL HAVE TO TAKE UP WHEN YOU GET BACK. I'M A NERVOUS WRECK."

So Wayne gave up his contractually guaranteed 10 percent of the profits in exchange for a flat fee of $100,000. Pappy would be able to make his film. In Ireland. In Technicolor.

"Duke came to work," said Maureen O'Hara.

He knew his lines. He worked like a dog. He tried to make each scene the best he possibly could. He wanted to satisfy the fans who were coming to see the film. . . . He was kind, he supported people. A good man.

Ford used to put people "In the barrel." The one in the barrel would get hell all day long. Insults, just awful. Your heart would turn over for them, and you wanted to poke [Ford] in the nose. But it wasn't them he was after, it was some other actor on the set. He wanted to make the other actor unsteady, ready to do a certain kind of scene. And the other actors would be totally involved with you, mad for you, unhappy for you. And then he'd shoot the scene.

He was a totally perverse human being. If you said, "That's a green tree," he would say, "What the hell are you talking about. Green? That's purple." I don't know why he was like that, but he was. Roddy McDowall thought he was an angel, the kindest, most wonderful man that ever was. But for the rest of us. . . .

For instance, he pretended he couldn't see very well, but he actually had eyes like a hawk. On *How Green Was My Valley,* I was to do a scene in a kitchen with Walter Pidgeon, and Ford said, "No. I want the shadow from the back of the chair on the wall." *He* was lighting the scene, not the cameraman.

O'Hara approached her part of Mary Kate in *The Quiet Man* as if she were an earth princess. "What I aimed to do was keep her walking three feet off the ground. I wanted a suspended feeling, so that she'd never land on the soil."

Andrew McLaglen, the assistant director on the picture, asserted that O'Hara and Ford had an affair during the production. O'Hara indignantly denied it, asserting, "The man was old enough to be my father!" But Wayne seems to have believed it as well — he told McLaglen he just didn't understand how Maureen could kiss Ford, what with his pipe and his habit of chewing on a filthy old handkerchief.

O'Hara had favorite stories of the production that may or may not have had any relation to reality. "They did terrible things to me. Because I was a woman, they wanted me to cry foul. And I wouldn't, by God, not once. They gathered up the sheep manure, so I'd be dragged through it. They'd kick it in, and my gang would kick it out, but Duke and Ward would kick it back in. And there's no foul smell like sheep manure. Then Ford would give everybody instructions not to give me a bucket of water to wash up. And the odor would almost kill me."

Others have pointed out that sheep manure didn't have to be placed in the meadow, that it was there through a natural process, but O'Hara always persisted in her narrative of victimization.

The crucial scene of declaration in *The Quiet Man* is the love scene in the rain, where Thornton (Wayne) and Mary Kate (O'Hara) feel the tidal pull of desire. "Ford never really directed Duke or me," said O'Hara. "He would put us in situations, talk to us about the situation and let you work your way out of it. It was never, 'Put your hand here, raise an eyebrow, then wink.' He never did that. He hired people he knew could give him what he wanted. All of us, Ward, McLaglen,

George O'Brien, the people that knew him so well, before he opened his mouth, we knew what he wanted."

O'Hara pointed to her oft-told anecdote about Ford shooting a close-up of O'Hara's hair lashing her face on the beach.

The average director would have put the fan in front of me and blown the hair back from my face, but he put it off to the side so that the hair was lashing my eyeballs. Then he started yelling at me to keep my hands down and let the hair go across my face.

And I put my hands down and said, "What would a baldheaded old son of a bitch know about hair lashing across his eyeballs?" And I immediately thought, "Oh, God, what have I done. I'm going to be killed."

And in the flash of a second, I could see him check every face on the crew, up in the lights. And I saw him make his decision about whether to kill me or laugh. And he laughed. And the whole crew was relieved. So people laughed for five minutes. But there was that split second when he took everything in and made his decision about how to handle it. And I thought, "*That's a great director.*"

The company spent six weeks in Ireland in June and July of 1951. Screenwriter Frank Nugent said that most of it was spent in "a fine drizzle." Nugent counted four days of unbroken sunshine, while cameraman Winton Hoch insisted that there were at least six. No matter. Ford and Hoch contrived to make it look like clouds never moved over Innisfree.

Maureen O'Hara asserted that was all nonsense. "[Ford] always gave interviews about the terrible weather in Ireland, and how we only had two days of sunshine. It just wasn't true. It was one of the finest summers I ever saw in Ireland. I think we had one single day of rain on the location, and that day is in the film. When I run out of the cottage and through the stream and fall down, that was the only day of rain we had. And I wasn't acting, I was blown down by the wind. But the rest of the film was glorious sunshine, blue skies and puffy clouds. But in interviews . . ."

What was definite was that the company was headquartered at Ashford Castle in the village of Cong. Ashford Castle is, as Frank Nugent wrote, "a battlemented, turreted, Victorian pile built by the Guinness Stout people in the 1850s." Cong itself had no electricity until the film company brought it, but the town contributed the pubs, the churches, and the houses.

What with the profusion of Guinness and Irish whiskey, it must have been a tough shoot for the alcoholics on the picture, but Ford stayed rigorously sober. Wayne also was on his best behavior, except once, when he had an afternoon off and went to a pub and started drinking. After shooting ended for the day, Ford and Andrew McLaglen went looking for their star and found him in a condition McLaglen called "falling down drunk." Ford didn't seem overly concerned, but at midnight McLaglen took a sandwich and some milk to Wayne's room. He was already fighting a terrible hangover, but he was ready to go by seven the next morning.

As usual, when a film was made during the summer Wayne took his kids with him. "I was only eleven," remembered Patrick Wayne, "but the experience made a huge impression on me. Mike and I were there for six weeks and my sisters were there for two or three. The people in Ireland are so friendly, and we had time to sightsee — 'tomorrow we're going to Galway,' they'd say. We had a lot of opportunity to see Ireland beyond the locations.

"In 1975, I went back, and nothing had changed at all. I remembered everything about every place I had gone. And I found that they played *The Quiet Man* every afternoon at four o'clock at Ashford Castle."

Ford had a bad day or two during the location shoot over his frustrations with O'Hara. With Ford sulking in bed, Wayne directed a section of the steeplechase race and a scene of O'Hara walking home from the beach. Herb Yates was visiting the location and when he saw the rushes, Wayne told him, vis à vis *The Alamo,* "You see, I know how to direct."

"The son of a bitch said, 'Maureen O'Hara walking up from the beach is not the same as filming the battle of the Alamo,' " Wayne remembered. "I always said he had no taste, and I was right. I knew where to put the camera and I knew how to work with the lighting cameraman, and all there was to know. It doesn't matter if you're directing a small scene or a big scene, you still have to know where to put the goddamn camera. But Yates knew nothing about filmmaking."

The critical and public response to *The Quiet Man* was mostly rapturous, although *The New Yorker* landed on the same qualities that have irritated a minority of viewers ever since. "The people are not only cute, but quaint, and the combination, stretched out for something more than two long hours, approaches the formidable . . . the master who made *The Informer* appears to have fallen into a vat of treacle." John Ford won his fourth Oscar for Best Director, and the film returned worldwide rentals of $5.8 million — the biggest hit in Republic's history.

In Cong today, *The Quiet Man* is an industry, and the 400 villagers put on *Quiet Man* festivals and John Wayne look-alike contests. They even went to the trouble of rebuilding White O'Morn, so tourists would have something to visit.

Throughout his period of frantic activity in the late 1940s, Wayne always kept one eye on *The Alamo*. Active preparation began in December of 1947, when he took two round-trip tickets and a $500 advance from Republic to scout around San Antonio for likely locations. Traveling with him was Pat Ford, John Ford's son, who would complete a 131-page outline — actually more of a first-draft script — in September 1948.

Pat Ford's script begins abruptly, but manages to avoid speeches about freedom. It makes a feint at a love story between Davy Crockett and a Mexican girl, and creates a fair amount of the characters and dramatic incidents that would eventually populate Wayne's movie, including successful raiding parties and the characters of the Beekeeper and the Parson. (It also gives a subsidiary character the spectacular death Crockett has in the final version.)

Contrary to Wayne's later story of wanting only a small part in order to concentrate on directing, Davy Crockett is clearly written for him: "Soldiering is a trade, Bub," Crockett says in the cadences of John Wayne. "Just like harness making. Or gunsmithing. And fights are won by the man who's best at his trade. Can you remember that? . . . You'd better, because from now on you'll be learning that trade. It's a hard one to master. Not many people have." Overall, it's a solid first draft, leagues ahead of the average Republic script.

A year after that, Wayne spent a week in Mexico looking for a more economical way to shoot the picture than could be had in the States. As always, Yates rode a tough herd on expenses; Wayne had to assume all costs for the trip over $500.

By this time, there were noticeable strains in the Wayne-Yates relationship; it took Wayne several years to receive his full 10 percent of the gross on *Wake of the Red Witch* and *Sands of Iwo Jima,* which cumulatively amounted to about $300,000. (Yates's position was that Wayne had to produce as well as act in his Republic films in order to get his percentage.)

When the Feldman agency checked with Wayne, he said he wasn't going to do anything so pathetic as write an angry letter, that he would get his 10 percent "or else." "I guess he meant by 'or else' he would tear the studio down or kill somebody," wrote the Feldman agency's Sam Norton. Yates eventually paid Wayne the money. Then there was Wayne having to give up his percentage in order to get *Rio Grande* and *The Quiet Man* made, gestures that ended up costing him somewhere north of $700,000.

Wayne never groused about it publicly, but late at night, with a drink or two in him, he would vent. "I get so mad every time I think about the money that this son of a bitch [Ford] cost me," he said. "He is such a fucking bad businessman. I said to him once, I said, 'For Christ's sake, when you make a deal, please, once in a while let me in on it if you're making the deal.' "

By 1951, Wayne was getting the distinct feeling that Yates was shying away from *The Alamo.* As *The Quiet Man* got under way, Wayne wrote Yates a multi-page letter of grievance. He was perturbed about the studio not anteing up as it should have for *The Bullfighter and the Lady,* pointed out that he had enlisted Jimmy Grant to do a rewrite in exchange for 5 percent of the profits, and then had enlisted "the best director in the business" i.e., Ford, to use his cutting talents to straighten out what Wayne called "a bad job of direction."

After all this, Wayne found that the picture was not credited as "A John Wayne Production," but, rather, "Herbert J. Yates Presents." Wayne demanded his proper credit and closed by saying, "I want you to stop misconstruing my cooperation and fellowship as stupidity."

In mid-1951, Yates asked if the script for *The Alamo* was ready. At this point, only four of Wayne's contractual seven pictures had been made and his contract was up in seven months. The budget for *The Alamo* had been locked at $1.2 million, even though in Wayne's own estimation, and that of many others who read the script, it was a $3 million picture. On August 28, Wayne wrote a letter charging that Yates and his organization were engaged in a backdoor sabotage operation — that Republic had killed a deal to make the movie in Mexico, even though the budget wouldn't allow it to be made in America.

Wayne's sense of grievance boiled over again regarding the costumes. Wayne had gotten estimates for leather uniforms made in Mexico for

$15 apiece against a $150 weekly rental from Western Costume. A Republic employee named Baker had replied, "We'll take care of that, Duke — we'll check what they can be made for down there and what they can be made for up here and decide which is best."

Wayne was enraged at Baker "talking down to me as if I were a child, or with no regard for what I had just a minute before stated." He concluded by writing, "I can't spend all my time at this studio fighting with people who do not understand or recognize the needs of Class A pictures."

In September 1951, Yates sent Wayne a six-page letter of his own, enumerating several main points: he regarded Wayne as being overly kind in his choice of associates, people he regarded as being far below Wayne's own standards. (This was a veiled but justified swipe at Grant Withers, whom Wayne had made associate producer on *The Bullfighter and the Lady*.) Yates then pointed out that he had paid James Edward Grant $30,000 for a screenplay that had not yet been delivered. So far, so good.

Yates then went off topic by making the highly dubious claim that Republic had lost money on two previous John Wayne productions (*Angel and the Badman* and *The Fighting Kentuckian*), that *The Bullfighter and the Lady* also looked like a loser, and that he had only made that film because of Wayne's unyielding enthusiasm. The clear implication was that *The Alamo* was likely to be more of the same.

Wayne's contract with Republic was due to expire on January 14, 1952, but the two men left the door open for *The Alamo*. Yates grudgingly increased the proposed budget to $1.5 million, with locations to be done in Panama. Then he stalled again, and on October 16, Wayne wrote yet another letter, this time more resigned than angry. "Every time it comes to making a picture, there's a hassle," he wrote, listing all the junkets he had made for pictures he hadn't even starred in, all he had done for the studio, including giving up his percentages on *Rio Grande* and *The Quiet Man*.

"So I repeat: I will make *The Alamo* if we start on it immediately — or I will forget it. It's up to you. . . . I might also add, Herb, that if I am disappointed in this instance, I will never make another picture at Republic."

Wayne had been at Republic for as long as the studio had existed; he had proven his loyalty over and over again. But Herbert Yates hated expensive films — *The Quiet Man* verged on being too rich for his blood, and *The Alamo* as Wayne envisioned it was going to cost more than *The Quiet Man*.

Finally, the two men got into a shouting match in Wayne's office, which ended when Yates stormed out, followed closely by Wayne. A half hour later, Wayne came back into the office and told Mary St. John, "Pack everything. We're moving." A truck would be there shortly.

Mary started packing, and just about the time the van arrived, Yates came back into the office, demanding to see Wayne. "He's gone," St. John said. Yates's jaw was working furiously on a plug of tobacco; a bit of the juice was lodged in the corner of his mouth. He ordered St. John to stop what she was doing, and she refused. "Who are you working for, him or me?" he demanded. "Wayne," she replied. She grabbed her purse and walked out of Republic, never to return — just like her boss.

Wayne left behind dozens of westerns distinguished only by his presence, some not bad costume pictures, and two pictures with Ford that have never stopped playing — *The Quiet Man* and *Rio Grande.* For Republic, there would be seven more years of diminishing returns, but the company was doomed by Herbert Yates's unwillingness to manufacture anything but downmarket goods at a time when downmarket goods were moving to television. A relationship that had begun in 1935 was over.

And then Yates did something truly reprehensible. He simply purloined the basic idea of the Alamo, which was in the public domain, commissioned a new screenplay, and produced a knockoff entitled *The Last Command* that took some small advantage of the public's rage for all things Davy Crockett in the wake of the Walt Disney–Fess Parker TV shows. Richard Carlson played Travis, Sterling Hayden played Jim Bowie, Arthur Hunnicutt played Crockett. It was a tawdry stunt even for Hollywood.

There were cards exchanged for birthdays and Christmas, but Yates and Wayne apparently never saw each other again.

In December 1951, with Republic disappearing in the rearview mirror, Wayne and Robert Fellows formed Wayne-Fellows Productions. James Edward Grant was invited into the fold for a salary plus a percentage of the profits of each film he wrote, as well as 5 percent of overall company profits.

Their first hire was a young man named Tom Kane, a naval veteran of World War II who had served in the South Pacific. Kane had been working as a story analyst at Paramount, where his office was a cubicle with a sofa, a chair, and a typewriter on a desk. Paramount wanted very clinical descriptions of properties, much like high school book reports, and Kane wanted out. Kane's sister in Evanston, Illinois, suggested he talk to an acquaintance of hers named James Edward Grant. Grant never returned Kane's calls, but the analyst persevered and got Grant's home phone number. They set up a meeting, and when Kane walked in, John Wayne was there, surrounded by scripts and books piled knee-high all over the room.

"Who's going to read this crap?" asked Wayne rhetorically.

Kane was offered the job as story editor for the new company. At Paramount he was counseled to think long and hard before he left a secure job. Paramount wasn't going to go out of business, but a crazy actor with an independent production company? They were likely to make one picture and fold.

On the other hand, Kane thought that working for a crazy actor would be a lot more fun and promise a lot more autonomy than Paramount. He took the job. Wayne-Fellows bought an office building right off Sunset Boulevard at 1022 Palm Avenue.

Tom Kane went to work for John Wayne in December of 1951. The first production meeting Kane attended made him wonder if perhaps the people at Paramount hadn't been right. The meeting was at Wayne's house in Encino; Fellows, Grant, William Wellman, and a few other people were there. Kane was anxious to see what a high-end production meeting was like, but the conversation began with the subject of bath towels — it seemed that the towels at the Lakeside Golf Club were good, but not as good as the ones at Hillcrest.

It would have been one thing if they were kidding, but they were serious, and the pressing matter of the absorption and comparative softness of the towels at various Los Angeles country clubs took up a lot of time before there was any consideration of a script. Kane found the entire experience both funny and relaxing; he realized that these were not gods he was dealing with, but people with quirks and eccentricities like everybody else.

He had to assert himself quickly. Kane was asked to read a new script by Grant. Kane didn't like it and told Wayne so.

"You think you know more about scripts than Jimmy Grant?" asked Wayne.

"Well, if he thinks this is a good script for you, then I guess I do," said Kane. Wayne gave him a dark look and Kane figured his days at Wayne-Fellows were numbered. But Wayne passed on the script, and Grant never did sell it.

Soon, Wayne-Fellows Productions arranged a financing and releasing agreement with Warner Bros.

The crazy actor was serious.

■ ■ ■ ■

PART THREE:
1952–1961

■ ■ ■ ■

"People identify with me, but they dream of being John Wayne."

— JAMES STEWART

"Screw ambiguity. Perversion and corruption masquerade as ambiguity. I don't like ambiguity. I don't trust ambiguity."

— JOHN WAYNE

CHAPTER ELEVEN

In the early 1950s, John Wayne was everywhere. He would reliably appear in two movies per year, and from 1949 to 1955, there was also a line of John Wayne western comic books selling a million copies every month. Then there were the John Wayne cowboy pistols and western outfits marketed as competition for the Hopalong Cassidy/Roy Rogers/Gene Autry lines.

It seemed the whole world loved John Wayne, or at least the whole world that wasn't politically liberal in its beliefs. Actually, a lot of liberals liked him, and even the occasional socialist.

The renowned film historian Kevin Brownlow was growing up in a London of relentless postwar deprivation. Despite their wildly different political views he said, "A lot of us austerity-struck blokes after the war would like to have *been* John Wayne. He was one of the most charismatic of the leading stars; even his voice was magnetic. He was admirable in the way he took John Ford's bullying and emerged triumphant. And he had a splendid sense of humor. I loved John Wayne, and would happily watch him in anything."

Brownlow pointed out how the richest characters of old Hollywood — wonderfully vital people right out of richly imagined fiction — were often incredibly right-wing. Merian C. Cooper, John Ford's partner in Argosy Productions, once told Brownlow that "I would rather every man, woman and child in America die than live under a welfare state." Brownlow's sense of emotional allegiance to Wayne could be echoed not just in Europe, but in Latin America and Asia as well.

For the first ten years of his career, Wayne had been mostly unlucky and out of step with the prevailing trends in Hollywood. But his luck had turned, and decisively so; Henry Luce's American Century now had an American hero to speak for it. Wayne's projection of heroic masculinity neatly coexisted with Hollywood's increasing commercial and — eventually — cultural dominance, not to mention America's own increasingly expansive sense of itself.

Some of Wayne's contemporaries in the movie industry didn't necessarily share in the general enthusiasm. Paul Nathan, publicity man and later associate producer for Hal Wallis, read the script for an MGM western called *Vengeance Valley* and reported to his boss that the lead was "a typical John Wayne part. Slow-thinking, slow-moving and very heroic." (Wallis contractee Burt Lancaster played the part.) But that was fine, because John Wayne wasn't working for Hal Wallis, he was now working for John Wayne.

Wayne-Fellows gave its main partner an office to go to, which was a good thing as he increasingly needed to get away from Chata — her drinking was spiraling out of control. "The longer they were married, the more of a problem it became," said Mary St. John. "The mother was long past saving, and Chata was not far behind. I don't

360

know if it was the drinking, but she seemed to age unusually fast. Her complexion got worse, and she lost that quality — a kind of innocence — that she had in the mid-forties."

Problems with Chata had accumulated during 1951. She and Wayne separated in December of that year after a set-to in Acapulco that began — she said — when he threw a glass of water in her face, she retaliated with a bucket, and he responded with a bottle of rubbing alcohol. Around that same time — he said — Chata passed out on the beach after a midnight swim and had to be carried to a nearby café, where she spent the night on the floor covered by a tablecloth.

The marriage finally hit the rocks in May of 1952, following an argument at a luau in Honolulu that involved Robert Fellows and a sportswear manufacturer. Wayne threw a couple of pillows at her, and she flew back to Los Angeles. A day or two later, Wayne was sitting on the bed to lace up his shoes when he noticed a little sliver of gold at his feet. There he found a pin from Hilton Hotels. Putting two and two together, he deduced that Nicky Hilton had also been sitting in the same place doing the same thing and had lost the pin from his sport coat.

Game on!

If the marriage to Chata was a train wreck, it was a train wreck that attested to Wayne's remarkable powers of compartmentalization. During their marriage, he made *She Wore a Yellow Ribbon, Fort Apache, Rio Grande, Red River,* and *The Quiet Man* — a good portion of the movies that constitute his best work as an actor.

Chata hired Jerry Geisler to handle her end of the divorce. Wayne's first offer was 15 percent of his gross earnings, $14,000 in bonds, their home in Mexico, half the proceeds from the sale of the Encino house, a $12,000 bank account, a piece of his oil leases, and two cars. All told, she would be up for about $80,000 in the first year after the divorce, and $35,000 to $40,000 thereafter. She turned it down flat. Then he offered about $325,000 paid out over nine years. Chata countered with $12,500 a month for the rest of her life. No deal.

Chata's complaints were specific:

1. Wayne had a temper and was liable to yell, swear, and bang doors when in bad humor. Once, enraged because there weren't enough towels in the bathroom, he heaved towels all around the stairway and corridor.
2. In Mexico, after a party, he had called her "an obscene name" and threw a glass of water in her face, followed by the bottle of rubbing alcohol.
3. At Budd Boetticher's house in Mexico City, Wayne and his cronies departed for a stag party. Wayne returned with a large hickey on his neck.

At one point, Chata even accused Wayne of hitting her. He denied it. "I have never in my life struck Mrs. Wayne. But there have been many times when I have had to protect myself from her temper. I have held her hands and I have held her feet, but only to protect myself."

With the newspapers full of competing tales of marital abuse, the rest of the family was mortified. (It's not hard to imagine satisfied "I told you so's" on Josie's part.) Michael would show up at school and the other kids would ask him, "Why is your father treating your mother that way?"

"She's not my mother," Michael would say through tightly compressed lips.

So the Wayne-Fellows office became a get-away as well as a boy's clubhouse for cronies from the old days, the men who had worked with Wayne when he was making $150 a week and a sandwich per day. Bob Steele and Grant Withers were always around, and usually left with a check — around the office, this was known as "shaking the money tree." An old directorial hand of no distinction named D. Ross Lederman, who had made a couple of Wayne's early B westerns, was also hovering and would eventually be made associate producer — actually second unit director — on a Wayne production entitled *Ring of Fear.*

One day, after Grant Withers left with a check, Wayne asked Tom Kane how much a pair of alligator shoes cost. "About $150," said Kane. Wayne exploded. "How come that son of a bitch wears fucking alligator shoes? I never had a pair of alligator shoes in my life and I make a lot of money. I just can't see it. Now, here he is around here getting dough off me wearing his alligator shoes. There's something the matter with the whole frickin' setup."

Wayne's instructions to Tom Kane about suitable script material were basic. Wayne was more interested in movies with Wayne than he was in movies without Wayne. He told Kane to look for westerns, but whatever he found, "don't make me ordinary. Just don't make me ordinary."

"I didn't know exactly what he would do," remembered Kane, "but I knew pretty well what he wouldn't. He didn't like long speeches, not because he couldn't deliver them, but he didn't like that. He would let the other guy have that . . .

363

lay off this crap on co-stars. They liked having a lot of dialogue."

First among equals was Jimmy Grant. "The Grants lived right around the corner from us," remembered Gretchen Wayne. "[Mike's dad] was in Encino, but Jimmy and his family were in Toluca. There was a country club called Lakeside, and Jimmy belonged, Mike's dad belonged, Bogart, Howard Hughes, Bob Hope, a lot of the actors from Warners and Republic."

But Jimmy Grant was not a good golfer — his temper kept getting in his way. "He was terribly irascible," said Gretchen Wayne. "He'd throw his clubs. He'd break his clubs. Of course, now everybody is so piss-elegant they don't think of doing that, but that's the way Jimmy was."

On March 21, 1952, Wayne-Fellows contracted with Warner Bros. for two pictures: *Big Jim McLain,* a Wayne vehicle based on a *Saturday Evening Post* story entitled "We Almost Lost Hawaii," and *Plunder of the Sun,* an adventure movie that was slotted for somebody else. *Big Jim McLain* was made cheaply and quickly — the picture started shooting April 27, 1952, and was in theaters by Labor Day in order to guarantee a profit.

Fellows gave an interview outlining the philosophy behind the new company: "Our format is basically the same simple one that originally made our industry the greatest entertainment medium in the world. We start with a story that's about something tangible. We're not going to make outdoor dramas necessarily, but we do recognize the fact that film fans want to break through the confines of four walls when they are seeking entertainment.

"We haven't any tricks up our sleeves, nor do

we have any dreams of collapsing all the major studios. On the contrary, our idea is to make money, a good deal of it, through offering the kind of entertainment that will lure people into the neighborhood theaters."

Jimmy Grant was working on the script of *McLain* and took time off to give an interview about his friend. When asked why he thought Wayne was so popular, Grant said, "Lots of guys think Duke is a big, dumb lummox. He isn't. I've written half a dozen scripts for the guy and he can pick out the holes in them faster than I can. He's a good cameraman, a sensitive director, and if a stunt man won't work a stunt, he'll do it himself. He says he can't act his way out of a hat, and his success is just one big lucky fluke. But don't kid yourself."

Some people at Warners were bothered by the script of *McLain;* it was about investigators for the House Un-American Activities Committee in Hawaii, and the script had them enthusiastically engaging in all manner of illegality — wiretapping, intimidation, breaking and entering. "I think this could play in a *Maltese Falcon* manner and with cooperation from the writers could be shaped so as to avoid any legal pitfalls," wrote one story analyst.

Just before the picture started shooting, Warners sent out a synopsis that stated the picture was about a Texas cattle buyer who followed "a trail of excitement" to Hawaii. Robert Fellows later acknowledged that the studio didn't "wish to play up the fact that we were making an anticommunist film. The studio didn't want to scare off exhibitors. A lot of them got burned in the past with anticommunist pictures that didn't do much business."

After the picture was finished shooting, Warners' sales department immediately began pressing Wayne to speed through the editing, but production people warned them off: "The only hitch which I think you should be forewarned about is Duke Wayne saying that if it needs a few more days . . . work after the preview, he will not sacrifice the picture in order to make a precise August 16th date. . . . I know for a fact . . . that he is the kind of actor who rears back at any show of the quirt. He is also a very honest man about his own work and very critical thereof."

The previews were good, not great: "good in spots, except for the too, too obvious propaganda (and I am NOT a Commie)" wrote one member of the audience. Another commented, "[Stephen Vincent] Benet would turn over in his grave the way he was quoted," and "one wonders about the future of this country when this sort of tripe passes for Americanism."

Actually, this sort of tripe was quite widespread. It was a time when conservatives were angry (conservatives are always angry) and liberals were nervous (liberals are always nervous). Mark Armistead, an associate of John Ford's during World War II, had gone into the camera rental business and felt it necessary to present Cecil B. DeMille with a check for $1,000 — the amount Armistead had been paid for his cameras by the producers of the left-wing film *Salt of the Earth*. Giving the money to the Motion Picture Alliance, on whose behalf DeMille accepted the money, was the only way Armistead could maintain ideological purity.

Warners promoted *Big Jim McLain* with a tagline that seems more amusing sixty years later than it did at the time: "He's a Go-Get-'Em Guy for the U.S.A. on a Treason-Trail That Leads Half-a-World Away!" The critical response reliably divided along political lines. The Hearst columnist Lee Mortimer wrote that "It combines thrills, excitement, suspense, sock comedy, high adventure, blood and thunder, tender romance, patriotic emotion, the lure of the tropics AND John Wayne, all in one huge soul-satisfying package and at the regular admission prices." He ended by calling it "one of the best movies ever made."

The *New York Post*'s Archer Winsten called it, "One of the worst movies ever made." (The *Post* was a liberal newspaper back then.) Another critic referred to its "storm trooper patriotism" for the way it pointed an accusing finger at intellectuals — the communists include a biologist, a psychiatrist, a labor leader, and a labor relations counsel.

Overseas, the strident anticommunism of *Big Jim McLain* was not the selling point it was in America. In Italy, the title was changed to *Marijuana,* and the dubbed soundtrack altered to make Wayne an agent looking for drug smugglers.

Wayne-Fellows' obvious intent was to start their company with a success, and it worked. The net profit of *Big Jim McLain* was $261,641. Wayne-Fellows was also in for 47.5 percent of the foreign income. (The not bad *Plunder of the Sun,* in which John Farrow directed Glenn Ford, was less successful, but eventually went into profit.)

Fellows and Wayne gave every evidence of trying to build a company with a wide foundation; in October 1952, they were in talks to make a comedy starring Sid Caesar and Imogene Coca, the current TV comedy rages. Also in the pipeline was a TV series to star Alan Hale Jr., and there were also discussions about a radio version of *Big Jim McLain* to star James Arness and Doe Avedon.

Right after *Big Jim McLain,* Wayne was back at Warner Bros. returning to the passion of his youth — in *Trouble Along the Way* he played a football coach who shapes up a team and saves a Catholic college about to go under. It was a variation on the cozy Catholicism of *Going My Way,* and the director was Michael Curtiz, beginning the downhill slide that marked the last ten years of his career.

The movie was shot under the title *Alma Mater,* and Wayne thought the change killed the picture's chances. "[*Trouble Along the Way*] made it sound like the story of an oil truck which had busted a rear axle going up Cajon Pass," he said. "Who would buy a ticket to that?" The movie cost $1.6 million and had world rentals of $2.5 million, so it made a little money, albeit not as much as Wayne thought it would have under the original title.

But *Trouble Along the Way* was trivial compared to what was happening off-camera. While the marriage to Chata was crumbling, Wayne had taken a trip to South America, where he met Pilar Pallette Weldy, a young actress from Peru, whose husband, Richard Weldy, styled himself as a big-game hunter. She was shooting a movie where she did a dance scene by firelight. She was still out of breath when she was introduced to Wayne.

"That was quite a dance," he said, looking her over appreciatively. They had dinner. "I was a very good guitar player," she reminisced. "Near the end of the evening I played guitar and sang and

Wayne listened and he was entranced." The next day he sent her a beautiful new guitar. Wayne came back to America and told Bö Roos that Pilar was very attractive, very nice, and "very normal." Roos undoubtedly sensed another domestic disaster in the offing.

Wayne was not a man who enjoyed isolation, domestic or otherwise. Soon, Pilar was divorced and moving to Los Angeles. She was one of five children of a Peruvian senator. Her quiet, aristocratic childhood was occasionally interrupted when the family would have to go into exile in Chile or Argentina when her father's party was out of power.

Like so many conveniently cast-off spouses, Richard Weldy disappeared into the mists of time, until September 1956 when he shot Robert Harrison, the publisher of *Confidential* magazine, shortly after the magazine ran a story about Wayne and Pilar. The incident took place in the Dominican Republic, and the two men supposedly ran into each other by accident, after which, Weldy explained, "the gun fell from my hand. It accidentally went off and hit Harrison in the shoulder. "All in all, a great many accidents to befall a professional hunter, but Harrison declined to press charges.

Wayne didn't want to just set up Pilar as his mistress in Hollywood, so he followed the time-honored tradition of movie producers. On February 20, 1953, the Los Angeles *Herald Express* ran a picture of Wayne and Bob Fellows signing what they claimed to be the twenty-three-year-old Pilar to a contract. "The South American charmer recently completed her first picture, *Sabotage,* filmed in Peru. . . . Miss Palette will alternate her acting between Hollywood and Lima, Peru. Her first American film is a recently completed story, as yet untitled, which affords her a singing, dancing and dramatic role." But there was no recently completed story, nor would there be.

Wayne was still beset by guilt over his treatment of Josephine. Before he introduced the new wife-to-be to his four children, he told Pilar, "He's still angry at me," referring to Michael. "I'm afraid he always will be. It breaks my heart. I let those kids down. Don't expect too much from them at first. They haven't forgiven me yet."

Gretchen Wayne eventually met Pilar at Jimmy Grant's house, on the dock by the lake. "She was a tiny thing who wore a taffeta suit and high heels — a strange thing to wear in the daytime. Her hair was naturally curly, and she always wore high heels because she was short. In the early years, she overdressed. He loved sportswear — casual slacks, sweaters, cashmere, leather jackets. He would say to her, 'Why can't you dress more like [Wayne's daughter] Toni?' But Pilar gradually developed her own taste and style."

And then Pilar became pregnant. Wayne told his lawyer to ram through the divorce from Chata — money was no object. But Chata wouldn't be rushed.

Wayne delegated the excruciating decision to Pilar. He told her that if she wanted to have the child, he would stand by her and suffer the consequences. But she knew the scandal would destroy Wayne's career — Ingrid Bergman's affair with Roberto Rossellini was only a few years in the past. She decided to get an abortion, an act, she recalled, that "almost destroyed" her.

Wayne still had a loose agreement with RKO, but dealing with Howard Hughes was always chaotic. Wayne was the complete professional, and Hughes's sloppy procedures and catch-as-catch-can attitude toward commitments drove him up the wall. "My racket isn't writing letters any more than answering them promptly is yours," Wayne began a letter to Hughes. "I must get some serious beefs off my chest. . . . At the other studios and for my own company . . . I seldom get involved on a picture for more than eight to ten weeks overall. I am paid top terms for that time. At RKO, I wind up giving six months of my time . . . and it's hectic, uncomfortable and unpleasant time . . . for a fraction of the compensation paid me by the other studios. You can resolve this by paying me what the others do for the two pictures I owe you."

Wayne went on to complain that contractually the studio was obligated to provide a suitable story by March of 1952. Five months after that, he hadn't heard a word so took a job with another studio. Wayne's two-picture commitment for RKO had been hanging over his head for nearly three years at this point, and both pictures should have been completed a year earlier.

RKO's loss was Warners' gain, for Wayne was demonstrating considerable commercial power for the Burbank studio. Besides the success of *Big Jim McLain,* and the middling *Trouble Along the Way,* the equally ordinary *Operation Pacific* would earn nearly $4 million in rentals.*

* The sole distinguishing moment in *Operation Pacific*

371

Given the ongoing difficulties at RKO, it made perfect sense that, in November 1952 Wayne-Fellows entered into a very ambitious long-term deal with Warners.

The company agreed to make eight pictures within thirty-six months, four with Wayne, four without. *Island in the Sky* would be the first picture. Warners would advance $2,000 a week for office expenses, which would be charged to the negative costs of the pictures. The non-Wayne pictures would cost around $600,000 each, while Wayne's would cost more, the specifics to be worked out later.

After eight years, ownership of the pictures would revert to Wayne-Fellows, provided that Warners had recouped all its costs, plus an adjusted 37.5 percent fee for foreign distribution. Any pictures that didn't recoup stayed with Warners. At the same time, Charlie Feldman floated yet another opportunity past his client — a deal with RKO for five pictures that would pay Wayne-Fellows 50 percent of the gross for the entire world after the pictures doubled their cost. As Feldman knew, this was potentially a bigger proposition than the Warner deal, but it didn't

---

arrived during production, when a repairman showed up to install a new air compressor on the set. It was Ralph Bushman, formerly Francis X. Bushman Jr., whom Wayne had doubled in his first movie appearance in 1926. "I know you, but I don't expect you to remember me," said Bushman. Wayne took a long look, then stuck out his hand. "Sure I do," he said. "Your name's Bushman and I doubled for you on my first movie job."

happen, either because it was simply too ambitious coming on top of the Warners arrangement, or because Wayne didn't want to tie that much of his professional future to Howard Hughes and RKO's distribution.

The Warners deal was going to be profitable only if Wayne-Fellows could contract with efficient, experienced directors. Once again, Wayne's sympathy with industry veterans came into play, as he entered into serious discussions with Leo McCarey to direct one or more of the pictures.

McCarey was an ardent Catholic anticommunist; he and Wayne probably met in the Motion Picture Alliance. Despite his alcoholism, McCarey was one of the most respected directors in the business, with such accomplishments as *Ruggles of Red Gap, Duck Soup, Make Way for Tomorrow, The Awful Truth, Going My Way,* and *The Bells of St. Mary's.* As such, his perks were considerable. Among other things, McCarey had the right to approve all ads and publicity and approve all final sales contracts on his pictures.

The prospective McCarey deal ultimately fell apart, but Wayne signed contracts with similarly efficient veteran A list directors — John Farrow and William Wellman, the legendary "Wild Bill" who had made *Wings, Public Enemy,* the original *A Star Is Born,* and *The Story of G.I. Joe,* among many others.

During 1953 alone, Wayne-Fellows shot and completed *Island in the Sky, Hondo, Ring of Fear,* and *The High and the Mighty.* Wayne's grim childhood had shaped an adult who would always be hustling, a man who was far more comfortable working than relaxing. In May 1953, Wayne wrote Jack Warner's assistant Bill Schaefer that he and

Bob Fellows wanted to lease a vacant lot the studio owned in Mexico City and build a car wash on it. He offered 800 pesos a month, or about $88, plus 2 percent of the profits. Schaefer noted at the bottom of the letter that the property was worth 2,500 pesos, or about $275 a month. A Mexico City car wash was not going to be the difference between a comfortable or impoverished retirement, but that was irrelevant. Wayne was always in search of income.

The new contract with Warners made Wayne-Fellows the talk of the industry. Wayne gave an interview explaining that "I've profited by the mistakes that friends of mine — stars, directors, and producers — have made with their own companies. Other companies have failed because they haven't been able to buck the big companies. They make deals that look swell on paper. But when they finish up they're taken for all kinds of hidden charges. You just can't make a go of it unless you can keep the companies from piling up the costs on you." The grim experiences of John Ford's Argosy Productions and Howard Hawks's Monterey Productions were obviously on Wayne's mind, but he and his partner would also eventually be victimized by the core problem of independent producers.

Island in the Sky, the first film made under the eight-picture deal with Warners, cost $962,000, earned $2.4 million in world rentals, and was more or less unseen for fifty years because it reverted to Wayne, after which Wayne and his son Mike sat on it. It's one of William Wellman's finest films, far outstripping the more commercially successful *The High and the Mighty.*

"I never had a more difficult location in my life," said actor James Lydon. "There were five actors working in fourteen feet of snow in Donner Pass and Donner Lake. And the only way everybody could get from the hotel five miles away to the location was a Greyhound bus. We parked on the side of the road and then a Snowcat that held about twenty-five people took us to the location. Cast, crew, electricians, everybody. They would drop us off in the snow about a quarter to eight in the morning and pick us up about five or 5:15 in the afternoon, when the light would start to fade.

"We didn't even have chairs, because where are you going to put chairs in fourteen feet of snow? So mostly we stood up for a dozen hours. For meals, the Snowcat would take us back to the Greyhound bus, where we ate."

The valley, which was six miles from Truckee in the Sierra Nevadas, served as an airplane runway during the summer, stretched out flat for six thousand feet, and was surrounded by pine trees similar to those in Labrador, where the picture was set. But they were shooting in February, and it was miserable.

"Duke was a love, as usual," said Lydon. "Wild Bill Wellman was no cinch to work for, and when things would get tough, Duke would say, 'Now, now, come on, everything's fine . . .' He was a peacemaker. He never put on his boss hat. He was a very kind gentleman."

The appalling conditions forced Wellman to ramrod the shoot in an even more ruthless fashion than usual. He did 114 setups on location; seventy-three of them were done in one take, and only five location shots needed more than two takes. The picture started shooting on February 1 and finished on February 25, nine days ahead of schedule. Interestingly, Robert Fellows was never on location and was not a presence on the interiors either. Wayne functioned as the line producer as well as the star, and Lydon said he was "a very competent, quiet, easygoing boss."

Lydon was accustomed to martinets, but *Island in the Sky* was his first and only go-round with Wellman.

John Ford on the set did exactly what he said he did in interviews. He said, "Come in the scene, say your words and get out. I don't want fancy shots and sunspots and zooms. I want that camera to be unnoticeable to the audience. If I need a close-up I'll punch it in, but I leave the camera alone." He was a master at playing a scene in masters or full shots.

But Ford did not keep it all to himself. Ford would chew on his handkerchief and mull things over. Sometimes he'd spend half an hour just thinking, and everyone would wait. Ford was not a shouter; he would just say something and we'd do it.

Wellman . . . Wellman was *enthusiastic.* He had his day's work in his mind when he walked on the set in the morning. He would talk to the cameraman, they lit it. Everything was pre-planned, and there was no room for discussion whatever. He didn't do a lot of takes, you did it his way and that was it. He knew what he wanted and he would go and get it.

I had a scene where I was supposed to break down and cry in front of the other men. I wanted my character to be silent in the interior of the plane, but Wellman said he wanted me to scream it out. In the rehearsal I did it my way, but he made me scream it out anyway.

Neither Ford nor Wellman was a cinch to work for, but I can only tip my hat to Duke. He wasn't like what he was on the screen. On-screen, he was a strong, strong American leading man, [but] I always remember him sitting at Oliver Hardy's feet, in awe of a star that he didn't consider himself to be on the same level with.

Given the speed with which Wellman and Wayne made *Island in the Sky,* the picture couldn't help but be profitable, but Jack Warner wasn't prepared for its quality. "Ran *Island in the Sky* last night with Wellman Bob [Fellows] and boys," he wired Wayne on April 29, 1953. "This is one of the most important pictures have seen in long time. Believe will have as much impact as *Dawn Patrol* and *Wings.*" A couple of months later, Warner's opinion was confirmed by a preview and he again wired Wayne: "Had wonderful preview *Island in the Sky* last night. You and all concerned are to be congratulated. If you were here you would have been as proud as we were." Charlie Feldman also chimed in, writing it was "a wonderful, wonderful film. It still lingers in my mind, after these many days."

But praise from the studio boss was not about to nudge Wayne into a supplicating posture. On September 18, 1953, he wrote a letter to Jack Warner grousing about the fact that he and Bob Fellows had personally spent $3,000 for a party after the premiere, with plenty of TV and still cameras and reporters present, only to find that Warner Bros. had already opened the picture in some areas of the country before the news about its quality could get out.

"I was under the impression that when you have a class picture, it is a good idea to get the publicity in the people's minds before it is released for grind runs. I know it doesn't have the news value or the selling possibilities of something like *The Robe,* but . . . when you have the critics on your side, it would be a good idea to play the picture for a week or so in one place and let the news travel before it goes into the grind."

On one level, *Island in the Sky* is old-home week; showing up in small parts are Bob Steele, Andy Devine, Harry Carey Jr., and Paul Fix. On another level it's a very personal story for both its director and its star — an essay on their idea of courage. The story is simple — a transport plane goes down in Labrador in uncharted territory. The film cross-cuts between the five-man crew struggling to survive and the men who are searching for it. Wellman narrates the film himself, quietly, intently, from the inside of a pilot's sensibility, and mixes in a stream-of-consciousness voice-over from Wayne's character, so the audience knows his uncertainty and fear — things he can't afford to show to his men.

This terse minor masterpiece is directed and played with precision and force.

By the time *Island in the Sky* was in previews, Wayne was in Mexico wrestling with *Hondo,* a heat wave, and an intransigent 3-D camera. *Hondo* derives from a Louis L'Amour story that is quite different from the film. The bulk of the original story involves Ches Lane, who searches for a young wife named Angie on the Texas plains to tell her that her husband was killed while trying to protect a stranger in a saloon fight. Ches is captured by Apaches and fights his way to their respect. The Apaches deliver him to Angie, suggesting that he is strong and brave and will be good for her.

Jimmy Grant improved the story in innumerable ways. He made Angie's husband a skulking brute who is himself killed by Hondo, thereby creating suspense as to how she'll react when she finds out the brave stranger with whom she's falling in love killed her husband. Grant gave Hondo and the Indian chief Vittorio a relationship of grudging mutual respect, and he gave Hondo a dog who mirrors his owner's self-reliance and lack of need for others. In many respects, it's a model creative adaptation — everything Grant did sharpens the conflicts and strengthens the characters.

But making a movie with a largely untried technology on a distant and primitive location is a recipe for trouble, especially when your camera is malfunctioning. *Hondo* was shot in the summer of 1953 in Camargo, Mexico, five hundred miles south of El Paso, a hundred miles from Chihuahua. It was the biggest thing ever to hit Camargo's seventeen thousand inhabitants, but for everyone else it was concentrated hell.

The temperature never went below a hundred, and occasionally went twenty degrees past that. Sam, Hondo's scruffy dog, was actually played by Lassie, covered with Fuller's earth to make him look bedraggled. Since the ground was too hot to walk on, Lassie was outfitted with leather booties to wear between shots. Some of the enterprising Camargo locals kidnapped the dog and held him for ransom; after the ransom was paid, he was returned unharmed.

Adding to the difficulties was the fact that the film was being photographed in 3-D by what Warners was calling their "all media" camera, a five-hundred-pound behemoth mounted on a special truck with an elevator platform that could rise thirty feet and could shoot film simultaneously in 2-D, 3-D, flat, or in the widescreen ratio of 1:85. "We had a wonderful first day," Wayne wrote Jack Warner, "if that monster got what we pointed it at."

In that era, 3-D was photographed on two separate 35mm negatives by two cameras that approximated the angle and distance between two human eyes. When projected with Polaroid filters mounted in front of two 35mm projectors running in precise synchronization onto a silver screen, the effect on the audience — also outfitted with Polaroid glasses — was stereoscopic imagery. It was hard enough to shoot in the studio, but on a dusty location it was particularly stressful.

On June 17, Wayne wrote Jack Warner complaining that it took an hour and a half to get a simple two-shot because of the huge camera. What they needed, he told Warner, was the just-off-the-assembly line new 3-D camera that made setting up shots much easier. "We are throwing away what we think are values in composition because of the cameraman's worries from the talks he's had with the front office," wrote Wayne. "He's worried about his reputation."

Wayne begged for the second camera so that they could save what he estimated would be about three hours of production time a day. Wayne wrote that at this rate *Hondo* would take forty-five days to make, about a third longer than the original estimate, all because of the difficulties they were having with the camera.

On June 18, Jack Warner wired Wayne that the new 3-D camera would be on its way in a week and he could keep it and the old one for a week to ten days.

Then Warner moved on to the matter of the rushes. "Saw three reels second group dailies tonight. Everything very good except director is not moving you and Geraldine [Page] close enough to camera. Everything seems to be too far away. Must have usual over shoulders close shots individuals and tight twos in three dimensional pictures so we can see people's expressions and everything else. . . . All of this fundamental in making a picture which am sure Farrow you cameraman know. Best wishes . . ."

Wayne quickly responded: "Farrow has done everything but play music to try and get camera in for close shots . . . cameraman is over-cautious for fear front office will scream eyestrain. Will show cameraman your wire."

The harried cameraman was Robert Burks, a staff cameraman who had been trained on the nascent 3-D technology. Wayne thought Burks was good, but he also realized that Burks's ultimate allegiance was to Warner Bros., not Wayne-Fellows and not *Hondo*. A further complication was that the unit had to travel from Camargo, Mexico, to El Paso, Texas, to see their rushes, which they couldn't do every day, so they spent their entire time in Mexico on tenterhooks waiting for Jack Warner's reaction to the rushes in Los Angeles.

Wayne's leading lady was Geraldine Page, a fine actress but an eccentric person. Among those eccentricities was a hesitance about the use of soap and water. "She thought that was cute, walking

381

around smelling like a goat," said Tom Kane. Page was rooming with Mary St. John, who was made unpleasantly aware of Page's shoddy hygiene. St. John endured it for a time, but finally she explained to Page that the next day's work was the love scene between her and Wayne. "I strongly suggest you bathe tonight. It's better that I tell you, because he'll tell you, and he'll tell you in front of the whole cast and crew." Page took St. John's advice.

It was Wayne's first film with John Farrow, who proved to be a good director, but one who was excessively class-conscious. One morning he asked Wayne what he had done the night before.

"I went out with the boys," said Wayne, meaning the stuntmen.

"Well, you shouldn't do that," said Farrow.

"What do you mean?" said Wayne. "They made me what I am."

Until he began delegating duties to Michael Wayne around 1960, Wayne was always a hands-on producer, and *Hondo*'s 3-D technology forced him to be even more vociferous. "Every morning, when he would be hung over, he would have a screaming fit," said Geraldine Page. "He'd yell at somebody until he got hoarse. He would pick on some technical point, and he was always right."

Page also noticed the peculiar gravitational pull of a great star, the way they attract sycophants and hangers-on. "Everybody tried to be Duke's right-hand man and his favorite. It was like the stories you hear about the old court days. Everybody was trying to slice everybody else's reputation in the Duke's eyes. There was tremendous, tremendous competition."

It was a time of convulsive upheaval in the movie

business. Movie attendance had been plummeting since the end of World War II, and the studios were counting on 3-D and widescreen processes to stop the descent. Charles Feldman wrote Wayne and told him about a recent dinner with "Herr Warner." While Warner was still "overboard" about 3-D, "for the first time he said, 'CinemaScope will absolutely clean up.' Everyone's opinion seems to be that once *The Robe* and the other Fox pictures are released, there will be a mad rush by everyone to get CinemaScope."

The *Hondo* crew finally got the second camera from Los Angeles, but it wasn't long before Warners began agitating to get it back so they could use it for another 3-D production. (Clearly, the studio felt that time was of the essence regarding the fad for 3-D, which indeed turned out to be the case.)

Right after the second camera got to the location, the original camera broke down. They got the old camera fixed and held it in reserve in case anything went wrong with the new camera, which was both easier to use, lighter, and less prone to breakdown.

Stuck in Mexico under terrible heat and with technical problems to match, Wayne finally exploded. "I am goddamned sick and tired of every time I come in from location to have my Production Department say that you want that other camera," he wrote on July 7. He went on to inform Jack Warner's assistant Steve Trilling that he had no intention of sending the camera back before the unit returned from location. "If you don't want to cooperate in this, just call me up and tell me to bring the camera back and I'll bring it back and cancel our relationship."

Having opened with anger, Wayne closed with logic. Warners had told him they had no more camera motors for the cameras in Los Angeles, the spares were down in Camargo with *Hondo,* and they certainly couldn't afford to risk losing their spare motors. The second camera would be of no use to anybody in L.A. anyway.

He closed by telling Trilling to go right ahead and show the letter to Jack Warner. He had the second camera, he needed it to make the film in something close to an expeditious manner, and nobody was going to pry it loose from his grip.

Ward Bond was working on the picture, and Geraldine Page said that Wayne's and Bond's conversations tended to center on philosophy and politics. "John Wayne would talk so sensibly, while Ward Bond was just an oversimplifying bully. John Wayne, I feel, was a reactionary for all sorts of non-reactionary reasons. He would always say such sensible human things; he was so quick about everything, mentally as well as physically."

Page came to feel that the cornerstone of Wayne's personality was an honesty that demanded honesty in return. "He hates all kinds of hypocrisy and folderol. He's a terribly honest man, and that comes across on the screen, underlined by the kind of parts he plays. One of his first mottos, I think, is always to be the hero to the people around you. Wayne has a leadership quality, so that people revere him."

Page would be irritated by Wayne's disparaging remarks about Stanislavsky and New York actors, but he would always back off when he sensed Page was about to explode. " 'Aw, Geraldine, you're not mad at the old Duke, are you?' And I would melt and say, 'No.' Then I'd go back to the motel and say, 'What have I done? I'm so stupid. I'm the same as everybody else, I get taken by that charm, that tremendous charm.' I just loved him."

Wayne retained his unusual sensitivity to the crew, probably because of the years he had spent as one of them. The company had been shooting at a dry lake bed when a storm blew in. The Americans abandoned the location and left the Mexican crew to take care of the equipment. Hours later, Wayne was worried about the Mexicans, who were spending the night outside in the cold. He woke up the caterer, and the two men put together coffee, sandwiches, and bottles of tequila. Duke and the caterer took the food out to the location where they ate, drank, and sang with the crew until it was time to go back to work.

While Wayne was coping with 3-D, he was also coping with his divorce. In the middle of 1953, Chata was living in an Encino house that Wayne was renting for $1,354 a month. A preliminary hearing got under way in the last week of May 1953. Wayne's accountant testified that out of every $500,000 Wayne earned, he had about $50,700 left after taxes and living expenses. $155,000 would go for professional expenses, $187,200 for federal income tax, and $15,300 for child support. Wayne's net worth, according to the accountant, was a mere $160,000, and his liabilities amounted to $394,075. Wayne himself testified that he hadn't seen a paycheck in years — his money went directly into the coffers of Bö Roos's Beverly Management Company. Wayne was also paying his mother-in-law $650 a month because, supposedly, he had promised to support her when he married Chata. (The mother-in-law stipend was ended by the court.)

Interestingly, the court filings revealed that Chata received $150 a week from Republic Pictures between 1942 and December of 1953 despite the fact that the studio had never called her to work as an actress — about $78,000 in all. This was the sort of minor payoff that studios indulged in all the time, putting a useless relative or mistress on the payroll in order to keep a star happy. Some of the money might even be funneled into the star's accounts without the IRS being any the wiser. That a chronically cheap outfit like Republic would fork over nearly $10,000 a year for services that were being rendered not to the studio but to a star shows just how important Wayne had been to the studio.

Other arcane sidelights of studio finances came out. RKO had loaned Wayne $100,000 at 2 percent interest so he could buy his house; the loan was being repaid by monthly deductions from his salary. Wayne also testified that he was carrying about $8,120 in bad debts, among them loans to Bob Steele and Grant Withers, which he didn't expect to be repaid.

Wayne regularly attended the court hearings, mostly maintaining a stoic facade except one time when Chata's attorney said to the judge, "But your honor, what if I can prove that John Wayne is a liar?" Wayne turned red, smashed his fist down on the guard railing and partially rose from his seat. After a few moments, he left the courtroom for a cigarette.

By July, Chata was indulging in exotic divorce theater. With her claimed "unlimited charge accounts" long gone, and her car repossessed over an unpaid liquor and grocery bill of $2,367, she drove a battered pickup truck to a court date. "Why doesn't someone ask her if the only time she ever drives this truck is to court?" Wayne asked reporters during a break. Then a little girl put a note in his pocket. It was from her mother, asking him to consider the child for a part in a movie.

Under questioning, Wayne talked about his encounter with a stripper, which led to the infamous hickey. "We were making the picture *Bullfighter*. One night it was arranged to go to Mr. Boetticher's home. It was so-called stag — the only one I ever went to in six years of marriage, incidentally. We had drinks. A man sat down at the piano and out came a strip tease girl. It was a very dull affair. Armida [the stripper] did not speak English and she was not having a good time. I was sitting on the sofa talking to [Andrew] McLaglen and she came around behind and bit me on the cheek. I stood up and showed anger the best I could. I said, 'What can I tell Chata?' They said, 'Tell her the truth. We were all here.' "

Wayne said he then went to the Tail o' the Cock restaurant, had a sandwich, and went home and told his wife what happened. " 'That's pretty strange,' she said."

Chata admitted in court that out of $89,613 she and Wayne spent in the first six months of 1952, $56,103 went exclusively for her needs. There was another hearing in which Chata's demand for $9,350 a month was reduced to $1,100 a month. Likewise, she asked for $40,000 for her lawyers. She got $10,000.

After the session, Wayne smiled and signed autographs for the teenagers that had packed the courtroom and applauded the verdict, while Chata sobbed as she drove away from the courthouse in a Cadillac that had mysteriously replaced the pickup truck.

Judge William R. McKay was clearly not enamored of either side. "From the fact that this preliminary hearing took 15 days," he said, "it can be surmised that the trial may be a very long one."

Chata went on to claim that Wayne had an affair with Gail Russell while he was shooting *Angel and the Badman.* Chata said she nearly shot him when she mistook him for a burglar when he staggered in after a night with Russell. The only thing that stopped her, she said, was that her mother recognized Wayne. (Mamacita was still living with them.) Wayne testified under oath that he and his wife had struggled over the .45 she owned.

The charge against Russell particularly infuriated Wayne, because he felt she was blameless. "I took her home from a set party because she had no other way of getting home. . . . Since when is it a crime to be gallant?" Russell's version of the same event: Wayne and James Edward Grant had given her a $500 bonus for her work on *Angel and the Badman.* "John took me home after the party. He had celebrated too much and apologized to my mother for his condition. He called a taxi. My brother helped him into the taxi and he left about 1 A.M. The next morning he sent my mother a box of flowers with a note of apology for any inconvenience he might have caused her." Russell said she was considering a lawsuit against Chata.

Wayne testified that Chata regularly drank herself into a stupor and made his and everybody else's life miserable. Wayne said that he had gotten a call at four in the morning. "Duke, please get up here and get your wife, she is dead drunk." When he did nothing, he got another call at 5:30.

"Duke will you come over here and get this woman out of my house?"

Wayne also testified that he had found out that Nicky Hilton had spent a week at his house. Entered into evidence was a sheet of paper on which Chata had doodled "Esperanza Hilton," "Chata and Nick," "Chata Hilton," and "Mrs. Nick Hilton." When he was asked about his reactions to his wife's doodlings, he replied, "I went into the bathroom and vomited."

Things were clearly accelerating toward mutual assured destruction, which seemed fine with both parties. "I should have my day in court," Wayne told reporters. "She has done all she can do. If the case was settled now, people would think it was because of what she has said."

Finally, on October 28, mutual victory was declared, and both parties were granted a divorce, because, said the exhausted judge, "it seemed eminently proper." The divorce terms were heavy. Wayne was obligated to pay Chata a total of $470,000 — $150,000 up front, $20,000 to clear various debts, and $50,000 a year for six years. Chata signed quit-claims on two homes — Wayne's residence at 4750 Louise Avenue in Encino and the house Chata had been living in at 4735 Tyrone Avenue in Van Nuys.

Shortly after the divorce was granted, Mary St. John called Tom Kane one Sunday and asked if he had any plans. It seemed that Wayne's lawyers had worked out a lump sum payment to Chata of $375,000 that would wipe out all his obligations. They needed someone they could trust to lug the cash down to Mexico. A couple of other people went instead of Kane, but that money, and the savings it represented of $100,000, was the end of

Wayne's relationship with Chata, who continued drinking until her early death in March 1961.

Tom Kane wondered about Wayne's reaction to his ex-wife's death and asked George Coleman, Wayne's driver. Coleman reported that Wayne never said anything about her death — there was no response whatever.

Wayne's vulnerability to an inappropriate, obviously predatory female like Chata when he was already middle-aged indicates a basic naïveté in his character. That character was formed early, as was his belief system. He was a hard-smoking, hard-drinking man by college, a conservative by the Depression, and his attitudes never altered by a millimeter. He tried marijuana but it didn't do anything for him, tried opium but it didn't affect him.

After the divorce from Chata was final in October 1954, Wayne married Pilar a month later. They would have three children: Aissa in 1956, John Ethan in 1962, and Marisa in 1966. Their mother was over twenty-five years younger than their father.

By the time *Hondo* finished shooting, public interest in 3-D had begun to fall off. Among other things, it was very difficult to maintain precise synchronization between two projectors running two reels of film, and if there was as much as a frame or two difference between the two projectors, the result would be audience eyestrain and headaches. Further complicating matters was the September 1953 premiere of *The Robe* in CinemaScope, an anamorphic widescreen process that didn't replicate 3-D, but did excite audiences the way the 70mm projection of *The Big Trail* had more than twenty years before.

Hondo was quickly edited and trade-screened in November. A studio minion reported back to Jack Warner: "*Hondo* screening last night drew excellent reaction. . . . These people plainly enjoyed the film and their appreciation and the good word they gave the picture at its conclusion seemed genuine. Picture played well throughout with no out of place laughs. [Geraldine] Page being accepted okay."

The night of the *Hondo* preview Wayne, Bob Fellows, Jimmy Grant, and Tom Kane were at Lucey's restaurant, adjacent to Paramount. It became apparent that Wayne was no longer listening to the conversation. Everybody followed Wayne's gaze and saw a teenaged Mike Wayne escorting his mother into the restaurant.

"That's the finest woman I've ever known," Wayne said. He would never forgive himself for selfishly blundering into divorce, especially considering how his second marriage turned out.

In order to maximize revenue, Warners announced that *Hondo* would be available in conventional prints as well as 3-D. *Hondo* was released at the end of November 1953, and was an enormous hit in both formats. Produced for $1.32 million, it returned worldwide rentals of $5.9 million — one of the highest-grossing films of the year.

Contrary to the general belief that it played most of its engagements in conventional 2-D, *Hondo* seems to have been among the last 3-D films to be widely exhibited in that format. Until February 1954, almost all bookings of *Hondo* were in 3-D; after that, it began playing smaller suburban theaters and drive-ins that were not equipped for

3-D. It was the second-highest-grossing 3-D film of the 1950s, after Warners' *House of Wax.*

The film begins with an arresting, quintessential Wayne image: a lone man carrying a saddle, accompanied only by his dog, walking out of the desert. Wayne is lean and looks spectacular. ("I was physically and mentally at my best when I was 45," he would say decades later.)

Hondo Lane is an Army scout who has an uneasy relationship with creatures with two legs, a marginally easier one with creatures with four legs. "Sam's independent," he says of the dog. "He doesn't need anybody. I want him to stay that way. It's a good way to be." Self-reliance is the keynote of his belief system; he's a libertarian: "I let people do what they want to do," he says.

Hondo doesn't own Sam, but has more of a partnership with him. He appraises the Indians as having "a good way of life, but it's gone now." End of discussion. You get the feeling that if Sam were to get a better offer, it would be fine with Hondo.

But *Hondo* is also the story of how a man who thinks he doesn't need anybody realizes that he just might need a family. He finds one ready-made after he has no choice but to kill the husband of Angie Lowe, a sturdily unglamorous frontier wife.

"I am fully aware that I am a homely woman, Mr. Lane," says Geraldine Page (playing Angie), who wasn't homely at all, just not a prodigious beauty, which in Hollywood means you're homely. The line might seem cruel if it wasn't part of the overall clinical nature of Hondo — the character as well as the film. It's why the film is probably the best movie Wayne ever made that wasn't directed by John Ford or Howard Hawks.

Page, who is as out of her element as her character, is one of the reasons the film works as well as it does. If Maureen O'Hara had come striding furiously out of a sod hut, the narrative would have been obvious, but Page gives the film an emotional credibility that would have been lacking if the part was more conventionally cast.

James Edward Grant's primary flaw as a writer was a lack of subtlety — he tended to clobber story or character points with a sledgehammer — but the script for *Hondo* is not just lean and epigrammatic, it's also graceful. Grant expertly communicates the mingled attraction and repulsion Angie feels for the Indian chief Vittorio, played by the Australian actor Michael Pate. He also captures the respect between Hondo and Vittorio — two men bound by a ferocious, mutually shared sense of honor.

The film runs a lean eighty-three minutes — a short running time minimized reel changes, which was important in a dicey system like early 3-D. The problems that plagued the production are occasionally obvious — some shots have a fuzzy focus, and the heat of the location was made worse by fill lights used to fully illuminate faces for 3-D effect.

Shortly after *Hondo* was released, *Mad* magazine came out with a parody of the movie. Bob Morrison, Tom Kane, and Mike Wayne were sitting in the office chortling at the magazine when Wayne walked by. He looked at the magazine and said, "There's nothing funny about this. You guys make your living on western films."

So much for *Mad* magazine; so much for laughter. Wayne generally enjoyed poking fun at his own image, but could get touchy when other people did it. "He was very tenacious about protecting his identity as a western, macho he-man," said the photographer Phil Stern, who became a good friend for a number of years. "He would not allow anyone to make fun of that except himself."

As part of the promotion for *Hondo,* Wayne made what seems to have been his first extensive television appearance other than a brief bit on *Art Linkletter's House Party.* Wayne appeared on *The Colgate Comedy Hour* in October 1953. The show was a big-budget, all-star spectacular with revolving hosts: Eddie Cantor, Jimmy Durante, Donald O'Connor, Martin and Lewis, Abbott and Costello.

Wayne's episode is gleefully under-rehearsed, rather in the manner of the later Dean Martin show. Wayne comes on and looks thoughtful while a voice-over tells us his thoughts à la *Strange Interlude:* "Why does [Durante] want to see me? Probably wants me to be on his television show. Why did Gary Cooper have to be out of town?"

Later in the skit, after a long pause, Durante asks him, "Who's got the next line, you or me?" Wayne breaks up and says, "You! We gotta work together."

Throughout the show, Wayne carries on manfully even though he seems to have only the vaguest idea of what he's supposed to be doing, which turns out to be singing a little, then switching his body language to the feminine when his voice becomes a soprano. The critics weren't impressed — *Variety*'s review said, "[Wayne] was unsure of himself and awkward in his lines and movements but Durante covered his nervousness by making a few fumbles with him. But with JD a goofed line is always good for a big laugh."

During that same trip to New York, he made an appearance on the Milton Berle show, during which he insisted that he was not one of those actors who go on TV just to plug a new movie. Every time he turned around, there was a big electric sign on his pants flashing HONDO.

"It got big laughs, but I felt embarrassed, kind of humiliated" said Wayne in retrospect. "I thought I had made a fool of myself. I felt I was basically a movie actor. I didn't belong in television." Wayne didn't feel secure playing comedy unless he had rehearsed it with a director he trusted. That, and TV's habit of burying the director in the control room a mile away from the actors, unnerved Wayne.

Besides that, there was the issue of prestige; at this point, TV had the aura of the B movies in which he had been mired for a long, long decade.

Wayne-Fellows was set up as a complete studio operation. Aside from associate-producer/brother-of-the-star Bob Morrison, the company had its own art director (Al Ybarra), production manager (Nate Edwards), and cameramen (Archie Stout and William Clothier).

Clothier had worked for Bill Wellman as far back as *Wings* in 1927. John Ford had offered Clothier a lieutenant's commission in his unit during the war, but Clothier had taken a captaincy in the Air Force instead, where he shot *The Memphis Belle* for William Wyler. Unusually, Ford didn't hold the rejection against Clothier and hired him to shoot second unit on *Fort Apache,* where he told him he was "too good to be a second cameraman."

Wayne would hire Clothier as a cameraman for

reasons both personal and professional. "Bill Clothier was like my father," said Michael Wayne. "He was independent, wasn't a joiner. For a long time he didn't belong to [the American Society of Cinematographers], and to get nominated for an Oscar you had to be a member. But Bill could do anything you wanted. He could get beautiful shots *and* keep to a schedule. A lot of cameramen take days to get their shots, but that's not filmmaking, that's waiting for shots."

In 1953, Wayne told reporters that in three years' time he intended to be producing four pictures a year and starring in only one. He was even signing contract players — James Arness, for instance. By that October, he was angling to sign Ronald Colman to star in *The High and the Mighty*.

Wayne had adopted some of John Ford's production grace notes for his own; as on Ford's films, Danny Borzage would serenade the cast and crew with his accordion during breaks. Otherwise, Wayne demanded a high standard of professionalism. "The men around me are doers, not talkers," he said. "I won't tolerate a free loader." Unless, of course, the freeloader happened to be named Bob Steele, Grant Withers, or Bruce Cabot, who could turn the Wayne-Fellows offices into something resembling fraternity row.

Wayne quickly found out that producing was a lot of work, not to mention a lot of hassles, most of which couldn't be delegated. When *Plunder of the Sun* got under way, Bob Fellows told him, "We've got a little problem here with [Glenn] Ford." (Wayne was always having problems with people named Ford . . .)

It seems that Ford had asked, "What do you people plan on giving me for a present when the picture's over?" This was an ominous question coming from a star who had a reputation for being extremely tight with his money. "What's he mean?" asked Wayne, who came from a tradition that said your paycheck was the only gift that mattered.

Fellows went on to explain that Ford wanted some sort of offering indicating the beloved status he had within the company, and Fellows had a sinking feeling that it was supposed to be a major offering. "Well," sighed Wayne, "we don't want to start a picture with an unhappy actor. Ask him what he wants. Give it to him."

Fellows went back to Ford, holding his breath during the conversation. What if he wanted a yacht? But Ford had decided he wanted a 16mm camera for home movies.

After the picture was finished, Wayne-Fellows had to send somebody over to Ford's house to get his wardrobe back. Evidently the camera was insufficient.

The money continued to roll in . . . and roll right back out. Besides the Culver City Hotel, Bö Roos and Wayne now owned a piece of a tennis club in Beverly Hills and some oil wells in Texas. Wayne also started a shrimp business in Panama with Roberto Arias, the husband of Margot Fonteyn, and there was an import-export business in Peru, called Pasador — Spanish for shoestring.

On those infrequent occasions when he wasn't making a movie, Wayne lived a life of relaxed conviviality. At John Ford's house, there would be parties, and Wayne would have to sing for his supper, which was the occasion for much merriment because Wayne had to pretend he couldn't sing.

"He had to sing purposely off-key," said Maureen O'Hara, "because that's what Ford would enjoy. And everybody would scream with laughter. Duke would sing 'Mary's a Grand Old Name,' and seeing him stand there hat in hand, with Ford making signs to listen for whenever he went off-key was all part of the game.

"Mary Ford would roll her eyes to the sky and say, 'Lord, we're gonna have an all-Irish night.' She enjoyed it but always pretended not to, and overfed us all. Mary was a lovely, lovely, lovely lady. She took a lot of guff from him. Most every time I made a film for Ford, my name would be 'Mary.' "

"Jack Warner was a very contradictory kind of character," remembered the director Vincent Sherman, who worked at Warner Bros. for more than twenty years. "On the one hand, he would make poor jokes about everything and seem to be not very deep about anything. Jack was the clown of the family and they didn't respect him. They liked him, but they didn't really respect him. On the other hand, he had a good nose about what made a good story for a good film. In many ways, he was very clever."

There was a great rivalry between Jack and Harry Warner, which was amplified by the death of their brother Sam in 1927. Sam had been equally respected by both brothers, but with him gone there was no one to be the arbiter, and Jack and Harry settled down to a war of attrition that lasted for more than a quarter century. Eventually, Jack euchred Harry out of the studio by negotiating a deal whereby they would both retire, then buying both his and Harry's stock in a backdoor deal.

"Jack Warner was a rude, crude moneymaking fool," snapped James Garner, who worked for him for years and heartily disliked him. "In most things, he had bad taste. He invited me to go to the Oscars and sit at his table. My wife is sitting next to him and he starts telling dirty jokes. He had a filthy mouth. So I got my wife and moved to another table. Bill Orr, his son-in-law, who ran television production for him, was at the next table and I told Orr that if his father-in-law ever again asked me to go to a function with him, I wasn't going to go. 'And,' I said, 'if you're afraid to tell him, I'll tell him.' "

Harry Warner's hobby was real estate — he bought a lot of property in the San Fernando Valley. Jack's hobbies were horses and girls. "There were times when Jack would reveal his humanity," said Vincent Sherman. "During one of the labor strikes, I remember he said to me, 'You can't blame these guys. They come in, they bring their box of tools, they work hard, they don't make much money and they see us come to work in limousines and make big money. You have to expect them to resent it.'

"Once, Jack said, 'I don't know why I go to all this trouble fighting with actors. My brother is in real estate, makes more money than I do and doesn't argue with anybody.' "

Jack never found much to argue about with John Wayne. Wayne showed up sober and ready for work. He made his movies on time and more or less on budget, and they made money. But another part of the bond between the two men was their politics. When Roosevelt's New Deal had been ascendant, Jack had been happy to run with the nimble foxes of the New Deal, but in the early 1950s Jack was happy to mount a horse and chase those same foxes.

"Once," said Vincent Sherman, "Jack called me into his office during the Red Scare and told me that one of the committees had questioned him. I can't prove it, but I think it's one of the reasons he let me go. You were on a gray list and he was trying to get rid of everybody that was on it, even if the only thing you had done was vote for Franklin Roosevelt."

Hedda Hopper was still acting as the Madame Defarge of the Red Scare, castigating her ideological opponents and coddling her friends. Hopper's own belief system was revealed when Jackie Robinson was scheduled for an interview at her house, and she yelled out to her cook, "Maude, if you see a nigger around the house, don't be scared. It's only Jackie Robinson!" Robinson, who had arrived a few minutes early for his appointment, overheard her. A few years after that, she said that the protests against Disney's paternalist — at best — *Song of the South* were the result of "several Commie groups," and she led a successful effort to get a special Academy Award for James Baskett, who played Uncle Remus in the film.

By this time, there was something of a schism in the Motion Picture Alliance. Leading one side was Hopper. On the other was Wayne. The screenwriter John Lee Mahin was a lifelong conservative and a member of the Alliance, and he put it this way: "You can't get into any political situation without attracting a few crackpots, and we had our share of those. . . . I can remember the people that found a Communist behind every tree and under every bush, and it seems that half our time was spent calming these people down, saying, 'Well, no, he's not a Communist, he's a liberal — a good, honest liberal. And there's nothing wrong with that.'

"Duke, of course, was very liberal in his attitude toward people's ideas. He would listen to anyone and draw his own conclusions. He came under attack, of course, because he was the president of the organization, but he was always the voice of reason and responsibility in the group."

Mahin fingered the extremists in the Alliance as Ward Bond and Jimmy Grant. When John Ford was making *The Long Gray Line* in West Point, Ward Bond would head over to a bar across the street from the location and watch the Army-McCarthy hearings. Bond knew McCarthy, and, according to Mahin, Wayne had Bond pass a message from him to the senator: "You're going to have to name names because you're just throwing out accusations and innuendo and not producing any facts, and you're making everybody look bad."

"I personally think McCarthy did more harm to the anti-Communist movement than anybody ever could have on the face of the earth," said Mahin. "He was a fool, just an absolute fool."

"Duke really went into the work of the organization," remembered Borden Chase. "He became president [and] . . . he was no *front*. Duke had guts. We had a split in the group — The once-a-communist-always-a-communist group and the group that thought it was ridiculous to destroy some of those, who, say, joined the party in the '30s in Nazi Germany. Duke and I were in the latter group."

Ward Bond was still acting as a clearing agent

for HUAC. "My agent at the time told me I had to go up and talk to Ward Bond," recalled Vincent Sherman.

I got his address and made an appointment. He kept me waiting almost an hour. I told him that I'd never been a member of the Communist party, that I was a left-leaning Roosevelt Democrat. Perhaps I subscribed to some of the same causes, because I thought the cause was right, but not because it was communist in origin.

And Bond listened and said, "Well, it's not only that. We've got quite a few things against you."

"Well," I said, "tell me what they are. I can tell you yes or no as to what I believed."

He went on to say that one of the members of the party had said I had a great deal of influence, and that "you may not have been a card-carrying communist, but you had a lot of influence in the top echelon." And I said that was ridiculous.

I didn't get to know Bond too well; he didn't behave very nicely, to me or anybody else.

John Ford's place in all this is hard to ascertain. Ford loved Bond because he was the designated class clown, but he also thought Bond was on the dim side. Vincent Sherman, who knew Ford through the Directors Guild, said, "He was a very independent Irishman. I had the feeling that he didn't really give a damn about politics. I certainly never heard him make any pro-McCarthy remarks, or anything like that.

"I also had the feeling that Wayne wasn't that much in favor of some of the things that were going on; I think he was in over his head and knew it. I knew Wayne a little, and his attitudes were more liberal than many people thought. We were introduced by Howard Hawks, and I always got on well with Hawks, who was also right-wing, but not active about it. He was a good director and a straight shooter."

During all this, Wayne publicly insisted that all the Alliance was doing was promoting a different point of view than "the excessively liberal one." Wayne estimated the membership of the Alliance at about two thousand, and said that the group had no interest in being the "policeman of the industry. We merely want to inform the people how we stand."

Budd Boetticher said that Wayne went so far as to have some of his co-workers vetted. "They were really American," he said. "The only people they were against were the guys that weren't in their group — everybody. The Jews, the Catholics, the Blacks, whatever — they were wrong, these guys were right. They fly the America flag and blow the bugle. And I mean, they were brutal.

"Of course, I never had anything to do with that . . . I only lasted two days as a Tenderfoot Scout. I never join anything."

Boetticher went on to tell a story about a 6 A.M. phone call from Wayne. " 'Bood? The Duke.' I said, 'Hi, Duke, how are you?' He said, 'You're clean.' I said, 'I'm what?' He said, 'You're not a Communist.' I said, 'You son of a bitch. I hope it cost you $20,000 to find that out.' "

In later years, Wayne would say that "I think those blacklisted people should have been sent over to Russia. They'd have been taken care of over there and if the Commies ever won over here, why hell, those guys would be the first ones they'd

403

take care of — after me."

A friend of Wayne's who sounds a lot like John Ford offered perhaps the pithiest summation of his politics: "Hell, Duke didn't know anything about the menace of Communism. All he knew was that some of his friends were against them."

CHAPTER TWELVE

William Wellman and John Wayne were united by vast stores of enthusiasm — each of them could get worked up over a story, an actor, a movie — their own or somebody else's. Wayne was particularly gung ho about *The High and the Mighty,* a gripping story about a plane bound from Honolulu to San Francisco that develops a cascading series of mechanical problems culminating in a burned-out engine and the likelihood of running out of gas over the Pacific.

Wayne originally wanted Spencer Tracy for the part of the older copilot who brings the plane in against all odds, but the trade papers announced that MGM wanted $500,000 for Tracy's services. This was a grossly inflated figure — MGM had just accepted $250,000, about double Tracy's actual salary, for a loan-out to Fox for *Broken Lance.* Wellman said that he and Tracy had lunch, after which they shook hands on the deal. Then Tracy backed out of the picture.

It's far more likely that Tracy simply didn't want to work with Wellman — the two men had had a fistfight nearly twenty years earlier over a crack Wellman made about Tracy's onetime lover Loretta Young. It's also possible that Tracy was uneasy about working for Wayne, who may have been too closely associated with his Loretta Young period.

Wayne then tried unsuccessfully for Gary Cooper or Henry Fonda, after which he decided to play the part himself. Wayne cast Robert Cummings for the copilot role, more or less because Cummings actually was a pilot, but Wellman wanted Robert Stack and Wayne acquiesced. William Boyd turned down a part, and MGM wouldn't loan out Keenan Wynn and Lionel Barrymore, so parts that had been intended for them were played by the less expensive alternatives of Sidney Blackmer and Wayne's old pal Paul Fix.

In fact, the list of people who turned down parts in *The High and the Mighty* was extensive. Wellman took runs at eminent actresses such as Joan Crawford, Bette Davis, Ida Lupino, Barbara Stanwyck, Ginger Rogers, and Dorothy McGuire. Mostly, they rejected the film because the parts were too small. Claire Trevor and Jan Sterling got the jobs.

The High and the Mighty had one great attraction as far as Jack Warner was concerned: it was going to be economical. Eighty percent of the film took place inside an airplane, and the exteriors were almost all second unit.

William Clothier was the cameraman on the aerial scenes, and captured the culminating shot of the runway lights forming a cross. "I didn't know what I had until I saw it through my lens," Clothier remembered.

It was a pretty good shot. Two nights later, Bill Wellman calls on the phone. "I have just seen

406

the greatest goddamn shot that was ever made for any goddamn picture in the world."

"Which shot is that?"

"That shot coming into the airfield! It's going to make our picture! These people have come across the ocean, they're flying on the vapor in the gas tanks and all at once the airfield opens up in the form of a cross." He raved for five minutes. Then Duke got on the line. "Bill, it's the damndest thing I've ever seen."

Playing the ingenue was a young actress named Karen Sharpe, whose credits consisted of a couple of five-day wonders at Monogram, the most successful of which was *Bomba and the Jungle Girl*. "Wellman directed my test," remembered Sharpe. "I was very prepared, and we shot the scene, where I think I'm pregnant. Now, if Bill Wellman didn't like you, everybody down the block knew about it. And if he did like you, the same people knew about that, too. And when we finished the scene, he said, 'My God, Karen, where have you been? You're it. This girl is fantastic!' He never even looked at the footage."

Sharpe remembered that *The High and the Mighty* "was a Wellman film all the way down the line. Duke may have been producing, but he was like any other actor on the set. He knew his lines, stepped in, and did it. He was very professional. I noticed that when I was working, he would come and stand close to the camera and watch me." Soon after the film wrapped, Wayne signed Sharpe to a contract.

A young actor named William Campbell was featured as a brash young aviator who holds Wayne's character in contempt. It was a difficult part for Campbell to play, simply because he was in awe of Wayne, and he had particular trouble with a scene where he had to humiliate Wayne for being old and passé. "I thought to myself, *Jesus Christ, I'm going to be tongue-lashing John Wayne.* And we did it in very close quarters. It just went phenomenally well. . . . When Wayne worked with you, he never would be, or could be, threatened by any other actor, unlike some others.

"Some actors weave a scene to make their character more important. Wayne never did that. He knew what he was doing, always knew his lines. . . . He had a problem in that he was so big, so overpowering. It didn't matter who had the authority in a scene; Wayne was always bigger. That's why he always seemed so comfortable lounging in the background, letting others have all the good lines. Inevitably the eye is drawn to him."

Wayne was worried about his own performance, but Wellman wasn't. "Do you mean to tell me you don't think you were good in that?" Wellman asked after Wayne requested another take. "You couldn't ask for anything better."

Robert Stack remembered that "Wellman scared the shit out of me; he scared the shit out of everybody. But he was a marshmallow. He was working on a scene with Doe Avedon, and he said to her, 'Jesus Christ, can't you walk straight?' 'Mr. Wellman,' she said, 'you've got me so scared my knees won't work!' And he said, 'Oh, don't take me seriously.' Wellman was never cruel, but he kept enough pressure on me, particularly in the scenes in the cockpit, for the realism of the situation to always come through."

Sharpe remembered the picture as "a very happy

set, except for the fact that people were scared of Wellman because he could be very boisterous one way or the other." Wayne had Wellman's director's chair embroidered with the ironic words, "Sweet William."

Wellman had a habit of photographing the first rehearsal, and a lot of times there was never a take beyond that. "One take and that was it," said Sharpe. "He loved everything I did, and every shot I was in was the first take." One critic visiting the set called Wellman the fastest director since W. S. Van Dyke II, and, among A list directors it was probably true.

Wellman was gung ho about the picture, about CinemaScope, about WarnerColor. "If we're gonna make 'em bad, we're gonna make 'em bad with everything there is," he bellowed. This gusto explains how Wellman was able to shoot a very long film (147 minutes) in little more than six weeks, from November 25, 1953, to January 11, 1954, including a week in San Francisco, the Goldwyn studios for interiors, followed by two nights of wrap-up work at the Glendale Airport.

Pilar was hanging around the set, and Wayne asked Sharpe if Pilar could stay in her dressing room. Sharpe was from Texas and had numerous Hispanic friends, so she and Pilar got along famously.

As the picture went into the cutting room, Wayne supervised the editing himself, eventually cutting five close-ups of himself that he thought were unnecessary. Warners was very high on the picture, and so was Wayne. Billy Wilkerson of *The Hollywood Reporter* caught Wayne and Wellman at their best after the two men watched the final version of *The High and the Mighty* for the first time.

His description of the conversation captures the bond between the two men, as well as the personal qualities that enabled them to sustain forty-year careers.

Wilkerson ran into them at a restaurant and they adjourned to Wayne's house, where the conversation lasted until 3:30 in the morning. Wilkerson didn't "remember a more entertaining and inspiring evening since the old days of Henry's on [Hollywood] Boulevard, when most of the picture-makers used to sit around at night and talk — pictures.

"Both Wayne and Wellman have been around a long time, both have been successful. However, from their conversations you would think they were two kids just starting out in the business, fighting and pushing every minute to get ahead, revealing in their seeming amazement the wonderful accomplishments of others and hoping to match those accomplishments. They had praise for every name brought into the gab and, above all, praise for the business that made it possible for unknowns to become great personages in such a short span. They had logical excuses for some failures — theirs and others — with never a knock, never derision, *always* enthusiasm."

When *The High and the Mighty* was released in May 1954, the critics were impressed. *The Hollywood Reporter* called it "highly entertaining, widely appealing and handsomely mounted . . . one of the great pictures of our time." The studio gave it a lavish premiere at the Egyptian Theatre in Hollywood. Wayne invited Karen Sharpe, who was thrilled to be the date of Tab Hunter. "I met Tab for the first time in the limousine on the way to the premiere. When we got out of the car, the fans went nuts for him, and he introduced me to the world of Hollywood premieres. I had no idea how lucky all this was. And at the end, when the lights went down and the movie started, Tab looked at me and said, 'Loved meeting you, I gotta go. I'm making a film and I have to get back to the studio.' So Robert Fellows escorted me to the party at Ciro's, where I sat between him and Jack Warner."

Wellman's directorial gusto led him astray, and the forcefulness he usually brought to scenes of elemental struggle or combat was pitched a bit too high for a character-driven emotional drama. What *The High and the Mighty* needed was some of Howard Hawks's terseness. Wayne stands out because everybody else is lunging for an Oscar nomination and he's playing a calm professional in a calm, professional manner. The dramatic problem at the core of the film is basic — the plane either has enough fuel to get to its destination or it doesn't — but the script invents personal crises for each and every character, which doesn't ratchet up the tension so much as get in the way.

It's essentially a decent blood-and-thunder melodrama whose primary attributes come down to William Clothier's aerial photography and Dimitri Tiomkin's thundering score, which even lends a spiritual dimension to the proceedings. But commercially speaking *The High and the Mighty* was the right movie at the right time and one of the biggest hits of its year — a cost of $1.4 million, world rentals of $8.1 million, and a lot of money in the pockets of Wayne, Fellows, and Bill Wellman, who had a third of Wayne-Fellows' profits. With the exception of a single TV broadcast in the late 1970s, Wayne kept the film out of circulation for decades, which gave the film the patina of a lost classic that it didn't really deserve.

The huge back-to-back hits of *Hondo* and *The High and the Mighty* put Wayne at the top of his profession, not just as an actor, but as a producer. The only problem to be found in their first two years of Wayne-Fellows' operation was that the company was having trouble controlling costs. Warners had advanced $750,000 to make *Big Jim McLain,* which ended up costing $825,544; likewise, *Island in the Sky* cost $66,815 more than the $900,000 Warners had advanced, despite the fact that Wellman had shot the picture in twenty-six days — a full ten days under schedule. After four starring pictures (*Big Jim McLain, Island in the Sky, Hondo, The High and the Mighty,* and the non-Wayne film *Plunder of the Sun*), Wayne-Fellows had spent $258,859 in excess of studio advances.

Fellows explained to Jack Warner that part of the problem was that they had no prior experience in figuring out their overhead costs, which they had concluded ran about $100,000 yearly. Also, their ambitious production plans meant that the pictures had been hurled into production without accurate budgets, which accounted for the average 7 percent overrun.

On the other hand, although Wayne-Fellows had no obligation to make two consecutive Wayne pictures, or to keep him exclusive, they had made three Waynes in a row, and he had refused all other studio offers. Not only that, but on one picture Wayne had cut his salary. (Fellows had been drawing only $21,000 salary per picture.)

All this was fixable and more or less part of the movie business. Besides, the profits from *Hondo* and *The High and the Mighty* obliterated Jack

Warner's concerns. But a Wayne-Fellows production called *Ring of Fear* was a real problem, and so was the emerging alcoholic spiral of Jimmy Grant.

Ring of Fear was a circus movie with the head-spinning cast of Clyde Beatty, Mickey Spillane, and Pat O'Brien. Spillane was a crude, bumptious hack who liked to sit around the Wayne-Fellows offices kibitzing. When he noticed some Hemingway, Faulkner, and Dos Passos books on the shelves, he said, "These guys are all bums." Only half joking, he began reeling off his sales figures compared to Hemingway and Faulkner and triumphantly concluded by saying, "I've sold more than all those guys put together."

Spillane had gotten lucky with Mike Hammer, but that wasn't enough; he wanted to be a movie star too, and Jimmy Grant took him on. "We felt by using James Edward Grant we would get a good script and a good job of direction for bargain prices — we got neither," complained Fellows. The studio advanced $677,613 for the picture, and Grant spent $706,701. That wasn't the primary problem — for their money, Warners had gotten a picture that was unreleasable.

Fellows described the job Grant had done as "a bad job, or no job at all." As Fellows wrote to Wayne, "his behavior has shaken . . . confidence in our judgment and made a dent of alarming proportions in the dignity and respect we had heretofore enjoyed in the industry. We have become the target of a certain amount of ridicule." Fellows went on to point out that they had given Grant 5 percent of company profits for "finding available stories and ideas and proposing such stories and ideas be acquired, and performing

413

such other services as the corporation may request of you. None of these services has he performed."

Grant had 3 percent of *Big Jim McLain* and 5 percent of *Ring of Fear.* Fellows suggested discontinuing Grant's vice presidency and his overall 5 percent of company profits. Instead, give him 5 percent or 10 percent of *Hondo,* and pay him on a per job basis thereafter. Grant knew he was in trouble and responded with a letter to Wayne that he admitted was a rambling mess. He defended *Ring of Fear,* saying, "The picture may be bad but it is not nearly as bad as Bob has convinced you [it is.]" He went on to say that the only two pictures Wayne had loved in the cutting room were *The Fighting Kentuckian* and *Island in the Sky* — "both failures," which wasn't really true. He accused Fellows of being a "grade B Svengali" and said that if Wayne followed through on the plan to take away Grant's title and percentage, "the man I thought was my best friend [would be] giving a perfect imitation of my worst enemy."

Wayne responded to Grant like a big brother exhausted by an errant sibling. "I feel that you have not been abused, but pampered," he wrote, before accusing Grant of never finishing scripts. In twenty-three months with the company, Grant had doctored *Big Jim McLain* and written *Hondo* — the only two acceptable properties he had been connected with. He had talked Wayne-Fellows into buying *White Gold,* a story that had been done as a silent movie by its author, William K. Howard, a once promising director undone by alcoholism. Two years later, nothing had been done with the story.

Wayne pointed out that Grant had five months to polish the script of *McLain* before they started

414

shooting and was still writing scenes the day they finished the movie. Why? "You were out playing with dames and getting drunk."

On *Hondo,* Wayne judged Grant's first draft to be "fair," with about five great scenes, but then he dropped the ball, never writing an ending or a payoff scene for the girl. Wayne further pointed out that he had gotten Grant $25,000 from Warners and $35,000 from RKO for jobs that didn't even figure into the money that the company had paid him.

Wrapping up his summation to the jury, Wayne said that Grant had received $184,359 in two years, not counting a salary for his secretary, and in that time he had written a couple of non–Wayne-Fellows scripts that went on the market and didn't sell. Wayne concluded by writing, "You haven't the talent of John Ford nor the charm of Huston. You're no fun to be with any more because you're bitter and vulgar and uninteresting in your conversation."

As castigating letters go, it's a small masterpiece — rigorously logical and well argued, a reminder that Wayne's early ambition had been to be a lawyer and a strong indication that he would have been a good one.

Two days later, Grant wrote Wayne a rambling reply. He had spent seven weeks on *Sands of Iwo Jima,* and Yates had only paid him for two, etc. He reiterated his fears that once word got out that he'd been pulled off *Ring of Fear* he'd be dead in the industry, and again said that Wayne was being swayed by the evil machinations of Bob Fellows, who had become Grant's designated bête noire.

That same day Wayne, his patience clearly at an end, wrote back to Grant saying that "You take

415

up too much of the time that should be spent in thinking of our business." Robert Fellows then wrote Wayne a long letter that basically said, "It's him or it's me." Grant had evidently compared himself to William K. Howard and Fellows thought that there might be something to the analogy. "Liquor got to Bill — and it seems to have pinned Jimmy down too. . . . Jimmy, like all hack writers, will work only when he is hungry. Creative writers do not kiss ass around Hollywood, sucking the life blood out of stars and friends: they go to out of the way places and spend a year or two or three writing. Often they miss, sometimes they hit — but always they WRITE. I for one am sick and tired of this horseshit of Jimmy being a creative writer. . . . It is my opinion that right now Jimmy is a sick miserable little man. It is further my opinion that he is mentally sick and needs the kind of help neither of us can give him."

And then Wayne caught Grant in a lie. Grant had said he only had liquor on the set of *Ring of Fire* one night. Wayne produced bills proving that liquor had been provided for sixteen nights on location in Phoenix, not to mention a $205 liquor bill at the hotel where the company was staying. Wayne followed that up with a memo noting that A. B. Guthrie, the Pulitzer Prize–winning author of *The Way West,* had stopped in to pick up a check for a story he was working on for Wayne-Fellows and told Wayne that he had been unable to work with Grant for three weeks because he was "very disturbed and drunk."

The company drafted a severance agreement giving Grant 5 percent of the net profits of *Hondo.* He would be advanced $500 a week, said sum to be deducted from his percentages, and the company gave him back the rights to the story he had been working on. Wayne-Fellows even gave him 5 percent of the net profits on *Ring of Fear,* assuming there were any. His 5 percent of the company's overall net profits would be discontinued, however. None of this was to be made public.

As was his wont, Grant took all this very dramatically. He wrote a note to Wayne, apologizing for suddenly bolting from a dinner engagement. "I knew suddenly that if I stayed for one more fraction of a second I was going to make a fool of myself. A line of dialogue had sprung full-born into my mind and I knew that if I didn't run away I would say it just as I turned to you. The line was, 'Almost all men have shaken hands with their pallbearers; very few with their embalmers.'

"Jimmy."

Grant maintained his office at Wayne-Fellows headquarters, but he and Wayne stopped speaking. Instead, they wrote insulting letters to each other. Grant's were full of literary allusions, and Wayne would call on Mary St. John or Tom Kane to help him spice up his responses.

Jimmy Grant would eventually climb back into Wayne's good graces, largely because he joined Alcoholics Anonymous and stopped drinking. Grant dated his sobriety from his firing but it was evidently intermittent until about 1957, when he gave up alcohol once and for all with the help of a psychiatrist. Wayne never truly wavered in his devotion, but others believed that Grant didn't really bring much to the table besides camaraderie. "The most remarkable thing about Jimmy Grant," said the stuntman Jack Williams, "was that he played chess with Wayne for over twenty years, and managed never to win a game! *That* was the genius of Jimmy Grant."

After Wayne-Fellows signed Karen Sharpe, she made one picture for the company, *Man in the Vault*. After that, she sat around collecting her paycheck and getting restless. "I knew I was never going to work with Duke, because I was too young, or too much the ingenue, or too something, and they were paying me for no work. So I went to Duke and said, 'Can I ask you something? I'm too young to play opposite you and I would like to do something that's not acceptable as things stand. I'd like to do some live TV. I'm getting offers for it, and I've done a lot of theater and I would love to get a chance to explore things. Would you let me go?'

"And Duke said, 'Absolutely, I think you should do it.' And gave me my release. And I had some wonderful experiences on the *Hallmark Hall of Fame* and other shows. And that was typical of him — I liked him a lot, even if he was a conservative Republican. I never felt I had to have an appointment to talk to Duke; he was a very generous man, very down-to-earth. I admired him for that, and still do. And I admire him because he stood up for what he believed and made no bones about it. His beliefs were the opposite of mine, but he always had the courage to take a stand."

Wayne-Fellows found that maintaining a large contract list was fraught with peril. Among the other contractees was the pneumatic Anita Ekberg. She was only earning about $10,000 a year, but the company spent a lot of money on Ekberg's publicity, dental work, clothes, etc. In three years, from 1954 through 1956, the company spent $72,186 on Ekberg, and in that same time period she earned about $70,000 for her professional services.

For the rest of 1954, Wayne-Fellows had planned *Track of the Cat* (a Well-man movie with Robert Mitchum), *Blood Alley* (an adventure movie with Wayne), *The Sea Chase* (another adventure movie with Wayne), and *The Quality of Mercy,* a script by Ben Hecht for which Wayne wanted Kirk Douglas. But when Hecht's script came in, Wayne was appalled. "It reads like a poorly written B picture script to me," he told Warners.

At that point, Wayne was in Hawaii making *The Sea Chase* with John Farrow, and his sour mood wasn't helped by a return of the nasty ear infection that he had picked up years before on *Reap the Wild Wind.* Also irritating him was the fact that the studio had booked him into a hotel rather than his preferred private residence. Wayne estimated that the hotel had a hundred guests, and the first night he must have had his picture taken with twenty-five of them, and signed at least sixty autographs. He was tired and needed a house. "Perhaps some actors can walk away from people and not be friendly and gracious," he wrote. "I cannot — not only because of my own personality, but business-wise I cannot afford it."

The Sea Chase ended up proving something that every filmmaker finds out the hard way: you work just as hard on mediocre pictures as you do on the good ones — sometimes harder. The picture had been written and rewritten since 1951 by: Bolton Mallory, James Warner Bellah, Andrew Geer (the author of the original novel), Frank Nugent, and John Twist. Wayne was never completely happy with the script, as is evidenced by some undated notes he dictated:

"Long dialogue at the beginning was just words and didn't give real character to the people. . . . Criticized Ehrlich [Wayne's character] being so unnecessarily ruthless . . . shouldn't be such a stickler for little things and doesn't like his petty remarks and actions toward Kirchner. . . . He really is an unromantic bore . . . just a cold, commercial guy."

Five weeks of locations off Hawaii were followed by more weeks in the studio at Burbank. When the picture wrapped, it had cost $3 million, but it got out alive; domestic rentals totaled $6 million, with a further $1.7 million from foreign markets, making it one of the ten highest grossing films of the year.

The Sea Chase was hampered by a lack of chemistry between . . . everybody. Wayne's co-star was Lana Turner, and their relationship was no more than polite. "The sparks often fly between leading men and their leading ladies," said Tab Hunter, who was co-starring, "but I felt a layer of wool between them. Wayne wasn't like Bob Mitchum, who had that twinkle about him and was a devil with women. Wayne was more like Gary Cooper, who was always very professional."

Wayne told Hunter that he liked his performance, and for a time there was some talk of Wayne-Fellows taking over Hunter's contract from Warner Bros., which would have been fine with Hunter — as he put it, "Wayne-Fellows was doing good projects and I respected Wayne."

Hunter observed Wayne as a producer before he worked with him as an actor and found him "the quiet producer, not a producer in your face. In meetings, he would state what he wanted and expect things to be carried out, as they usually were."

Hunter respected Wayne — up to a point. "He was a consummate pro, which I admired, but . . . at bottom, a football jock. . . . I don't like macho bullshit. But with Wayne, what you saw was pretty much what you got. He was a straight shooter, similar offscreen to what he was on-screen, which is what makes a great screen personality. Great stars never entirely lose their identity, they just expand or contract the balloon according to the character and the performance."

Cameraman William Clothier didn't think much of the picture, or of John Farrow, who spent a lot of time trying to get Lana Turner into bed — not really such a lofty ambition. "Bill Clothier was a very honest, direct, talented man," said Hunter, "and he had Farrow's number immediately. Farrow had a lecherous quality; there was something seedy about him. I wasn't mad for him; as a director he didn't stand out, although he knew his shots and knew what he wanted. With the exception of Bill Wellman, who I loved, the directors that were the most important to me came out of live TV — Frankenheimer and Lumet."

Wayne's demeanor on the set was neither overly respectful to Farrow nor overtly disrespectful. "Wayne would do what he would do and he did it damn well," said Hunter. "Gary Cooper was more gentle, more of a quiet soul — but I found Wayne fascinating. He knew what he wanted and you had to be on your toes. He was a good man to be around for young kids starting out. He was friendly, but all business — a powerhouse actor."

The Sea Chase permanently soured Wayne on John Farrow; Wayne said that "He took a great story and made a dime novel spy story." Jack Warner appears not to have cared for *The Sea Chase* either; his notes are cuttingly brief: "Speed it up."

Ring of Fear was still hanging fire. Wayne knew that it needed extensive retakes to make it releasable; he and Bob Fellows estimated that said retakes would cost another $115,908 on top of the $700,000 that had already been overspent. Wayne persuaded William Wellman to do the retakes, not for his usual $10,000 a week, but for free. He also promised to cut Wellman in on Wayne-Fellows' profits if he could somehow make a facsimile of a silk purse out of a genuine sow's ear.

"My father wasn't really a director," said Colin Grant, "and he would have been the first to tell you. DeMille's *The Greatest Show on Earth* had made a fortune, and my dad thought he could make a fortune with another circus movie. He really wanted to make the movie; I don't think Duke wanted to make it at all."

Wellman sailed in with a writer, rewrote the script and reshot a lot of the picture without credit. The picture actually made money and Wayne showed his gratitude by giving Wellman 10 percent of the profits for eight years.

On June 1, 1954, Wayne-Fellows Productions became Batjac Productions — the name of a trading company featured in *Wake of the Red Witch*. In the film, the name was spelled Batjak, but, as Michael Wayne explained, "one of the legal secretaries who was examining the documents thought that there was a typo in the word 'Batjak.' She wondered if it should be 'Batjack,' so she called Robert Fellows and said, 'Is there a "c" missing from the company title?' And he said, 'No c.' But she thought he said, 'No, c.' So she typed it 'Batjac.' "

When the document was prepared, the mistake was noticed, but Wayne said, "I liked it better with a 'k' but leave it as it is. It's no big deal."

A month after the name change was official, Bob Fellows began agitating for better terms from Warner Bros., specifically on foreign receipts. Batjac's contract with Warners was due to expire in March 1955, and at this point Batjac's pictures were financed 100 percent by Warners, with profits split 50-50 after the studio recovered a liberal interpretation of its costs. But unhappiness with the way Warners was allocating money from foreign markets led Fellows to start sniffing around for other releasing deals.

And then there was the matter of *The Alamo.* Wayne was still determined to make it, although it hadn't been a quid pro quo when the Warners deal had been negotiated. Quietly at first, then more vocally, Bob Fellows began to agree with Herb Yates and Jack Warner. Why not get Ford, or Hawks, or someone with experience in massive action scenes to make *The Alamo*? Jesus Christ, Bill Wellman was right across the hall! Fellows probably saw the company's cash surplus disappearing overnight on a picture nobody but Wayne was sure Wayne could direct.

Fellows's opinion rankled his partner. Then there was Fellows's behavior around the office. He fell in love with his secretary and told his wife he wanted a divorce. She turned for support to Wayne, who didn't believe it was any of his business. As far as Eleanor Fellows was concerned, that meant Wayne approved of his partner's behavior. He didn't, but neither was he about to get in the middle of someone else's domestic meltdown, having just survived one of his own. Eleanor kept hounding Wayne until he halfheartedly agreed to attend a mediation session with the couple, but he left early after telling them that they had to solve their problems themselves.

Fellows got his divorce in 1955, and to pay for it he had to sell half of his interest in the films he and Wayne had made together, an amount estimated as $500,000. Fellows would be out of the company as of January 1956, after which John Wayne would be in total control of both Batjac and his career.

In the breakup Fellows got 10 percent of the net income from the company's pictures to the extent that said income exceeded $2.34 million. He also got the contract of Anita Ekberg, as well as two scripts: *The Quality of Mercy* by Ben Hecht, which was never made, and a Burt Kennedy adaptation of an Elmore Leonard story that became *The Tall T*. After Fellows left Batjac, he produced only two more movies: *Screaming Mimi* and *The Girl Hunters,* in which Mickey Spillane made another bid for stardom.

Wayne redoubled his efforts to set up *The Alamo.* It wouldn't be for Republic, and it wouldn't be for Warner Bros. But make it he would.

William Wellman's *Track of the Cat* emerged as a strange, attractively arty western shot in color but with only Robert Mitchum wearing anything other than earth tones.

Wayne liked Mitchum, even though the actor was not a producer's best friend. The locations for

Track of the Cat were in Olympia, Washington, where a high school girl interviewed Mitchum for the school paper while some of the Batjac people stood by.

"Do you have any hobbies, Mr. Mitchum?"

"Yes, I do."

"Well, what would you say is your principal hobby?"

"Hunting."

"Well, what do you hunt in particular?"

"Poontang."

A rustling sound from the Batjac people.

"I never heard of that."

"Well, it's an elusive, furry little animal."

Wayne was hired to play Genghis Khan in *The Conqueror* for Howard Hughes, but not before the usual series of charades that always attended anything requiring Hughes's signature. A fleet of seven Chevrolets pulled into the Batjac offices on Palm Avenue. They were all the same, with the backseats ripped out and no whitewalls. Hughes got out of the third Chevy from the front and came into the office. "Everybody's got to get out of here, got to get out of the building before we can complete the negotiations," he announced.

Wayne ordered everyone out, except for the woman at the switchboard. "What about her?" asked Hughes. "She's got to answer the phones," said Wayne — an exception Hughes accepted. Hughes and Wayne went into an office for about twenty minutes. In the meantime, everyone except the woman at the switchboard cooled their heels in the parking lot.

Finally, the two men came out and Wayne got in the third Chevy with Hughes. The fleet went west on Sunset, then made a hard right into the hills and was lost to sight. The next day the office was clamoring to know where the caravan had gone.

"You won't believe it," said Wayne, who seemed resigned to the madness. "We went up in the hills and then came down out of the hills and headed for Culver City. We eventually went down some alley there and in the back door of an abandoned laundry that Hughes must own. Anyway, his people had a key to it, and we went in there and that's where we signed the contract."

Wayne had estimated that RKO's constant postponements of its commitments to Wayne had cost him around $1 million, because he had held himself ready for weeks every year for three consecutive years and turned down a lot of work. Hughes agreed to pay his star an extra $100,000, but there were still more postponements, which led to problems with the schedule of *The Sea Chase,* which led to Warners threatening to charge Wayne for the delays.

Now Wayne was really angry. He wrote Hughes a letter saying that "$100,000 does not even start to make the necessary adjustment." Hughes wanted to settle up after *The Conqueror* was shot, but it wasn't Wayne's first rodeo. He sent a wire to Hughes at his headquarters on Romaine Street in Hollywood, with two more copies addressed to Hughes at RKO saying that "I insist it be done right now." He must have gotten what he asked for, because *The Conqueror* went into production that same month.

Although the picture was shot between May and August of 1954, the release was held up when Hughes sold off RKO and its library to General Teleradio for $25 million in July of 1955. For a time, Wayne harbored feverish fantasies about buying RKO from its new purchasers for $5 million, with the two unreleased Wayne pictures costing another $5 million. Charlie Feldman talked sense to him, but Wayne always had a burning urge to be wealthy and he kept returning to the RKO idea.

In January 1956, Hughes bought back *The Conqueror* and the still unreleased *Jet Pilot* for a whopping $12 million. *The Conqueror* was released in February 1956, *Jet Pilot* in October of 1957 — nearly eight years after it had begun shooting.

In 1957, Wayne again told Feldman to look into a deal to buy RKO, which had just closed. Feldman took the time and trouble to write a detailed two-and-a-half-page single-spaced letter about why that was a very bad idea: "Everything points to RKO getting further out of the business rather than getting into active production."

The Conqueror is one of those unusual pictures that really is as bad as its reputation. It features some of the most jaw-dropping dialogue in movie history. Nothing is clearly stated, but inverted to the point of gibberish. Instead of "I don't doubt it," the line becomes "I doubt it not." As Genghis Khan, Wayne is defiantly miscast, but the dialogue would defeat anybody: "Know this woman: I take you for wife," announces Wayne just before he forces himself on Susan Hayward, who spends the movie heaving her admittedly enticing chest while looking sullen. Clearly, she had read the script.

In outline, and probably in intent, the film is a throwback to a Jon Hall/Maria Montez epic of the 1940s, except on a much larger scale and played for complete seriousness. Hughes's sense of scale always trampled his nonexistent taste, so the film, like all of his later productions, is a leaden howler, dismally dull whenever the cast isn't struggling with the dialogue. *The Conqueror* is completely unaware of its own absurdity as the world's biggest Ed Wood movie.

Hayward decided a location affair was the perfect antidote to the script and the boring location of St. George, Utah. One night, after drinking too much, she stumbled across the street to the house where Wayne and Pilar were staying and challenged Pilar to a fight. Later, while shooting a love scene, Hayward stuck her tongue in Wayne's mouth. All this didn't stimulate Wayne; rather, it irritated him. "That goddamn bitch just stuck her tongue halfway down my throat," he raged to Mary St. John, while never saying a word to Hayward.

Wayne seems to have known what he was involved with; he referred to the film as his "Chinese Western," but otherwise plowed through manfully. "His camaraderie impressed me very much," said the actor Gregg Barton, who was in the film. "He played hard, he worked hard, and was very responsible."

He probably played too hard. For one of the few times in his career, his carousing affected his mornings. Gregg Barton remembered that at breakfast Wayne's hands were shaking so badly he had to rig a handkerchief around his neck as a pulley to raise his coffee cup to his mouth. Wayne made jokes about it, but must have realized it wasn't really a joking matter, as it didn't reoccur.

The sole bright spot of *The Conqueror* was the presence of Pedro Armendáriz, a close friend since *Fort Apache,* who was playing Genghis Khan's blood brother. Armendáriz and Tom Kane cooked up a practical joke based on Armendáriz's firmly held belief that Pilar had the upper hand in Wayne's marriage. Armendáriz objected to Pilar's dachshund having the run of the Wayne house, up to and including sleeping on the bed. "Dogs are great," Armendáriz proclaimed, "but you don't have them in the house. They stay outside. You play with them in the yard." Armendáriz decided to steal the dachshund. With the dog stashed in a room at a motel, Armendáriz and Kane went back to the bar, confident in the inevitability of the explosion.

The next morning, Armendáriz asked an obviously exhausted Wayne what was the matter — he looked tired. Hadn't he slept? "Ah, that damn dachshund ran away or something. Pilar's all upset and had me up climbing around the hills trying to find him."

Armendáriz and Kane got the dog out of the motel room and tossed him over the fence of the house where Wayne was staying with his family. The dog's magical reappearance satisfied everyone, and neither Armendáriz nor Kane ever summoned the courage to tell Wayne the true story.

When *The Conqueror* was released, the publicity ("The Warrior Who Shook the World! This Tartar Woman Matches His Fury with Flame . . . Meets His Fire with Ice! . . . Mighty in Scope . . . Mighty as the Man Whose Conquests Changed the Face of the World!") claimed that the film cost $6 million. Actually it cost $4.4 million, with Wayne earning $250,000 for the privilege of thoroughly embarrassing himself.

RKO mounted a huge advertising campaign, complete with color ads in the Sunday supplements and a Dell comic book adaptation. The picture eked out domestic rentals of $4.5 million. Amazingly, it actually got some good reviews: the Los Angeles *Herald-Examiner* said that "for sheer magnitude, wild beauty and thrilling action, *The Conqueror* stands in a class by itself!"

The only reason *The Conqueror* and *Jet Pilot* had even trace elements of commercial viability was Wayne's presence. In later years, Wayne gave the impression that he put up with Hughes because he aroused the actor's pity. "He used to call me up and say, Would I meet him . . . and then I would meet him and we'd go up for a ride and he'd talk about the studio and talk about a lot of things and ask my advice and I got to where I started feeling sorry for this guy."

Then it dawned on Wayne that it was ridiculous to feel sorry for a man rich enough to do anything he wanted in a world eager to sell itself to the highest bidder. "He was a very, very shy man," said Wayne. "I was conscious that he was embarrassed by people, [who] don't embarrass me a goddamn bit."

Wayne had gradually come to believe that Bill Wellman was the answer to Batjac's problems, which were the same problems that every other independent in the business had: manufacturing reliable commercial films at a price so low that even expert bookkeeping couldn't hide all the profits.

Other people at Batjac weren't so sure. One day Tom Kane came into his office to find Wellman furiously opening and closing the drawers in Kane's desk.

"Are you looking for something, Bill?"

"Yeah. I'm looking for some pipe tobacco. You

got any?"

"As a matter of fact, I do." Kane went over to the drawer where he kept his pipe tobacco and brought it out.

"Goddammit," Wellman said, "I don't want to be indebted to you, you son of a bitch." He stalked out of the office without the tobacco.

"Wellman had a terrible temper," said Michael Wayne. "One time at our office they were taking some publicity pictures with [stunt flier] Paul Mantz. Wellman and Mantz had known each other for years, but they were having some sort of disagreement, and Wellman suddenly sucker punched Mantz and knocked out a tooth. Wellman was scrappy — he would throw the overhand right. You never knew what Wellman was going to do."

Wellman was assigned a Batjac production entitled *Blood Alley* that was to star Robert Mitchum and began shooting on January 2, 1955, after two months of preparation near San Rafael, California. Mitchum was again reuniting with Wellman, the director who had made him a star in *The Story of G.I. Joe.*

But Mitchum was drinking and feeling obstreperous. George Coleman, the transportation manager, refused Mitchum permission to take a bus full of people to San Francisco for a party. "Mitchum started bouncing on a gangplank and blew [Coleman] right off the plank," remembered Michael Wayne. "After that, we couldn't find Mitchum; he wasn't at the hotel the next morning."

Wellman was in no mood for such juvenalia. He overnighted a letter to the studio. There was a forty-five-minute meeting with Mitchum during

431

which he refused to apologize. "Me? Push any-body? Who told you that?" he asked with a straight face.

So Mitchum was fired, which undoubtedly felt good, but was no joke with the picture about to start in a day or two and most other major leading men either working or with impossible schedules. Batjac tried for Humphrey Bogart or Gregory Peck, but neither was available. Wayne suggested Burt Lancaster, but no dice. William Holden? Not available. Kirk Douglas? Working. Fred MacMurray? Not big enough.

The clock was ticking — Wellman estimated he could stall for two weeks by using doubles for long shots or shooting around the leading man. "If we can't get anyone else I suppose I'll have to do it," grumbled Wayne, "although I really don't feel up to it." He was battling a flu he had recently picked up in New York.

Wayne had little choice but to rush to San Rafael and step into the void, thereby upsetting Pilar, who had been looking forward to having her husband to herself. Lauren Bacall had been all set to work with Mitchum, and was nervous about the change in her leading man. She was an ardent New Deal Democrat, a fan of Adlai Stevenson, and Wayne's reputation as a Red baiter preceded him. As it turned out, she didn't have to worry.

"I was apprehensive, when I first met him, about what he might discuss politically," Bacall remembered. "But of course . . . he never brought up anything. He never embarrassed me, he never inflicted his own thinking onto me, he never backed me against a wall and made me feel uncomfortable."

A little more than a week after Wayne took over

the lead in *Blood Alley,* he also had to take over the direction when Wellman got the flu. And a couple of weeks after that, there was a wild party at a Stockton bar that resulted in five members of the company being jailed, with one requiring hospital treatment. Wayne, who seems not to have been at the party, had to bail everybody out.

After a lot of difficulties, *Blood Alley* finally got made and was released in October 1955. It's not much of a picture — Paul Fix plays a Chinese elder — and Wayne has some impossible monologues addressed to God, whom he refers to as "Baby" when he's imprisoned by the "Commies." It's a picture that would have been every bit as bad with Mitchum, and it's just possible Mitchum decided discretion was the better part of valor.

Blood Alley was a flop, with worldwide rentals of $3 million against a cost of $2.5 million. Wayne and Wellman never worked together again. "They were so much fun together," remembered William Wellman Jr. "They were like two college boys, patting each other on the back, so excited about things. They had similar personalities in terms of their enthusiasm for the movie business. And similar senses of humor."

But there had been some tension between the two men. With truculent patriarchs like Ford, Hawks, or Henry Hathaway, Wayne would listen to instructions, nod, and say "Yes, sir." But increasingly, and for the rest of his life, with other directors it wouldn't be that simple. The problem stemmed from Wayne's ambitions.

"Wayne wanted to be the filmmaker," said William Wellman Jr. There had been no problems on *Island in the Sky,* but there was a single incident on *The High and the Mighty,* when Wayne made some comments that Wellman interpreted as directorial in nature and that got his back up.

Wellman announced "If I try to do your job, I would look just as silly as you do trying to do mine. You're bigger and stronger, but if you continue with this I will take your face and I will make a character actor out of you."

Wellman wasn't kidding. "My dad had a darker side than Wayne had," Wellman Jr. said. "Wayne liked to get along with people; my father, not so much." Wayne quickly backed down, the two men finished the picture, but Wellman held a grudge, as he was wont to do.

Wayne kept trying to get Wellman to make a picture with him for years, even after Wellman retired. He sent Wellman the script for *The Comancheros,* but Wellman didn't like it. A few years later, when Wellman was thinking about coming out of retirement to make *The Flight of the Phoenix,* he had mellowed to the extent of calling Wayne and asking him to co-star with Joel McCrea. They both said yes, but the project fell apart and Robert Aldrich eventually made it with Jimmy Stewart.

To the end of his life, everything Wayne said about Wellman marked him as a fan. "He's a wonderful old son of a bitch," Wayne told me when the topic of Wellman came up. "He had a metal plate in his head [from World War I] and he'd go around belting all these big, tough guys, and they'd be afraid to hit him back for fear they'd kill him. Wild Bill Wellman, a wonderful old guy. A fine director. Didn't delve into character as much as some.

"I'll tell you the difference between directors: Hawks has tremendous patience with people. Ford won't hire you unless he knows he can get it out of you. Wellman figures you're a pro and doesn't bother you as an actor. If you don't deliver, he'll simply cut the part down. It's that easy."

As for Wellman's feelings about Wayne, well . . . "When I put a tribute together for my dad on *The Merv Griffin Show,*" remembered Wellman Jr., "I called Wayne and he gave me clips from *The High and the Mighty,* and he wasn't giving those out to anyone. And on the show when Griffin asked my dad about John Wayne, he started talking about his 'fairy walk.' And I just shrank in my chair. So at the commercial break, I said something to him, and when they came back my father said he wanted to talk more about Wayne, and he called him the greatest star in the business.

"But the truth is that my father spent the rest of his life lambasting him. I would say, 'Dad, look at the films you made together.' But he held a grudge and I don't know why. I just can't believe it was that incident on *The High and the Mighty* all by itself."

Wayne's relationship with Mitchum was entirely free of such undertones. Despite having had to fire Mitchum, there was no animosity, and Mitchum would pop in and out of Wayne's life more or less according to the state of his marriage to Pilar, who had a single ongoing complaint about her husband's friends: they drank too much. "After a while, it got tiresome being around drunks," she said.

In the late 1950s, Mitchum and his wife were invited to a party at Wayne's house. Pilar was still angry at Mitchum for forcing her husband into eight weeks of unscheduled work on *Blood Alley,* but she was determined to be cordial. As Mitchum

435

and his wife, Dorothy, came through the door, Pilar was there to greet him. "Boy," Mitchum said, looking down the front of her dress, "do you need a new bra."

Pilar hit the roof and ordered the Mitchums out of her house. When she told her husband what had happened, he managed to keep a straight face.

In early 1955, Wayne and Pilar were going to take a quick Mexican vacation, and then he would be back at Warners for a western for his Coach.

William Wellman called Wayne's screen character "a nice guy with a special touch of nastiness." That nastiness had been called on occasionally — *Red River, Sands of Iwo Jima* — but it was the Ford western that would make special demands, that would obliterate the actor's innate likability and replace it with something far more dangerous.

The Ford picture was called *The Searchers.*

CHAPTER THIRTEEN

The middle and late 1950s were a golden period for Wayne — nearly everything he did made money, and, with occasional exceptions, almost everything he did was good, too. This was probably why he rejected a gilt-edged offer from William Paley to star in the TV version of the hit radio show *Gunsmoke.* The money on offer was about $2 million guaranteed, not to mention partial ownership of the show, but Wayne turned it down, instead off-loading Batjac contract actor James Arness onto the project. He was only being consistent; a few months earlier, NBC had offered him a deal to finance all or most of his pictures and give Wayne 100 percent of the profits in return for exclusivity for Wayne on NBC shows.

This offer sent Charles Feldman into a tizzy and he advised Wayne to give it serious thought. Feldman told Wayne to talk to David Selznick, Sam Goldwyn, and Walt Disney. But Wayne didn't feel comfortable with television. A few years later, he would turn down another lucrative TV offer from Allied Artists to host a *John Wayne Theater* — seventy-eight half hours. "I don't think the price is right, nor that I have the time," he grumbled.

Out of friendship for Arness, Wayne offered to

introduce the first episode of *Gunsmoke,* and on September 10, 1955, he was as good as his word: "Good Evening. My name's Wayne. Some of you may have seen me before. I hope so, I've been kicking around Hollywood a long time. I've made a lot of pictures out here — all kinds, and some of them have been westerns. And that's what I'm here to tell you about tonight, a western. A new television show called *Gunsmoke.* No, I'm not in it — I wish I were though, because I think it's the best thing of its kind that's come along, and I hope you'll agree with me. It's honest, it's adult, it's realistic. Now when I first heard about the show *Gunsmoke,* I knew there was only one man to play it — James Arness. He's a young fella and may be new to some of you, but I've worked with him and I predict he'll be a big star. So you might as well get used to him, like you've had to get used to me. And now I'm proud to present my friend Jim Arness in *Gunsmoke.*"

It was a typically generous Wayne gesture for a friend, one that imparted added value to a series that had not yet earned a reputation. Arness played Sheriff Matt Dillon for the next twenty years. A month later, in October, Wayne shot a half hour TV episode, entitled "Rookie of the Year," in five days, for a show called *The Screen Directors Playhouse.* He got $5,000 for the job, although he would undoubtedly have passed it up had anybody but John Ford been directing. Ward Bond and Patrick Wayne were also featured in the TV show, which Ford handled with his customary dispatch: ten to twenty setups a day, usually finishing between 2:30 and four in the afternoon.

"Rookie of the Year" was a straight favor for

Pappy Ford, but for his next film with Ford, *The Searchers,* Wayne was getting a good payday. He received $250,000 plus 10 percent of the rentals after Warners recouped their negative cost.

Ford and screenwriter Frank Nugent made a full roster of changes in Alan Le May's novel, many aimed at streamlining the cast and narrative. In the novel, Ethan's name is Amos, there are two boys in the massacred family instead of one, the kidnapped Debbie falls in love with Marty, and it is not blinded Comanches who wander amongst the winds after death, but scalped Comanches. And one other thing: Amos dies in the end.

From the first day of production on *The Searchers,* Wayne assumed a different attitude. Normally, he was the most amiable of co-workers, but Ethan Edwards required him to access the darkest part of his character, and he couldn't turn it on and off. "My father was able to become his character," said his son Patrick, who played a small part in the picture. "During filming, I was in the presence of Ethan Edwards, not my father. When it was over, my father was back." Likewise, Harry Carey Jr. remembered that Wayne "had a blanket over him in that film, a mood that was pretty strong and he carried it around with him 24/7. He didn't joke around at all on *The Searchers,* and Duke had a good sense of humor."

The picture had been shooting for a couple of weeks when Natalie Wood reported to the location in Monument Valley. She didn't have any scenes scheduled for her first day, so she spent it sunbathing, appreciably darkening her color. When John Ford saw her, he was angry — he wanted to emphasize the lightness of her skin as a contrast with the Indians — and he let her know he was angry as only Ford could.

That he was arguably the greatest American director impressed the young — seventeen years — actress not at all. "Go shit in your hat!" she told him, just before storming off.

That night, there was a knock on her hotel room door.

"Who is it?" she asked.

"Mr. Ford."

The door opened slightly, just wide enough to admit a long arm, at the end of which was a hand holding Ford's rumpled hat. He turned it upside down and shook it, just to show there was no shit in evidence. Ford and Wood patched up their differences, although she was never terribly enamored of him. Her experience with Wayne was considerably warmer. "She thought he was a very nice man," said her husband, Robert Wagner.

Throughout the shoot, Ford streamlined Frank Nugent's script, trimming exposition, cutting dialogue, eliminating explanations. In the novel, the center of the story is Martin Pawley; Amos Edwards has no particular desire or even intention to kill his niece, but Ford and Nugent introduced racial rage as the central motivation of the search, and they also made Martin a "half-breed" so as to make Ethan's unease with miscegenation central in the narrative.

The Searchers was previewed in San Francisco on December 3, 1955, on a double bill with Rebel Without a Cause (there were giants in those days . . .). Jack Warner's assistant Walter MacEwen thought that the picture, although "brutal in spots to the point of being daring," was a great success and reported back to his boss how it went:

440

The Searchers is a very big picture and was previewed to an enthusiastic audience. . . . I don't believe we lost more than 2 or 3 people who probably just had to go . . . the picture has a great pictorial beauty which came through with great clarity on a very big screen, no doubt aided by the fact that it was photographed on the double-size negative of VistaVision. . . .

Wayne has never been better, in a rugged, sometimes cruel role, and the audience is with him all the way from his opening shots. . . . Wayne's name on the main title got a tremendous hand.

The whole picture has a real feeling of bigness and honesty, as if you were actually witnessing how the pioneers lived on the frontier. . . . I do not believe that there are any major deletions to be made.

The initial reviews would be respectful but not overly enthusiastic. *Variety* wrote that *The Searchers* was "an exciting western on the grand scale" but also complained that "there is a feeling that *The Searchers* could have been so much more. It appears overlong and repetitious at 119 minutes." There was one exception to the prevailing response. William Weaver, the critic for the *Motion Picture Herald,* wrote, "*The Searchers* is one of the great ones — one of the greatest of the great pictures of the American West," and went on to compare it to *The Covered Wagon* and *Shane* and said that Ethan Edwards was "possibly the best all-around Wayne role he's ever had."

Wayne went on the road to sell *The Searchers*. He spent two and a half frantic days in Chicago, humping it from 7:45 in the morning until eleven at night, doing everything from radio shows to luncheons for the movie editors at the four Chicago dailies, to accepting the first poppy of the annual Poppy Day Association from the Rojieck triplets.

The Searchers went on to considerable financial success, earning $6.9 million (as of 1959) against a cost of $2.5 million. But 1959's profits have paled as the film has gone on to become a perennial, revered by critics and audiences alike for its vast formal beauty, its uncompromising treatment of a main character ravaged by racism, and the fearless intimacy between actor and character.

Ethan Edwards is a mysterious figure. He's carrying a lot of money, which is never explained, and the Reverend (Ward Bond) says of him somewhat obliquely that Ethan "fits a lot of descriptions." Mainly, Ethan identifies with the thing he hates: Comanches.

The conflict in the movie, which is far more important than the actual plot, in which Ethan figures as an agent of disruption as well as reconciliation, is not between Ethan and society, but between Ethan and Ethan. Ethan has to be respected, but he can never be understood. His fury is not exactly unmotivated, but it is irrational. You can, as Garry Wills does, point to Ethan's loss of the woman he loves to his brother, loss in the war, loss of his comrades, loss of the woman he loves to an Indian he hates. Yet none of that quite explains the blast furnace of rage and guilt that Wayne unleashes — unafraid, unapologetic.

Ethan is a racist, openly contemptuous of Martin Pawley for being part Cherokee. Not only that, he's a murderous racist, committed to killing his own niece because she has become the squaw of the Indian chief Scar, who killed Debbie's father and mother — the woman Ethan clearly loved.

Yet the roots of Ethan's racism are unexplained. It's clear that he hated Indians long before things became personal. Ethan just *is*. This mystery at the heart of the character's darkness forces the audience to sit up and wonder, to make its own best guess about what comes next, and about just what Ethan is capable of.

In his malevolent determination to kill his niece because she has become a contaminated creature, as well as in the fury that Wayne expresses, largely without dialogue, the actor goes further than he ever had before or ever would again, and in the process he brings something new to his persona.

As Glenn Frankel wrote, "This was the heart of Wayne's art. He came on direct, angry, and unbending, daring you to test him and prepared to deposit your ass on the ground with a punch to the jaw. Yet there was a certain sadness to the whole enterprise. Wayne's character seemed to be constantly looking back, searching for something — a way of life, a code of honor — that had ceased to exist."

And he also brought something new to the western, a genre that seamlessly encompasses all the great American themes — the trek west, the shifting balance between individual independence and communal alliance, and the challenges of technology: the stagecoach, the telegraph, the railroad. It's a genre about ceaseless change.

Ford and Wayne introduce a particularly virulent racism into the equation, not as something to be vanquished (Delmer Daves's *Broken Arrow*), but as something to be assimilated. They also access a profound truth: Ethan is an outsider who can never be anything but an outsider, the sort of hard man mandatory for the taming of a nation or the waging of a war, but who cannot live in the aftermath, in a calmed environment.

As one critic noted, "Ford goes very far with Ethan. . . . A central character who spews racist invective at every opportunity, who mutilates the bodies of the dead . . . and [scalps] an adversary, even though he did not 'earn' that warrior right by killing him himself, who slaughters buffalo in an insane rage just to deprive Indians of food, and who is out to murder a child?"

And this, ladies and gentlemen, is the hero.

Ford knew he could get away with it because Ethan was being played by John Wayne; he knew that Wayne had the strength to play profound psychological weakness — *The Searchers* is a Conradian tale in which an outward quest is really a metaphor for inner definition.

Ford and Wayne invite the audience to take Ethan as an extension of Hondo, as *the* John Wayne type — a completely competent loner of utter integrity, the only man capable of accomplishing the necessary task. As Randy Roberts and James Olson wrote of Ford's landscapes and Ethan's emotions, "Such landscapes and feelings trivialize religion, language and culture, because strength matters more than faith, action more than words, individual men more than women and families." If it wasn't such an insistent part of the fabric of the film, the audience could glide by the character's murderous racism. But they can't, because the dramatic movement of *The Searchers* is dictated by hate.

In the middle and latter stages of Wayne's career, his characters' fierce single-mindedness is often indicated by his refusal of the erotic: Tom Dunson holds himself aloof from emotional involvement in *Red River,* offering a woman a chance to bear his child only as a financial transaction; Ethan Edwards refuses to indulge his repressed passion for his brother's wife in *The Searchers;* Tom Doniphon renounces the woman he loves in *The Man Who Shot Liberty Valance* because another man is better for her. Among all the stars of his generation, only Wayne could consistently get away with this recurring motif of renunciation because only Wayne could believably play men who only needed themselves.

Ford emphasizes Ethan's vehemence, his harshness, his inscrutability. At times, Ethan is like some creature from the id, a walking representation of the enormous cost of repression. And at the film's conclusion, as Ethan lifts Debbie over his head — a moment not in Frank Nugent's script — duplicating a gesture from the first moments of the film, he emphasizes the tidal pull of family. As he cradles her like a child, he murmurs, "Let's go home, Debbie," and the film moves toward reconciliation and toward its legendary ending.

Ethan's symbolic aspect might be why Ford has the other characters move around Ethan in the film's final scene as if he isn't there — Ethan has become a ghost in a darkness he can't dispel. No one thanks him, no one acknowledges his existence. Now that he's completed the task only he could accomplish, now that the darkness is gone, so is Ethan, left to wander in the winds.

Harry Carey Jr. was on the set when Ford shot the ending.

The big man standing alone in the doorway, the red desert stretching out behind him. The other players in the scene, which included my mother, had passed by the camera, a joyous moment. Debbie was home at last, brought there in the arms of the man in the doorway. Uncle Jack told Duke that he was to look and then walk away, but just before he turned, he saw my mother, the widow of his all-time hero, standing behind the camera. It was natural as taking a breath. Duke raised his left hand, reached across his chest and grabbed his right arm at the elbow.

My father, Harry Carey Sr., did that a lot in the movies when Duke was a kid in Glendale, California. It was Duke's tribute. He'd spent many a dime just to see that. He stared at my mother for a couple of beats, then turned, walking away into loneliness across the red sand. The Jorgensen cabin door slowly closes.

It's a daring shot. As cinematographer Winton Hoch observed, "We had a vertical doorway and a horizontal frame. But here again, you're bold and you gamble and it is a shot that Jack wanted. He had his reasons." More subtly, Wayne's walk is different in the last shot. He no longer moves with his purposeful, graceful stride; as the door closes, he's almost staggering, aimless. For the first time, Ethan gives evidence of not knowing where he's going.

Wayne always had a thrilling command of physical rhetoric — the one-handed cocking of the rifle in *Stagecoach,* walking malevolently through the longhorns at the climax of *Red River.* But his work in *The Searchers* is even more expressive: when Ethan sees the burning cabin of his brother, Ford cuts to a low-angle shot of Ethan on his horse. Wayne unholsters his rifle by flinging it behind him, the scabbard flying off behind the horse, then brings the rifle back, all in one fluid motion. It's a moment that takes longer to describe than it does to witness — the piercing beauty that movies were made for.

Some of these movements were Ford's (lifting Debbie over his head); some were Wayne's (holding his elbow and ambling away as the door closes). That Wayne was capable of carrying off these bravura moments is his actor's glory — he had been what Brecht would call an "epic actor" before, and would be again, but the greatness of this performance is in going all the way with such a largely indefensible human being, who embodies what D. H. Lawrence referred to as the essential American soul: "harsh, isolate, stoic and a killer."

Besides his rage, Ethan has intelligence, faith, unexpected flashes of generosity, loyalty, purpose, audacity, skill. That's the way he's written, but Wayne brings a touch of something else: the hope of redemption. And Ford and Wayne brilliantly suggest the stifled sexual desire at the core of his racist obsession.

In the past Wayne had gotten close to the power he summons here, but either the script or the director had let him down. But in *The Searchers,* his life as a man coalesces around his gifts as an actor: the residual bitterness he carried from growing up in a brooding, recriminatory household; the years of working in films he felt were degrading, that led to him being ignored, scorned, or condescended to, of being sloughed off by the industry he respected. And, perhaps, guilt over his own mistakes. Here he summons his rage and pours it into a vehicle that can contain it — barely.

Wayne never puts any comforting space between the character and the actor. He never asks for our sympathy. Wayne *understands* this distressed and distressing loner. Ethan has seen a lot of ugliness — in the breaking of the land, in the war, in the acts of the Indians, in himself. But he stops just short of the one unforgivable act, and in the final image, embodies resignation as well as a plaintive loneliness — the same towering power that brings Debbie home also makes a domestic connection impossible.

Tom Dunson and Ethan Edwards personify the peculiarly American resistance to settling into the soft lap of family or community — in another time or place they might be outliers, living off the grid. But the genius of Wayne is that they don't seem completely alien to us; rather, they're part of us.

Here, at his best, Wayne is something rare: a fearless actor exposing wildly varied aspects of himself with skill and energy. That so many people persisted in their sneering dismissal of Wayne's acting ability is their shame — had they no eyes? As the critic David Overbey once observed, the naive and romantic Ringo Kid of *Stagecoach* is a long way from the sentimental and socially integrated Captain Brittles of *She Wore a Yellow Ribbon;* the existential exile of *Hondo* has little in common with the disillusioned Tom Doniphon of *The Man Who Shot Liberty Valance.* Likewise, the bitter Tom Dunson of *Red River* is a long way from the life-embracing gusto of Rooster Cogburn in *True Grit.* All different men, with entirely different psychological foundations and behaviors.

There is always a sense with most commentators on Wayne, even the favorable ones, that his politics are regarded as an embarrassment in relation to the power of his acting. But Wayne's acting is not a thing apart; it is, rather, constantly informed by his politics. Wayne's personal stubbornness and the authority of his belief system are the foundations for the obstinance essential to Dunson, Edwards, and Doniphon.

Wayne is the anti-Brando — the latter's knack for the unconventional choice, and his welcoming of the potential chaos of the improvisational moment indicate his deeply antiauthoritarian bent as much as ten labored biographies. As early as *The Big Trail,* Wayne's character almost always has a sure and certain knowledge of the right thing to do, and is indifferent to or impatient with the squabbling that goes on all around him. Indeed, the central dramatic conflict of the last half of Wayne's career was between his character's rigid belief system and a society that rejects it.

"Wayne was never — despite the endlessly repeated words of his eulogists — a vision of what Americans dreamed themselves to be," wrote the critic Terry Curtis Fox. "He was a vision of what Americans wished their past had been. He was a man who had no place in the modern, psychological world, and every bit of his performing presence told us that. He needed age for this conflict to become apparent."

Wayne did all this without words. Indeed, words got in the way because they were too specific. There was always something going on behind Wayne's assurance, something suggested by his physical grace, but it was never explicit. "He could *suggest* a past," wrote Fox, "— through a glance, a turning of the head, a shying away of the body

— but he would never *reveal* one."

Years later, musing about Ethan Edwards, Wayne touchingly theorized that the film's power derived from the point at which Ford chose to end it. He even speculated with optimism about what happened after the door closes: "I don't see any reason why Ethan couldn't have snapped out of it. . . . I'm sure that he went off and got on his horse and went into town and had a few belts, and somebody said, 'That land your brother homesteaded is getting close to — you know where the old burned-out building is?' 'Yes.' 'Well, the railroad is right close to there now and it's worth some money. Why don't you go out there and start growing some wheat or put up some corrals and make a siding there and buy cattle and sell them.' Somehow or another a man as strong as that man . . . isn't going to quit."

Maybe. Maybe not.

The Searchers is Wayne's greatest acting achievement. If Brando's triumphs were the external life of Stanley Kowalski and the internal lives of Terry Malloy and Vito Corleone, then Wayne combines all of them into Ethan Edwards. The sheer size of the part, and Wayne's portrayal of it, also signaled a quantum change in his screen dynamic. Ethan Edwards is so implacable and menacing that he's too large for any genre but the western at its most mythical.

In so many ways, *The Searchers* is a summation for its director, for its star, and for the western. The question hanging in the air for Wayne, as well as for the genre he represented, was simple: What now?

Mary Brown, before she was Mary Morrison and the mother of John Wayne.

The house Clyde Morrison was renting in Winterset, Iowa, when his eldest son was born on May 26, 1907.

The Morrison family circa 1914, shortly before they moved to Glendale, California. (Note gun and holster on Clyde.) From left: Duke (the dog), Duke (the boy), Bob, Molly, and Clyde Morrison.

Marion Morrison (second row, fourth from left) as vice president of the junior class at Glendale High in 1924.

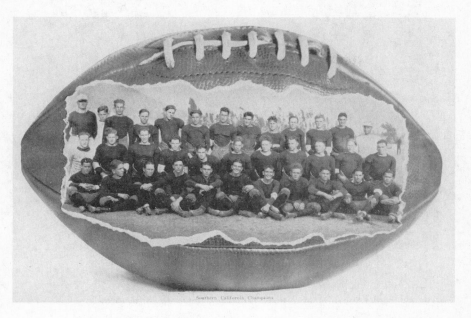

Big Man on Campus: Duke Morrison (bottom row, center) with his teammates on the Glendale High team that was Southern California high school champs, and below in the school yearbook.

A heretofore unknown Duke Morrison/John Wayne appearance in a two-reel comedy from Educational Studios entitled *Seeing Stars,* shot in 1927.

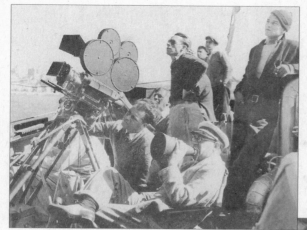

A young prop man/bit player named Duke Morrison (far right) watches John Ford direct *Men Without Women* (Fox, 1930). *(Joe Musso Collection)*

The newly minted young star in 1930's *The Big Trail*.

With ever-present off-screen cigarette on the set of *The Big Trail,* sitting next to Fox production head Winfield Sheehan (with cigar) and director Raoul Walsh. *(Courtesy of the Academy of Motion Picture Arts and Sciences)*

After the failure of *The Big Trail,* Wayne became a jobbing actor in anything that would pay a salary, including serials. *Hurricane Express* (Mascot, 1932) starred Wayne, along with players Ernie Adams (far left) and stuntman Glenn Strange (holding onto Wayne's leg), who later played Frankenstein's monster at Universal. *(Joe Musso Collection)*

A too-carefully posed barroom brawl from *The Dawn Rider* (1935) with Wayne facing off with stuntman Yakima Canutt. *(Joe Musso Collection)*

Looking like the star he would become, circa 1936. *(Courtesy of the Academy of Motion Picture Arts and Sciences)*

In 1939's *New Frontier*, one of the Republic Three Mesquiteers westerns, with Ray (Crash) Corrigan and Phyllis Isley, soon to be renamed Jennifer Jones. *(Joe Musso Collection)*

With Claire Trevor in *Stagecoach* (1939).

The cast of *Stagecoach* rehearsing. From left: John Carradine (in profile), Andy Devine, Berton Churchill, Donald Meek, George Bancroft, John Wayne, Claire Trevor, and unidentified pianist.

With his first wife, Josephine, and Claire Trevor at a costume party circa 1940. *(Courtesy of the Academy of Motion Picture Arts and Sciences)*

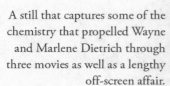

A still that captures some of the chemistry that propelled Wayne and Marlene Dietrich through three movies as well as a lengthy off-screen affair.

With Harry Carey
Sr., yet another father
figure/mentor in
*The Shepherd of the
Hills* (1941).

A snapshot from Wayne's
three-month tour of New
Guinea and related areas
during World War II.

With his second wife, Chata (right), and her ever-present mother.
(Courtesy of the Academy of Motion Picture Arts and Sciences)

Pedro Armandariz, Harry Carey Jr., and Wayne in John Ford's *Three Godfathers* (1948).

With Montgomery Clift in Howard Hawks's *Red River* (1948).

As the haunted Sergeant Stryker in Republic's *Sands of Iwo Jima* (1949).

As Nathan Brittles in *She Wore a Yellow Ribbon* (1949), with Victor McLaglen, Ben Johnson and George O'Brien.

The blended Wayne family: Wayne, his second wife, Chata, and the children from his first marriage: Michael, Melinda, Patrick and Toni.

Wayne the Cold Warrior, with Walter Pidgeon and Ward Bond at an American Legion event in Miami in 1951.

With Maureen O'Hara in *The Quiet Man* (1952).

With Lassie as Sam the
Dog, in *Hondo* (1953).

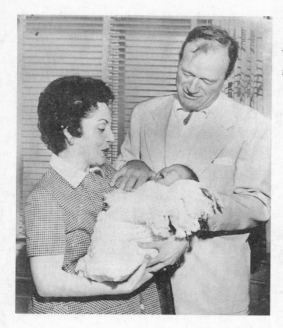

With third wife, Pilar, and their new daughter, Aissa, 1956.

As Genghis Khan with Susan Hayward in the Howard Hughes howler *The Conqueror* (1956).

As the implacable Ethan Edwards in John Ford's *The Searchers* (1956), with Monument Valley in the background, and Harry Carey, Jr., on the left.

Bringing Debbie (Natalie Wood) home in *The Searchers*, with Jeffrey Hunter alongside.

With Angie Dickinson in Howard Hawks's *Rio Bravo* (1959).

The set for *The Alamo* in Brackettville, Texas, just before filming began.

On the set of *The Alamo,* with cameraman and strong right arm William Clothier.

As Davy Crockett in *The Alamo.* This is the photo that served as the basis for the image of Wayne on the Congressional Medal of Honor awarded him in 1979.

With John Ford on the set of *The Alamo* (1960).

About to face down Lee Van Cleef and Strother Martin in John Ford's *The Man Who Shot Liberty Valance* (1962).

An extended Wayne family gathering, January 1966.

With Robert Mitchum in Howard Hawks's *El Dorado* (1967).

Directing *The Green Berets* (1968).

"Fill your hand, you son of a bitch!" As Rooster Cogburn in *True Grit* (1969).

Accepting his Best Actor Oscar for *True Grit* from Barbra Streisand.

John Ford visiting Wayne and director Mark Rydell on location in New Mexico for *The Cowboys* (1972).

In his dressing room at CBS, August 1972, photo by the author.

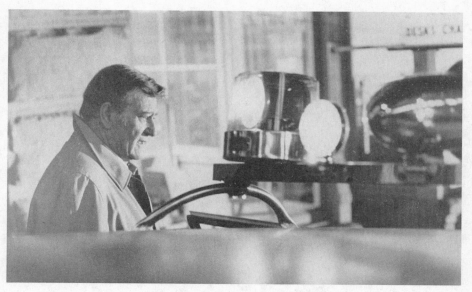

In *McQ* (1974), an indifferent stab at the then-popular rogue cop genre.

With James Stewart in *The Shootist* (1976).

The last public appearance, at the 1979
Oscars, a few months before his death.

CHAPTER FOURTEEN

In November 1955, Wayne wrote Ford a particularly chatty letter. Pappy was relaxing in Hawaii after finishing the editing on *The Searchers,* and Wayne had just seen the picture for the first time, calling it "just plain wonderful," although he wasn't crazy about Max Steiner's score. He thought the picture featured great performances and had a raw brutality but his character never became what he dreaded creeping into his portrayals — petty or mean.

Wayne had a great contractual opportunity at Warners, and another at RKO, but if he signed up with them he wouldn't be able to do the picture Ford was planning at MGM about the aviator/screenwriter Frank Wead (*The Wings of Eagles*). "It's more important for me to be in a picture with you, career-wise — for my health — and for my mental relief."

Being a movie star was hard enough, but Wayne was also doing quality work as a producer. In later years, Batjac became essentially a service organization for John Wayne, but in the 1950s the company made quality pictures that didn't star the owner.

Take, for instance, *Seven Men from Now,* a great little western directed by Budd Boetticher and written by Burt Kennedy, who was brought to Batjac by Paul Fix.

Seven Men from Now was a far superior script to everything Wayne was making around the same time, with the single exception of *The Searchers,* but Wayne farmed it out anyway. He was just finishing the Ford picture and didn't want to do another western about revenge.

Initially, the script went to Gary Cooper, but Cooper passed. At that point, Wayne developed a strange enthusiasm for Richard Egan, telling Jack Warner "this is the most manly guy I've seen on the screen since Gable." Fox wanted $50,000 for Egan's services, and Wayne felt it was a good deal, if only because in five years the picture could be rereleased when Egan was an even bigger star.

But Jack Warner had a better eye for leading men than Wayne and down-played Egan. He thought that *Seven Men from Now* had the potential to be another *High Noon* "if you can get the right lead" and counseled a cool head until the right ingredients were assembled. The script was finally accepted by Randolph Scott.

"Duke [gave] me a beautiful script called *Seven Men from Now,*" said Budd Boetticher. "I read 35 pages of it at lunch and I had never read anything this good. I walked back and John Ford and a very handsome young man and John Wayne were sitting on Mr. Ford's couch. I was allowed to call [Ford] Jack; everybody else called him Jesus or Coach. Terrifying man. I walked on the set and said, 'Duke this is the best thing I've read in my life. I want to do it.'

"He said, 'Well, you couldn't have read much of it in an hour for lunch.' I said, 'I read 35 pages, I don't have to see another thing and I would give anything in the world to meet this author.' He said, 'Mr. Burt Kennedy, Mr. Budd Boetticher.' " It was the beginning of a superior group of westerns written by Kennedy, directed by Boetticher, and starring Scott. As Burt Kennedy remembered, "I wrote 'em for Duke, but Randy made 'em. They pretty much shot the scripts. Sometimes things would happen, someone would hit their head or do something by mistake and they'd leave it in and call it a director's touch."

For the leading lady, Wayne hired Gail Russell. She hadn't worked in several years — there had been some arrests for drunk driving — although she still looked lovely. If Boetticher was initially resistant, he was soon won over. "I think [Wayne] was more fond of Gail Russell than any of them," Boetticher said. "And I think Duke had a crush on her. I think she was the one leading lady that he really cared about in anything but a professional way."

Russell behaved during production, but got terribly drunk at the wrap party and disappeared. Budd Boetticher believed that Andy McLaglen was in love with her; McLaglen spent three days traveling around Hollywood trying to find her. By the time she was located, Russell's stomach was so swollen it looked like she'd swallowed a football. *Seven Men from Now* was Gail Russell's last movie; she died in 1961 at the age of thirty-six, in an apartment surrounded by empty liquor bottles.

At Batjac, Burt Kennedy learned the business under the loose tutelage of Jimmy Grant, who was once again in Wayne's good graces. "I stole so much from Jimmy that people thought he stole from me." Kennedy started off at Batjac for close to nothing and rose to $1,000 a week. "After I had a few successes under my belt, Duke would loan me out to Warners and to Fox, and Duke and I would split the overage. It worked out fine.

"Duke . . . always said he cut his throat because he didn't make [*Seven Men from Now*]. Despite the fact he gave Budd two big breaks, he and Budd weren't buddies. If Duke liked you, he could be rough with you. If he didn't like you, he'd dismiss you. He learned everything he knew from Ford. Duke spent his whole career getting even with directors as revenge for the tough times that Ford gave him."

Boetticher and Kennedy remembered Randolph Scott as a tremendous gentleman with a dry sense of humor. And rich. Very rich. "One day at Lone Pine I walked out to get on horseback and exercise," remembered Boetticher. "Randy had a rocking chair that he didn't need. . . . He was rocking back and forth reading *The Wall Street Journal.* And I walked out and he said, 'Budd, the most terrible thing happened to me.' And I said, 'What happened Randy?' He said, 'Three of my new oil wells blew out.' I said, 'How many came in?' He said, 'Eleven. But damn it, you shouldn't lose an oil well with today's technology.' "

Burt Kennedy said, "[Randolph Scott] was wonderful for Budd to work with because Randy liked the way he came off the screen in Budd's pictures — as a tough guy, which he wasn't." The later Boetticher-Scott pictures were made for budgets of around $400,000 to $500,000. "They were fourteen-day pictures," said Kennedy. "I wrote them to the money, for very few interiors because interiors cost money. You have to rent

454

space and decorate the sets, and that was money we didn't have."

But *Seven Men from Now* was made under Batjac's deal at Warners and they could spend more money. It cost $719,000 and amassed world rentals of $1.6 million — a decent profit-making venture. Around this time, Batjac also started up a subsidiary corporation called Romina that produced a couple of pictures for United Artists, among them *China Doll,* directed by Frank Borzage — another one of the great old-timers that clustered around Wayne hoping for a last hurrah. But Borzage hadn't made a picture in ten years and *China Doll* was fairly expensive — $1.14 million for the negative, prints, and advertising, with world rentals of only $860,592. "Borzage had been hanging around the studio for a long time," said Bill Clothier. "I think Duke had promised him something. It was a lousy picture, but it was a pleasure working with [Borzage]."

Other Romina pictures also failed: *Escort West* ($872,059 cost, $777,991 worldwide rentals); and *Gun the Man Down* ($269,780 cost; worldwide rentals of $325,180).

It was clear that most Wayne productions that didn't star Wayne trended toward loss. What made it worse was that Jack Warner's accounting games had a way of turning small winners into big losers. William Wellman made a sweet little dog story for Batjac called *Good-bye, My Lady,* with Brandon De Wilde and Sidney Poitier. William Clothier photographed the picture and said that "Wayne got into a beef with Warner about the costs of a picture Wayne had made; Warners hung us on that one too. Warners promptly threw away the rest of the pictures . . . we got a good screwing, because of the way Warners released the picture." *Good-bye, My Lady* cost $900,000, and had world rentals of $677,000.

Still, the profits spun off by *Hondo* and *The High and the Mighty* had given Batjac a comfortable war chest, and Wayne knew what he wanted to do with it. But Jack Warner was no more enthusiastic about *The Alamo* than Yates had been.

"Jack was funny," said Angie Dickinson, who was under contract at Warner Bros. for a number of years. "He was funny because he wasn't funny, but he was always trying to be funny, and that struck me as funny. As a producer, Jack didn't have great vision; he could take care of himself and his studio, but he wasn't Arthur Freed. Not long before he died, I saw him and told him, 'Jack, you never knew what to do with me, did you?'

"And do you know what he said? 'Well, you got an awful lot of red in your hair.' "

Batjac packed up and left Warner Bros., although Wayne and Warner maintained a friendly social relationship. A rundown of the Batjac productions reveals that Wayne was a careful, effective producer. He started the pact with the cheaply made *Big Jim McLain,* which, at $750,000, cost precisely half of what *Operation Pacific,* his previous film for Warners had cost.

The money continued to roll in with *Island in the Sky, Hondo,* and *The High and the Mighty.* Even the overtly arty *Track of the Cat* didn't lose much money. But according to Warners' bookkeeping, *The Sea Chase* lost money, as did the dismal *Blood Alley,* in spite of the fact that the former earned rentals of more than $7 million and the latter rentals of $3 million — very solid figures for the period. Consistent returns like this were why financiers would follow Wayne anywhere; good or bad, there was a financial floor beneath which a Wayne picture did not go — then or now, the most valuable thing a star can bring to a picture.

Despite the largely positive results of the Batjac-Warner alliance, Wayne always felt that he had been badly used by the studio; that some of his movies were far more profitable than the studio would admit. He was almost certainly correct. "Nobody came out with a sizable profit from doing any deal with Warners," said the producer-screenwriter Niven Busch, who believed Jack Warner was the Zen master of double-entry bookkeeping. "They had the most foolproof, plate-steel accounting system in the world. I still don't know, and I don't think anybody else does, how they do it."

The general feeling of being had was probably why Wayne turned down an overture from Jack Warner at the end of 1956 to buy out Batjac. Years later, Wayne and his son Michael were at the studio for a meeting, when they ran into Jack Warner. "You really oughta bring Batjac back to Warner Bros., Duke," Warner said. "You should be here, where you can be fucked by friends."

Wayne was an indulgent boss, but he was strangely absentminded. Every early-arriving employee of Batjac grew used to finding Wayne sitting on the steps of the Palm Avenue building, reading the morning paper and waiting for someone to let him in because he'd lost his keys.

John Ford was renting an office in the Batjac building, and every once in a while Katharine Hepburn would drop by to visit Ford, with whom she had a love affair in 1936–1937, during and after the production of *Mary of Scotland*. Hepburn always adored Ford, and he returned the favor, but that didn't mean she was willing to suspend her strongly held views of social propriety.

"You people have no pride," she announced one day to anyone that would listen. "That Venetian blind right behind you there. It's broken! It hangs down. It's never been fixed. If it wasn't broken down you'd never find this place." And with that, she stormed out.

Wayne was amused by Hepburn's temperament, but he himself was much milder — unless the subject was politics. When it came to the public he always kept the lid on. Because of his image, drunks or belligerents would frequently challenge him to fights, which he always managed to avoid. Ray Kellogg, a stuntman and second unit director, was with Wayne at the casino on Catalina one time when a man standing next to them in the men's room suddenly said, "I'll can your ass." Kellogg said the man would have to go through him first, but the guy persisted.

Finally, Wayne said, "You probably could knock me on my ass; I can see you're a real tough mother. I'll tell you what we'll do. We'll arm wrestle. How about that? We'll arm wrestle first, see who's stronger."

The man said okay, so they tipped a wastebasket over to serve as the table. Unfortunately, the wastebasket was rusty and their elbows went right through the bottom. Both men's arms got stuck until Kellogg pried some of the torn metal loose. The entire experience ended with the man offering to buy Wayne a drink, and Wayne accepting.

There were a fair number of relatives on the Batjac payroll, although, with the possible exception of his brother, Bob, they all had to earn their positions. Bob was there only because of Mary Morrison. As far as the relationship between Wayne and his mother, nothing had changed.

"Mary was salty and sharp and tough," said Gretchen Wayne.

They were actually a lot alike. He could never please her. He tried, but he couldn't. With his mother, it was always, "Why isn't Bob making more money? Why isn't Bob producing your pictures?" Bob was her baby. Bob would take off for Mexico and go drinking. Bob was Bob; you couldn't help but love him, and everybody did. He was one of the boys, a great sense of humor, never a nose-to-the-grindstone type of guy. And that's okay — someone has to be the lifeguard, and in that family the lifeguard was Bob's older brother.

He was always crazy about his father, always said he was the kindest, gentlest, nicest man. But Mary. . . . She was *tough.* I'm sure she just ground the hell out of Clyde. I never heard about Clyde drinking, but he didn't have any drive, while Mary worked for the phone company, Mary worked for political campaigns, Mary smoked, Mary drank. I think Mike's dad was intimidated by her. But then, he was never aggressive with women. He was respectful; he was reserved. He never bounded into the room and played the Star.

In June of 1956, Wayne signed a deal with 20th Century Fox to make three pictures for a total fee of $2 million, the money to be paid out at the rate of $200,000 per year for ten years for tax reasons. Not only that, but Fox agreed to pay Charlie Feldman's commission. Wayne had director approval — a partial list of approved directors included Henry King, Henry Hathaway, Jean Negulesco, Walter Lang, and, interestingly, Edward Dmytryk. This deal, the highest flat fee ever negotiated for a movie star up to that time, set off the usual chest clutching among executives and gullible journalists about whether the industry could afford such salaries. (Only actors' salaries are questioned, never executives'.)

What was not generally known was that there was also an agreement with Fox for a fourth picture, with Wayne's compensation set at $175,000 against 50 percent of the gross, which, had it been publicized, would have undoubtedly caused aneurysms. Actually, the money was not far out of line with what was being paid to comparable names. Bob Hope was getting $200,000 and 50 percent of the profits, Marlon Brando and Gregory Peck were both asking for 75 percent of the profits of their pictures. "How much further can it go?" asked The Hollywood Reporter.

As it turned out, quite a bit.

The signing of the deal with Fox got a lot of attention, especially from traditionalists such as Sam Goldwyn, who decried the increasing industry reliance on the star as the single most important component of the industry. Wayne didn't feel a bit guilty.

"After 30 years in this business, the pendulum finally has swung to the actors — and everybody hollers," he said. "We're only getting the money that used to go to the relatives of the studio bosses. . . . When I used to turn out those old westerns you see on television every day, I was getting $75 a week and doing my own stunts. The pictures cost about $11,000 and made big profits. Those same profits built Beverly Hills mansions for a lot of people who would have been on relief if their uncles hadn't been movie moguls."

But Wayne never got on a high horse where Charles Feldman was concerned. Through all the years that Wayne was the biggest box office star in the business, meetings with his agent were always conducted at Feldman's office, never at Wayne's.

The Wings of Eagles is one of John Ford's strangest pictures. Initially a labored, drably shot service comedy in which everybody is twenty-five years too old for their parts, it slowly morphs into the story of an absent father and an alcoholic mother who are oddly characterized as the salt of the earth despite their huge character flaws, finally ending as a genuinely moving story of personal regeneration. It's less like the carefully plotted stories we're used to seeing in the movies than the messy, random progressions of life itself.

James Stewart was first considered as the star of a biography of Frank "Spig" Wead, a Navy pilot during World War I who helped devise the "baby" carriers and revitalized the Navy's air operation between the wars. After a fall, Wead was rendered a paraplegic and became a screenwriter for John Ford (*Air Mail, They Were Expendable*) among others, until his death in 1947. In outline, it was a story of personal heroism transmuted into professional heroism.

Early correspondence about the script indicates some of the problems. "There is no love story," complained one writer, "and that is the problem. Mrs. Wead, soon after she knew his back was

461

broken and he would remain a hopeless cripple, took her two daughters and left him. The men in the Navy are bitter about this and feel it is better left unsaid, although Mrs. Wead is dead now."

Dore Schary's MGM was bedeviled by declining attendance and corresponding budget cuts. In the early stages of development, the studio was considering using black and white stock footage, tinting it and blowing it up into CinemaScope proportions, in the hopes it would get by. When John Ford came onto the picture, corner cutting was over.

The script and some of Ford's direction can be criticized, but there can be no criticism of Wayne's performance in the latter half of the picture. He even goes without his toupee, although his performance is so intense that few people notice. (When Maureen O'Hara has a late-film reconciliation scene with Wayne, she affectionately kisses his bald spot.) If, after *The Searchers,* there remained any question about Wayne's bona fides as an actor, you need only look at this garbled, touching movie — a textbook example of the credibility a great star can bring to a part.

Frank Wead is written to conform to the Wayne model of self-determination; when he's told that the doctors need the permission of next of kin to operate, he snaps, "*I'm* my next of kin." For several reels after that, we never see Wayne's face — just the top of his head and his huge, immobile body as he lies facedown in a hospital bed struggling to regain movement in his feet. Ford is gambling that he can take away any actor's most valuable tool and not lose the audience. As usual, he was right.

Wayne brings a total emotional commitment to

Wead's grueling rehabilitation, and Ford even indulges in an amusing self-portrait, as Ward Bond plays a querulous Hollywood film director named John Dodge, who has pictures of Harry Carey and Tom Mix in his office.

Like *The Long Gray Line,* Ford's elegiac movie about West Point's Marty Maher, who was an alcoholic and, reputedly, a wife beater, *The Wings of Eagles* avoids some of the more unpleasant truths about its subject. Maureen O'Hara, for instance, found the real Spig Wead unpleasant and mean. "Two minutes after you were in the door, he knew just where to place the knife and twist it," she remembered. O'Hara always brooded over the deletion of a couple of scenes depicting Wead's wife's decline into alcoholism — cut, she said, because Wead's daughters objected.

But if Ford was cornered by his own sentimentality into celebrating a man with darker corners than his friend wished to acknowledge, Wayne's performance nearly redeems the enterprise. "He had authority," said Maureen O'Hara of her favorite co-star.

He had credibility. He had manliness. He had his humble — he didn't have that overpowering actor's ego. And you liked him and you couldn't help liking what he was doing. He had the magic. And don't forget that the magic doesn't always photograph.

When I was a young girl in England, there was an actress who was so beautiful I would literally gasp when I saw her at the studio. Googie Withers. And when I saw her on film, it wasn't there. Her beauty didn't register.

But with certain people — Duke, Henry Fonda,

Jimmy Stewart, old Spencer Tracy — the magic just goes through the lens onto the film. Just standing still, there's a presence. Duke was a fine, fine actor. But when people accept someone totally, and believe them totally, they don't think to call them an actor. But that's what Duke was, a fine actor.

Unfortunately, one of Wayne's best performances was in a movie that takes too long to find its center. Ford shot the film efficiently in forty-seven days on location in Pensacola and Hollywood at a negative cost of $2.6 million, but the picture only earned domestic rentals of $2.3 million. The loss totaled $804,000.

Legend of the Lost, Wayne's next picture, was a co-production between Batjac, Dear Film, and United Artists. The studio initially stalled on making a decision about the picture, which provoked one of Wayne's trademark letters of irritation. The total budget was $3 million, but UA's investment was a modest $1.75 million. Wayne was budgeted for only $250,000 with the rest of his salary deferred. Wayne's letter to UA's Robert Blumofe pointed out that Batjac was offering the company a picture with Sophia Loren, one of the top stars of Europe ("I'm of pretty good standing in the United States . . .") as well as a director named Henry Hathaway.

"The deal is either worth it or it isn't," Wayne wrote. "I see no room for negotiation. . . . I would appreciate an answer 'Yes' or 'No' by the first of the week."

The original script was by Robert Presnell Jr., who was married to Marsha Hunt, Wayne's co-star in the forgotten B western *Born to the West.*

After a notable career at MGM, where she was being groomed as a potential replacement for Myrna Loy, Hunt was dropped by the studio and eventually blacklisted. When she was making *The Happy Time* for Stanley Kramer, she was told she could be cleared of the charge of Communism if she would take out a full page ad in the trade papers. "I said it was like taking out an ad saying 'I don't beat my wife,' " she remembered. "You can't disprove a negative. I held out and continued not working."

Presnell worked with Henry Hathaway on the development of the script. "Hathaway and his cigars came over a few times, and the cigar slinging went on," remembered Hunt. "Boy, were they pungent!" Shortly before the film got under way, Wayne invited Presnell and Hunt to his house in Encino for dinner. It was a working dinner, not a social dinner. "Wayne wanted his character to be more monosyllabic," remembered Hunt. "I don't know if it was about breath control, or whether he was just concerned about his image as a man of few words, and not feeling comfortable with an articulate role. My husband wrote wonderful dialogue and I would have thought it would have been refreshing for Wayne to be more expressive. But Wayne wanted it simplified.

"He was a good host. There was no trace of animosity about our differing politics. He showed no particular interest in me; I was invited out of courtesy to my husband. He was a nice man, not a perfunctory man. We had some brief talk about what he hoped for out of the changes. And that was the end of it."

It certainly was. Either Presnell resisted the changes or his changes were deemed insufficient, so Ben Hecht was called in and made the required alterations. Rossano Brazzi came aboard for $135,000, while Loren got $200,000.

Legend of the Lost filmed in Libya in February 1957. The location was hellish — "The Sahara desert during the day," wrote cinematographer Jack Cardiff in his memoirs, "was a shimmering, ferocious furnace, but at night so numbingly cold that it was like being in cryogenic suspension. We slept in every garment we possessed, a couple of pullovers, as many socks as we could manage, overcoats — everything."

And Hathaway was . . . Hathaway, "screaming maniacally at those who left footprints in the sand, until we were all afraid to move." Cardiff glumly remembered what Hathaway had told him in pre-production: "If you want to be a son of a bitch, be a good one."

Wayne wanted Pilar to accompany him to the location, which was Pilar's idea of hell. She explained that their daughter Aissa, who had been born in 1956, was too young for the inoculations she'd require to come to Africa. Pilar didn't want to leave her with a nurse. Wayne insisted that the nurse could handle the situation, so Pilar trooped off to Libya to find that her accommodations consisted of a mud-plastered room whose dirt floor had to be watered down every morning to keep dust to a minimum.

Wayne and Loren never established much simpatico; he believed she was having an affair with the married Brazzi, even though she was engaged to Carlo Ponti. Wayne wrote a letter outlining the location's difficulties to Billy Wilkerson of *The Hollywood Reporter:*

We are working at an oasis in the middle of the Sahara desert, 400 air miles from Tripoli. This little village is completely isolated from the rest of the world; no radio, telephone; no modern facilities. We bunk in tents. In the day it's sunburn hot, at sundown the temperature drops to around 30 degrees. . . .

We move out of this village each morning at five in four and six wheel vehicles equipped with special desert tires, all flown in, and we move around until Henry Hathaway finds a background he wants and we start to work; finishing with that, we dash off to another location. It's bitter cold when we leave and just as cold when we return to our base of operations around 9 at night. . . . I would not have missed this location for anything, but when I leave it, I'm certain that I would never want to make it again.

The picture was scheduled for fifty days in Libya, with the interiors to be done at Cinecittà in Rome. The North African locations were in a place called Gaudemes, also a lost Libyan city named Leptis Magna that had only recently been uncovered. They were shooting at Leptis Magna when it was reported that Wayne tore a couple of ligaments in his left foot after a fall. He wired Charles Feldman not to worry; it was only a "painful ankle strain."

John Ford's intuition told him the film was in trouble, and he wrote a letter to Wayne. "I hope Pilar is well. I called the house and the baby is fine. She is calling Ward 'Papa.' " Another Ford letter was more expansive; he told Wayne that he had no particular interest in making a picture for Hecht-Hill-Lancaster. "They asked me about it.

467

Natch, I made no commitments. Remember, this is Jack speaking, and you're Duke. You're the guy that makes commitments — at bars, lunch, tables, steam baths, airplanes, George V hotel, at Batjac, at Romanoff's . . ."

A few months later, another Ford letter arrived, the main purpose of which seemed to be the venting of steam. Ford had made a tentative deal with Orson Welles to play the part of Frank Skeffington in *The Last Hurrah,* and as soon as the trade papers announced it, Harry Cohn at Columbia received a packet supposedly documenting Welles's "communistic or subversive activities (alleged). . . . These were sent by an actor who had said all over town that he was to play the part — a Ward Bond. . . .

"You know my very decided views on Traitors, Commies, fellow travelers and such like — you also know my integrity in making films + also my ideas of justice — you are not guilty until proven so (and the jury is not necessarily Ward Bond)." Ford closed the letter by noting that Welles had missed a meeting because "of a slight fever upset etc. So fuck him. Coach." Below that was a P.S.: "Fuck Bond too."

Ford suggested that Wayne play the part of Frank Skeffington. What was surprising was that Wayne gave it serious thought, although it would have meant breaking his boycott of Columbia Pictures and Harry Cohn. But Wayne was leery of being rushed into the deal by Ford — Feldman was already talking to Columbia about "a big-scale tax carry forward corporation" for several pictures. Ultimately, Spencer Tracy played Frank Skeffington — a much better choice than either Welles or Wayne.

The result of the Libyan agony was a picture of no distinction whatever save its visuals, thanks to the talents of the great Jack Cardiff, who lavished attention on each composition as if he were making a much better movie.

"When I finally saw the film in New York," remembered Marsha Hunt, "I wept. I wept for my husband's script, which was nowhere to be found. It seemed to have been savaged. A little later, I met Sophia Loren by chance. She was doing *Houseboat* and I was doing some little independent picture, and there we were at the same restaurant. I mentioned that my husband had written *Legend of the Lost,* and she looked puzzled at his name. And I thought, 'Uh-oh.' "

Hunt's career never regained any traction, but she always resented people who regarded her as a victim of the blacklist.

"I never had this attitude of people who've never met me who summarize my career. 'Poor thing, she never made it.' The truth is that I never wanted to be a big star. It was a motion picture, you did your best on it, and gifted people worked with you. Someday it's got to be said that I was the happiest actress in town because I never got any two roles alike. I got challenging characters to play; I was blissful at Metro doing starkly different things because that is what I became an actress to do."

When it came to the blacklist, Hunt drew a line between hard-core conservatives and people who informed for reasons of career. "I know what [Wayne] was doing was arrogant and unfair and damaging and awful — all those things. But I have to respect conviction. He was absolutely sure he was right. I once ran into Roy Brewer, who was a great ally of John Wayne's in that period. And Brewer and I concluded about each other that we both were following strongly held conviction. They just happened to be opposing convictions. Wayne didn't do what he did for economic reasons. He was up to mischief about other people's lives and careers, but I could hate that without hating him. I guess I'm just not an angry person."

Legend of the Lost returned only $3.6 million in rentals to United Artists.

In 1957, Wayne attended a studio preview of *Lust for Life,* the florid Vincente Minnelli movie about Vincent van Gogh. Afterward, there was a party at Merle Oberon's house where Wayne motioned Kirk Douglas onto the terrace. "Christ, Kirk," he began, "how can you play a part like that? There's so goddamn few of us left. We got to play strong, tough characters. Not those weak queers."

"Hey, John, I'm an actor," said Douglas. "I like to play interesting roles. It's all make-believe, John. It isn't real. You're not really John Wayne, you know." Douglas remembered Wayne looking at him oddly, but not for the reasons Douglas imagined — that he really thought he was John Wayne.

In Wayne's own mind, he was Duke Morrison. John Wayne was to him what the Tramp was to Charlie Chaplin — a character that overlapped his own personality, but not to the point of subsuming it. And Wayne was emotionally committed to playing nothing but John Wayne parts, so that he would never, ever have to go back to being Duke Morrison.

At this point, Wayne was juggling a couple of possible properties. One was a movie about Heartbreak Ridge, written by the actor Barton MacLane; another was "Thunder in the South," about the Civil War, and there was "Earthquake McGoon," a story about a Chinese adventurer by Corey Ford and A. S. Fleischman.

Instead, in December 1957, Wayne went to Japan to star in *The Barbarian and the Geisha,* the first of the three films for Fox. It was the story of Townsend Harris, the first American envoy to Japan. The director was John Huston, and the picture was problematic from the beginning. An early script, from December 1956, describes Harris as "a Robert Mitchum type," but as written he's more of a John Wayne type; a still earlier script contained a reflective character that could have been played by Spencer Tracy.

In years to come, Wayne blamed Huston for the entire debacle, explaining that he signed on to a fragmentary script purely to work with Huston. Whereupon Huston, instead of working on the script, took off for four months in Mexico, digging up pre-Columbian art and staying out of the country to avoid taxes.

The surviving memos from Fox production chief Buddy Adler to Huston prove that Adler was a smart executive with a good story sense and Huston was more interested in his images than his story. After reading the script by Charles Grayson, Adler wrote Huston, "I feel that on the whole the script: a. lacks emotional impact; b. there is a lack of depth to certain characterizations; c. there is very little excitement in the love story." It simply wasn't as good as it could be.

Adler pointed to *Sayonara,* a Marlon Brando picture that was just about to be released and would prove a smash hit. *Sayonara* had an inter-racial love story and a script by Paul Osborn that worked; the Townsend Harris script didn't. Harris had evidently been an alcoholic, and Adler was fine with not making him an alcoholic, "but we have to make him *something.* What do we know about Harris in this script? Only that he has had a post in China; that he has no family or marital ties; that he has a quick temper; that he is brave and he is determined to do a good job. That is all very admirable but it is not enough."

A week later, Charles Grayson had done some rewriting that was an improvement, but Adler still felt the script lacked depth to go along with the premise and the setting. It's probable that Huston felt that the gaps in the characterization would be filled by the presence of John Wayne; that, as is often the case, the personality of the star would make up for the impersonality of the character.

As soon as he showed up in Japan, Wayne presented Huston with thirteen pages of notes about the script. He was evidently ignorant of the fact that Huston had recently walked off David O. Selznick's production of *A Farewell to Arms* because of the unceasing flow of memos. Huston took Wayne's notes, but never read them or referred to them.

When Pilar arrived in Japan just before Christmas, she found her husband furious. "I ask him what's on tomorrow's shooting schedule," Wayne groused, "and he'll tell me to spend more time absorbing the beauty of the scenery and less time worrying about my part. When I tell him I can't memorize the script unless I know what we'll be shooting, the bastard says, 'Don't worry, we'll improvise.' "

Wayne saw no reason to be discreet with reporters. "After a couple of weeks out here with no action, I had to make up my mind whether to quit and go home and let them sue me, or stay and trust in God and Huston.

"I decided to stay. Anyway, I was in too deep to get out. . . . Mister Huston is on a Japan kick, and as I see it he wants me to walk through a series of Japanese pastels."

Wayne expressed his contempt in a letter to John Ford: "It's a little frustrating trying to arouse the . . . sleeping talent of our lead, Mr. Huston, who wears the clothes of an Irish country gentleman. Maybe I'm prejudiced, but I'd say without the manner." Wayne's only consolation for what he was correctly convinced was a disaster in the making was the opportunity it gave him to buy some Japanese art, which decorated his homes for the rest of his life.

Angela Allen, Huston's script supervisor, ascribed the breach between the men to a complete lack of shared outlook. "They had nothing in common. John Wayne loathed him. He used to say, 'I'm gonna kill him!' I said, 'I'll fix up the appointment, what time do you want to come?' But he didn't want to be left alone with Huston. He was very regimented and could only go in one way. Very professional, but he wasn't that bright."

Huston was always a sucker for visual experimentation, and his original intent was to hire an all-Japanese crew so the film could reflect some of the beauty of Japanese films such as *Gate of Hell*. But Fox wanted the film shot in CinemaScope, and the studio wanted a cameraman experienced in the format. It wasn't an excuse that made much sense, but Huston capitulated and used Fox's

473

Charles Clarke, who had worked in Japan before.

By December 20, the picture was a whopping eleven and a half days behind schedule. Fox's Sid Rogell wrote a letter to Charles Clarke imploring speed. "Anything you can do to speed things up or to suggest eliminations will, of course, be important steps in the right direction." Besides the lagging pace, nobody could figure out what to call the picture. Wayne's suggestion was *Pine and Bamboo,* symbolizing East and West, which Huston liked a lot. Buddy Adler and the sales department were horrified. Among the alternates were *First Ambassador, East Is East, The Kimona Curtain,* and *Geisha*! — the ideal title for a Samuel Fuller movie.

When the studio came up with *The Barbarian and the Geisha,* Huston cabled Adler, "Are you serious? If so I am changing my name, too." Huston assuaged his irritation by embarking on an affair with co-star Eiko Ando.

Wayne spent his off-hours stewing and working on the script for *The Alamo.* When the unit returned to California, Wayne leaned on Buddy Adler, who ordered Walter Lang to reshoot five or six scenes in April of 1958. (The remade scenes: Harris explains about his credentials being in limbo; after Okichi has been ordered back to see Harris; Harris packing up to leave Japan; in the marketplace; Harris burns the house.) One scene was remade because Wayne thought his sideburns were unattractive, another because he thought he looked too old, and a couple were redone, explained producer Eugene Frenke to Huston, "to give [the character of Harris] some vitality."

In short, Wayne took over postproduction. When Huston wrote his memoirs over twenty years later, he was still angry at being outweighed by a movie star: "When I brought it back to Hollywood, the picture, including the music, was finished. . . . It was a sensitive, well-balanced work. . . . John Wayne apparently took over after I left . . . and when I saw it, I was aghast." Later, Huston told a writer, "It was really a fucked-up proposition."

The film was a miserable financial failure, earning $2.5 million in domestic rentals against a cost of $3.4 million, although it can be viewed with considerable pleasure as one of Huston's visual experiments (*Moulin Rouge, Reflections in a Golden Eye*). Dramatically, it feels garbled; after all of Buddy Adler's complaints, Townsend Harris still seems to appear out of nowhere, with no back-story and no motivation for coming to Japan. And there are bewildering continuity gaps — the scene that moves the geisha Okichi from the status of spy to mistress is nonexistent.

Years later, Wayne said that John Huston was the single biggest mistake of his career in terms of directors, and grew agitated at the mere mention of Huston's name. "I found it impossible to make any contact at all. When I look back at his career, Bogie and his dad helped him get started. Outside of *Moulin Rouge* and *Asphalt Jungle,* I don't think he's made anything worthwhile when they weren't there to help him."

Wayne thought Huston wanted him to play Harris with the stiff demeanor that Gregory Peck brought to Ahab in *Moby Dick.* "There was no life in [Peck]. Then I started to work with Huston and found out that was how he was going to have me play this drunken, riotous man, Townsend Harris, who had a great love of people. He had me started out dressed like Abe Lincoln and

475

everybody knows I'm John Wayne. He had scenes where the Americans caused an epidemic of typhoid — wonderful chances to have me be something more than a textbook illustration. But no.

"There was a scene where the Japanese won't sell us food, so I wanted to go out and come back with fish. The kids ask me where I got it, so I take them out and show them how to fish. There were all sorts of things he could have done to make us human beings, but he was only concerned with his tapestry, which he thought was more important than the human story. Huston? You can have him!"

In June 1958, Wayne made a live appearance on the NBC series *Wide, Wide World* for a segment about the western. John Ford, Ward Bond, James Arness, James Garner, and a dozen other stars past and current were scheduled to appear on the show that was being broadcast from a western set in Newhall built decades earlier by Trem Carr and that Wayne knew all too well.

The night before the show Wayne had been drinking with friends. Seven A.M. came, and no Wayne; eight o'clock, and no Wayne. Finally, at nine, Wayne showed up, hungover and struggling.

Ford was furious and berated Wayne for being unprofessional and holding up rehearsal. Wayne just kept his head down, scuffing his toe in the dirt and saying, "I'm sorry, boss." "You're going to pay for this and you're going to pay for it hard all the way," Ford snarled. He ordered Wayne to go all the way to the end of the western street and walk toward the camera while delivering a speech about westerns.

Wayne was searching for the words on the first

rehearsal, so Ford ordered another rehearsal. Back they went to the end of the street. And again. This went on for about six long, hot rehearsals. About twenty minutes before the show was to go on the air, Ford took Gene Autry aside and told him to help Wayne out a little, but under no circumstances was he to tell Wayne that Ford had suggested it.

Autry was no stranger to carousing and always had a supply of adult beverages on hand. He brought Wayne a Coke that had a little something extra in it. Wayne didn't want a Coke. Autry insisted he try the Coke. "He took it and said, 'Not bad, not bad.' So we went ahead then and did the show and after it was all over, Wayne came over and he said, 'Look, you saved my life. I don't know whether I could have made it or not.' "

Wayne's four children from his first marriage were starting their own lives. Twenty-year-old Toni married Don La Cava, a Loyola graduate, in May 1956. Wayne gave the bride away, then sat in the second pew with his former wife Josie. Pilar did not attend the wedding. Officiating was Cardinal McIntyre, who read an Apostolic Benediction from Pope Pius XII. Attending were such notables as Bob Hope, Ray Milland, and Ward Bond.

Wayne's oldest son, Michael, married Gretchen Deibel in 1958. They had met when they were both fifteen, on a blind date at Gretchen's school, Immaculate Heart, where Toni — a friend of Gretchen's — was also a student. (Mike was going to Loyola.) It was a square dance, but neither of them could square dance, so they sat there the entire night and talked. From then on, remembered Gretchen, "We were off and on sweethearts.

I spent my life with him; I knew my father-in-law when I was a teenager."

In those early days, Gretchen always addressed Wayne as "Mr. Wayne," which was fine, but once she and Mike were married, something else seemed to be called for. "Call me Dad," he suggested, but she was too intimidated by his size and presence. "Call me Duke" was the next suggestion, but Gretchen couldn't manage that either.

In short order Gretchen got pregnant and presented Wayne with his first grandchild. At that point, he told Gretchen, "Call me Granddaddy," which sounded all right to her. She called him Granddaddy for the rest of his life.

Jim Henaghan, Wayne's publicist, was another one of the raucous Irish characters he enjoyed. Henaghan had been around a long time — he had been a columnist for *The Hollywood Reporter,* not to mention the first husband of Gwen Verdon, and he had also written some admiring articles about Wayne for the fan magazines — a fairly common way for a publicist to earn his keep since the silent days. (See, for example, *Modern Screen,* October 1954, and *Motion Picture,* November 1956.)

Reputedly, Henaghan could drink Wayne and just about anybody else under the table. Once, the two men were in Acapulco watching the cliff divers leap off a ledge and plummet two hundred feet, just missing the jutting rocks below.

Henaghan turned to his boss and said, "I bet you a round of drinks I could do that." Wayne said it was impossible, that Henaghan would only get himself killed. Nevertheless, he took the bet.

Henaghan went down the steps, around a corner

out of sight, found a diver and paid him to wear Henaghan's swimming trunks. From a distance, all Wayne could see was a man with Henaghan's build in Henaghan's trunks climb out onto the ledge and make a perfect dive beyond the rocks.

After the diver swam back to shore, Henaghan and he switched trunks again. Henaghan jumped in and out of the water, then climbed back up the steps to be greeted as a conquering hero. "You son of a bitch, you really did it!" exclaimed Wayne, who bought drinks for everyone on the patio.

Howard Hawks and Wayne had both disliked Fred Zinnemann's *High Noon,* the former for what he regarded as a lack of professionalism on the part of Gary Cooper's Sheriff Will Kane, the latter for its liberal allegory. As Hawks put it, "I didn't think a good sheriff was going to go running around town like a chicken with his head off asking for help, and finally his Quaker wife had to save him." Hawks wanted to make a western with the precisely opposite point of view — a lawman who feels it's a matter of pride to count only on other professionals.

It was a good idea for a western, especially since Hawks was coming out of a bad period. He hadn't worked since the disastrous *Land of the Pharaohs,* Wayne hadn't made a western since *The Searchers,* and his most recent films hadn't exactly been a string of triumphs.

Rio Bravo looked like money from the beginning, even though it took a long time to come together. The screenwriters were Leigh Brackett and the seventy-year-old Jules Furthman working in tandem — the latter contributed the name Feathers for the leading lady, also the name of the female lead in Furthman's 1927 script for Josef von Sternberg's *Underworld* — which, coincidentally, also involved a man attempting to sober up his best friend.

But the early script drafts weren't a revision of the *High Noon* formula at all. The original story was called "El Paso Red," and, while the opening sequence in the story is fairly close to the film, the plot itself is different from the finished film. The main character, Chance, and his sidekick — in the original story he's named Eddie, not Dude — are bringing in a bunch of horses along with a wagon train from Mexico. The plot hinges on a prominent rancher who is killed and whose daughter goes missing, and a sheriff who is afraid to do anything until Chance and Eddie/Dude decide to help.

Leigh Brackett's first draft retains most of the original story, but loses the Dude character. By the time of the estimating script the basic plot is in place. The script ends with the following:

146 Int. Feather's Room Day
   As Chance unlocks the door and comes in, Feathers is waiting . . .
      *

(This scene was censored before it went to mimeo. Until we get another one, supply your own.)

Wayne was the only actor considered for John T. Chance, but the rest of the cast was up for grabs. For Dude, the choices, in order, were: Frank Sinatra, Robert Mitchum, Spencer Tracy, James Cagney, Tony Curtis, Burt Lancaster, Kirk Douglas, Glenn Ford, Cary Grant, William Holden,

Montgomery Clift, Henry Fonda, Van Johnson, Dean Martin, and Richard Widmark.

For Colorado: Frank Gifford, Michael Landon, Earl Holliman, Richard Jaeckel, Rod Taylor, Murray Hamilton, Stuart Whitman. (Ricky Nelson, who played the part, was obviously an afterthought.)

For Feathers: Rhonda Fleming, Jane Greer, Martha Hyer, Beverly Garland, Carolyn Jones, Piper Laurie, Julie London, Sheree North, Janis Paige, Barbara Rush, Ruta Lee, Donna Reed. (Likewise Angie Dickinson.)

Once again, Hawks pillaged what had worked for him before. The indolent young gun Colorado was yet another riff on Billy the Kid in *The Outlaw* and Cherry Valance in *Red River*. But, as Todd McCarthy wrote in his wise and authoritative biography of the director, Hawks was still on top of his game: "The dialogue in the finished film is uniformly smarter, more assured, and insolent than that in the final screenplay."

Hawks also devised the great opening sequence that so brilliantly defines the characters and the situations without dialogue: A sweaty, bedraggled Dude (Dean Martin) sidles into a bar looking for a drink. A man disdainfully throws a coin into a spittoon. Dude is thinking about going after it when Sheriff John T. Chance (Wayne) stops him. Chance turns to deal with the man who threw the coin in the spittoon. The humiliated Dude slugs Wayne from behind. Burdette (Claude Akins) beats up Dude while others hold him. When someone tries to stop Burdette, he shoots the man down in cold blood.

Two minutes have elapsed, not a word has been spoken, and we're already deep into foundational conflicts about which Hawks is so secure he spends half the picture ignoring them — an extraordinary economy that couldn't have been devised by anyone who hadn't worked in silent film.

Once his cast was set, Hawks shot his movie in sixty-one days, six days over schedule, from May 4 to July 23, 1958. Under the contract he signed on April 1, Wayne was paid a flat $750,000 for his services, spread out in one payment of $250,000, two payments of $175,000, and one payment of $150,000 — one payment a year for four years, from 1958 to 1961. (Spacing out the money was a means of avoiding the heaviest income tax percentage.)

For the rest of the cast, Dean Martin got $5,000 a week for ten weeks, with two weeks added for postproduction. If Hawks had known how Martin felt about John Wayne westerns he could have gotten him for free. "I remember third shows at the Copa where [Dean would] speed up so as not to miss the three A.M. showing of John Wayne in *Red River* or *Stagecoach,*" remembered Jerry Lewis. "In fact, I'll swear: as much as Dean loved the ladies, when the fun was done, he preferred being left alone to watch his westerns or read his comic books. Women always seemed to need the kind of attention he wasn't much interested in giving."

Ricky Nelson got $3,500 per week with a ten-week guarantee, and Angie Dickinson got $833.33 per week with a twelve-week guarantee. The two payroll surprises were Walter Brennan, who got $10,000 a week for five weeks, and Ward Bond, who got $3,333 a week for six weeks, even though his scenes could easily have been photographed in a couple of days.

Wayne's salary for *Rio Bravo* represented a financial diminishment, since he had been getting a percentage of the proceeds since Republic. He was willing to take less money when working for Ford; it's possible that he was doing the same thing because of his affection for Hawks, whose Armada Productions was in for 30 percent of the profits.

After Martin was cast, Wayne began to think seriously about his character. "Martin gets all the fireworks, doesn't he?" he asked Hawks, who had to agree. "What do I do?" he finally asked.

"What would happen to you if your best friend had been a drunk and he was trying to come back — wouldn't you watch him?" asked Hawks. Wayne knew all about working with drunks; he thought about it, nodded and said, "OK, I know what to do."

As he moved into the latter stages of his career, Wayne would often express the same basic anxiety, especially with complex scripts — that he was the hub of the wheel but didn't actually have a lot to do, or even much of a character to play, and just how the hell was he supposed to be interesting for 120 minutes? It was basic actor's fear, the rough equivalent of Spencer Tracy's neurotic attempts to try to back out of nearly every movie just before shooting started. It was also somehow touching in that Wayne seemed unaware of the compelling strength he could project without trying — the innate quality that Hawks and Ford relied on.

Hawks chose Arizona's Old Tucson for the primary location, and did a lot of construction, building an entirely new main street about four blocks long that bisected the old, pre-existing pueblo structures and included twenty-six buildings, not counting the large warehouse that was blown up in the film's climax.

Wayne is relaxed, commanding, unflappable. In a direct riposte to *High Noon,* he wants no help from well-meaning amateurs. In one of the great dialogue exchanges of the movies, he outlines his meager troops:

1. A drunk.
2. A crazy old man.

"That's all you got?" asks Ward Bond.

"That's *what* I got," says Wayne.

John T. Chance is a self-sufficient man who inspires others to rise above their own acknowledged shortcomings. Beneath the surface it's a very democratic movie — a small community of friends in which each individual shores up the next. Crude readings of Wayne's persona accuse him of mindless cheerleading for American might. It would be more accurate to say that Wayne embodies the American experiment far more than he does American power, if only because he never avoided dramatizing the potential that experiment had for going wrong.

Howard Hawks didn't have a lot of ideas, but the ones he had were solid: play comedy as fast as possible, underplay drama as much as possible, make the girl as tough as the leading man. Mainly, Hawks believed that if something worked once, it would work at least three more times. Angie Dickinson has the same part that Lauren Bacall had in *To Have and Have Not,* complete with thinly paraphrased dialogue, and Ricky Nelson rubs his nose with one finger, just like Montgomery Clift in *Red River.* As for Wayne, in a charming in-joke, he wears a belt buckle that sports Tom Dunson's brand from *Red River.*

Angie Dickinson had to test for the part, not opposite Wayne but opposite football player Frank Gifford, who was moonlighting from the New York Giants while recovering from an injury. Hawks gave Capucine, Charles Feldman's mistress, pro forma consideration for the part of Feathers, but he didn't want an accent in his movie. Also, Capucine had an aristocratic air that was at odds with Hawks's taste in women. (Feldman would finally get his way when he stuck Capucine in *North to Alaska* a year later.)

Dickinson had already worked for Wayne indirectly when she made *Gun the Man Down,* the James Arness western that Andrew McLaglen had directed for Batjac a couple of years earlier. She had also done an unbilled bit with Wayne in a George Gobel vehicle at RKO entitled *I Married a Woman.*

None of these films was going to earn her a starring role opposite John Wayne. "I had done one good movie, *Cry Terror,* with James Mason," remembered Dickinson. "It was made in '57, came out in '58 and I was damn good. I could see I had something to stick around for." Auteurists might also point to Samuel Fuller's *China Gate,* but Dickinson insisted that the Fuller movie was barely seen.

Dickinson actually got *Rio Bravo* through an episode of *Perry Mason.* Chris Nyby, who had been Hawks's film editor as well as the credited director on *The Thing,* had been directing *Perry Mason* and told his former employer to take a look at the startlingly sensual young actress.

"Chris's recommendation meant that I was more than actress #47 coming through the door," said Dickinson. "It was serendipity." Also working

485

in her favor was the fact that Dickinson had a mind of her own. One day Hawks played a song that he liked called "Tiger by the Tail," and asked Dickinson if she liked it.

"No," she said.

"Everybody always says 'Yes' to me," mused Hawks, but Dickinson could see that he was pleased by her refusal to acquiesce. "I think it surprised him; Howard liked to be surprised."

Dickinson joined the company in Old Tucson, where Hawks, Wayne, and Dean Martin threw a dinner in her honor. When they got down to work, Wayne didn't offer her any coaching, as he often did with young actors, because "with Hawks around he didn't have to coach. But Duke was incredibly patient with me. My scenes were well written, but they were tough to play. It was on the page, but you don't know how hard to press."

Dickinson's problem was that she was playing the sexual aggressor — a part she wasn't used to. "Wayne is better when the girl is forcing the issue," said Hawks, comparing it to the way Clark Gable forced the issue in a love scene. "If you've got a love scene in a Wayne picture, you adjust it to his personality. He just wouldn't be effective if he were aggressive toward a woman. Partly that's because of his size. He's too big to be a Rover Boy like Gable was."

"We didn't shoot that many takes, but we rehearsed a lot," said Dickinson. "And never once did Duke say, 'Jesus Christ, can't she just do it?' Never once did he appear to be impatient. And for a star of his caliber, working with a green actress, that was remarkable. Never, not for a second, did I feel he didn't approve of what I was doing."

486

On-screen as well as off, Wayne was always slightly abashed when confronted with a strong woman, and Dickinson's Feathers is definitely somebody he can't quite handle. She backs him up, metaphorically and literally. "His characters are not adorable," said Dickinson, "but in those scenes, he was adorable."

Like Feathers, Hawks knew when to press and when to relax. As Dickinson and Wayne were shooting the last scene in the picture, where she forces Chance to admit he loves her, Hawks told her, "Try it again, and in the middle start crying."

"Crying wasn't in the script," said Dickinson. "And that's the take he used." Dickinson remembered that Hawks "had a way of wanting you to do something very special. Yet he would not tell you how to make it special. He wanted you to come up with it by yourself. And therefore it would be special. If he told you, it wouldn't be special. . . . He wouldn't tell you very much; he would just leak out a little of what he wanted, and you had to play with it."

In Hawks's world, which largely derives from Hemingway's world, the worst thing you can say to another human being is "You're not good enough." Because of this ethical stand, it was daunting for Dickinson to go up against Wayne and Hawks. "I was not really ready for it. It worked, but I was in over my head, and Hawks was very good. He just stuck with me and didn't give up. Those were very tough scenes to do."

It was a happy set, because there was a mutual respect between Wayne and Hawks, even though they were totally different men. "Hawks was complex and Duke was simple," said Dickinson. "Hawks wanted excitement in his life, and Duke didn't, particularly. They bore more respect than love for each other."

Dickinson watched Wayne with an eagle's eye. "When a movie is rich there's so much to take from it — a lot of colors. But a rich movie takes a lot of work and finesse. As an actor, Duke was not Al Pacino, who I imagine looks at a scene and thinks of a dozen different ways to play it before starting to narrow down the options. Duke went on instinct. Which is not to say he wasn't intelligent. He was, and well informed too; there was nothing casual about him or his approach to the work, or to his life. He was determined and solid in his beliefs."

Wayne and Dean Martin got along well and would play chess, but there wasn't a deep simpatico. "Dean was a Democrat, and that might have been part of it," said Dickinson. "But Dean wasn't a talker. He could be in a group for a long time and not say a word. At all. Forever. He was unschooled and shy; the intelligentsia would make him insecure. He was always difficult socially."

Dickinson was conscious of a strong mutual attraction between herself and Wayne. She had grown up watching John Wayne movies, and had been astonished by his rugged beauty as a young man. When they made *Rio Bravo,* he was married and she was involved, but she believed that "in another world, on the right island, yes, we would have ended up together. In later years, whenever we saw each other, there was always a special warmth. Did I find him sexy? More romantic than sexy — the sort of man you fall in love with rather than fall into bed with. He wasn't aggressive with women. He was always very respectful, and a gentleman."

Rio Bravo is as much of an anthology as it is a movie. Walter Brennan is back playing the ornery old coot, Wayne the granite wall, and Ricky Nelson the barely-out-of-adolescence baby-faced killer. (The picture's great originality is in beginning to set Dean Martin's character as an amiable drunk.)

Rio Bravo has enormous charm, but the picture goes on for an unconscionable 141 minutes — one song maybe, but two? Nevertheless, *Rio Bravo* was one of those pictures that everybody saw, and that almost everybody liked. Made for $3 million, it had world rentals of $10 million, and it proved that Wayne's reach as a star was not bound by the Atlantic and Pacific oceans — its foreign take was $4.5 million, just a little short of the domestic gross of $5.4 million.

Although the picture is more than slightly baggy and can't build up much suspense, Todd McCarthy correctly points out that it represents perhaps the most direct expression of the director's interests: "self-respect, self-control, the interdependence of select chosen friends, being good at what you do, the blossoming of sexual-romantic attraction — as demonstrated by characters utterly removed from the norms of routine existence." And because Wayne was finely attuned to "the interdependence of select chosen friends" as well as a philosophy of personal excellence, it naturally provided him with an arena in which he shone.

But for Wayne, *Rio Bravo* was more or less a job of work, for his attention was increasingly centered on *The Alamo*. Potential partners were circling — even Jack Warner was suddenly attentive: "I was going to come down to the set to see you this afternoon late," he wrote Wayne a few days before the end of production on *Rio Bravo,* "but when I phoned was told the company had finished for the day . . . have been seeing almost all the dailies and the film looks great. I feel we will really have a very important picture."

He then got down to brass tacks: "[Louella] Parsons had a story in her column today that Clint Murchison and a group of Texans were going to finance your Alamo film. Is there any chance of our company getting this for distribution?"

What with Batjac's experiences in the recent past, it wasn't hard for Wayne to resist Jack Warner's overtures. He had been happy there, he had made a great deal of money there, and he would return and make more money. But Warner Bros. was entering a bad period. "Jack got to the point where he wasn't buying properties unless he felt it could be a big, successful film," said Vincent Sherman. "Contract people were let go. Raoul Walsh was there as long as anybody, but eventually he left too. Jack didn't know what to make exactly, and he didn't want to spend a lot of money unless he thought a project couldn't miss — *My Fair Lady,* for instance. He didn't know which way the business was going, and he got gun-shy."

Victor McLaglen died in 1959, the first major figure of the Ford stock company to go. He had watched his son's progress through the ranks with eagerness and pride. Andrew McLaglen had moved from being an assistant at Batjac to directing quality TV westerns such as *Have Gun, Will Travel* and *Gunsmoke,* and had tentatively begun a career in features by the time of his father's death.

Wayne remembered that "[Vic] would always come to me and say, 'How's he doing? How's the boy doing? How do the other guys your age feel about him?' Always worrying about the boy." In a few years, Wayne would give Andrew his break into the big time.

That same year, Grant Withers committed suicide. Wayne had carried him financially for years, and even gotten him a job at Universal guiding celebrities around the lot for $200 a week. But Withers's alcoholism and the accompanying physical problems finally overwhelmed him. Typically, Wayne blamed himself, but only because he had been too benevolent. "It's all my fault. I made it too easy for him. If the guy had to go out and goddamn go to work or something, maybe he wouldn't have done it. But I let him keep up his half-ass standard of being a big shot around town. I made it too easy for him."

Shortly after *Rio Bravo* ended production, Wayne gave an interview to UPI's Vernon Scott that centered on his financial difficulties. "I've been acting for almost 30 years, and never come close to amassing a fortune," he said. "I'd like to take it easy for a while, but I can't. I have to work to keep my head above water. By the time I pay off alimony, my business agent, manager and raise five kids, I'm lucky if I break even. I keep working because I need the money."

Wayne continued to be alarmed at the state of the industry he loved. He was particularly upset about the Tennessee Williams film *Suddenly, Last Summer,* with the homosexual Sebastian being cannibalized by native urchins. Wayne said the

491

film was "polluting the bloodstream of Hollywood."

He committed to a group of films that would be made nearly back to back in order to build up cash reserves for *The Alamo*. *The Horse Soldiers* was a picture that Martin Rackin and John Lee Mahin ginned up with John Ford before they brought it to the Mirisch brothers. The latter had raised themselves out of Monogram by renaming the company Allied Artists and producing William Wyler's *Friendly Persuasion* and Billy Wilder's *Love in the Afternoon*. Leaving Monogram/Allied Artists behind, the Mirische's decamped for United Artists, where they would be organization mainstays for the next fifteen years.

The Horse Soldiers was a Civil War picture, and with Ford's interest, which generally translated to John Wayne's interest, it quickly became what the industry likes to term a Go project. At his first meeting with Ford, Walter Mirisch asked about a leading man. "Well, Duke. Duke," said Ford. Mirisch breathed a sigh of relief but pointed out that the picture was mostly exteriors and would have to be made in the spring or summer, and it was already the fall of 1958 — not much time to lock in a script and the services of major star. Ford wasn't alarmed. "When I'm ready, he'll be there," said Ford. In due course, Wayne was there. Wayne and William Holden each signed on for $750,000 plus 20 percent of the profits; Ford was in for $200,000 and 10 percent of the gross.

Hiring on as an actor was William Wellman Jr. He had known Wayne for years; when he was a young boy, his father took him to Johnny Indrisano for boxing lessons, who also instructed Mike and Pat Wayne in the manly art of self-defense while their fathers looked on.

But *The Horse Soldiers* was William Wellman Jr.'s first time on a Ford picture, and the experience left him shaken, especially because of what it did to his idea of John Wayne. "I liked John Wayne. I was a fan. I thought he was a god. And the fact that he would take the abuse from Ford. . . . I mean, people would turn away. It was cringe-making. Ford would say things like, 'You're nothing but a goddamn cowboy. You couldn't act your way out of a paper bag.' And that was for starters. And Wayne just took it. He never spoke back. Ford was like his father, he had given him his career. Eventually Ford would stop, and Wayne would just pick up where he had left off and go on. It rolled off him, or seemed to."

One day Ford tried the same thing with Holden, who came over and stuck his finger in Ford's chest and said, "Don't ever do that again. If you ever do that again, I don't care who you are and how old you are, I will pick you up and throw you in the river."

"Ford hardly talked to Holden after that," remembered Wellman. "Ford was never mean to women, always treated them with respect and courtesy. It was actors and men that he would go after.

"Now, Ford liked my father, and my father liked him. They were friendly, but I was afraid to get close to him, because he got angry with me my first day on the picture. I was whistling, and Ford turned suddenly in his chair and looked at me and all work stopped. And I stopped whistling and everybody turned to go back to work. Later, someone told me, 'Don't ever whistle around the Old Man. And don't laugh or sing or tell any stories unless he instigates it.' So I just stayed clear of him."

The Horse Soldiers would be marred by the death of stuntman Fred Kennedy, who broke his neck doing a simple horse fall. Ford and Wayne had worked with Kennedy for years and both were devastated. Ford lost interest in the picture.

If *The Horse Soldiers* was a missed opportunity for Ford, it must have been a nightmare for Wayne. Pilar had been beset by insomnia for some years, a function of anxiety at being plucked out of Peru and tossed into the highest reaches of Hollywood life. She had begun taking Seconal to sleep and gradually became addicted.

On location in Louisiana, Pilar ran out of the pills and began an inadvertent drug withdrawal. Her mouth went dry, her breath was short, her heart began pounding wildly, she began to hallucinate. The episode culminated in Pilar slashing her wrists. Wayne hired a private airplane and nurses to get her back to California while he stayed in Louisiana. There was nothing else to do. There was a movie to be made.

"I liked Duke Wayne a great deal," said Walter Mirisch. "A very decent, professional man, no nonsense. He came to work, he knew his lines. He was approachable, he didn't throw his power or prominence around. And a tremendously underrated actor. He gave many extraordinary performances — *Red River, The Searchers* — but he had to wait until the end of his career for an Oscar.

"I thought he was good on script, although my only experience with him was through Ford, and his whole relationship with Ford was so screwy. I was on the set one day when Ford made some kind of disparaging remark to him: 'Get over

494

there, you dumb cluck' or something like that. It bothered me, and later I said to Duke, 'Why the hell do you let him talk to you like that?'

" 'Aw, that's just the Old Man,' he said. 'He doesn't mean it. Forget about it.' But I didn't like it."

Nineteen fifty-eight had been devoted to three movies and to preparation for *The Alamo*. Nineteen fifty-nine would be devoted to one movie only. As Wayne wrote in August of that year, "my career, my personal fortune, and my standing in the business are at stake."

CHAPTER FIFTEEN

By now, everybody in Wayne's inner circle could list all the reasons not to make *The Alamo*. There were a dozen financial concerns Bö Roos could cite and John Ford had more objections: Wayne was too old, had never directed, and the story of the Alamo would be one hell of a complicated production to use as a learning experience. Wayne turned a deaf ear to all of this. He had made up his mind, and when he arrived at that point he could be every bit as focused as one of his obsessive characters.

In 1956, Batjac had outlined a distribution deal with United Artists in which UA would front $2.5 million of the budget in return for distribution rights. Batjac had to match the funds. Wayne had to abandon his plan to play a cameo as Sam Houston in order to play a major part and add some box office insurance. He chose Davy Crockett, then had to find someone equally commanding for Sam Houston. He eventually settled on his old contractee James Arness, now a huge TV star on *Gunsmoke*.

Wayne asked Andy McLaglen to set up a meeting with Arness, which he did. Wayne brought his entourage over to the *Gunsmoke* set after shooting one day to ask Arness to be in the picture, only to find that Arness had skipped out on the meeting. "Jim powdered," remembered McLaglen. "He absolutely did not show up for the meeting. He totally powdered."

Wayne was understandably furious, and never really forgave Arness for his flagrant disloyalty. "Get that other guy you work with," he snapped at McLaglen, meaning Richard Boone, the star of *Have Gun, Will Travel.* So Richard Boone played Sam Houston.

Besides casting difficulties, there were money problems. The proposed budget of $5 million wasn't anywhere near enough to make the movie Wayne was planning. In search of additional funding, he approached Texas governor Price Daniel, who introduced him to Texas businessmen who were anxious to counter the negative, nativist image that George Stevens had given the state in 1956's *Giant.*

In June 1958, Clint Murchison agreed to invest $1.5 million in incremental amounts, under the condition that he was in line to get his money back after UA but before anybody else was repaid. He was also charging 6 percent per year interest, and demanded that Wayne receive no personal salary for making the movie. All this and 5 percent of the net profits. He also capped his investment at $1.5 million; any further monies were Wayne's problem. What all this meant was that Batjac's own investment could not be recovered until both UA and subsidiary investors got their money back.

Wayne would later estimate that besides Batjac's contractual contribution, he dropped in $1.2 million of his personal funds — more or less all the ready cash that he had in the world.

Since 1956, he had been looking for a place to shoot his movie cheaply, which led him to consider Mexico and Peru. But those locations were submarined by the problem of finding sufficiently skilled professionals to staff the picture and the fact that distance added costs.

One man was convinced that the movie needed to be made in Texas, and that man was James T. "Happy" Shahan, the mayor of Brackettville, Texas, a town of 1,800 hardy souls one hundred miles west of San Antonio. It just so happened that Shahan owned a 22,000-acre ranch in Brackettville that he believed had all sorts of possibilities.

Parts of *The Last Command,* Herbert Yates's underhanded attempt to preempt Wayne's dream project, had been shot in nearby Fort Clark, although the set Republic built was only a small L configuration on the ranch of Louis Hobbs — the Alamo chapel itself had been a matte painting. Shahan believed that Brackettville was the perfect location to build a more expansive set.

At this point, Wayne was planning to shoot in Durango, Mexico, where he had already set the local people to work making authentic adobe bricks to use in constructing the sets. But beginning in 1955, Shahan set siege to Wayne. As he put it, they started talking in the spring of 1955, "and we argued until September, 1957."

That summer, Wayne sent Nate Edwards, the Batjac production manager, to examine Shahan's ranch. Edwards arrived in late June, and Shahan took him around Kinney County. Edwards liked Fort Clark, because it could billet a large crew, but they needed something more for the actual Alamo set. After several days of looking, Edwards hadn't seen anything that would work.

On the last day of Edwards's visit, Shahan had to double back to his ranch to cut out some cattle. Shahan and Edwards pulled into the ranch as the sun was setting. As they drove past Shahan's house and onto the flatland where the cattle were corraled, Edwards told Shahan to stop his truck. Why, he wanted to know, had Shahan not brought him here before? On July 1, one week after Edwards returned to Hollywood with photographs of the proposed location, Wayne called Shahan and told him he was on his way to Brackettville.

"When?" asked Shahan.

"Tomorrow," said Wayne. After Wayne saw the location, negotiations were quickly accomplished. He would make his movie in Brackettville. What seems to have closed the deal was Shahan's willingness to serve as the construction ramrod on the project. "All I want is an architect, your art director and that's all," he told Wayne. "I can do the rest."

Wayne thought it was an empty promise until Shahan introduced him to a round little man named Chato Hernández, whom Shahan said could handle the construction. Wayne drew himself up to his full height and said, "Chato, can you build an Alamo?"

"Mr. Wayne, can you make a movie?" replied Hernández.

Set construction got under way in February 1958, with production planned for September. Eventually, the sets spread over four hundred acres of land. Wayne had hired Al Ybarra as the Batjac art director because of the work Ybarra had done for Ford on *The Fugitive* in 1947. "When John Wayne saw it," Ybarra told the film historian

499

Frank Thompson, "he was in love with the picture, the way it was done. He liked particularly the fade-out scene, and I designed the fade-out scene. . . . He says, 'Look, one day I'm gonna do a story on the Alamo. I want you to be my art director.' "

Ybarra was the art director on *The High and the Mighty, Hondo,* and all the other Batjac productions while he kept working on *The Alamo.* When it finally came time to start building the set, Ybarra had the benefit of nearly ten years of thinking and planning.

The facade of the Alamo was built of stone, with most of the wood cannibalized from derelict buildings at Fort Clark. Only the chapel was reproduced to exact scale — the rest of the compound was constructed at about 75 percent actual size — and even then Ybarra cheated a little. The humped gable on the facing of the chapel wasn't actually there when the battle was fought, nor were two upper windows that were added in 1850.

Ybarra went down to Mexico and bought old handmade iron hardware, then brought in 150 Mexicans from across the border to make adobes. Four months after construction began, a rainstorm washed away fifty thousand adobe bricks that had been drying in the sun. Parts of the set representing old San Antonio also disappeared. After the rains, Ybarra had his crew dig drainage ditches around the entire set.

Even with the flash flood, Ybarra was on schedule, but the September 1958 production date came and went because Batjac had a cash shortfall that resulted from buying out Robert Fellows's share of the company. Wayne realized that the filming had to be postponed for an entire year.

500

Wayne called Shahan and told him to stop building the set, but Shahan said he couldn't stop. He decided to take over financial responsibility for the construction himself, and got a loan for $100,000 that was co-signed by Wayne.

As if all this wasn't enough turmoil, at the end of 1958 Wayne terminated his professional relationship with Bö Roos's Beverly Management Corporation. Although Wayne would always claim Roos had cheated him up, down, and sideways, after a thorough investigation nothing illegal was found. Most of the money Wayne had given Roos to invest had been flushed down the toilet of bad real estate, overpriced Mexican hotels, dry wells, and management fees. Lots of management fees.

Another financial hit came with the Panamanian investments Wayne had made through Roberto Arias, the husband of Margot Fonteyn and the son of the former president of Panama. Arias was, first, a charmer, and, second, a rogue. Rampant infidelity was not unusual for a Latin male, but Arias took it a step further. In April 1959, Arias fled Panama, which led to Fonteyn being arrested for purportedly plotting against the government. Wayne claimed that "Tito" (Arias's nickname) "never talked politics and I never heard him say anything about overthrowing the Panamanian government."

What made it awkward for Wayne was the discovery of Arias's suitcase that held an envelope with Wayne's address. Inside the envelope was a memorandum to Wayne outlining a "schedule of funds totaling $682,850 given to or drawn by Tito Arias in connection with his Panamanian operations in which you are involved." The memorandum went on to specify that $525,000 had been turned over to Arias personally.

The implication was that Arias had diverted some of Wayne's investment monies into political activities against the Panamanian government. Wayne said that the charges against Arias were "ridiculous."

Before all this happened, Wayne estimated that he, Arias, and Arias's brother Tony had about 70 percent of the shrimp business in Panama locked up. It all came tumbling down when Tony Arias was killed in an airplane crash, and his brother fled the country. Wayne estimated that he lost $500,000 in the resulting debacle.

While Wayne went off to make *The Barbarian and the Geisha, Rio Bravo,* and *The Horse Soldiers* in rapid succession, Al Ybarra and Happy Shahan kept going. The Alamo set eventually took more than a year to build out of wood, limestone, and thousands of handmade adobe bricks. Ybarra had to install ten miles of wiring, and Batjac fronted the cost of fourteen miles of gravel and tar roads, as well as a four-thousand-foot runway at nearby Fort Clark, where the unit would be housed.

The isolation of the location forced Wayne into great expense. At the height of the production, about 2,500 people would be living and working around Brackettville, so Batjac had to have deep-water wells dug and twenty miles of sewage lines laid into mammoth cesspools. In addition, a series of dikes and dams were constructed to turn a lazy prairie creek into a decent sized river. Giant corrals were built to house the one thousand horses and three hundred longhorns needed for the production.

The longhorns posed a particular problem; they were practically extinct by 1959, and the herd had

502

to be put together in small numbers. Each animal had to be insured for $1,500, and they were driven to Brackettville from ranches elsewhere in Texas.

Throughout 1959, Wayne made a series of visits to the Brackettville location to check out Ybarra's set as it grew. During his final walk-through before production, Wayne noticed that Ybarra had placed a small cross on the very tip of the chapel. Wayne stared at it for a while, then said, "Take that down." After it was removed, he stared at the front of the chapel some more, then said, "Gimme something allegorical. We need something up there — maybe a larger cross."

Ybarra thought about it for a few minutes, then told the crew to place a large cross on top of the chapel, only at an angle, as if it had fallen over. Ybarra wasn't happy about the substitution — he felt the fallen cross was out of scale — but Wayne wanted something allegorical, and he got something allegorical.

Ybarra didn't attempt to accurately reproduce the San Antonio of 1836. Although Mexican towns of the time were constructed around plazas, Ybarra's San Antonio is more or less a conventional western town, with dusty streets and parallel lines of buildings.

Wayne's passion for the picture continued to lead him into a series of bad deals. Besides the fact that UA's investment was small considering the overall budget, and both UA and the additional investors were due their money before Batjac could recoup, the set he was building at great cost became Happy Shahan's property when the picture was finished. (No wonder Shahan was happy.)

But Wayne believed that the picture had to be

done right if it was going to be done at all, and he wasn't about to let niggling financial considerations derail him. He even laid a railroad track into Shahan's property to drop hay for the horses and feed for the livestock.

Among the people he consulted about the picture were the historian J. Frank Dobie, and former vice president John Nance Garner, who, Wayne told Hedda Hopper, "was the only man in his administration with enough guts to stand up against FDR" — a comment that disappeared between the interview and the printed version.

By June 1959, Wayne was negotiating with Todd-AO to shoot his film in the 70mm process, but he realized that he needed still more money. He began canvassing for additional investors and the McCullough Tool Company seemed interested. On June 30, he wrote them a long letter outlining the project's financials. The production cost was listed as $4.5 million, with an additional $1 million for advertising and publicity, $1.5 million apiece for the cast as well as distribution costs. With this — grievously underestimated — math, the break-even point on *The Alamo* was forecast to be $9.6 million.

He then outlined the returns on the three previous Todd-AO spectaculars: *Oklahoma!* had returned rentals of $11 million, *Around the World in 80 Days* had returned about $27 million, while *South Pacific* was at $10 million and still playing.

Donning the cap of Max Bialystock, Wayne went on to feverishly assert that the worst-case scenario for *Oklahoma!* and *South Pacific* was that investors would get their money back, plus 6 percent interest, plus a profit of about $600,000. If *The Alamo* turned out to be a real smash like *Around the*

504

World in 80 Days, "my adding machine's broken. . . . Under these circumstances, it seems to me that the million dollars and completion guarantee from your group is a safe investment." The inference, of course, was that Todd-AO was some sort of commercial safety net that would bring the picture home no matter its quality.

In New York, Todd-AO cleared their corporate throats and announced that they had . . . *issues.* On July 8, George Skouras, brother of 20th Century Fox's Spyros Skouras, wrote Wayne that the board of Todd-AO would have to read the script before it agreed to honor Wayne with its 70mm cameras. A week later, Skouras wrote, "To be frank, I am not enthusiastic over the script. I find the first 112 pages more or less anemic."

At this point, Skouras was under the impression that John Ford was going to direct the picture, but even that didn't cut any ice: "I don't believe, however, even in the hands of John Ford, that the story incorporated in the script has the ingredients of a road show Todd-AO picture." A few days later, Charles Feldman talked to Skouras, who told Feldman that if Wayne persisted with Jimmy Grant's existing script the film would be a fiasco.

Wayne responded with both a letter and a telegram. The former quoted John Ford's opinion of the script — "thrilling" — and went on to enumerate the displays of showmanship he was planning. He said that he would reproduce John Singer Sargent's *El Jaleo* as embodied by José Greco and his troupe during the night raid on the Mexican army. "Picture that being used just as a background to a suspense sequence in which a group of our men are sneaking through enemy lines, and you will realize the scope of our artistic planning in this picture."

After a few days of intense lobbying with Skouras, Feldman sent a memo to some associates in his agency outlining the situation. George Skouras hated the script and believed it would bankrupt Wayne. But his brother Spyros, the chairman of Fox, with whom Wayne was in serious business, pleaded with his brother and finally wore him down. Spyros Skouras even said that Fox would pay half of the guarantee that Todd-AO was demanding. "If Spyros didn't put it in a personal basis — brother to brother — George would have said 'no,' " reported Feldman.

But George Skouras wanted a guarantee that John Ford would direct key scenes. Feldman had raised this chimera earlier in the year, in February, when he wrote Spyros Skouras that "in all probability there will be a codirector who may not get credit for the personal scenes and of course a second unit director for the big battle scenes." Since everybody in the industry associated Wayne with Ford, they assumed Ford would be the uncredited co-director.

Feldman's opinion was that nothing else mattered but getting Skouras to sign on the line which is dotted — "once you sign the *papers,* you needn't be *concerned,* as I will handle it." (Feldman's emphasis.) Spyros Skouras finally offered to have Fox take the picture over from UA if it came to that.

While all this was going on, Clint Murchison made noises about pulling out his investment. Murchison had agreed to advance $2 million, an extra $500,000 over his initial investment, in return for a bump in his share of the profits to 15 percent. Then Murchison got cold feet. Wayne wrote that he could probably find the extra $500,000 elsewhere, but Murchison's $1.5 million was crucial; there wasn't enough time to raise it elsewhere, and postponing the picture was impossible.

Batjac forwarded a balance sheet which showed that the company's assets totaled $707,344, while the liabilities amounted to much less; there was a surplus of $242,943. Most importantly, the Batjac film library, which included *The High and the Mighty, Hondo,* and ten other pictures, was carried at a net value of only $27,655. Attorneys regarded the financial potential of the library for reissue and television to be, conservatively speaking, $500,000. They were Batjac's own attorneys, but they were still grossly underestimating the library's value.

On July 3, 1959, Murchison's attorney wrote Wayne that the commitment would be honored. But Wayne's massively scaled historical spectacular was still underfunded. Wayne and everybody else knew that he was going to have to ante up more money.

The final shooting schedule, dated August 21, called for sixty-six days, an improbably short schedule considering the scale of the picture. While final preparations were going on through the summer of 1959, Wayne and Jimmy Grant were polishing the script, with Grant beginning yet another rewrite — the twelfth! — in May. When he finished, the script had expanded from 106 pages to 156 pages.

As the final version of the script was being completed, Wayne received a letter from Raoul Walsh, which was accompanied by a still from *The Big Trail* showing Wayne astride a horse with

507

the Grand Tetons in the distance.

"Have been looking over some old stills and ran across the enclosed," wrote Walsh. "Thought you might enjoy meeting a dashing young plainsman.

"Read in the trade papers that you are going to direct *The Alamo* and also play in it. This is a pretty tough assignment but with all the experience you have had I know of nobody better qualified to become a director. So I'll be rooting for you. And if you take the advice of an old wrangler, do not start the picture until you have a finished script to your liking."

Walsh had intuitively determined the primary problem of *The Alamo.* Wayne's years of thinking about the project had resulted in a prolix script.

The script would be the focus of critical dissatisfaction then and now, but Happy Shahan insisted that Wayne's original ideas were actually much stronger than what finally emerged. "I have to defend Wayne. It definitely wasn't Wayne's fault as much as it was the writer's. . . . I was there during arguments when Wayne wanted to do what history said and Grant said, 'Hey, who knows about that? Nobody but Texans.' . . .

"You gotta remember one thing: Wayne was very loyal to his friends."

Shahan's version of events was confirmed by Al Ybarra, who said, "[Wayne] should have done more cutting, eliminating [the scene in the woods where Crockett sends the girl home] and also eliminating the scene in the Cantina. That didn't mean a damn thing. . . . When guys were down there on that kind of a hardship and with a potential war on their hands, they don't mess around with feathers on their noses. . . . His writer, Jimmy Grant, talked him into that. And he

508

talked him into the love scene which should never have been left in the final cut."

The script became "way too wordy," according to Gretchen Wayne. "They never shut up. No wonder they lost — the Mexicans could have come over the walls while they were all talking. But Granddaddy wanted to get his points across, and it was his picture and he could do what he wanted."

Wayne was blinded by his dream. Concerned that United Artists' limited investment would correspond to a limited enthusiasm for the picture he hired Russell Birdwell as Batjac's personal publicity man for *The Alamo*. Birdwell was a legendary figure who had supervised publicity for Selznick's *Gone With the Wind,* as well as Howard Hughes's *The Outlaw.* Not coincidentally, Birdwell had also been born in Texas.

Birdwell's affinity for the bold began early; he had been a reporter at the sensational New York *Daily Mirror* in 1927 when he scooped the world with the story of Lindbergh's takeoff for Paris. Birdwell had enormous energy, a lot of charm, and wasn't hampered by excessive amounts of taste.

Wayne's plan was that Birdwell would work in tandem with UA's own publicity apparatus on *The Alamo,* but UA immediately resented the idea of Birdwell's interference, mostly because they regarded his ideas as old-fashioned ballyhoo that, given the seriousness of the picture, was in atrocious taste. The conflict that resulted undoubtedly damaged the picture.

Wayne was pleasantly surprised when Frank Sinatra expressed interest in the part of the chilly, driven William Barret Travis. "Frank came over," remembered Wayne, "he talked to me about the Travis part, he knew Travis as well as I do." But Sinatra was booked up for the next year, and Wayne couldn't afford to put off production and pay interest on the loans.

Wayne offered Richard Widmark his choice of either Travis or Bowie, hoping he'd take Travis. He took Bowie and a salary of $200,000. That left Travis, for whom Wayne recruited Laurence Harvey, hot from the previous year's *Room at the Top*. Harvey came on board for $100,000.

Wayne not only personally hired every actor, he personally hired every stuntman. A twenty-seven-year-old Texan named Dean Smith was doubling for Dale Robertson on *Tales of Wells Fargo* when Olympic decathlon champion Bob Mathias took him to meet Mike Wayne and Bob Morrison. Smith had won a gold medal on the 1952 Olympic team with Mathias, who made *China Doll* for Batjac while Smith was playing for the Los Angeles Rams.

"I told them I could ride and jump with anybody," remembered Smith, "and that I wanted to go back to Texas and work on something dealing with Texas history. While I was there with Bob and Mike, I also met Tom Kane. And then guess who walked in?"

Wayne remembered Smith from the Olympics and the Rams. After a brief conversation, he turned to Mike and his brother and said, "Let's take this kid to Texas. He needs to go back home."

Over in Culver City, a young assistant director at MGM named Robert Relyea had just been fired for mouthing off to the head of production. He had never worked anywhere but MGM, so was understandably worried. That afternoon, his phone rang: "Bob Relyea," announced a familiar voice. "This is John Wayne."

"Yeah, and I'm Attila the Hun," said Relyea as he slammed the phone down and wondered which of his jerk friends was teasing him. The phone rang again, and again it was that unmistakable voice. "If you're done fucking around . . ."

The next morning Relyea left for Brackettville to work as John Wayne's assistant director on *The Alamo.* It was now late August 1959, and William Clothier was making test shots of the set under varying angles of light with the 70mm Todd-AO camera. Wayne went down a month before shooting to get used to the location and the sets.

"When we walked on the set for the first time," remembered William Clothier, "Duke said to me, 'We have no angles here.'

"What do you mean we haven't got any angles?'

" 'We haven't got anything to shoot.'

"Well, this is the set of *The Alamo,* they spent a million dollars building this damn thing. I said, 'Duke, you got all sorts of angles.'

" 'Well, show me one.'

" 'Well, over here, you shoot through the stairway.'

" 'Show me another one.'

"So I showed him half a dozen. Then he says, 'What if I'm out in the middle of a street?' I said 'We got props; we got wagons, we got cannons, we got cows and horses, we got all sorts of things.' You have to set it up to frame on something. You put something in the foreground. Anyway, he scratched his head and said, 'I never thought of that.' Well, he'd never directed a picture, either."

To a great extent, Wayne hired John Ford's crew,

except for Wingate Smith, Ford's assistant director for decades as well as brother-in-law, and a man Wayne didn't care for. Relyea's status as an interloper worried him — needlessly. The department heads, as well as all the members of the Ford stock company, turned out to be extremely courteous to the assistant director.

Once he saw the set, Relyea suggested to Al Ybarra and Wayne that the walls of the Alamo be built a bit higher, but Wayne wouldn't hear of it. "I want to see thousands behind every wall," he said. His ambition was laudable but expensive, because every time the camera did a reverse, people had to be moved to fill up the vast spaces visible beyond the low walls.

Just before production got under way, Wayne estimated that about $1.1 million was already spent. Once the cameras started turning, the weekly charges would range from $200,000 to $350,000, depending on the number of people before the cameras. That money did not include much salary for Wayne, who was making only Directors Guild minimum ($13,000 and change). Wayne was working for what he fervently hoped would be the profits. He was up for 7.5 percent of the gross, to be deferred until all the first and secondary loans were repaid. In case the loans were not repaid, then Batjac would pay him 7.5 percent of its net proceeds, although his compensation was limited to $100,000 in any calendar year, in order to avoid a huge tax bite.

On Wednesday morning, September 9, 1959, production began on *The Alamo* with an 8 A.M. blessing from Father Peter Rogers of St. Mary's Catholic Church in San Antonio. "O, Almighty

512

God, centuries ago, Thou raised a magnificent mission — a harbor for all, of peace and freedom. This was The Alamo. Today, we ask Thy blessing, Thy help and Thy protection as once again history is relived in this production."

Wayne had been waiting more than twelve years for this moment, and he was completely prepared. "Duke knew that script backwards," said William Clothier. "He knew every line better than the actors did. In the morning we'd have our breakfast together and go out on location and discuss every shot we were gonna shoot that day, and figure out which we should start with and when we should do such and such a shot for the light.

"Wayne was always on the set. He was the first on the set in the morning and the last to leave in the evening."

One production problem that immediately presented itself was a result of Wayne's insistence on physical realism — the interior sets had been built without movable walls or ceilings. This meant that Clothier had to struggle to keep his lights out of the shot. A more easily solved problem was Wayne's tension, which manifested itself with him silently mouthing another actor's words while he was in the same shot. Clothier grew used to cutting the camera and telling Wayne to stop moving his lips.

After a couple of weeks of production, Wayne wrote Charles Feldman that "we are working like hell, but the cast is wonderful and the backgrounds are magnificent. [Richard] Boone did a wonderful job . . . [and] I can't tell you how beautiful the weather is here. We haven't had one unusually hot day."

But soon after that letter, Wayne's anxiety

ramped up, and for a good reason. Right after lunch one day, John Ford walked onto the set. "He plunked himself down in the director's chair and stopped Duke's scene," remembered William Clothier. " 'Jesus Christ, Duke, that's not the way to do it . . .' "

The company at large was flabbergasted, but Wayne had known he was coming. Ford's participation had been whispered about for some time, before and during the start of production, perhaps as a result of the bogus agreement with George Skouras. In July 1959, *The Hollywood Reporter* had written that "scenes in which Wayne appears will be directed by John Ford."

The night before Ford showed up, Wayne had taken Clothier aside and ranted: "Goddamn it. I want to make this picture and I don't want Ford directing. What the hell am I going to do?" Clothier thought for a moment then offered up a solution.

"Look, I've got a big crew here. Let's give the Old Man a second unit." Wayne loved the idea, so Clothier got a crew together, and actors who weren't scheduled to be used in the next couple of days.

The next morning, Wayne called the production's twenty-seven stuntmen together. "Gentlemen, I want to tell you something. Old Man Ford's coming up to visit and I know he's going to ask for a camera. And I'm going to give it to him. And I know that he's going to ask for you guys to do stunts. And you're gonna do them. But, whatever he shoots, I'm telling you now, none of that will be in the picture. So do what you want, it makes no difference, but it's not going to be in the picture, because all they have to do is find out

514

in Hollywood that Old Man Ford shot a scene or something, they'll say, 'Well, he shot *The Alamo.*' And this is not going to happen!"

John "Bear" Hudkins was one of the stuntmen, and he remembered, "We thought Ford was gonna burn [the] place down. Oh, he did everything. We had fires; we had jumping horses; we had falling horses; we were falling off walls and everything with the Old Man just sitting there and shooting, and we knowing that they weren't even going to use this."

"Ford went out and shot stuff that couldn't possibly be used," remembered Clothier. "It didn't have anything to do with the picture we were making. I don't think we used three cuts that the Old Man did. It cost Duke over $250,000 to give Ford that second unit."

Ford would amble around and occasionally announce what he was going to do. "Duke needs close shots," he said. "He's got a lot of long shots." He went about shooting what he called "three-footers," quick details of action. Occasionally, he would get involved in the long shots as well. For a master shot of the aftermath of the battle, with dead men and horses lying on the ground in front of the Alamo, Ford wandered around, kicking dirt on a hat, moving the corpses into more compositionally attractive positions.

Ford would come down for a few days, go away for a week or two, then come back. "I don't think he directed anything in the final film," said Bob Relyea. "Ford would go off into a corner of the compound and shoot a couple of stuntmen fighting with nothing behind them, and we were shooting scenes with thousands of people. You couldn't cut Ford's stuff in. At night, Ford would get

515

together with Ken Curtis and Wayne and play poker till one or two in the morning. The next morning, he'd fly out."

One night, Ford was watching while Wayne directed a scene where the men go outside the fortress to steal cattle, during which Dean Smith did a standing jump over a horse. "It was a terrific shot," Smith remembered. "I was standing there afterward when this old man walks up to me. He had on white buck shoes, cream colored slacks, a blue blazer, a slouch hat and an eyepatch. He pulled up the patch and looked at me.

" 'Son,' he said, 'I've done lots of westerns and I never saw a man jump over a horse like that. You didn't even use a trampoline. My name's John Ford. You hear of me working, you come and see me. You got a job.' " Smith would work for Ford on *Two Rode Together, Cheyenne Autumn,* and *How the West Was Won.*

Smith believed that Ford came down to Brackettville with the thought that Wayne would throw up his hands in abject gratitude and hand him the picture. "But he found out that Duke had learned more than he thought," said Smith.

One day, word was sent to Relyea that Ford needed an assistant director. Relyea was feeling tired and grumpy, so he sent Mike Wayne. Ford was Pat Wayne's godfather, but he and Mike were never close.

"Duke had a very strong admiration for Mike, who was a lot like he was — bright, hardnosed and short-tempered," said Relyea. "And Pat was an actor, with his SAG card tattooed on his chest." It wasn't long before Ford started mimicking what he thought Mike sounded like around his father: "Dad, can we put the horses here? Dad, how

516

about the cannons?" Mike responded in kind: he pulled a handkerchief out of his pocket and began tearing at it with his teeth — Ford's primary nervous habit when directing.

"At that point, Ford went apeshit and started screaming bloody murder," said Bob Relyea. " 'You little dumbbell!' So I had to get Ford a different assistant director. It was kind of funny."

Ford's presence on the picture was unnerving for Wayne, as well as everybody else. "Ford was always courteous to me," said Relyea, "but you could cut the air with a knife whenever he was around. I'm not a psychiatrist, but it seemed to me that in a lot of ways he was getting back at Duke. It felt like it was unwritten that if *The Alamo* ever got made, that Ford would direct it. And then one day Duke must have said, 'How about lunch? And by the way, I'm going to direct *The Alamo*.' And I think the hurt was so deep that Ford never got over it.

"It was a strange kind of love/hate relationship. I think Ford wanted Duke to succeed with the picture, but he couldn't quite forgive him for not wanting him to direct it. Or perhaps Ford genuinely didn't think the picture could succeed without him."

But *The Alamo* was more than a movie for its director; it was a personal crusade that explained Wayne to Wayne — the patriotism, the single-mindedness that could result in compromised marriages. It would also, he believed, explain America to the world.

Occasionally, Ford would sit there while Wayne was in a scene. Richard Widmark remembered that after one scene between him and Wayne, Wayne asked him if it was okay for him. Widmark said yes, then Ford growled, "Do it again!"

"*Why*, Coach?" asked Wayne.

" 'Cause it was no damn good," said Ford.

They did the scene again.

In his career as an assistant director, Robert Relyea would work with, among others, William Wyler, Robert Wise, Richard Brooks, and John Sturges. In his estimation, "Technically, Wayne was the best director I ever worked with. He understood cameras, he understood editing, he understood lenses. What was wanting was communication with the actors. He was so gruff and short on patience that I don't think he even knew he was gruff. If he had a weakness as a director, it was communication with the actors. The rest of the stuff he knew. Certainly, he knew *exactly* what he wanted. Completely. More so than anybody else I ever worked with. His abruptness was part of his nature. He simply had a short temper."

Relyea found out just how short Wayne's temper could be during one night's shoot. Something wasn't working that the electricians had promised to have working. Wayne wasn't in a great mood to begin with — the weather was cold and rainy, and now the electricians were falling short. He began picking up rocks and throwing them at the offending electricians.

"They were standing on ladders at the time," remembered Relyea, "and he picked them off as if he was Sandy Koufax. He had a hell of an arm." Wayne undoubtedly felt better for expressing his dissatisfaction, but the next day *The Alamo* had need of twenty new electricians, because all the old ones had quit.

He was everywhere, all the time. Instructing

518

some Mexican extras who were supposed to come in through a hole in the wall, he ordered, "You men, pour in here. Fill it up. Hold your rifles at high port. Get back in there. Get a gun. Come through with these men. Round up those guys sleeping in Bejar." When a costume needed fixing, he yelled "Wardrobe!" When nothing happened, he bellowed, "When I call, somebody say 'Yo!' "

Wayne took special care of his twenty-seven stuntmen, each of whom was earning about $1,000 a week. One of the few accidents involved Rudy Robbins, who was on horseback for a shot in which he was herding longhorns toward the mission. Robbins's saddle began slipping, his foot wedged in the stirrup and he got hung up. The horse tried to throw him, but Robbins was still stuck. After being dragged facedown for a hundred yards, Robbins finally worked loose, but his nose was broken, not to mention jammed full of pebbles and sticks.

Wayne and stunt coordinator Cliff Lyons dreamed up one shot that called for a group of stuntmen playing Santa Anna's cavalry to leap a barricade in a line only to be simultaneously mowed down and roll over with their horses. It was difficult, dangerous and expensive. Each of the eight stuntmen got $100 for the jump and $250 for the rollover — stunt work is à la carte.

There were inconveniences. The publicity office at Fort Clark caught fire, destroying payroll records, correspondence, and files. Some actors who weren't working, such as Ken Curtis and John Dierkes, manned firehoses and tried to get as many file cabinets as possible out of the office. Later, a flu virus swept through the company, and

80 percent of the cast and crew got sick.

The shoot was marred by a couple of tragedies. There was a car crash that killed two crew members, as well as a civilian. A local girl who had made some forays into San Antonio theater was playing a small part and doing quite well. Wayne gave her more screen time and told her that if she was serious about acting, she should come to Hollywood and he would introduce her around town. She told her boyfriend about the offer, he became violently jealous, grabbed a butcher knife and killed her.

But a big movie is like an ocean liner — nothing stops it short of total disaster. During one shot, a cannon recoil rolled a wheel over Laurence Harvey's left foot. He maintained his composure until Wayne yelled "Cut," then let out a scream of pain. The foot swelled up, but Harvey refused to go to the hospital and hold up shooting. Instead, he dipped his injured foot in successive buckets of hot and cold water until the swelling went down. With his foot wrapped, Harvey just kept working. This show of raw guts endeared Harvey to Wayne and the rest of the crew.

Wayne had agreed to pay Jim Henaghan $100,000 or 2.5 percent of the profits of the picture for his services as unit publicist. Henaghan was importing a lot of newspapermen, but Mary St. John said he was also importing hookers to keep the writers entertained. When Wayne found out, he was personally offended and had it out with Henaghan, who departed the picture and Wayne's employ.

The overriding problem of the production was that Brackettville and Fort Clark were simply too small to hold the 450 people making up the cast and crew. "Brackettville had a gas station, a Frosty Freeze, and a liquor store," remembered Bob Relyea. "The liquor store did very well. Fort Clark was an army base where Custer had been the last listed commander. Their mess hall became our mess hall, and Custer's quarters became Wayne's.

"But there was simply no place to go. San Antonio was hours away. We shot six days a week. By the time you got to Sunday evening, it was like the Friday night fights. People would say things like, 'Not another goddamn steak. I'm sick of steak!' It was just too long of a shoot to put that many people in a small town."

Relations between Wayne and Richard Widmark broke down completely. "Dick was one of the most professional men alive," said Bob Relyea, "and I considered him one of the nicest men in his field as well. He was always courteous to everybody. If Dick asked if he could fly out on Sunday, I could always let him go, because I could count on him being in makeup at seven in the morning on Monday. His word was gold.

One night shoot, we were breaking for lunch about three in the morning. Dick came up behind Duke, touched him on the sleeve and said, "I want to talk to you about tomorrow night's scene."

Duke was touchy about being tugged at and he snapped, "Not now, you little shit."

And Widmark said, "Fine!" and jumped in front of Wayne and put his fists up. And Duke turned to me and said, "What's the matter with him?"

"He wants to fight."

"Why?"

"You just called him a little shit."

521

Wayne drew back. "I did not! Why would I say that?"

While all this explaining was going on, Widmark was waiting for Wayne to put up his fists. Relyea finally calmed Widmark down and got them both into the mess hall. Wayne was still insisting he had never called Widmark a little shit, while Relyea was insisting he had.

"I can't believe it," Wayne finally said, concluding with, "feisty little shit, isn't he?" just loud enough for Widmark to hear. "I didn't think we were ever going to get through the night," sighed Relyea. "The sad part about it was that Duke's respect for Widmark as an actor was enormous. Duke admired him. But Dick thought Duke was a big bag of wind, and he was bored with him and the picture."

Things were much better with Laurence Harvey, if only because Harvey settled into the role of class clown. Harvey was a gourmet and had fine wines, champagne, and caviar shipped to the middle of Texas, all of which he would enjoy in the middle of the commissary tent. Wayne had admired Harvey's courage, and now he came to admire his style. He also thought Harvey was hilarious. The photographer Sam Shaw, who was covering the production, remembered that "Harvey, in the middle of all the tough guys, the cream of the Hollywood stuntmen, the tempers, the heat, would go over to Wayne, tweak his cheeks and call him 'Dukey.' "

"Duke teased him all the time, called him 'the English fag,' " said Bob Relyea. "*To his face.* And Larry would laugh and say, 'Where do I stand? Tell me where to stand.' They got along fine. Larry was an awfully good actor, and dedicated to doing the best job he could. He couldn't have cared less about the insults."

At the end of one of Harvey's scenes, the crew broke into applause. Jimmy Grant was standing nearby and snapped, "Don't look so smug, Laurence. They're applauding the writing, not the acting." Harvey looked at Grant and said, "Quiet, James, or I will give you a big kiss and all these Texans will be sure you are a fag."

Wayne would give line readings, which made Relyea and the actors bite their tongues. Once he even showed Linda Cristal how he wanted her to walk to a carriage, complete with a little sashay. Once or twice he snapped, "Be graceful — like me, goddammit."

"Duke's only problem as a director is that he feels every actor should be able to do a scene the way he can do a scene," said William Clothier. "He'd be pushing [people] and screaming. I must have told him 50 times, 'You don't know how lucky you are; relax and be patient. Other people can't do what you can do." The one actor that Wayne treated with great politeness was Richard Boone, but then Boone was notoriously truculent.

The Screen Writers Guild went on strike while the picture was shooting, and Jimmy Grant had to stop working. It could have been a blessing in disguise, and Grant wrote a note to Wayne suggesting that if he needed a line to cover an actor's move, he should just write it himself. "All the fans tell me they love you because you say such honest, straightforward things right out of your own balding, pointed head."

But it was only a question of time until Jimmy Grant brought the spotlight back to where he

523

needed it to be — on Jimmy Grant. After a disagreement with the president of Batjac, Grant wrote Wayne a memo quitting the picture and the company. "Don't let this upset you for a moment," he wrote. "I have served my purpose on this picture — and well, I think. I'm proud of the job. And this incident will not affect in the slightest my personal attachment to you. It will not dim the almost sexual joy I have experienced from having my stuff put on the screen by a director who had an instinctive and intuitive understanding of the values."

This was the last thing Wayne needed to concern himself with, but he managed to put out the fire and keep Grant close. There were those who wondered why. Happy Shahan said that Grant "was an opinionated guy. He wrote a lot of good scripts. But when he made up his mind that he wanted it this way, he fought to get it. I liked James Edward to talk to; I argued with him all the time about the historical Alamo. Wayne knew what was right, but he let Grant out-talk him."

Wayne's main creative partner on the picture was cameraman William Clothier. "He listened to Clothier and respected him," said Bob Relyea. "And Clothier was a solid guy; technically, he was one of the best cameramen in the world." Clothier certainly worked magic when he had to. One great shot showing thousands of Mexican soldiers on a hillside was done with optical trickery. The troops first filled a third of the shot, with two thirds of the image blacked out. Clothier moved the same soldiers over and put them on horses, then unblocked the lens. The same group then moved further still and this time played artillery. "It looks like we had a pretty good-sized army there . . .

but we had three times more people on the screen than we ever did on the set." (The largest extra call appears to have been 1,800, for the final assault.)

"The picture was hard," said Bob Relyea.

The nature of the piece was a couple of thousand extras. And we shot forever. People died of old age. And I must say, Duke never went off on me. He did get joy out of calling me "Bobby." Somebody had told him I hated being called Bobby, so of course he had to do that.

The shooting was efficient. Some of the picture was storyboarded, but not much. All of it was storyboarded in Duke's mind and we didn't vary from that much. He would never argue about practicality or logistics. If I told him we were getting deep into gold [overtime], he'd say okay. His preferred method was to do his master shot, then move in. He didn't do a lot of takes, but he wasn't a one-and-out kind of guy. He would stay with a shot until it was right.

He wasn't difficult. It was the picture that was difficult.

The only real moment of tension between the two men came on one of the dreaded night shoots. The production was busing in extras for the next morning, and Wayne and Relyea rounded a corner around two in the morning in deep discussion. A large woman was standing there, and she couldn't have been any more startled by the sudden appearance of Jesus than by the presence of John Wayne. She began yelling, *"John Wayne! John Wayne!"* and then in a frenzy she started picking up pebbles and throwing them in Wayne's face.

Wayne was used to strange reactions, but he'd never gotten one like this before, and he just stood there and stared while the woman kept scooping up pebbles and tossing them at him as some sort of love offering. The image was so incongruous that Bob Relyea first began to laugh, then lost all control and fell to the ground in hysterics.

When Relyea got his wind back, he looked up to see Wayne coldly staring down at him.

"Are you finished?" Wayne asked.

"I'm sorry. It was just that the image was so hilarious."

"Well, if you're finished, and if you feel like it, you can get up off the ground and we can continue discussing what we're going to shoot."

During this conversation, the occasional stray pebble was still bouncing off Wayne's face. As they turned and walked away, Wayne pirouetted, took off his hat and made a low, sweeping bow to the hysterical woman. He didn't speak to Relyea for the next three days unless it was absolutely necessary.

Relyea believed that Grant's occasional presence was not productive. "Duke gave me the impression that Grant would not make changes in the script that Duke needed or thought he needed," said Relyea. "I wouldn't say they were on the outs, but Duke would say things like, 'I need a scene here,' and Grant would say 'Sure' and do nothing about it."

"There really weren't any [production] rewrites on that script," said Burt Kennedy. "I did a little work on Richard Widmark's part, but that was about all. . . . Jimmy was a good writer and good writers don't want to work; after a certain point, he wouldn't work on that script.

"The problem I always had with the script was that it's a big historical picture and they brought in a romance that didn't make any sense at all. I thought we should spend more time on the back-stories of the men at the Alamo so you'd feel some loss when they were killed." It's entirely possible that Grant was simply written out — he'd been on the picture off and on since at least 1950.

Between the difficult location and the problems of the production, Relyea's health began to suffer. Late one night, the noise from his air-conditioner woke him up. He got up to turn it off, but he fell down and blood started pouring out of his mouth. He lay on the floor until he felt stronger.

The company doctor examined him and told him an ulcer had broken. "Let's see if you can make it through the night," the doctor said, prescribing shots of warm cream. At two in the morning, Relyea was feeling pretty good until he went down again. The nearest hospital was in a border town called Del Rio, where he was given thirteen pints of blood.

Things got increasingly ragged. During night shoots the actors and crew had to contend with thousands of crickets that were so thick you couldn't see the ground. Then there were the rattlesnakes — the high count for a night was sixteen — and skunks. Makeup man Webb Overlander said he counted thirty-two one day; Wayne had to hire someone who did nothing but catch skunks all day long.

Wayne stayed healthy — he was medicating himself with poker, whiskey, and tobacco, lighting cigarettes nonstop off the stub of the previous one — but he lost a fair amount of weight during the shoot. "He believed in the picture so much," said

Relyea. "Rightly or wrongly, he thought the story of the Alamo was an example of America at its best — that Americans should be able to hold off ten times their number for thirteen days because dammit, that's the way we are.

"But if he had a couple of drinks, he would start talking about how he was going to be in the poorhouse when it was all over. And then he'd brighten a little and say, 'But then nobody else in the poorhouse has ever made a $14 million dollar picture.'"

Relyea accompanied Wayne when he flew to Clint Murchison's ranch to repay Murchison's seed money. On the way back, Wayne said to Relyea, "He's no gambler. He's not gracious. He took my personal check." And then he sighed and looked out the window. "The only son of a bitch who's going to be broke is me," he said.

By the second week of November, just as Wayne was to begin shooting the all-important battle scenes, a wire arrived from United Artists. The film was about to use up its budget, and the studio estimated that Wayne would need an additional $400,000 to finish the picture. UA refused to advance the money, which left Wayne no choice but to kick in more of his own money.

Cliff Lyons got credit for the second unit direction, but Dean Smith remembered that Wayne directed a lot of the battle. "Scenes like jumping horses over the barricade, Duke was right there. He was an action man and he knew every move the stuntmen knew. Duke Wayne wouldn't ask a stuntman to do anything he wouldn't do himself. We all liked him, we knew he wanted the best, and we loved and respected him."

528

For much of the shoot, Pilar was there with the children; Bob Relyea thought the relationship seemed strong. One night, there was banging on Relyea's door. It was one of the company saying he needed a plane to San Antonio. It seemed that he had said something negative about Pilar at dinner, or Wayne thought he did. The man's nose was now resting on the side of his face.

Wayne seems to have been sensitive to Pilar's isolation. Karen Sharpe, the ingenue of *The High and the Mighty,* was visiting her father in San Antonio, and the two drove over to Brackettville for a visit. After an exchange of pleasantries, Wayne asked Sharpe if she would take Pilar shopping. "You know how they treat Hispanics," he said, the implication being that being accompanied by a beautiful blonde would insulate Pilar from racist exchanges. "I said I certainly did understand," recalled Sharpe. "I could never stand Texas because it's such a reactionary place."

On December 15, after eighty-three days of production, seventeen days over schedule, Wayne wrapped principal photography on *The Alamo.* He had shot 560,000 feet of film and lost more than twenty pounds. Cliff Lyons spent a few more weeks shooting close-ups of the battle that would be spliced around scenes of the principals. With that, the film went into the cutting room for ten months of postproduction that featured Dimitri Tiomkin's epic musical score spread over a running time that eventually encompassed three hours and twelve minutes.

"After it was all over," said Relyea, "I liked Duke. It was hard not to. Being an assistant director on a picture like *The Alamo,* you worry about everything — shooting, what people do when

529

they're not shooting, everything else. But I could always count on Duke being prepared. Sometimes hungover, but always prepared. And organized. And definite. It was always, 'Yes,' or 'no.'

"Everybody took direction from him. You can tell when a director is organized and has a point of view. If he's got that, unless you're totally opposed to that approach, it's a relief. The cameraman knows where to put the camera, the actors know where to stand. And you could tell he knew what he was doing. If Duke looked at a set and said, 'We'd better go with the 75mm lens,' he was always exactly right. People pick that up quickly and say to themselves, 'Right or wrong, at least we have leadership.' A film set is mainly about leadership, and Duke had that."

Soon after returning to Hollywood for post-production, Wayne unburdened himself of his anger about the diseased state of the current cinema in a windy statement that was probably written by Russell Birdwell: "Filthy minds and filthy words and filthy thoughts have no place upon any motion picture screen." Wayne went on to enumerate the ways in which *The Alamo* would serve as the antidote:

I think we are all in danger and have been for a long time of going soft, of taking things for granted . . . [of] forgetting the things that made this a great nation.

The best reminder that has ever happened in the history of the world in my opinion is what took place at the Alamo in San Antonio, Texas. It was there that 182 Americans holed up in an adobe mission fought for 13 days and nights against 5,000 troops of the Dictator Santa Anna.

These 182 men killed 1,700 of the enemy before they were slaughtered because they didn't think a bully should push people around.

I'm glad to play a part in the making of a motion picture that is true and real and which I believe will present some of the most inspiring and entertaining subject matter that has ever been put on the screen.

Postproduction on *The Alamo* was done at the Goldwyn studio on Formosa Avenue. One day, Laurence Harvey came in to wrap up his dubbing. After an hour or two, Wayne got bored and said, "Let's go over to Lucey's." The autograph hounds sniffed out Wayne and before long he was signing menus, napkins, and all manner of scrap paper. While everybody was asking Wayne for his signature, nobody was making a fuss over Harvey.

"How come nobody ever asks you for your autograph?" asked an amused Wayne.

"If we were in London, it would be just the opposite," said Harvey. "They'd be coming after me, and they'd say, 'John Wayne? Eh . . .' They're *much* more sophisticated over there."

"They had a great relationship," remembered Tom Kane. "Larry wasn't afraid of Duke. He'd tell him off and Duke loved that, instead of people kissing his ass all the time." What was supposed to be a break from the rigors of the dubbing room turned into an all-night party, in which Harvey introduced Wayne to the brutal pleasures of the Bullshot — vodka, beef consommé, and lime.

On January 18, 1960, Wayne wrote a letter to UA president Arthur Krim informing him that Russell Birdwell — who was being paid over $200,000, counting expenses and office overhead,

531

for a year of work between November 1959 and November 1960 — was to be in charge of the publicity campaign for *The Alamo.* "The emphasis," wrote Wayne, "is going to be on publicity and not on paid advertising."

Krim grudgingly agreed, but UA's ad and publicity budget for the picture had been set at $415,000, with $125,000 of that already spent. Birdwell's close-to-the-vest style of operating meant that there would be unavoidable duplication of effort, not to mention much corporate irritation.

All of Wayne's financial troubles didn't lessen his belief in the picture he had brought back from Brackettville. In March 1960, Wayne received an offer to sell his percentage in the picture for what James Edward Grant called "a huge capital gain." He turned the deal down. Grant had a percentage of the profits, and would also have made a sizable chunk of money from the sale, but said that he was happy with his friend's decision. Grant wrote that he believed his piece of the action would bring in so much money that he would be able to afford to start drinking again, although he hoped "[I] will have some sense enough not to." That same month, a production memo carried the negative cost of the picture at nearly $5.3 million, almost $800,000 over Wayne's initial budget.

Ahead lay more editing, the musical score, print costs, and a massive publicity campaign. More money was going to be needed. Accordingly, in April an agreement was set up with Bank of America for yet another loan, a maximum of $700,000 secured by the Batjac film library. Once again, Batjac agreed that all the other investors, including the Bank of America, were to be repaid before Batjac could recoup its own investment.

Attached to the loan application was an itemized list containing the purpose for each dollar of the loan. Included was $55,000 for Frankie Avalon and $25,000 for Richard Boone, both of whom had evidently done their stints without being paid. (*Variety* reported that Wayne bought Boone a Rolls-Royce for his contribution.)

Also budgeted was $117,000 for the writing and recording of Dimitri Tiomkin's score, and, oddly enough, $100,000 for John Ford. But Ford's files don't show him doing any preparation or research work, nor do they show any disbursements from Batjac. Dan Ford, the director's grandson and executor, says, "Ford didn't do enough to ask for money. I'm sure it was a cover," i.e., the money designated for Ford was actually being used for other expenses.

Batjac was now in a nearly impossible financial position. At this point, the negative cost of the picture, plus prints and advertising, meant that it would have to return rentals — what the movie company gets after the theaters have deducted their share — of something like $15 million to reimburse the UA, the McCullough Tool Company, and the Bank of America loans, which didn't even take into account the money Wayne had personally thrown into the bucket. (Clint Murchison had already been repaid.) Not only that, but Batjac had given away 10 percent of its net profits to McCullough and Murchison.

Essentially, *The Alamo* had to be one of the fifteen highest grossing pictures in Hollywood history or there was going to be a lot of red ink on Batjac's accounting books.

The publicity drums began to beat in the summer of 1960. There was a hugely expensive ($152,000) three-page fold-out ad in *Life* magazine on July 4, headlined "There Were No Ghost Writers at the Alamo," which made a tenuous connection between the flacks working for the two presidential candidates of 1960 and the lack of same at the Alamo. "There were no ghost writers at the Alamo. Only men. Among them Colonel David Crockett who was 50 years old, Colonel James Bowie, 40; Colonel William Barret Travis, 26.

"These men left a legacy for all who prize freedom above tyranny, individualism above conformity." It was signed by Wayne and Grant, although it had been written by Birdwell.

In May, Wayne started shooting *North to Alaska,* another one of his 20th Century Fox commitments. In between shots, he worked on the final editing and release plans for *The Alamo.* Wayne ordered two hundred Bowie knives as gifts for reporters at the San Antonio premiere, and a series of full-page newspaper ads for thirty-five papers in twelve cities. The ad budget for the premiere cities alone was $353,393.

Wayne began screening the rough cut for friends and family. John Ford responded with a blurb for his pal: "This is the most important motion picture ever made. It is timeless. It's the greatest motion picture I've ever seen. It will last forever — run forever — for all peoples, all families, everywhere!" The exclamation point was presumably Birdwell's addition.

Director George Stevens came on board too: "When the roll call of the great ones is made, *The Alamo* will be among those few by which the films of the future will and must be measured. There are images in *The Alamo* that will haunt you and inspire you for a lifetime. *The Alamo* is among the screen's finest literature — a classic."

By August, Jimmy Grant had succeeded in hypnotizing himself: "I have to admit that I am now married to Birdwell's estimate of an *Alamo* gross in the neighborhood of a hundred million dollars," he wrote. He asked Batjac to pay out his profits at no more than $50,000 a year, so as to avoid tax nightmares.

But by September, a month before *The Alamo* opened, Wayne was depressed about Batjac's financial position. Everything Wayne and his company owned was either spent or mortgaged. On September 24, Grant wrote Wayne a long letter outlining his ideas for cutting back the company overhead so that the company could survive while waiting for the profits to roll in.

At this point, Batjac's overhead was about $450,000 a year. Grant suggested that Wayne get rid of the accountant ($24,000 a year), then furlough production manager Nate Edwards ($26,000 a year), who wouldn't be needed for at least a year — the company had no immediate production plans after *The Alamo.* Cut one or two other people, and for God's sake knock off free coffee and phone service for out-of-work actors. As for Bob Morrison ($15,000 a year), Grant suggested cutting his salary in half, and letting him pick up work as an assistant director on television.

Then Grant kicked into high gear: sell the Batjac building, rent some space, keep Mary St. John, a few others, rent help when you need it, and lower the yearly costs to $75,000–$100,000 a year. Failing that, Grant suggested that Wayne make two Batjac pictures back to back that would at least cover the company overhead, preferably two scripts by James Edward Grant. (Grant's was not a subtle personality.) Either way, Grant counseled speed: "The grave awaits much more suddenly than we ever expect . . ."

The fate of Batjac hung fire for several years, and Charles Feldman did a good deal of spade-work to insure the company's survival. At one point, there were conversations of varying degrees of seriousness with Columbia, Fox, and Seven Arts. The rough outline of the deal with Seven Arts was a purchase price of around $3 million for the Batjac assets — the film library, the company's percentage of *The Alamo* — plus a four-picture deal with Wayne.

Feldman was having health problems, and he was worried about himself and his client. Wayne was in the middle of bouncing from *The Alamo* to *North to Alaska* to *Hatari!* to *The Comancheros* with hardly any time off between pictures, in order to replenish his cash reserves. "I am very concerned about you, Duke, and your not getting a holiday and working week after week practically for the past year. This must be remedied. . . . Please take care of yourself and again take care of your health."

The deal with Seven Arts would have wiped out all the debt and given Wayne $1 million in the bank, but he didn't pull the trigger. Batjac was a large part of his identity — it meant he was more than an actor for hire, and losing it would have meant far more than an acknowledgment that his idée fixe had cost him his company.

Instead of selling out, he handed the company over to his son Mike, who embarked on a strategic and successful series of maneuvers that kept the company alive. Wayne maintained Batjac as a production entity for the rest of his life.

By the fall of 1960, the publicity drumbeats for *The Alamo* would have terrified the bravest man behind the mission walls. United Artists sent out what was believed to be the world's largest press release — actually the film's production notes. They ran to 184 pages and weighed in at two and a quarter pounds. Ten thousand of them cost $14,752 to print and $3,500 to mail.

The Alamo premiered in spectacular fashion in San Antonio on October 24, 1960, as the culmination of three days of Alamo-centered hullabaloo. There were round-the-clock appearances by Wayne and the rest of the cast, uniformed high school bands, a symphonic concert of Dimitri Tiomkin's score, a group of trail riders from 130 miles away, and a column of U.S. Marines who reenacted the seventy-mile march of Alamo reinforcements with a banner that read "Come And Take It." There was also a three-hundred-foot-long cake in the shape of the Alamo, which Wayne helped cut with a Bowie knife.

ABC aired a special entitled *The Spirit of the Alamo* that amounted to a one-hour commercial. There was a tour of the set in Brackettville, Laurence Harvey recited Shakespeare, Frankie Avalon and Chill Wills sang, and Wayne and Richard Boone extolled the virtues of Texas in particular and America in general. There was even an interview with the ninety-two-year-old John Nance Garner that *Variety* termed "rather painful."

A couple of days before the premiere, Wayne admitted to Hedda Hopper that he thought the picture was too long. He also said that the picture could wipe him out. "When I say we spent $12 million, I'm leveling. I've got everything I own in it. I borrowed from banks and friends. Take a look at one scene and you'll never be able to count the thousands of people. . . . But I'm not worried. This is a darned good picture — it's a real American history, the kind of movie we need today more than ever. It'll make money for years to come."

Wayne did press in Los Angeles, he did press in Texas, he did press in New York. For Wayne, all the publicity was worthwhile, because he felt compelled to speak out on politics and, increasingly, movies. There were more and more movies — *On the Beach* and Robert Rossen's *They Came to Cordura* — that aroused his ire. He told *The Hollywood Reporter* that he objected to a "trend in certain quarters of Hollywood to glorify all that is degrading in a small percentage of disreputable human beings."

Warming to his subject, he said he didn't see how they got Gary Cooper to make the Rossen picture — Coop was always going off the reservation and making a movie about fear instead of resolution. By comparison, there was *The Alamo,* "a film made up of men and women who believed that in order to live decently one must be prepared to die decently."

Also upsetting him was the way he felt America tentatively addressed other world powers. "Why don't both our presidential candidates emphasize that this is the greatest nation in the history of the world?" he asked. "When the world was flat on its back, what brought it back? American money and American energy, our humanitarianism and our sense of social responsibility for friend and foe alike."

The reviews of *The Alamo* began rolling in, and they were good, not great. Opinions were not radically different than they have been ever since — a splendid physical show with majestic battle scenes marred by too much didactic palaver. "His action scenes are usually vivid, his talk scenes are long and unusually dull," wrote Bosley Crowther of *The New York Times,* while *Variety* said, "The picture is too talkative at times. . . . In undertaking production, direction and thespic participation, Wayne may have spread his talents out too thin for best results."

"A great deal that goes on in the first two-thirds of the film," wrote Philip Scheuer of the *Los Angeles Times,* "might have been scissored to advantage — not so much because it is incompetent, irrelevant or immaterial as because it is corny."

The Alamo received the signal honor of a parody in *Mad* magazine, in which "John Wayde" narrates the story of the making of the movie: "As we all know, the longer the picture nowadays, the greater it is," says Wayde by way of introduction. "Well, we had a greatness problem right from the start. Namely, how to add three hours to an exciting half-hour assault on the Alamo by the Mexican army. One way was to pad the time with lengthy speeches about freedom . . ."

As far as Wayne's friends — and quite possibly Wayne himself — were concerned, all this was delayed retribution for the activities of the Motion Picture Alliance. "The word of mouth was that [*The Alamo*] was a dog," said Borden Chase. "This was created by the Communists to get back at Wayne. Then there were some bad reviews inspired by the Communists. Of course, I wouldn't say that all criticism of *The Alamo* was Communist-inspired, but some of these movie reviewers, who are only liberals, have some best pals who are Communists."

The vast left-wing conspiracy helped to focus United Artists' doubts that *The Alamo* was not really a road show (reserved seat) picture, if only because Wayne's audience did not consist of sophisticates in big cities who traditionally attended such movies. Business the first week was very good, mostly sellouts, then started drifting downward. With grosses not holding firm, United Artists also wanted to cut the picture in order to squeeze in more shows per day.

Batjac wanted to stick with the road shows because it was to their economic advantage — UA's distribution fee for the road show was only 15 percent versus 30 percent for general release. Conversely, UA wanted to rush the picture into general release because it was to *their* economic advantage. Then there was the fact that the film wouldn't be able to break even without the premium pricing of reserved seats. Also contributing to the studio's attitude was the unpleasant fact that UA's investment was less than Wayne's, which meant that UA had less of a commitment to maximizing revenue than did the star-director.

The other shoe dropped very quickly. On November 4, only a few weeks after the premiere, *The Hollywood Reporter* announced that Wayne was cutting the film to about two and a half hours for a general release, a trim of about thirty minutes — an admission that the film was too long and wasn't pulling the desired audiences. Although UA announced that the shorter running time wouldn't mean any change in the reserved seat engagements, everyone in the business knew that was only temporary.

Wayne had just left for Tanganyika to make *Hatari!* for Howard Hawks, so Mike Wayne and editor Stuart Gilmore cut thirty-one minutes out of the picture. It's not uncommon to lop off the beginning and ending of scenes in such cases, in order to get to the drama more quickly, which Mike and Gilmore did. But they also changed the order of some scenes, and in the film's final battle scenes there are several shots without dialogue that were also trimmed, probably because doing so wouldn't upset the sound mix.

Some of the scenes that were cut take place just before the final assault, as the men contemplate what they know will be their deaths. Laurence Harvey had more screen time in the uncut version, and many of his scenes were truncated. Likewise, Wayne's death scene is more protracted and slightly more violent in the uncut version. The primary difference between the two cuts is that the road show version is an authentic epic, while the edited version feels more like a very long western.*

* The original negative was cut to conform to the new 161-minute length, and the trims and deletions were destroyed. For over thirty years, the original version of the film was generally thought lost, until in 1991 a single 70mm print was found in Toronto and used as the master for laser disc and VHS release. Unfortunately, by the time DVDs and Blu-rays came in, the

Jimmy Grant wrote Wayne that UA was making contracts for the general release of *The Alamo* in March, and glumly noted that they didn't seem to be planning any sort of campaign to counter the underwhelming business of the road shows. "We have no stick to threaten with, and we have no one on our side to wield it if we had one," concluded Grant.

By December 12, the writing was on the wall, and in large letters. "There doesn't seem to be any sense in my flailing the ghost of *The Alamo*," Grant wrote Wayne. "I think you'll agree with me that [United Artists] have no intention of letting the picture ever break even."

It was becoming clear that *The Alamo* was going to be, at best, a lot like the battle it dramatized: a moral victory perhaps, but otherwise a bloodbath. Grant recommended hiring outside auditors in order to bring suit against United Artists. "It dawns on me that this is a morbid Xmas communication, but it ain't only in Africa that things are tough."

A day later, Grant talked to distribution executives at Paramount and others who told him that the general feeling in the industry was that *North to Alaska* (which Fox had unhelpfully rushed into release a few weeks after *The Alamo*) "is kicking hell out of us. The public can see Wayne for a buck, so why should they pay three or four?"

70mm print had likewise deteriorated. The masters used for the laser disc and VHS were unsuitable for the increased definition of DVD or Blu-ray, so those obsolete systems remain the only way Wayne's expansive vision of the film can be seen.

It was true; Charles Feldman wrote Wayne that "*North to Alaska* business is exceptionally good. . . . It was the hottest picture around the country during the Thanksgiving weekend."

Wayne's delight in the success of the Henry Hathaway picture must have been severely muted, but Feldman was doing the best he could for his friend. Fox offered Feldman 25 percent of the profits of *North to Alaska* for his packaging services, but he rejected that as "unsatisfactory." Feldman wrote his client that whatever Fox paid him, the money would go to Wayne.

In the first week of January 1961, Jimmy Grant's instincts about United Artists were borne out when UA's Seymour Poe wrote Mike Wayne that there was no possibility of the Chinese Theatre, nor any other of the prestigious theaters on Hollywood Boulevard, for the general 35mm release of *The Alamo.*

UA was going to rush the picture into general release Easter weekend, with some territories — Florida, for instance — scheduled for the end of February. This meant that the road show would be pulled within two to three months of the premiere — a clear sign of failure. UA further cut the ground out from Wayne by telling *Variety* that this release pattern had been its preference all along, but they had gone along with the reserved seat engagements "on Wayne's insistence."

It was the first open acknowledgment of the internecine war that had been going on for nearly a year over the film's publicity and release, which was only exacerbated when Russell Birdwell announced that the general release version had been cut. "In my opinion, this is absolute suicide, and every experience in the industry proves it," wrote UA's Roger Lewis to Birdwell. "You can't tell people that they are buying the cut version even if you justify it by saying it has improved the picture. It merely plants the conviction that there was something wrong to begin with, or that they are not getting their money's worth."

Soon after the New Year, Wayne anted up money yet again, this time for an ad campaign for Oscar nominations. Birdwell wrote UA's Roger Lewis complaining about the studio's treatment of the picture, asserting that they had allowed the movie to fall into obscurity over the Christmas holidays. Lewis responded with a bridge burner:

This is sheer, unadulterated bull, and you know it. Obviously, you feel that without your master touch, nothing good can happen. This may salve your ego, but does not square the record. . . . There is no evading the money that was spent, $1.3 million up to opening in eight situations — a record high in the entire history of the motion picture business — not the fact that most of that was spent under your direction, in a manner you defined or decided and sometimes without our even being consulted. . . .

Did it or does it occur to you that perhaps you did something wrong . . . and how do you square the fact that in those areas where you had little or no part in the campaign — London, Paris, Stockholm and Japan — where we were able to do the job as we believed it should be done — the picture is a smash. . . . I must make it clear that I cannot and will not work with you on the old basis nor will I tolerate any longer the kind of assaults on the people in my organization that you have perpetrated in the past.

Then, just to derail whatever slight momentum the picture might pick up, Chill Wills got into the act by taking out trade ads masterminded by someone with the Perelman-esque name of "Bow Wow" Wojchiechowicz, who turned out to be the ex-husband of gossip columnist Sheilah Graham.

One of Bow Wow's ads featured copy that said "We of the Alamo cast are praying harder — than the real Texans prayed for their lives in the Alamo — for Chill Wills to win the Oscar as Best Supporting Actor — cousin Chill's acting was great." It was signed "Your Alamo cousins." Next to Wills's ad was one by Groucho Marx that read, "Dear Mr. Chill Wills, I am delighted to be your cousin, but I voted for Sal Mineo."

"Wayne went ballistic when Wills took out those ads," said Bob Relyea. "He just thought they were in the worst possible taste." Wayne was furious as only John Wayne could be furious. He bought an ad disassociating himself from Cousin Chill's definitive display of hubris: "I wish to state that the Chill Wills ad published in the *Hollywood Reporter,* of which we had no advance knowledge, in which he wrote, or permitted to be written, that 'we of the Alamo cast are praying . . .' is an untrue and reprehensible claim.

"No one in the Batjac organization or in the Russell Birdwell office has been a party to his trade paper advertising. I refrain from using stronger language because I am sure his intentions were not as bad as his taste."

Campaigning for Oscars is generally done through surrogates; it's considered bad form for a nominee to let their desperation show. Wayne believed that Wills's gauche appeals adversely affected the picture's chances for Oscars.

The Alamo was eventually nominated for seven Academy Awards, including Best Picture, which provoked some carping articles from critics. In the *Los Angeles Times,* Philip Scheuer wrote, "I find it almost impossible to understand why *Pepe* and *The Alamo* should have captured seven nominations apiece. They are two of the least distinguished films representative of the 'art' that have ever been shown at advanced prices on a prestige basis."

After the expenditure of $90,819 in Oscar ads, *The Alamo*'s seven nominations resulted in precisely one award, for Best Sound, although it might justifiably have also won for Dimitri Tiomkin's score and William Clothier's cinematography.

The Alamo has been castigated for not being faithful to the sketchy historical record, in a far more vociferous manner than have other historically fanciful films — Ford's *My Darling Clementine,* for instance — a difference probably stemming from enduring grudges over Wayne's politics.

But Wayne never intended the film to be a documentary; rather, it was supposed to be *emotionally* true, a stirring ballad, a call to arms that would revive America's combative strength. As Frank Thompson wrote, Wayne's intentions were to create "an ode to a heroic era, aimed at a generation that didn't seem to believe in heroes anymore."

Although Wayne studied at John Ford University, where the image always took precedence over the

546

word, in *The Alamo* characters are positioned more by speech — lots and lots of speech — than they are by action, although the superior attitude of Laurence Harvey's Travis is visually emphasized by usually staging his scenes so that he's literally above the men he's addressing.

Harvey gives the best performance in the picture because he alone is able to rise above the script's needlessly explicit exposition — introductory scene after introductory scene with people standing in the background, not to mention irrelevancies such as a cantina dance solo that, just as Wayne promised Spyros Skouras, re-creates John Singer Sargent's *El Jaleo.* (Disastrously, the first half of the picture has virtually no action.) Harvey's Travis is icy and arrogant, but he's also compelling, and the actor doesn't have to wade through Jimmy Grant's faux-backwoods dialogue ("You don't get lard 'lessen you boil a hog.").

Richard Widmark gives a surface performance that indicates his lack of interest; the three leads don't seem to be in the same movie. Conversely, a lot of the supporting actors come on too strong, in Hollywood's best get-out-of-the-way-and-give-me-the-Oscar fashion. Wayne cast his actors well, but he didn't — or couldn't — sculpt the performances.

Once the film moves into its second half, it comes alive. While Wayne's blocking of the interior dialogue scenes is often unimaginative, he has a real feel for epic compositions and action, even if he's oblivious to emotional reality — when Linda Cristal's Flaca tells Crockett she loves him, he responds with a speech about right and wrong.

The battle scene is first-rate, full of fire and sweep and vistas of violence, and there's an effec-

547

tive tag at the end, as the sole survivors — a woman and her little girl — leave the ruins and the bodies behind while Santa Anna doffs his hat in respect. Helping out is Dimitri Tiomkin's music score, which continually gives the film a spaciousness and grandeur that is absent until the film's climax.

Oddly, there's an internal inconsistency that neither the film nor most critics ever address: Travis insists on defending the Alamo at all costs, while Bowie counsels a guerrilla cut-and-run strategy. Every time the defenders leave the fort, they win, but then they troop back to the Alamo so they can die. Since there's really not much emphasis placed on living under siege, Travis's insistence on staying in the fort makes no dramatic sense and seems self-defeating.

Wayne had been vociferously representing his political and social viewpoints since *Big Jim McLain,* so the Mexicans are less a brown peril than they are the faceless minions of a totalitarian dictator bent on subjugating people who want to be free. In other words, Communists. But Wayne's deep affection for Mexico and its people wouldn't have allowed him to promote negative stereotypes, so Santa Anna's handsome spokesman is played by none other than the legendary matador Carlos Arruza.

"I think that the directorial job Duke did was excellent," said Bob Relyea. "It's just that he couldn't sit down with an actor like Willy Wyler could and talk about a performance. He would just blurt out something, or yell. And the conversational part of directing cannot be completely ignored.

"Duke could make *The Alamo,* but Duke could

not make *The Searchers,* where you're frightened by the shadow of an Indian. Look at *The Searchers.* It should be required viewing in every film school, so young people can see just what images can look like and how much can be communicated by them. But the truth is, I don't know if John Ford could have done a better job with the script of *The Alamo* than Duke did." Burt Kennedy believed that Wayne was stretching beyond his emotional capabilities. "Duke didn't have the patience to be a director," Kennedy said. "He had a short, short fuse. It's hard to be a good director if you're not patient."

Wayne's attitude toward the film in later years never changed — pride in getting it done and a stubborn refusal to acknowledge in any way that the film fell short, although he would admit, in a roundabout way, that "Everybody made money from it but me. I was so anxious to make the picture that I made bad deals all down the line." As with most dream projects, it was more about the doing than the result. "There was such a strong feeling of accomplishment on my part, that I don't mind the money business too much."

As for Happy Shahan, he rebuilt the parts of the set that had been blown up during the battle sequences and opened it as a tourist attraction called Alamo Village, which he rented out for a succession of westerns and miniseries: *Two Rode Together, The Alamo: 13 Days to Glory,* and *Lonesome Dove.*

After a year or so of release, United Artists' official figures maintained an $8 million domestic gross for *The Alamo* (Wayne told me that the film grossed $10 million). Before the film was released, Wayne had estimated that the film would have to gross $17 million to break even. By comparison, Billy Wilder's *The Apartment* grossed $9.3 million domestically, while Otto Preminger's *Exodus* grossed $8.7 domestically, and neither picture cost anywhere near what *The Alamo* did.

An undated financial worksheet in the Batjac files headed " 'Alamo' Comparison of Costs & Grosses" gives what seems to be the most comprehensive overview of the financial realities. The picture's negative cost is listed as $6.56 million, with an additional $2.5 million for advertising, $1.5 million for prints, $1.2 million for interest, $250,000 for "misc. charges," and $175,000 for Todd-AO. The total: a whopping $12.2 million. Domestic road show gross was a dismal $693,000, while the domestic general release gross was $6.8 million. The foreign road shows were more successful, amassing $1.1 million, with a foreign general release gross of $6.12 million. UA's total worldwide distribution fee added up to $4.8 million, which, added to the $12.2 million negative cost, means that the total cost and distribution fee came to $17 million. The total worldwide gross came to $15 million, leading to what the worksheet tallies as a loss of $2.048 million. Wayne's comment that he had to gross $17 million to break even turns out to have been absolutely correct.

Relative to the hopes of its maker, *The Alamo* would have to be regarded as a financial disappointment. Wayne gave away too much and didn't control his costs. Also, it's clear that a number of people who were far less idealistic than Wayne saw him coming and adjusted their appetites accordingly.

UA certainly made out well, almost doubling its

$2.5 million investment from their distribution fee. But Wayne signed off on contracts stipulating such things as royalties for Todd-AO amounting to 3 percent of a theater's net receipts. (Todd-AO was guaranteed $250,000 in royalties, with a $50,000 advance.)

Had Batjac spent $1 million for advertising instead of $2.5 million, and controlled its print costs — Wayne always believed the $1.5 million for prints was "exaggerated" — the picture would have broken even. Wayne said that a realistic possible profit of $2 million was eaten up by what he termed "extraordinary miscellaneous charges," plus added costs tacked on by UA's foreign distribution, plus random interest.

Well, maybe.

The finances of *The Alamo* were the focus of several forensic accountings over the next five years. After a certain point, i.e., after they were assured a tidy profit, UA threw in the towel; it made flat sales to certain countries for small change: $16,000 for Turkey, $5,500 for Iceland.

But there was also an underlying problem: Batjac was on the hook to UA for other movie loans in addition to *The Alamo*. UA had financed Batjac's *China Doll, Escort West* — both with Victor Mature — *Gun the Man Down,* and *Legend of the Lost* — losers all.

The result of this pile of aggregate debt was that Batjac owed UA $2.5 million, and this did not even take into account the money Batjac owed the McCullough Tool Company.

As early as 1965, UA made some overtures about reissuing the picture. One executive wrote, "it would be a crime to think about television until we had had at least one mass theatrical run for the picture."

Mike Wayne was agreeable, so long as there was an even split of the gross between Batjac and UA, with Batjac's share to go toward retiring the McCullough debt, which was still outstanding. Mike was willing to give UA ownership of the Victor Mature pictures if they could work out an accounting dispute that Mike estimated as amounting to between $150,000 and $200,000.

The deal took more than a year to come to fruition. By 1967, UA was still carrying *The Alamo* as $2 million in the red, so Batjac made the decision to wash its hands of the picture and sell its 16.5 percent for $500,000 and forgiveness of the debt. UA now owned the picture outright, and promptly reissued *The Alamo* in the shortened general release version. Over the next year the movie brought in another $710,000 domestically and $160,000 foreign. The eventual gross from the reissue was estimated at $1.2 million.

At the same time, the studio licensed the picture to television along with ninety-four other UA pictures, for $115 million. The amount allocated for *The Alamo* was fuzzy, although it wouldn't be surprising if — purely coincidentally, of course — it would have been about $2 million, thereby finally putting the picture decisively into the black. United Artists paid off the debt to McCullough in 1969, just about the time the tool company went into receivership.

That was the end of John Wayne's financial involvement with *The Alamo;* his emotional involvement was another thing entirely. Ultimately, *The Alamo* went into profit, but not for Wayne and not for Batjac.

The Alamo was a film that was born only because

of John Wayne's total dedication and will. But it fought him every inch of the way.

CHAPTER SIXTEEN

The financial failure of *The Alamo* wasn't the worst thing that happened to John Wayne in 1960.

Ward Bond had chafed for years at the fact that he wasn't a star, but he finally realized his dream when *Wagon Train* went on the air in September of 1957. Playing Major Seth Adams, a riff on his portrayal in John Ford's *Wagon Master,* this showcase for Bond's avuncular but firm personality granted him what he had always wanted: magazine covers and a star's salary.

Bond's late-life success came with a stinger — a highly competitive younger man as a co-star. Robert Horton had heard all about Bond's strong dislikes. "Ward had many reputations," remembered Horton, "but his main reputation was being anti-black, anti-Spanish, and of course anti-gay. And maybe anti-democratic. Ward had lots of qualities that weren't admirable."

Bond and Horton had an uneasy relationship from the first meeting, even though Horton thought Bond deserved an Oscar for his performance as John L. Sullivan in *Gentleman Jim* and told him so.

Initially, everything was fine. "Ward was very compatible and very warm," remembered Horton. "Then he said, 'Let's go across the street to Dupar's.' Well, we went over there and had a bite to eat and we talked and there was no antagonism. But you know how, when you meet somebody, you can tell pretty quickly if you're going to be long-term friends or not? That's exactly what happened with Ward. It just wasn't going to be a friendship."

In the very first episode of *Wagon Train,* Horton had a scene of conflict with Bond, a scene about two men of equivalent strength working toward the same goal in different ways. But the scene was cut from the pilot before it aired — the first of a long list of Bond's political power grabs.

"He acted like a despot," said Horton, "as if *Wagon Train* was his own particular vehicle. In some ways, he had reason to feel that. It was based on a movie he had starred in, and he was starring in the show as well. But he thought he ran the show."

There was only one instance of overt conflict between Bond and Horton. Horton was directed to do something that he felt would violate his character and he resisted. Bond overheard the exchange and came riding over on his horse. "How dare you tell this man you don't want to take his direction?" he yelled at Horton.

Other than that, the two men maintained a steely courtesy. But Virgil Vogel, one of the show's primary directors, told Horton that Bond was doing everything he could to get rid of him. If Horton had a good line, Bond would go to Vogel about cutting it; if Horton had a good scene, Bond would try to have it cut. "It was very petty," said Horton, "and it never worked." Bond was also telling the men on the show that Horton was homosexual — which he wasn't.

As the first year of *Wagon Train* closed out, Bond's anger grew intense. He wanted the show to be all about him, but Horton had captured the young fans. "He had top billing, but I was getting five thousand fan letters a week and Ward was getting fifty," said Horton. "That played on him. That said, although I knew we didn't get along great, there was really no obvious sense of anger between us."

As the first season ended, Bond told MCA, the producers of *Wagon Train,* that he wouldn't work with Horton anymore. There was a formal meeting at the producer's office, where the brass made an introductory speech about how big a hit the show was. We — the studio — can't afford to let personal views put the show off the air, and that could happen, etc. We all stand to make a lot of money, so let's let bygones be bygones, etc.

Bond was firm: "I won't work with him anymore."

The producer asked Bond what he didn't like about Horton. "I don't like the spurs he wears," said Bond.

"I'll get rid of them," said Horton.

"I don't like his horse either," said Bond.

Horton said it was fine if Bond didn't want to work with him; he was going to leave when his contract was up anyway. And then Horton said that he didn't appreciate Bond spreading rumors that he was homosexual. The meeting broke up in disarray. Both men remained adamant.

At the next production meeting, the brass announced that the two men didn't have to work together; that Bond would front half the shows and Horton the other half, and scenes between them would be kept to a bare minimum. And for the next couple of years, that was the way it was.

By the end of 1960, *Wagon Train* was in its fourth season and still a top ten show. In some respects, stardom hadn't changed Bond much; he still lived on twenty-three and three quarters acres in Coldwater Canyon that he had bought in 1946, where he lived with his wife, Mary Lou, surrounded by handmade Early American furniture and a couple of Labradors named Joe and Angus. Mary Lou Bond was generally known as "Maisie," and had lived with Bond for years before John Ford had enough and told them to get married and be quick about it.

The house contained Bond's proudest possession, a plaque from the Freedoms Foundation at Valley Forge he'd received in 1959. It commended Bond for "steadfastness, courage, and clarity of thought in the face of personal abuse and vilification by advocates of the alien, atheistic doctrine of world socialistic communism."

The heavy workload of a weekly hour-long TV show hadn't stemmed Bond's drinking. He would start his day in the makeup chair with what he called a coffee royale — coffee and whiskey. On the set in the morning, there were Bloody Marys or screwdrivers, which he referred to as his "daily vitamins." Lunch would be carried by both red and white wine, and in the afternoon there was a cooler that held a six-pack of beer, which he refused to share with anybody. At 5 P.M., Bond would declare, "Goddamn it, the sun's going down, it's time to have a real drink," which meant whiskey or bourbon.

In most respects, Bond was an open book — his drinking and his politics were all generally known.

But Bond also had his secrets. For one, he was epileptic, which is why he hadn't served in World War II. For another, he was taking Dexamyl tablets — time-released speed — in an effort to keep up with his workload. John Ford knew about the pills, and was deeply concerned.

All this contributed to the fact that Bond seemed much older than his chronological age of fifty-seven — as the fourth season of *Wagon Train* got under way in the fall of 1960, Bond's hair was turning from gray to white, his gut was even more prominent, and his voice was unusually raspy.

Whatever his failings, Bond's emotional intelligence made him lend each part a touch of humanity. "He was an excellent actor," said Horton. "He was instinctive and very, very good. His choices were almost always dead-on. If the director had a different choice for him, he would take it instantly and not argue about it. And he was very professional and well prepared."

Bond pulled off a considerable coup when he got John Ford to direct an episode of *Wagon Train* in May of 1960. Ford's show was called *The Colter Craven Story,* and featured a brief appearance by John Wayne as William Tecumseh Sherman. It's the story of an alcoholic doctor whose will to stay sober is revived by Major Seth Adams (Bond) telling him the story — in flashback — of General U.S. Grant. It's recognizably a Ford film, with dark-hued photography and a flashback structure that foretells *The Man Who Shot Liberty Valance.*

In November 1960, Bond made plans to go to Dallas to appear at half-time of a Cowboys football game as a favor to a friend. The night before he went to Dallas, he was in his dressing room, which he shared with co-stars (and former stuntmen) Terry Wilson and Frank McGrath. Robert Horton came in looking for McGrath, but he wasn't there.

Horton told Bond, "You know, Ward, we've had our differences, but we can agree on one thing: this script stinks." Bond smiled and put his hand on Horton's shoulder.

"Bobby," he said, sounding for all the world like Major Seth Adams, "we don't have any goldarn differences."

The next day, Bond was taking a shower in his hotel room in Dallas when he was stricken with a heart attack. He collapsed against the bathroom door, and by the time the ambulance crew got there, he was dead.

Terry Wilson broke the bad news to Wayne: "Hold on," blurted Wilson by phone, "Ward just dropped dead." Wayne and Wilson both began crying. The funeral was two days later, at John Ford's Field Photo Farm, where Bond was laid out in an open casket. Among the attendees were Wayne, Gregory Peck, Adolphe Menjou, Jane Darwell, Monte Blue, Harry Carey Jr., Terry Wilson, Frank McGrath, and Robert Horton. John Ford was there but was too upset to speak.

Harry Carey and Ken Curtis sang "He Was There" and "Come, Come Ye Saints." After the service, Wayne came up to Terry Wilson and asked him what the studio was going to do about the show. Wilson said he didn't know.

"I'll tell you what you do," said Wayne. "You go back tomorrow. You tell those guys if they want me to come in, I'll make two or three of the shows for them as a guest appearance thing . . . until they can get somebody [else] to do it."

Wilson relayed the offer to MCA, but they

thought that Wayne would unbalance the show; they carried on with the existing cast for some months. In March 1961, they finally cast John McIntire as the leader of the wagon train, without ever explaining what had happened to Major Seth Adams.

After the funeral, Wayne delegated Terry Wilson, Mark Armistead, and Ray Kellogg to spread Bond's ashes around Catalina. The men loaded up with a bottle of scotch, a bottle of bourbon, a bottle of gin, and a bottle of vodka. Each one of them tossed a handful of Ward into the ocean around Cherry Cove, then took a drink. By the time Ward was dispersed, they were thoroughly lubricated.

The only untoward thing was the fact that Bond had been cremated wearing his stainless steel watch, and there were recognizable pieces of the watch amongst the ashes and bone fragments. Terry Wilson kept the pieces of the watch as a souvenir of his friend. Bond's 1956 will left most of his property to his wife, but he left Wayne his favorite shotgun — the same gun that Wayne had shot him with years before.

On November 23, Wayne watched the episode of *Wagon Train* that Ford had directed. When it was over, he turned to Pilar and said, "There will never be another Ward Bond. I remember telling him, a hell of a long time ago, that he was too damn ugly to be a movie star. But I was wrong, Pilar. He was beautiful where it counted — inside." And then he began to cry, his huge body shaking with grief as the tears poured out of him.

It took Wayne a long time to process his grief at Bond's death. "I had never seen him so preoccupied, so quiet, so depressed," said Mary St.

John. "He lost fifteen pounds . . . because he didn't want to eat. It was as if someone had cut out his heart."

Bond's death got Wayne thinking about his own inevitable end. He came to the conclusion that "funerals are so medieval — I don't want one. John Ford has a little clubhouse in the valley. Harry Carey, Ward Bond — they were buried out of the chapel there. I will be too."

In 1959, a candy manufacturer named Robert Welch established the John Birch Society, named after a Baptist missionary murdered by Chinese Communists in 1945. The Birch Society was against taxes, welfare, the United Nations, the fluoridation of water, and Supreme Court chief justice Earl Warren. Above everything else, they were against Communists, who, they believed, were behind all the above. The FBI regarded the Birch Society as a "fanatical right wing" group with "utterly absurd viewpoints."

In June 1960, an informer, rated by the FBI as "reliable," listed the members of the Beverly Hills chapter of the Birch Society as including John Wayne, Adolphe Menjou, Hedda Hopper, Morrie Ryskind, and Ronald Reagan. Nobody has ever confirmed Reagan's membership, and it's unclear if the FBI believed it. But the president of the Birch Society did confirm that Wayne, Menjou, and Ryskind were members.

Wayne ultimately became uneasy about the Birch Society because of its campaign against fluoridation, not to mention Robert Welch's conviction that Dwight Eisenhower was a "dedicated conscientious agent of the Communist conspiracy."

"What a bunch of horseshit," he told a friend. "Ike was not my favorite politician, but he sure as hell wasn't a Communist."

Wayne had not been shy in complaining about what he regarded as confiscatory tax rates, as well as producers who couldn't produce, and the ethical swamp of modern — as of 1960 — Hollywood. And some producers weren't much happier, in large part because of movie stars such as John Wayne.

"Actors are now directing, writing, producing," complained Darryl Zanuck. "Actors have taken over Hollywood completely with their agents. They want approval of everything — script, stars, still pictures. . . .

"Now, I've got great affection for Duke Wayne, but what right has he to write, direct and produce a motion picture? What right has Kirk Douglas got? . . . My God, look at Brando with *One-Eyed Jacks*. My God, he's still shooting!"

Wayne read Zanuck's comments and steamed. But before he could exact his pound of flesh, he had to make some money, which is where *Hatari!* and *The Comancheros* came in. *Hatari!* is one of those movies that was probably more fun to make than it is to watch. Highly regarded at the time, nobody talks about it anymore. It's more or less Hawks's *Rio Bravo* formula: a group of likable characters interacting at inordinate length in a picturesque setting — Africa.

Hawks wanted to emulate John Huston and make a picture in Africa for years, and after the success of *Rio Bravo*, he decided it was time. Wayne came aboard for $750,000 plus 10 percent of the gross after the picture earned $7.5 million, i.e., theoretical break-even. The long location work in Africa meant that the picture was bound to be expensive, so Paramount refused to pay for another big star opposite Wayne. A provisional budget was set at $4.25 million, but that proved illusory. Base camp for the story about men who catch wild animals for zoos was set up at Arusha, about sixty miles west of Mount Kilimanjaro, on the eastern edge of the Serengeti.

Hawks told the cast and crew that they were privileged to be going on the most expensive safari ever, and he expected steady nerves and a lion's energy. Unfortunately, nobody had proffered copies of the shooting script and the actors began to panic. They knew that Wayne had worked with Hawks before, so they descended.

Wayne heard everybody out, then explained a few things. "Listen kids, I've shot a hundred movies. Well, the greatest directors, including Hawks, never handed me a script. . . . You just have to trust them. If you're good, they'll show you to your best advantage day by day."

Production got under way on November 28, 1960, and continued to mid-March 1961. Wayne didn't want to use any doubles for the dangerous scenes with the wild animals and did a lot of the work himself. Pilar and Aissa were there for the first few weeks of shooting, and Wayne was relaxed and happy. Getting out of the country and away from the flailing of *The Alamo* was undoubtedly good for Wayne's disposition.

One night Wayne and Red Buttons were outside their tents playing cards. Over Wayne's shoulder Buttons saw a leopard walk out of the bush and begin moving toward them.

"Duke, there's a leopard walking toward us,"

Buttons noted.

Wayne didn't turn around, merely said, "Buttons, see what he wants."

Elsa Martinelli, the female lead, found Wayne to be a complete gentleman; she played chess with him and enjoyed cooking pasta for him and Hawks. Martinelli also claimed that after his wife and daughter left the location, Wayne began a discreet affair with a blond woman who lived nearby, but if it happened it was so discreet it was unknown to everybody else on the production.

A lot of interesting people visited the set — William Holden, Rosalind Russell, the advertising guru Ed Lasker, and even the director Pier Paolo Pasolini, who came to talk to Martinelli. At one point, the publicity people inveigled Wayne into shooting an elephant for a photo op. While Wayne would say that "there's no particular thrill in killing an animal," he did enjoy an occasional bird-hunting jaunt with Bill Clothier or Webb Overlander. He also allowed as how the African environment, filled with the sounds of savage animals in the morning and night, did awaken certain atavistic impulses. "You take a different attitude than you did when you were at home saying, *'Well, I'd never shoot a little deer.'* "

Back in Hollywood, Leigh Brackett stayed with the film for the studio work, writing scenes that would tie the African footage together. She observed the star's humor and professionalism: "I remember his working with the baby elephant in the scene at the end of *Hatari!,* when the critter gets on the bed and it crashes down. They tried about 18 takes, and he said, 'He's doing it right. I'm not.' The elephant had his cues down perfectly, but it was Duke who was blowing it. He's a much more complex person than people give him credit for being."

Hatari! opened in June 1962 with an insane running time of 159 minutes, completing Hawks's transition from the fastest director in Hollywood to the slowest. In most respects, it's a lazy picture, albeit with a first-rate score from Henry Mancini. Hawks is doing the mixture as before, with one new wrinkle that would be present in all of his later pictures: beautiful young women who can't act.

It's a strange, amiable ramble, with overly broad comic relief. Yet, by some strange alchemy, by the end of the movie there exists a palpable affection for all the walking, talking clichés.

Wayne thought the movie was okay, but overlong: "We should have done something so two or three of the sequences would have been different. You know, you just can't ride out and catch animals the same frigging way all the time . . . it needs to have a variety of approaches and [Hawks] let the second unit do it and they didn't know how to handle action. . . . Shit, we did everything the second unit did." By the end of 1964, the film had amassed domestic rentals of only $4.7 million, although it went into profit in the 1970s.

Wayne enjoyed making the picture, but it became less enjoyable after he again had trouble extracting his overage from Hawks and Paramount. Wayne had agreed that Hawks was to have twelve weeks of his time, which later became fourteen. But as the shoot kept going and going, Wayne found himself budgeted for twenty weeks — five months, "which is about as much as a fellow can be asked to give."

Paramount claimed that Hawks had said Wayne

wouldn't want any overage. *Au contraire,* said Wayne. "I would appreciate hearing from you on this subject," wrote Wayne to Hawks. "I certainly want to keep my relationship with you a pleasant and fair one."

Paul Wellman's novel *The Comancheros* first entered Wayne's orbit in 1953, when Charles Feldman sent him a copy of the book, which had been purchased by George Stevens. The director eventually sold the property to 20th Century Fox in 1959 for $300,000 as part of the deal to make *The Diary of Anne Frank.*

Originally, the film was planned for Gary Cooper and Burt Lancaster as a follow-up to their very popular *Vera Cruz;* after Cooper died the western was reconfigured for Wayne as part of his three-picture deal with Fox. Charlton Heston was originally set as Wayne's co-star, but after *Ben-Hur* Heston wasn't about to take second billing to anyone, so the studio downshifted.

Stuart Whitman was making *Francis of Assisi* with Michael Curtiz in Italy when the director gave him the script for the western. "There's a hell of a role in there for me," Whitman said the next day.

"I think the part is cast," replied Curtiz. "But when you get back to Fox, check and see." It was indeed cast, but Curtiz told Whitman he would prefer him to the actor that had gotten the job, and told him to go talk to Wayne, who was shooting the interiors for *Hatari!*

"I went over and walked behind him as he was going into his dressing room," remembered Whitman.

"What do you want?" asked Wayne.

"I want to play Monsieur Regret."

"Oh, you do?"

The two men spent about twenty minutes together and Wayne ended the conversation by telling Whitman, "You've got the role."

When production began in the summer of 1961, Whitman could see that Curtiz was not in good shape; he had been diagnosed with cancer and had begun fading toward the end of *Francis of Assisi* as well. Working as a third assistant director was the future screenwriter Tom Mankiewicz, the son of director Joseph L. Mankiewicz. The young man's primary assignment was to pick up Wayne every morning at six at the house he was renting in Moab. The first day of the picture Mankiewicz was in the coffee shop of the Apache Motel where most of the company was staying, killing time until he was due to pick up the star.

At 5:40 A.M., Mankiewicz was just about ready to leave when he heard a clanking sound behind him. He turned around to find Wayne, fully costumed and made up, complete with spurs.

"Are you the fella who's supposed to pick me up?"

"Yes sir, Mr. Wayne."

"Well, I like to drive myself with my wardrobe and makeup guys. I know this valley pretty well by now. I'll get there."

"Yes, sir."

Wayne then noticed the John F. Kennedy button that Mankiewicz was wearing. "I'd take that button off if I were you. We don't advertise Socialists on my set." And then he broke into a big John Wayne grin, just to let Mankiewicz know he was kidding — more or less. Mankiewicz decided to downplay his political sympathies for the duration

567

of the shoot.

Mankiewicz found Wayne to be kind and caring, a leader who projected camaraderie, although occasionally gruff. After a few weeks, Wayne told Mankiewicz to call him Duke, and the young man knew he had arrived.

Wayne's warmth was in contrast to Curtiz, who was, said Mankiewicz, "an arrogant prick." Curtiz sneezed into tablecloths, he sunbathed nude at the hotel. He might have been dying, but that didn't mean he was going to stop pushing everybody's patience to the utmost, as he had done all of his life.

Although Wayne had approved Curtiz's hiring, the two men didn't seem to like each other. The unease that Mankiewicz noted might have had something to do with Curtiz's plans for a scene involving a cattle stampede. For the occasion, several dozen of Wayne's own longhorns had been rented. Curtiz told second unit director Cliff Lyons that he wanted the cattle to go over a five-foot drop, then scramble up the other side. Lyons told him that some of the cattle would surely break their legs.

"Don't argue with me, just do it!" snapped Curtiz, walking away.

Mankiewicz asked Lyons if he was going to go ahead and kill John Wayne's cattle.

"Fuck it," said Lyons. "Curtiz is the director. If he wants to commit suicide, that's up to him."

Mankiewicz was young and foolish, so he went over to Curtiz and asked him if it wouldn't be a good idea to call Wayne and run the idea by him first. Curtiz grabbed a gun from an extra's holster, fired a blank at Mankiewicz, then fired him.

That night, as Mankiewicz was packing up in

his hotel room, the phone rang. "I heard what you did out there," said Wayne. "Thank you. I'm going out to see what that Hungarian piece of shit is doing with my cattle. See you in the morning."

"I don't think so, Duke. He fired me."

"Hell, by the time I'm through with him he won't even remember that. See you tomorrow." Mankiewicz showed up for work the next day, and Curtiz didn't say a word.

Every day after lunch, Curtiz would fall asleep in his chair. The crew would put up umbrellas to protect him from sunburn and place wet chamois cloths around his neck. Wayne would simply pick up directing where Curtiz had left off.

"Duke could see what was happening, took the reins and took over," said Stuart Whitman. "That went on for a couple of days while Mike was there, then Mike disappeared to go into the hospital. Duke directed about half of the picture."

Stuntman Dean Smith, who was doubling for Whitman, said, "Duke directed *more* than half of *The Comancheros*. During the final battle, I ran and scissor-jumped onto the back of the horse, spun him around and jumped him over the fence. Duke directed all of that battle, every damn bit. He was a really good action director."

Ina Balin's first scene was a small one with Wayne, where she tells him her father is a captive and Wayne says, "Let's go."

Wayne set the shot up and said "Let's shoot it."

"Excuse me," said Balin, "but aren't we going to rehearse first?"

"What's to rehearse?" Wayne wanted to know. "You say, 'They've got my father' and I say 'Let's go.' "

"Well, I don't know, maybe it's because I'm

from the stage and I'm used to rehearsals."

Wayne drew himself up to his full height, amplified by the two-inch heels on his boots. "Let me tell you something, little lady. I've worked with stage people before. I've worked with Miss Geraldine Page of the New York stage. Best goddamn part she ever had. *Hondo.*" He turned to Bill Clothier. "Shoot the rehearsal," he ordered.

Balin said that her father was captured, Wayne said "Let's go," then paused and said, "Cut. Print. See how easy this is?"

Choreographing and shooting large-scale action sequences for a location western, balanced with ongoing money worries in the wake of *The Alamo* spurred Wayne's nervous energy, not to mention his smoking. Dean Smith remembered looking at Wayne's hand one day — the fingers were yellow from nicotine.

Smith believed that hiring Curtiz at the end of his career, and getting the old Republic hand George Sherman assigned as producer, was Wayne's way of doing people favors. "That's the way those guys were — loyal. If they liked you, they would go to bat for you, even if you hadn't been doing all that well lately."

William Clothier said that the situation was a trifle more complicated than that. "Duke and George Sherman grew up together working at Republic for $75 a week and all the horses you could ride. They were old friends. Duke didn't understand old Mike Curtiz very well and I must say that he didn't try very hard. On top of that, James Edward Grant, Duke's favorite writer, wrote the story. Mike was just plain outnumbered and I felt sorry for him."

"Duke was a terrific director as long as you did

what he wanted you to do," said Whitman. "Shooting with him was very easy, although Ina Balin worked from the Method, and that pissed him off. Before each shot, she'd dig down and get emotional and he was a little impatient. 'Get the goddamn words out,' he'd mutter to himself."

Whitman found that you couldn't help but talk politics with Wayne. The chess games went on between setups, but he didn't play for money. "He was nice and easy to be with, and we got along great. In fact, he told John Ford, 'You gotta use this guy.'" Ford never got the chance to use Whitman in a picture but the two men became friendly anyway. "I would go over and visit with him when he was sitting in bed watching baseball. His wife also liked baseball. She'd come in whenever someone got a hit."

It was Wayne's production to do with as he pleased, which meant it was tightly run. The crazy-eyed Jack Elam was playing one of the heavies, and won a pair of camera-trained vultures in a poker game with their handler. Elam promptly tried to up the price the vultures were being paid from $100 a day to $250.

Waiting in the hot sun for the vultures to be placed on the branch of a tree, Wayne was informed of the sudden hike — a threatened vulture no-show! He promptly strode over to Elam's trailer and banged on the door.

"You get those goddamn birds up in that tree right now or one of their heads is gonna be sticking out of your mouth and the other head out of your asshole."

Elam gulped. "Putting them in the tree right now, Duke, they're moving even as we speak."

Despite a meandering narrative, *The Coman-*

cheros is enlivened by strong action scenes and a particularly malevolent Lee Marvin showing up half scalped. The picture is far better than most of Michael Curtiz's late pictures, with typically splendid photography from William Clothier and propulsive music from Elmer Bernstein. The overall quality probably has to be ascribed to Wayne's effective handling of the action sequences. (The film was partially remade a few years later as *Rio Conchos,* with Anthony Franciosa in the Stuart Whitman part and Whitman himself in the John Wayne part.)

The back-to-back western hits of *North to Alaska* and *The Comancheros* served as the matrix for the rest of Wayne's career in the genre. With the occasional ambitious exception — *The Man Who Shot Liberty Valance, True Grit, The Shootist* — Wayne would focus on what the historian John McElwee calls "comfort westerns." He would make them until he — and the genre — were on their last legs.

■ ■ ■ ■ ■

PART FOUR:
1961–1979

■ ■ ■ ■ ■

"I won't be wronged, I won't be insulted, I won't be laid a hand on. I don't do these things to other people, and I require the same from them."
— *THE SHOOTIST*

CHAPTER SEVENTEEN

In March 1961, John Ford paid $7,500 for Dorothy Johnson's short story "The Man Who Shot Liberty Valance." The story is identical in theme to the film Ford made, but differs in most particulars. For one thing, Johnson's dialogue is much flatter — there's no "when the legend becomes fact, print the legend" here. Bert Barricune — renamed Tom Doniphon for the film — acts as a sort of fairy godfather to tenderfoot Ransom Stoddard, not only killing Liberty Valance for him, but goading him on to all his other accomplishments as well, so that Hallie, the woman who rejects Barricune for Stoddard, can be happy. Ford shifted the story so that Doniphon isn't rejected, but instead hands off Hallie to Stoddard, because he's a better match for her. Ford's last great film once again involves Wayne's character denying himself a relationship with a woman.

Ford set the film up at Paramount, but because of star salaries the days when a Ford western could be knocked off relatively cheaply were long past, which must have galled him no end. Wayne was getting $750,000 and James Stewart $300,000 against 7.5 percent of the gross apiece. (Ford was paid a comparatively minor $150,000, but he had

25 percent of the profits.) The total budget was $3.2 million — a great deal of money for a black and white (at Ford's insistence) western made almost entirely in the studio.

Once again, Wayne serves as the film's core, making rage and disappointment palpable, another man surrounding a dark, isolated heart. Valance can be countered only by Doniphon; both men understand how fragile the rule of law really is, albeit from different sides of the equation — they're opposing catalysts.

In a fury about his lost future, Doniphon burns down his house and very nearly himself. The house reveals how much Doniphon wants to get away from the self-sufficiency that everybody else admires — he yearns for domesticity.

He's an authentically tragic figure — a man who does the right thing knowing that, for him, it is the wrong thing, but does it anyway — perhaps for the greater good, perhaps because Hallie would be destroyed if Stoddard dies. He does all this, then slides into the shadows, unremembered and unmourned — the man who actually shot Liberty Valance. (In this sense, the ending is eerily similar to *The Searchers.*)

With his secret revealed, the falsity of the town and of Rance Stoddard's bonhomie is revealed — it's all based on a lie. In *The Searchers* and *Liberty Valance,* the men needed to master the wilderness are the same men civilization must expel, and if society is to benefit from the sacrifice, then legend must take precedence over truth.

For the most part, gallantry had been a keynote quality of Ford's westerns ever since the beginning, but in *The Man Who Shot Liberty Valance* the prevailing mood is overwhelming sadness. In movies as disparate as *The Grapes of Wrath, My Darling Clementine,* and *The Searchers,* Ford had nudged his characters toward a final ascendance to myth. In *Liberty Valance,* he begins with myth and methodically dismantles it on the way to a mournful irony, utterly undercutting the newspaperman's aphorism that has become so famous.

At the heart of all the characters is powerlessness. Tom Doniphon lets Stoddard have his woman, his town, his West, while Stoddard is helpless before the psychotic Valance and the strong Doniphon. The only true agent of power is time itself, and it does terrible things — the gap between the firmly idealistic young Stoddard and the bloviating windbag he becomes is heartbreaking. Stoddard, Hallie, and Link Appleyard are all haunted, and everything is changed, changed utterly — except for the desert.

Other than Doniphon, the characters get what they thought they wanted. The result is that Doniphon is dead and everybody else is profoundly unhappy. Welcome to the twentieth century.

Ford celebrates America's history, rituals, and communal values, but he also articulates the contradictions. Like many Ford films, *Liberty Valance* focuses on the need to subordinate individual needs to a collective good; unlike other Ford films, *Liberty Valance* questions whether the sacrifice is justified.

What makes the film possible is Wayne's emotional size, which corresponds to the way his athlete's body could suggest finely shaded tonalities of character and loss. Not that he thought of it that way, or was comfortable with what Ford was asking of him.

Wayne's idea of himself always involved action, movement. He complained to Peter Bogdanovich about Ford's habit of throwing juicy acting moments to other actors. *The Man Who Shot Liberty Valance* was worrisome because James Stewart's Ransom Stoddard is the fulcrum of the plot and, for 99 percent of the picture, is also the man who shot Liberty Valance.

"Hawks [also] does it all the time, he just says, 'Oh, well, Duke will get by,' and he gives everybody else everything to do. Well, Ford was doing that with me. Thank Christ, he thought of me kicking that steak out of the guy's hand. And then he was going to cut out the scene at the end, of me coming back to Stewart and saying, 'Get in there, you sonofabitch.' He said, 'The scene isn't important, and then you're walking out.' And I said, 'Oh God, Jack.' He said, 'Well, we'll ask Jimmy,' and thank Christ he asked Jimmy and Jimmy said, 'Oh, Jesus, Jack, he needs this scene.' . . . I'm sure he knew that he had to do the scene. . . . The kicking the steak and the last scene gave me enough strength to carry him [Wayne's character] through the picture."

Actors don't always know what's good for them. Wayne's obliviousness to his innate power is rather touching. So is the fact that, after having his cage rattled by John Ford for more than thirty years, he was still sincerely worried that Ford would cut one of the most important scenes in the picture.

Wayne's discomfort derived from the fact that he was surrounded by actors who tended toward the florid — Andy Devine, John Carradine, Edmond O'Brien — and Wayne's character didn't have center stage, even though he's unquestionably the hero of the story. As Dan Ford points out, "James Edward Grant wouldn't have written *Liberty Valance* that way." Which is perhaps why, for the only time in his career, Grant was called in on the next collaboration between Wayne and Ford — to make sure that Wayne's character stayed center stage and didn't have to risk Lee Marvin stealing two movies in a row.

Despite the film's self-evident qualities, Ford had entered that stage of critical overfamiliarity where every film was regarded as inferior to the ones before it. *Variety* complained that *Liberty Valance* could lose twenty minutes. Bosley Crowther in *The New York Times* called it "odd," while Ernest Callenbach in *Film Quarterly* bewilderingly called it a "sinister little fable" with "crypto-fascist" tendencies.

One Mike Herr, writing in *The New Leader,* eagerly seized an opportunity to make a fool of himself. "Ford has been making bad pictures for so long that it makes me wonder if he has ever been better than he is now. . . . I have not liked a Ford picture since *My Darling Clementine,* and that was about 20 years ago . . . It is a thoroughly boring movie; a western with less feeling for the West than one finds in any given episode of *Gunsmoke* . . . an actionless, colorless, humorless embarrassment that is atrociously acted."

Overseas, it was immediately greeted as a major work. The London *Observer* found it "bathed in Ford's talent and affection," and *Cahiers du Cinéma* delivered a riposte to Ernest Callenbach and said it was "anti-fascist."

Happily, time has been kinder to *Liberty Valance* than would have seemed possible in 1962. The picture returned worldwide rentals of more than $7 million, although the domestic receipts were only $3.1 million, below Wayne's norm. Clearly, American audiences had grown to like Wayne triumphant, not as a moody alcoholic who dies offscreen. But the picture has never stopped playing in the fifty-odd years since, and is still capable of sparking serious debate. As *The New Yorker*'s Richard Brody noted about the film he called "the most romantic Western [and] also the greatest American political movie," the movie follows the path laid out by the ending of *Fort Apache:* "Ford shows both the rousing myth and the humbling truth — about the extralegal violence on which law is based, about a glorious political career, and about love."

Darryl Zanuck had staked what was left of his career, not to mention his studio, on *The Longest Day,* an adaptation of Cornelius Ryan's bestseller about the D-Day invasion. To hedge his bets he was determined to infuse the picture with stars. He began pursuing Wayne in mid-1961, enticing him with the size and importance of the project. "I am writing this from a little village in Corsica where we have been shooting amphibious landings with the Sixth Fleet," wrote Zanuck by way of introduction. He explained that the script was a joint undertaking by Ryan, James Jones, and Romain Gary, and he was spending the summer supervising the huge battle sequences being directed by Andrew Marton, Elmo Williams, and Gerd Oswald. By the winter, he would be shooting the dialogue sequences.

Initially, Zanuck wanted Wayne to play Brigadier General Norman Cota — the part eventually played by Robert Mitchum — and he went after Wayne with fervor, sending in script rewrites in order to entice a star he had thoroughly alienated with his remarks about overreaching actors.

"I don't want you because you look like Cota (which actually happens to be the case). I don't want you because of your box office status (which I certainly don't underestimate). I want you because I believe in these six episodes you can characterize Cota, and symbolize what he stood for."

Wayne was interested, but noncommittal. In September, Zanuck set James Jones to rewriting the Cota scenes, but Wayne continued to make himself scarce.

Zanuck continued with the cajolery: "I am shocked to learn that you are going to be with Charlie [Feldman]. I advise you to change your plans immediately as Charlie is a lost fish in Europe. The main difficulty lies in the fact that he cannot determine in advance what gal he is going to take out to dinner — so he usually ends up eating alone."

In December, Zanuck cabled Feldman that William Holden — another Feldman client — had decided not to play Lieutenant Colonel Benjamin Vandervoort and he wanted Wayne to play the part. After much back and forth, Wayne settled for $250,000 for ten days work — a huge payday, especially considering that many stars were working for $25,000 apiece for the honor and prestige of appearing in such an important picture. Not only that, but Charles Feldman extracted special billing — everybody else was listed alphabetically, except for "And John Wayne" at the end of the cast list.

Despite the traces of bad blood between the two men, Zanuck had no intention of delegating the direction of his biggest star to any of the film's polyglot roster of directors. (Besides Gerd Oswald, Andrew Marton, and Ken Annakin, Bernhard Wicki was directing the German footage). Zanuck directed all of Wayne's scenes himself, as he did with some other key actors.

Wayne and dialogue director Mickey Knox became fairly good friends, despite Knox's left-wing politics. Knox would occasionally take issue with Wayne's defense of the blacklist, but he remembered that "Wayne never showed any disrespect or anger when listening to me."

The headquarters for the Normandy location was the Malherbe Hotel in nearby Caen. In Paris, Wayne was reunited with Stuart Whitman, who was sent to the location to deliver twelve boxes of cigars to Darryl Zanuck. After taking delivery, Zanuck asked Whitman if he wanted to go to work, and the actor was promptly cast in Wayne's scenes.

"It was late January or early February, and we were all freezing our asses off on the location," remembered Whitman. "None of us could figure out how that son of a bitch Wayne could be so strong, so impervious to the cold. It didn't seem to be bothering him at all.

"So one day I followed him into his dressing room and I discovered that he had handwarmers built into his underpants so that they covered his kidneys. They kept his kidneys warm, folded newspapers in his shoes kept his feet warm. And he made sure I promised not to tell anybody else what he was doing."

During production, there was a party thrown by a local duchess, who had a slight scar on her face from a dueling mishap, which Whitman thought was extremely sexy. At one point, Whitman walked into a bathroom and discovered the butler sitting on the bidet while being straddled by the hostess, who was vigorously bouncing up and down. He promptly backed out and closed the door.

A minute later Wayne came around the corner and Whitman beckoned him over. Whitman opened the door and Wayne and Whitman observed the butler and the hostess going at it.

"We walked down the hallway just choking with laughter," recalled Whitman.

It was a long way from Winterset, Iowa.

Unfortunately, the shoot was not all ribald fun and games. A friend of Whitman's had just opened a restaurant in Paris and invited the actor to bring some guests for a visit. Whitman was good friends with Robert Ryan, who lived a few doors away from him in North Hollywood. Whitman also invited Wayne, without knowing that the two men had a visceral dislike of each other's politics.

"Bob was very liberal, and of course Duke was very conservative. We all sat down at this table and it didn't take long before both of them stood up and started to go for each other. I grabbed hold of Ryan and someone else grabbed Duke." It would have been an interesting fight; Wayne outweighed Ryan by forty or so pounds, but Ryan had been a heavyweight boxing champion at Dartmouth and a Marine drill instructor during World War II.

Later, Whitman asked Ryan what set him off. "Those fucking Republicans," he said. "The day before I left to do this film, someone set off a bomb in my doorway and the door got blown off." Ryan blamed the John Birch Society, and he was in no mood for a typical Wayne crack about "goddamn liberals." Within a few days, Wayne and

Ryan had repaired the breach; Mickey Knox reported that they even went on a weekend bender together and reported for work on Monday morning only slightly the worse for wear.

In his ten days of work, Wayne shot eight crackerjack scenes for *The Longest Day,* and he even does some expert but unnecessary exposition ("We're on the threshold of the most crucial day of our times . . ."). *The Longest Day* was critically hailed and a great hit, but the script is inadequate to the drama, as almost any script would be. It's a film with a couple of great sequences — the parachute drop into Sainte-Mère-Eglise, the Pointe du Hoc climb — more than it is a great film.

Another glorified guest appearance entailed five days of work for John Ford in the Cinerama production of *How the West Was Won.* Wayne played an ahistorically oversized — but accurately unkempt — William Tecumseh Sherman for little glory and the modest fee of $25,000. (Part of the movie's impetus was that a lot of the profits would go to St. John's Hospital in Santa Monica, so the all-star cast worked cheaply to keep costs down.)

By this time, Ford had largely despaired of inclusion, let alone contentment, and his episode of *How the West Was Won* is all about leaving and longing. In the wake of the bloodbath of Shiloh, even U.S. Grant (Harry Morgan) is full of despair, which leads to Sherman's pep talk: "Doesn't matter what the people think. It's what you think, Grant."

In later years, Wayne seemed slightly embarrassed about *Donovan's Reef:* "[Ford] never should have used me in that picture," Wayne told me. "He should have picked some young guy. It didn't require much of him. All he had to be was a good-looking young guy, and I wasn't young enough."

Actually, a number of people connected with the picture seemed embarrassed by it. "Ford hired a friend of Wayne's, James Edward Grant," said William Clothier, who photographed the film. "Jimmy wrote a script and Ford hated it. He got another writer [Frank Nugent] and changed the whole damn thing. They called it *Donovan's Reef.* You've got to blame the Old Man for things like that. Just plain bad judgment."

Actually, Ford hired several writers; Edmund Beloin is credited with "screen story," Nugent gets billing over Grant, and no less than James A. Michener was credited with the original source material in publicity handouts but not on the film itself.

The problem is not so much the picture — it's a ragged but loving Quirt and Flagg movie mostly made on the island of Kaui between late July and September 1962 — it's that it's relentlessly caricatured. It does have some compensations — among other things, Ford uses his ship the *Araner* in the movie.

The film has one beautiful set piece, a Christmas pageant that once again brings out Ford's great gift for ceremony. And yes, Wayne and Marvin are too old for their parts — Wayne had arrived at the same conclusion as Cary Grant: he was simply too old to get the girl.

Wayne and Lee Marvin pursued their usual ration of after hours drinking, as well as comparing notes about literature, which led Marvin to exclaim, "You're not the illiterate, uneducated ignoramus you'd like people to think."

"Neither are you," said Wayne. "Let's keep it to ourselves or we'll ruin our image."

Dorothy Lamour went back a quarter century with Ford, to *The Hurricane,* but she and her husband had moved to Baltimore years earlier and she was more or less retired. "John [Ford] called and asked me to do the picture and right away I said, 'I don't know where I can find Hawaiian clothes in Baltimore.' And John said, 'That's all right, Mary has a closet full of them.' " Lamour played much of the picture wearing Mary Ford's mu-muus. She said that Ford "hadn't mellowed too much, but he was a darling man."

Lamour was stunned one day when Wayne actually yelled back at Ford — an unheard-of occurrence. When Lamour asked Wayne about it later, he explained that Ford's thinking simply wasn't what it had been, and that his eyesight was also compromised. Wayne was checking out the rushes every day to avoid embarrassment, and he was feeling the strain. He finished by telling Lamour that he loved Ford too, and he was sure things would work out.

But everybody noticed a difference in the Coach. William Clothier told stories about Ford wanting to work a short day, not wanting to venture far from his hotel room on location, and even making tentative moves toward settling for something less than top-notch photography — the foundation of his art.

The reviews ranged from mildly favorable to what-the-hell-happened? One critic said that "the screenplay . . . is almost primeval in its foolishness." *Donovan's Reef* cost $3.4 million, earned worldwide rentals of $5.7 million, and didn't go into the black for decades. Besides his salary,

Wayne got 10 percent of the gross after recoupment.

The film's reputation has risen somewhat in the intervening decades, but it's probably best regarded as a paid vacation for a director who had long since earned one.

As with many of John Ford's extended family, Wayne had a boat, the *Nor'wester,* a seventy-three-foot motor sailer which increasingly struck him as insufficient. "There was no pride of possession," was the way he put it.

Between Ford's *Araner* and his own *Nor'wester,* Wayne had had a lot of sailing experience, but he had always yearned for something grander — something with huge diesel engines. So, in 1962, Wayne finally scratched the itch and bought a boat. Not just any boat — a minesweeper commissioned YMS 382 by the Navy when it was built during the war. The Navy sold the ship in 1948, and it cruised the Pacific Northwest for a number of years until it was bought by Wayne's friend Max Wyman.

Wayne was a guest on the boat when Wyman traveled through the Princess Louisa Inland Waterway. "Well, we had a wonderful time," remembered Wayne. "There were three couples on board, but nobody ever got in anyone else's way . . . and the comfort of this thing was just great."

Wyman used the boat only once a year or so. Mostly it just lay at anchor in Seattle. Wayne told Wyman he'd like to buy the boat, and a deal was quickly consummated. The price was $116,000, and then Wayne spent even more to remodel it to his specifications. He called it the *Wild Goose.*

The *Wild Goose* wasn't a trim thing of beauty like Ford's *Araner,* but rather 136 feet of form following function. She was made of Douglas fir, drew nine feet, with a twenty-five-foot beam and twin diesel 500 horsepower engines. When the Navy had her, she held four officers and twenty-nine enlisted men, but as a private vehicle she carried a crew of six, slept twelve, and cruised nicely at 11 knots.

Her appointments included two chattering Teletype machines — one for AP and one for UPI — a barbecue outfit, a wine cellar, and a 16mm projector for watching movies. The pilothouse, master stateroom, and a small two-bunk cabin were all on the top deck, while the main salon, a small head, the engineer's cabin, a double guest cabin, and the galley, forward of which was the only enclosed dining area on the boat, seating up to eight, were on the main deck. The ship had five deep freeze refrigerators, with enough space to keep the ship fully supplied for a two-month cruise.

In 1965, Wayne renovated the master stateroom to make room for his king-sized frame. It was located directly behind the wheelhouse, and it had six feet, eight inches of headroom. That was all to the good, but the added weight on top of the ship meant that the *Wild Goose* was even more inclined to roll than she had been. With stability that crew member and later Captain Bert Minshall remembered as "marginal," the crew dropped eight-hundred-pound sacks of cement into the bilge to steady her. The boat dropped down six added inches in the water, which helped, but over the years the cement broke loose and caused problems with the bilge pumps.

The master cabin had a color TV and a small library with some of Wayne's favorite books, and the chessboard was always set up for a game. Hanging on the sides of the boat were a sixteen-foot Boston whaler and a seventeen-foot British dory for excursions. The atmosphere was comfortable, masculine, and far from ostentatious. For the next sixteen years, until just before Wayne died, the *Wild Goose* was kept at Berth 54 at the Lido Yacht Anchorage.

Bert Minshall, who went to work on the boat in 1963, believed that Wayne was far less a cowboy at heart than he was a sailor.

"He liked to fish for giant salmon," remembered Minshall. "Forty- and fifty-pounders. He'd do that from sunup to sundown. He also liked wahoo, tuna, marlin, and lobster, but he was a fanatic about salmon." Wayne would put about 100,000 miles on the ship every year, with his favorite destination being north of Vancouver, where he liked to fish.

"The first time we met, I was wearing brand-new Top-Siders," remembered Minshall. "We were shooting the breeze and then he suddenly spat on my shoes. I guess I looked confused, because then he put his hand on my shoulder and said, 'Always spit on new shoes for luck.'

"Well, okay."

Minshall was from Liverpool, and became popular with the Wayne family because of his tireless energy and the fact that he was a good nanny for the children. Wayne adored them, but felt he was too old to tend them personally and handed them off to Minshall when they were on board. "It gave him a chance to relax, play bridge, go over his scripts."

589

Typically, Minshall would swim with the kids and man the boat pulling the water skis. Once in Acapulco, Minshall was towing Marisa on a plywood sled he had constructed, with the other children in the boat with him. Wayne didn't like the look of the jury-rigged sled and yelled out, "I'm gonna shoot four people if Marisa gets hurt on that thing!"

That put an end to the festivities, and the next day Wayne came up to Minshall and apologized. Wayne told Minshall he should call him Duke, at least when he was off the ship, but that came hard for the sailor.

Over his years with Wayne, Minshall became familiar with the actor's fury, which was sudden and complete, but also transient. He also grew used to his apologies. "It's my damn Irish temper," Wayne would say by way of explanation. When Minshall's parents visited from England, Wayne invited them to the house and cheerfully posed for pictures with the awestruck couple. For that matter, he didn't mind Minshall bringing his camera on trips, good-naturedly griping that he ought to be getting a performance fee if Minshall insisted on taking home movies. The *Wild Goose* would occasionally be chartered out to friends, and Otto Preminger used the boat on-camera for his lamentable *Skidoo.*

Contributing to Wayne's enthusiasm for the *Wild Goose* was the fact that it could be used for parental leverage. "I need the space for six kids and the six grandchildren and the wife, that makes fourteen people already," he explained. "A boat's the only place I can relax and forget about my work. And I like to have my kids around me. You know how kids are. The only way you can have

590

them is if you have something they want that no one else has. It was the same way with me. I love my mother and my father, but you make your own life and don't see your parents much unless they have something extra to offer."

In the winter, Wayne would sail for Mexico, in the summer for Seattle, with occasional weekends in Catalina. Few movie people were to be seen on the boat — only co-workers such as Claire Trevor, Dean Martin, Maureen O'Hara, and Hugh O'Brian were welcome. Mostly, he favored friends who were businessmen — a car dealer named Chick Iverson, or, for that matter, the boat's ex-owner, Max Wyman.

Wayne made sure that Pilar didn't succeed in her occasional attempts to redecorate the ship to her specifications. He once told an overenthusiastic interior decorator, "I don't want my boat turned into a goddamned French whorehouse." On board, Wayne would read and engage in marathon sessions of gin or bridge. In the early years aboard the ship, he drank brandy on the rocks, but in the mid to late 1960s he switched almost exclusively to tequila, which remained his drink of choice for the rest of his life. As with everybody else who watched Wayne drink, Minshall was amazed at his capacity. No matter the volume, he always remained on his feet, "coherent and coordinated. He never got seasick, but didn't pretend he was more of a sailor than he was, either. I never once saw him take the wheel."

Like all boats, the *Wild Goose* was an expensive toy. The ship's original captain was named Pete Stein, a wild man with a drinking problem who was once thrown overboard by a steward he had just fired. Wayne didn't mind Stein's occasional benders, saying, "I don't trust a man that doesn't drink."

"He couldn't stand to be alone," remembered Bert Minshall, "so even if we were only going to Catalina, he'd invite two other couples and play bridge all day. Every once in a while, he'd take a little five-minute break and dive off the stern to cool off. And every single time he'd come to the surface and say, 'Jesus Christ, it's cold.' It didn't matter if the water was 80 degrees — 'Jesus Christ, it's cold.'

"He'd go out fishing in the morning, come back in the afternoon, go back out, back for dinner, then back out until it was dark. He'd hire professional guides to find the hot spots where the fish were. He'd come back with gunny sacks full of fish."

On one trip aboard the *Wild Goose*, Batjac story editor Tom Kane was puzzled by the presence of a man who was introduced as Joe Roe. Kane thought he knew everybody in Wayne's circle, but he had never met him before. Not only that, Wayne treated Roe as if he was a dear friend. Kane asked Mike Wayne about Roe, and Mike didn't know any more about him than Kane. Finally, Kane asked Wayne.

"Joe Roe kept me from starving," he explained. It was just after Harry Cohn had fired him from Columbia and blackballed him. "I couldn't get a day's work. I literally was not eating." But Joe Roe owned a restaurant on Sunset and Gower, right across the street from Columbia, and he grubstaked Wayne to three meals a day for as long as it took to get back on his feet. Once Mascot hired Wayne for the serials, he repaid Roe for all the meals, but didn't think it was quite enough.

Years later, he had Mary St. John track the man down. Roe's restaurant was gone, as was his money, and he was at the veterans hospital in Sawtelle. Roe jumped at the chance to go on a fishing trip, and when he came back from the voyage Wayne gave him a box of fancy lures as a keepsake.

Perhaps because he worked in a business that was always convulsively unsettled, Wayne took great solace in familiar faces. Among the Batjac staff was a crusty man named Al Podlasky, an accountant who lost an arm in a streetcar accident. Wayne had met him at Republic when he was making the Three Mesquiteers pictures. Wayne asked Podlasky for a new pair of boots, as his had holes in the bottom and he was getting pebbles in them.

Podlasky was reading *The Hollywood Reporter* at the time. As Wayne finished his request, Podlasky folded the paper up and handed it to Wayne. "Stick that in there," he said.

Wayne remembered thinking, "You old son of a bitch, if I ever get a company of my own, you're the first guy I'm going to hire to protect my money." As far as Wayne was concerned, the one-armed accountant had a job for life.

Things were changing everywhere, and not necessarily for the better. Grant Withers was gone, Ward Bond was gone, and Jimmy Grant was now a mainstay of Alcoholics Anonymous.

After a few years of hibernation, Batjac was reactivated for *McLintock!* — one of Wayne's more personal films. It was an obviously commercial project, and the reason United Artists got distribution was that Batjac still owed the company $700,000.

In August 1962, Batjac and UA made a deal in which Batjac would repay the studio out of the gross receipts for *McLintock!* To maximize profits, the budget was kept to a very low $2 million. Wayne took no salary, only a percentage: 5 percent of the gross up to break-even, the first $700,000 in profits, and 10 percent of the gross thereafter. After recoupment, Batjac took 10 percent of the gross and 75 percent of the net, and the film negative was to revert to Batjac after five years.

In return, UA released the Batjac film library that had served as collateral for *The Alamo* loan and Charles Feldman agreed to make a good-faith effort to convince Wayne to play the title role in *Mister Moses,* a project UA was very high on. (Robert Mitchum played the part, to no great public or critical response.)

For $100,000, Mike — who became the executive producer on Batjac pictures — and his dad hired Maureen O'Hara for the part of McLintock's estranged, continually outraged wife, a part she could have played in her sleep. (Some thought was also given to Deborah Kerr — who was twice as expensive as O'Hara — and Susan Hayward.)

Mike's mandate in producing the picture was to cut costs whenever possible without cheating the picture. Mike's father wanted Henry Hathaway to direct, but Hathaway's price was $100,000 and a percentage. Mike hired Andrew McLaglen to direct for a flat $25,000, and so on down the line — not Dimitri Tiomkin but Frank De Vol, etc.

The film had a fairly comfortable fifty-nine-day shoot, but costs were rigorously watched. Although UA was releasing the picture, Batjac shot the interiors at Paramount. A month before shooting began, Paramount's Frank Caffey wrote a memo stating that Batjac was "promised complete autonomy. . . . It is of the utmost importance that we watch every expenditure and make sure it has been OK'd by the Batjac office, as they have had some very unhappy experiences at Warners."

Everybody remembered the film as a pleasant experience, with Wayne always hovering. For a scene where doubles for Wayne, Yvonne De Carlo, and Maureen O'Hara were to tumble down stairs, Wayne said he didn't want stuntwomen doing the shot. "Why not?" asked Polly Burson, who was supposed to double for De Carlo.

"Someone might elbow or knee you in the breast or someplace," Wayne grumbled. "I just don't want to risk it."

"Duke, I just did an outside stair fall at Universal with no pads on," said Burson.

"Well, that's fine," he said, "but you're not going to do it for me." Two small stuntmen in drag doubled for De Carlo and O'Hara, while the stuntwomen stood by and got paid anyway.

Andrew McLaglen had been born in London in 1920, but came to California with his father at the age of five. He met John Ford for the first time when he accompanied his father to the Arizona locations of *The Lost Patrol*. By the time he was fifteen he was making 16mm home movies with his friends at the Cate prep school in Santa Barbara. He first met Wayne around the time he was nineteen, when Wayne had just finished *Stagecoach*.

McLaglen attended the University of Virginia because it had a good boxing program and his father had been an excellent boxer in his youth. Beginning as a clerk in the production department of Paramount, McLaglen then graduated to second assistant director, then first assistant, in which capacity he worked on *Sands of Iwo Jima* and *The Quiet Man.*

He'd been under contract to Batjac, where he worked mostly as an assistant director and had produced *Seven Men from Now* with Bob Morrison. Wayne had guaranteed the bank loan for *Man in the Vault*, McLaglen's first feature in 1956. After *Gunsmoke* went on hiatus after its first year, McLaglen directed James Arness in the low-budget Batjac western *Gun the Man Down,* with Angie Dickinson.

Arness recommended McLaglen to CBS, who signed him as a staff director. Over the next six years, McLaglen directed ninety-five episodes of *Gunsmoke* and over a hundred episodes of *Have Gun, Will Travel,* not to mention *Rawhide, Perry Mason,* and whatever other CBS shows came along. He also directed one of his father's last movies.

By the time Wayne gave McLaglen the nod for *McLintock!* he was a highly professional and experienced budget-minded director. And because he had been brought up at Wayne's knee, the always affable McLaglen was also unlikely to tell his old mentor when he was settling for second-best.

Also joining the Batjac family was a young man named Luster Bayless, the son of a Mississippi sharecropper, who was hired to help out on the production department of *McLintock!* Bayless would become Wayne's primary costumer for the rest of his career, and he remembered his favorite star's measurements all his life: "chest 49, hat 7 3/8, shoe 10 1/2 D — he had small feet."

McLintock! began production on October 25,

1962, and wrapped on January 10, 1963. Playing McLintock's daughter was Stefanie Powers, a young actress under contract to Columbia, who had never encountered a similar environment before and only occasionally would in the future.

"If you worked for Batjac," Powers remembered, "you were moving into the Wayne family, which was an offshoot of the John Ford family. It was utterly and completely a family, a club.

"Nobody was forgotten. We had Ford's Indians from Kanab, Indians I had seen as a kid growing up at the movies. There was a small part of a train engineer, and they hired Bob Steele, who had been a big western star I saw at matinees. There was a sense of loyalty, a sense that Duke never forgot people with whom he had rapport."

It was an adjunct of the Ford family in all sorts of ways. Every morning Danny Borzage would play the accordion in the makeup trailer. "From top to bottom, it was a mentorship," said Stefanie Powers. "Old stuntmen were teaching young stuntmen how to do their jobs, and the same stuntmen were teaching me the tricks of the trade, like how not to eat dust. The abiding word was generosity."

Coexisting with the generosity was Wayne's innate competitiveness. One day on the set, Wayne grew irritated with Maureen O'Hara's approach and growled, "C'mon, Maureen, get going. This is your scene." O'Hara replied that she was trying to go 50–50. "It's your scene," repeated Wayne, "take it," then added, almost under his breath, "If you can."

McLintock! was the first film to be entirely produced by Michael Wayne, and he and his father kept their relationship entirely professional.

"There was no father and son scrapping," said Stefanie Powers. "If they had any disagreements, it was private; Duke made sure that Michael maintained his dignity."

Pat Wayne was also in the film, and Melinda Wayne was hanging around the set as well. Pilar — "an ice queen" according to Powers — was on location for a while, then left, and Pat Wayne and Powers were assigned to keep Wayne company. If he was lonely, they would play chess with him, and Powers found that "in any state of inebriation, he could cream you."

Andy McLaglen wasn't directing the picture by himself. "It was a collaboration," said Powers. "Andy deferred to Duke. Wayne was there for every rehearsal of every scene, he did every offstage line in every scene he was in — he never abandoned an actor. There was not a shot of that movie he didn't attend."

McLaglen would rehearse a scene, and Wayne would point out "If you moved the camera over there, the actors can move without a cut." Wayne's suggestions were invariably followed. Wayne offered the young actress only one tip: "It's all in the eyes."

For a scene in which Powers had to ride out fast, the production had hired a local palomino instead of an experienced motion picture horse. The palomino fell and threw Powers, and when her eyes were able to focus, she looked up at John Wayne. He was in tears, carefully putting his jacket under her head.

"Did you get that on film?" she asked, which cemented their relationship. She would be invited regularly to the Encino house for screenings.

One day the word came down that Andy Mc-

Laglen was sick and someone else was going to take over. The company sent a car to the airport to pick up the substitute director but the car came back empty. The substitute had taken a cab instead.

The entire company was standing at attention as the cab advanced from the far distance, a puff of smoke on the dirt road to Nogales. When the cab arrived, the door slowly opened, and a sneakered foot stepped tentatively out, followed by a head covered with a filthy old hat, followed by the rest of John Ford. Wayne walked over to lend a hand, but Ford slapped the hand aside and walked over to Bill Clothier standing by the camera.

"Bill," said Ford, "let's go to work."

It was all terribly impressive for everyone but Stefanie Powers. "I was peeing myself with fear. I was the only person on that set who had never worked for him." Ford never turned on her, but he didn't turn on the charm either. He was mostly just gruff. "Duke and Maureen called him Pappy. He had such total patriarchal power that everybody around him was reduced to the level of a child."

Ford shot for three days, a lot of footage around the house in Nogales, entrances and exits and some entire scenes. Aside from the mortal fear engendered by Ford's aura, for a young actress "it was a dream experience," remembered Powers. "Duke had a very poetic soul, an interestingly sensitive side to go along with his great moralism. And he did love his ladies. I found him adorable. The entire experience was a cherished part of my life."

"He was a marvelous actor," said the character actor Ed Faulkner, who worked with Wayne in

599

McLintock! and a batch of pictures afterward. "A lot of what he did was movement and timing. For a scene at a train station, he said, 'Let me show you something. Make your turn like this — watch how I do this.' And it worked. He was very good to work with. He'd run lines and seldom gave you specific directions. I just loved working with him."

The production was enlivened by the presence of "Big" John Hamilton, a restaurateur from San Antonio. Despite his size, Hamilton possessed a high, squeaky voice and a Pekinese named Buck. He also drove a specially modified Cadillac that held several tanks of booze in the trunk so he'd never be without. Wayne cast Hamilton as a man who tries to break up a fight.

The brawl in the mud pit was shot over four days, from November 16 to the 19. During the sequence the weather turned cold — the temperature was about forty-two degrees. Some stars would have insisted the scene be postponed until the weather warmed up, but Wayne wasn't about to complicate what needed to be an efficient production.

Nineteen stuntmen were employed, but both Wayne and O'Hara took the slide in close-up. The mud pit wasn't actually made of mud, but of bentonite, which was much slicker than mud. "Good God, Duke," said O'Hara, caked in the horrible chemical mixture, "this bloody stuff is like bird shit!"

Wayne disagreed. "It's like snot!" he said.

As *McLintock!* wrapped production, Jimmy Grant wrote Mike Wayne a Dutch uncle letter in commiseration at having to once again deal with United Artists. "This town is full of independent producers," wrote Grant. "They come and go like the bait on which the big fish feed, swelling in here by the millions and going out with the tide. Everyone deposits his sad tale of his UA experience before he goes. No one, but no one, has ever made five cents with a UA deal."

But *McLintock!* was a hit, if a muted one because much of the profit went to pay off Batjac's indebtedness to United Artists. *McLintock!* cost $2.1 million, earned domestic rentals of $4.5 million. Adding in foreign monies meant that the debt to UA was paid off, with a little left over. Batjac was out of debt and once again owned its film library. They were back in business.

McLintock! has been aptly described by Leonard Maltin as a "boisterous, rowdy comic western," as it eventually becomes a rough — very rough — variation on *The Taming of the Shrew.* It completes the transition of Wayne's character from disenfranchised outsider to a monied, occasionally belligerent ("Don't say it's a fine morning, or I'll shoot ya' " is McLintock's first line) land baron — an extension of Wayne's politics, and his respect for his own accomplishments.

McLintock is proudly paternalistic, has a passion for chess, and what he regards as an appropriate loathing for government bureaucrats and seedy politicians. The film is a virtual anthology of Wayne's social views, including a certain propensity for ethnic caricature — the querulous proprietor of the general store is named Birnbaum — not to mention his sense of humor.

"What does 'reactionary' mean?" asks one character of McLintock. "Me, I guess," he replies.

Despite a blatant steal of the ending of *The Quiet Man,* with Wayne chasing and humiliating Maureen O'Hara, albeit without the earlier film's careful dramatic justification, the film is never as irritating as it might be because of its expansive good humor — a mélange of familial and political philosophies, comic fights and Indian rights, all of it slammed over with good humor.

Mike Wayne always had a soft spot for the picture because it proved to both his father and the industry at large that he was the businessman his father had been looking for. John Wayne had spent nearly ten years looking for someone to effectively run Batjac, and the best candidate had been underfoot the entire time. Mike Wayne ran Batjac for the rest of his father's, and his own, life.

McLintock! was shot in part at Old Tucson, a 320-acre western town located in the middle of a 29,000-acre county park. The town had been built by Columbia for its 1940 film *Arizona,* and had been run since 1959 by Bob Shelton, who built a soundstage that brought even more productions to town. Shelton played host to Wayne numerous times; among other pictures, *El Dorado* and *Rio Lobo* would be shot there, and Shelton became a good friend.

Shelton's first film as proprietor of Old Tucson had been Sam Peckinpah's *The Deadly Companions,* with Maureen O'Hara. Shortly after that, Shelton was in Tucson giving a luncheon talk to a Rotary club. When he returned to his office, a secretary told him there was a film company looking around the location.

Shelton went out to the plaza area and met a production manager who said, "The Boss is around back, by the Mission." They went over to the Mission and when Shelton approached a large man standing in front of the building, the Boss turned around. It was John Wayne. "I almost crapped my pants," remembered Shelton, "because I had been a big fan since the days of the Three Mesquiteers. He was big as life, and just as blustery."

"I want to put a building here," Wayne told Shelton, "and I want to put a false front on that building over there. Now, what are you going to do for me?"

"Well," replied Shelton, "I got an old pocket-knife, a used Cadillac, and a wife who plays good bridge. You can have 'em all."

They laughed, shook hands — "it was like grabbing a Virginia ham" — and that was the beginning of the friendship. "He was a gregarious, loving kind of guy," said Shelton. "He enjoyed everybody and everything. He had very good friends in Nogales: the Wingfields — Ralph Wingfield and his wife. Great, wonderful people. He and Wayne became acquainted when Duke made *Red River* and Wingfield supplied some cattle for the picture.

"Wing had a big spread, and a hacienda type house in southern Pima County, near Nogales. He created a suite of rooms for Duke, reserved just for him. Duke would come there quite frequently; between pictures, Duke would loaf at Wing's. We used to play gin rummy all day, drink some tequila, then go into Nogales and whoop it up at night. In the morning, he'd go off to work. A great professional."

When he was in production in Old Tucson, Wayne would remain in the vicinity because he liked to stay at the same place as the crew. A Wayne picture shot six days a week, and there was usually some sort of activity planned for Sunday — Wayne's idea of hell was an empty afternoon with nothing to do but watch television. There would be parties at Bob Shelton's house, or the Arizona Inn, or the Tucson National Country Club. When Shelton's stepson got married, Wayne went to the reception.

Being with John Wayne in Arizona, or, for that matter, anyplace, was not unlike being with the pope in Rome — everybody knew him and everybody that didn't know him wanted to meet him. "He had a partner in Stanfield, Arizona, who was in the cattle business with him, a man named Johnson. Duke owned a couple of ranches. And we'd do trips to all these places just to say hello. I drove him all over hell's half acre looking for locations. Everywhere he went, there were people he knew. And everywhere he went, people gravitated to him like you wouldn't believe."

"A man named Johnson" was Louis Johnson, a little beer keg of a man who was born in 1919 and who provided Wayne with one of his few lucrative investments. In 1958, Wayne borrowed money to buy four thousand acres of land south of Phoenix that was earmarked for cotton farming. Johnson owned land adjacent to Wayne's, and Johnson was getting four bales of cotton out of an acre when everybody else was getting only two and a half — if they were lucky. The two men cut a deal to have Johnson manage Wayne's fields. Johnson kept on making four bales an acre, so in 1960 the two men became partners.

Johnson was one of the few businessmen in Wayne's life who was better than his word; at one point, at a time when Wayne was incommunicado because of *The Alamo,* Johnson personally guaranteed a $500,000 loan in order to bring in a bumper crop.

In 1961, Wayne and Johnson combined their acreage into a single operation and plowed all the profits back into the operation. The cotton was eventually replaced by the 26 Bar Ranch in 1964, where they became leading breeders of purebred Herefords on twenty thousand acres, with another thirty thousand acres rented from the Forest Service.

Both *Hatari!* and *The Man Who Shot Liberty Valance* had been single-picture deals with Paramount. But now Wayne entered into a six-picture contract with the studio. There was talk in the trade papers of a ten-picture deal, with the money to be paid out up front, indicating Wayne was still in financial straits from *The Alamo,* but the contractual evidence indicates that the deal was for six pictures. The cash crunch, however, was real; Wayne was earning only $500,000 a picture — well below his already established market value.

The deal was for seven years, from August 6, 1962, to August 5, 1969. The first picture was *Donovan's Reef,* with the producers being charged $750,000 for Wayne's services, with $30,000 a week overage after twelve weeks. (The $250,000 difference per picture appears to have been Paramount's guaranteed profit on the long-term deal.) The pictures (*Donovan's Reef, Circus World, In Harm's Way, The Sons of Katie Elder, El Dorado,* and *True Grit*) were, on the whole, a strong lot, and Paramount sweetened the deal by giving Wayne a share of the copyrights on *Katie Elder* and *True Grit.*

The deal gave Paramount some much needed

security, because the studio was in rocky shape and about to get rockier. The problem, according to studio head Howard W. Koch, was that Charlie Bluhdorn, whose Gulf & Western Corporation bought the studio in 1966, was "bright, funny, and liked broads" but didn't have a clear idea of what he wanted from a studio head.

Koch took the studio over from Martin Rackin, and would later be replaced by Robert Evans. As Koch remembered it, "I came into it for two years and three months and thought about committing suicide twice. I never met so many hateful people in my life."

Koch was hampered by a lot of production deals that had been made before he took office. Jerry Lewis's appeal was fading, but Paramount was committed to producing and releasing his pictures, each of which was grossing less than the one before. Worst of all, however, was the deal that had been cut with Otto Preminger just before Koch came on board. "Preminger — that dirty son of a bitch. He made seven pictures [actually five] for us, all losers. He took advantage; he looked down on me. He was totally unlike someone like John Ford, who was a leader, who got you involved. Ford was one of those guys with every scene in his mind, completely prepared.

"I looked at Preminger's first picture, then looked at the contract. He could do any picture he wanted up to a certain budget point. Nobody could do anything to it. Even *In Harm's Way* got fucked up and never did the business it should have. I should have just killed him."

As Koch knew, directors come and directors go, but John Wayne went on forever.

CHAPTER EIGHTEEN

The Romanian-born producer Samuel Bronston made a splash in 1961 with *King of Kings,* a remake of DeMille's silent classic. That had been followed by *El Cid* (a great hit) and *The Fall of the Roman Empire* (a great flop), all of which were financed via country-by-country advances secured by money from DuPont interests. Now Bronston and Paramount had a deal for *Circus World.* Paramount's share of *Circus World* amounted to an investment of $2.5 million (shades of UA and *The Alamo*!). Bronston wanted John Wayne, and Paramount was agreeable to making *Circus World* part of its overall deal.

There were problems from the beginning, because the failure of *The Fall of the Roman Empire* had put Bronston in severe straits. (Paramount was concerned when Bronston failed to make a contractual $5,000 pension payment for Wayne.) James Edward Grant had bought a ranch in Merced, near Yosemite — six hundred acres, four hundred head of cattle. What with ranching's high overhead, Grant was always up for making some money. With Wayne's deal for *Circus World* set — his co-stars were to be David Niven and Claudia Cardinale, but Niven was soon replaced by Lloyd

Nolan — and the script in chaos, Wayne asked Grant to go over to Madrid, where the film was to be shot, and help. Grant didn't really want to go — *Ring of Fear* seems to have permanently soured him on circuses. But Bronston upped the ante by offering Grant a three-picture deal. Grant instructed his agent to ask for a ridiculous amount of money, which Bronston gave him.

Once he got to Madrid, Grant saw that there was trouble afoot. Grant would go over to Bronston's house for dinner, where he noticed that the producer's collection of famous paintings was shrinking — Bronston was selling assets to raise short-term cash.

Grant found himself beset by all manner of problems: the script, the Bronston organization, and Frank Capra, the prospective director of *Circus World*.

Grant believed that Bronston "is an absolute genius at raising money and peddling pictures" but had comparatively little interest in their production. Grant found the Bronston organization a rat's nest of competing interests, with everybody playing courtier to Bronston, the better to feather their own nest. Of all the problems, the worst was Capra.

Wayne had originally told Paramount to push hard for Henry Hathaway, with Capra as second choice. But Paramount wanted to hold Hathaway in reserve for a Paramount picture that, as it happened, was never made, so Capra was hired — a great director years past his greatness.

What set Grant off was Capra's treachery over the script. "I, who should be inured to treachery, having worked with Hungarians, have just had a terrific shock. This prick Capra has been having daily singing sessions with my grandchildren and eating and sleeping at my house and at the same time has been putting a Sicilian stiletto between my shoulder blades."

Grant discovered that Capra was writing the script behind Grant's back, had circulated copies to the top brass, and had told the brass that Grant was on a free ride; that he didn't actually write anything, just checked scripts for Wayne, who then forced the studio to put Grant's name on the script.

Grant then found that Capra's script actually incorporated some of the material Grant had been writing. "It's as if you put shit and honey in a Waring blender. His stuff is so incredibly old-fashioned that Duke comes out sometimes as Harold Lloyd, sometimes as Oliver Hardy and sometimes as . . . Stan Laurel. When you read this thing it is easy to understand why this guy hasn't had a hit since [screenwriter] Robert Riskin died."

Grant went to Philip Yordan, Bronston's production ramrod, whom he referred to as "my one-eyed Jew" (Yordan had eye problems), who banished most of Capra's acolytes. But there was still the problem of Capra. During a meeting Capra informed Grant that no matter what he or anybody else put in the script, Capra was only going to shoot what Capra had written. If anybody didn't like it they could take a walk. "It's amazing that a guy with a track record of ten flops in a solid row can be so insanely egotistical, but he is," reported Grant.

For his part, Capra looked at Grant and saw a familiar Shakespearean character. "I didn't realize [that] when you took on Duke Wayne you took on a small empire," wrote Capra in his memoirs. "And part of that empire was a personal writer by the name of James Edward Grant. Jimmy Grant was . . . a writer who attached himself to a male star and functioned as that star's confidant, adviser, bosom playpal, baby sitter, flatterer, string puller and personal Iago to incite mistrust between his meal ticket and film directors, especially name directors."

According to Capra, Grant announced that "all you gotta have in a John Wayne picture is a hoity-toity dame with big tits that Duke can throw over his knee and spank, and a collection of jerks he can smash in the face every five minutes. In between you fill in with gags, flags and chases."

This does sound like something Grant would say, but he was undoubtedly trying to make himself look like the only sane man in an insane situation — at one point he fantasized about Batjac taking over the Bronston organization. Then there was the hard fact that *Circus World* was ridiculous material for a director who was just trying to hang on, and, most recently, hadn't been able to turn the trick with *A Hole in the Head* or *Pocketful of Miracles* — stories more or less in his wheelhouse. Capra was under the impression that it was 1940 and he was coming off *Lost Horizon, You Can't Take It with You,* and *Mr. Smith Goes to Washington.* But in the Hollywood — or Madrid — of 1963, John Wayne had far more power than Frank Capra.

Phil Yordan was willing to fire Capra, but only if it was absolutely necessary — for one thing it would cost $150,000 to make Capra go away; for another, Yordan was concerned that Wayne would take a walk unless they could land an acceptable replacement director. But Capra was gone from the picture in January 1963, and Henry Hathaway got a phone call from Wayne. *Circus World* needed a director. After what Hathaway remembered as a week's work of rewrites with Ben Hecht, Hathaway flew to Madrid and found that he couldn't stand Grant, whom he termed "a phony."

Phony or not, Grant put his finger on the core problem of the Bronston organization when he observed, "These people are all promoters and are only anxious to get the show on the road and get on to the next promotional gimmick. They really don't give a damn who's in charge as long as somebody is making some kind of film and as long as there is huge production in it."

While Hathaway and Grant frantically rewrote, Wayne sailed the *Wild Goose* across the Atlantic to Spain. He would always remember the trip as the biggest thrill of his nautical life. They went down the Baja coast, through the Panama Canal and the San Blas islands, with stops in the Caribbean. In Bermuda, a hotel mogul named Cooley came aboard and mentioned that he'd always wanted to make a voyage across the Atlantic.

Wayne knew a cue when he heard one, and told Cooley the only thing standing between him and his dream was a pair of deck shoes. Unfortunately, Cooley turned out to be a bad sailor, and the crossing encountered some miserable weather. "We had gale forces on us for four days," remembered Wayne. "For 14 hours we were going to 45 degrees! This fella Cooley just lay back there in a blanket, the waves cleaning up after him. When we finally got to the Azores, and he put his foot on that ground, if they hadn't had an airport on that place, he'd still be living there. I don't think he'll ever get on another ship as long as he lives!"

Initially hired as the romantic lead in the picture was the young Australian actor Rod Taylor, who was coming off *The Time Machine.* Taylor had accepted the part on the basis of Wayne, and hadn't read the script. When he got to Spain, he discovered that there was nothing in the script for him to do.

"Why don't you write something?" asked Hathaway. At that point, Taylor politely bowed out, to be replaced by John Smith. "I met Duke when he was with that monster Henry Hathaway," remembered Taylor. "And I was so surprised at how he liked me and showed it. I didn't feel that I would fit with him comfortably, but we immediately liked each other."

For Wayne, *Circus World* was little more than a paycheck, but it introduced Taylor into Wayne's orbit. Soon, John Ford cast Taylor as the star of *Young Cassidy,* his biographical film about Sean O'Casey, and Taylor found himself drawn toward the inner circle. "Working with Ford gave me a certain cachet in Duke's eyes. He had such an emotional thing about Ford. I honestly think that he was still intimidated by Ford, and Duke was always amazed that Ford didn't scare me. I didn't give a shit, I just liked the man. In any case, he took it for granted that I was in the family. He wanted to keep me around as a sort of mini-McLaglen.

"Duke's great joy in life was to beat the shit out of me in poker. I never truly won. He was a good chess player, but he was also a good poker player — stud and five card. He played for the pleasure of the game and he played as long as there was a bottle of Conmemorativo on the table, because he insisted it didn't give him the hangover whiskey did. He *hated* to lose — the old jock thing."

Production on *Circus World* began at the end of September 1963 on an overly idealistic schedule of seventy-three days for the main unit and thirty-nine days for the second unit. Wayne was contractually bound to work until December 18; after that he was entitled to $30,000 a week overage. But there were weather problems at locations in Toledo — the location was flooded out at one point — and the film went far over schedule.

Wayne was quickly alienated by co-star Rita Hayworth, who was chronically late, didn't know her lines, and was surly to the crew. That experience may have been what led him to give his children a lecture about how to treat people: "Never lose the common touch. Never think anyone is better than you, but never assume you're superior to anyone else. Try and be decent to everyone, until they give you reason not to."

The picture had been shooting for two months when John F. Kennedy was assassinated. Wayne had been a Nixon man, but he had a sneaking affection for Kennedy — he knew an Irish rogue when he saw one. Wayne had sent congratulations to Peter Lawford when Lawford's brother-in-law was elected, and also sent a telegram to the president after his inauguration speech, calling it "thrilling."

Years later, in a wide-ranging conversation that touched on his own realization of how he had assumed a position of secular leadership that had once been monopolized by politicians, Wayne said, "You didn't have to be a Kennedy fan to be decimated by his assassination. It was a time to rethink a lot of things we believed; I had to re-affirm to myself my belief in man. John Kennedy could have been good — he was just beginning to realize his responsibilities. The Bay of Pigs taught him a great deal, like living up to his word. . . . Potentially he was a leader [but] we never had a chance to find out.

"There are so many people who can no longer look to politicians, but they've begun to look at me . . . so I've got an obligation."

Oddly favorable words, but this was also a period in which Wayne was quietly engaging with many on the Hollywood left. He and the politically liberal Paul Newman exchanged "Dear Duke/Dear Paul" letters and books. Wayne sent Newman a book by a conservative writer, and Newman sent Wayne material by Herman Kahn. Neither seems to have changed the other's mind, but they enjoyed jousting with each other.

It would be pleasant to report that Jimmy Grant's take-charge attitude somehow saved a dicey project from going off the rails. Pleasant, but inaccurate. Bronston's organization was going down, and so was *Circus World*. In March 1964, just after production had ended, news broke about the ruptured partnership between DuPont and Bronston. "It looks like there are a lot of problems ahead," wrote Paramount's Frank Caffey to Bronston production supervisor C. O. Erickson. He didn't know the half of it.

Grant was still in Spain keeping Duke and his son Michael apprised of the situation, and of worrisome developments with Duke's brother, Bob Morrison, who was also in Spain. Morrison had gone over to work on *Circus World* and felt that

Henry Hathaway had knifed him out of an associate producer's credit. His response was to drink heavily.

Wayne's response to all this was, said Grant, typical: dig in his heels and "defend the indefensible," in this case Hathaway, who Grant thought had first manipulated Morrison, then knifed him.

Like many dry drunks, Grant was finely attuned to other people's alcohol intake, which in Bob Morrison's case was huge. "Morrison looks dreadful," he wrote to Mike Wayne. "He is the color of Spanish toilet paper and wears the expression of a man going down for the third time. He drinks all night every night with that bunch of bums . . . and then nips all day to keep alive."

On top of all this, Grant had seen about an hour of *Circus World.* It was awful, "but what is worse is that Duke is bad. He has so many violent reactions when there is nothing to react to that I am very much afraid a lot of critics will single him out for some of the knocks."

When the movie was finally completed, people were appropriately mortified. *Circus World* is beautifully designed by John DeCuir, even though Bronston's financial troubles are made obvious by one or two recycled sets from *The Fall of the Roman Empire.* A shaky sense of production is indicated by an intermission in a film that only runs 135 minutes.

Wayne plays Matt Masters, who runs a combination circus/Wild West show around the capitals of Europe; his adopted daughter is Claudia Cardinale, complete with unexplained thick Italian accent, his lost love is Rita Hayworth. Before the inevitable reconciliation, there's some thinly motivated spectacle — most stirringly a large ship capsizing and a fire sequence directed by Richard Talmadge — interspersed with some pretty good circus acts.

That's on the positive side. On the debit side are some of the worst process shots of the sound era and a script that Herbert Yates would have rejected as old-fashioned. (The hash is explained by the credits: "Screenplay by Ben Hecht, Julian Halevy, James Edward Grant, from a Screen Story by Philip Yordan and Nicholas Ray." And that's not even counting whatever Frank Capra contributed, or the blacklisted Bernard Gordon, whose credit was restored in 2000.)

Jimmy Grant tried to take his name off the picture, but his agent told him not to be stupid, leave it there for future residuals, of which there were none. The reviews were dire: *Time* wrote that "Cinerama . . . magnifies a meager tale beyond all reasonable proportions. To sit through the film is something like holding an elephant on your lap for two hours and 15 minutes." Produced for slightly less than $8 million, North American rentals were $3.5 million.

Circus World was the second consecutive Bronston flop, and his Madrid studio completed its slow-motion collapse. Bronston spent the rest of his life in court, battling people who wanted the money he had promised them. Grant received $50,000 for his work on *Circus World* — less than he had been promised, more than he deserved.

For several years, Wayne had been troubled by a hacking cough, the result of his four- and five-pack-a-day smoking habit. On a voyage to Mexico's Coyote Bay aboard the *Wild Goose,* Wayne wanted to go water skiing, but it went badly. Getting up on the skis was difficult for him, and afterward he was badly winded, then beset by a coughing attack. He never went water skiing again.

One day, as he opened his fifth pack of cigarettes and lit a fresh unfiltered Camel off the butt of an old one, he looked at his nicotine-stained fingers. "So maybe it's six months off the end of my life," he said. "But they're not going to kill me."

Wayne felt that he owed George Stevens a favor for the director's favorable blurb for *The Alamo,* so he appeared in a much derided cameo in Stevens's *The Greatest Story Ever Told.* The two men had agreed to the cameo in 1960, five years before the film was actually released, on the basis of a handshake. "I can use an earthquake, or a big storm to show the conversion," Stevens told Wayne, "but I want you to capture it in your face." Wayne played a centurion at the Crucifixion and had only one line: "Truly, this man was the son of God."

A more meaningful part arrived with Otto Preminger's *In Harm's Way.* The bulk of the picture was made in Hawaii, with only ten days scheduled for the studio in Hollywood. Casting Wayne made perfect sense given the story: Rockwell Torrey, a naval captain, is estranged from his wife, but his son enlists against his mother's wishes — the same plot as Ford's *Rio Grande,* but transposed to World War II.

Preminger surrounded Wayne with a great cast: Kirk Douglas, Patricia Neal, Dana Andrews, Burgess Meredith, Franchot Tone, and, as Wayne's son, Brandon De Wilde.

As with Ford, as with von Sternberg, Wayne easily coped with the authoritarian Preminger. "He had my respect and I had his respect," he said. "He is terribly hard on the crew, and he's terribly hard on people that he thinks are sloughing. But this is a thing that I can understand. . . . I come ready and that he appreciated."

On the first day of production, Wayne marked an article in what Preminger said was a "reactionary" magazine and gave it to Preminger's chauffeur with instructions to have his boss read it. Preminger was a liberal Democrat and dropped the magazine without reading it. That day, he took Wayne aside. "Look, John, anybody over 30 has made up his mind about politics. You know where you stand politically, and I would never succeed in trying to convert you. I would not even try. So you shouldn't try to convert me to your opinions. Let's agree not to talk politics and we'll get along very well."

And so they did. Preminger said that Wayne was "the most cooperative actor, willing to rehearse, willing to do anything as long as anybody."

Wayne had never worked with Kirk Douglas before, but while they were never close emotionally or politically, they meshed on-screen. "We would usually have dinner together only once or twice during the entire shooting of a movie," Douglas wrote in his memoirs. "And yet we got along quite well." Douglas was not so sanguine about Preminger, who he thought was a bully and a mediocre director.

Beneath the surface high spirits, people watching Wayne saw something very wrong. "He *looked* ill," remembered Tom Tryon. "He was coughing badly. I mean, *really* awful. It was painful to see and hear, so God knows what it was like for him. He'd begin coughing and he wouldn't stop and it

618

sounded just horrendous. He'd begin coughing in the middle of a scene and Preminger would have to stop filming. If it was anybody else, Preminger would have yelled some kind of abuse at him, but he never yelled at Duke."

Pilar had accompanied her husband to Hawaii and was alarmed, but Wayne refused to acknowledge that anything was amiss. "Soon everyone was aware of his deteriorating health," she remembered. "Everyone but him. He refused to see a doctor while we were on the island."

Most of the film was shot aboard a heavy cruiser, the USS *St. Paul*. Tom Kane, the Batjac story editor, casually mentioned that he had served on the ship during the war. "I not only served on it, I put her in commission," said Kane. "I was a plank owner." Wayne became very attentive and wanted to know all about Kane's service on the ship. Kane hadn't been on board very long, he explained, because the *St. Paul* was commissioned in the spring of 1945. It had been clear to Kane that the war was almost over — the *St. Paul* and other ships cruised up and down the coast of Japan and encountered little opposition other than an occasional kamikaze mission. Kane stayed on her until the end of the war, and the *St. Paul* was right next to the USS *Missouri* in Tokyo Bay when the peace terms were signed by General Douglas MacArthur.

Kane sensed that Wayne felt he had missed out on being part of history, "even though he had tried very hard to get into any branch of the service."

On the last day of production, Hawaii's governor gave a party for the cast and crew and Preminger presented each guest with a lei made of red flowers. "At last you are showing your true colors," grinned Wayne.

The climactic naval battle scene of *In Harm's Way* was hampered by intercutting miniatures with actual ships, which made the differences in scale all too apparent. "The special effects . . . were terrible and phony," remembered Kirk Douglas. "I said, 'Otto, you can tell they're goddamn little toy boats. There's nobody on deck. Couldn't you have at least put a couple of toy soldiers on the ship?' "

Preminger brought the film in eleven days under schedule, but *In Harm's Way* still cost $8 million and earned domestic rentals of only $4.2 million. It did better overseas, but was still a loser. Finances aside, it's a watchable hunk of Palmolive made up of bits and pieces from other, better movies. It features some well-written characters, notably Dana Andrews's vain careerist naval officer, and there are intimations of anti-Semitism in Torrey's son's disinclination to fight "Mr. Roosevelt's war."

Wayne actually doesn't do much except be a leader of men and be obviously amused by Burgess Meredith's witty performance. But he brings a thoughtful, unsentimental quality to some reflective scenes with Patricia Neal as a loving nurse — the best moments in the picture.

In June 1964, Wayne agreed to make a western entitled *The Sons of Katie Elder* as his next picture at Paramount. The property had been bouncing around the studio since 1955 until Hal Wallis took it up, initially for director John Sturges and star Burt Lancaster, who thought it was a routine western with unsympathetic characters. Dean

Martin was always penciled in for the second lead, but everybody from James Stewart to Charlton Heston was considered for the role of John Elder until Wayne signed on. It was a good deal — $600,000 plus one third of the profits and one third ownership of the negative. Henry Hathaway agreed to direct the picture for $200,000.

Wayne hadn't seen a doctor in two years, and his cough was terrible. Since *In Harm's Way* had finished almost two weeks early, Pilar insisted he get a check-up. The examination was done at the Scripps Clinic in La Jolla, where X-rays were taken. The next day he was back at the clinic, when a technician came in. Wayne wanted to know if they were going to take still more X-rays. "Well, you know, we could go on taking them from every angle, but it's pretty obvious; I don't have to do any more."

Wayne was confused. "It certainly looks like it's there," the technician continued.

"What's there?" asked Wayne.

"Didn't they tell you? Cancer."

There was a tumor the size of a golf ball in his left lung.

It was one of those moments when the hearing suddenly disappears and there's a sudden coldness in your fingers. "I sat there, trying to be John Wayne," he remembered years later.

Wayne thought of several things simultaneously. His children, mostly, and how to tell them. And he thought of Pedro Armendáriz, his old friend who had committed suicide the year before after a fatal cancer diagnosis. He couldn't think how he was going to tell his mother, who had refused to see *The Alamo* because he died in it.

He was suddenly conscious of something that

other people had always taken for granted as a primary part of his personality — his embrace of life. "People resist death," he would say in retrospect. "There is a little pull that begins somewhere in you that begins wanting to stick around a little bit longer."

In the next couple of months, and for the rest of his life, he would have cause to experience that pull a great deal. The strange part was that, aside from his cough, he didn't feel sick, so he couldn't quite believe he might be dying. That came later.

It was September 13, and he was supposed to start *The Sons of Katie Elder* on October 20. The next day, Wayne invited Hal Wallis to his dressing room at Paramount. As soon as he walked in, Wallis knew something was wrong. Henry Hathaway was there, and so was Michael Wayne.

"Well, Hal, I'm going to hit you with it," he began. "I've got the Big C."

Wallis sat there in complete shock. "All he could say was 'What?' " remembered Wayne. Wallis asked Wayne if he was going to have radiation treatments. "No. None of that stuff. I'm going to have the lung removed. I'm checking in for surgery tomorrow morning." Wallis remembered that "he said it matter-of-factly, much as one might say that an ingrown toenail was going to be removed."

Wayne said that he knew Wallis would want to recast the picture. He thought Kirk Douglas would be good in the part. Wallis protested that he didn't want to do that, that he would postpone the picture until Wayne could do it. Wayne said he didn't know how long he was going to be laid up; it might be as long as six weeks.

Wallis told him that the would wait as long as

necessary. The stunned producer went back to his office and sent a telegram to his associate producer Paul Nathan: "Due to unforeseen circumstances, we are going to have to postpone the start of *Katie Elder* until possibly sometime in the middle of November and it might be even a little later. This I will not know for about a week."

Wayne needed to talk to people who had beaten cancer, but in 1964 there weren't that many of them. Fortuitously, one was Henry Hathaway, who had survived colon cancer more than ten years before. He told Wayne that his odds were good — something Hathaway couldn't really have known — but also counseled him that the surgery "is no piece of cake. We're not young men anymore; expect to be tired and expect the recovery to take longer than you think. You're gonna be sore as hell."

Scripps recommended that Dr. John Jones at Good Samaritan Hospital in Los Angeles perform the surgery. Jones examined the X-rays and said that the tumor was too big to go in from the front; he would have to go through Wayne's back, which would make it easier to look for evidence of metastases. On September 16, Wayne was admitted to the hospital for what was announced as an ankle injury; a few days later, the story was that he was under treatment for a lung abscess.

On the morning of September 17, Dr. Jones sliced into Wayne's chest under his left breast and continued under his arm and around his back — a twenty-eight-inch incision. He moved the diaphragm and stomach aside, removed two ribs, and got down to the business at hand. What Jones found in the lung was an obviously malignant tumor the size of a chicken egg — very large, but with a well-defined border between it and the surrounding tissue, which meant that it might not have spread. Jones removed the entire upper lobe of the left lung.

The surgery took six hours and went well, but a few days later, Wayne had a coughing fit and ripped all of his stitches loose. And then he began to swell up. First his throat, then his face, then his hands. Edema. He was tranquilized, but not so much that he couldn't tell something was very wrong. When he scratched his face, he could tell it was the shape of a basketball. He believed the swelling was the cancer; he believed it was the end.

"I lost interest in everything; I didn't say a word when they told me they were going to operate again. . . . Air got into my whole system and when [my children] looked at me their faces told me I'd had it."

But the doctors insisted that they had gotten the cancer, and the swelling was just fluid. They'd fix it. Five days after the original surgery, they operated again. This time he was under the knife for an additional six and a half hours. The broken stitches were repaired and holes were opened in his side to drain the fluid. "It looked like they had lawn hoses in my side," Wayne remembered.

On October 7, three weeks after entering the hospital, Wayne left under his own power — barely. Pictures show him smiling but drawn; he had lost a lot of weight. There was an election coming up on November 4, and he managed to summon the strength to do a half hour national TV show promoting Barry Goldwater.

Back home, Wayne lay in bed, staring at the ceiling and contemplating his mortality. He had promised to show his children the scar if they wanted to see it, and they all did. Up to this point his publicists had misled the public, at least partially because Wayne was terrified that accurate reports of the situation would render him unemployable. "I'll never work again if they find out how sick I am," he said. "If they think an actor is sick, they won't hire him."

While the patient was battling cancer, edema, and depression, Hal Wallis held firm in his determination to make *The Sons of Katie Elder* with Wayne and nobody else. Joseph Hazen, Wallis's financial partner, gently suggested he switch leading men — what about Mitchum or Holden? "If we hold onto *Katie Elder* to assist John Wayne's recovery," wrote Hazen, "and he is recovered to start production after the 1st of the year, you will be running into a terrific production jam on all the other projects. I do not see why we should box ourselves into that situation if an out presents itself at this time."

But Wallis refused to back down; when Wayne called him on October 26 to check on the status of the project, Wallis told him that he was putting the picture off until after the first of the year. A week later, Paul Nathan again nudged Wallis about recasting the part, but Wallis again refused; he wouldn't go back on his word. Wallis demonstrated a remarkable degree of personal integrity for a man usually regarded as a cold fish, one, moreover, who had no prior professional or personal relationship with Wayne.

Paramount wondered if it would be able to get insurance on Wayne, which caused a flurry of memos from Wallis to Paramount and back. Paramount told Wallis that if they couldn't insure

Wayne, hiring him would have to go before the executive committee. Wallis told them the matter had to be decided now, before the examination. He told the studio that Dr. Jones, who had performed the surgery, had just looked at some new X-rays and they were completely satisfactory — there was no reason Wayne could not go back to work in January. Jones offered to talk to the insurance company in order to convince them that Wayne was insurable.

The exam took place and Wayne was indeed insurable, albeit with the high deductible of $25,000 plus 2.5 percent of the final net insurable cost. But Wayne continued to struggle with post-surgical depression; he began to refer to the cancer as "the Red Witch," after *Wake of the Red Witch.* For years, whenever he was due for a check-up, he would say, "Well, I'm going down to La Jolla to see if the Red Witch is waiting for me." For years, the X-rays would be clear and he would say, "Well, the witch wasn't there this time."

Depression was unusual for Wayne, but it might have been one of the things that stimulated him into going public with his illness. Just before New Year's, he gave a series of interviews in which he outlined the story of his cancer, always emphasizing the importance of getting regular check-ups. Wayne was among the first celebrities to tell the story of surviving cancer — besides Henry Hathaway, William Powell had also gone through major cancer surgery and lived, but the news had been stifled by MGM.

To a degree that the public never knew, cancer would be a consideration for the rest of Wayne's life, especially in terms of breathing difficulties that would become part of his daily reality. Then there was his newfound status as a public survivor, a status he took very seriously. On December 22, Wayne sent a telegram to Nat King Cole, who had just been diagnosed with lung cancer. "Sorry to hear you've joined the club but it can be whipped," Wayne wrote, then mentioning that he'd just listened to Cole's "The Christmas Song" and thanked him for the joy he had brought into the world. He closed by saying "Keep punching." Cole died a little less than two months later.

As Wayne prepared to go to Mexico to make *The Sons of Katie Elder,* assistant director Michael Moore wrote Hal Wallis, "I have had a complete oxygen tank with mask . . . put on the property truck to be with us at all times. Also, I am taking a small, portable outfit which the doctor will have with him at all times. I feel this is good insurance for John."

On January 3, just a few days before Wayne left for Durango, a burglar broke into the house in Encino. He had taken a cab to the estate before he broke in. Wayne grabbed a loaded .45 and chased the robber out of the house, but then he couldn't find him. When the police arrived, they found the thief hiding by the basement door. As they were leading him away, the incompetent crook asked Wayne for a favor: would he pay the taxi driver? Wayne told the police to wait, got a $20 bill and gave it to the thief, who gave it to the taxi driver.

"I felt sorry for the cabbie," he explained to Mary St. John. "The poor bastard's working the night shift and I thought he might have to cough up the fare himself. Anyway, maybe the whole thing's symbolic. We've decided to sell the house and get out of this shithole of a Los Angeles."

After nearly a four-month postponement, on January 6, 1965, production began on *The Sons of Katie Elder* and continued for the next forty-six days at a cost of $3.19 million.

Wayne was nervous because of his diminished lung capacity; as he put it, "I had just got over that cancer operation and I thought I could hear myself breathing all the time." Then there was Henry Hathaway, who refused even to think about coddling his star. "Old Henry was very thoughtful of me, of course. Since I was recuperating and all. He took me up to 8,500 feet to shoot the damned thing and the fourth day of shooting he had me jumping into ice water. Very considerate.

"We had to jump off a bridge into the water and swim across the February River to escape from the heavies and God, that water was cold! The rest of the guys had rubber suits to take the shock away, but I'm so big, they couldn't get one to fit under my clothes. I didn't think I'd ever catch my breath."

Later, struggling with the high elevation, as he would for the rest of his life, Wayne was shooting a night scene that involved him riding up a street. "I'm waiting for Hathaway to get a long shot and let it go at that because, damn it, I'm hurting. Well, he makes me ride right up in the foreground, right up to the camera, get down off that horse the way Duke Wayne's supposed to get off a horse, tie the reins and walk out. . . . I'm calling the SOB every name I can think of under my breath."

With another director, Wayne would have rebelled, but he knew that Hathaway was doing it for a reason. Toward the end of his life, Wayne would call Hathaway "the meanest man in the business. He worked me like a goddamn dog. And you know something? It was the best thing ever happened to me. It meant I got no chance to walk around looking for sympathy." Hathaway's lack of nurturing was therapeutic — maddening, painful, but therapeutic.

Throughout the production, Wayne talked about his experience with cancer to anyone that would listen. He hadn't been so scared of dying, he said, as of being helpless. "That feeling . . . of being a burden to your family. That's what hit me hardest of all. . . . I just couldn't see myself lying in bed, not being able to help myself — no damn good to anybody. That, to me, was worse than the fear of dying."

"I told [the public about the cancer] because I know how much solid hope my recovery could bring to many poor devils in the same fix," he said. "And if it encouraged people to get regular checkups, it would save lives. More men ought to listen to their wives when they beg them to get checkups."

To all appearances, Wayne was in fine fettle, throwing ascorbic acid lozenges in his mouth and washing them down with mezcal he kept in a half gallon jug, then proclaiming "Goddamn! I'm the stuff that men are made of." Dean Martin, working in his second movie with Wayne, was affectionately amused. "He's two loudspeaking guys in one. Me, when people see me, they sometimes say, 'Oh, there goes Perry Como.' But there's only one John Wayne and nobody makes any mistakes about that."

Mostly, it was old-home week, the atmosphere

in which Wayne always felt most comfortable. Earl Holliman, a Hal Wallis contractee who was playing one of Wayne's brothers, was the outlier. He had always loved Wayne on-screen, but this was his first time working with him. He found Wayne "a wonderful person" and "lots of fun," but he was dismayed by Wayne's compulsion to be the Big Dog. "He had to be the macho man. He had to have more drinks than the next guy." Holliman also found Wayne "a bit of a bigot in conversation."

When the production moved to Del Rio, George Kennedy joined it. Kennedy had worked on *In Harm's Way,* and would also work with Wayne in *Cahill U.S. Marshal.* Kennedy matched up well with Wayne, if only because he was six-one.

"Duke was Duke," recalled Kennedy. "Very bright. I worked with and dearly loved Jimmy Stewart, and I worked with Burt Lancaster and Paul Newman. Heavyweights. But Wayne was on a different planet. If you put him in a group with other movie stars, the eye went to him, and that is the ultimate marker of respect. He was John Wayne. He was very real. It didn't matter if he wasn't Olivier; Olivier wasn't John Wayne."

One day during a lunch break, Wayne took off his shirt to get some sun, and Kennedy was stunned by the expanse of the angry purple scar from the recent surgery.

Kennedy proceeded to be even more stunned when Wayne lit up a cigar.

"Duke, look at yourself. You look like a railroad track from here to Duluth, and you're smoking?"

Wayne sighed, took a drag. "I can't stop," he said.

Publicly, Wayne loudly proclaimed his abandonment of tobacco, but that was a lie. When I met him in 1972, he was smoking small cigars, as if they were less damaging than unfiltered Camels. He occasionally smoked large cigars as well. Other times, he would chew tobacco.

Psychologically, he was addicted. "He used to die when he saw Jackie Gleason take a drag on a cigarette on TV," remembered Gretchen Wayne. "He'd say, 'Boy, he really knows how to smoke a cigarette.' He inhaled it deeply; you didn't think the smoke would ever come out."

If cancer hadn't nudged him off tobacco, there were other, subtler changes, most of which were only noticeable to the people who had previously worked with him. He seemed less sure of himself on a horse — "He did not want to take a chance of letting a horse get out from under him, so he rode a shorter rein," said the stuntman Dean Smith. "He wanted to be sure that he didn't get bucked off or fall from one of those big horses."

Also joining the company was Dennis Hopper, who had had a legendary run-in with Henry Hathaway years before on *From Hell to Texas.* "We argued all day and had a wonderful time at dinner," Hopper remembered.

He was a primitive director — he rarely moved his camera, the movement came from the actors — and he gave me line readings that were imitative Brando crap. I'd try to reason with him and he'd snap, "Kid, that's dinner talk." I walked off the set three times.

One day he pointed to a huge stack of film cans and said, "Kid, I own 40 percent of 20th Century Fox stock, there's enough film in those cans to shoot for three months, and we're gonna film this scene until you get it right."

I don't know how many takes we did. I say 86 because I was really 86'd when we were done. But Hathaway wore me down and got what he wanted, and then he told me, "You'll never work in this town again." And the word went out and I didn't make a major Hollywood picture for several years.

Hopper went to New York and studied with Lee Strasberg, then came back and did TV. By 1964, Hopper had married Brooke Hayward, the daughter of the late Margaret Sullavan. "She was an actress Hathaway and Wayne respected as a good, honest woman. They knew Brooke and I had a baby girl. They talked it over and decided I should be working. And we all got along fine."

Hopper took pains to be on his good behavior with Hathaway and decided to fish for a compliment. "See what a better actor I am now?" he said to Hathaway after a take.

"You're not better, just smarter," snorted the director.

Hopper liked Wayne, "But it was a strange relationship. He thought of me as his house Commie. He'd get agitated about something and shout, 'Where's Hopper, that little Commie bastard?' and try to involve me in a political debate.

"And he would take time to teach me little acting tricks. He would say, 'Dennis, if you break your line in the middle — for example, 'They went . . . thataway — they can't cut away from you.' And I would think, 'Well, that works if you're John Wayne.' Anyone else, they'll get cut out."

As the picture wound down, so did Wayne. He

got one of the bad colds that would increasingly plague him, and he was still coughing. By late afternoon the oxygen inhaler was usually set up by his chair on the set. And he was increasingly sensitive about his age and appearance.

"That guy," he groused about one reporter who he felt had stabbed him in the back. "I admit I'm balding. I admit I got a tire around my middle. What man 57 doesn't? Big news."

Wayne took a break in the interviews about his cancer to pay eloquent tribute to the genre that had defined him. "Westerns are art. They've got simplicity, and simplicity is art. They deal in life and sudden death and primitive struggle and with the basic human emotions — love, hate, anger, fear. In Europe they understand that better than we do over here. . . .

"Take a horse. A horse is the greatest vehicle for action there is. . . . Put a man on him and you've got the makings of something magnificent — physical strength, speed where you can see and feel it, heroism. . . . There's a simplicity of conflict you can't beat. Westerns are our folklore and folklore is international."

The Sons of Katie Elder emerged as a fully formed, entertaining western, well directed and well acted. Because of the public's curiosity about how Wayne would look after his cancer operation, the film was also a considerable hit, earning domestic rentals of $6 million even though the story would just about have sufficed at Monogram — a ranch is stolen from the parents of the titular sons, who have to fight to get it back. But the impeccable production, the stars, and a slew of great character actors keep the picture airborne. Cinematographer Lucien Ballard even makes the scrubby area around Durango look picturesque.

Henry Hathaway, by this time a director who stuck strictly to his narrative, pauses to let his camera lovingly observe Wayne walking for ten seconds at a time — an ineffable image of grace. The loose amble of *Stagecoach* had altered to a very specific walk — arms raised at the elbow, trunk leaning slightly forward, leading with his narrow hips, often coming to rest with a hip cocked in the contrapposto pose of classical Greek statuary. The youthful beauty had faded, but Wayne compensated for that and his extra girth with a continuing Apollonian grace — movement in a mythic rhythm.

CHAPTER NINETEEN

Wayne's triumph over cancer only increased his stature as the unkillable American ideal. Not everybody took his image as seriously as he did. Terry Southern said that Stanley Kubrick offered Wayne the part of the apocalyptically crazed cowboy eventually played by Slim Pickens in *Dr. Strangelove.* "Wayne was approached and dismissed it immediately," said Southern.

But Wayne always considered himself a working actor, and he remained on the lookout for parts that didn't require a full-scale commitment. Shortly before the cancer had been discovered, Wayne helped writer-director Melville Shavelson set up a movie about Mickey Marcus, an American Jew who had fought with the Haganah to found Israel. Shavelson was amused, because, as he noted, "If God set out to print a million photographs of Jewishness, he would use John Wayne as the negative."

But Wayne was enthused by the freedom-fighting foreground of the story. "You could call Jerusalem the Jewish Alamo," said Shavelson. "You out of your mind?" snorted Wayne. "That picture lost so much money I can't buy a pack of chewing gum in Texas without a co-signer. Let's not remind anybody."

Shavelson asked Wayne to appear in a small part in the picture, to which Wayne agreed, but he went further than that. He personally called Kirk Douglas and asked him to look at the script. Batjac took a profit position in the picture, which was financed by the Mirisch Corporation for United Artists.

Unfortunately, *Cast a Giant Shadow* failed to earn back its negative cost, and there were no profits for Batjac.

Just as Wayne was recovering, Jimmy Grant began to feel ill. He went to a doctor in Madrid, who couldn't find anything, so he came back to California and to UCLA, where he was diagnosed with cancer.

James Edward Grant died in 1966. After the funeral, Wayne told Colin Grant that his father had been his best friend. It was a lovely thing to say, but Wayne's special gift was that all of his friends could plausibly believe the same thing. The family didn't forget Jimmy's widow; Pilar regularly sent a limo to bring her to the house for lunch.

Jimmy Grant's last script, *Support Your Local Gunfighter,* was made five years after he died. He was prolific and successful to the end — and beyond.

Originally, Newport Beach was supposed to be just another California seaside community, but by the late 1920s the bay was being dredged and a seawall was constructed. By the 1960s, it was one of the most exclusive beach and boating communities in the world.

Wayne had customized the house in Encino to his specifications and most people believed he didn't really want to move but was doing it for Pilar. Tom Kane came to the Encino house one day and found Wayne on his hands and knees with a tape measure and a legal pad. He was measuring his den. "Just let me finish this and I'll be right with you," he said. "I'm going to reproduce this room in the house in Newport Beach exactly as it is here."

"Duke was essentially a family man," said Tom Kane. "He'd do anything to try to keep a family and a marriage together, such as [the] move. He was not too happy about leaving Encino, but he did it anyway."

The Newport Beach house — 2688 Bay Shore Drive — was remarkable primarily for its location: at the water's edge, facing Balboa Island. The house itself, like many extraordinary houses on the Malibu and Santa Monica oceanfronts, was nothing special from the outside. Inside, the eleven-room, seven-bath house blossomed as you moved toward the bay view.

The interior was an unexpectedly stylish compendium of travels and accomplishments, decorated largely with furniture and objects Wayne had picked up on his travels — he enjoyed shopping for antiques, and he made a habit of taking a few favored possessions with him whenever he went on location, to dress up a hotel room and make it feel more like home. The house had furniture from Madrid, antiques from Colorado Springs, figurines from Kyoto. The living room had a fire-engine–red coffee table and a stone fireplace wall that held attractive modern art and a gilt-bronze Buddha. The dining room featured a Baccarat chandelier and a mirrored wall, before which was a Nepalese statue of a deity.

"Wayne bought out the original woodcut blocks from a Buddhist temple," remembered photographer Sam Shaw. "The prints of the wallpaper were made from these woodblocks. He gave me a print. A beautiful Japanese print. Rice paper. With eight tones of black and one red."

Wayne's office was paneled, with a fireplace, a small collection of guns, some Harry Jackson sculptures, and a collection of kachina dolls that he had collected during his forays into Monument Valley. There was a bar in one corner, and a draft beer dispenser — a gift from Budweiser. Elsewhere in the house, there was also a hidden screen and projector for the screening of films.

"Wayne took the western very seriously," remembered Sam Shaw.

He had an immense library on the west. He absorbed the west, was steeped in western folklore. He did scholarly studies on the west. You know, I'm a professional photographer, and Wayne, an actor, showed me the work of Edward Curtis, an early photographer of American Indians. Wayne had a rare portfolio edition, printed by J. P. Morgan, which he bought for $3,000. Bought before Curtis became accepted by the art world. . . . It was Wayne who introduced me to Curtis, a photographer sympathetic to Indians.

Wayne was cultured; very charming, polite, elegant. Not from what we heard and read about him, but in the confines of his home. Not even in his friendships with his fellow filmmakers, but in the confines of himself. . . . But on the set, for the press, he played a guy rolling in the mud.

Shaw was from New York and had been born with the name Arshawsky — a die-hard Jewish liberal. After a number of political set-to's, Shaw said to him, "You're not the reactionary they say you are."

"I'm a reactionary?" asked Wayne, managing to keep a straight face.

"Yes. From where I come, everybody looks upon you as the leader of the wolf pack."

"Sam, I'm not the leader of the wolf pack. I'm not a reactionary."

"No, you're not. You're a real strong trade union guy. What you are is a Bull Mooser."

"What's a Bull Mooser?"

"Like Harold Ickes and Theodore Roosevelt. Honest, uncorrupted American conservatives. Dedicated American citizens."

Prominent in his office was what Wayne called his "Fifty Years of Hard Work Wall," featuring plaques and honors deriving from his career, as well as a faded photo of Wayne, John Ford, Henry Fonda, and Ward Bond displaying a sailfish caught near Cabo San Lucas in the 1930s. There was a picture of Barry Goldwater, another of Richard and Pat Nixon and Wayne, signed by the president. Another picture was signed by Dwight Eisenhower. There were Winchesters in display cases, and some Remingtons, including a 1901 Remington picturebook. Some Charles Russell bronzes. An 1855 pepperpot pistol.

There was an autographed picture from Ronald and Nancy Reagan that said, "Duke, we love you," as well as a piece of polished wood from the deck of the battleship *Arizona.* In time, pride of place on the Fifty Years of Hard Work Wall would be given to his Academy Award for *True Grit.*

Outside, a long dock rocked gently with the waves.

A new house in a new town mandated new friends. Cecilia deMille Presley had been raised by her grandfather Cecil B. DeMille, so she wasn't intimidated by movie stars. She had a long marriage with a real estate developer named Randy Presley and had been a friend of Mike Wayne's when they were both children. But it was only after Wayne moved to Newport that she got to know him as an equal.

"Duke would bring his backgammon set to the Balboa Bay club to kill time while Pilar played tennis," she remembered. Randy Presley would always give him a game. The Presleys would be married for over fifty years and part of their relationship involved merciless mutual teasing. They were playing bridge with Wayne one day, when Cecilia told her husband, "Randy, you played that well, for a lay-down."

Wayne broke up and said, "If I ever said that to Pilar, I'd have to leave the fucking house."

Wayne grew to love the Newport Beach house because he loved the sea. "Look at that changing scene out there," he once exclaimed. "You know, a view like you have in Encino doesn't mean anything after you've lived there for a while but here — God, it's beautiful. It's hard as hell to work because you start looking at this and pretty quick your mind just eases off into numbness."

But it was more than that. In the mid-1960s, Newport Beach was a seaside village of only 36,000 people, with few markets or restaurants.

In many respects, Wayne was replicating his fond memories of Glendale, except on a higher economic stratum. Where the Encino house had been a comparatively sterile walled enclave, Newport was wide open to the sea; the smell of freesia, orange blossoms, and night-blooming jasmine were as regular as the salt air.

Wayne could sit out on the back veranda for hours, watching the water change color as the sun shifted. Along with the new house came a new dog, a Samoyed named Frosty, who would eat breakfast on a chair beside his master, who fed him strips of bacon. Wayne happily spent the rest of his life at the Newport Beach house.

An arbitrator's decision about Wayne and Bö Roos's business dealings finally came down in September 1964. He stated that "Each have a unique ability to create complex business and personal problems for themselves. . . . Each communicated orally by preference and apparently shun or are inexpert in writing techniques."

This lack of written documentation created havoc not only in their business dealings but in the arbitrator's attempt to resolve problems. Batjac had agreed to pay Roos 2.5 percent of its net profit before taxes. The arbitrator decided that, while Roos owed Wayne various sums for repayments of loans, notes, and other fees, Wayne also owed Roos money on his percentage, as well as fees due Roos for *The Barbarian and the Geisha, Rio Bravo,* and *The Horse Soldiers.* The Solomonic decision concluded that Roos owed Wayne $31,613.66; Wayne owed Roos $94,601.78.

Nine months later, in June 1965, Wayne sued Roos for $500,000, asserting that an original investment of $144,468 had been devalued by Roos's pillaging the funds for unauthorized travel, entertainment, and granting of discounts to friends, relatives, and various airline hostesses. Joining Wayne in the lawsuit were cowboy star Rex Allen, Frank Belcher (Wayne's attorney), and Roberto Arias. They wanted damages, and they wanted the court to declare them the controlling owners of various hotels.

Despite the legal proceedings, Roos and Wayne maintained a semblance of friendly relations. When Wayne would run into Carolyn, Roos's daughter, he would always come over and give her a big hug, and end by saying something nice about her father. But the days when the two men socialized were over.

As far as Wayne's finances were concerned, he still paid alimony to Josie, and the overhead for Pilar and his second family was around $200,000 a year. Add in the upkeep for the *Wild Goose,* his private helicopter, agent's fees, and tax bracket, and it's obvious that Wayne's output of two pictures a year was as much a financial imperative as professional preference.

People assumed Wayne had a great deal of money, and the temperature could drop very quickly if people asked him why he kept working at such a pace: "What makes you think I don't have to work? Have you checked my financial statements? If you did, you'd know that if I'm going to continue to live this way, I do have to work. Maybe I should be in a position where I don't have to work, but I'm not."

One day Wayne had looked out over his house with a water view and said, "I wish I could afford all this and enjoy it too. I can afford it, but it's hard to find time to enjoy it."

But that was what amounted to a philosophical reverie. When he was what actors like to call "in the moment," he gave every evidence of enjoying it very much. He would burst through the front door, bellowing "Hello the House!" and there would suddenly be an electrical charge of energy. The children would come running into his arms, ingesting his specific odors — Camel cigarettes, Neutrogena soap, Listerine.

The man described by family members was close to the man millions saw on the screen, except when he wasn't. He wasn't as calm as he was on-screen, was in fact frequently irascible. He was innately restless, often pacing back and forth like a caged cat, seldom staying in any one spot longer than it took to smoke a cigarette.

"A lot of the time, he played a stranger, an outsider, the strong, lonely type," remembered Michael Wayne. "He wasn't really like that at all. My mental picture of him is children and grand-children crawling all over him at Christmastime. He loved kids, loved to be married, loved to decorate houses. Once he said to me, 'I've been married all my life.' I looked at him and then he said, 'Well, not to the same woman, but I've been married all my life.' " There were other contradictions. Mike learned to ride not from his father, but from stuntmen. John Wayne didn't particularly like horses and insisted "I don't get on a horse unless they pay me."

As a father, said his oldest son, he was "generous, affectionate, interested, but he was also, you know, the discipliner. He commanded a lot of respect." His oldest sons had identical schooling:

643

Cathedral Chapel Parochial Grammar School, followed by Loyola High School, followed by Loyola University.

Wayne believed in self-reliance for the boys; Mike never got an allowance and had to pay for his own clothes, his own car, everything except tuition, which was covered by his father. His children learned their father's quirks early — when he would start to get irritated, for instance, his breathing would quicken, like a locomotive expelling steam. For his first two sons, their father believed in corporal punishment. "He was always fair, you could always depend on a square shoot, and all of that," said Mike, "but if he said to do something, that was it. Do it or else. You get the hell beat out of you. I'd say we were pretty well regimented. We were just told to mind all our elders and that was it, and if we didn't we'd get the hell beat out of us."

He was completely competitive; his sons thought of him as a poor winner. He'd cheat — in gin, he'd lay down a four, five, and seven and hope you didn't notice the six was missing. "To me, to lose a game of cards or to win a game of cards, doesn't mean a thing," said Mike. "It's a very important thing to my father to win at anything. And then to needle everybody."

It was his nature to be generous. He liked pants with a little watch pocket in the front, and in that watch pocket he would keep $100 bills folded up to the dimensions of a postage stamp. These would be used for tips and handouts, or for walking around money.

His years of working on film sets had given him a detailed eye for clothing and appropriate styles. "Duke never, never asked what size a woman was," said Mary St. John. "He would meet the wife of some associate one time and a month or two later see some dress in a catalog and say, 'You know, Mary, I think so-and-so would like this. Order a size seven.' "

Generally, he was cordial and welcoming to reporters, but if a writer seemed unprepared, or in some way antagonistic, God help him. One hapless rookie began by telling Wayne that he thought his real career began with *Red River.*

"That's not a question, it's a theory," retorted Wayne. "You want me to sit here like a dummy and nod my head while you put words in my mouth."

The rattled writer tried to regroup. "When you made *Stagecoach* . . ."

"Start somewhere else," snapped Wayne.

On his desk at home he kept a small plaque that said "A Kind Word." If someone asked him if he wanted anything — a sandwich, a drink — he'd almost certainly reply, "Yes, and a kind word."

He disliked routine, liked to eat. A lot. Breakfast at a restaurant would often entail six eggs and four orders of bacon, and when the waitress would ask how he wanted his eggs, he'd say, "Looking at me." If breakfast didn't come quickly enough, he'd start with little packages of saltines, after first slathering some butter on them.

He didn't like milk, except with a breakfast dish he enjoyed: a piece of toast placed in milk, with an egg on top of that, topped off by a sprinkling of sugar. "It's a cake, unassembled," he would beam. Another culinary guilty pleasure was peanut butter, with a little bit of jelly. "Pilar doesn't like it," he said. "She thinks peanut butter is uncivilized."

He kept several checkbooks scattered around the house, and whenever he needed a check, he'd tear it out of the nearest book without recording anything. As a result, balancing his checking account was impossible, and he never had as much money as he thought.

His favorite lunch was steak and tomatoes, his favorite dinner was steak and lobster, the steak charred on the outside, red on the inside. If he was at home, he tended to be a light drinker; Pilar insisted he couldn't even have a cocktail before dinner, unless he was with some of his cronies, in which case it was an odds-on bet that the competitive drinking would extend into the next morning. He liked to pretend that he didn't get hangovers, but he did. On particularly bad mornings, his heart would pound and he'd yell, "My heart, my heart. Pilar, I'm gonna die. Pilar, where are you? Goddamn it! I will *never* drink again. *Pilar!*"

He instructed his children on the importance of concentrating on a goal, whatever it might be. "When I'd ride horses or motorcycles," remembered his son Ethan, "he'd tell me not to focus on that hole, rock, or bump. 'Look where you want to go, not at what you're trying to avoid,' he'd say. 'Or else you're going to hit it.' . . . He always moved forward . . . He always stayed positive."

The children hated to see their father leave for location, because they knew he'd be gone a long time. "He'd always say, 'All right boy, see you in October,' or whatever it was," remembered Ethan, "and [then] he'd say, 'God willing and the river don't rise.' I got this horrible feeling inside! My stomach would drop every time he'd say it. Why'd you have to say that? And he'd hit the gate and I'd see him leave, and I'd think, 'Don't go!' Oh, my God. What does that mean? 'God willing and the river don't rise.' I just didn't get it."

Between Wayne's charisma, his huge physical presence and his energy, he could be overwhelming, but his absence could be more overwhelming, when the house became deathly quiet. His daughter Aissa hated it when her father left to make a movie, so he took her aside once and told her, "Every night I'm gone, honey, I want you to look at the stars. Wherever I am, I'll look at them, too. And no matter how far apart we are, we'll know we've looked at the same stars."

The little girl's neediness derived from her father; for years, whenever Aissa would walk past him, he'd need to be kissed and be told she loved him. "You have to kiss me before you can cross by," he would say. When he was out of town on a picture, he'd call or send telegrams, reminding the kids he was their father.

Harry Carey Jr. said that he was "a marvelous father. Broadminded. Didn't try to affect his kids' opinions. He loved them very much." That said, it wasn't easy being one of John Wayne's kids, because the bar was set high. "A B in school didn't exist," sighed Michael Wayne. "To be second-best didn't exist. If you were in a race, you had to win. He gave of himself that way and he thought everybody should do that."

"He was a friendly man for the most part," said Dan Ford, the grandson of John Ford. "He was never a nasty drunk. I'd have to say that what you saw was pretty much what you got. And the relationship between he and my grandfather never changed. Late in my grandfather's life, Duke was sitting with him. My grandfather turned to him and said, 'You're doing too much TV. Get off.'

"And Duke said, 'Yes, sir.' That was it."

"He was always frightened of Ford," said Harry Carey Jr. "He was more scared of him than I ever was. I got to know the old man really well, and Duke didn't have to be that scared of him, but he was."

For most of his life, his energy was volcanic. When he was working, he would wake up around 4:30 or five in the morning; when he was at home he was up by dawn. Because he didn't like to be alone he would wake everybody else in the house by seven. When he arrived back home after shooting a movie, he'd be a homebody for all of a week or so, then get restless and bored and expect everybody to drop everything and do what he wanted to do.

He regretted being a slow reader, but took pride in the fact that he remembered everything he read. His two favorite novels were both by Sir Arthur Conan Doyle: *The White Company* (a favorite of John Ford's as well) and *Sir Nigel.* Other favorite writers were Agatha Christie, Raymond Chandler, and Rex Stout. For nonfiction, he liked either political or military history, and anything by Winston Churchill — next to John Ford, his hero. Occasionally, he'd say something that indicated the range of his reading — if he decided to pursue a business proposition, for instance, he would smile and say, "Barkis is willing," after the character in Dickens's *David Copperfield.*

He was deeply superstitious — a hat on a bed would provoke an angry outburst at the miscreant who had put it there, and if a playing card turned face-up on the table, the owner would have to stand and circle his or her chair three times. Nobody could pass the salt to him; they would have to put it on the table, at which point he'd pick it up. He was also deeply sentimental, but made it a point not to throw compliments around promiscuously, unless the subject was John Ford.

The years of studying Ford, of being showcased by his genius and enduring his abuse, had left their imprint and he had adopted some of the director's peremptory traits. Ford's habit of ordering attendance became part of Wayne's own personality, even though Wayne would get irritated when Ford did the same thing to him. Once when Wayne and the actor Ed Faulkner were on location, Faulkner was just getting ready to go to bed when he got a call.

"What are you doing?"

"Well, I'm going to bed."

"Well, the hell you are! The chessboard is set up." Faulkner manfully trooped over to Wayne's room and played till dawn.

Besides the *Wild Goose*, Wayne's primary extravagance was a personal helicopter, which could make the trip from Newport Beach to Hollywood in twenty minutes, as opposed to an hour and a half on the freeway. What Wayne regarded as extreme expenses for the helicopter became an issue as his relationship with Don La Cava, the husband of his daughter Toni, and the man who had been managing Wayne's finances since Bö Roos, blew up. Gretchen Wayne remembered that one day her father-in-law concluded La Cava had managed his money poorly.

Wayne "wanted to kill" La Cava, but Michael said that John Wayne was not going to kill the father of his grandchildren. Wayne went to Cecilia Presley, who ran the Cecil B. DeMille estate, and told her he had a problem. "Get him out," counseled Cecilia, "and put Toni's money in a trust."

Eventually, La Cava and Toni separated. Toni put up a wall and never discussed it, while Wayne would, but only with family and close friends. The upshot was that Michael took over his father's business affairs for the rest of his life.

The family unpleasantness didn't change things overmuch. Wayne refused to alter his lifestyle and simply made more movies. "I can make a million dollars by stepping onto that horse," he pointed out, "and I can make two or three pictures a year."

As he aged, he put on weight and grew grumpy when he had to lose fifteen or so pounds for a picture. As soon as a picture was finished, he'd put the weight back on, and between Halloween and New Year's he'd add even more. He enjoyed personally shopping for Halloween candy — black and red licorice, Tootsie Rolls, and something called Abba-Zabas, which consisted primarily of peanut butter and toffee. What the trick-or-treaters didn't eat, he would. In addition, the family grew accustomed to his midnight snacks of salami, baloney, bacon, "any kind of heavy red meat," as his daughter Aissa remembered. (Given Wayne's passions for nicotine, cholesterol, and tequila, the fact that he lived to be seventy-two has to be considered a testament to his remarkable stamina.)

His politics hadn't altered one millimeter. People on unemployment were apt to be labeled "layabouts." "Obviously, government is the enemy of the individual," he said. "My feeling about life is that you're put here and you have to make your own way. Our country used to be small enough so that a man who'd proven himself and who had some understanding could get himself sent to Congress and the people back home would just go on about their business believing that whatever he'd do would be good enough for them. . . . Now though, we've got this democracy and the politician kowtows to whomever wants the most . . . the politician appeals to the popular vote, that being the mob vote."

He remained on the lookout for signs of untoward political sympathies. "[Dean] *Rusk* was with Stilwell when they made that coalition government in China. *Rusk* was with Truman and told him, after he'd had the guts to go to war with the Communists not to go all the way. *Rusk,* he was the one who wouldn't fight the thing all the way in Cuba. And now, Rusk, *Rusk,* he's putting up a coalition government with the Commies in Laos. How many mistakes are we going to let the s.o.b. make?"

He knew he was the biggest star in the business and he surveyed his situation with a great deal of objectivity. "I've reached a point in my career where it's really hard to get parts to fit me any more. Like Coop [Gary Cooper] and Gable, they'd reached a maturity where they shouldn't be playing with these younger girls, and it quite obviously affected their audience. Nobody's that good an actor."

Nor did he have illusions about unlimited power. "Stars are valuable only to get people inside the doors," he told one studio executive, by way of explaining that a bad picture can't be propped up by any actor, no matter how popular.

He maintained a lingering sense of disgruntlement over his long exile in B pictures and the fact that he had had to do it all himself. "I never had a build-up by a major studio, like Cooper and Randolph Scott. Paramount spent lots of money on them, and I had to come up the hard way, with exposure to the kids . . . ten years in those quickie pictures."

Of course, that long exposure to a youthful audience also meant that he and the audience grew into maturity and old age together. One of his best friends said that in the deepest recesses of his conscience Wayne still thought of himself as "a stagehand who got lucky."

The old stagehand had some very well-developed ideas about the movie business, ideas that he had learned at the feet of John Ford. He would point to *Red River* as a standard story of father-son conflict that could have been set in a factory or a drawing room or even another country. But placing it outdoors, against the background of a nineteenth-century cattle drive, gave what was actually an intimate character conflict an epic sweep that elevated the material.

"Get it out of doors," he would demand. "Let some fresh air and sunlight into the story. Give your cameraman a chance to photograph something besides walls and doors and tea tables. Don't let your story expire for lack of air."

When the four children from his first marriage fell in love and got married, he wouldn't allow Pilar to attend the ceremonies. "It's not appropriate," he said. Those were occasions for him and Josie to come together and celebrate the raising of their children without awkwardness. "Duke respected Josie, and she respected him," said Gretchen Wayne. "They supported each other when it came to their children and whatever decisions they made were made together. Because of that, the kids all turned out well."

What Pilar thought of this restriction is unknown. After her depression of the late 1950s, the marriage had settled down and seemed to be in decent equilibrium, but there were those who had their doubts — about Pilar, and about Wayne's taste in women in general.

For a time, Wayne and Pilar were happy; they had three children together — children he loved passionately. And then, gradually, he and Pilar weren't happy. "He was terribly unlucky in marriage, but he never understood why," said Maureen O'Hara. "Neither did I. I thought he was wonderful, although there was never anything between us. His first wife, Josie, was a sweetheart. The second — well, let's just say she died of a heart attack in Mexico. The third was the mother of his last kids. They were all Latin women with slightly different temperaments, but he was really marrying the same woman every time."

Gretchen Wayne saw the central problem as clashing desires. "He wanted a normal life and family, but he also wanted a piece of arm candy who would look great when they went out. All three of the women he married provided the arm candy — they looked great."

Some people close to Wayne — Harry Carey Jr., for instance — thought he should have married someone like Mary St. John, his devoted secretary, who was smart, tough, and loved him, although not romantically. Gretchen Wayne thought that unlikely. "Mary St. John would never have put up with him."

"I knew Josie, and I knew Chata, and I knew Pilar," said Harry Carey Jr. "Chata and Pilar were very different; Pilar was much more intelligent and more grounded. Chata — that was physical more than anything else.

"But Duke never married anybody with brains, not really. It baffled me why he married the women he did. His wives weren't good company; they weren't someone you could gab all night with. And his wives were always tough on him. He wasn't henpecked, but he did put up with a lot. I don't think he was ever buddies with any of his wives like I am with Marilyn."

But the subtle misalliance of his third marriage didn't propel him into affairs the way it had twenty-five years before. Perhaps residual guilt over the divorce from Josie acted as a brake, or perhaps he had just learned his lesson. "There were women that were crazy about him," said Harry Carey Jr., "and he didn't fool around. His brother did. Bob would boff them, but not Duke."

He enjoyed mentoring young actors, often giving them advice worthy of a life coach. When he met Michael Caine in the lobby of the Beverly Hills Hotel, he pointed at him and said, "What's your name?"

"Michael Caine."

"That's right. I saw you in that movie, what was it called?"

"Alfie?"

"That's right."

Wayne put his arm around Caine's shoulders as he guided him across the lobby. "You're gonna be a star, kid. But let me give you a piece of advice: talk low, talk slow, and don't say too fucking much."

Caine was grateful, said thank you, and then Wayne said, "Call me Duke. And never wear suede shoes."

Caine had been taking it all in just fine, but the last sentence threw him.

"Why not?"

"Because one day I was taking a piss and the guy in the next stall recognized me and turned towards me and said, 'John Wayne — you're my favorite actor!' and pissed all over my suede shoes. So don't wear them when you're famous, kid."

After a quarter century in the movie business, Wayne had been nominated for an Oscar only once, for *Sands of Iwo Jima.* "What'd I do with an Oscar anyway? It'd just clutter up the mantel." Although he pretended he didn't care about the critics, he read all of the major reviews of his pictures as a matter of course, and if he felt badly used, he'd get angry. "That son of a bitch," he'd mutter. "I've been in this goddamn business for fifty years. He's never been in front of a camera in his life. What the hell does he know about acting?"

But he pretended that reviews mattered either not at all or a lot less than the verdict of the public, to whom he was invariably charming and helpful. Patrick Wayne remembered that having lunch with him in public was a series of interruptions by admirers asking for an autograph. Pat asked his father if it ever bothered him.

"If they didn't want to come up, how do you think we could have gotten this lunch?" his father said.

As a result, Wayne had a horror of allowing his craft and technique to show. "It's not being natural," he explained in one of the few times he discussed acting seriously. "It's *acting* natural. If you're just natural, you can drop a scene. You've got to do it so the plumber sitting out there, and the lawyer next to him and the doctor don't see anything wrong."

To those people who always said he just played himself, he would retort, "It is quite obvious it can't be done. If you are yourself, you'll be the dullest son of a bitch in the world on the screen. You have to *act* yourself, you have to project something — a personality. . . .

"I have very few tricks. Oh, I'll stop in the middle of a sentence so they'll keep looking at me, and I don't stop at the end, so they don't look away, but that's about the only trick I have."

Another time, he emphasized how important it was for him to play the truth of a scene. "If someone starts acting phony at a party, you go out and get a drink and the hell with him. But if I start acting phony on the screen, you gotta sit there. Pretty soon you're just looking at me instead of feeling with me."

Wayne was a member in good standing of a pre-Method generation of actors whose general intent was, as James Cagney put it, "Look the other actor in the eye and tell the truth." His primary limitation was a psychological commitment to naturalism. "Duke . . . had to do everything real," said Henry Hathaway. "There wasn't anything in Duke that would allow him to pretend he was something. He couldn't be French, he couldn't have an accent. . . . It wasn't a question of acting, it was a question of reality."

Wayne theorized that stage training could be a handicap rather than a help in movie acting. "If a kid came to me to ask me how to prepare for a screen career, I guess what I'd say would be to go to school, learn to handle liquor, mix with people, get into trouble, work in lots of different jobs and

656

always remember his reactions to things and people. That's the best equipment in front of a camera."

In other words, acting for Wayne was accurately replicating responses to life experiences. Nothing more, but nothing less. That sounds constraining, but it was typical of that generation of actors. Henry Fonda, an actor generally granted greater range and respect by the critics than Wayne, said precisely the same thing about himself: "I can't play anything except someone that I can believe myself to be," Fonda said. "I can play period American, but I can't do something classical in the sense that the minute I start to read poetry, then it's phony. And if I feel phony, I'm dead."

Actors working with Wayne for the first time were unprepared for his intensity. "He locks his eyes onto you and practically yanks the emotions out of you," said one. Morgan Paull, who worked with George C. Scott in *Patton,* said that the experience was not dissimilar: "They look you right in the eye. Right into you. Both are very intense actors."

An alpha male on the set and off, he turned docile before other alpha males — Ford, Hathaway, DeMille. "You are just paint as an actor. If a director uses your color well, that's fine." But if the director was someone less assertive, Wayne would make it a point to help mix the colors himself. "He couldn't help himself," said Gretchen Wayne. "If you bought a house, Grandaddy would tell you where to put the lights, he'd tell you where to put the couch in the living room. He had opinions on all of that."

If he was making a movie during the summer, he made it a point to take his children on location. He was particularly attentive to his second family, and was unhappy when Aissa, Ethan, and Marisa weren't around. If one of them was out of the house when he came home, he'd wander around looking for them. "Where is Ethan? Does he know I'm home? Where is he? Damn it, I would like to know where Ethan is . . ."

With the children of his third marriage, all he had to do was show his disappointment to bring them back in line. "I've spent 50 years building up a name in this business," he would say; the responsibility of the children not to screw that name up was implicit.

"I don't really ask very much of them," he said once. "I guess the main thing is that they never lie to me or their mother — or to themselves. I've told them that I'll always help them if they get into trouble as long as they don't lie. But the minute they lie, they lose my respect. And I can never remember any of them doing it."

There were a few house rules: the kids had to check in every day at 5:30, and if they were going to be late, they had to call. He believed in being demonstrative; he was always picking them up and hugging them, kissing them on the lips, including his sons.

When it came to his daughters' weddings, he would listen as they told him what they wanted, and then offer them a choice: a check for the amount the wedding would cost or he would pay for the wedding. They always opted to have him pay for the wedding, which he thought foolish. "Who expects the young to be practical?" he said with the practiced wisdom of someone who had been broke for a long time.

When his children were young, he tried to attend as many school events as possible. Gretchen Wayne remembered a time in high school when Toni Wayne had been elected to some position, and her father came and stood at the back of the auditorium. "He was always very polite and proper about things like that," Gretchen remembered. "He didn't want to take over the room by his presence; he was not aggressive in any way." As his children became adults, he tried to stay out of their lives unless there were money troubles, and then he would intervene.

Because his married children always had to make Christmas stops at in-laws', Wayne decreed January 15 as a mutually convenient "All Family Day." That was the day they got together around the tree and exchanged gifts. "Christmas was a big deal," remembered Gretchen Wayne. "Toni had eight kids, Patrick had two, Michael and I had five, Melinda had five. Grandaddy would ask me beforehand what the kids wanted and then do his own shopping for the grandchildren. The house was decorated with more stuff than you can imagine, and there would be gifts for us as well.

"He loved his family, loved the holidays, loved to celebrate. He was also a great catalogue shopper. When he died, we found a closet full of stuff he'd ordered from catalogues and hadn't gotten around to either giving or returning."

Mail order packages would arrive in bunches, ten or twenty at a time. Wayne would sit there with a child on his lap and they'd take turns opening the boxes. Tom Kane believed it all had to do with the deprivations of his childhood.

The Christmas tree in the house at Encino had gone all the way to the ceiling. At the house in Newport he would decorate the pier and the *Wild*

Goose. "He went as far as personally addressing the little stickers that went on the packages even though he had three secretaries available to do that stuff," said Tom Kane. "He liked to do it himself."

Wayne was usually in Newport for the holidays, and took great pleasure in the Festival of Lights, a flotilla of carolers in colorfully decorated boats who sailed up and down the channel in front of his deck. Wayne would erect a tent over his flagstone patio and hire an orchestra. The railing on the sea wall would be covered with holly and Christmas lights, and the *Wild Goose* would be anchored in the middle of the channel in case any of the guests wanted to go aboard. Typical guests would include Wayne's brother, Bob, Mike, Patrick, Toni, and Melinda Wayne and their spouses. Other invitees might include UA executive Robert Blumofe, perhaps Ricardo Montalban and his wife, Andy Devine, Buddy Ebsen, Claire Trevor and her husband. One year, Rod Laver and Roy Emerson made an appearance at the party as a special treat for the tennis-crazed Pilar.

Amidst all the Christmas bounty, there was one consistent shortfall. There wouldn't be any presents for Michael. "Pilar was wonderful to me, terrible to Michael," said Gretchen Wayne. "Grandaddy would look around and ask Pilar where Michael's present was, and she would say, 'Oh, I forgot.' So he would go get a bunch of cash and give it to Michael; Michael didn't really care, but what did bother him was that his father was bothered by it.

"The problem was that Michael didn't think his dad should have married Pilar, and she picked up on it. He didn't want to see his father get married again; he just thought it wasn't in his father's best interests. Grandaddy liked to play cards with Pilar, but she wasn't of the same intellectual background. She wasn't up on politics; she would rather play tennis. He would talk to me about what was going on in the Republican Party, and she couldn't have cared less. It simply wasn't interesting to her. She had her coterie of friends — the nouveau riche who played tennis, then lunched."

Wayne's grandchildren were a special case, and he never stood on ceremony with them any more than he did anybody else. His grandson Matthew Munoz, a Catholic priest, remembered taking an outboard to the Newport Beach house with a friend when he was a teenager. The boys docked, got out, and walked up the pier, only to discover that there was a formal party going on, with everybody in tuxedos and gowns.

Matt was wearing only swim trunks and was prepared to be thrown out on his ear, but his grandfather was delighted to see him. "His whole face lit up," remembered Munoz. " 'Hey you guys! How you doing?' Well, he threw me up on his leg, didn't even dust me off, he was so proud of me. And I had probably trampled sand through the house. . . . 'But get back before [Matt's parents] find out.' So my cousin and I stayed for a while longer and then left. But Grandpa never told my parents about us visiting. It was a little secret between us.

"Part of his charm was his earthiness. He spoke what he believed, whether you liked it or not. And yet he saw himself as just another guy doing a job."

People were surprised by how solicitous Wayne

was of others, of how he would go out of his way to please them. "He liked to walk down Fifth Avenue in the morning, just when the stores were opening," said Gretchen Wayne. "He'd wave and say 'Hi,' but he learned never to stop, otherwise he'd get mobbed. But he always had a touch with people. In social situations, if someone wanted to take his picture, he'd squat down a little, so they'd be on the same level; he was always very kind about things like that."

Beginning in 1951, with *The Quiet Man,* and continuing for the rest of his life, he indulged in a beau geste of ordering personalized coffee mugs for the cast and crew of each of his films. These mugs would say, "To xxxx from Duke" on one side, and on the other would be a scene from the film, or a line of dialogue. Wayne would rough out the artwork himself, then give it to an artist for the final version. The cup from *The Searchers* shows two horsemen in the desert with an Indian spear alongside them and underneath, "That'll be the day." On the other side is "The Searchers."

Conversely, it was hard to buy for John Wayne. One day at Bullock's department store, Tom Kane ran across a huge wastebasket, about three feet tall, emblazoned with red, white, blue, and gold American eagles. Kane knew Wayne would love it, so he had Bullock's ship it to his house.

A few days later, Wayne stuck his head in Kane's office. "You're off the hook" he said. "You're off the hook for Christmas, you're off the hook for my birthday, you're off the hook." Wayne kept the wastebasket on *The Wild Goose* for years.

"He really didn't give you a lot of rules, do's and don't's," said Patrick Wayne, his second-eldest son.

He knew the difference between right and wrong. He valued honesty, reliability, trustworthiness, and friendship — character things more than anything else.

Most of what I gleaned about acting was by watching him, seeing how he prepared and went about his business. The standards and goals I set were self-imposed by his presence.

In hindsight, it wasn't that hard being his son. He didn't put that many demands on you. He could accept very little and be a dear friend forever, with few requirements. But if you crossed the line, it was hard to get back into the fold. The big things were honesty and loyalty. Consistency was a big thing with him. He didn't really make demands of anybody else that he didn't make of himself. He had a temper, and if he blew up, he would apologize just as loudly and in front of just as many people.

Usually, the competitive edge was stifled when Wayne was with his family, but not always. "I used to play chess with my dad a lot, and I never fared very well," said Pat Wayne. "But there was this one particular time when I won three games in a row. He started to set the pieces up again and I said, 'I'm tired, I don't want to play again.' And he followed me around with the board for hours, trying to get me to play with him again. And finally I agreed and we sat down and he slaughtered me."

His relationship with his mother remained unrewarding. Every year he sent his mother and her second husband on a vacation. One year, it was an around-the-world, all-expenses-paid trip. When they got back, Wayne greeted them and wanted to hear all about it. Sidney Preen, Wayne's stepfather, raved about the trip and thanked him profusely. Molly just complained — the flights were tiring, the service was bad, etc. Wayne's response was a visible deflation. After he left the room, Mary St. John asked Molly, "Don't you think you could be a little nicer to him sometimes?"

To which Molly Morrison Preen replied, "I don't give a damn about him."

As sentimental as he was about family and friends, some things left him cold. One day a man came to the Batjac office with two copies of the 1925 Glendale High School yearbook. His wife had been in the class that year, they had two copies and they thought Wayne might like one. No charge.

When Wayne came in, he was handed the yearbook. He leafed through it casually, as if it were an old issue of *The Hollywood Reporter.* "God, there sure were a lot of ugly broads in our class," was all he said as he put the book down. At the end of the day, one of the Batjac people handed it to him to take home.

"Nah, I don't want it," he said. "You want it? Take it."

"He couldn't have cared less about that kind of thing," said Gretchen Wayne. "He never saved anything from his own career. Michael saved posters, Michael saved wardrobe pieces. If the house had burned down, Granddaddy would have said, 'Is everybody OK? Then let's move forward and build another house.' One time Michael had a fire in the garage. He lost some pictures, and tools for woodworking and electrical work. He mourned it for 20 years. His father wouldn't have cared about that at all."

Working or at ease, he was a creature of routine. If he was at home he would spend the morning writing letters and business correspondence, the early afternoon talking business or scripts. Later in the afternoon, he and Pilar might go to Laguna Beach and trawl through antique shops — he could spot a Georgian table or Tiffany lamp at twenty yards. Or he might go to the Big Canyon Country Club, looking for a game of chess or bridge. Dinner would be with the family, with perhaps a screening of a movie.

He exuded much of the self-confidence of his screen character. If he walked into Tom Kane's office and found a script on Kane's desk that he didn't want anything to do with, he would simply flick it on the floor without saying anything. He'd do the same thing with a hat on a desk if he didn't like the person it belonged to. In the 1960s, bumper stickers started appearing saying "John Wayne for President." His brother, Bob, shook his head and said, "No. Emperor. He wouldn't go for that four-year re-election stuff. It would have to be for life."

Although Wayne felt he was a true liberal in the sense of being in the liberal arts, as well as being open to listening to other ideas and opinions, political parameters were enforced. "None of his kids were Democrats, not that I can think of," said Gretchen Wayne. "If you didn't vote the way he did, you had better know why. After Grandaddy died, one of my kids voted for Clinton and another one voted for Ross Perot. Michael couldn't believe it, but they had their reasons so he couldn't argue with them."

Even his children found the relationship with

John Ford curious. "His relationship with Ford was a much different relationship than father-son," said Patrick Wayne. "It was a mentor relationship. He forever held Ford up and gave him total credit for his success and for giving him the opportunity to be where he was in the business, which may have been less than true. I think my father would have been a success at whatever he chose. He was driven and focused and ambitious. But the opportunity was presented by Ford and continued to be, although it would become awkward at times. He wasn't that submissive with anyone else."

With the crafts people, the filmmaking rank and file, Wayne's status was always high. "He holds no malice," said George Coleman, a jack-of-all-trades who also worked as Wayne's driver. "He knows I'm a Democrat. With some people you'd either have to switch or you wouldn't be working for them, but not Duke. He never turns to anybody and says, 'You're just a laborer, what do you know?' He'll say, 'This man has something to say, let's listen. Maybe he has an idea we can use to make this job better and faster.' He never belittles anybody."

"If you had an opinion about something, he wanted you to state it," said the character actor Ed Faulkner, who made six pictures with him. "He did not like yes-men. Even if he disagreed with you, he'd want to hear your argument. And he might say 'I don't agree with you,' but he would always let you say your piece. Which was not always the case with the people around him. With Bruce Cabot, for instance, things were either black or white. And if Bruce disagreed with you, he'd turn and walk away, just snub you. Duke would always let someone say their piece."

The shy and uncertain boy, the young actor who wanted to play every kind of part, now implicitly demanded that his parts be modeled on the man he had become. "The only difference between Grandaddy on the screen and Grandaddy in the room was in his wardrobe," said Gretchen Wayne. "What he projected was the man. His basis for his career after a certain point was that he would not trick or cheat the public in any way. 'Those are the people that put the food on my table,' he would say, and he had the utmost respect for them. Early on, he played light comedies, but as his role grew, as he played a military man in World War II, he began to understand what the public expected of him — a man who was heroic in the way he dealt with life. That was the consistent element in all of his films. Even *True Grit*."

More than anything else, he believed in loyalty. If Wayne came to believe someone could be trusted he would take them aside for a heart to heart: "If you ever want anything, anything at all, call me. Don't call Mike. Don't call Mickey [Rudin, his lawyer]. Don't call Jack [Gordean, his agent at the Feldman office]. Call me. I mean money too. Any amount you want. I'll give it to you. It's important you know you have me behind you."

John Wayne.

CHAPTER TWENTY

Rod Taylor was up for the co-starring part in a Wayne picture called *The War Wagon* at Universal, but Kirk Douglas read the script and liked it. Since Douglas was under contract with Universal, *The War Wagon* would use up one of his commitments. Wayne went to Lew Wasserman about Taylor, but the studio prevailed and Douglas played the part for $300,000 plus 15 percent of the gross after break-even until he got a total of $675,000, after which he got 10 percent of the worldwide gross in perpetuity.

The War Wagon was directed by Burt Kennedy. "The only reason *The War Wagon* was a hard time," said Kennedy, "was that Duke started me — picked me up off the street. Kirk Douglas said in his book that I was afraid of Duke. Hell, everybody was afraid of him."

Art director Alfred Sweeney built a western town in Durango, Mexico, in six short weeks. When it was finished, there were twenty new, beautifully aged buildings of wood and brick supplementing some pre-existing structures. The saloon and a mining company office featured detailed interiors that could be used for cover sets in bad weather.

The picture got off to a rocky start when Douglas showed up with a costume that included a flamboyant ring worn over a black leather glove — an expert attempt at scene stealing, as well as a test for the young director. Wayne's response was instantaneous: "If you don't get that faggot ring off that sonofabitch, I'm walking off the picture right now!"

Kennedy obediently walked over to Douglas and said, "Don't you think the ring is a little much, Kirk?"

"No, I think it's just fine," Douglas replied. "What do you think?"

"It's great, just great," said Wayne. (Reaming out a director was one thing, reaming out another actor on the same level as him was quite another.) Later, Wayne sidled up to Douglas and asked, "You're going to play it in that effete fashion?"

"John, I'm trying not to let my effeminacy show." (The nature of the relationship can be gauged by the fact that Douglas always refused to call Wayne "Duke.")

Durango would become Wayne's favorite place to shoot movies and hang out. There wasn't really much to do other than drink, play golf — there was a good nine-hole course — and drink some more. The airstrip had no lights, so planes had to land and take off during daylight hours. "Duke loved it," said Harry Carey Jr. "People didn't bother him there. They weren't movie-conscious. You could go shopping without being bothered."

But other people weren't so thrilled. You couldn't drink the water, and there was a sign that appeared in all the bathrooms of the very modest hotel where the production personnel were lodged: "Please Shake Out Your Boots Before

Putting Them On." The sign referred to the preference scorpions have for hiding in warm places. For Wayne and the stuntmen, this was the Real Thing; for a lot of other people, it paled next to locations in the south of France.

Wayne and Bruce Cabot shared a house on location. On Saturday nights they drank. One night Cabot came back from a night out to find Wayne weaving through the house. "Sleep well," said Wayne. "There's very few of us left." He went into his bedroom, then came back out again. "You know," he said, "there weren't too goddamn many of us to start with!"

Howard Keel was playing a comic Indian and remembered that his main problem was staying sober, while all about him the stuntmen were drinking and being serviced by hookers from a private house. After a month, Keel began to think longingly about being serviced himself, so decided to fly home to his wife for the weekend. Wayne didn't like it, but he let him go.

In Keel's memory, Wayne was the director and Burt Kennedy was strictly the writer. William Clothier remembered how Wayne took over on the set one day, grabbing Keel and showing him how he thought Keel should play a scene. Keel was struggling with dysentery and didn't take kindly to being manhandled.

"I'm watching this," remembered Clothier, "and Keel started to get pretty red. After the scene was over I went to Keel and said, 'I saw your reactions . . .' and before I could say anything [else] he said, 'If he puts his hands on me again, I'm gonna clobber that son of a bitch.'"

The next day, word filtered down to Wayne that Keel had been upset and Wayne came over to him.

"I think you're a damned good director," said Keel, "and I like and respect you. But I don't like being pushed around. I'll do anything you like, but don't push me. I've got a bad temper. I'm not as good at brawling as you are. I only have one good arm, and if I lose my temper, I'll not brawl with you, I'll try to kill you."

Wayne looked at Keel and said, "I'm sorry, kid. I understand." Wayne and Keel ended up friends; Wayne would ask him to appear in *The Green Berets,* but Keel was booked for a theater tour and had to turn the job down.

Bill Clothier had seen Wayne manifest control before and understood it. "Duke doesn't mean anything by it, it's just the way he is. That doesn't change the fact that he doesn't have any business putting his hands on people. When Duke's working with Ford he comes up and says, 'OK Coach, what do I do?' Ford says, 'You walk over to the horse, get on and ride out.' Duke will then walk over to the horse, get on and ride out. When he's working with another director, it doesn't happen that way: 'Goddamn it, I'm tired. I don't want to get on the horse.' That's the way it works.

"Duke hasn't patience with anybody. His own family, other actors, anybody. If you've got a big-name star, he'll keep quiet. He wouldn't think of telling [Robert] Mitchum how to play a scene. Bill Holden too. But you take another actor . . ."

Not all of Wayne's suggestions had negative results. One day he was watching Kennedy shoot footage of six horses pulling the massive War Wagon down the street. He walked over to Kennedy and asked him if he remembered the ominous rumble that preceded the earthquake in the MGM movie *San Francisco.* That sort of thing would be good for their picture. Start the wagon further back, before the camera picked it up, and the soundtrack could precede it with a low rumble. The suggestion was used in the picture to great effect.

Robert Walker Jr., the son of Jennifer Jones, Wayne's co-star in *New Frontier* at Republic, was also appearing in the movie. The younger Walker had only been in movies a few years, and was a good friend of Dennis Hopper and Jack Nicholson. He was part of a very different generation who would view Wayne with occasional hostility. Nevertheless, Wayne went out of his way to make the young man feel comfortable.

"He defined the word 'professional,' " remembered Walker. "It was really the last of Old Hollywood. He was in control, but he didn't micromanage things. I never felt intimidated by him, I felt comfortable with him. I felt he would take care of things and that things would be all right as long as he was around. He had confidence and security and he gave everyone that worked for him that same confidence."

Walker remembered a slightly different chain of command than Howard Keel. "Duke was the boss, but he let Burt Kennedy set things. Burt consulted him on the setups. But the way it was written, it was almost as if the picture made itself, as if it didn't need any direction, or even a whole lot of supervising. The cameraman, the crew, the costumers, they were all the best. The grips, the wranglers, the stuntmen, they all loved being there and they all respected Duke tremendously and loved him. He was the presence that kept it all together."

For Walker, it was a kind of paid vacation. He

would grab a horse and ride up above Durango and sit in the canyons and watch the lizards. Down below, the stuntmen chased the War Wagon. He'd sense when he was needed and he'd make his way down in time for his shot. Wayne was still climbing onto his horse, but if any serious riding was needed, Wayne's double, Chuck Roberson, was called upon.

Wayne said kind things about Walker's father, and commented about how much his son resembled him. "For me, John Wayne was a grandfather figure; he reminded me of my grandfather, Phil Isley — there was a kindness there, although there was no question that he was the boss. But Duke didn't lord it over you or make you feel small or insignificant. He was very kind and supportive of everybody. He didn't give advice. He just set an example by the way he behaved on a set. I always knew instinctively what to do, but if I hadn't, I could have learned just by watching him.

"John Wayne? I had the pleasure, the honor of working with him."

Kirk Douglas and Wayne had good chemistry on-screen, although Wayne was mightily irritated when Douglas was late to work one morning — a cardinal sin in Wayne's theology. "We're waiting for our star," he said sarcastically.

It had to be difficult navigating between two alpha males, but Burt Kennedy did his best. "Duke was tough but he was good," Kennedy said.

You had to go to the mat with him. On *War Wagon,* there was a shot where he's at a bar, and it's the first time the audience sees Kirk. Duke said, "You'll never use this shot." He didn't

673

want to do the shot, but he was just being contrary. The thing about John Ford that actors resented was that he was tough on them. But actors really love that. They're like children — actors want discipline, and they want praise. Duke would get mad at me and say, "You never tell the actors they're any good."

I never saw the guy blow a line. Ever. As big as he was, Duke never forgot making those five-day westerns, and he had an entirely different attitude about work as a result. He was like Bill Clothier, the wonderful old cameraman. You want a cameraman who's inventive, but not too inventive. Bill was great, and he was in his 60s when I worked with him for the first time; his camera operator was ten years older than he was. And they both could go longer than the young guys. Young crews are spoiled; the first thing they say is, "Are we gonna work late?" You never heard that from Bill or Duke.

Kennedy came to believe that Wayne had superb instincts about movies, knew when a scene wasn't working and often knew how to fix it. "It was uncanny how he could put a finger on something." The problem, however, was that while he may have always been right about the problem of a given scene, he could be very wrong in the way he *presented* his argument. If you didn't agree with him, you were wrong.

"I remember, after *The War Wagon,* he went to make *The Green Berets.* People asked me, 'Are you going to direct *The Green Berets?*' And I said, 'I'd rather *join* the Green Berets.' "

Dean Smith, who was working on the picture as a stuntman, said that the problem was really very basic: "If you were directing Duke, you had to be smarter than him. That's all. He was an aggressive guy who knew what he was doing. He was so stout in his own character, and a lot of people are not that confident. My grandmother had a saying that applied to Duke: 'He had a steel backbone and a wire tail.' He was tough. He would stay out there all day with us stuntmen. He'd rather work with the stuntmen than be at the hotel. He loved making pictures and he liked the people. He expected you to be just like him and do what was expected of you. But I'll tell you, if you're going to ride into a battle, you want to ride with Duke."

Another stuntman, Hal Needham, noticed that by this time Wayne had to husband his energies, especially for fight scenes — the cancer surgery had left him with a limited energy. "He just couldn't do a whole bunch," said Needham. "If we did a fight scene and needed a close-up, he could do a half dozen punches and do them well, but after that . . ."

The War Wagon emerged as a quintessentially brawny entertainment, the essence of late-period Wayne, complete with a thundering Dimitri Tiomkin score and an unusually strong supporting cast that included Keel, Walker, Keenan Wynn, and, as the heavy, Bruce Cabot, half of whose $1,000 weekly salary was garnished by Los Angeles marshals, for reasons that remain unclear.

The War Wagon cost $4.2 million, a couple of hundred thousand over budget because of weather. It returned domestic rentals of about $5.5 million and it went into profit in mid-1973, when it passed $10.7 million in worldwide rentals — two and a half times negative cost.

Overall, *The War Wagon* was a good-sized hit,

but Wayne knew the picture's value precisely. "It isn't a cold picture, but it lacks any real warmth, any getting inside the characters. But there are some tremendously funny scenes in the picture and Kirk Douglas is great in it. . . . There is a nice little love story, but outside of that we're just two big roughhouse characters. But . . . that sort of thing did all right for Victor McLaglen for quite a few years, you know."

Although Howard Hawks's *El Dorado* wasn't released until the summer of 1967, it was made in late 1965 and early 1966. Leigh Brackett believed that her script was the best of her career, but there were several problems. Hawks was coming off two dismal flops (*Man's Favorite Sport?* and *Red Line 7000*), and John Wayne's character died in the end. Hawks, as had been conclusively proven by *Red River,* was allergic to unhappy endings and retreated to something he knew would work, if only because it had worked before: he had the script rewritten until it became an uncredited remake of *Rio Bravo.*

Although Wayne had fired Robert Mitchum off *Blood Alley* ten years before, there were no hard feelings. Hawks called Mitchum to offer him the part. "Bob, how about a western with Duke Wayne?"

"Sounds great. Where are you going to shoot it?"

"I thought we'd do it in Old Tucson."

"Good — I like that too. What's the story?"

"Oh, no story, Bob. Just character. Stories bore people."

"You never knew which Mitchum was going to show up," said the writer-director Andrew Fenady, who made pictures with both Wayne and Mitchum. "If Mitchum was with people that didn't know what they were doing, or weren't pros, he'd say, 'OK, I'll hit the marks and say the lines.' If he was working with someone he thought had depth and character and know-how and cared about what they were doing, he'd give a performance. Mitchum was a mirror; he reflected what was around him. He was highly intelligent, wrote poetry, and was a fine writer as well. He could discourse on almost any subject, from cattle to Communism. He was an interested party, as long as you didn't bore the shit out of him."

It was a pleasant production but a ragged one, because Hawks was making a lot of it up as he went along. Johnny Crawford remembered the pace as "totally relaxed and ponderous." One day, when the company was preparing to shoot Crawford's death scene, Hawks looked up at the sky and said, "It looks like the sun's going to be behind the clouds for quite awhile." He and Wayne promptly jumped into a car and headed for Nogales. The rest of the company stayed on location, just in case, but nothing else got shot.

Wayne still liked Hawks and Hawks still liked Wayne. Hawks told one journalist that the two best actors he ever worked with were Wayne and Cary Grant. "Duke is the easiest to work with; Cary Grant is facile. Duke and I have a lingo — I want to do things his way. With Cary, we change things. Duke knows when something is wrong; he's got an instinct. . . . It took him so long to realize he was a good actor. Mitchum and Ann Sheridan were the same way, but they didn't get really good pictures. You have to be lucky.

"Duke got into four or five good ones — *Yellow*

Ribbon, Iwo Jima, Red River — and it made him. Nobody's good in a bad picture and everybody's good in a good picture."

The result of all this mutual admiration was that after four days of production Hawks was two days behind. By Christmas, he was twelve days behind schedule — he was shooting only about one and a third pages of script a day instead of the scheduled two and a third. Seven actors who thought they had finished their jobs were called back for retakes. By the time *El Dorado* finished in late January, the picture had been shooting for eighty-four days, an astonishing twenty-four days over schedule — a huge overrun for a small-scale movie that didn't present any production problems.

It didn't faze Mitchum, of course. Soon after the picture started in Tucson, Mitchum showed up at lunch with a teenager from a local high school or, perhaps, college. "Fellas, I'd like to introduce what's-her-name here. She'll be with us for the entire picture. She's my new drama coach." And she did indeed shadow Mitchum through the location shoot.

Mitchum and Wayne got along well, although they were wildly disparate personalities. Wayne was having his toupee fitted when he asked Mitchum, "Goddamn it, Mitch, when are you gonna let me direct you in a picture?"

"Duke, that's all you do anyway," replied Mitchum.

For a couple of months after *El Dorado* was finished, Wayne and Mitchum became the Huck Finn and Tom Sawyer of the Hollywood drinking set. They crashed a party Ray Stark threw to welcome Barbra Streisand to Hollywood. The two men stumbled around Stark's garden bellowing,

"We want to meet Barbra!" although neither of them had previously evinced a taste for show tunes.

Their friendship gave Mitchum some good Wayne stories. Some of them were false — Mitchum said Wayne wore four-inch lifts in his shoes — and some of them were probably true, as with a time at the Batjac office when Wayne was in a fine fury, bellowing at the staff and even knocking over some chairs. Then he went into his office, slammed the door, and pulled out a bottle. "You gotta keep 'em Wayne-conscious," he grinned.

Mitchum insisted Wayne wasn't anywhere near as square as he liked to pretend. When a friend who smoked pot with Mitchum asked if Wayne ever got high, Mitchum said, "Duke will do anything. He'll do it all."

When *El Dorado* was finally released in the summer of 1967, it did well, although nowhere near as well as it would have had Hawks made it more expeditiously. The film had originally been budgeted for $3.8 million, but the cost rose to $4.5 million. The film earned good domestic rentals of $5.2 million, and was a hit overseas as well. Three consecutive successful westerns (*The Sons of Katie Elder, El Dorado,* and *The War Wagon*) swelled his coffers — Wayne declared his 1966 income at $1.6 million, with deductions of $947,367.77.

Another frequent offscreen companion around this time was Rod Taylor. Once, Wayne idly asked Taylor what he was working on. "The second of two pictures with Doris Day," he replied.

"Jesus Christ!" Wayne exploded. "I would crawl over the mountains of Beverly Hills on my hands and knees if I could do a movie with Doris Day!"

Taylor thought he was being sarcastic, but gradually realized Wayne was serious. "All that macho bullshit, all those men's men that he played, and what he really wanted was for someone to offer him a romantic comedy." Despite his narrow focus on playing men with a code, it appeared that the wish he had expressed to Ollie Carey twenty-five years before was still lurking about.

Taylor invited Wayne to one of his marriages at a church in Westwood. As Taylor walked down the aisle, there was Wayne, sitting next to Pilar in the pew reserved for friends. Taylor scanned the room while the music was swelling. The men were smiling, the women were dabbing at their eyes. But Wayne was shaking his head slowly from side to side, as if to say, "No way, no way in hell."

"What made it worse was that he turned out to be right," said Taylor.

One day during the *El Dorado* shoot at Old Tucson, Bob Shelton came home to find Wayne, James Caan, and John Ford gathered around the table playing bridge with Shelton's wife. Shelton was shocked, not because of the bridge — Wayne loved to play cards — but because of Ford's presence. "I knew Ford was in town, but I didn't know why — he hadn't come to the set at all."

Ford's last several pictures had been failures: *Cheyenne Autumn* had been a critical and commercial disappointment. He started *Young Cassidy* but had gone on a bender and been unable to finish it, and *7 Women* had been a disaster. If he had been fifty, he could have ridden it out, but Hollywood is brutal on old directors with consecutive flops, no matter how eminent they might be.

John Ford would never make another movie, and the only way he could see Duke was socially.

That was fine with Wayne, not so fine with Ford, who chafed at the inactivity. Wayne had felt that Ford's powers were diminishing, and he hadn't gone to see *7 Women,* sensing that it would make him unhappy. For the next several years, until Ford's declining health made work impossible, Wayne tried to dance around Ford's occasional attempts to inveigle him into a picture. Often, Wayne would use Mike and Batjac as an excuse: "I'd love to do it, Pappy, but Mike's got me all tied up." Although the two men were never close to being estranged, the sense of distance that was geographically imposed after Wayne moved to Newport Beach became slightly emphasized.

In 1966, the producer Martin Rackin did an indifferent remake of *Stagecoach,* but not before giving an interview in which he said that he thought Ford's original was old-fashioned. After the Rackin version came out, the producer was at Wayne's house, when Ford dropped in without warning. There was an awkward moment, followed by Ford glaring at Rackin and asking Wayne, "Mind if I hit this SOB in the mouth?"

For one of the few times in his life, Wayne refused a direct request from Ford. "Not in my house," he said. There was a stony silence for some minutes, but Wayne worked overtime at playing the genial host and managed to effect a rough reconciliation.

Beginning in November 1967, and continuing for the next eighteen years, the Bar 26, the cattle ranch Wayne co-owned with Louis Johnson, would hold a sale for the ranch's red and white Herefords. The Bar 26 raised about four hundred bulls each year, with the top 125 being sold at auction. Each year the Bar 26 sold about fifty two-year-old bulls, twenty-five heifers, and forty special bulls, all for high-end breeding purposes.

Wayne loved the event and usually attended, partially because he genuinely loved the environment, not to mention Johnson and his wife, Alice, partially because a personal appearance ginned up sales.

"Duke and I had an agreement," Johnson would remember. "Anytime he came east of the Colorado River, I paid the expenses for him and his guests. When I went west of the Colorado, he paid mine. Sometimes he tried to see how many friends he could bring with him." On those occasions when he came alone, Wayne would stay at the Johnsons' house, which he always entered by yelling, "I love this house and everybody in it." In time, the farm was named the Red River Land Company.

A less lucrative but equally rewarding event involved USC awarding him an honorary Doctor of Fine Arts degree at the June commencement. "Sportsman, responsible citizen and patriot, as well as motion picture star, Mr. Wayne is certainly one of the most famous living alumni of this university," said Raymond Sparling, a member of USC's Board of Trustees. "In a medium of imagery, he has faithfully portrayed to hundreds of millions of persons throughout the world the authentic spirit of the pioneering American. In the medium of life, he is, in fact, the rugged man of courage, strength, honor, humor and generosity who has contributed so much to the character and to the perpetuity of this land."

■ ■ ■ ■

By the mid-1960s, the marriage to Pilar had grown increasingly problematic, although Wayne didn't seem to want to split up, perhaps because a third divorce would have been too embarrassing. The age difference was unimportant at first, when passion served as a bridge. Later, when a man slows up and might need to be tended, it seems to have become an issue. Mainly, Pilar was increasingly restless with the highly ordered life Wayne led. He could languish on the *Wild Goose* while she got bored after a few days; he loved nothing in life more than holing up in Old Tucson or Durango and making a western, but there was nothing for her to do while Wayne was shooting his movie. How much tennis can a woman play?

Complicating things was her *grande dame* personality. "Duke had something about distant, austere women," said Stefanie Powers. "Perhaps it went back to his mother. Bill Holden's mother was like that — not warm or cuddly. She had three boys and wouldn't let them play inside the house. She was uninvolved in her children's lives. And Bill ended up marrying Brenda Marshall — the same kind of woman as his mother."

From her point of view, Pilar was just bored, and her feelings were probably not much different than those of the late, unlamented Chata, who had told one reporter, "My husband is one of the few persons who is always interested in his business. He talks of it constantly. When he reads, it's scripts. Our dinner guests always talk business, and he spends all his time working, discussing work or planning work."

683

"Pilar was very introverted," said Rod Taylor. "By the time I got to know him, Duke's attitude toward her was a respectful, Spanish family relationship with the wealthy woman of the house. I felt no emotional intimacy at all. I think Duke's male friends were far more important to him than his female friends."

Even though the marriage to Pilar was approaching in-name-only status, Wayne had little interest in the traditional *droit du seigneur* of the movie star. "He was never flirtatious or overly interested in actresses," said Rod Taylor. "He turned a blind eye to punks like me who were always scouting around."

Bob Shelton, from Old Tucson, also felt a slight chill emanating from Pilar. "I have no authority to have an opinion, but here it is: she was more movie star-ish than he was. In the early days, she traveled with him and she was always with him. And then she gradually grew tired of it, and sort of began enjoying her own celebrity status. And she quit traveling with Duke, which is not a good sign because in that business you need to stay close together.

"Each of them was respectful of the other, but I felt no warmth."

Trophy wives want to play, and Wayne wanted to work. And, as with Josie, Pilar's friends were not really his friends. Once, a friend of Wayne's was visiting at the house when the doorbell rang. Wayne looked out from behind the drapes and suddenly put his finger over his mouth. "It's some friends of Pilar's. If I open the door, they'll want to talk the whole goddamn afternoon." Wayne and his friend hid in the room until the visitors went away.

No matter how petulant he could be, his employees stayed with him for decades, the same way the public did. The reasons are best conveyed by a story told by Tom Kane, whose wife, Ruth, was in the Motion Picture Home dying of cancer. Wayne was close to Kane, not particularly close to Ruth.

One morning at 9:15, Kane's phone rang. It was his wife, sounding like she did before she got sick.

"My God, you sound great," said Kane.

"Well, how would you feel if you woke up in the morning and John Wayne was standing by your bed?" She went on to explain that Wayne had stayed for more than an hour talking to her. Before he left, he had brushed her hair.

Kane vowed then and there that he would never let anything Wayne said or did interfere with their relationship. When Ruth died, Wayne came from Newport to Burbank for the 8 A.M. funeral Mass. Wayne drove himself to the funeral, which was potentially dangerous because he was a terrible driver — recklessly fast. But he got to the church in one piece, even if he did park halfway up on the curb. He put his arm around Kane, who leaned against him. "Things will never be the same again," Wayne told him.

Charlie Feldman had been experiencing bouts of bad health in the midst of producing films. His latest was *Casino Royale.* Since it involved no fewer than five directors, any cohesive approach was impossible, and Feldman was exhausted. "I've been through the most harrowing experience that I have ever been through since I've been in the business," he wrote Wayne in October 1966. "Not a moment to myself, not a moment to write a letter, not a moment to pick up the horn. . . . I was so ill at times I didn't know whether I could finish the film. . . .

"Dear Duke, please take care of yourself," closed Feldman. "Though I am not a faggot, I close this note with a big kiss and all my love to you, Pilar and your wonderful family." Charles Feldman died in 1968, but Wayne stayed with the agency after Feldman's death.

The genesis of *The Green Berets* seems to have been an encounter Wayne had on the USC campus. He was there to discuss a benefit for a children's hospital and was taking a stroll with Mary St. John when he saw students protesting the Vietnam War.

What got my goat was that these students were heckling a young marine, a corporal, who was going by and heading for his car. He walked with his back straight as a rod, and he wore his uniform with pride. Then I noticed that where his right arm should have been there was only an empty sleeve which was neatly folded and pinned back.

Turned out he was one of the Ninth Marine Brigade which were the first ground troops America sent to Vietnam. He had a chest full of medals and ribbons. He said his drill instructor had taught him to ignore impolite civilians. He said, "You don't give them the satisfaction of noticing them." I waved to him as he drove away. And my blood was boiling.

I ran over to the students and I was just so angry, I drummed my fists into their goddamn table and I said, "You *stupid* bastards! You *stupid* fucking *assholes*! Blame Johnson if you like. Blame Kennedy. Blame Eisenhower or Truman or fucking goddamn Roosevelt. But *don't* you blame that kid. Don't you *dare* blame any of those kids. They *served*! Jesus, the kid lost his *arm.* I mean what the hell is *happening* to this country?

The first concrete sign of *The Green Berets* was a December 29, 1965, letter from Wayne to the distinguished director George Stevens. "My company and I want to make a motion picture about the war in Vietnam," Wayne began. "It will have the scope, integrity and dignity required by the subject matter. . . . Our film about the exciting new unit fighting in Vietnam will be as American as 'apple pie' and as harshly against the 'beard and sandal' brigade as possible."

Stevens was no co-religionist of Wayne's — he was a New Deal liberal. Wayne was writing him because Stevens's son was working in the Johnson administration and Wayne knew he would need help from the Defense Department.

Wayne also wrote President Johnson, while George Stevens Jr. spoke to Johnson's assistant Jack Valenti, who made sure Johnson saw Wayne's letter. Valenti advised Johnson to give Wayne what he wanted: "Wayne's politics are wrong, but insofar as Vietnam is concerned, his views are right. If he made the picture he would be saying the things we want said."

Wayne opened his offensive by telling Lyndon Johnson that, while he, Wayne, supported the war, he knew it was not popular. It was important that the people of the United States as well as the rest of the world understand why it was important to be there.

"The most effective way to accomplish this is through the motion picture medium. Some day soon a motion picture *will* be made about Vietnam. Let's make sure it is the kind of picture that will help our cause throughout the world."

Wayne wanted the cooperation of the Defense Department, just as they had helped on *The Longest Day* and *Sands of Iwo Jima.* Unsure if Johnson was a movie fan, he recapitulated his career, slightly exaggerating by saying he had been a star for thirty-seven years, then closed by quoting some of Jimmy Grant's dialogue from *The Alamo,* about how a man who gets in the habit of goring oxes gets his appetite whetted. "And we don't want people like Kosygin, Mao Tse-Tung, or the like, 'gorin' our oxes.' "

Three weeks later, Bill Moyers, special assistant to the president, wrote Wayne saying that President Johnson did indeed remember *The Alamo* and understood the reference. However, whether or not the Defense Department could offer assistance depended on the script. A month after that, Wayne replied to Moyers: "We feel confident that the finished script will be one that adheres closely to the thinking of President Johnson . . . regarding the role being played by the U.S. fighting men in Vietnam."

The Green Berets, then, was always intended to illuminate the administration's — and John Wayne's — view of the war. The American involvement in Vietnam fit right into Wayne's worldview — Communism had to be fought everywhere it surfaced, whether Hollywood or Southeast Asia.

In June 1966, Wayne went to Vietnam to work

on a documentary for the Defense Department that he was narrating. "I'm going around the hinterlands to give the boys something to break the monotony," he said. He was amused by the urchins of Saigon, who immediately recognized him and called out "Hey you! Numbah one cowboy!"

In time, Wayne would make trips to all four of the combat areas of Vietnam, and most of the forward camps, purely by himself and without any accompanying entertainment units. During one of the visits, he received a Montagnard bracelet from a Strike Force under the command of Captain Jerry Dodds. The Montagnards were mountain tribesmen who had fought for the French during the Indochina war and were currently working as mercenaries for the Americans in Vietnam, usually as the defenders of isolated camps in the highlands or elsewhere.

Wayne was deeply moved and wrote a letter saying that he hadn't removed the bracelet since it was bent around his arm. Indeed, the bracelet can be seen on Wayne's wrist in several movies of the late '60s.

Working from Robin Moore's book, James Lee Barrett completed a first-draft script of *The Green Berets* in August 1966, to which the Pentagon strenuously objected. Barrett's script involved a Special Forces unit going into North Vietnam on an offensive mission, which was forbidden for the Green Berets. Mike Wayne didn't tell his father about the rejection. "I was actually afraid to because he would have said, 'You dumb son of a bitch!' " Barrett went on a research trip to Vietnam, and came back to do a second draft. The Pentagon objected to some specifics, and a third draft was soon under way.

By the end of March 1967, the Pentagon agreed to assist Batjac, provided specific modifications were made in the script. Mike Wayne and Barrett made the changes. In April of 1967, Jack Valenti wrote Wayne that the Defense Department had approved the script of *The Green Berets*. "I urged them to go all out on equipment and material co-operation. Let me know if you run into road blocks. Good luck." Michael Wayne wrote George Stevens to thank him for his help.

The Green Berets was to be the second picture on a two-picture deal Wayne had with Universal (the first was *The War Wagon*). In many respects, Wayne was making the same deal John Ford had been forced to make for *The Quiet Man* — an overtly commercial film in exchange for a far dicier personal project.

The Green Berets was penciled in to begin shooting in the late spring of 1967, but after stalling for a few months Universal backed out of the project, ostensibly because of changes the studio wanted to make in the script, but mostly because they got cold feet. Batjac quickly moved the picture over to Warner Bros., with production scheduled to start in August.

Ed Faulkner hadn't worked with Wayne since *McLintock!* and asked his agent about getting him an interview for *The Green Berets*. His agent couldn't do anything, so Faulkner sat down and wrote a personal letter. "Like yourself, I've worn a Stetson long enough. Maybe a change in hats is called for." He signed it and sent it over to Mary St. John. Five days later, Faulkner's agent called and asked if he had talked to Wayne, because a script for *The Green Berets* was on the way to Faulkner.

At this point, the picture had a budget of $5.1 million and a sixty-two-day schedule. Okinawa was being considered as the primary location, but the Huey helicopters needed for the movie wouldn't be available from Japan until the end of the year. The Department of Defense preferred a Fort Benning location because it would involve fewer personnel. Besides that, the terrain, they said, was similar to Vietnam.

Wayne finally agreed to Fort Benning. The Pentagon handed over five acres, on which Batjac spent $171,000 building a Green Beret camp, which was left intact for training purposes. Batjac also spent $305,000 in salaries for personnel, 80 percent of which was to off-duty or furloughed soldiers. In return for the Pentagon's land and equipment, Batjac was charged a grand total of $18,623.

Wayne was acting in the picture for $750,000 plus 10 percent of the gross over $7.5 million. For directing the picture, he was paid an additional $120,000. Co-director Ray Kellogg was on board for $40,000 for twenty-two weeks' work, second unit director Cliff Lyons was getting $1,000 a week, and cinematographer Winton Hoch was getting a total of $17,500.

Wayne cast George Takei, who had just finished the first season of *Star Trek,* as a South Vietnamese officer who relishes killing Vietcong. Takei stifled his ambition and told his prospective director that he was opposed to the Vietnam War.

"I respect your opinion, George," replied Wayne. "I know a lot of people feel the same way. David Janssen and Jim Hutton, who are also in the movie, feel as you do. But I want you guys in this movie because you're the best actors for the job. I need your help. I'll need your ideas to make this a good movie. And I'll try to do what I can to make this a good movie."

Takei remembered that Wayne was "forthright, persuasive and charming. After all, he *was* John Wayne." The picture started shooting on August 9, 1967, and they were on schedule until August 21, when the heavy rains that are always a part of summer in the South began. They were four days behind by September 1, and Warners informed them that the picture was $187,000 over budget. Mike Wayne responded that they were still within the final $5.6 million budget.

Wayne was averaging between six and nine setups a day, slow but not unreasonable for a picture of this size, but he continued to fall behind schedule. Warners was increasingly worried about the film. Wayne had an eye infection and put off shooting his own close-ups, which the studio interpreted as a lack of coverage. But a simple phone call would have cleared up that problem.

Late in the first week of September, the trade papers announced that Mervyn LeRoy, the venerable Hollywood pro who had directed pictures great (*I Am a Fugitive from a Chain Gang, Five Star Final*) and far from great (*The Bad Seed, The Devil at 4 O'Clock*) was on his way to Georgia to "assist" (*Variety*) or to "handle the direction" (*Boxoffice*) of *The Green Berets*.

LeRoy was a legend around the Warners lot because he had been married to Harry Warner's daughter. He had been one of the studio's mainstays in the 1930s until decamping for MGM and $10,000 a week. LeRoy's compensation under his current Warners contract was $3,000 a week, $200,000 a picture, and a whopping 15 percent of the profits — a figure that attests to his familial relationship with Jack Warner.

LeRoy's contract ran until March 1973, and it had a clause that said only Jack Warner could produce one of LeRoy's pictures. (Jack Warner had sold his shares of the company to Seven Arts Productions in November 1966 for $32 million, but he was still running the studio.)

Just as *The Green Berets* was getting under way in Georgia, Jack Warner was editing his personal production of *Camelot,* and downshifting to the status of an independent producer. With Jack Warner preoccupied, the Seven Arts people may well have been trying to use *The Green Berets* as one of LeRoy's commitments, with Batjac taking the fall for his salary.

According to LeRoy, Seven Arts was simply nervous. They told him that he had a free hand with the picture — if he wanted to shut *The Green Berets* down, he could. All this certainly suggests concerns that transcended missing close-ups.

The upshot of all this was that by the end of September, Fort Benning had nearly as many directors as soldiers. Ray Kellogg and Cliff Lyons were directing a unit for scenes that didn't have any of the main actors in them; Wayne was directing the main unit; Mervyn LeRoy was . . . around. *Variety* reported different stories at different times — Wayne was directing the scenes he wasn't in, or, alternately, LeRoy was directing the scenes that featured Wayne. David Janssen told *Variety*'s Army Archerd that LeRoy directed Wayne and Janssen in their first scenes together.

LeRoy's claim that he worked for five and a half

months on the picture is more or less borne out by the documentation — he followed the picture all the way through the dubbing of Miklos Rozsa's score — but the testimony of the people that worked on the movie indicates he was functioning more as an associate producer than a director.

"Mervyn was a nice man," said Ed Faulkner, "but he didn't do much. He was there looking over Duke's shoulder. He may have said things to him privately, but he didn't make a lot of noise publicly." David Janssen said that LeRoy "just went through the motions to keep Warner happy. And anyway, he didn't want his name on the credits."

"Duke directed the dialogue scenes," said Faulkner. "And he certainly directed all the scenes I was in. Cliff Lyons was coordinating the stunts, and Ray Kellogg was directing the second unit. Often Wayne would be blocking a shot and Winton Hoch would say, 'Duke, you're supposed to be in this shot. Where are you?' Wayne would nod at Faulkner, who had been nicknamed "Deacon," and say, "The hell with it; let's get the Deacon in there."

Cameraman Winton Hoch had done landmark work for John Ford on *3 Godfathers, She Wore a Yellow Ribbon,* and *The Searchers,* but he left the distinct impression that this last reunion with Wayne was not his favorite shoot: "There were three directors on that show, Ray Kellogg, John Wayne and Mervyn LeRoy, and it's a little difficult to work with three directors."

Despite the production pressures, Wayne remained the father figure on the set. "On August 21," remembered Ed Faulkner, "my wife was scheduled to deliver my fourth and last daughter.

694

I told my wife, 'I don't know where I'll be, but I will try to call you every day at noon L.A. time, 3 P.M. Georgia time.' I told Jim Hutton about all this. Duke knew that my wife was pregnant, but he didn't know about our plans to stay in touch.

"On August 21, we were twenty miles outside of Columbus [Georgia]. I had finished lunch, there was no way I could get to a phone, and I was worried. And suddenly I felt this big arm around me. It was Duke. 'Aren't you supposed to be making a phone call?' he asked me. He turned around, and there was the production manager with a Pontiac wagon with a bubble top. And they broke every traffic record in Georgia to get me back to my apartment to make my phone call at 3 P.M."

With all the pressure, Wayne was chewing tobacco. When people would raise an eyebrow about the tobacco, he'd respond by saying "That can't hurt me." Occasionally, someone would offer him a cigar and he'd always accept it.

Georgia in August and September is no time to shoot a movie — if it's not broiling, it's raining — and the production was still running behind, but not a great deal; production manager Lee Lukather estimated that the picture was about one third finished: "We have had seven full days of sunlight and two half days. The rest have been overcast. Tremendous rain storms, etc. . . . Duke, Kellogg, Mervyn LeRoy and everyone have been working their hearts out, but when the weather doesn't cooperate, we are lost."

Lukather said that theft was rampant, so the production had to post guards on every set so that trucks, wheels, tires, and lumber wouldn't disappear. In addition, the promised military vehicles from the Defense Department hadn't shown up, so the production had to rent them, along with Teamsters. Nevertheless, wrote Lukather, "Duke has the strength of a Lion and the patience of a saint to do the job that he is doing."

Wayne kept up a reasonable pace. He lost fifteen pounds over the course of production, but was constantly on the move, and no more liable to suffer in silence than he had been on *The Alamo*. "I want it black in the background," he yelled during the shooting of the night battle scene. "We're going to come back here every goddamn night until I get it black in there!"

Besides the heat, the rain, and the studio, Wayne was also having trouble with Aldo Ray, whose drinking problem, he had been assured by Ray's agent, was in the past. As soon as Ray was firmly established in the picture — i.e., it would be prohibitively expensive to reshoot his scenes — he fell off the wagon with a resounding crash. At one point, Ray was so drunk he couldn't stand up to act. There wasn't anything Wayne could do other than give Ray's dialogue to other actors.

It was a long slog of a shoot, from August to November on location, then back to Warner Bros. in Burbank for a week or two of studio work. The last scene of the film was shot at Point Mugu in Malibu, which is why, for the only time in history, the sun sets in the east.

When production wrapped up in December 1967, *The Green Berets* was eighteen days over the scheduled seventy-two-day shooting schedule, at a final cost of $7 million. As soon as the picture was finished shooting, Warners tried to add $150,000 to the budget by assessing Batjac for the services of Mervyn LeRoy, but Mike Wayne was adamant, reminding Warners that "it was [their] agreement . . . in which the salary, expenses, charges, etc. relating to Mervyn LeRoy would not be charged to the production cost of *The Green Berets.*" The tab for LeRoy was to be an ongoing dispute between the studio and Batjac, with the amount in question rising to $162,000.

As the picture wound its way through the postproduction process, Wayne was already on the defensive, without ever acknowledging it. In January 1968, he wrote a piece for the *Los Angeles Times* saying that his purpose in making *The Green Berets* was "to make an exciting motion picture about the bravery of the men in the Special Forces, not to make a controversial film about the war. . . .

"When I was in South Vietnam, I was awed by the varied accomplishments required of these men but one qualification they all share: courage. Danger is with them every moment, but they face it as a necessary part of the work they are proud of doing."

A few months after *The Green Berets* wrapped production, Wayne began shooting *Hellfighters* on location, with Casper, Wyoming, doubling for Venezuela. The film was based on the life of Red Adair, who put out thirty-five to fifty oil fires every year with an insanely risky technique he devised himself — a metal drum filled with one hundred to five hundred pounds of solidified glycerine, a jelly that was pure high explosive. The barrel was attached to a long crane and the entire apparatus backed into the fire until the barrel was in the center of the fire. Adair bailed out of the crane as the barrel was detonated with electrical caps implanted in the jelly. The resulting explosion consumed all available oxygen near the well for a few seconds, which generally extinguished the fire.

All very impressive, but the original script for *Hellfighters* by Clair Huffaker wasn't much, and after John Lee Mahin did a rewrite, it still wasn't much. But Lew Wasserman had offered Wayne $1 million and 10 percent of the gross, which eradicated his doubts about the material. As soon as *Hellfighters* was finished, Wayne hurled himself into promotion for *The Green Berets,* which was released in June 1968 to some of the most scathing reviews ever dumped on a major star.

Michael Korda called it "immoral . . . a simple-minded tract in praise of killing, brutality and American superiority over Asians." Even the trade papers got in on the stomping. *The Hollywood Reporter* said it was "a cliché-ridden throw-back to the battlefield potboilers of World War II, its artifice readily exposed by the nightly actuality of TV news coverage . . . clumsily scripted, blandly directed, performed with disinterest."

But the keynote piece was Renata Adler's review in *The New York Times.* Adler called Wayne "a filmmaker of truly monstrous ineptitude," and that was just for starters.

It had not occurred to me until I saw *The Green Berets* that I had not seen a film in many months which unequivocally, unironically endorsed violence — not even war — just violence. There have been cruel, vicious, messy films all over the place but . . . everyone is or pretends to be laughing or tongue in cheek. . . .

The Green Berets are not of an average 60 years of age, do not parachute about as in World

War II, spend hours at nightclubs a la Fontaine-bleau, set virtuous Vietnamese ladies to seductions, abduct V.C. officials in the night with the help of montagnard crossbows, drugs and a most ridiculous balloon and string, so that passing aircraft can yank them off into the sky; Vietnam is not full of artifical foliage and white birch.

There is clearly a certain out-of-touchness here — an insanity, an arrogance. . . . The film is a travesty and a falsification, and a foolish romantic falsification at that.

In its first six months of release, *The Green Berets* grossed $8 million — a million more than it cost. *Variety* reported that the film eventually took in about $10 million domestically, and $8 million abroad. Internal Batjac correspondence indicates that the figure for worldwide rentals, i.e., net to the studio, was $12.5 million — a success, but not an overwhelming one. Mike Wayne wrangled with Warners for years about their profit accounting, or, rather, their non–profit accounting.*

In retrospect, Wayne believed that the critics made a mistake. "They overkilled it," he told the military historian Lawrence Suid. "*The Green Berets* would have been successful regardless of what the critics did, but it might have taken the public longer to find out about the picture if they hadn't

* Of the $12.5 million, Warners wanted to allocate $9.8 million for distribution fees and expenses, leaving a grand total of $2.7 million to apply to the negative cost they tallied at slightly more than $7 million. This meant that Wayne's great-grandchildren might have been able to collect his 10 percent of the profits, but nobody else.

made so much noise about it."

In terms of Wayne's directorial career, *The Alamo* has many defenders, but *The Green Berets* has none. Disregarding its politics — no easy task — the film is flatly lit, with lots of zoom shots. It seems that there are a great many pine trees in Vietnam, and the troops that fought the war were indeed largely left over from World War II — a sergeant named Muldoon, a scrounger, a lovable orphan. With the exception of a well-done night battle scene that gradually turns into morning, the direction is in a utilitarian style that puts the politics front and center. *The Green Berets* makes *The Alamo* look like *The Best Years of Our Lives*.

Nevertheless, both Wayne and Jack Warner were proud of the picture; in February 1969, Mike Wayne forwarded a certificate of appreciation he had been given by the American Legion. Jack Warner wrote back, "I am extremely pleased that this picture has performed so well at the box office and so many people throughout the country have seen it so they can get some idea of the devotion to duty that characterizes the men in the Special Service unit.

"My kindest regards to you and your father. Sincerely, Jack."

In sum, *The Green Berets* was a reasonable commercial success, but a critical disaster that convinced most of the moviegoing audience under the age of thirty never to see a John Wayne movie.

But Wayne was more interested in pleasing the audience he had than he was in broadening it. "All I know," he said, "is that it gave me great pleasure to pass [the financial success of the picture] on over to Universal where at the last minute they reneged. I let them off the hook, but they wouldn't let it go at that. They kept telling everybody that the picture couldn't make money, that it wouldn't go foreign, that it was an unpopular war. What the hell war isn't unpopular?"

The critics were right in that Wayne's mind-set, the way he saw the movies and the audiences who paid to see them, had a way of reducing the moral grays of a strange war to black and white. "It's Cowboys and Indians," Wayne said. "In a motion picture, you cannot confuse the audience. . . . I'm not making a picture about Vietnam. I'm making a picture about good against bad. I happen to think that's what's true about Vietnam."

Verbally, Wayne was always blunter than he was as an actor, or even as a producer; he knew full well that he had often depicted Indians, to take his own example, as complex, honorable men — *Hondo,* for instance. But when he was cornered by a press that he never entirely trusted, he disingenuously pretended, first, that his picture wasn't political, second, that he was only following the simplifying traditions of the movies.

If *The Green Berets* hardened the hearts of many in the American moviegoing audience, in Europe there was a more modulated attitude. The French director Bertrand Tavernier enjoyed provoking his left-wing friends by telling them Wayne was a far more intelligent actor than the reliably left-wing Marlon Brando — that Brando, at the zenith of his Hollywood power, had specialized in terrible movies and ridiculous accents. Wayne, on the other hand, had consistently used his power to make good films, including some that nobody ever talked about, such as *Wake of the Red Witch* or *Shepherd of the Hills.*

Years later, after spending time with some of

Wayne's directors and many actors who worked with him, Tavernier would go even further. "I know he was right-wing and *The Green Berets* is lousy and embarrassing. But some of his opinions were more complex (about the treatment of the Indians, the Mexicans) than he was given credit for. Furthermore, many actors told me he was more open, more generous with other actors, including black people, than many 'liberal' stars. He was also more respectful of bit players, more democratic."

In August 1968, Wayne spoke at the 29th Republican convention in Miami. On the fifth day he made a speech that was headlined "Why I Am Proud to Be an American."

Looking dapper in a dark blue pinstriped suit, Wayne began by saying,

I'm about as political as a Bengal tiger. . . . I have a feeling that a nation is more than just government, laws and rules. It's an attitude. It's the people's outlook. Dean Martin once asked me what I wanted for my baby daughter, and I realize now that my answer was kind of an attitude toward my country. Well, he asked me this on election day and the bars were closed anyway, so he had a lot of time to listen and I told him. . . .

I told him that I wanted for my daughter Marisa what most parents want for their children. I wanted to stick around long enough to see that she got a good start and I would like her to know some of the values that we knew as kids, some of the values that an articulate few now are saying are old-fashioned. But most of all I want her to be grateful, as I am grateful for every day of my life that I spend in the United States of America. . . .

I don't care whether she ever memorizes the Gettysburg Address or not, but I want her to understand it, and since very few little girls are asked to defend their country, she will probably never have to raise her hand to that oath, but I want her to respect all who do.

I guess that is what I want for my girl. That is what I want for my country, and that's what I want for the men that you people are going to pick from here to go shape our destinies.

The convention chose Richard Nixon and Spiro Agnew to shape the nation's destiny.

By now, Mike Wayne was running Batjac smoothly, and his father had grown to respect his eldest son. "I could get John Wayne to read a script without putting up a million dollar offer," remembered Mike. "I was always in competition for him with other studios, but I could get a free read. He was used to seeing finished scripts; I would never give him anything unless it was a complete treatment, or a complete script. As far as his being the boss, he was the boss on any film he was on. In movies, the most important element eventually becomes known and gets his way. Running Batjac wasn't any harder [for me] than it would have been for anybody else."

Left unsaid was the fact that it wasn't any easier either. "The fact that he was so professional made it easier, but there was never any doubt about where the muscle was. That was the good thing and the bad thing about John Wayne: he dominated everything he was associated with because of his charisma, his star energy."

John Wayne was gold-plated as far as the Hollywood studios were concerned because he guaranteed a bottom — something very few stars can do. A Wayne picture rarely did less than $4 million in domestic rentals and could go much higher. Since Wayne films rarely cost more than $4 million to shoot, there was almost no downside risk. "He wasn't a guarantee of success," said Mike, "he was a guarantee against failure."

His price for the pictures he made after *The Green Berets* was $1 million against 10 percent of the gross. First up was a project he had wanted to produce himself. Batjac was after it but so was Hal Wallis. Wayne didn't care who produced it because he knew that nobody could play the main character better than he could — a one-eyed lawman named Rooster Cogburn.

Chapter Twenty-One

The word about *True Grit* was spreading even before the novel was published. "Dad was on vacation on his boat," remembered Mike Wayne, "and he came back into town. I had just gotten the galleys of *True Grit.* He was in my office, and I was just about to hand him the galleys when the phone rang. It was Henry Hathaway. Before I handed him the phone, I put my hand over the phone and said, 'I'm on this *True Grit* project. Don't commit to it.'

"Hathaway started talking to him about *True Grit*; he and Hal Wallis were bidding on it and so forth. When the conversation was over, I handed him the book. He read it and told me, 'I think it's great, and I hope you get it. But no matter who gets it, I'm gonna play that part.' "

Author Charles Portis chose Wallis for two reasons: he had liked some of Wallis's westerns, and Wallis upped the ante by also buying Portis's novel *Norwood*. "I bid $300,000 and Wallis bid $350,000," said Mike Wayne. "I was out-moneyed. I was paying my father a million against 10 percent, and he did *True Grit* for $500,000 [actually $750,000] against one third of the profits. And I asked him, 'Why are you taking less money from Hal Wallis than from me?' And he said, 'Because Wallis is a better producer than you, and I'll make more money with a third of the profits.' And he was right, but I didn't want to hear it."

Wallis was determined to make the movie, with John Wayne or without. (Some thought was given to Robert Mitchum or Walter Matthau for the role.) But Paramount, where Wallis made his pictures, was leery, especially at such a high cost for what was, after all, a western, not to mention giving Portis 2 percent of the gross in excess of $10 million. Wallis promptly took the project to Fox, which impelled Paramount to reconsider, which led Wallis to back out of Fox with apologies to Richard Zanuck.

For the part of Mattie Ross, Hal Wallis wanted Mia Farrow against Hathaway's preference for Sally Field. But Wallis felt Field's Flying Nun background (she was the eponymous main character of this television program) worked against her. Wallis ran through some other options including Jaclyn Smith ("Too pretty"), Jennifer O'Neill ("Tall, inexperienced"), and Geneviève Bujold ("if Mia Farrow turns it down").

Farrow had more or less agreed to take the part, then went off to London to do *Secret Ceremony* with Robert Mitchum and Elizabeth Taylor. She told Mitchum that her next picture would be for Henry Hathaway, and he told her to avoid the experience at all costs — Hathaway was a son of a bitch and she would hate him. Farrow then made the outlandish request that Wallis replace Hathaway with Roman Polanski. When Wallis rejected that idea outright, she bailed. Time was short; by this time, Wallis only had about a month before the start of production. Then he saw Kim Darby on a TV show and hired her quickly, paying her $75,000 — the same money he was paying Glen Campbell to play the Texas Ranger.

As production got closer, Wayne got jumpy — he didn't have a handle on how to play Rooster Cogburn. For one thing, there was the matter of the eyepatch. "I'm not gonna wear that patch on my eye," he told Henry Hathaway. "No way will I wear a patch."

He was, of course, nervous because the part was out of his comfort zone and hadn't been specifically tailored to his screen character by one of his in-house screenwriters. (Hal Wallis had assigned the script to Marguerite Roberts, a good writer married to the blacklisted John Sanford.)

Hathaway knew how to gentle the fractious old stallion. He wasn't simply going to tell Wayne what to do — only John Ford could do that. He got some clothes from wardrobe for Wayne to try on in front of a cheval mirror. Hanging on the hinge of the mirror was an eyepatch.

Wayne went through the fitting, eyeing the patch, saying nothing. When it was all over, he said, "You're a pretty smart son of a bitch. No way, no way."

At the second fitting, the patch was still there and Wayne was still calling Hathaway a smart son of a bitch. "The trouble with — you put that on and you can't see anything, and on a horse . . ."

Hathaway said, "Look, Duke, if you try it on, you'll see that instead of it being a patch, I've got black gauze there. You can see through it perfectly. It's almost as if there was no patch. On top of that, for the closer shots, I have a finer gauze. Not until I take a big close-up will I use one that's completely blank. So you can see at all times."

"You got gauze in there?" Wayne asked, gingerly putting on the patch. He turned and looked at himself in the mirror, then turned around to Hathaway. "Shall I try on a coat?" he said.

"He got to kind of like it," remembered Hathaway.

Hathaway wanted to make the picture a fairy tale, so certain key things needed to be elevated to physical perfection. "I looked for weeks, literally, for that natural arena surrounded by aspen trees where the final shoot-out takes place," remembered Hathaway. "I shot it from up high on purpose, so it looks like . . . knights jousting. . . . It worked. It was a fantasy that I couched in as realistic terms as possible."

For Charles Portis, the script was wrong, Wayne was wrong, and the locations were wrong. Portis thought that the dialogue needed rewriting because the book's dialogue — a lot of which had been transplanted into the script — was from the point of view of an old woman telling the story retrospectively. Portis also disliked the beautiful Colorado locations because it wasn't his native Arkansas, where he had set the story.

With the tact that endeared him to hundreds of actors, Hathaway thoughtfully responded to Portis's concerns: "In Arkansas, nobody's been ten miles from their house in their whole fucking lives. And when they see the picture they'll be happy to know that some part of Arkansas looks like that." Wallis and Hathaway stayed with Marguerite Roberts's adaptation.

Wayne had never been a conventional leading man, i.e., one dependent on his looks. He had at times been fatherly through most of the 1950s and 1960s, but *True Grit* would enable him to slide comfortably into the role of a feisty grandfather for the final stage of his career — men who were getting old, were admittedly past their prime, but still possessed of sufficient skills to do the job — any job.

Henry Hathaway asserted his authority on the first day of production, when he gathered the company around him and announced that there would be only two hard and fast rules: no discussions of politics, and no discussions of cattle. (Wayne's successful Hereford operation meant that he disputed the quality of any competing breed.)

It wasn't long before someone from Texas announced that longhorns were preferable to Herefords. Wayne thought that was a highly debatable point, but the debate was quickly cut off because Hathaway fired the Texan immediately.

Off the set, Hathaway was a charmer who drank good wine, knew art and architecture, lived in a gleaming white modern house, and could talk knowledgeably about nearly any subject. He had been married to his wife, Skip, for a long time, and his secret burden was her alcoholism.

But on the set, Hathaway remained a martinet who had developed an unholy hatred for plastic cups. In Hathaway's mind, a gust of wind might blow a plastic cup in front of the camera and ruin a take. Holding a plastic cup on a Hathaway set was like holding a live hand grenade on anybody else's.

"Old Henry would eat anybody's ass out," remembered stuntman Dean Smith, who was doubling Robert Duvall on the picture. Smith was covering for Duvall during the shot in which the wounded Duvall slowly slides off his horse. But

Smith caught his chaps on the saddle horn and got hung up.

"Even the horse was trying to help me," he remembered. "And you could hear Hathaway hollering for a thousand miles. Duke was laying there with a horse on his leg, and he looked at me and said, 'Pay no mind to that son of a bitch.'"

Wayne was used to Hathaway, but Robert Duvall wasn't, and Duvall had a large hunk of true grit in him. He didn't like being yelled at, and one day he blew sky high at Hathaway, screaming, "I can't do this goddamn scene like Martha Graham!"

"Duke was sitting there with his mouth open," remembered Dean Smith. "We all were. God, Bob erupted right in Hathaway's face. It was something!"

"You have to have discipline," Hathaway asserted near the end of his life in explaining his theory of running a set. "It's like a father with a big family. What do you do if a kid gets out of line? You've got to whip him or pretty soon all the kids are wild. Well, making a picture involves a mighty big family, and there's a lot of money involved, so I don't let things get very far out of line."

When Kim Darby started shooting the picture, she had just given birth to her first child and was simultaneously beginning divorce proceedings against her husband. Naturally, she was distracted. Hathaway hadn't wanted Darby, which was bad enough, but on top of that he didn't particularly like her.

"My problem with her was simple. She's not particularly attractive, so her book of tricks consisted mostly [of] being a little cute. All through the film, I had to stop her from acting funny, doing bits of business and so forth."

Complicating things was the fact that Darby was scared of horses; Hathaway had to use stunt-woman Polly Burson wearing a Darby mask for most of the picture. Darby estimated that she was actually on a horse for perhaps five minutes of the finished picture.

Surrounded by an angry director, a nervous actress, and the inexperienced Glen Campbell, Wayne took the reins between his teeth the same way Rooster Cogburn does in the climax of the film. "He was there on the set before anyone else and knew every line perfectly," said Kim Darby.

Joining the picture for seven days to play a doomed heavy was Dennis Hopper, who was taking a break from editing *Easy Rider*. Hopper had come to love the director who had driven him to distraction on *From Hell to Texas*. "I studied his films when I began directing, and I realized he was a very pure filmmaker." Working on *The Sons of Katie Elder* in Durango five years before had given Hopper the idea for *The Last Movie*. "For the movie, Henry had built fake facades in front of real houses! And people there were still riding horses, and they still wore guns. And I wondered what they would do when they walked past these facades once the film crew had gone." Hopper would eventually offer Hathaway the part of the director of the film within the film in *The Last Movie,* but his doctor wouldn't let him work at the high elevations in Peru. Hopper hired Sam Fuller instead.

Near the end of his own life, Hopper took pride in a couple of things: when Henry Hathaway died in 1985, Hopper went to the funeral of a man who had first been a tormentor, then a mentor. "I

711

was one of about seventeen people at the Rosary. He wasn't a beloved man, and he had outlived most of his peers."

That and one other thing: "In both of the films I made with John Wayne, I died in his arms."

Five weeks into the shoot, Wayne wrote Hal Wallis a letter from his quarters at the Lazy IG Motel in Montrose, Colorado. There was a general feeling that the film was working well and was going to be a hit, and Wayne had heard rumors of a possible reserved seat release. He asked Wallis to think about it before a summer general release. He closed by saying that he didn't really know much about distribution, but was throwing the idea out on behalf of a picture he believed in. "I'm sure this one is going to make those theater owners 'fill their hands.' "

The locations in Montrose were nearly six thousand feet above sea level, causing Wayne his usual difficulty with his breathing, but he didn't flinch, except for the day they were shooting his mounted charge against Lucky Ned Pepper's gang. For his close-up, with the reins between his teeth, twirling and cocking his rifle one-handed as he bore down on the outlaws, Wayne was not sitting on a horse, but on a saddle mounted on a camera car. The still man took some shots of Wayne on the contraption, and the actor stopped, leveling his rifle and the pistol at the still man and firing blanks at him.

"If they'd been real bullets the guy would have been dead," remembered Glen Campbell. "He got down, ran the guy down, took the camera, took the film out of it and called [him] numerous names. The still man was gone after that."

He was always going to be in the John Wayne

business, always going to be protecting the franchise.

At the end of the Montrose shoot, they shot the tag of the picture, the last scene in the cemetery with Wayne and Darby. They couldn't get the whole scene done in one day, and when they came back in the morning to finish, they found it had snowed during the night. Hathaway quickly decided to reshoot the entire scene to take advantage of the snow.

Gary Combs, a stuntman who was working the picture, said that Wayne was slower than he had been, because of the elevation, but he did the jump himself for the freeze frame that ends the picture.

"It's not an easy thing for an actor to do, to ride a jumping horse. But [stuntman Chuck] Hayward took his old sorrel horse Twinkletoes, and we made a low jump and we set the camera low and Duke ran the horse down there and jumped over the thing which was probably about two feet high. It was a nice jump. . . . He was game for anything."

By the time the picture got back to the studio for the interiors, Kim Darby was telling Hal Wallis she would never work for Hathaway again. John Wayne was another matter. "He was wonderful to work with, he really was," said Darby. "When you work with someone who's as big a star as he is . . . there's an unspoken thing that they sort of set the environment for the working conditions on the set and the feeling on the set. And he creates an environment that is very safe to work in. He's very supportive of the people around him and the people he works with, very supportive.

"He's really a reflection, an honest reflection, of what he really is. I mean, that's what you see on

713

the screen. He's simple and direct, and I love that in his work."

Patrick Wayne visited the set at Paramount. "It was a courtroom scene, and they were doing a close-up of my dad on the witness stand. Hathaway was going nuts, pacing around and screaming. I had brought a friend of my dad's over to the set, and Hathaway turned around and looked at us. 'I want silence on this set, and I don't care who the fuck you're related to!' he yelled. And neither of us was saying anything.

"My dad just rolled his eyes."

"Acting in the movie business is not limited to actors," observed George Kennedy. "Ford, Hathaway, Preminger, all those men were good directors, but they were also performers in their own right. They would do things for effect, to make them more important. Are they in charge? They better be, or I assure you that the actors will walk all over them."

Wayne gave Roger Ebert an interview during the production of *True Grit* and he told the critic that he thought the film was his first good part in twenty years. Ebert's eyebrows shot up, but Wayne persisted. "I've gotten damn few roles you could get your teeth into and develop a character. . . . I haven't had a role like [Rooster Cogburn] since *The Searchers.* And before that, maybe Sgt. Stryker [in *Sands of Iwo Jima*] or *She Wore a Yellow Ribbon,* another great Ford picture. Just look at *The Quiet Man.* Everybody was a character but me."

While the picture was shooting interiors at Paramount, there was a photo shoot featuring all the stars who were working on the lot: Barbra Streisand, Clint Eastwood, Goldie Hawn, along with Wayne. Kim Darby was sitting on the curb watching the photo shoot when Wayne saw her. "Hey kid," he said as he walked away from the shoot, lifted her off the curb and carried her over to the shoot, putting her in the center of the picture. "How wonderful was that?" she asked over forty years later.

True Grit began shooting on September 5, 1968, and finished on December 6, a couple of weeks over schedule (Darby got sick and missed three days, among other things) and a final cost of $4.5 million, $470,000 over budget. But nobody at the studio complained, because from the first rushes all the way through postproduction it was clear that they had a winner; the only question was how big the picture would be.

Wayne hovered over the picture, taking a look at a rough cut five weeks later, then dictating a memo to Wallis about the editing. He told the producer that he didn't think Kim Darby hit her stride until her character's meeting with Rooster. The quicker they could get to the scene with Lawyer Daggett after the death of Glen Campbell, the better off they'd be, and he thought the editor needed to give Strother Martin another two or three feet of his close-up in that scene. He was alarmed by the absence of the shot of Kim Darby uttering the film's title line when Rooster charges the four outlaws.

Mostly, he thought the picture had been edited too tightly: "I plead with you to lengthen the looks in two or three of the intimate scenes. . . . It's too big a picture to cut because of expediency, like a television show."

In May 1969, a few weeks before the picture was released, Wayne wrote to Marguerite Roberts thanking her for her "magnificent" screenplay, especially for the beautiful ending in the cemetery that she had devised in Portis's style. He closed by telling her, "Please write once in a while with me in mind."

When it was released in June 1969, even critics who had excoriated Wayne for *The Green Berets* realized that the actor had long since transcended categories and politics. "I never thought I would be able to take John Wayne seriously again," wrote Vincent Canby in *The New York Times.* "The curious thing about *True Grit* is that although he still is playing a variation on the self-assured serviceman he has played so many times in the past, the character that seemed grotesque in Vietnam fits into this frontier landscape, emotionally and perhaps politically too."

Not everybody liked Kim Darby — Stanley Kauffman said she was the dullest discovery since Millie Perkins in *The Diary of Anne Frank,* and Penelope Gilliatt in *The New Yorker* stupidly said that the final scene in the graveyard was "offensive . . . a coarse piece of opportunism."

Some critics felt that Wayne's performance was little more than expert self-parody, a tongue-in-cheek exaggeration of all the roles Wayne had played over the previous forty years. But those who had known him and worked with Wayne knew that Rooster Cogburn's charge into four heavily armed outlaws was a metaphor for the values of the actor playing him. "This was as factual a rendition of Duke's attitude toward life and death as a government report on the national deficit," observed Melville Shavelson. "Maybe more factual."

True Grit brought Wayne his second Academy

Award nomination as an actor. Wayne's relation-ship to the Academy Award was slightly touchy. As early as 1954, he was pointing out that he had been nominated only once, for *Sands of Iwo Jima.* "Usually, I attend the Academy Awards to be on hand in case one of my friends, who is not in town, wins an Oscar and I can accept it in his behalf," he said with a touch of asperity. "I have received awards for Gary Cooper and John Ford. No one — including me — ever has collected one for John Wayne."

He was up against strong competition (Richard Burton for *Anne of the Thousand Days,* Peter O'Toole for *Goodbye, Mr. Chips,* Dustin Hoffman and Jon Voight for *Midnight Cowboy*). Since Hoffman and Voight would cancel each other out, Wayne believed that Burton was the likely winner. When the two ran into each other before the Awards rehearsal, they agreed to have a private party at the Beverly Hills Hotel no matter who won.

After Barbra Streisand announced Wayne's name as the winner, he walked up to her and whispered in her ear, "Beginner's luck." Then he stepped to the microphone: "Wow. If I'd known that, I'd have put on that patch 35 years earlier. Ladies and gentleman, I'm no stranger to this podium. I've come up here and picked up these beautiful golden men before, but always for friends. One night I picked up two — one for Admiral John Ford, and one for our beloved Gary Cooper. I was very clever and witty that night — the envy of even Bob Hope. But tonight I don't feel very clever, very witty. I feel very grateful, very humble. And I owe thanks to many, many people. I want to thank the members of the

717

Academy. To all you people who are watching on television, thank you for taking such a warm interest in our glorious industry."

Back at the Beverly Hills Hotel, Richard Burton was depressed and made a gloomy prediction: "Thirty years from now, Peter O'Toole and I will still be appearing on talk shows plugging for our first Oscar." As a matter of fact, Burton would die fifteen years later without having won an Oscar, and thirty years later O'Toole would still be plugging, until he received an honorary Oscar in 2003.

Hours after the ceremony, Wayne banged on Burton's door, thrust the Oscar statue at him and said, "You should have this, not me." (Actually, Burton was robbed for *Who's Afraid of Virginia Woolf?* not *Anne of the Thousand Days,* as Wayne had been robbed for *Red River* and *The Searchers,* performances for which he wasn't even nominated. Turnabout is fair play.) The two men spent the rest of the night drinking. Burton found him "very drunk but, in his foul-mouthed way, very affable."

True Grit was the right movie at the right time. It washed away the ideological bitterness wrought by *The Green Berets* and presented Wayne apolitically, as a beloved anachronism, creaky but indomitable. It was a role he would play, with some variations, for the rest of his life — not a culture warrior, but an old man dredging up enough strength for one last hurrah.

Wayne had certainly done more subtle acting than Rooster Cogburn, but few of his performances were quite as enjoyable — the actor's pleasure transfers to the audience. And in the scene where he talks about his isolation from his family, the reason his only friends are a Chinese

718

man and an insolent orange cat named General Sterling Price, he reveals a sense of loss that was all the more touching because it was usually concealed by masculine bravado — the same combination of elements that made Frank Sinatra a great singer.

True Grit was an enormous commercial and critical success, earning rentals of slightly more than $14 million. As of September 1970, Wayne's profit percentage from *True Grit* had earned him another $788,000 on top of his salary. It would be Wayne's last massive commercial success, the reasons for which were contained in a brief exchange with a man from *The Hollywood Reporter.*

"Westerns are different today," said the reporter, referring to *The Good, the Bad and the Ugly* and *The Wild Bunch.*

"Not mine," said John Wayne.

The only negative experience relating to *True Grit* was Paramount's hasty decision to sell the film to television in September 1969, while it was still in the theaters and before Wayne got his Oscar. Joseph Hazen, Wallis's partner, and also a participant in the profits, wrote a steely letter to the studio pointing out that there was a good chance that Wayne would win an Academy Award for the picture, in which case *True Grit* would have a substantially higher broadcast value than would otherwise be the case.

"There is nothing to be gained by making a sale of *True Grit* now," Hazen wrote, further pointing out that the picture was going into profit only three months after release. "As 662/3% owners of the profits from the network telecast of *Grit,* it is our deep conviction and strong feeling that Paramount should neither offer nor sell *True Grit* to the networks at this time, and that it should definitely and positively await the results of the Academy Awards *before* it offers the picture for network showing."

But Paramount sold the picture anyway, for $1.1 million, about the same as the first-run prices for *The Sons of Katie Elder* and *Rosemary's Baby.* Wayne and Wallis were both incensed, and they continued to feel that way even after the license fee was increased to $1.54 million. Wallis, Hazen, and Wayne sued and eventually got a settlement for more money.

For those who knew Wayne, *True Grit* always had a special place. "Rooster Cogburn — that *was* Duke," said Cecilia deMille Presley. "He was the kindest teddy bear in the world. Unless you did something wrong. Then you best step back."

True Grit also contained the prism that would slightly distort the final stage of Wayne's career, in which he would be not only the star of his movies but their subject. With the marginal exception of *The Cowboys* and *The Shootist,* the succeeding Wayne films — *The Undefeated, Chisum, Big Jake,* etc. — were not movies with individual identities so much as they were John Wayne movies, in which the star's persona was identical from film to film. This presentation suited Wayne, suited his ego and his idea of himself, and it also suited his audience.

"For my father, the studio and the producers were not the boss," said Mike Wayne. "The fans were the boss. He felt he worked for his fans. He played bigoted, terrible guys, but bigoted, terrible guys with convictions. Every man he played had a code and never deviated from it during the film. If he was a mean son of a bitch, that's what he was. And he would never trick his audience. Surprise yes; trick, no."

That audience was extremely loyal, but it was also finite, and Wayne's refusal to try to expand it meant that it would stay finite, before it inevitably began to shrink.

The Undefeated had been purchased by Warner Bros. back in 1961. In the mid-1960s, there was a screenplay by the old hand Casey Robinson for director Henry King, but Warners sold the property to Fox, who ordered up a rewrite from James Lee Barrett. The picture was expensive — $7 million — partially because of its pricey co-star Rock Hudson, but coming on the heels of *True Grit* it seemed like a good bet.

Wayne's co-star Lee Meriwether was lodged in a hotel in Baton Rouge, when most of the other major actors had houses. Marian McCargo found out and invited her to stay with her in her rented house. The two women threw a party for the cast and crew, which involved two days of cooking. Everybody pitched in — stuntman Hal Needham cooked chicken livers. Wayne ended up in the kitchen with a few friends — Ed Faulkner and Dobe Carey.

After everybody else had gone home, Rock Hudson stayed behind to help McCargo and Meriwether clean up. The women were washing dishes, Hudson was drying, and Wayne was sitting at the kitchen table finishing off his drink. With the dishes finished, Hudson said, "C'mon, Duke." Wayne rose and staggered a bit. Hudson steadied him and the two went through the front door. When Wayne staggered again, Hudson put his arm around Wayne's shoulder and the two men walked to the end of the block, while Meriwether watched and wished she had had a camera.

Hudson is the most famous example of a closeted movie star, and he was still working at it. Meriwether remembered that Hudson was "the best dancer ever," and came over to her at a party. "Are you happy?" he asked.

"Yes, I am."

"Are you happy at home?"

"Why, yes I am," she replied.

"He was flirting with me," remembered Meriwether. "I honestly didn't know he was gay."

Wayne did know, and was flummoxed by the vagaries of sexual identity. "Look at that face," he said admiringly to his daughter Aissa, who was visiting the set. "What a waste of a face on a queer. You know what I could have done with that face?" To someone else he would say about Hudson, "It never bothered me. Life's too short. Who the hell cares if he's queer? The man plays great chess."

The gay man flirted; the straight man didn't. "It was all business," says Meriwether. "Duke was a journeyman film man. He was very relaxed and didn't need to rev up for a scene. When it was time to act, he just started acting. He knew what he wanted to do with a scene, and he did it.

"It was a fantastic lesson in film acting. Natural, comfortable, easy. He was comfortable in his own skin and he didn't have anything to prove. He tended to be the same take to take, but if something was thrown at him, he could go with it. He didn't ad-lib much, but he could adapt; he was flexible."

On the set, someone asked Wayne the secret of acting. "Listening," he said. He was as good as his word. "He didn't show you he was listening," says

722

Meriwether, "he just listened."

In spite of the goodwill on the set and a pleasant atmosphere, *The Undefeated* didn't return its investment, running up a $2.4 million loss for Fox. Part of the reason was a sequence involving a stampede of horses. Horses are generally easy to control in a staged stampede because they're run toward a corral and they're usually not bright enough to head off on their own. But on *The Undefeated,* the stampede was staged with three thousand horses. "When we got through shooting the stampede, we had 2,940," said William Clothier. "Somewhere we lost 60 horses. . . . Those damn horses took off like goats. We had horses all over Mexico."

The first time Andrew Fenady saw John Wayne was in 1951. He was newly arrived in Hollywood and drove around town to see all the studios — "Even Monogram. I was wondering if I would ever get into any of those places." One day on Barham Boulevard, right by Warner Bros., a large man was walking across the street against the light and was nearly run down by Fenady.

"You dumb bastard, watch where you're going," yelled John Wayne.

Years later, after Fenady had hits on television such as *The Rebel,* the editor Otho Lovering came to Fenady's doorway with John Wayne in tow. "Ya see, Duke, there it is," said Lovering, pointing to a large poster of Wayne as Hondo with Sam the dog, curving down from the ceiling to the floor of Fenady's office. Wayne nodded and said, "That's one of my favorite pictures. It comes back to me in three years."

The two men were favorably disposed toward

one another, so Fenady began working on a story based on the career of the cattle baron John Chisum while Wayne made *Hellfighters, True Grit,* and *The Undefeated.*

When Fenady was finished, he had both a ten-page outline and a forty-page treatment. Mike Wayne read the ten pages, as did Tom Kane, the Batjac story editor. Both liked it, and Fenady was told, "Duke wants to talk to you about it. Tell him the story. He doesn't want to read it."

So Fenady trooped onto the *Wild Goose* and began telling the story. "Mind if I smoke?" asked Fenady. "Not if you blow it my way," said Wayne. After five or six minutes of Fenady's recitation, Wayne stood up and walked out of the salon, saying "Turn 'em loose." Mike whacked Fenady on the shoulder. "You're in," he said. "He wants you to do it."

Chisum is a typical example of Wayne's producing style in the final phase of his career. Fox signed an agreement to make the picture in July 1968, but the preliminary budget came in at $5.3 million instead of the agreed-upon $4.5 million. Mike Wayne cut $450,000 out of the budget, but Fox passed anyway. This was in July 1969, and *The Undefeated* wasn't released until October, so Fox's lack of enthusiasm couldn't have been based on that film's failure.

Richard Zanuck told Mike that Fox's situation had changed considerably in the year since they had made the deal — New York was giving him a hard time about making deals on which Fox had only a marginal chance of making money, and things just generally didn't look good.

Luckily, Warner Bros. had been happy with the financial results of *The Green Berets,* and Mike moved *Chisum* there in a matter of weeks. *Chisum* went into production in October. Mike Wayne and Andrew Fenady made *Chisum* for $4.5 million on a forty-five-day schedule. $1 million of the budget was apportioned to Wayne, with Fenady getting $100,000 and a percentage for his script and production. The picture came in five days under schedule. "It was a textbook production," said Fenady. "We made a lot of money."

Robert Mitchum's son Christopher was acting in the picture, and Wayne's affection for the father rubbed off on the son. One day, Wayne rode up to Christopher Mitchum and said, "You know, you should have played Billy the Kid." (Geoffrey Deuel was playing the part.)

Wayne soon invited Mitchum to play chess, but the younger man couldn't believe what he was seeing. "He had huge hands," remembered Mitchum, "and for the first couple of days we were playing, he'd reach out to move a piece with his fingers, and his thumb would slide a rook over. And I'm looking at this thinking, 'My God, the man's cheating at chess.' I didn't know what to do. And of course, he was creaming me because he was getting two moves to every one of mine."

Mitchum complained to Ed Faulkner, who explained, "Tell him to knock that crap off. He's just playing with you."

"Just like that?" asked the queasy Mitchum.

"Yeah, just tell him to knock it off."

The next time Wayne moved a rook with his thumb, Mitchum swallowed and said, "Excuse me, Duke, but you're cheating."

"Well, I was wondering when you were going to say *something,*" Wayne said. "Set 'em up. We'll play again." With Wayne reduced to one move at a time, the games got competitive. When Howard Hawks visited the set, Wayne introduced him to Mitchum and suggested that Hawks consider him for a part in a western the two men were planning.

Most of the offscreen entertainment on the picture was supplied by Forrest Tucker, who was playing the heavy and had a high director's chair outfitted with a couple of saddlebags. In one of the saddlebags was a fifth of Ballantine's, which Tucker would start drinking at breakfast and finish by lunch. After lunch, he turned to the other saddlebag, which had a bottle of vodka or gin. That would be empty by the time the company broke for the day. In spite of such Homeric consumption, nobody ever saw Tucker drunk.

As always, Wayne was exuberant, although there was one flash of rue. The mornings are cold in Durango, and when Wayne and Tucker had to finish shooting a fight scene left over from the day before in very chilly weather, Wayne looked at Tucker and said, "Aren't we getting a little old for this?"

Fenady noticed a couple of displays of temper. "He was not nuts about Teamsters, and one time he blew up because something wasn't there and he blamed the Teamsters. And he blew up at Forrest Tucker once. In spite of his drinking, Tucker never missed a line. But Duke got mad at him because Tucker went to the assistant and pointed out that he wasn't scheduled to work for the next six days. He wanted to take three or four days off. The assistant said OK, and I said 'No, we might need him.' "

Tucker wanted the time off to go to Chicago and make a lucrative personal appearance, but it might have thrown the production off for one day. Wayne was adamant and confronted Tucker, who had been a friend since *Sands of Iwo Jima.* "Are you a professional, or are you not? You signed on to do this show. We're shooting Saturday. *You're* shooting on Saturday. *I'm* shooting on Saturday. We as a *company* are shooting on Saturday. Because that's what we all signed up to do." Tucker worked on Saturday.

Andrew Fenady noticed Wayne's way of reading a script: "He only read the dialogue, never the descriptions. Descriptions he skimmed." The first time Wayne opened the script, his eyes fell on a line another character had about Chisum: "He thinks his boots is filled with something special." Wayne didn't like the line, so out it went. After that, Fenady was afraid Wayne would run rough-shod over the dialogue, or bring in another writer, but he found the actor very respectful of good dialogue, and even given to removing unnecessary lines from his character.

"There's a scene where Chisum is opening up a general store. Someone says that the next thing is to open a bank. 'Why not,' was the line, 'all it takes is money, and I got plenty.' And he said, 'McFenady' — he always called me McFenady — 'I don't need to say that.' " And he took himself out of a scene . . . entirely. He was the most gener-ous actor."

Fenady noticed the easy working relationship with Andrew McLaglen. "When Duke worked with Burt Kennedy, it was 'Don't put the camera there. Put it here. *Here!*' And it had been the same thing on *McLintock!,* Andy's first picture with Duke. But by the time we made *Chisum,* there was never a strained word between the two.

Chisum was really an easy shoot. And Duke told me, "McFenady, this is the most pleasant picture I've ever made."

One morning Mike Wayne gave the company a 9 A.M. call, which meant the crew call was 8 A.M. As usual, Mike drove to the location with McLaglen and Fenady. It was 8 A.M., the sun was up, but there was only one lonely, large figure standing in the middle of the set. He wasn't happy.

"Who is the smart son of a bitch who gave a nine o'clock call?" Wayne demanded, looking right at his son.

"I did," said Mike Wayne.

"Well, tomorrow, it will be 8 A.M."

"When that sun broke, he wanted to start shooting," said Mike Wayne. Habits left over from Monogram and Republic persisted.

Besides his $1 million salary, Wayne was getting 10 percent of the gross, plus 15 percent of the gross TV sales — a very rich deal, commensurate with the great box office and critical success of *True Grit*. Ben Johnson got $30,000, Forrest Tucker $75,000, and Bruce Cabot $17,500. *Chisum* was a success, although not compared to *True Grit*. By 1974, it had earned world rentals of $9.6 million.

Wayne and Howard Hawks had been talking about another western for a good six months, and Hawks found financing from Cinema Center, a production arm for CBS. When the cast and crew arrived in Cuernavaca for the location work for *Rio Lobo,* Hawks had about eighteen pages of material. "It wasn't a script," said Ed Faulkner, "it was a fragment. Hawks did a lot of the writing down in Cuernavaca, although I'm sure he had some collaborators." This wasn't unusual for Hawks — he had made a lot of good pictures writing a day or two in front of shooting — but he had passed the point where he could pull off that particular high-wire act.

The altitude at Cuernavaca was difficult for Wayne, and Chuck Roberson was called upon to do almost any shot involving action. Otherwise, he was the same old Duke. The young actor Peter Jason remembered his first day on the set, when Wayne greeted forty Mexicans, walking up to each of them and shaking their hand, greeting them by name. "It was very impressive to watch the real guys do it. As opposed to today, when nobody even knows who the hell's on the set."

Rio Lobo began to go off the rails fairly quickly, and Hawks couldn't bring himself to admit that he might be the problem. "Wayne had a hard time getting on and off his horse," he complained. "He can't move like a big cat the way he used to. He has to hold his belly in. He's a different kind of person."

Actually, Wayne was in better condition than his director. One Monday morning, the company was ready to shoot but there was no Hawks. They scoured the set, and everywhere else they could think of. Finally, someone went to his hotel and found the director relaxing by the pool. He had lost track of time and thought it was Sunday.

In March 1970, just a few weeks into *Rio Lobo,* Wayne had to fly home — Molly Morrison had died at the age of eighty-one. She had always been formidable, and she didn't get any less so as she aged. Bob Morrison would die that year, too, from lung cancer. On the ride over to visit his brother in the hospital, Wayne railed to his children, "You

729

know what your uncle did? He's got a tube in his throat, and the stupid sonofabitch is inhaling cigarettes through *that*."

Wayne soldiered on. His energy was good — Dean Smith said he was "still as tough as an old boot" — and he still loved to play chess. Near the end of every shooting day, he'd say to Ed Faulkner, "Doing anything tonight?" If the answer was no, he'd say "We'll have dinner and play chess."

Some nights, a small group of actors that included Faulkner and Chris Mitchum would be invited to dinner at Wayne's rented house. The company had a 6 A.M. call, so the actors had to get up at five, but Wayne would say, "Well, why don't we go up to the Tropicana and see the girlie show?" Soon, there would be three cars lined up to transport the actors to the Tropicana, where tables would have been cleared in advance, surrounded, as Chris Mitchum remembered, "by 30 glaring Mexicans . . . who'd been thrown off their tables." The group wouldn't get back to their rooms until three or four in the morning — just in time to shower, shave, and go to work.

In June 1970 Wayne received an invitation to go to Las Vegas for a benefit that featured the astronauts that had landed on the moon. The astronauts had been asked whom they wanted to meet, and their answer was: John Wayne.

Wayne told Bob Shelton that he'd go if Shelton would go with him, and the entire twenty-four-hour experience gave Shelton a ground-level view of just what it was like to be John Wayne. By the time the benefit rolled around, *Rio Lobo* was shooting in Hollywood. Shelton went there with an overnight bag and at the end of the day they got on a private jet to Vegas. The plane was supposed to land and taxi to the private terminal. "Don't worry," said the pilot, "nobody knows you're coming, and we're taking you to the private terminal."

The plane taxied over to the corner of the hangar where Shelton observed thousands of people clustered around, including some on top of the hangar — a mob scene. Wayne wasn't appalled — "he expected it," remembered Shelton, and he gave Shelton some of the autographed cards he always carried, so Shelton could pass them out.

At the Frontier Hotel, the beautiful people were out in force and also mobbed Wayne. If he was uncomfortable or in an awkward moment, he would pull his earlobe, which was the signal for Shelton to come over and say "The governor wants to speak to you."

Glen Campbell was appearing at the hotel, and Wayne said he'd like to take a peek at the show. Campbell was in the middle of his set, but his conductor told him who was in the audience, and Campbell introduced Wayne from the stage. The lights went up and people swarmed Wayne. The lights went back down and Shelton watched with amazement at people crawling down the aisle on their hands and knees to get an autograph.

Wayne had made Shelton promise to get him on the 7 A.M. flight because it was imperative that he be back at the Newport Beach house by 8 A.M. It wasn't business, it was Pilar. "If I don't get there in time, it's a death sentence," he grumbled to Shelton.

Wayne and Shelton were given a large suite with a bedroom on either side. They finally got to bed about four in the morning, but not before Shelton left a 5 A.M. wake-up call.

The call woke up Shelton and he went into Wayne's room to rouse him. He just followed the clothes — a shoe, another shoe, pants, then underwear. Wayne had simply shed his clothes on the way to bed. With one hour of sleep, Wayne bounced right up and the two men went off to breakfast. They made the flight, and Wayne was back home in time to avoid domestic unpleasantness.

The interiors for *Rio Lobo* were shot at Studio Center in Hollywood, the renamed Republic Studios lot. Someone asked Wayne where his dressing room had been in the old days and he snorted, "Dressing room? I didn't have a dressing room. I had a hook."

Joining the company for a bit part was George Plimpton, then at the height of his success as an Everyman attempting fish-out-of-water experiences, which he memorialized in books, or, in this case, a TV documentary. Wayne enjoyed teasing the writer by mispronouncing his name, or referring to his popular book *Paper Lion* as *Paper Tiger.* Plimpton observed the care with which Wayne made a movie — his pleasure in being on the set at all times instead of hiding in his trailer. And he also overheard, as he was meant to, some of Wayne's oft-stated political views, which struck him as paradoxical. How could a man who listened so intently, who was a first-class bridge player, a very good chess player, a man with an obviously fine mind — Plimpton listened to Wayne recite John Milton from memory — how could that man's politics be so rigid and simplistic?

The movie industry was much on Wayne's mind. He gave an interview to *The Hollywood Reporter* in which he vented his pessimism about the industry. "The Jack Warners, Harry Cohns and Louis B. Mayers were men with a certain integrity, whether for business reasons or not, and they cared about the future of the industry," he said. "Now we're afflicted with fast-buck producers cashing in on pornography and depravity, and there's no leadership to stop them."

He was convinced that the movie industry as it was constituted in the early 1970s was a house of cards. "I see pay-TV in the not so distant future and this, I think, is how it will work as far as those who make it are concerned: At the moment, we know our feature films will show in theaters for from one to a couple of years, and then, after quite a while, they go on the air. But pay-TV is going to work differently. We'll do the feature films, all right, but we'll pull them out of the theaters in three to six months, hold them for another three months, then show them on pay-TV. And it won't be the tiny screens we show them on now.

"See that over there?" he said, pointing to a movie screen of about three feet by five feet. "That's what's coming, you mark my words, and it'll be the death blow of dirty X-rated pictures, which have just about run their cycle anyway." Except for overlooking home video, and the human appetite for pornography, he got it right, up to and including the time element.

When it was released in December 1970, *Rio Lobo* proved to be flaccidly written and shot, shakily acted by almost all of the supporting cast — a careless old man's movie capable of lowering the spirits of the most ardent auteurist. Some idea of the messiness of the enterprise can be gauged by the casting of a Mexican actor to play a Confederate officer, which is explained by giving the character a French mother and a Mexican father from New Orleans.

Structurally, it's a mess — the film's first half hour has almost no relation to the rest of the film — and even William Clothier's camerawork is perfunctory. The only charming moment passes almost unnoticed — a wanted poster for one Hondo Lane brightens up a sheriff's office.

"*Rio Lobo* doesn't look like a Hawks film," wrote critic John C. Mahoney. "It hasn't the relationships of a Hawks film. It hasn't the sound of a Hawks film, the wit, mocking, contrapuntal and over-lapping dialogue. . . . Nor does it have the cast and performances, having an even poorer ensemble of actors than those corralled for *Red Line 7000*."

The film's only attributes were a good opening sequence of a runaway boxcar, and Wayne, who knew the picture was terrible. "*Rio Lobo* is bad," he admitted to one writer off the record. "Hawks made the mistake of doing too much of the writing." He went on to remark on Hawks's habit of playing off writers against each other. "Both Ford and Hawks could direct . . . but Hawks couldn't write. He never should have tried. That was pretty obvious by *Rio Lobo*. He'd become sort of aloof and I guess there have been too many showings in Paris of his films. He's feeling that he's a cult now."

Rio Lobo brought in $4.25 million in domestic rentals against a cost of $5 million — in twentieth place for movies that year. "Anybody else would have made it, [it] wouldn't even have been released in LA," said Tom Kane. "It would be Rod Cameron [and it would play] somewhere down in Sweetwater, Texas."

John Ford was now retired. Every once in a while, he'd make an appearance at one of the colleges around town, as with a January 1970 turn at USC. The future screenwriter John Sacret Young was there, and he remembered that Ford "looked like a big man who had lost his bigness. Age and ill health had eaten it away."

Ford called the camera "this wonderful looking monster," and told the kids to "forget about it. Get a good cameraman and work with the people. Shoot their eyes. You can express more with the eyes than with anything else." Someone asked him about French cinema, and he grumbled, "All they do is get in and out of cars." He said that Dudley Nichols and he had the same idea about scripts — that there should be a "paucity of dialogue."

"In just his choice of words there is the flavor he imbued," wrote Young in his notes. "This self-created image, now deeply ingrained, of a big, slouching roughneck of an Irish New Englander slipping in the word 'paucity.' It is funny and more."

Five months later, Young attended the annual Memorial Day service at the Field Photo Chapel, which had been moved to the grounds of the Motion Picture Home. It is a small white building with four pillars in front and an antique pulpit. There are nine rows of benches and a sign that says, "Here dead lie we/Because we did not choose/To live and shame the land/From which we sprung," followed by the names of the men of the Field Photo Service who had died in the war.

Ford was in uniform, with seven and a half rows

of bars. He was smoking a Tiparillo, but put it aside as Ray Kellogg helped him put on his sword. "Every year the same sword," Ford muttered.

Mike was making deals. Wayne was continuing to spread himself very thin and was enjoying every minute of it. But when he was with his family, he was totally there.

"Because he worked so much, and he worked with my dad, it was different than with kids whose grandparents grew up around the corner," said Michael Wayne's daughter Alicia McFarlane. "It was like he was out of town a lot of the time. We would see him if he was in town, or around the holidays — Thanksgiving and Christmas. Occasionally he would surprise us; our house was in Toluca Lake, and he would drop by with the biggest box of candy I've ever seen."

McFarlane remembered him as "a wonderful grandfather, a grab-you-and-throw-you-up-in-the-sky grandfather. It's a credit to my parents that we didn't have a big concept of who he was, or his impact. To us, he was our grandfather. We went a few times to visit him on the set, and we figured out what business he was in, but we were kids — we weren't watching old movies.

"I have a great photo of the two of us sharing an Oreo cookie — he's handing me the part with the icing on it. He was a doting grandfather, and he didn't mind having kids around the house — he already had dogs."

Alicia loved to sneak into her grandfather's office when nobody was around and look at his collection of kachina dolls, then browse through the hundreds of books that were neatly lined up on the shelves. Wayne's library was unfocused, but with an emphasis on his business. He had first editions of *The Searchers* and *True Grit,* novels by Zane Grey, stories by Bret Harte, coffee-table books of Frederic Remington and Tom Phillips.

There were conservative-oriented books on politics, pop fiction (*Jaws, Centennial*) and some very un-pop literary fiction: Nabokov's *Lolita.* There were books on Hollywood westerns, a signed copy of Darryl Zanuck's biography, unsigned copies of books about Spencer Tracy, Montgomery Clift, and Marilyn Monroe, as well as compatriots such as Raoul Walsh and Edward Dmytryk. He had a surprising taste for Tolkien, with hardcovers of all the *Lord of the Rings* novels. His musical tastes centered around Frank Sinatra, Dean Martin, Peggy Lee, Doris Day.

Mike and Gretchen's son Chris was born prematurely in 1967 and had to have open heart surgery when he was five. He would occasionally mention to his grandfather that he wished he was bigger, so he could play football. "You're healthy," Wayne would say. "That's the main thing."

"The house in Newport was a neat place to be," said Alicia, "and it was a pure delight to go there. Pilar would say, 'We're all going to the toy store!' Looking back as an adult, it must have been a pain in the neck, but Pilar was great; she spoiled us."

If the grandchildren were at the house, the evening's entertainment would consist of a double feature — the first picture was for the kids, the last for the adults. Alicia felt she'd finally come of age when she was allowed to watch the second feature: *Le Mans,* with Steve McQueen.

"My grandfather made this movie called *Trouble Along the Way,* where he had a little singsong in his voice when he talked to the little girl. That's the way I remember him talking to me when I was little. When I got bigger, it was 'How are you doing in school? How are your grades?' I was a very average Joe in school, so I didn't look forward to those questions. He very definitely wanted to know what was going on in our lives."

Alicia's favorite memory of her grandfather involved a huge trampoline Wayne installed in his yard. "All of us were out there, and he came out and got on the trampoline and started jumping high into the sky! He was so much bigger than the rest of us, so he went higher than we could. All of his kids and grandkids were there, popping up into the sky, and he was right in the middle of them, going higher than anybody else."

About this time, Wayne began to combat what he saw as his younger children's lack of interest in the family. He decreed that dinner would be at 5 P.M. every day, with mandatory attendance. But the kids were teenagers, didn't want to be there, and even Pilar seemed to resent the command performance. "Asking about our lives, he'd allow us to answer, then he'd wind up issuing lectures," remembered Aissa. He was harder on Ethan than the girls, and hit him once or twice for lying, when all the girls would get was a lecture.

But Ethan was a boy, and a chance for Wayne to make up for the mistakes he'd made with Mike and Pat, as well as a chance to mitigate the mortality he felt gaining on him. "He's mine and I want to be with him," he said of Ethan. "He'll be 14 before I know it and something happens [then]. They start to drift away and they don't come back until their thirties. At 30 they realize what father-hood is. My oldest boys are in their 30s now and they've come back. But with Ethan I won't be here when he's 30, so I've got to love him now."

The girls tended to get a pass. For Christmas 1972, nine months after Aissa turned sixteen, Wayne gave her a yellow Porsche 914. She lent the car to a boyfriend, who wrecked it. She returned home at dawn to find Wayne in his pajamas, pacing in the driveway, furious because he thought she'd be home by 2 A.M. Wayne gave her the silent treatment for a day, then came into her bedroom. "If I gave you what you deserved," he said, "I'd have to ground you forever. So let's just forget it."

CHAPTER TWENTY-TWO

Wayne's TV appearances began increasing in the 1970s. In June 1971, he went to Monument Valley to shoot a CBS special called *The American West of John Ford.* He wasn't happy about the fact that he was only paid scale, but he did it because Ford's grandson, Dan, was producing the show and Ford asked him to appear. It was Ford's last trip to the location he defined in the world's consciousness. As the two men reminisced about Ward Bond, Ford said, "Oh God, rest his soul. The only bad thing about this trip is that I miss him."

Bob Shelton was putting together a promotional film for Old Tucson when he heard Wayne was in Monument Valley shooting the documentary. Shelton got a small crew together and flew over. Shelton and his film crew handed over some prepared questions they wanted Wayne to respond to. He took a look at them, then threw them over his shoulder.

"Where's the camera?" Wayne asked. And then he rattled off five minutes of footage, extolling the benefits and history and pleasures of Old Tucson and all the great pictures he had been lucky enough to make there.

"We got in the plane and flew home," said Shelton. "I would have to say that John Wayne was what every young boy wants to be like, and what every old man wishes he had been."

Among Wayne's appearances were spots on the popular *Rowan & Martin's Laugh-In,* also done for scale — $210. He liked Paul Keyes, the head writer, who also wrote for Dean Martin's TV show. (For one *Laugh-In* appearance he dressed up as the Easter Bunny; another involved him holding up a red, white, and blue daisy and reciting, "The sky is blue, the grass is green, get off your butt and be a Marine.")

In late November 1970, Wayne hosted *Swing Out, Sweet Land,* written and produced by Keyes and executive-produced by Bill Harbach, whom Wayne had first met while shooting *They Were Expendable.*

The show ran ninety minutes, cost Anheuser-Busch $1.4 million, and serves as a time capsule of a special kind of show business hell. Lorne Greene plays George Washington, Rowan and Martin are the Wright Brothers, Lucille Ball is the Statue of Liberty, Dan Blocker is an Indian who sells Manhattan to Michael Landon's Peter Minuit, and Bob Hope and Ann-Margret entertain the troops at Valley Forge.

Dean Martin plays Eli Whitney — cotton *gin* — get it? The Doodle-town Pipers sing a choral version of the Declaration of Independence, there are laugh tracks for the comedy bits, and Wayne played himself as an *Our Town*–style narrator who framed the show and introduced the scenes.

NBC handed the show to Harbach and his partner Nick Vanoff, who were already producing

741

the highly successful *Hollywood Palace* series. "It was the biggest show we ever did," remembered Harbach. "We shot for two weeks, and there were hardly any problems. We told [Wayne] our ideas for the show and he said 'That sounds fine.'

"Wayne was a pro. He'd ask, 'What time tomorrow, Boss?' and I'd tell him and he'd be there fifteen minutes early. He was very outgoing, and had this deep enthusiasm under the skin. Anything you needed him to do, he did. Of course, he was to the right of Charlemagne."

The trade papers found the show mawkish — "a star-studded, often awkward, seldom amusing extravaganza . . . a massive name-dropping mélange [with] a few bright spots," wrote the critic for *Variety*. But the ratings were huge; NBC estimated that about 77 million people watched the show, once again proving Wayne's command of his audience, as well as his knack for seamlessly spreading his brand.

An ancillary reason for the show's existence was revealed in the credits: the copyright for the show was held by John Wayne.

As with many politically committed people, seeing the nation move in the opposite direction from his own orientation had a residual impact on Wayne. Although he talked about how much he hated politics and politicians — his preferred phrase was "fucking politicians" — he obsessively returned to the subject of the deadly path America was on. At the same time, he was at pains to refute the prevailing image of himself as an intellectual troglodyte. "I came into this business from the University of Southern California, where I was taking a pre-law course. I had gone to Glendale

742

High School, from which I graduated with a 94 average. I could say, 'isn't' as well as 'ain't.' "

On college professors: "It takes 15 years of kissing somebody's backside for a professor to get a chair somewhere and then he's a big shot in a little world, passing his point of view on to a lot of impressionable kids. He's never really had to tough it out in this world of ours, so he has a completely theoretical view of how it should be run and what we should do for our fellow man."

On Vietnam: "I would think somebody like Jane Fonda and her idiot husband would be terribly ashamed and saddened that they were a part of causing us to stop helping the South Vietnamese. Now look what's happening. They're getting killed by the millions. Murdered by the millions. How the hell can she and her husband sleep at night?"

On government: "I don't want any handouts from a benevolent government. I think government is naturally the enemy of the individual, but it's a necessary evil, like, say motion picture agents are. I do not want the government . . . to insure me anything more than normal security."

On Manifest Destiny: "When we came to America, there were a few thousand Indians over millions of miles, and I don't feel we did wrong in taking this great country away from these people, taking their happy hunting ground away. We were progressive, and we were doing something that was good for everyone."

On identity politics: "The hyphenated American is ridiculous. But that's what we have to put up with. I think that any person that's in the United States is better off here than they would be where they came from."

On the women's movement: "I have always felt

743

that women should get exactly the same salary for the same work that a man would. And I assume and presume that is gradually coming to pass. Mainly because women have been individual enough to step out and become lawyers and do these different things.

"But I think it's ridiculous for the studio to have a woman be a grip on a set. There are certain standards of hard work that are expected of a grip that a woman can't cut. That doesn't mean that she couldn't direct the picture if she had the talent to do it. But I mean, there's a lot of men that couldn't go in and be a grip, because they're not capable of the physical effort required to perform that job."

On Richard Nixon: "The Cronkites and the Sevareids and the rest of you guys are out to get him just because a bunch of jerk underlings acted stupidly. The President is too great a man to be mixed up in anything like Watergate."

On the dark night of the soul: "There's that hour when you go to bed at night, before you sleep, when you're alone. That's when you have time to think over your past and that helps you shape up your attitudes toward people, toward situations. If you lose your self-respect, you've lost everything."

The simmering irritation that some of the public felt about Wayne's social and political opinions came to a boil when Wayne sat down for an interview with *Playboy* that was published in May 1971: "With a lot of blacks, there's quite a bit of resentment along with their dissent, and possibly rightfully so. But we can't all of a sudden get down on our knees and turn everything over to the leadership of the blacks. I believe in white supremacy until the blacks are educated to a point of responsibility. I don't believe in giving authority and positions of leadership and judgment to irresponsible people."

That was just for starters. Carl Foreman and Robert Rossen had done things "that were detrimental to our way of life" by making *High Noon* ("the most un-American thing I've ever seen in my whole life") and *All the King's Men* respectively, and he would never regret "having helped run Foreman out of the country." The men that gave him faith in his country were men like Spiro Agnew. Douglas MacArthur "would have handled the Vietnam situation with dispatch."

Some of the *Playboy* interview was funny — after comparing modern producers to whores, he said, "Why doesn't that son of a bitch Darryl Zanuck get himself a striped silk shirt and learn how to play the piano? Then he could work in any room in the house." But the truculence overwhelmed the humor.

Wayne had voiced many, if not all, of these opinions in print before, but not in the pages of *Playboy* at the height of its influence. The year before, he had told *Reader's Digest* that "the way to stop [Vietnam] is to call Russia's Kosygin and say that the next time a Russian-made gun is turned against us, we'll drop a bomb right on him. They tell me everything isn't black and white. Well, I say why the hell not?"

Wayne loosed his most breathtaking blast of imperialist rhetoric in the not exactly obscure pages of *Life* a few months after the *Playboy* article: "Your generation's frontier should have been Tanganyika. It's a land with eight million blacks and it could hold 60 million people. We could feed India with the food we produced in

Tanganyika. It could have been a new frontier for any American or English or French kid with a little gumption. Another Israel! But the do-gooders had to give it back to the Indians."

The *Playboy* interview inflamed the bruises left by *The Green Berets,* although it was both an amplification and a distortion of Wayne's feelings. While Wayne didn't care for the 1964 Civil Rights Act — he felt it violated the rights of property owners — he blamed white supremacists for the civil rights movement. The Fifteenth Amendment, he believed, clearly gave everybody the right to vote. "If blacks had been allowed to vote all along," he told Mary St. John, "we wouldn't have all this horseshit going on. George Wallace is part of the goddamn problem, not the solution."

The novelist P. F. Kluge, who wrote the cover story for *Life* that contained the inflammatory quotes about Africa, found something other than his expectations, something other than an imperialist dinosaur. "My strategy for the story was whether or not the end of the west meant the end of his career," Kluge remembered. "And I found a level of articulation that I had not expected. The description he gave me about Monument Valley rose to the level of elegy, which I wasn't sure he had in him. There were depths of memory in him that surprised me. All of those stars of that generation had been interviewed to death and pawed over and worn smooth. His ability to articulate and come up with something fresh surprised me."

The interview was done on a transcontinental flight from New York to Los Angeles, with another day at Wayne's house in Newport Beach. Kluge was delighted to find that the local Budweister distributor had supplied Wayne with a tap, and

746

the two men started drinking, which is when Wayne sailed into politics.

"He was really invested in his politics. I had to acknowledge that this was not bullshit, this was from the heart. And he had a need to talk about it; it wasn't a potted right-wing speech that he had given before. He was generating feeling when he spoke to me.

"I liked him. Kind of. Yeah. But there was a considerable gap of disagreement there. And you didn't know how far you could go before you pissed him off."

The hangover from the *Playboy* interview lasted for decades. A year after it was published, Wayne was made the grand marshal of the Rose Bowl Parade. The USC *Daily Trojan* opined that the selection of Wayne was "a gross insult to Blacks, to American Indians and to Americans of any race who believe in equality. John Wayne is a blatant racist."

The pot was kept bubbling when a reporter for *The Advocate* asked Wayne about gay rights. He clearly hadn't been expecting the question, because he paused to think. "I think gay people . . . personally . . ." he began. "You know, I'm an older man, and I've been thrown in a lot of experiences, and I have a feeling that it's abnormal and it's certainly not the natural way we were put on earth. So I see no reason to jump with joy because somebody is gay, and I don't see any reason for waving a flag for all the wonderful things gays have done for the world . . . any more than you'd say, 'Oh, boy, hooray for the tuberculosis victim!' It's abnormal to me.

"Now, as far as having them live their own life, I feel that a man has a right to live his life the way

747

he wishes — as long as he doesn't interfere with me having my rights. So I have nothing against them, but I certainly see no reason to jump with joy about it."

It hardly needs to be pointed out that Wayne was a man of his time, embodying the attributes of a small-town Edwardian boyhood and a good many of the prejudices as well. Once, in a discursive conversation, he expounded on his sense of fair play. "I didn't know about Jews, niggers or Japs as minority groups until I went to college. At Glendale High we had 'em all — and on the football team if any guy called the Japanese fella a Jap we took him off the field, but not until the bunch of us took our turns at 'em. We all shared the fact that we were poor and struggling and there wasn't time to show prejudice. We only felt together."

In his own mind, Wayne was a true democrat, if not a Democrat, but at the same time he was oblivious to matters of terminology and tone. "His language reflected his background and his class," said P. F. Kluge. "But that wasn't him. I know a lot of people like that. I'm from New Jersey, and people from New Jersey speak roughly about other races. But they're all in the same neighborhood and rubbing against each other and giving each other a ration of shit and having a beer. Wayne would give a fair shake to people he encountered."

Increasingly journalists baited Wayne with questions that were predominantly social in nature, and he couldn't resist responding. The vast majority of the interviews he faced now focused on politics and sociology, at which Wayne had presumably developed an expertise through his portrayal of frontier values. The interviews set

748

Wayne's public image as a reactionary in amber.

What seemed at the time to be paleoconservatism has since become Republican orthodoxy, as with Wayne's essential mistrust of government, expressed when he wrote, "Government has no wealth, and when a politician promises to give you something for nothing, he must first confiscate that wealth from you — either by direct taxes, or by the cruelly indirect tax of inflation."

Wayne's politics made it easier for those who didn't share his beliefs to refuse to engage with the truths he told as an actor. If Wayne was an ignoramus, if he was a war-mongering hypocrite who never served in the military, if he was an actor in a dying genre like westerns, then he didn't have to be taken seriously as a craftsman, let alone an artist.

Many New York critics went to town. Pauline Kael wrote, "The world has changed since audiences first responded to John Wayne as a simple cowboy . . . now, when he does the same things and represents the same simple values, he's so archaic it's funny. We used to be frightened of a reactionary becoming 'a man on horseback'; now that seems the best place for him."

But there was a corresponding undercurrent of respect and love from literary writers like Joan Didion: "When John Wayne rode through my childhood, and perhaps through yours, he determined forever the shape of certain of our dreams. . . . When John Wayne spoke, there was no mistaking his intentions; he had a sexual authority so strong that even a child could perceive it. And in a world we understood early to be characterized by venality and doubt and paralyzing ambiguities, he suggested another world, one which may or may not have existed ever but in any case existed no more."

In many respects, these dueling dialogues about Wayne's value and meaning continue in another century, with the subject long dead.

In 1971, Wayne made some inquiries to some friends in the White House. As a loyal Nixon man, he wondered if he deserved better than he was getting at the callused hands of the IRS. Wayne had recently received a bill for back taxes of $251,116 for the years 1964–1966. White House counselor John Dean instructed John Caulfield to look into the matter of celebrity audits, and Caulfield discovered that Wayne was by no means being singled out — Jerry Lewis had been hit for $446,332 between 1958 and 1960. "The Wayne complaint," wrote Caulfield, "when viewed in the attached context, doesn't appear to be strong enough to pursue."

There were plenty of acting offers, some more interesting than others. Robert Aldrich wanted to team Wayne and Katharine Hepburn in a script called *Rage of Honor,* about an old cowboy alienated by industrial development in California in 1929. Aldrich sent the script to Hepburn, who replied, "I can't think of a single thing to say about that script which would not be insulting to it — especially to you — Good God — Blood and pomposity — Rotten police and butchered horse —You're hard up?"

Wayne's business interests remained slightly ramshackle, if only because his criteria for a deal continued to involve the personal more than the professional. He was told about a German ship that had been scuttled in Acapulco Bay and was believed to be full of mercury. He promptly bought the salvage rights, only to find out that the only thing the ship contained was rust. He'd tell the story on himself, roaring with laughter.

"Grandaddy wanted to be in business with his pals," said Gretchen Wayne. "It was like every guy wants to own a bar, you know? He would go to Michael about a project and say, 'These guys are going to do this, they're going to do that . . .' And Michael would say, 'Really? And how much are they putting in, and how much do they want you to put in?' And Grandaddy would grumble and walk out the door.

"Michael was a businessman, he was shrewd, he wouldn't spend more than he had and he always negotiated for the better deal. Michael's dad recognized this and would say, 'Well, I don't have a college education like you do.' But Grandaddy was smart in that he always knew how much he could afford to lose, and he wouldn't go beyond that."

Wayne hired an old acquaintance named Joe de Franco to run a company called Separation and Recovery Systems Inc., which separated oil from water. De Franco had worked at Studebaker for years and Wayne had long respected him as a solid businessman. Once the two got reacquainted Wayne offered him the job of running the company. De Franco inspected the operation and thought it could be made profitable, but it was severely underfunded.

"I'm going to have to use you, Duke," he told the owner. "Why not?" Wayne replied, "Everybody else does." For the next year or so, de Franco marched Wayne into luncheons with prospective investors, who eventually included, among others,

Robert Abplanalp, the Nixon crony who had gotten rich by inventing the aerosol valve. In addition to the investors, de Franco got some government grants.

When he was done, de Franco had raised about $3.5 million, with his salary coming out of what he had raised and his piece of the business. Separation and Recovery Systems operated out of Irvine, California, and de Franco built it up to successfully operate in such far-flung locations as Norway, Sweden, and South America.

De Franco's impression was that the company was one of the few that Wayne owned that was successful. Mike Wayne kept Separation and Recovery Systems going for years after his father died, not selling it off until the mid-1980s.

"I found Duke to be super," said de Franco. "If you were a smart-ass, he had a temper. Mostly, though, he was thoughtful and praiseworthy. He was appreciative, and he delegated, although sometimes he would micromanage — like when he'd play bridge."

Although Wayne's bad memory for names was legendary, de Franco found that his memory for business details was highly retentive. De Franco would go to Wayne's house every Friday for a business conference, and often on Sundays as well, because de Franco would cook a big Italian dinner.

Like many people around Wayne, de Franco found Pilar "very self-centered. She had that 'Look at me' attitude." Wayne and his wife rarely argued; when they did it was over some social event that Wayne didn't want to attend. "She'd get huffy and go in the other room and close the door, and he'd go after her and apologize," said de Franco. "He also thought she spent too much money, but he never complained about it.

"He was a good father in that he set a good example. He was attentive. He would get upset because Aissa's grades were usually terrible. God, he'd be so proud of how she turned out — going to law school and becoming a successful attorney. He's beaming down at her, believe me."

After *The Last Picture Show* and *What's Up, Doc?* Peter Bogdanovich was the hottest director in Hollywood, but he nevertheless accompanied his girlfriend Cybill Shepherd to Miami, where she was shooting *The Heartbreak Kid.* With time on his hands, Bogdanovich decided to turn his hand to the western he had always wanted to make. Summoning Larry McMurtry, the author of the novel and co-screenwriter of *The Last Picture Show,* they set to work on a western that would unite all of John Ford's great leading men: John Wayne, James Stewart, and Henry Fonda. Bogdanovich and McMurtry called the script *The Streets of Laredo.*

"What we had planned was a sort of last adventure," remembered McMurtry, "after which they would be over, as would the Old West." With quality scripts being thin on the ground at the moment, Stewart and Fonda both signed on, if a trifle reluctantly. "They wanted," wrote McMurtry, "the last adventure to be a wild success, not a dim moral victory of the sort we had planned for them."

As for Wayne, he circled, delayed, and finally said no. Unlike Stewart and Fonda, Wayne had plenty of work, but other than that nobody could quite figure out why he passed. "Maybe he didn't like it that James Stewart got to play the more

753

poetic character," ruminated McMurtry. "Maybe he didn't like Peter, or the script, or because he was tired of playing the competent grump yet one more time."

Actually, Wayne liked Bogdanovich well enough — "He likes the things I like," was the way he put it — but there was definitely a context to Bogdanovich's script that bothered him. "It's kind of an end-of-the-West Western," Wayne told Bogdanovich, "and I'm not ready to hang up my spurs yet."

"But you don't die in it," Bogdanovich offered.

"Yeah, but everybody else does," replied Wayne.

"I just don't like the story," he confided. "I like Bogdanovich. He's a good student of all the directors that mean anything to me. But I don't go for his story . . . and Bogdanovich can be almighty stubborn about it." There was no getting away from the fact that *The Streets of Laredo* was a western about the Death of the West, and since the West was more or less synonymous with John Wayne, he wasn't overjoyed by the implications.

When Bogdanovich wasn't around, Wayne was more specific: "It just wasn't a good part. Peter had written a good part for Fonda and some fun lines for Jimmy, but I was a whiner. Why the hell should I do that? . . . Peter said, 'This is a great part.' I said, 'To you, not to me.'"

Bogdanovich put on as much of a press as he could, even sending Wayne a handwritten letter ("This can be a beautiful movie and not a downbeat one, as you fear . . ."). But Wayne's mind was made up. All this would have been understandable if Wayne was buried beneath quality scripts, but he was mostly engaged in time passers. As a last resort, Bogdanovich told Wayne that John

Ford said he should do it, but Wayne retorted, "That's not what he told me." Years later, Barbara Ford told Bogdanovich that her father told Wayne to turn it down, while simultaneously telling Bogdanovich it was a great script.

The Streets of Laredo hung around Warner Bros. for a number of years, but it was generally felt that Wayne was the only man who could carry the increasingly dicey genre to any kind of box office, and once he passed on a project, it stayed passed. McMurtry let the project go, then rethought it, refocused some of the characters and the plot, and wrote a novel called *Lonesome Dove.* When it was made into a great miniseries years later, Robert Duvall played the part that had been written for Wayne, and Tommy Lee Jones played the role designed for James Stewart.

The cancer surgery was now a part of the dim past. Wayne had regained most of his strength, although there were still things he was leery of. Water skiing, for instance. One day off Catalina he thought he and Bert Minshall should go scuba diving. Minshall wasn't sure it was a good idea — Wayne's wind wasn't good, and he still coughed a lot — but they jumped off the back end of the boat anyway and went down twelve to fifteen feet looking for abalone.

"I could see he was having problems," remembered Minshall. "He goes back to the surface and I follow him, and he tears his mask off and says, 'Goddamn it, I'll never have any more fun!' And that was the last time he went diving."

The young man who had once swum, dived, and body surfed with animal joy was now hemmed in by physical limitations, to which he would never entirely reconcile himself. "He got grouchy," said Minshall. "Near the end he was very short-tempered."

For a Batjac production called *Big Jake,* Wayne reached far back into the past and hired George Sherman to direct. Sherman had been a mainstay at Republic in the 1930s and 1940s, and at Universal in the 1950s, but had never planted a flag in A pictures and hadn't directed a theatrical picture since 1966. Batjac got Sherman for the bargain price of $50,000, with options for four more pictures that were shared with CBS.

Big Jake was written by the husband-and-wife team of Harry Julian and Rita Fink, who had previously collaborated on *Dirty Harry,* and who injected the western with harsher violence than was customary for Wayne. The plot involved the kidnapping of the grandson of a cattle baron named Jacob McCandles. Even though it's 1909, and McCandles has long been estranged from his family, he's regarded as the only man sufficiently fearless to get the boy back.

Sherman began shooting the picture before Wayne showed up in Durango, Mexico. When he arrived, he asked Harry Carey Jr. how Sherman was doing. "Okay," said Carey. Wayne looked at the rushes, then sought Carey out. "I thought you said he was doing OK. He's doing shit!" The result, said Pat Wayne, was that "My dad directed *Big Jake.*" Dobe, as Carey was generally known, said that Wayne strengthened the dialogue and re-choreographed the shoot-out at the end of the picture.

Wayne filled *Big Jake* with family — his son Pat, Harry Carey Jr., Richard Boone. Dobe Carey showed up with a bushy beard he had worn on his previous picture, and was told to keep it. The beard was darkened to indicate that copious amounts of tobacco juice had dripped down into it. "You look like the Cowardly Lion," Wayne cracked one day. In fact, Dobe, as Carey was generally known, chewing tobacco throughout the shoot, as was Wayne — Red Man was giving him his nicotine fix.

One day Dobe was snoozing on his lunch break when he was awakened by the *thunk* of a large body landing in an adjacent chair. He looked over to discover Wayne sitting there. "Jeez, I miss your dad," he said. "I loved that old man. Even if he was a Democrat."

One Sunday night at sunset, Wayne was sitting in a rocking chair on the porch of the house where he was living when Mike Wayne came bustling by. "Come up here, sit down and look at this sunset," Wayne said. Mike said he couldn't, there were things he had to straighten out for the next day's shooting. "Let me tell you," Wayne said, "the work will be there. This sunset isn't going to be there. It will never be there again." In telling the story, Mike Wayne concluded, "He had balance in his life. He was in sync with the world around him."

Mike Wayne was always proud of the deal he made for *Big Jake,* and it's easy to see why. The film was fully financed by CBS for its theatrical arm Cinema Center Films, at a budget of $4.3 million, but Batjac owned the picture. Mike called it "the best deal I ever made in my life, and it also made the most money. Just phenomenal. The script was better than the film, but it really played."

The cast budget for the picture clearly shows

that special consideration was given to actors in the Batjac family. Wayne got his usual $1 million and a percentage, Patrick Wayne got $25,000. Dobe Carey got $1,000 a week, Bruce Cabot got $2,000 a week with an eight-week guarantee, and Maureen O'Hara got $30,000 for the small part of Wayne's estranged wife, a character originally offered to Susan Hayward, who had a scheduling conflict. Richard Boone got $90,000, with $5,000 of that salary diverted to a school he helped support in Hawaii. (Wayne knew that the roster of actors who could go up against him was not large; the second choice for the part appears to have been Gene Hackman.) Ethan Wayne, in his first screen role, earned $650 a week, with his father signing the contract for the minor. As for the crew, the venerable William Clothier got $2,250 a week.

A very interesting casting choice that didn't happen involved Jeff Bridges playing Wayne's son. Mike Wayne and George Sherman decided on Bridges after what Mike remembered as "fifty-five interviews, twenty-three readings, and three tests." Batjac agreed to pay Bridges $1,750 a week for eight weeks, but he ultimately turned down the film. CBS didn't like Chris Mitchum, Bridges's replacement, but Batjac lobbied until the studio agreed. Production began on October 10, 1970, and wrapped fifty-five days later, three days under schedule, at a cost of $4.39 million.

The most startling thing about *Big Jake* is its violence — at one point, Jake's dog gets hacked to death, and a man takes a pitchfork to the face — but it was somehow rated PG. At times, the self-reliance of the Wayne character coarsens to something approaching the ugly — when he's not slugging his sons for insubordination, he's humili-

758

ating them.

But the audience didn't mind. The casts of these later pictures were mostly the same, the saloon brawls were from central casting, and so were some of the character beats: Jacob McCandles is as relentless as Tom Dunson, he's embarrassed when he has to put on his reading glasses, just as Nathan Brittles was in *She Wore a Yellow Ribbon,* and when somebody tells him, "I thought you were dead," he responds with "That'll be the day." It's also a little sloppy; at one point, Wayne mispronounces "ostentatious" as "ostentious." There was no retake.

Despite all of this, *Big Jake* was a success, returning domestic rentals of $7.9 million. In 1971, the sixty-four-year-old Wayne was the number one box office star in America, in front of Clint Eastwood, Paul Newman, Steve McQueen, and George C. Scott.

Big Jake was released in May of 1971, and Chris Mitchum and Wayne went on *The Tonight Show* to promote the picture. Mitchum had been working for the passage of Proposition 13, an environmental initiative to clean up Los Angeles harbor and set pollution controls. Wayne preceded Mitchum on the show, and when Mitchum brought up his work for the environment, Wayne and Mitchum engaged in an apparently playful back-and-forth about the supposedly left-wing politics behind the movement. The exchange resulted in a flurry of publicity and letters to the editor to the general effect that being conservative does not have to mean turning your back on the environment.

Wayne never spoke to Mitchum again. "I don't know if he decided I was a Commie, or if he was just mad that he'd gotten involved in something with me and because of it received some negative fallout," remembered Mitchum. He wrote Wayne several notes trying to repair the damage, and when Wayne fell ill a few years later sent him a letter saying he was only an hour away and was ready for a chess game anytime. There was never a response.

"It really hurt me, because the man was more of a mentor and a father to me in the business than my own father was. . . . He did nothing but give me support. He took me from a two or three line role to co-starring with him. He basically made my career. And to have it end that way has always been a great sadness in my life."

For his next picture, Wayne opted for something more demanding than the pictures he had been making, something closer to the epic. *The Cowboys* began life as a novel by William Dale Jennings, an Army veteran who in 1950 co-founded the Mattachine Society, the first modern gay organization in America.

Jennings's novel concerned Wil Andersen, a Montana rancher who has 1,500 head of cattle that he needs to get to the rail head at a time when every available hand is off pursuing a gold strike. His only alternative is to hire a crew of kids, ages ten to fifteen, to help him drive the cattle four hundred miles. Andersen's brand of tough love gets the boys started on the maturation process. He and his crew are waylaid by trail scum and he's killed, but the boys summon their resources to take revenge on the killers and finish what Andersen started.

It's a good, often poetic novel that spins off the traditional movie convention that certain problems can only be solved by slaughter. It quickly sold to the movies because of its interesting combination of ingredients — a little bit of *True Grit,* a little bit of *Hondo,* quite a bit of *Lord of the Flies.*

Jennings wrote several drafts of the script, which was then punched up by the husband-and-wife screenwriting team of Irving Ravetch and Harriet Frank Jr. What Jennings did not want was for it to be made into a John Wayne western — he had written it with George C. Scott in mind. In this, he was of the same mind as the film's director.

"I did not want John Wayne for *The Cowboys,*" said director Mark Rydell. "But Warners was heavily invested in John Wayne, with whom I was at polar opposites politically and emotionally and every possible way. I did not admire him. But he seduced me mercilessly. 'I promise you I will do the best job I possibly can,' he said. 'Let's not talk about anything but acting. Not politics or religion, just acting.' He completely won me over and I agreed he should play the part."

Wayne compared the film to *Goodbye, Mr. Chips* and *Sands of Iwo Jima* — an older man molding young men, although in the case of *The Cowboys* it was unwillingly.

"He came on board and didn't talk politics or religion or any anti-Semitic horseshit," said Rydell. "But I consciously surrounded him with a different crew and actors than he was used to. None of his cronies were on the picture. I cast Roscoe Lee Browne. Allyn Ann McLerie, who played his wife, had been blacklisted. It was my private joke. I wanted him not to be comfortable because I didn't want a standard Wayne performance; I wanted to agitate him off the mark of his usual performances."

For the boys, Rydell split the cast down the middle; half the kids were skilled horsemen who had never acted before, and half were actors who had little experience with horses. Preproduction was largely given over to teaching young actors how to ride and young riders how to act.

From the first, Wayne was happy with the script and the cast. "He sensed competitiveness from the actors and that made him competitive," said Rydell. "He was the first on the set and the last to leave. The kids adored him, climbed on him as if he was a playground. And in the end he impressed me tremendously."

One day John Ford and his grandson, Dan, showed up after making a special trip via the Super Chief from Los Angeles to Santa Fe. Ford dropped by the set in a limousine and gave Rydell one crystalline bit of advice: "Don't let 'em give you any shit."

Wayne was living in a large ranch house with a couple of hippie girls he had picked up hitchhiking on the drive to New Mexico. "Duke was not known for being a particularly tolerant man," said Dan Ford, "but he asked these two good-looking girls if they wanted jobs, so they took care of the house and cooked for him. They were great-looking and funny, and he enjoyed having them around." Also staying at the house was Wayne Warga, a writer for the *Los Angeles Times,* who was ghosting a prospective autobiography for Wayne.

On a Saturday afternoon, Ford and Wayne sat around reminiscing about old times. Wayne complained to Ford about the considerable wind on the location, and the old director perked up. "I hope they're using it," he said. Wayne said they were using so much of it that it took him most of the night to get the dust out of his eyes.

Amid random fulminations about the Teamsters from Wayne ("I think Hoffa's organization was designed to fuck up a scene in the picture"), inevitably the subject of Ward Bond arose. Ford asked if Wayne had ever gotten back the guns stolen from his house in a recent robbery. "I got everything but the good shotgun," said Wayne.

"The one that shot Ward in the ass?"

"That's gone . . . I wish he was around so I could shoot him again."

Ford was slowly recovering from a broken hip incurred by tripping over some laundry on the back porch of his house in Bel Air. He wasn't very mobile and wasn't feeling well. Wayne invited Ford and his grandson to go out for dinner with him. Ford passed because he was tired, so Wayne asked Dan if he wanted to come alone. But Dan said he was going to play some cards with his grandfather.

A little shadow moved over Wayne's face — he wasn't used to being rejected. The real reason Dan skipped the dinner was that he had recently returned from Vietnam and had no interest in talking about any aspect of the war, which emphatically included *The Green Berets,* a film that he and every other Vietnam veteran he knew thought "was a complete piece of shit."

The set for *The Cowboys* was about eight miles outside Galisteo, a one-horse village with two shops, a gas station, and a dirt floor bar called La Fonda that was locally famous for their margaritas. Wayne was in fine fettle, listening to Frank Sinatra's "September of My Years" in the car on the way to the location, arriving at least forty-five minutes before his call. Referring to Rydell's *The*

Reivers, Wayne told the director, "I can't believe it took you 100 days to shoot a picture with two guys, a kid and a car."

"I can't believe it either," said Rydell.

Occasionally, the elevation caused him to feel tightness in the chest and he would cough. "God, I hate not to feel good," he would say. As was obvious by the repeated playing of the Sinatra album, age and time were on his mind. His ghosts were gathering, and he knew it.

After the shooting day was done, there was a shower, a massage, one big drink, and dinner. On several occasions he went into the kitchen and mixed up a spicy chili soufflé. He went to bed early, and was again working his way through the writings of Winston Churchill, whom he could quote from memory. If he wasn't reading Churchill, he was browsing through mail order catalogues.

Dealing with the young actors in the picture brought out the gentleness and consideration that modulated his temper. "It's never easy for a young man to talk to an old man unless the old man paves the way," he said. "It's much easier for me to start a conversation with a younger person than the other way around. I try to communicate sooner than other people do."

But Mark Rydell didn't grasp Wayne's patriarchal imperative. On the day they started the cattle drive scene, Rydell gave the stuntmen a 5:30 A.M. call. Wayne arrived on the set an hour later and was upset to find everyone else in gear. "I want to have the same damn call as the stunt guys," he told Rydell.

That was the day Wayne chose to challenge Rydell. "There were the kids, the stuntmen, hundreds of head of cattle, five cameras, and I'm up on a camera crane," remembered Rydell.

You don't start cattle by saying "Action!" you start by pushing them, and cattle move slowly. I didn't want to waste a lot of film by rolling before the cattle started moving, but Wayne was impatient and had decided that it was time to go. He called for the camera to start, and I just lost it and started screaming.

"Don't you ever do that! I haven't rolled the cameras. I'll tell you when to go."

It was not a wise thing to do. Everybody was there, everybody was watching and he was humiliated.

He looked at me and went back to his spot and I rolled the cameras and he did the scene. And then he got in his car and drove back to Santa Fe. And as the camera crane came down, the crew filed by me and shook my hand, as if they were saying goodbye.

That night at the production office, there were four calls from Wayne. I thought Andy McLaglen was going to be there the next day. I may have been producing and directing, but he was John Wayne. One call to Warners and I was gone. So we met and had dinner and that's when he told me that the only people that treated him that way were me and John Ford. He was very respectful.

In retrospect, I was wrong; I shouldn't have lost my temper and shouted at him in front of everybody. But he ultimately respected the fact that I had stood up to him.

He was extremely competitive and, in his way, a very private man. Bruce Dern and Roscoe Lee Browne were younger, hotter actors, and he was damned if he was going to be thought of as any less than they were. He wanted to make sure that I understood that, in his mind, he and Gary Cooper had developed realistic acting in westerns.

One day on the set, he and Roscoe were trading lines of poetry from Keats and Byron. I was amazed at his erudition. He loved Roscoe and told him, "You're the first nigger I've ever met with a sense of humor." It sounds bad in the telling, but it was said jokingly, lovingly, one friend to another.

In the end, he gave a great, loving performance. His feeling for children surprised me; he was amazing with them, and he encouraged them. It taught me a lesson: how many people with whom you agree politically are jerks? And how many people with whom you disagree politically are attractive human beings? He knew I hated his support of the blacklist and was much more liberal than he was, and he laughed about it.

Wayne liked Rydell but thought the picture could have been better. "I was too strong for this young man," he said a few years later. Specifically, Wayne felt that Rydell botched Wil Andersen's death scene. "He played everything off the heavy, and I had no chance to show the audience that what I was doing was trying to save these kids' lives. . . . Give me an *opportunity* to play the scene. Those kids were crying when I played the scene, but the audience wasn't crying with them because they weren't in the mood for the scene when it started."

It wouldn't have taken much to fix the scene,

766

and Wayne made his suggestions, but he said that there were "so many sycophants around [that] had said, 'Oh, I think it's great, it's great, it's great.' When a guy is directing a picture, that's his picture. I can only tell him what I think, and if he wants to do it the other way, then goddamn, I'm getting pretty good money to do what he says. Only one man can paint the picture."

A good picture, not a great one, *The Cowboys* cost $4.8 million and brought back domestic rentals of $7.4 million, with Wayne receiving $1 million and 15 percent of the profits.

Wayne had thought about writing a memoir for a number of years and got as far as a series of reminiscences with the fan magazine writer Maurice Zolotow that were later cannibalized for a biography. In 1971, Wayne again made tentative steps toward a book when he began dictating to Wayne Warga.

They got as far as fifteen hours of tapes and five chapters before Wayne began to get uncomfortable, specifically about the chapter devoted to John Huston and *The Barbarian and the Geisha*. He wanted his anger to show, but he also wanted the chapter to be funny and he didn't want to hurt anybody's feelings. He threw the chapter out because, "If there's one person out there who might think it's petty of me to pick on Huston, then I don't want it in the book."

Wayne would invite Warga on the *Wild Goose* for what were supposed to be working vacations on a book that was tentatively titled *What Hat, Which Door and When Do I Come In?* Not a lot of work got done.

"I want you to see what it's like to be around

767

me, and don't worry about the goddamn book," said Wayne. They were somewhere in British Columbia when Warga casually mentioned that he'd never seen a glacier. Nothing would do but that Wayne charter a seaplane that landed by the *Wild Goose.* Off they flew to take pictures of a glacier from the air.

Wayne told Warga that he always wanted to be Fred Astaire, and he demonstrated by launching into "Putting on the Ritz." He danced, remembered the writer, "with all the grace of a freight elevator." He also told Warga that he'd like to make something besides westerns, but people didn't come to him with those kinds of stories, and he'd accommodated himself to the industry's perception.

Warga was being paid $10,000 plus 25 percent of the royalties, but Wayne pulled away and the project gradually atrophied. Warga found him "a richly complicated man, far more intelligent than he was given credit for, easily hurt, very witty, very literate, naturally friendly, and often in conflict with the world's image of him. He worshipped his children. He was a very bad businessman and a very loyal friend."

Ultimately, he shied away from the memoir for the same reasons he shied away from *The Streets of Laredo.* "He . . . felt," wrote Warga, "that the day he wrote The End for his book it might also mean the beginning of the end of John Wayne."

Wayne had known for decades that to stay in the business at a high level required constant vigilance. Robert Relyea, the assistant director on *The Alamo,* became a producer later in the 1960s, notably on *Bullitt* and other pictures made by Steve

McQueen's Solar Productions. One day on the Warners lot, as Wayne was preparing *The Cowboys,* he sidled up to Relyea and put his arm around him. "You got a project?" Wayne inquired. "Well, when you're looking for an actor, think of your old friend."

"He was partially kidding, but, in his John Wayne way, he was also partially serious," said Relyea. "At the time, his private helicopter was parked on a pad right outside my office window."

About this time there came to be a sense within the youthful population of the industry that Wayne was falling behind the times. Strictly speaking, it was true.

Tom Kane told a story about a time when Wayne was fishing on the *Wild Goose* in Mexico when Lee Marvin pulled up alongside him. "Hey Duke!" Marvin yelled. "Did you ever go fishing with a Jew?" Marvin was referring to his fishing partner Keenan Wynn. Wayne began talking about a nice little part in an upcoming picture that would be good for Marvin, and the younger man chuckled.

"What are you laughing about?"

"You said it's a nice little part. I don't do little parts anymore, Duke."

"What do you mean?"

"Well, Christ, I'm a big star like you are. I get a million dollars a picture."

"You what?"

"Yeah. I did *The Dirty Dozen* and it made more money than anything in the last 20 years. I was the lead and that's what I get now."

Wayne was puzzled by this and thought Marvin was pulling his leg. "What did we pay him on that

Randy Scott picture we made?" he asked Tom Kane.

"$16,000," replied Kane, who got the distinct impression that Wayne never believed Marvin got a million dollars a picture.

If Wayne was falling behind the times in some aspects, he was still susceptible to majestic film-making. "I loved *The Godfather,*" he enthused. "It was just terrific. It had such a wonderful feeling [for] Sicilian or Italian family life even though it had the murderous stuff in it. Marlon Brando was just great. The way he played with his grandson, Jesus, he looked like he was ninety years old. He used that light make-up over the beard to get that sallow effect. Great. But his attitude was what made it."

In 1972, Tom Kane got a phone call from a friend at MGM. The studio had just bought a bestseller called *The Man Who Loved Cat Dancing,* and there was a part in it that was perfect for John Wayne — a man who gets out of prison after twenty years for killing his wife, an Indian squaw.

Kane read the book and agreed that it was a perfect upper-range vehicle for Wayne. He made some calls, and found that not only had MGM not discussed Wayne, they weren't interested. MGM wanted a younger, more au courant star — they eventually made the picture with Burt Reynolds.

Kane never told Wayne about the book, because he didn't want Wayne to say, "I love it," only to have him find out that MGM didn't want him. "I was never going to put him in that position," remembered Kane. "And I didn't."

Many of Wayne's friends felt similarly protective of him on the personal level. They thought he was utterly devoted to his children, but many had come to the conclusion that he was badly used by his wife. Cecilia Presley respected Pilar as a mother, but was less enthusiastic about other aspects of her personality.

"The difference between them — well, there were a lot of differences between them, but the main one was that he had a wonderful sense of humor about himself. You could make fun of him and he'd take it. She had no sense of humor about herself. None. She was the sort of woman who didn't want to go on the *Wild Goose* because she'd get her hair mussed. If he liked you, Duke didn't care if you were a busboy or the president of the United States. He was not a snob . . .

"The problem was that he couldn't have fun with Pilar. But he loved her and wanted to keep the marriage going and really tried to be a good husband. He would follow her around and sit there while she played tennis or shopped, and she loved to shop. It was kind of pathetic."

Cecilia and Wayne would sit and drink and talk and drink. One day she asked him who had been the greatest one-night stand in his life, the single most exciting sexual episode. "Oh, Christ, Citzie . . ." he demurred. But she kept after him and finally he cast his mind back and smiled. "Rome. The Excelsior Hotel. Dietrich. I took her on the staircase."

Wayne tried to be a family man, and mostly succeeded, but there were rumors for years about a single affair with a legendary co-star. "He and Maureen O'Hara had a long affair," said one good friend. "They would meet in Arizona, at the ranch he owned with Louis Johnson. It went on for years, before and during his marriage to Pilar."

771

Other people scoffed at that possibility, among them Harry Carey Jr. "Maureen and Duke off-screen didn't have anything going on like the attraction between Duke and Gail Russell. They were good friends, that's all . . . Duke took marriage seriously." Likewise, Andrew McLaglen, who said that "I think [Wayne and O'Hara] respected each other a great deal. I think they liked each other. There was nothing personal ever between them, but that's the way it is sometimes — that makes the best screen relationships, people that don't really know each other on a personal level, but they can sure act it."

O'Hara always denied any romantic connection with Wayne, but Christopher Mitchum, who worked with them both in *Big Jake,* asserted that "Duke was truly in love with that woman."

But if Wayne and O'Hara had an offscreen connection every bit as strong as their on-screen connection, why didn't he marry her when he had the chance?

"Because Maureen was strong and tough and he probably didn't think he could control her. He married women he thought he could control. Then he found out he couldn't."

Wayne became far more a part of the community in Newport Beach than he ever had in Encino. Part of it was the thriving boat culture of the area — there are around ten thousand yachts in Newport Beach, and the *Wild Goose* had become as important to Wayne as the *Araner* was to John Ford.

But it was more than recreational. Wayne was in love with the sea, or as much as his innate impatience would allow him to be. "When I die," he told his family, "I don't want to miss the ocean. I want to stay here. That's why I don't want to be buried. I want to be cremated when I die. Then take me out and scatter me over the ocean. Because that's where my heart is."

He felt at home in Newport Beach because of the culture, but also because there were no cameras, and no intrusion on his space. "It was conservative, it wasn't plastic, it wasn't about celebrity glitz," said Tom Fuentes, the chairman of the Orange County Republican Party from 1984 to 2004. "Culturally and politically, he was apart from all that. This was a retreat from the Hollywood crowd."

Wayne was a fixture at the Balboa Yacht Club, and at the fundraising activities of the Orange County Republican Party. Orange County had originally been an agricultural district of Catholics and Hispanics, but in the 1960s and 1970s, the area grew by more than 100,000 people a year, most of them urban conservatives, on the way to the present population of 3.5 million — more people than six states.

Traditionally, Orange County was where California Republicans needed a 200,000-vote margin to offset the liberal Democratic enclaves in West Los Angeles and San Francisco. If he wasn't working, Wayne could always be counted on to lend his celebrity and presence to Republican fundraisers.

"His participation was always generous," said Tom Fuentes. "If we had an event and we needed a draw to rally the troops, a crowd-booster, he was very approachable. We only had two or three Republican celebrities in the area — there was Duke, then Buddy Ebsen, and perhaps Andy Devine. It didn't have to be anything huge for Duke to participate; one afternoon, we had a party to sign the nominating papers for a county supervisor who was running for reelection. I was in the kitchen and there was a knock on the door. I opened it and there stood John Wayne.

" 'Hello, I'm John Wayne,' he said. He always had the humility and modesty to introduce himself." Wayne rarely contributed money but Fuentes believed that his presence was more valuable than cash.

Wayne drove himself around Newport in an unpretentious dark green 1973 Pontiac Safari station wagon that had been slightly modified by George Barris, who raised its sunroof six inches, so that Wayne had headroom. (The Safari also included something unusual for the time — a telephone with two channels.) The local grocery store became known as "Duke's Safeway," because he would occasionally be seen doing some grocery shopping there. He would also regularly drive his children to school and pick them up, or take them for drives along the Coast Highway.

Aissa remembered that "He was always the one that got us out of jams and protected us and everything. He was security for all of us and if we needed help at school or something, my dad always had good, sound advice. He sat down and really talked to us, but he wasn't so unreasonable that you couldn't even talk to him about something. He was a real support day to day, so you never got too far out of line, because he was around."

Wayne enjoyed his days and nights at the Balboa Yacht Club, which was formed in 1948 and overlooks the channel. The club was eventually rebuilt, greatly expanded, and now resembles a

Las Vegas hotel, but when Wayne was alive it was a glorified beach club, the structure supported by telephone poles.

When Wayne was in Newport Beach, he would come in for breakfast about three times a week, for dinner once or twice a week. On Wednesdays he played cards in a clubroom near the spa. In the early years of his membership, Pilar was there also, playing tennis constantly, outfitted in layers of white to protect her skin.

The dining room was open until eleven at night, and once Wayne didn't feel like going home. He made a date with George Valenzuela, a Mexican dining room captain he was friendly with, to meet up at a nearby restaurant in Costa Mesa. "Keep it open, and I'll be there," Wayne said. "You buy the first round and I'll buy the rest."

Valenzuela picked up a few more waiters and busboys and their wives, until there were about eight couples in all. He told them that John Wayne was coming to drink with them, which provoked a dubious response. But Wayne showed up as promised and started buying rounds.

"He loved tacos," remembered Valenzuela, who went to work at the Yacht Club in 1969. "The food at his parties was always salsa and guacamole. He liked me because I liked to drink and talk. He'd talk about filming in Durango and the things that happened. He just loved Mexico. 'If I'm in Mexico, then I'm happy,' he told me. He didn't speak Spanish often, but when he did he spoke good Spanish, not gringo Spanish. He was always the same simple guy."

Wayne particularly enjoyed the annual employee party at the club, when the membership donned red jackets and waited on the staff. Wayne wore a particularly large jacket and took George's station, and the waiter pronounced himself satisfied with the actor's service. "George loved him and vice versa," said Tom Fuentes. "He had that kind of personality and openness, and a total lack of prejudice."

Gretchen Wayne thought that in many ways the second family made more demands on Wayne's energies than he was capable of meeting. "He was more like a grandfather to the second group of kids," she said. "He was working, he was away, he was tired and then he got sick. Ethan once said, 'All I remember about my father are his bags in the hall ready to leave. And he was always mad at me.' And I said, 'That's because you were a jerk to your sisters.'

"The child that was closest to him was Aissa. When she got her real estate license, he was so proud. She was getting her first apartment, and he said, 'Let's go shopping. You have to look professional. You'll need a nice blazer.' And then he helped her furnish the apartment, which he could do very well. He had a good eye, good taste and loved the decorative arts.

"Grandaddy came from a tough background and was very concerned about presenting well; he always believed it was important to have your shoes shined and to dress as well as you could afford. Those were the things that were important to Mary Morrison, and she passed it on to him."

When Ethan was little, his father would pick him up and sit him on the railing of the boat. Ethan would be scared of falling, so his father would say, "What do you think I'm going to do? Drop you? Lean back!" So Ethan would lean back over the ocean in the middle of the night, while his father held his arms tightly. "See, I'm not gonna let you go," he'd say.

When Ethan was older, he and his father would just stand on the prow of the ship, looking out at the ocean. "The ocean looked like *Victory at Sea.* We'd just stand out there and look around. I miss that."

A young actor-turned-writer named Robert Osborne came to Wayne's house for an interview about Wayne's childhood. After a bit of talking, Wayne offered Osborne a drink. It was only about two in the afternoon, but few people said no to John Wayne. Osborne opted for a scotch and soda. So did Wayne.

After sipping his drink, Wayne began to warm to his subject — not horses, but Hollywood phonies. "You know, the problem with this business of ours is that too many people pretend to be something they're not. Take Roy Rogers."

"Roy Rogers?" echoed the confused Osborne.

"Yeah, Roy Rogers. He wasn't a cowboy. He was a goddamn country singer from Ohio."

Wayne launched into a long story about the two men making *Dark Command* for Republic in 1940. There was a gala premiere and parade in some town, and Roy Rogers got more applause than either Wayne or Claire Trevor.

"I didn't care about me," Wayne said, now thoroughly worked up, "but Claire Trevor was a great actress. And Rogers wasn't any actor, Rogers was barely a singer! And they applauded *him*!"

Roy Rogers was a very pleasant, unassuming man who never worked for John Ford once, let alone more than a dozen times, but that didn't matter to Wayne. Neither did the fact that, with the exception of Ben Johnson, there weren't any real cowboys working in front of Hollywood cameras in the 1940s and 1950s. Wayne's lubricated disquisition proved only that, in everybody's life, no matter their accomplishments or their place in the world, there is always some tender place where they feel they've been slighted. Even if they're John Wayne; even if they're pretending to be angry on someone else's behalf.

Chapter Twenty-Three

He was still making movies because they were there. "In Michael's mind," said his wife, Gretchen, "*Chisum, Cahill* and *The Train Robbers* were all the same picture." Finally, there was a part of sorts for Rod Taylor, or there was after Wayne instructed Burt Kennedy to write an extra scene for him and Ben Johnson in *The Train Robbers*. It was shot in Durango, Mexico, from March to June 1972.

The deal with Warners specified that the picture was not to cost more than $4.5 million. Burt Kennedy was getting $62,500 for his script and $80,000 for directing, Mike Wayne was getting $150,000 for producing, and his father was getting only $200,000 guaranteed, plus 10 percent of the gross up to $5 million, 15 percent thereafter. There was also a "consultant's fee" of $125,000, but the diminishing guarantee was a clear indication of the way Warners was beginning to regard westerns . . . and John Wayne.

Wayne was on location every day from early in the morning until five in the afternoon. On the way back to the hotel in a van, he would take a quick nap. That and dinner refreshed him sufficiently for a long night of drinking and storytelling with Rod Taylor. He was smoking little cigars again. Someone worked up the nerve to ask if he wasn't afraid of killing himself. "We are all under sentence of death," he replied. "Bet you don't know who said that? Whittaker Chambers."

If the subject turned to politics, he'd usually get angry about what he saw as misfeasance, malfeasance, or nonfeasance, but, as one writer observed, "He was always happy to see the cook and waiters. He was always happy to see the cast. He was always happy to drive out to the location. . . . In the immediacies of everyday life, in what he was doing and living, he seemed to relish everything, the simple ordinary things, the fried eggs over easy and the toasted rolls and the wonderful Mexican coffee. And he relished every morning he was working."

At work, remembered Taylor, "He did what he wanted to do. Burt was very gentle with him. Duke wanted a free rein." At night, there were the poker games — Taylor remembered more poker than filming. Mike was there, Taylor was there, Kennedy would sit in on a few, and a few wranglers. "Anybody who could lose a dollar was there," said Taylor. "He played for the pleasure of the game and he played as long as there was a bottle of Commemorativo on the table. When it came to conversation, movies were off-limits. And one of the last times I was at his house, I was looking at this monstrous wall of trophies and honorary diplomas. It was an enormous display, and on the bottom was a line of my uncashed checks, nicely framed, from all of our poker games."

Politics came up occasionally, and Taylor found that you didn't have to be conservative to be well regarded. "I would call him an Old Nazi, and he didn't care. He didn't change his mind about anything, but he didn't care because he didn't have rules or regulations about who was entitled to be his friend. He loved Nixon. Jesus, how do you do that? Reagan I can understand, but Nixon?"

One night Taylor and Wayne were invited to the home of two well-to-do brothers who helped the company scout locations outside Durango. "We got stuck at this thing talking bullshit for hours, and finally we staggered away. There was no car waiting. I didn't know what time it was. So I staggered into an adjoining gym, where there was a sauna and a rubbing table, and he staggered off to his bedroom.

"I woke up the next morning to this masseur Duke had, an old ex-pug. 'Rod, you can't do this to the old man,' he said. 'He's not as young as he used to be.'

" 'Fuck you! He handcuffed me to the fucking sofa until we finished the tequila!' "

Wayne's age was finally beginning to show. He had what Taylor remembered as "lapses," when the energy would flag and he would lie down in a dark room. "He was just kind of ill. If you walked in, he would say, 'Who the fuck is there?' Occasionally, there was a sense that he was harboring his energy. He would sometimes lose his balance on the set. I would say he was slightly infirm."

Once Wayne said something about John Ford that struck Taylor as odd. "He seemed a bit disgusted about one thing — he believed Maureen O'Hara had fooled around with Ford. He was disappointed in her, not Ford. He said, 'Jesus, that face, and that mouth, and his pipe . . .' "

Given his age, and medical past, many actors might have backed off a little, but Wayne was still scheduling pictures a year ahead of time. "I don't think Duke had any alternative to making movies," said Taylor. "In between pictures was not a pleasant time for him, which is why he would have had difficulty in a marriage — he could not get a lot of happiness out of just being together with a woman. His only answer to not having anything to do was to make another movie. He didn't bet on the horses, didn't have a baseball team that he liked. Making movies was exciting; in between movies was the boring part of life."

Taylor found that, as with any actor, you had to get on a wavelength with Wayne. "You alter the game of tennis to suit your opponent, and he enjoyed that — the back and forth. With other people he could be very impatient — one day he told another actor, 'Why don't you learn your fucking lines?' right on the set, in front of everybody — but he was fine with me, even if I changed things. And I think that was because I had been under the baton of Jack Ford, which meant that I knew what I was doing."

The Train Robbers was cameraman William Clothier's final picture. He was seventy years old and had been thinking about quitting for some time. "I like turkey, I have it at Thanksgiving and New Year's but I don't want it seven days a week," was the way he explained it. "If I'm working on a picture at Batjac, I'm picked up at six in the morning to go on location. Duke and I are either the first or second ones on the set. We work until the sun goes down, then I have to go into town to see the rushes. Hell, it's strenuous to get up at 6 A.M. if all you do all day is sit in a rocking chair!"

Clothier's decision also derived from a gradual disinclination to listen to any more of Wayne's constant discontent. "Duke loves the movies but lately it just wasn't fun making pictures. I went to Duke and said, 'Goddammit, Duke, don't yell at me.'

" 'I wasn't yelling at you.'

" 'Well, you were looking at me while you were yelling.'

" 'I was yelling at that stupid goddamn director.'

" 'Well, go tell that stupid goddamn director and stop taking it out on everybody else.' "

Wayne and Clothier were like an old vaudeville team — they had been working together since *Fort Apache,* so long they could finish each other's sentences, and they could also say things to each other that would have been mortally offensive had they come from anybody else. "Old Duke is like my brother . . . but it just wasn't fun anymore."

Also contributing was Clothier's realization that the pictures Wayne was making were programmers, pure and simple; the creeping lack of ambition was irritating. *The Train Robbers* had an excellent cast and is beautifully photographed, but Mike Wayne realized the problem when he said, "I worked very hard on *The Train Robbers* to try to make it into something, when basically the story wasn't that good. I was trying to make up for the story in production values and cast."

So the beauties of *The Train Robbers* are far more physical than behavioral or emotional. And as with *Big Jake,* there's an unpleasant atmosphere of enforced hero worship — the other characters are always admiring Wayne's character, as if the star was feeling insecure. The film is only ninety-one minutes long, but feels longer.

The Train Robbers cost a little more than $4 million and earned rentals in North America equal to its negative cost, with another $1.9 in foreign receipts. Adding in television brought the total rentals to $6.4 million. Warner Bros.' calculations carried the film's break-even at 2.5 times its negative cost, meaning the film had to return $10.5 million to break even. Add in the usual studio financial legerdemain, and Warners carried *The Train Robbers* as $7.57 million in the red.

As the scope of the failure became clear, Burt Kennedy, who wrote and directed the film, sent Mike Wayne a note: "Really feel rotten about 'Train Robbers' falling on its ass. Guess it just wasn't any good." In truth, the films that were making real money weren't westerns. *The Godfather* had earned $86 million, *The Exorcist* $82 million, *The Sting* $78 million. There were no parts for John Wayne in any of these movies, or in the world they were about.

The Train Robbers finished shooting in June 1972, and in November, Wayne was back in Durango for the eighth time shooting a film called *Wednesday Morning,* released as *Cahill U.S. Marshal,* directed by Andrew McLaglen. Wayne's contract again reflected the studio's insecurity about westerns. He was working for a percentage of the gross; on *Cahill* he got 10 percent of the gross up to break-even, 15 percent thereafter.

As with all Batjac productions, *Cahill* was a very smooth operation; budgeted at $4.4 million, after a little more than two weeks they were four days ahead of schedule, and the picture finished two full weeks under schedule and nearly $600,000 under budget. Unfortunately, audiences don't go

784

to movies to marvel at the efficiency of the production. A year and a half after it was released in the summer of 1973, Warners estimated the world rentals for *Cahill* as $6.2 million, including TV sales, which was even less than *The Train Robbers* estimate of $6.4 million.

Cahill is about a marshal with mildly delinquent kids who are black-mailed by a hardened criminal. It's not good, but it's not terrible either. Mainly, it's listless and crudely characterized. Wayne knew it wasn't as good as it could have been: "The theme was a good theme," he said. "It just wasn't a well-done picture. It needed better writing. It needed a little more care in the making."

Andrew McLaglen's relationship to Wayne was complicated. "Andy was a great big guy, a wonderful man, but very unassuming and laid-back," said William Wellman Jr. "He wasn't at all like Wayne. On the set, it appeared that Wayne was in charge, and, in fact, Wayne was in charge. But at the same time he respected Andy and liked him and they got along. But you knew who was the boss."

Perhaps it would be fair to say that McLaglen, Burt Kennedy, and the other men who directed Wayne for Wayne's own production company knew they were there to serve their star. Conversely, on a picture directed by Ford, Hawks, Hathaway, or Wellman, Wayne was there to serve the director and, by extension, the picture.

"I'm amazed by actors who can direct themselves," said Mark Rydell. "It's oppositional; the two skills are in direct contrast to one another. An actor has to live in the moment. If he's really good, he doesn't know what happened during a take. On the first day of shooting *On Golden Pond,* Henry Fonda and Kate Hepburn turned to me after the first take with faces like nineteen-year-old kids. They had become lost in what they were doing, and were unable to evaluate what happened. Which is the appropriate way for an actor to work. If they're judging themselves, then their concentration is not where it belongs."

Mostly, *Cahill* is product, and it shows the extent to which the declines of Ford, Hawks, and Hathaway adversely affected Wayne's career — they had always demanded more of him than he demanded of himself. Without them to nudge him forward, he was content to bask in the familiar, and the familiar won't sustain the career of a sixty-five-year-old movie star. Westerns were dying precisely because of movies like *The Train Robbers* and *Cahill.*

It was while Wayne was wrapping up *Cahill* at the studio that he ran headlong into what might have been. Mel Brooks was at Warners working on the final draft of *Blazing Saddles,* which at the time was called *Black Bart.* Walking through the commissary, Brooks saw John Wayne having lunch and realized Wayne would be hilarious as the Waco Kid — the part eventually played by Gene Wilder. Brooks walked over, introduced himself and asked Wayne to read the script.

"He knew who I was," remembered Brooks, "he had seen and loved *The Producers.* Before he could change his mind I slammed the script on the table and said, 'Please read it at your convenience — like in the next hour.' "

Wayne said he'd read it that night and Brooks could meet him at the commissary the next day. "I met him at the same table at the same time the next day, and he said, 'I read it and found myself actually laughing out loud. It's much too rough and raw. I could never be in a movie that used the N-word, or that had such low-down dirty talk. I'm sorry I can't be in your movie but I promise you I'll be the first one in line to see it.'

"And that is the true story of Mel Brooks, John Wayne, and *Blazing Saddles*."

Cahill U.S. Marshal was Wayne's last picture at Warner Bros. The association that had begun in the early 1930s with the Leon Schlesinger productions constructed around old Ken Maynard footage and had slammed into high gear with the hugely successful Batjac productions of the 1950s limped to an end. There was no recognition of all that Wayne had meant to the studio. Even a few months after *Cahill* was released, in the executive meetings presided over by John Calley, John Wayne's name never came up. It was as if he had never existed.

There was clearly a gradual erosion in Wayne's box office. Simply put, the public would come out for something perceived as special — *True Grit, The Cowboys* — but bread-and-butter westerns such as *The Train Robbers* were now difficult to make profitably.

There have been dozens of theories to explain the apparently permanent decline of the genre. The writer-director Larry Cohen had a novel take: "What killed the western? Burt Kennedy and Andy McLaglen killed the western. They made dozens of them, one after the other, none of them very successful, none of them that good."

While Wayne had moved effortlessly from picture to picture, John Ford sat in Bel Air and stewed. "Ford used to like me," said Burt Kennedy. "He would say, 'You and Duke had some

787

rough times. Duke's got the big head now.' Ford wasn't bitter, he was angry. But that's what they do to you in this town. You make two bad pictures, it's over. It happens to all of us. You get to the point where you don't make as many pictures and you have too much time on your hands. You're not retired, you're just not hired."

Early in 1973 it was announced that Ford would be the recipient of the first American Film Institute Life Achievement Award. There was really no other choice — for one thing, he was the only director to have won six Oscars, universally recognized for his great accomplishments. For another, he was dying of cancer.

All the surviving Ford actors and crew attended. Publicly, they all paid tribute to the Old Man, but some of them hadn't forgiven him. "He kept sending me messages that weekend that he wanted to do a picture with me," remembered Charlton Heston, the chairman of the American Film Institute. "But Hank Fonda told me, 'You wouldn't have liked it. He was a mean son of a bitch.' "

Wayne thought about the best way to pay tribute to his mentor and father figure, and decided on a full-page ad in *Variety.* In Wayne's looping, graceful handwriting, the message read, "Dear Coach, Thanks for a wonderful and eventful life. Duke. John Wayne, 1973."

At the ceremony itself, Wayne seemed tongue-tied; he cut his own speech short with an abrupt, "I love him; I could say more." After the ceremony, there was a receiving line, with Ford in his wheelchair and Wayne standing impassively behind him. When everybody had filed by and congratulated the honoree, Wayne pushed Ford's wheelchair up the ramp and out of the empty ballroom.

Four months later, Ford was on his deathbed. On August 30, 1973, Wayne arrived at Ford's Palm Desert house. "Hi, Duke, down for the death-watch?" asked Ford. "Hell, no, Jack," said Wayne. "You're the anchor — you'll bury us all."

"Oh, well, maybe I'll stick around a while longer then."

But Wayne knew — Ford was terribly emaciated. "He looked so weak," said Wayne.

Then Ford said, "Duke, do you ever think of Ward?"

"All the time," said Wayne.

"Well, let's have a drink to Ward." So Wayne got out the brandy and gave Ford a sip and took one himself. "All right, Duke," said Ford. "I think I'll rest for a while."

John Ford died at 6:35 P.M. the next day, August 31, 1973. An American flag was draped over his body and his life was toasted with a glass of brandy. Then the glasses were broken.

The funeral mass was held at the Church of the Blessed Sacrament in Hollywood. Ford's mahogany coffin was covered by the tattered flag from the Battle of Midway — a battle he had photographed with a handheld 16mm camera. Jean Nugent, Frank Nugent's widow, attended the funeral. Barbara Ford was drunk. "Hi, Jeannie," she said, "I'm looking for Duke, I gotta find Duke." Jean Nugent told her it was her father's funeral, but that didn't help.

"In came the procession," remembered Jean Nugent, "and there was Duke, and I thought he was going to drop dead. He was beet red and could hardly walk." Wayne had obviously been crying heavily. Jean Nugent sat there thinking about John Ford — what a tough taskmaster he had been; how when he and Merian Cooper cashed out of Argosy Productions, they didn't send her husband even a bottle of scotch; how Ford had once told her husband he had only been to three funerals in his life: his father's, his brother's, and Harry Cohn's, because "I wanted to make sure the son of a bitch was dead."

A young makeup man, an ardent Fordian named Michael Blake, also attended the funeral and watched Wayne and a group of stuntmen place Ford's coffin in the hearse for the procession to Holy Cross Cemetery in Culver City. Wayne left the church with Pilar on one arm and Mary Ford on the other. Tears were streaming down Wayne's face. That this giant sequoia was vulnerable to shattering grief, not just on screen but in life, affected Blake, who began sobbing as well.

The funeral procession wound its way to Holy Cross, where Ford was laid to rest near his brother, Francis. Wayne went home to contemplate the definitive end to the best chapter of his life.

"Jack Ford was the one true friend I had," said Wayne after Ford's death. "Jack was the person who had the greatest influence on my life. I don't think I can ever be close to anyone again. I miss that man. Right now I feel lonely. Jack and I didn't need a lot of words. Sometimes we went fishing and we would sit for hours without speaking. We rarely tried to force our personalities on each other. It was a case of knowing you had a friend to turn to. That man was everything to me."

"Ford was so defiant," said Darcy O'Brien, the son of George O'Brien. "I doubt that he ever gave himself to anybody. Can you imagine John Ford in therapy? He was *so* untouchy, *so* unfeely. It would have been very embarrassing had he ever attempted to tell O'Brien or Wayne how much they meant to him. Maybe Ford gave himself to Mary — who knows what they talked about in private? Maybe there was an intimacy there beyond our cliché understanding of marriage.

"But I think John Ford was his movies."

With westerns faltering, it was time for something else. *McQ* was an attempt to catch up to an audience that increasingly felt Wayne was old (cowboy) hat. He had turned down a lot of pictures over the years, usually without regrets. He had turned down *The Dirty Dozen* solely because it was going to be shot in Europe and Pilar was pregnant and he was concerned that the shoot might run into Pilar's due date. He had turned down *Patton,* although since he was a huge admirer of George C. Scott's performance he had no regrets.

But *Dirty Harry* had passed through Batjac, and Wayne had also turned it down. "I made a mistake with that one," he said, ignoring the fact that it would have been an entirely different movie with John Wayne and his house director than it was with Clint Eastwood and his house director. Wayne wasn't crazy about the script for *McQ,* believing that the basic plot was ordinary and that the dialogue was lackluster. But, as he explained, "I haven't made a movie in over six months, and this one is better than most of the junk they've been sending me."

After giving some consideration to Jud Taylor, Stuart Millar, and Don Medford, Batjac actually hired an A list director, but John Sturges was now an A list director on the downhill slide, preoccupied with things that interested him more than the movies — designing a boat, for instance. Sturges's price to direct the picture was $206,000.

McQ shot from June to August 1973 in Seattle and the Olympic Peninsula, the setting for the car chase finale. One of the attractions was that the main character lived on his boat, which meant that Wayne could stay on board the *Wild Goose* while the picture was on location.

Wayne was in a bad mood during the shoot — the noose of Watergate was closing around Nixon's neck. And beneath the affectionate magazine profiles Wayne's life was growing increasingly complicated.

Wayne and Pilar had stopped sleeping together around 1968. Pilar had increasingly staked out a life for herself that had little or nothing to do with her husband. Aside from her passion for tennis, she had converted to Christian Science. As a goodwill gesture, Wayne went to church with her once, but he fidgeted throughout the service. He thought the religion was "too extreme" and didn't understand what on earth his wife was looking for.

He also thought Christian Science was impractical. Once, Aissa got diarrhea and asked Mary St. John what she should do. Mary told her to see a doctor and get some medicine, but Aissa double-checked with her father. He agreed with St. John, but told his daughter not to tell her mother. If, God forbid, Pilar found out her daughter had consulted a doctor, tell her the advice came from Mary St. John.

St. John had been working for Wayne since 1946, and was leaning toward retiring; among other things, she was unhappy about the increasing amount of time she had to devote to being a go-between for Wayne and Pilar. St. John's replacement was a young woman named Pat Stacy, who was hired from the accounting firm of Arthur Andersen. Initially, her duties focused on Wayne's business, personal, and fan mail. Wayne felt it was imperative to honor fan mail requests for photos and such. "He feels," Mary St. John explained to Stacy, "that the fans were responsible for making him a star and keeping him a star, and he's not about to ignore them now. Remember — he's *adamant* about that."

Stacy found that, as a boss, Wayne "required perfection." He was "sensitive, very affectionate, tough if he had to be, had a temper which exploded easily but was over within five minutes. He didn't hold a grudge and had a terrible time with names." And, she noticed, he was terribly restless. "Duke just had to be doing something all the time."

Stacy was thirty-four, relaxed, reasonably efficient, good-looking but not beautiful. But she didn't have St. John's knowledge of the industry or her institutional memory. Tom Kane began to get phone calls from Wayne, with a long list of questions that ordinarily would have been St. John's purview — "What's the name of the little boy in *Trouble Along the Way*?" and so forth. Stacy came to Seattle for the shooting of *McQ*, and Bert Minshall made a pass at her, to no avail. "She was after bigger game," he chuckled.

For the Seattle shoot of *McQ*, Wayne brought his chef from Hollywood, so that the oysters Rockefeller, trout stuffed with crab, and cherries jubilee were just as he liked.

He was smoking cigars, and he was inhaling. "I don't know how in hell you can smoke them without inhaling them," he said. Between the run of indifferent movies, and the indifference to his health, it seems obvious that Wayne was, on some level, no longer willing to make the sacrifices necessary to stay alive, physically or at the box office.

A couple of weeks into the picture, Pilar came with Marisa for a quick visit. Wayne was first delighted, then angry when Pilar left almost as quickly as she had arrived. After Pilar returned to Newport Beach, he and Pat Stacy went to a charity premiere of *Cahill U.S. Marshal* and then to a restaurant.

Everybody was feeling good by the time they got back to the *Wild Goose.* According to Stacy's recollection, she was headed back to her cabin when Wayne took her gently by the arm and escorted her to his stateroom, where she spent the night. "It seemed like the most natural thing in the world to go with him," she recalled.

Shortly after he got back from the location of *McQ,* Wayne and Pilar had a major blowup. She wanted him to retire and spend time with his family — probably the only thing he could not, would not give her.

Wayne came into his daughter Aissa's room and sat down. Slowly, tears began rolling down his face. "Honey, your mother and I are having some serious problems. I love her so much, I love you, I love our family, but I have to work — you know I have to — to support us, and I know it's hard on your mother. She doesn't understand." There was no sobbing, just tears that kept coming faster and faster. John Wayne's seventeen-year-old daughter went over to her sixty-six-year-old father and held him while he cried.

A few days later, Pilar and Wayne separated. Pilar never had a bad word to say about him other than he couldn't or wouldn't adjust to changing times. "That man maybe was not perfect, but he was about 80% perfect," she said years later. "I liked the way he handled himself. I liked the way he treated people."

The underlying problem was the same in 1973 as it had been in 1958: "Pilar felt I was trying to smother her personality," he explained. As if all this wasn't complicated enough, Josie, Wayne's first wife, was also around Newport occasionally. "Josie had a lot of spunk," said Tom Fuentes. "In her mind, she was still married to Duke. But the two women were quite different. Josie was refined and sweet, in a Beverly Hills kind of way. Pilar was very Newport Beach."

Wayne and Pilar officially separated in November 1973. He was miserable about the failure of yet another marriage, but beyond that he was also lonely. "What does she want?" he would ask rhetorically. "I'd give her anything she wants." Joe de Franco concurred, saying, "He never saw it coming. I don't remember any anger at all; I remember disappointment." But Pilar had moved on, although not to the extent of a divorce. She recognized the residual power in being Mrs. John Wayne and wasn't about to let it go.

"She left and moved to Big Canyon," said de Franco. "They would see each other, exchange Christmas presents. I never heard him say an unkind word about her. He supported her in every way he could; he bought her a French restaurant in Corona del Mar."

It was a turbulent time emotionally, but he maintained his professionalism on the set. Julie Adams played McQ's divorced wife and found Wayne "a charming gentleman. He had a sense of humor." Adams and Wayne had never met, so after the introductions were made, they went off and rehearsed the scene just for themselves. "We rehearsed several times, and I felt we caught the undercurrent — two people who were both being polite, but who were in an awkward situation, conscious of all that they had felt for each other. We ran it a few times until we felt it was right." John Sturges made almost no suggestions. A few takes later and the scene was done. Wayne was undoubtedly aware of the resonance the scene had to his own life.

"He was one of those stars who came across on screen as the person he was," said Adams. "Many stars of the studio system did, because that was part of what the studios wanted. I worked with huge movie stars like Tyrone Power and James Stewart, and they were not radically different from how they came across on-screen. Ty Power was terribly charming, with the most exquisite manners, and my idea of heaven was to go to work with Jimmy Stewart every day. Their images were congruent with who they were as people. In that era, you were expected to bring your own personality as part of your screen personality.

"But the scene for *McQ* was a psychologically real scene, so my preparation was to erase my idea of John Wayne, Movie Star and see him as this big cop I used to be married to. John Wayne, Movie Star was also a lovely man and a very good actor."

The attributes of *McQ* were precisely those quiet domestic scenes between Wayne and Adams and

Wayne and Colleen Dewhurst, the latter played for gentle affection. Then there was the hardware — the Trans-Am Wayne drove, the massive machine gun so big Wayne had to cradle it in his arms.

But *McQ* can be filed under the heading of too little, too late. Wayne's cutting notes for the picture are perfunctory, as if he knew there wasn't much to be done: "Trim any close-ups of McQ in the morning after scene in Myra's [Dewhurst] . . . What does McQ see (his POV) as he looks from his car toward the hospital? . . ."

Even if the star had been a more modern figure such as Clint Eastwood, whose career was based on playing characters whose embrace of revenge had little or nothing to do with building or defending a tenuous civilization, in contrast to the pro-social heroism of Wayne; even if Wayne hadn't looked every week of his sixty-six years and been far too old for the part he was playing, *McQ* would have been an ordinary picture. "John Wayne," wrote Vincent Canby of *The New York Times,* "looks as if he should be celebrating his diamond jubilee on the force. . . . There's a scene . . . in which Wayne is required to pick a lock and his massive hands are so gnarled from years on the range that you get the impression of a bear trying to tie a shoelace."

Cheap, but not inaccurate.

Wayne no longer fit particularly well in contemporary stories. It wasn't just his image, although that was part of it, but his own preferences for contrasts of black and white behavior and morality that increasingly consigned him to nineteenth-century settings.

■ ■ ■ ■

Late in 1973, *The Harvard Lampoon* issued a challenge. James Downey, the president of *The Harvard Lampoon,* wrote Wayne a letter. "You think you're tough? You're not so tough. You've never pored through dozens of critical volumes on imagist poetry. You've never gotten your hands dirty with Corrasable Bond and corrector fluid. You've never had to do three papers and a midterm all for one course. The halls of academia may not be the halls of Montezuma, and maybe ivy doesn't smell like sagebrush, but we know a thing or two about guts.

"We challenge you to come to Cambridge and premiere that new movie of yours smack dab in the middle of the most intellectual, the most traditionally radical, in short, the most hostile territory on earth."

In his reply, Wayne wrote, "I'm sorry to note in your challenge that there is a weakness in your breeding, but there is a ray of hope in the fact that you are conscious of it. . . . I shall be most happy to stop by your campus on my way to London to visit the original college whose name you have assumed and whose breeding and manners you haven't been able to buy. May the Good Lord keep you well until I get there."

On January 15, 1974, Wayne showed up at the *Lampoon*'s headquarters on Bow Street, after first riding down Massachusetts Avenue in a tank borrowed from Fort Devens, manned by Army reservists from the 5th Cavalry. A few snowballs were tossed at him, but the crowd was friendly. He was wearing his toupee and a big smile.

At the ceremony, Wayne announced that "coming here is like being invited to lunch with the Borgias." Downey — later a writing stalwart of *Saturday Night Live* — narrated an account of the good old days when Duke Wayne had been a family friend.

"I guess the thing I remember most is the way he would kid us. I guess every visit he'd come and punch us in the mouth. He'd take a length of rubber tubing and crack us with it. Once, I was quite young at the time, five or six, but it seems like yesterday, he put my fingers in a drawer and then he kicked the drawer shut."

Sixteen hundred people gathered at the Harvard Square theater for an amusing Q&A:

"Is it true that since you've lost weight, your horse's hernia has cleared up?"

"Well, the weight was too much for him, so we canned him, which is what you've been eating over at The Harvard Club."

"They thought I was a horse's ass," he would say in retrospect, "but when they saw I was as honest about what I thought as they were about their beliefs, they came around. Then they went too far the other way. We stayed up all night drinking. I guess I was the father they never had."

On the one hand, the Harvard episode showed that Wayne could take a joke; on the other hand, it served as a decent promotion for *McQ,* which needed all the help it could get. Made for purely commercial reasons, *McQ* cost $3.24 million, $274,000 under budget, but stalled out at slightly more than $4 million in rentals in North America and $2.5 million in foreign rentals. The film went into profit in 1980 — a year after Wayne died. "He hated that picture," said Cecilia deMille Presley. "He told me, 'I shouldn't have done it.' " But shooting movies was better than hanging around the house.

Perhaps the stress of another failed marriage inspired another bad decision about a script. Shortly after Clint Eastwood made *High Plains Drifter* in 1973, Eastwood optioned a script by Larry Cohen entitled *The Hostiles* as a prospective vehicle for himself and John Wayne. *The Hostiles* involved a gambler (Eastwood) who wins 50 percent of a ranch owned by an older man (Wayne). The two men have to become partners, which is complicated by the fact that they can't stand each other. There's a battle coming that will destroy the ranch, so Eastwood, who knows about the situation, sells his half of the ranch back to Wayne, who's innocent of the underlying situation. At the last minute, Eastwood returns to help the older man fight off the hostiles.

Eastwood's Malpaso sent the script to Wayne's Batjac, with a note saying that Eastwood thought the script promising, albeit needing some work. Wayne returned it with a "No, Thanks."

Eastwood's option ran out, and shortly afterward he moved his production company over to Warner Bros., where he again optioned the script and again pitched it to Wayne. This time, Wayne responded with a letter complaining about the portrayal of the townspeople in *High Plains Drifter* — they did not, he said, accurately represent the spirit of the pioneers who had made America great.

Eastwood didn't write back, and once again the option expired, at which point Mike Wayne called Larry Cohen and asked if *The Hostiles* was available. "Are you kidding me?" asked Cohen. "You've held that script up for two years; if you want to buy it, buy it." Mike said that his dad was going out on the *Wild Goose* over the weekend, and he'd once again pitch him the script. Cohen sent over a copy.

On Tuesday, Cohen called Mike. "Well," Mike said, "Dad was sitting on the deck and he looked at the script for a few minutes and said, 'This piece of shit again,' and he threw it overboard."

Cohen had a sudden vision of his script floating on the Pacific Ocean, taking with it his hopes of a movie starring the two preeminent masculine role models of their respective generations. There was no further explanation of why Wayne didn't like the script, but that came during a conversation with Pat Stacy: "This kind of stuff is all they know how to write these days. The sheriff is the heavy, the townspeople a bunch of jerks; someone like me and Eastwood ride into town, know everything, act the big guys, and everyone else is a bunch of idiots." Perhaps it was the idea of being rescued by another character, perhaps it was simply tradition's discomfort with a more minimalist, modern star.

Soon afterward, Mike Wayne called Cohen with yet another offer. Would he be interested in working with Budd Boetticher on a rewrite of a script for Batjac? The money was okay, so Cohen agreed. The script, called *When There's Somethin' to Do,* involved Germans trying to infiltrate the Mexican military during World War I in order to build up a second front across the Rio Grande. Wayne's character was to lead a party that went across the border to fight the German influence in the Mexican army.

"I went in and worked for a few weeks with

Budd," remembered Cohen. "He was a very affable guy, very desperate to get a picture, which he hadn't had in years. Nobody would give him a job, and he was planning on directing the picture for Batjac."

In later years, Boetticher would be ambivalent about Wayne, but when he and Cohen were working on the script, he was completely positive. "He thought Wayne was great on-screen," said Larry Cohen, "because he was. He was a very good actor who didn't get the credit he deserved."

One day when Boetticher wasn't there, Mike Wayne said to Cohen, "Budd's not going to direct this picture." Cohen was thunderstruck. " 'Why string him along?' I asked. I just didn't know what to do. I didn't know how to tell Budd; he thought he was going to direct and that John Wayne wanted him to direct it. Every time I went into a meeting about the script I felt like I was betraying Budd. And I never did tell him the truth."

Cohen and Boetticher completed their draft, but it never got made, by Boetticher or anybody else. Cohen believed that Mike wanted to make the picture — "He didn't care what picture he made as long as he made something" — but that somehow a decision had been made that Boetticher would not direct.

Perhaps *When There's Somethin' to Do* would have been a good picture, but certainly *The Hostiles* would have been better than the standard-issue Wayne pictures of the period, if only because of the intriguing chemistry of Wayne and Eastwood. "Writing a John Wayne picture would have been the highlight of my career," said Larry Cohen. "But he did dull fucking pictures like *Cahill* and *The Train Robbers* instead of a picture with

Clint Eastwood. Can you imagine?"

It was becoming clear that for every recent great western such as *Once Upon a Time in the West* or *The Wild Bunch,* there was a comedy western such as *Cat Ballou* and *Blazing Saddles* that relentlessly ridiculed the genre.

As early as 1967, Richard Goldstein had written a prescient article about Wayne for the *Los Angeles Times:* "Duke sees the Western as an eternal form, solid and unchanging. He is dead wrong. The Western is a living mythology, and like all vital folklore, it evolves with the times. The American saga is a continuing story. The John Wayne hero is built to survive massacres, tidal waves and corruption. But it can never bear the erosion of style."

Westerns might have been dying, but the machine still had to be fed. The fish-out-of-water cop story *Brannigan* was shot in the summer of 1974 in England. The picture had the dual benefits of qualifying for production subsidies under the Eady plan, and for getting its star out of the country at a time when he was restless. "He was getting away from Pilar," said Gretchen Wayne, "and it was easy to go to England and make *Brannigan* at the same time."

After he arrived in London, Pilar flew over with Marisa, Ethan, and Aissa. She initially told Wayne that the children missed him, but many people in the family believed that Pilar was trying to effect a reconciliation. Since Wayne was living with Pat Stacy while in London, the situation was a lot closer to Ernst Lubitsch than John Ford. Although Wayne admired Lubitsch's films, he had no knack for equivalent social situations. He told Stacy that she had to move out of their rented house on

Cheyne Walk and into the Penta Hotel, where the crew was staying.

After several nights at the Penta, Stacy eagerly accepted an invitation from Luster Bayless to go shopping at Harrod's. Someone saw them leaving the hotel and word got back to Wayne, who promptly accused Stacy of having an affair behind his back. It wasn't true, but Wayne was very sensitive about the possibility.

A few nights later, Wayne invited Bayless and Stacy for dinner, so he could size up their relationship. At the same time, Pilar was eyeing Stacy trying to figure out what the attraction was. The day before Pilar was to fly home, Stacy worked up the courage to tell Wayne that if he wanted to go back to his family, she'd understand. "Don't ever talk about it again," he snapped.

Wayne took a few days off from the picture and flew Stacy to Paris. He ordered her to get a room at the George V, but it was summer and all the major hotels were booked solid. With the noblesse oblige of a Star, he instructed the cab driver to take them from Orly to the George V, walked in, and was given a suite.

The time in Paris cemented the relationship. Stacy remembered that as a lover, Wayne was "affectionate, considerate and gentle. If there weren't fireworks bursting in the air, we didn't care. Neither of us was a kid."

Brannigan was originally written by Christopher Trumbo and Michael Butler as a TV pilot for Telly Savalas. Jules Levy and Arthur Gardner, the producers, got the script and thought it was too good for a TV show. "And that's when the name John Wayne came in," remembered Trumbo.

But Trumbo was the son of the blacklisted

screenwriter Dalton Trumbo and the producers thought that might be a problem for Wayne. They called Mike Wayne and asked him if his father would object. Mike said no, but Levy and Gardner were still nervous.

Mike told his father that Trumbo was the son of Dalton Trumbo. Did that make any difference? "I only want to know if he can write," said Wayne. Wayne liked the script, but when revisions got under way — the story stayed the same, but the dialogue and some scenes were modified — Trumbo and Butler weren't called in to do them. In fact, Christopher Trumbo never met John Wayne.

For many of the blacklistees, Wayne remained a lightning rod, which became clear when Carl Foreman wrote a scathing article for *Punch* in August of 1974, which was reprinted in the Writers Guild of America magazine that December. The piece was in response to an interview Wayne gave in London about Foreman and "his rotten *High Noon.*"

"A week or so ago," Foreman began, "I was in the counting house, fondling the paltry residue of all that good old Moscow gold we used to get so regularly from Comrade Beria, back in those marvelous subversive Hollywood days."

Foreman pointed out that when Wayne had handed Gary Cooper his Oscar for *High Noon,* he had said, "Why can't I find me a scriptwriter to write me a part like the one that got you this?"

"He could have got me very easily, except that I was blacklisted in Hollywood and looking for work in England."

Foreman went on to recall his one and only meeting with Wayne, at Bö Roos's office on a

Saturday morning. "We were alone, equally uncomfortable, like two teenagers in a whorehouse, and the meeting began with old world courtesy and tact. . . . Good old Duke had given up his Saturday morning solely to help me hit the sawdust trail to political salvation.

"All that was required were a few public confessions, complete with breast-beating, and a reasonable amount of informing on old friends, passing acquaintances or absolute strangers, for that matter. Just a little cooperation, that was all, and I'd be working again."

Foreman refused, and Wayne said that if that was his final decision, he'd never work in films again. "It was a pity, he said, because obviously I wasn't a commie bastard, really, just a dupe." After calling the Motion Picture Alliance "a scurvy gang of character assassins," and Ward Bond a man "who could smell a Jew-commie a mile away," Foreman warmed to his task.

Ask him if there was ever a political blacklist in Hollywood, and he will look you in the eye and say, Oh, dear me, no, never. Or, if there ever actually was one, unbeknownst to old Duke, it was probably the commies who were trying to blacklist the real Americans, who naturally defended themselves and saved Hollywood, if not, for that matter, the nation itself. But no one was blacklisted, ever. . . .

Ask him what he thinks of Joe McCarthy, and he will tell you that, as near as he can remember, the Senator was a much vilified, much misunderstood, great, great American.

Ask him if it wasn't indecent, if not to say vicious, to break Larry Parks, live on TV, and then

806

destroy him forever in films and he will reply cynically (and untruthfully) that Parks, then at the height of his career, wasn't working much anyway. Or, at least, not as much as old Duke. Ask him if it isn't true that for quite a time you couldn't work in Hollywood unless old Duke, Hedda Hopper, Ward Bond and a cheapjack union boss named Roy Brewer passed on your "Americanism" and he won't remember any such thing. Or other things, such as suicides and broken homes and heart attacks and people dying long before their time, like John Garfield and Joe Bromberg and Robert Rossen and others.

Twenty-two years had passed, and Foreman had amassed huge success in England with *The Guns of Navarone* and *Born Free,* among others. He was still enraged. Wayne read Foreman's piece and called it "a scathing attack," although he also said that Foreman was "a helluva writer."

Neither Wayne nor Foreman was about to forget, and forgiveness seemed a long way off. Not all of the blacklistees went to their graves hating their opponents. Dalton Trumbo was alive when his son got screen credit for writing *Brannigan,* but they never discussed it. Trumbo senior was a pragmatist, but that wasn't the basis for his calm response.

"It wasn't really a concern of mine or his," said Christopher Trumbo.

Before the blacklist, all of those guys on both sides of the political question worked together. My dad worked for Sam Wood, the head of the Motion Picture Alliance, on *Kitty Foyle.* They were ideological enemies, but you can work with your ideological enemies because politics doesn't come up. It doesn't belong there. It happened all the time then and it still happens. My father's point about his work was always to appreciate what everybody brings to the project.

What my father always tried to zero in on was this: who was responsible? What power did individuals have? Nobody wanted to go before the committee and answer the questions positively or negatively. When people quit the Communist Party, they didn't rush off to the papers and offer up the names of the other people in the party. They were compelled to do that by a congressional committee who had the power to throw them into jail.

The informer is far down the food chain; my father wanted people to remember who the enemy really was. He didn't like informers, but the idea of focusing attention on the informer is a mistake.

One way or another, he was always trying to operate from principle, and when you do that you take the longer view. People focus on Elia Kazan, they don't focus on the Committee. Kazan didn't want to inform. Robert Rossen, same thing. Those men didn't change overnight; they didn't become different people.

Wayne replicated the certainty of his screen character by refusing to admit he might have been wrong or at least overenthusiastic in his participation in blacklisting through the Motion Picture Alliance. Those things he deeply regretted — his marital failures, his failure to serve — he kept resolutely private.

And he did indeed try to justify the Alliance's

behavior on retributive grounds. "It was the commies who did the first blacklisting," he insisted, pointing to Morrie Ryskind, a Pulitzer Prize winner for *Of Thee I Sing,* and longtime screenwriter (*A Night at the Opera, My Man Godfrey,* among others). Ryskind, Wayne insisted, was blacklisted by Dore Schary at MGM because of his anticommunist activities.

Schary responded by saying that Ryskind had been up for a job at MGM only once during Schary's tenure as studio head. Schary was willing to pay him $2,000 a week, but Ryskind asked for $3,500. Schary thought that was too much and the deal was never made.

In fact, MGM contract files show that Ryskind was employed by MGM twice: once in 1934 and once in 1935 to work on *A Night at the Opera,* along with an undated deal from the 1930s to buy the title *Strike Up the Band.* Ryskind was never employed at MGM during the 1940s, and had his last screen credit for adapting the Ginger Rogers vehicle *Heartbeat* in 1946 — before the blacklist wave broke.

Everybody wants to be the victim.

But unlike many on the political right, the personal always trumped the political for Wayne. Several years after Foreman's magazine piece, Wayne went to the popular Los Angeles restaurant Dan Tana's for dinner, and there was Foreman. The two men looked at each other, then quickly embraced as if they were old friends. Foreman called over his English wife and young child and introduced them to his antagonist.

Later, after they sat down to dinner, Foreman's wife asked him about the sudden change of heart. "He was a patriot," said Foreman. "I was a patriot.

He didn't do it to hurt me." As with Dalton Trumbo, Foreman made a distinction between those who acted out of political principle, and those who acted out of personal expediency.

The shifting alliances, residual anguish, and attempted moral equivalencies of the blacklist era are far more interesting and worthy of passionate response than *Brannigan.* Wayne's budgets had been averaging around $4 million, but *Brannigan* was made for $2.5 million, with Wayne getting $750,000 of that plus 10 percent of the gross after $7.5 million. The total script costs for four writers were a minute $50,000, Richard Attenborough got $60,000 to co-star, and director Douglas Hickox, primarily a director of commercials until he had made the entertaining *Theatre of Blood* in 1973, got only $50,000.

Wayne did some halfhearted promotion for *Brannigan,* hosting journalists at his house dressed in a natty blue blazer despite the fact that he had just gotten out of a dentist's chair. The tequila was uncorked, and the journalists responded by baiting the tired old bull. They asked him about Cambodia, they asked him about a recent biography that had (wrongly) suggested he was conceived out of wedlock.

"If my mother was alive, she'd have taken a horsewhip to the big stupid son of a bitch and run him out of town. And if I hadn't offered to do it for her, she'd have turned the whip on me."

When one of the reporters suggested suing, Wayne warmed to his core issue — the gap between the world he inhabited as a young man and still inhabited as an actor, and the world he saw around him. "That's the trouble with you people — you *sue* people. I think you ought to take it out in pieces of their body. We're becoming a nation of who-can-you-sue instead of what is decent and graceful and nice and clean. I just don't know how to think anymore. I don't know who I'm talking to or which one of you is a person who believes in a completely different world than the one I was brought up to believe in."

Finally, he tried to turn the subject back closer to the ostensible subject at hand — show business as a celebration of grace and style. He picked a book off the coffee table and began flipping through the pages. "Here is the most beautiful person I've known in my whole life," he said, pointing to a picture of Margot Fonteyn taking a bow after a performance of *Swan Lake.*

The tub thumping for *Brannigan* entailed an appearance on the popular CBS sitcom *Maude.* The premise wasn't bad — Maude, played by Beatrice Arthur, was a loudmouthed feminist, and the idea of her sparring with Mr. Conservative promised some laughs, somewhat in the manner of Sammy Davis Jr. kissing Archie Bunker on *All in the Family.* But the writers didn't follow through and had Maude go weak in the knees at the sight of him.

"I've spent thousands of hours in dark theaters loving you, Duke," she says.

Wayne looks roguish. "Was that you?" The writing, and the undying sitcom mannerism of braying the lines to the furthest reaches of the balcony submarined the show.

Brannigan offered the unappetizing sight of an apparently demoralized, overweight sixty-eight-year-old man playing a cop under the undistinguished aegis of a British B movie director. It was pure hackwork, and it got what it deserved. The North American rentals on *Brannigan* came to only $2 million — a flat-out flop.

With his own commercial appeal clearly on the wane, Wayne kept a wary eye on younger actors who were siphoning off his audience. He gave two primary rivals respect, if not enthusiasm. "I like most of what [Steve] McQueen has been doing and I think Eastwood has a chance. Peckinpah? Well, our business is all about getting attention. Peckinpah got the attention of the public by throwing away what I still think pictures are all about — illusion. He brought in realism. Capsules of exploding calf's blood for when a guy gets shot. Not my cup of tea."

But Wayne was a capitalist, and in a capitalist society public appetites have a way of being met. "I can't find fault too much with what these people are doing," he said. "If people want to see nude pictures, they're going to make nude pictures. If they want to see dirty pictures, they're going to make dirty pictures."

In most respects, Wayne had always functioned above public taste and studio politics, if not his own. He wanted to make a western — the public came; he played Genghis Khan — the public came. The public's taste conformed to Wayne's powerful personality and knack for delivering movies as the people wanted to see them.

But now he was older, heavier not just in body but in spirit. The image that he had built and sustained for nearly fifty years was working against him, at least in part because of his unflinching support of the most conservative causes — Vietnam, Nixon — which in turn bred hostile responses from the opposing camp who repeatedly characterized him, as Wayne put it, as "a caricature of a heavy in a Gene Autry western."

"On occasions . . . I have used sensationally bad English," he said,

but I've done it to exaggerate a point. Yet, there's a tendency, seemingly to have me drop my g's and to quote me in poor English *on every occasion.* I think that if they would go through the letters I have written — I write thirty or forty letters a day when I'm not on a picture — I don't think they will find the type of English they try to put in my mouth. I don't mind that. It's not irritating to me. I know how well educated I am and I also know how stupid I am, so anything they might do to set the picture doesn't bother my ego. . . .

The way the majority of them show their objectivity — if John Wayne rides down a street with Ann-Margret, their objective reporting will read something like this: "A balding, gray-haired old man with a rather heavy paunch is riding down the street with Ann-Margret." The objective thing only goes as far as I'm concerned. At least they could say, "with the beautiful Ann-Margret," but that's not the way it would be written.

He thought about playing General Douglas MacArthur in a biopic at Universal but finally turned it down, saying, "He was a magnificent man, one of the few people I really admire. But I don't honestly think there's a story in him. Maybe I'm wrong. I've blown enough films in my time." Despite a good performance by Gregory Peck, who was, in any case, more physically suited to the part than Wayne, the film failed.

After *Brannigan,* there was no doubt about Pat

813

Stacy's place in Wayne's life. "He was so lonely," said Cecilia deMille Presley, "and Pat Stacy was there." Pilar and Wayne would never sign divorce papers, according to Gretchen Wayne, "because he didn't want to be a three-time loser. And that way he never had to marry Pat Stacy."

Stacy would be Wayne's companion for the rest of his life, but there would always be a clear demarcation between her and the rest of the family. One day, Cecilia deMille Presley noticed an attractive picture of Wayne and Stacy on a desk and suggested he sign it to Stacy with a suitably loving inscription. "He looked at me as if I was crazy," remembered Presley. "And that told me everything. Pat was there, someone to keep him warm. But it didn't go further than that."

After Wayne's death, Stacy wrote a book that some in the family felt glamorized their affair to make it seem more than it was. Aissa said that Wayne was always slightly distant with Stacy whenever the family was around. If he had loved her that much, their reasoning went, he would have married her.

In September of 1974, Wayne once again donned his eyepatch and flew to Oregon for location work on *Rooster Cogburn,* a sequel to *True Grit.* Surprisingly, Hal Wallis's staff had made a preliminary list of people who could conceivably play Rooster, although Wayne was always first choice. Following him were Clint Eastwood, Paul Newman, Gene Hackman, George C. Scott, Steve McQueen, Marlon Brando, Anthony Quinn, Burt Lancaster, Richard Burton, Charles Bronson, Lee Marvin, Gregory Peck, Kirk Douglas, Charlton Heston, Robert Mitchum, and Rock Hudson. It was more or less a catch-all list of every leading man of the period, but Wallis got his first, his only choice.

Wallis's initial idea for Wayne's leading lady was Ingrid Bergman, who might have been a better choice than Katharine Hepburn, if only because Hepburn and Wayne were similarly assertive personalities who could cancel each other out. Bergman was softer, as well as sexier, while Hepburn's sexuality had long been subsumed by her expert playing of a succession of flinty spinsters.

Bergman didn't work out, which opened the door for other possibilities. Maureen O'Hara was considered, as well as Maggie Smith, Vanessa Redgrave, or Glenda Jackson. "We should talk about Bette Davis too," wrote Paul Nathan, Wallis's associate producer, "although I think she'd turn over the raft and beat the hell out of Wayne."

Wallis began negotiating with Hepburn, but Paul Nathan offered the wild card of a comeback from Loretta Young, who was Mike Wayne's godmother and still a friend of the family. Wallis drew a line through Young's name and scribbled "No thanks" on the memo. As the choices for his leading lady narrowed, Wayne decided to throw in his two cents.

In a surprising letter to Wallis that shows both his big-picture viewpoint and his knowledge of film history, he pointed out that Wayne and Hepburn together were no guarantee of success: "To the people under 30 years old the combination won't mean anything but two older people in a picture . . . so far no one has ever made a success of [a picture] about two old people — not even *Make Way for Tomorrow,* directed by Leo McCarey could stand the pressure."

He went on to say that someone younger — he mentioned Mary Tyler Moore — with some appeal to younger audiences might be a better idea. It was a typically logical argument, but Wallis wasn't deterred. Hepburn was signed that same month for $150,000, plus $100,000 deferred and 10 percent of the net profits.

Wallis again offered the director's job to Henry Hathaway, but Hathaway wasn't too sure — he thought the script, which had mostly been written by Wallis's wife, actress Martha Hyer under the name Martin Julien — "Marty" was Hyer's nickname, and "Julien" was her father's name — was close to self-parody. There were also some contributions from Wallis, while Charles Portis, the author of *True Grit,* did a polish on the dialogue. The result was a more or less blatant retread of *The African Queen* — Hepburn as a prim minister's relative stuck with a boisterous but resourceful drunk on a dangerous river voyage.

Wayne's notes on Hyer's script are dated May 6, 1974. This version of the script picks up Cogburn after he is no longer a marshal and is more or less the town drunk. Wayne took exception to seeing Cogburn falling that low. Beyond that, he thought that there was a lack of a point of view; he referred to the scene in *True Grit* where Rooster shoots a rat and talks about how the law can miscarry justice. He felt it was important that Rooster be able to justify his killing, as a way of asserting that he hasn't gone completely to seed. Wallis seemed to agree with almost all of Wayne's points, checking them off one by one, and the things Wayne objected to were indeed altered in the final script.

After thinking about it, Hathaway turned down the picture. Aside from the script, trying to handle both Wayne and Hepburn on a distant location just seemed like too much work for a man who was, as he liked to point out, quite wealthy.

At that point, Wallis began canvassing for a director. Wallis wrote Wayne telling him that George Seaton was working on a play, hence unavailable, and mentioned some alternatives: Lamont Johnson, Charles Jarrott, John Avildsen, John Moxey. Wallis lobbied hard for Dick Richards, who had made *The Culpepper Cattle Co.,* but Wayne resisted because of what he felt to be "a lot of bad taste" in the picture. There were many other possibilities, but at no time were the names of either Sam Peckinpah or Sergio Leone in the mix, indicating that Wayne, Wallis, or both of them felt they were unacceptable.

Wayne overcame his reservations about Dick Richards, but Richards couldn't overcome his reservations about the script. Tom Gries was also in the last stage of the directorial competition, but Wallis decided he didn't like Gries's penchant for multiple cameras.

Wallis deserved to be criticized for his eventual choice: Stuart Millar, a man who had directed precisely one picture (*When the Legends Die*). It was a lowball choice — Millar was only making $50,000 — indicative of Wallis's preference at this stage of his career for younger, cheaper directors, probably because they were less inclined to argue.

In the first week of September the cast and crew assembled for six weeks of location work in and around the Cascade Mountains near Bend, Oregon. Just before shooting started, Hepburn told Millar, "You realize, of course, that you are working with three bullies."

Faced with two bullies too many, Millar never had a chance.

Production got under way on September 4, returned to the studio on October 28, and wrapped two days later, six days under schedule. The only real mishap involved Wayne getting hit in the eye with a golf club swung by his daughter. Waiting for the swelling to go down took four days, and Wallis dropped a couple of scenes rather than reschedule them.

The working day habitually began with Wayne and Hepburn telling Millar how the scenes should be shot. Millar would groan and Hepburn would offer her nostrum of the day, which was borrowed from the script: "A sharp knife cuts the quickest and hurts the least." Hal Wallis joined the scrum by sending Millar memos complaining about coverage — too many setups per scene, with lines being dropped.

When Millar would call Wayne on his ad-libbing, Wayne groused, "I haven't said lines just as they were written in a scene since I worked for Mascot Productions." Wayne's main complaint was that Millar was indecisive and overshot. "Goddammit," he said, "we can say these lines just so many times before they stop making sense." Millar would say "Action!" and Wayne would grumble that he wasn't ready yet. Or Millar would say "Cut" and Wayne would say, "No! Keep going." The cameraman usually followed Wayne's orders. When Millar got flustered, Wayne would pile on: "Hey, Mister Director, you're supposed to say 'Action' aren't you?" At one point, Wayne fulminated that Millar was "a six-foot-six son of a bitch no-talent."

Hepburn's touchy mood might have been exacerbated by hip surgery she had undergone nine months earlier. She hated the way she looked and wouldn't watch rushes; she did her lipstick with a special mirror that blocked out her face so she wouldn't have to look at the lines and wrinkles.

"Katharine Hepburn was all over the place," said Mark Rydell, who would direct her in *On Golden Pond.* "She would give you much too much. You had to curb her, contain her." Millar couldn't contain either of them. Twice Wallis went to Wayne and offered to fire Millar, and twice Wayne said no; it would hurt Millar's career and Wayne said that if they all worked together and did what needed to be done they could make the best of it.

The relationship between Wayne and Hepburn could be characterized as a chaste infatuation. "I can honestly say I never met a man who worked harder or played harder than Duke," said Hepburn. "He was a total straight-shooter, decent, and fun. Just a natural. We were up in the Cascades, and some days we got on our horses and rode all day. Great fun. Big man. Small backside." (Hepburn mentioned what she considered Wayne's most delectable physical attribute whenever she was asked about him.)

Wayne gave her both front-handed and backhanded compliments. "Christ, she wants to do everything," he complained. "She can't ride worth a damn and I gotta keep reining my horse in so she can keep up. But I'd hate to think of what this goddamned picture would be without her."

Hal Wallis and Paul Nathan managed to convince themselves that everything was wonderful. "Have been loving the dailies," wrote Nathan to

819

Hepburn. "Truly excellent film on you and Duke. You both make sparks fly — each scene tops the previous, is so special and so fine. I'm very certain Hal and Martha have told you all of that, though."

Wayne and Hepburn more or less co-directed the picture, and Wallis thought it was just as well. (Millar never directed another theatrical feature.) But both stars were feeling their age. Work was now hard. One day on location, Hepburn asked Wayne, "Do you mind if I ask you a personal question? Do you hurt?"

"In every joint," was the reply.

On the last day of shooting in Oregon, Hal Wallis threw a party, but the weather had turned cold, and that, plus the elevation, caused Wayne to start wheezing and gasping. There was a canister of oxygen nearby, and he recovered, but it was a clear indication of the razor's edge Wayne had been walking since the cancer surgery eleven years before.

After *Rooster Cogburn* was cut and scored, plans were made for publicity, but Wayne begged off, telling Universal that he was still battling a viral pneumonia he couldn't shake, on top of which he had some business affairs that were going to involve months of effort. He told them that the male audience would come because of his presence, but they needed to get Hepburn to give them some time for publicity in order to draw the female audience.

In September 1975, a long-simmering series of perceived slights finally exploded and Wayne wrote a recriminatory letter to Hal Wallis — a laundry list of accumulated grievances. The proximate cause, it seems, was Universal's decision to move the release date of *Rooster Cogburn* from the summer to the fall.

Wayne accused Wallis of panicking when Wayne told him about his cancer eleven years before; Wayne accused him of using Paramount's money to outbid Batjac for *True Grit;* Wayne castigated him for the choice of Stuart Millar, and he made a preemptive strike on some of the particulars of a second sequel to *True Grit* that Wallis was already preparing.

Wallis responded with a four-page, single-spaced letter giving chapter and verse of why he was not at fault. He pointed out that Charles Portis's agent had announced that the price for *True Grit* was $300,000 plus a small percentage of the gross, and that in the event of more than one bid, Portis reserved the right to designate which company got the property. Wallis said that it was his understanding that Mike Wayne had actually bid $350,000, but that Portis had chosen Wallis to make the movie because he had liked a couple of Wallis's earlier westerns: *Last Train from Gun Hill* and *Gunfight at the O.K. Corral.*

"You got the deal and a 1/3 interest in the picture along with Paramount and myself and if that isn't a joint venture I don't know what is," wrote Wallis. As for the release date, Wallis pointed out that Universal was releasing *Rooster Cogburn* in the same month they had released *Airport* and *American Graffiti.*

The underlying problem was that Wayne had felt betrayed by Universal when they backed out of *The Green Berets* and he remained suspicious of their motives. "I had nothing to do with it," wrote Wallis of the *Green Berets* incident. "I was not even on the lot."

Wayne's letter had suggested that if Universal

821

did not want to give a fixed starting date for the next sequel, then Wallis should give him a guaranteed deal, i.e., Wayne would get paid whether the picture got made or not. Wallis didn't want to do that, because then he'd be holding the bag for a $5 million picture. Wallis pointed out that he had already been on location trips to New Mexico and Arizona, and Charles Portis was working on the script, which should certainly indicate good faith in the matter.

Wallis agreed with Wayne on one issue only: Stuart Millar. "I confess that was a mistake." He then reminded Wayne that twice during production he had offered to fire Millar but that Wayne wouldn't allow it.

What was most hurtful to Wallis was the suggestion that he had panicked about losing a cheap commitment from Dean Martin when *The Sons of Katie Elder* needed to be postponed. Wayne had no way of knowing that most of Wallis's organization had wanted him to hire another leading man to replace Wayne, and he had flatly refused.

"This is grossly unfair," an obviously hurt Wallis wrote, going on to say, "My only concern was for your well-being." He never defended himself by citing the list of employees who wanted him to hire another actor and be done with it.

Wallis closed by saying, "We have worked together on three pictures, all of them successful. I have enjoyed all of them and want to continue an association that gives me a great deal of pleasure. My principal concern is to make this thing work to your satisfaction and to get all other matters behind us."

Rooster Cogburn has come to be regarded as a missed opportunity at best, a reheated dinner at worst. Henry Hathaway filled the original film with beautiful, well-photographed locations; he knew, as did Ford and Hawks, that in a western the landscape is a character, and in *True Grit* the fluttering leaves of the aspen trees that surround the final shootout and the mantle of snow in the film's last scene lend intimations of mortality.

But despite the Oregon locations, *Rooster Cogburn* is perfunctorily photographed. Besides that, the film feels unshaped, little more than a succession of scenes. Budgeted at $4.6 million (Wayne got $750,000 and a percentage of the net), *Rooster Cogburn* brought in $7.5 million in rentals in North America, so it should have made a little money. But, relative to expectations, it was yet another disappointment.

It was now clear that a hero who had survived deep into a period devoted to antiheroes had finally been tripped up by time. The western was the genre that perfectly accommodated Wayne's particular gifts, but it was also a genre that was becoming extinct.

As a picture, *Rooster Cogburn* didn't live up to *True Grit,* but it did provide Wayne with a chance to meet and know Hepburn. She wrote him several starstruck letters. ("You are an extraordinary actor-man-spirit-creature . . . I am as goofy as a fan from Nebraska.") Befitting a woman who'd had relationships with Leland Hayward, John Ford, and Spencer Tracy, Kate Hepburn liked her men masculine and complicated. A magazine piece she wrote about Wayne is little short of a mash note:

"From head to toe he is all of a piece. Big head. Wide blue eyes. Sandy hair. Rugged skin — lined by living and fun and character. Not by just rotting away. A nose not too big, not too small. Good teeth. A face alive with humor. Good humor, I should say, and a sharp wit. Dangerous when roused. His shoulders are broad — very. His chest massive — very. When I leaned against him (which I did as often as possible, I must confess — I am reduced to such innocent pleasures) thrilling. It was like leaning against a great tree."

Having gotten the fluttery pleasantries out of the way, she got serious: "Politically, he is a reactionary. He suffers from a point of view based entirely on his own experience. He was surrounded in his early years in the motion picture business by people like himself. Self-made. Hard working. Independent. . . . People who were willing to live or die entirely on their own independent judgment. Jack Ford, the man who first brought Wayne into the movies, was cut from the same block of wood. . . . They seemed to have no patience and no understanding of the more timid and dependent type of person. Pull your own freight. This is their slogan. Sometimes I don't think that they realize that their own load is attached to a very powerful engine."

When Wayne was told that Hepburn said he reminded her of Spencer Tracy, he first circled, then encompassed that relationship: "She's some woman. A strong feminist and yet, you know, she worshipped her father. . . . Tracy was like a father to her, a god." He searched for the right words, then formed his arms into a circle. "He really enclosed her."

At Thanksgiving 1975, Wayne and Pat Stacy headed for Arizona to spend the holiday with Louis Johnson and his wife and attend the livestock sale. This time, he drove rather than flew. Cold sober, Wayne drove like he was drunk, swerving in and out of lanes and treating other cars as if they were the enemy.

When they finally got to Stanfield, Stacy was charmed by the Johnsons and in love with rural Arizona. Alice Johnson prepared a Thanksgiving feast, with special attention to the pies that Wayne loved — he thought Alice's pies were the best in the world.

Around this time, a reporter asked him if he still had any specific ambitions.

"Ambition? Son of a bitch, yes. I have an ambition, and that's to get up every morning still breathing." To another writer, he put it even more simply: "I'm very conscious that now I know more dead people than live ones. But I don't try to live back there. I try to live in tomorrow."

CHAPTER TWENTY-FOUR

Glendon Swarthout's novel *The Shootist* was bought before publication by the producing team of Mike Frankovich and William Self for $350,000. The price included a first-draft screenplay from Miles Hood Swarthout, the author's son. Frankovich and Self found financing from Dino De Laurentiis, who took all foreign rights in return for veto power over star and director.

Self flew to New York for a meeting with George C. Scott, who was starring in *Death of a Salesman.* Scott didn't think he wanted to do a western, but a meeting with Self and the nature of the part convinced him. Self returned to Hollywood to give Frankovich and De Laurentiis the good news about Scott, at which point they told him they wanted John Wayne. "Scott is not a western star," explained Frankovich, "and we know the low level of a John Wayne western. We know we won't go below that."

Wayne was officially cast on August 30, 1975, which gave the production plenty of time to fine-tune the script and production — the picture wasn't scheduled to start until the New Year. The problem came with Wayne's physical. Everybody knew about the cancer, but that had been more than ten years before. What wasn't generally known was that Wayne was beginning to have heart problems. It wasn't known because Wayne didn't want it known — he was afraid it would render him unemployable.

The insurance company must have gotten wind of the situation because it began backing away. Such was Wayne's desire for the part that he kicked in what Self remembered as $250,000 of his salary to help pay for his insurance.

If the actual state of Wayne's health had been known, he probably wouldn't have been insurable. Before *The Shootist* got under way, he began feeling bad, although nothing could be found. Then the doctors did a biopsy and found some cancer growing in his stomach. It was treated and went into remission, but by the time the picture got under way, he still wasn't feeling 100 percent. More importantly, he knew the Red Witch was in heat again.

Frankovich and Self thought about offering the picture to Howard Hawks, or another of the old guard, but the only actual offer went to Don Siegel, who had lifted Clint Eastwood to another level with *Dirty Harry* but hadn't directed many westerns. Siegel was coming off the dismal *The Black Windmill,* and there would be more stiffs ahead — *Telefon, Rough Cut* — but Self had worked with him on a TV pilot and been impressed.

Miles Hood Swarthout wrote several drafts of the script. He had a meeting with Siegel at Universal, and found the director preoccupied with trying to set up *Telefon* at MGM. "He wasn't fully engaged," said Swarthout. "I think in his mind *The Shootist* was a work for hire. Lenny Hirshan, Siegel's agent, was also Clint Eastwood's agent, and it was Lenny who got Siegel into the picture. Lenny told me that Siegel couldn't get along with anybody but Clint and was virtually unemployable because he spoke his mind so loudly.

"My greatest creative contribution came after I knew Wayne was cast. I got the book *The Films of John Wayne* and figured out that if we did a montage sequence with clips from his old movies, we could quickly sketch in the character's violent past. Siegel had started doing montages at Warners, and when I told him my idea, he said 'Great! Make a list of some of the westerns we could use scenes from.'"

Siegel wasn't completely happy with Swarthout's script, so he brought in Scott Hale, who had worked with him as a script supervisor. For Wayne, who wasn't sure he could trust Siegel, the director insisting on his own writer was a red flag.

But after an initial meeting or two, Wayne seemed to relax. He showed Siegel around his house and said, "Wanna buy it? It's all I've got left. Two lousy, crooked business managers done me in." Later, he told the director sadly, "All I wanted, for all the years I've worked, was to keep the status quo."

Wayne's take on John Bernard Books, the aging shootist of the title, was that "it's about a fellow who has a little more good than bad in him. That's the kind of character I like to play." But even after the script was polished, there were elements that he found objectionable. He didn't mind Books being diagnosed with a fatal cancer, but the obvious implication of a rectal examination to diagnose it struck him as obnoxious. Nevertheless, he let it pass.

Wayne didn't really dig in his heels until the ending, which was the same as the ending of the novel: the young boy, to be played by Ron Howard, kills Books. "He's mortally wounded," remembered Self of the script conference, "dying of cancer, in terrible pain. He looks at Howard, knows that he's always coveted his gun and says, 'Take my gun . . . but first kill me.' It was a mercy killing.

"We were all somewhat concerned about the ending — squeamish — but Duke was adamant. He felt the audience would react badly." Also, he probably felt that his character was acquiescing to malignant fate — a man with a code being outstripped by events. The ending was changed — the Howard character kills the man who kills Books, then throws the gun away in a renunciation of violence.

Once Wayne came on board, the rest of the casting proceeded smoothly. "Old Hollywood came to the rescue," said Self. "Jimmy Stewart came in and did his small part for Duke. We were not in a position to meet Lauren Bacall's usual salary, but she did the picture because of Duke." The reason was simple: "We all felt it might be his last film," said Hugh O'Brian, who played the gambler who takes on Books in his last gunfight.

At Siegel's suggestion, Wayne began to grow a mustache and a little patch under his lower lip. He hadn't liked the idea, but agreed to try, and during preproduction Siegel received a Polaroid of Wayne that had been taken in Mexico. He was sporting two weeks worth of a bona fide mustache and the soul patch. Scrawled on the Polaroid were the words, "I can't believe it. Duke."

With a budget of $8 million, half from Paramount, half from De Laurentiis, *The Shootist* got under way in the second week of January 1976 with location work outside Carson City. As Miles Hood Swarthout said, "It was hammer and tongs from day one."

"It started with a quote in the Carson City newspaper," recalled Ron Howard. "Don Siegel had given an interview and we were walking around while Wayne was reading the article out loud. 'Listen to this,' he said. 'Wayne is supposed to eat directors for breakfast. But if he tries to eat me, he'll get indigestion.'

"Wayne folded up the newspaper and looked at me. 'Why the fuck did he have to say that?' he said." That led into a long, fuming diatribe about how *Dirty Harry* wasn't all that good, that Europe liked Siegel a lot more than Americans did, somehow arriving at the injustice of *The Apartment* beating out *The Alamo* for Best Picture.

Howard already knew he wanted to be a director and found himself in what he called "an unbelievably privileged situation. Duke always referred to me as 'Old 21.' He respected the fact that I had come out of TV. Early on, he said to me, 'I came out of cheap westerns, and that was the TV of our time.' He liked the unpretentious work ethic of television, where you have to finish it by Friday."

Wayne and Howard had several important scenes together, and since Wayne was always willing to rehearse, Howard spent a lot of time in Wayne's trailer. Siegel knew Howard wanted to be a director, so Siegel was always answering Howard's questions about the craft. "I was in both of their good graces. And when the schism presented itself, I was afforded a little insight."

The elevation was 3,500 feet. Wayne quickly caught a cold, which, as was often the case after his cancer surgery, turned into a bronchial infection. The film was supposed to open with shots of Wayne descending on horseback from the high country, but that proved to be a bad idea; his faltering lung capacity wouldn't allow him to go any higher than the flatlands, so the film opened with unimpressive landscapes.

After an initial set-to when Wayne discovered that Frankovich and Self had hired a still photographer he hadn't approved, Siegel began directing. He got the shot for the main title, but as they segued to the scene of an attempted holdup that began the story, Wayne simply took over and directed the sequence himself. "He didn't do too badly," remembered Siegel with dry humor. "I wasn't welcome to have anything to do with it." At the end of the day, Siegel was embarrassed and despondent.

The next morning, Wayne called Siegel and asked him to come to his hotel room, where he apologized and said it wouldn't happen again. "The trouble is simply this," he said. "I have to work loose, or I'm no good." For that day and several thereafter, Wayne was docile. "Mr. Siegel, there's one director on this picture and thank God it's you," he announced to the cast and crew. "What's your pleasure?"

But Wayne continued to have trouble breathing. Several mornings he had to lie across a table while a physical therapist pounded his back to try to loosen the phlegm that was collecting in his lungs

— the same therapy cystic fibrosis patients have to endure. A couple of times he needed assistance to stand up.

Occasionally he was racked by spasms of coughing, and his voice was raspy from the cold and elevation. His stamina was not what it had been; he had to lie down in his trailer for twenty minutes at lunchtime. "I just don't seem to have the charge anymore," he grumbled. "But damn it, I'm 69 in May."

Contributing to the general malaise was a salt-free diet he'd adopted in an effort to get his weight down. He was also taking Lasix, a drug given to heart patients to drain water out of the system. The result was that everything was tasteless — "the goddamn lettuce tastes like grass," he complained. He was a virtual prisoner in his suite on the eighth floor of the Ormsby House hotel. He ventured down into the casino area precisely once, and managed only about three minutes at the craps tables before a crowd assembled and made further play impossible.

"He had one lung, and had trouble breathing at any altitude whatsoever," said Miles Hood Swarthout. "He had a nurse assigned to him twenty-four hours a day. Sometimes between takes he would take a hit from an oxygen tank."

The feeling was that once production got out of the cold and back to Hollywood the star would get his equilibrium, but until then everything was a chore. Wayne was irascible, and he lashed out at cameraman Bruce Surtees, who was supervising the laying of track for a moving shot: "You'd do a damn sight better if you concentrated on the lighting instead of fucking around with dollies, making the cast look like zombies."

At dinnertime, the conversation was about old times and old friends — Bogart, Hepburn, Tracy, Pappy Ford. One night, Wayne told Lauren Bacall about his salt-free diet, and she promptly snatched the olive out of his martini. During the day, Wayne groused about his age ("I don't mind being old, I just mind not being able to move") and advised Don Siegel on his camera angles.

On Sunday, Wayne invited Siegel and Carol Rydall, his script supervisor, to his suite to watch a football game and they shared some clams that a friend of his had just flown in from Seattle. But after Wayne advised them to bet the Steelers over the Cowboys, he said he wasn't feeling well and was going to bed.

"Wayne wasn't particularly reflective, at least not with me," remembered Bacall. "He loved to enjoy life, but he wasn't feeling well. One day he said to me, 'God, I can't drink, I can't smoke, life's no fun anymore.' But he was still feisty, ornery in a way. A very sweet man, actually. We got along very well."

Even though the company was working short days, often quitting around 3 P.M. Carson City was hard for Wayne. "They were resting Duke," said Ron Howard. "He never complained, except to say once, 'I only have the one lung.' " The company made it through the location work without any further trouble. There were no more explosions from the star, and his performance was consistently excellent. But the producers were worried.

"He was physically uncomfortable," remembered Self. "A lot of the animosity toward Siegel was due to Wayne's health. He would get tired, and say to Don, 'It's good enough.' And Don would say, 'I want another one.' That became an issue at times. Wayne thought we were over-covering a scene, doing too many takes. Duke would want to move on to another scene and Don would want to keep working. And Wayne being the professional he was, he would do it again."

The picture moved to the Warner Bros. back lot, where Robert Boyle converted a run-down west-ern street into a thing of beauty for less than $300,000. James Stewart came in to do his scene, and seemed glad to be back in the saddle, however briefly. But Stewart hadn't made a movie in five years, and his hearing was badly compromised. He couldn't pick up his cues quickly, which in turn threw Wayne's timing off. The two old pros rallied and pulled the scene off beautifully, but it was yet another reminder that the making of the movie was in some sense a mirror image of the story of the movie.

The tension between Wayne and Siegel contin-ued. Wayne told Tom Kane that Siegel didn't know how to cover a scene, that he was a TV director — over-the-shoulder close-up, cut to another over-the-shoulder close-up. He com-plained to reporters about what he felt to be the unnecessary claustrophobia of Siegel's vision. "Jack Ford used to tell me, 'Give 'em scenery, give 'em a scene, and give 'em action. Do it in any order you want, but don't try to give 'em a scene and scenery at the same time, and don't try to play action at the same time.' I can't tell you how many fellas I've worked with didn't realize that."

"Siegel had a short man's complex," said Swar-thout. "He was a little guy, and very feisty — a little bit of a martinet who wanted to do things his way: to follow the script he had laid out. Wayne didn't like to work that way. He wanted to improvise, change his lines, have a say in the casting. They were just complete opposites in the way they approached movies."

"The reality was that outside of one or two moments, I didn't actually witness much of anything," said Ron Howard. "But they simply weren't comfortable with each other. Siegel staged it, he directed it. He didn't abdicate and Wayne didn't mutiny, outside of a couple of flare-ups."

One of those flare-ups remained permanently engraved on Howard's memory — a scene between him and Wayne in a barn.

It was an important scene. Duke walked in. There were two things: the camera was on the floor looking up at Duke, who was supposed to be sitting on a bale of hay. The camera was on a dolly and there was going to be a microphone between his feet.

Duke sat down and looked at the camera and looked at Siegel. And sighed. And said, "Well, hell." And then he looked at the dolly grip and stared swinging his arms around. The grip didn't know what to do. Duke kept swinging his arms around, telling him to move the camera without actually saying it. And finally the grip moved the camera over in front of Wayne. And then Duke started moving his arm upward, telling him to raise the camera off the ground, so it wouldn't look up his nose and jowls.

And when that was done, he said, "Now let's shoot the goddamn scene." Throughout all of this, Don Siegel just stood there and didn't say a thing. I felt terrible for him. And after we'd done the scene and Duke had left, Siegel said to me, "The reality is that you bring everything you have to a movie, but three weeks into the picture you're a captive of the star. If they fire anybody, it's going to be the director. You have to make the decision."

That was the only time I saw Wayne take over completely. And ever since then, I've wondered what I would do if an actor did that to me.

Mostly, the relationship between Wayne and Siegel was like a bad marriage that neither partner wants to completely destroy. "There were these little flare-ups, and both guys were angry," said Howard. "Privately, I suspect there were words. They never kissed and made up, but both of them respected the work. It never held us up."

Despite Wayne's ongoing dissatisfaction, despite his physical problems, the picture was on schedule. "He was on time, he knew his words, he was ready," said Hugh O'Brian. "There was no bullshit with Duke; he was absolutely professional."

Wayne played chess a few times with "Old 21" and beat the hell out of the young man. "He was *so* aggressive," said Howard. "I played him well, but I couldn't come close to beating him. Dave [Grayson], his makeup man, could beat him, and Duke would stomp around and curse about it, but he wasn't really mad; he loved a good game."

Even though Wayne knew that cancer had him in its sights again, he moved resolutely forward, playing even the most dangerous scenes without a trace of self-pity. "Every now and then we would just be standing next to one another and he'd kind of just hold my hand," said Lauren Bacall. "One of the crew mentioned that it was a beautiful day, and he said, 'Every day you wake up is a beautiful day.' "

There were no such gentle reflections with Siegel, who became the target for all of the star's dissatisfactions and fear. After a while, Siegel began to look pale and beaten. He had worked with recalcitrant actors before, but never someone this formidable. Wayne would tell anyone who asked that Siegel was too rigid, that he was blocking scenes instead of letting them flow. Burt Kennedy or Andy McLaglen would have capitulated, but Siegel dug in his heels and the film settled down to a grinding series of disagreements and mutual bad temper.

"He couldn't *stand* Siegel," said Bacall. "He humiliated him in front of the [crew.] '*That's* your setup?' he would say." Despite the bad temper, Bacall didn't think any the less of either man. "Duke was a sick, dying man; Don was a damn good director."

If Wayne wasn't in the mood to talk, he would stay in his trailer and hunch over his chessboard, leaving the trailer door open. If he was feeling gregarious, he would interject himself into conversations or offer random opinions. Both his kindness and his bad temper were larger than life, as when a crew member walked between Wayne and a light as he was studying his script and he turned and roared, "Will you get the fuck out of the light?"

In many respects, John Bernard Books was a tricky part, and an unusual Wayne character — because the character is dying, he's of necessity focused almost exclusively on himself. Wayne was very concerned about the character becoming maudlin. He was also concerned that Siegel was

837

making the movie darker than it needed to be. Literally. Wayne was particularly irate over a scene where a couple of gunmen come through a window to try to kill Books. (One of the men was played by the director Robert Totten, Ron Howard's directorial mentor.) "He thought it was all too dark," said Howard. "He objected to both the lighting and the camerawork."

As the pieces of the film were cut together, it became obvious that Siegel's intimate approach to the picture was both intellectually and emotionally valid — he never lets us get very far from Books. John Ford would have undoubtedly been ideal, and would have given the film more poetry, but he was dead and Hawks and Hathaway were over-the-hill. Siegel's decision to make the movie an intimate chamber piece gave Wayne and his character a compressed power.

For Howard, *The Shootist* became an opportunity he hadn't expected. He had initially come to the picture a little dissatisfied with his part — he wanted to be a little less callow, a little tougher — but all that was swept away by a priceless learning experience.

"The only thing Duke told me about acting was something he said John Ford had taught him — not to take an emotion to its furthest extreme. Always leave the audience a percentage of the emotion to complete for themselves. If you have to cry in a scene, don't feel that you as the actor have to completely fulfill it. Hold a little back. And pacing. He cared a lot about pacing. He was very aware of rhythm."

Howard had already worked with other Golden Age stars such as Henry Fonda and Bette Davis, and, while he was a fan of Wayne he thought of him less as an accomplished artist than as a personality. But that changed.

When we ran lines, and he was sorting out his performance, sometimes there would be an awkward moment that was a little stilted — a speech that wasn't quite landing. And he would say, 'Let me try again.' And he would put that hitch in, that pause that he had in his speeches, and the line would suddenly take on power. He understood how to work with the rhythms of speech, to find a surprising nuance in the moment of the dialogue.

I had always thought those hitches were him forgetting his lines. Not at all. The opposite. It was a very particular tool — it was a way of putting the focus on an aspect of a verbal moment. And it worked in different ways. When I saw more movies of his in later years, sometimes it made him funny, and sometimes it made him vulnerable.

It was interesting, and it was art.

The one thing that united Wayne with Fonda and Davis was a ferocious work ethic. "They were who they were because they worked harder than anybody else, even into their seventies," said Howard. "Every scene was still important to them. Not in a neurotic, crazy way, but in a professional, caring way."

In particular, Howard found the difference between Wayne and Fonda instructive. "Fonda was more of a working actor, less of a star. He expected a certain amount of respect, but that was easily given because he commanded that naturally — there was a lot to respect. Fonda's attitude was, 'My job is to do the scene and I'm not gonna tell you how to do your job.' "

One day word spread that Clint Eastwood was going to visit the set, and Wayne began talking about the pictures Eastwood and Siegel had made together. "I remember this great moment," said Ron Howard. "Wayne wondered out loud what Eastwood's politics were. He'd heard he was conservative, but then he'd also heard he was liberal. And Don Siegel told him, 'He's very conservative.' And you could tell that Duke was much more excited about meeting him after that."

Hollywood had changed, the movies themselves had changed, but one thing hadn't changed: John Wayne needed to do what he had been doing for more than fifty years — work at the craft he loved more passionately than anything besides his children. A reporter asked him about his refusal to quit, and he said, "To stop would be to surrender. To give up." He understood his situation and had no illusions. "You don't beat it, friend," he said of cancer. "You stand it off."

Beset by shaky health, by a director he disliked, and by a picture that was leading him into places he wasn't entirely sure of, Wayne could be pettish but always there was his willingness to extend a hand.

"Anyplace I go in the world they treat me like a friend," he said, with satisfaction and some wonder. But now he found that one depressing subject — politics — had been replaced by another — his health. "I *hate* it. It's so *damn* irritating to feel bad when you haven't felt bad all your life. I have been abnormally healthy. Even when they told me I had cancer, I hadn't had any pain . . . *nothing.* They took the lung out and I was well again. Felt fine.

"But this last year, it's been one thing after another. . . . That's the worst thing about getting old — having to use your will power to drive yourself instead of natural physical energy. Before, it all came so easy. Now I have to push."

The bronchial infection was still plaguing Wayne and he began to wear down. Some days, it was a struggle to walk twenty feet. Again, he had to have his back pounded to clear his lungs. As Siegel moved into the crucial scene of the final gunfight, the set became increasingly tense. Wayne wasn't happy with Siegel's staging of his entrance into the saloon, but acquiesced. At one point, Wayne said, "You're really fucking this up," loudly, in front of everybody.

Siegel shot the beginning of the gunfight, but ran out of time and called a wrap. Wayne was visibly exhausted and said, "I've been waiting for you to wrap the moment I got here. See you all tomorrow. Don't drink up all the booze."

But when tomorrow came, Wayne wasn't there. Mike Frankovich told Siegel that Wayne was ill and they weren't sure when he would be back. The words "if ever" were hanging in the air. Frankovich wanted to know how much could be done without Wayne.

"A few days," Siegel replied.

"I heard Don say, 'We'll shoot around him,' " said Ron Howard. "And then he said, 'Of course, I have to root for his recovery.' "

So for a few days, Siegel staged the action with the other people in the scene: Hugh O'Brian, Richard Boone, and Bill McKinney. "He brilliantly shot around him," said Howard. "He staged

841

that entire shootout, and covered everybody first, including me, without John Wayne. Sometimes there was a double, but mostly there wasn't. He staged the whole scene without the protagonist."

Hugh O'Brian's death scene involved Books shooting him in the forehead as he peeked around the end of the bar. The bullet was to enter directly above the bridge of his nose. It was as harrowing an experience as any the actor ever had.

Today the shot would be done with CGI, but at the time the studio hired a marksman to shoot O'Brian with a rifle firing a red pellet that flattened on impact and resembled a bullet hit. The marksman was situated to the right of the camera, about ten feet away from O'Brian. They rehearsed the shot a couple of times, after which O'Brian went to Siegel and told him they better get it on the first take, because there wasn't going to be a second take.

"If he missed, he could put my eye out," remembered O'Brian. "The director knew it, I knew it, the marksman knew it. It was one of the most difficult things I've ever done. But he didn't miss."

And then shooting was suspended. There were some scenes still to be done — between Wayne and Bacall, between Wayne and Howard — but they couldn't be done without Wayne. This was all unheard of; Wayne worked hungover, he worked sick, he worked on impossible locations, he worked on pictures where the script was an embarrassment, he *worked*.

But not this time.

"It wasn't easy keeping his illness quiet," said William Self. "None of us talked about it, there was no gossip. It didn't get in the trade papers. And at this point it became obvious that this picture could be it for him."

As the days passed by, the producers quietly floated the idea of using a double for Wayne in order to finish the picture. Siegel hated the idea, but he was contractually obligated to make the movie with or without its star. Siegel finished shooting the gunfight with Chuck Roberson doubling for Wayne, which meant that you couldn't see Wayne's face as he engaged in the gunfight and as he died. The sequence would cut together, but the picture was obviously going to suffer from the substitution.

After two weeks, Wayne finally came back to work. He was pale but otherwise all right. When he asked what had been done in his absence, Siegel knew he was in trouble. They offered to take up part of the lunch hour by showing him the gunfight as it had been edited. Wayne nodded to Hugh O'Brian and said, "Watch the rushes with me."

The two men trooped off with Siegel, who must have felt like he was marching to his execution. "Duke agreed with the majority of the stuff he saw," remembered O'Brian. "The only thing that startled him was the way Siegel had shot the scene with the guy played by Bill McKinney, the town braggart. Duke — or Duke's double — shot him in the back as he's trying to get out the door of the saloon. And when he saw that, Duke jumped up. 'Wait a goddamn minute! I've never shot anybody in the back and I'm not going to start now.' "

For a man who had spent a lifetime personalizing his screen character, this was a negation of his belief system. "He was very clear that he felt this would violate his reputation as he meant to preserve it on film," said O'Brian. Siegel argued, but Wayne was adamant. Siegel finally gave in after saying that Wayne's insistence on the primacy of his image was "ridiculous and senseless."

Siegel and the producers agreed to reshoot the sequence so that McKinney was shot in the chest, and to remove the shots of Wayne's double. (Two shots of Chuck Roberson remained in the picture, because there was no way Wayne could do them himself: when Books vaults over the bar, and when he's shot in the back and tumbles to the ground.)

Although Siegel agreed to reshoot anything that Wayne wanted reshot, Wayne was clearly still angry. Siegel asked if Wayne would prefer another director. The actor ignored the question. "Let's shoot the dying scene first," said Wayne. "I'll go over this list of shots you've made and make up my mind what we should re-shoot."

Siegel carefully talked Wayne through his close-ups in the gunfight and his death scene, all of which went smoothly. A few less strenuous scenes followed, on an abbreviated work schedule. "The director and the producers were wise enough not to push Duke for a full day's work," said Hugh O'Brian. "They let him go home early, because they wanted to finish the film."

The picture finally struggled to its close on April 5, 1976, with Wayne and Siegel exhibiting the mutual exhaustion of two fighters who have pummeled each other for fifteen rounds without a clear decision. A few weeks later, Mike Frankovich brought a rough cut to Newport Beach for a screening. Wayne provided an audio commentary as the picture unreeled, a stream-of-consciousness ramble about the sets, the photography, and anything else that occurred to him.

He was pleased with the picture and his own performance, but his daughter Marisa began to cry during the ending and didn't stop when the lights came up. "Stop acting so silly," snapped Ethan. "It's only a movie. Dad is sitting right here next to you."

Paramount released the picture in July — too quickly. Wayne was angry, because he felt that *The Shootist* needed a more thoughtful publicity campaign. "Those people are putting all their damn time into *King Kong,*" he told Pat Stacy, referring to the De Laurentiis remake that Paramount was also releasing. "They think the Wayne movie will make it on its own. Well, it won't. People don't go to see a movie just because my name is on the marquee. Those bastards don't understand that. It used to be the case, but it's not the case anymore."

The reviews were mainly laudatory. *Variety* said that "the entire film is in totally correct balance, artistically and technically" and said that it was one of "John Wayne's towering achievements and his very best since *True Grit.*"

The *Newsweek* critic summed up the consensus by citing Wayne's "richness that seems born of self-knowledge; he lends the film a tremendous sense of intimacy and a surprisingly confessional mood. *The Shootist* is, in its own reserved way, John Wayne's singleminded statement about both the burden and the triumph of being John Wayne."

Some people complained about the self-conscious conflation of character and star. Molly Haskell in *The Village Voice* was one of the few nay-sayers, calling the picture "an artfully arranged memorial . . . a museum-like anthology of vignettes in one period-display set after another . . . some quite lovely, that never seem to connect."

Posterity has disagreed. "It was one of those pictures where nobody gets along but everything managed to work anyway," said Miles Hood Swarthout. "Wayne was playing a gunfighter at the end of his life, a man who's very full of himself, a very forceful guy. That character fit Wayne like a glove. But what made it work was his performance — a very sober performance, a very reserved performance. There was none of the bluster that you saw in so many of his films."

Wayne's performance centers on a stoic anguish. The basic idea of a famous man dying in a rooming house surrounded by strangers has a haunting resonance — nobody wants to die alone. But there is a quiet but nagging hole at the narrative heart of the movie that is never really addressed. Books decides he wants to go out with his boots on, so he invites three other gunmen to meet him in the saloon for a final showdown. One of them will be famous as the man who kills John Bernard Books.

But instead of essentially committing suicide, Books kills all three of them, dying only when he's shot in the back by a bartender with a shotgun, who wasn't in his equation. The irony is attractive, but there's no getting away from the fact that Books has provoked and killed three men who aren't guilty of anything except going up against John Wayne . . . er, John Bernard Books.

The Shootist earned rentals of $5.9 million in North America against its cost of $8 million. It did slightly better than that in the rest of the world. "I wouldn't say it lost money, but it didn't make any money," remembered William Self. "It would be fair to call it a disappointment. It's a

846

sad picture, and not a typical western; he dies at the end. Frankovich and I both had a percentage of the profits, and somewhere along the line I sold him my share. A few years later, I asked Mike Wayne how the Wayne estate was doing with the picture, and he told me they sold their percentage to De Laurentiis."

For Hugh O'Brian, it was a thrill just to work with the man. "I wanted that part in the worst way. I'm absolutely grateful to have worked with John Wayne. John Wayne refereed my first fight in the Marines and I was the last man he shot in the movies."

Oddly, Wayne wasn't even nominated for an Academy Award, although there were a smattering of ads in the trades headlined "Consider Duke Before You Vote." The difficulty of the film had been worth it on every level except the economic and, for some, the emotional. Months later, Don Siegel came up to Burt Kennedy at a restaurant, put his arm around him and said, "You're the only man that would understand."

CHAPTER TWENTY-FIVE

Besides his lung and heart problems, one of the things that had bedeviled Wayne on *The Shootist* was his prostate — he had to get up several times during the night to urinate and couldn't seem to empty his bladder. It's a common complaint for sixty-nine-year-old men, but Wayne was concerned about cancer. In November he went to the hospital for an examination, where it was found that he had an enlarged prostate that was restricting the flow of urine. Surgery was performed the first week of December 1976, and Wayne was relieved that there was no sign of cancer.

During the summer, he had made some time for the *Wild Goose,* with Pat Stacy in tow — they joined the ship in Acapulco, sailed up the coast to Puerto Vallarta. They'd swim, soak up the sun lying side by side on the deck, or take the dinghy to shore and go shopping. After that, there was a trip up to northwestern Washington for some salmon fishing.

His health seemed stable, but Stacy was worried about him. She gently suggested slowing down, and he leveled with her as he had with all the women in his life: "Pat, you've got to understand something. As long as a man has a project —

848

something to look forward to — there'll always be something important to him. He'll never really get old. If I had nothing to look forward to, I might as well be dead."

But the reality was that with successive commercial disappointments behind him, not to mention a serious illness that required an insurance claim, producers were not besieging Wayne with scripts. Over the next eighteen months, Wayne kept himself occupied with television.

As always when it came to TV, his feelings were ambiguous. "I don't know whether I love it or hate it," he said. "But there sure has never been any form of entertainment so available to the human race with so little effort since they invented marital sex.

"The worst part of it has been, I think, the adverse effect on family life. It kills off family conversation. And it's hard to get your children to read books. I became a confirmed reader when I was growing up in Glendale. I've loved reading all my life. Now I've got this daughter, Aissa, a very bright young lady — but it is a hard job to get her to read. Television's just too easy."

Wayne's core problem was that TV was too helter-skelter, but TV was also increasingly where his audience was. One of the more ignominious showcases was *An All-Star Tribute to John Wayne,* which ran on ABC in November 1976. It's a bizarre amalgam of stars, many of whom had nothing to do with Wayne: Charles Bronson, Glen Campbell, Sammy Davis Jr., Ron Howard, Lee Majors, Claire Trevor, James Stewart, Bob Hope, Rowan and Martin, Maureen O'Hara, Angie Dickinson, Henry Winkler, and Monty Hall. Totie Fields stands up and takes a bow.

Frank Sinatra hosted and the format was more or less that of the AFI Life Achievement Awards — an entrance by the star, who sits at a table surrounded by family and friends, with various people singing his praises, and a final heartfelt thank-you from the honoree. Wit was in short supply, although Bob Hope got off a decent line: "He's a symbol of the Old West, where men are men and women are women, and the way he walks he could fall into either category." Maureen O'Hara sang "I've Grown Accustomed to Your Face," which obviously moved Wayne, and he used notes for his own thank-you speech: "Folks out there, I want to thank you for the last 50 years of my career. I hope I can keep it up for another 50 years, or at least until I get it right."

The show is more or less a shambles without a clear purpose — *The Shootist* had already come and gone, so it couldn't even be rationalized as publicity for the picture. Wayne probably went along with it only because it was a charity event to raise money for the Variety Clubs. But in the deepest sense, he had never differentiated all that much between media — it was all show business to him. His career had not been built on consistently making discerning choices so much as a steady stream of appearances. Some would be good, and some wouldn't, but work was work.

By now, Wayne and Frank Sinatra were close friends. Sinatra and his wife, Barbara, visited Wayne in Newport Beach, where they would drink and josh each other. "They were buddies," said Barbara Sinatra. "I don't know why, because they were completely different in almost everything. But they liked each other a great deal, and they kidded a lot."

At this point, a couple of prospective pictures appeared on the horizon. Wayne was talked about for the role of an old IRA leader in the movie version of Leon Uris's *Trinity,* and Robert Aldrich offered him a part opposite Gene Wilder in *The Frisco Kid.* In the case of the former, the film fell through; in the latter, Wayne's health became an issue, and Harrison Ford played the part. The result of all this was that he had time on his hands — never a good thing.

In April 1977, looking slightly drawn from an unexplained weight loss but sporting a flattering pair of glasses, Wayne accepted the Asa V. Call award from USC, the school's highest alumni award. The presenter was Gene Clarke, whom Wayne had known since his Glendale days. "Gene and I have known each other since the beginning of time," noted Wayne in his acceptance speech, "which ain't just yesterday. I don't think of university days when I think of him. I think of Boy Scouts and sandlot football, Model T Fords with Ruckskell axles, Robert and Echols' Drugstore on Brand Boulevard, Pexi Eckles' older sister . . ." It was a touching tribute to yesterday from a man who preferred to live in today and tomorrow.

Wayne was beginning to take more and more medications. He began to believe that the doctors were treating symptoms rather than illness. Pat Stacy devised a chart and taped it to the bathroom mirror so he could keep track of when he had taken his digitalis, his digoxin, his allopurinol, his potassium, his Lasix.

He remained available for interviews. The English film historian Kevin Brownlow was making *Hollywood,* his series about silent movies, and enlisted Ollie Carey to call Wayne for an interview. Wayne enthusiastically agreed to talk about Harry Carey, John Ford, and silent movies. The interview was set for June 1, 1977.

When Brownlow's crew arrived, Wayne was dressed in slacks, open shirt, and a jacket with a rumpled collar. He was drinking out of a tall glass of colorless liquid. Deciding on the setup took a long time; Brownlow's co-director David Gill suggested the sofa, but Wayne rejected the idea. "You won't get a background worth a damn," he said.

Someone suggested that some of Wayne's Charles Russell bronzes could be raised on a two by four, and brighten up the background, but Wayne refused, saying the couch would still be too low. After more indecisive milling around, he tried to take charge.

"I mean, don't let me take over your job, but if I was shooting it, I'd start here" — he formed his hands into a film frame — "[and say] 'We visited John Wayne's house' — here he pointed at a statue with a Harry Carey–like pose in the other room — 'and we found a statue which was posed like Harry Carey' and so on. Now, that may not be what you want, but it's an idea." Brownlow sensed the years of torment Wayne must have endured while waiting to direct *The Alamo,* and not measuring up to Hollywood's expectations when he did.

No one seemed to like Wayne's idea, and the crew decided on the sofa. And then somebody asked for some phone books to raise the Russell statues. "That's it," Wayne said, his voice rising. "Telephone directories! I was trying to be helpful and I hardly get through talking when some guy cuts in with another idea. The people I'm used to working with don't act that way." With that, he petulantly stalked off to his office. "When you're ready, I'll be in here — *if* you're ever ready."

Brownlow took stock of the situation, which was on the verge of collapsing. He thought that Wayne might very well have a hangover, and liked to dish out a little John Ford, so long as Ford himself wasn't around.

Brownlow began to apply the soft soap, saying Wayne couldn't expect TV technicians to be the equal of a John Ford crew, and then asked Wayne if by any chance had he known the outlaw-turned-actor Al Jennings.

Wayne's face brightened. "Yes, very well."

Informed there was a lot of silent footage of Al Jennings, Wayne said he didn't know any had survived. "We were going to make a picture around '32 with him as my uncle." Wayne was soon telling one of his favorite John Ford stories — playing a member of the jury for Ford in 1928's *Hangman's House* and being carried away by Hobart Bosworth's (over)acting.

By then he was laughing and in a good mood. When the camera setup was finally arranged, Wayne approved. Just before the cameras turned, Brownlow asked Wayne if he had a high regard for Tom Mix. "Not so much for Mix," he said. Brownlow went on to talk about the research that had been done on Mix's life, and the resulting chasm between legend and reality.

"I don't think they ought to do that," said Wayne. "It takes something away from the people." He blamed the publicity departments. "They said I was an All-American. Christ! I went up to the publicity man and got him by the throat and said, 'You take that back!' Because it looked ridiculous. And I felt ridiculous with the fellows in my group."

When the camera finally turned, Wayne was funny, charming, completely entertaining. When it was all over, he noticed a gold bracelet on the wrist of one of the crew. "Where'd you get that from?"

"Vietnam."

Wayne was wearing the identical bracelet, and they began comparing notes. When some souvenir photos were being taken, a helicopter passed overhead and Wayne said, "Listen. A Chinook chopper. The sound of Vietnam."

As the crew filed out the door, Wayne said, "Thanks for showing me such respect when I teed off a little back there." In the car, everyone was excited; some of the men had been shaken by the sight and sound of an angry John Wayne, but one of the female members of the crew was near rapture: "Wonderful, sexy, so attractive."

November 1977 brought *Oscar Presents the War Movies and John Wayne,* an ABC special that mostly consisted of movie clips. The script was written by the *Los Angeles Times* movie critic Charles Champlin, who remembered that Wayne was unhappy about the inclusion of a scene from the 1949 Stanley Kramer/Carl Foreman production *Home of the Brave,* about racism in the military, because it did not reflect what he thought of as the reality of the American fighting man. Champlin said that Wayne watched a montage of his own valorous achievements in screen battle with wry humor: "I really was brave, wasn't I?"

In late 1977, the then burning issue of sovereignty for the Panama Canal came to a head. President Jimmy Carter wanted to hand the canal to the Panamanians, a move angrily denounced by right-wing Republicans, whose arguments could be synopsized as, "We built it, we paid for it, it's ours." What difference did it make that the original agreement called for it to be given to the Panamanians?

On November 11, Wayne wrote a private letter to Ronald Reagan in which he accused his friend of spreading untruths about the treaty. "I'll show you point by goddamn point in the treaty where you are misinforming people," wrote an infuriated Wayne. "If you continue these erroneous remarks, someone will publicise your letter to prove that you are not as thorough in your reviewing of this treaty as you say, or are damned obtuse when it comes to reading the English language." He signed the letter, "Duke" and copied it to President Carter.

Wayne then weighed in with a piece for *The New York Times* saying he thought the canal should be given to Panama. Wayne's full article, which was edited by the *Times,* veered wildly off topic near the end: "Quite obviously, there are some Communists in General Torrijos' administration as there have been and probably still are in ours. Back in the days of McCarthy, it was proven that a great number of people in our government were communists. For his high-handed manner with the use of the Committee, he was censored; but the truth of his findings were never questioned. . . .

"He does have his Escobar Bethancourt as we have our Andrew Young, neither of whom were elected. . . . A quarter century from now — when and if this agreement is carried out to the letter of the law . . . Escobar Bethancourt will be an old and forgotten character; and Young will probably be relegated to some posh job in our civil service from which he cannot be fired or taken care of by some liberal foundation as was [Alger] Hiss."

There was a script called *Cattle Annie and Little Britches* making the rounds, about two adolescent girls who joined the Doolin-Dalton gang in the waning days of the Old West. The plan was to cast a couple of unknown girls in the title roles, which necessitated a star for the part of Bill Doolin. Wayne was an obvious possibility, but he wasn't feeling up to it. The producers said they'd wait, but after a while began to canvass for other possibilities.

Features were getting harder for Wayne to make, but his overhead hadn't changed. He began to fret about the IRS, the expense of the *Wild Goose,* his medical bills, his flagging cash flow, and how he believed his money had been mismanaged by Bö Roos and Don La Cava. Aissa was attending USC, and her father gave her only $200 a month for an allowance — barely enough to get by.

So Wayne downshifted and agreed to make a series of commercials for Great Western Bank. (There had been an earlier, brief series of appearances for Datril, a pain reliever, but Wayne hadn't been happy with the ads and stopped making them.) As he told Aissa, "The truth is, I'm doing it for the money. . . . If Michael had been old enough to manage my money from the start, I'd never have had these problems. You've gotta find something you can fall back on Aissa. If I get sick, I don't know what will happen to you kids. It's not what you think it is, Aissa."

Great Western agreed to pay Wayne $350,000 for 1977, $400,000 for 1978, and $450,000 for 1979, with two one-year options after that. Along with the money he was getting from ABC for the TV specials, it was enough to keep the wolf from the door.

The bank received about thirty letters condemning it for hiring someone that the letters referred to variously as a reactionary or a liberal — many paleo-conservatives were still enraged by Wayne's support for the Panama Canal treaty.

The commercials started running at the end of 1977, and the bank was immediately gratified by the response. In December, the first month of the commercials, Great Western had a net savings gain of $8 million, even though December is traditionally bad for savings and loans because of Christmas withdrawals. January brought more good news, as Great Western recorded a $21 million net increase, most of it in over-the-counter passbook deposits from small investors.

What made the production of the spots particularly interesting is that most of them were directed and photographed by the great cinematographer and committed liberal Haskell Wexler. Wexler had a commercial company in partnership with Conrad Hall, and the two men had recently had success with ads for the Wells Fargo bank, which is how they got the job for yet another bank.

Wexler made a trip to Wayne's house in Newport Beach to discuss the commercials and was pleasantly surprised by the environment. "It was not a big, plush Hollywood house," said Wexler. "There was one room filled with awards; that room was a museum of a thousand awards. Otherwise, it was a homey, simple setup."

Wayne was aware of Wexler's politics. "He brought it up right off. He knew I'd been in Vietnam with Jane Fonda. 'I know where you stand,' he said. 'And I'm absolutely in favor of standing by our agreement with Panama and I'm taking a lot of guff from the damn right-wingers.' He gave me all his credentials of how he didn't go along with the nutty right wing. And then he showed me his station wagon with a big bump in the roof so he could sit in the driver's seat with his cowboy hat on."

The two men got along fine that day, although there was one small dustup on the first day of shooting the first commercial. Wexler had placed a horse in the background of the shot, and Wayne looked around and yelled "Cut! What makes you think you're a director, Wexler? That horse is a swayback. I don't want a swayback horse in the background of my shot."

Wexler was a good rider and knew a swayback when he saw one, but he had another horse placed in the background anyway. He could never figure out if Wayne was entirely serious or just asserting his authority.

Wayne's nineteenth-century attitudes reared up only once. The location was Oregon, and Wexler, as was his wont, had hired a couple of female camera assistants — he believed in integrated crews. One of them, Kristin Glover, had been working regularly in production for five years.

The crew had to cross a muddy field to get to the location, and Wexler decided he wanted to carry the Arriflex camera, which he owned, rather than delegate the job to one of the other crew members. Normally, the camera assistant would have carried it, but it was Wexler's camera and he was the boss. Wayne observed the director lugging the camera, but said nothing.

When he noticed that the crew included women,

Wayne muttered, "Does the crew still shower together?" Once they began working, Wayne completely ignored Glover, even when she was standing right next to him with a tape measure to check focus. Throughout the first day of the shoot, he refused to acknowledge her existence. "I was a nonentity," she recalled. "I just did my job and figured that was the way he was."

That night, Wayne invited Wexler and the crew to dinner. Kristin Glover was the first person to arrive at the restaurant, and Wayne was alone at the table. "Well," he announced, "I see that you can't carry a camera, so what are you good for?"

"Why Mr. Wayne, how rude," said Glover, teasing him. The rest of the crew came in, including a female assistant Glover was paying out of her own pocket.

During dinner, Wayne began baiting Wexler. "What we need is another good war," etc. Wexler figured the dinner was an extension of the shoot; since it didn't pay to antagonize the star, he didn't take the bait. Wayne then began a diatribe about women on film sets, specifically women who couldn't do the job, who took jobs away from men who needed to feed their families, and so forth. Glover sat there until she couldn't take it anymore.

"I have something I'd like to say," she announced.

"Well, go ahead," said Wayne.

"I was hired because I'm capable of doing my job. I take it seriously. I love it, I care about it, and I'm good at it." At this point, Glover's voice cracked. "And besides," she continued, "you're really hurting our feelings."

"I didn't cry," she remembered, "but I was on the verge."

Wayne's entire demeanor shifted. "I am so sorry," he announced to the crew, specifically to the women members of the crew. "I didn't mean to hurt your feelings. I apologize."

The next day, in front of the entire crew, Wayne came up to Glover and put his arm around her "so sweetly. He was a huge man, he just towered over me."

"I hope you're not still mad at me?" he asked her.

"I couldn't possibly have stayed mad at him," she said. "He was a chauvinist, and he couldn't help himself. *But he heard me.* I realized that he loved to start arguments, loved to debate, loved to tussle with people and challenge them. The rest of the time he treated me as an accepted member of the crew, worthy of being spoken to. I would have to call him a charming chauvinist."

"He was a great guy to work with," said Haskell Wexler. "It was a very important situation in Kristin's life to see a man of that stature in the film business who did good interactive things that showed in the work. It was good for her. After that initial dustup, he was charming to the girls. He responded to them, and they responded to him.

"I thought he would be tougher, and maybe a little mean. But my expectations were colored by prejudice. And I think maybe it goes with my getting older or maybe just being more mature. I don't think there are too many people I've come across that are all bad or that I hate. All of us have something to say that's worth listening to and paying attention to and acting well with. It doesn't mean we don't have principles of our own, it just means that it's not worth fouling up relationships.

"Kristin says Wayne was a charming chauvinist? I would have to say he was a principled reactionary."

Although the commercials didn't tax Wayne's endurance — a couple of them were completed in one take — he was very much cognizant of a health situation that was not apparent to anybody else: he was beginning to lose weight for no apparent reason, and was drinking protein drinks during the shoots.

"He was aware that his days were numbered," said Wexler. "It was nothing overt, but he would say things. I remember he told me, 'As lousy a director as you might be, Wexler, you might be the last one I work with.' "

The Great Western commercials turned out to be simply but elegantly produced, and surprisingly emotional. The messages are all heartfelt, the mood is intimate and gently retrospective, the sell is soft and dependent on Wayne's status as a trusted friend of the audience.

In one, Wayne stands among redwood trees, wearing his familiar vest and cowboy hat and having lost a fair amount of weight. "These trees have been around for a thousand years," he says. "It's a nice feeling to be around something that's been here a long time and is going to last." Another one shows him in front of the mountains of Lone Pine. "I rode out here about 50 years ago on a little dun horse and started a film career. A picture called *The Big Trail*. . . . In those days, a Great Western Savings Account would have come in pretty handy."

"I have a picture of the two of us," said Haskell Wexler. "Part of [the inscription] is that quote from Wayne: 'What makes you think you're a director, Wexler?' Thirty-odd years later, Kristin will still say that to me out of the blue. Whenever I see the people from that crew, we still talk about the experience of working with him."

For the first time in forty years, Wayne had time on his hands, so he looked around for make-work projects. When *The People's Almanac* asked him to rate the five best movie actors and five best movies of all time, he thought about it, then made his choices. For actors, he listed (from the top) Spencer Tracy, Elizabeth Taylor, Kathrine (sic) Hepburn, Laurence Olivier, and Lionel Barrymore. For the best pictures, he went with *A Man for All Seasons, Gone With the Wind,* Rex Ingram's *The Four Horsemen of the Apocalypse, The Searchers,* and *The Quiet Man.*

In February 1978, Wayne's voice began to deteriorate — it was raspy, and the low tones were disappearing. He was angry about his condition, angry about the lack of work, angry about the country. Although he liked Jimmy Carter personally, he felt he was weak and ineffectual. "The United States is losing its balls and its spirit," he complained. "It's gotten so crappy here, I can't stand to see it."

He began to talk about moving to Mexico. Why not? His marriage was broken, his career was frozen, his health was uncertain. He was ready to give up, and besides the Mexicans loved him. Baja, perhaps. He seemed to be serious and began taking lessons to improve his Spanish, although Michael would undoubtedly have hurled his body between his father and the door to keep him from abandoning America.

In March, Wayne and Pat Stacy attended Henry Hathaway's eightieth birthday party at the Bel-Air Country Club. It was one more reunion of Old Hollywood: Henry Fonda was there, Jimmy Stewart, Richard Widmark, Hal Wallis, William Wyler, Vincente Minnelli, Tony Curtis, Glenn Ford, Karl Malden, George Burns. Wayne announced that Hathaway was "the most irascible, most fascinating, most talented bastard." No one disagreed. He tried to take a spin around the dance floor with Hathaway's wife, Skip, but had to stop after a couple of minutes because he couldn't catch his breath.

There were a couple of mediocre job offers. Irwin Allen was preparing *Beyond the Poseidon Adventure* and wanted Burt Reynolds for the lead, while Warner Bros. was trying to convince Clint Eastwood to take the part. Then Wayne contacted Allen and said he'd be interested in the film, and Allen was thunderstruck. Having John Wayne would lift the film to another level.

However, when the initial script went out — it had the upside-down ship resting on top of an underwater volcano, and yes, the volcano finally exploded — Reynolds, Eastwood, and Wayne all turned the picture down. Around the same time, Steven Spielberg offered Wayne the part of General Joseph Stilwell in his film *1941.* Wayne invited Spielberg down to Newport Beach to discuss the script, then chewed the director out for wasting his time with a role that he felt was demeaning to the military.

"He didn't want me to make *1941,*" remembered Spielberg. "He said to me, 'You're making a mockery of a very serious time. . . . And I read your script. . . . I for one didn't laugh.' He gave me such a bollicking about it. We stayed friends although he was just disgusted that I would make what he thought was a very anti-American picture."

Robert Stack was happy to play the part, and his scene was a bright spot in a very bad picture.

The hoarseness got worse, and he was becoming extremely short of breath — his wind could barely support him through a sentence. After St. Patrick's Day 1978 he traveled to Boston for open heart surgery to repair a defective mitral valve. Mike Wayne's son Chris, who had had open heart surgery when he was five, called to tell his grandfather that "If I can do it, you can do it."

"Well, if I didn't have so many miles on me, I'd feel more confident," Wayne replied.

In fact, the hospital was not thrilled about the surgery; Wayne was about to be seventy-one, had one lung and chronic bronchitis. Open heart surgery under those circumstances had a failure rate of at least 10 percent, and nobody wanted to be responsible for killing John Wayne.

On the night of April 2, Wayne and the family went out to dinner at a private dining room at Maison Robert, a fine restaurant in downtown Boston. Wayne's doctor gave him permission to have one drink, so he ordered the largest martini in the house and raised his glass in a toast: "To the last supper." That put a lid on the evening, which was already filled with foreboding, but Joe de Franco saved it by altering the terms of the toast: "Last supper until Newport."

On April 3, the doctors cracked Wayne's chest, sliced into his heart, and replaced his mitral valve with one from a pig. When he woke up after the surgery, the doctor asked him how he felt. "I saw it was raining," he said. "I found myself wanting to roll in the mud." He admitted that he had been "scared, damn scared." There weren't a lot of parts for an actor without a voice. "Now, with that damn pig valve in me, I not only have my voice back but I go around saying 'Oink oink.'"

Back home, Wayne's recuperative therapy involved walking, a daily hike of at least a mile and a quarter. Afterward, he would sit on the deck of his house waving to yachts that sailed by. In the house, four secretaries had to be hired to handle the mail that had flooded in since his surgery. "They've opened 10,000 so far," he said. "And I can take you back and show you boxes with 50,000 more. Isn't that something? There's just no way I can answer them, but jeez, I'm really touched."

In May, he celebrated his seventy-first birthday. Joe de Franco was there, Pat Stacy was there, ten other close friends. But he didn't enter into the celebration, and he didn't even empty his glass of wine. He was listless during the following week, so he went to the hospital for more tests, which revealed hepatitis. That entailed six weeks of bed rest, more drugs, daily visits from a doctor. When Pat Stacy's birthday arrived, he was too sick to help her celebrate. A trip to Catalina aboard the *Wild Goose* seemed to perk him up, and he was better by the end of June. A month later, he surprised Stacy by taking her to the private showroom of Dicker and Dicker in Beverly Hills, where he presented her with her choice of mink coats for a belated birthday gift, then added a white fox boa.

As late as September, he was still slightly listless

from the hepatitis and rested for up to seven hours a day. But he hauled himself from Newport Beach to be honored at the Century Plaza for a Boy Scout testimonial dinner. Twelve hundred guests paid $250 a plate to honor Wayne, which amounted to more than $400,000 for the purchase of a camp at Lake Arrowhead that was named the John Wayne Outpost Camp. Merv Griffin was the emcee, and old friends such as James Stewart showed up as well. "If I could pick any man to be my brother," Wayne told Stewart, "I'd sure pick someone like you — rich."

By October 1978, it had been nearly three years since John Wayne had made a movie, and a sense of aimlessness had descended. The Utah Film Festival awarded him its John Ford Medallion, but he didn't feel up to traveling, so he asked Peter Bogdanovich to accept it for him. Bogdanovich brought the medallion to the Beverly Hills Hotel, where Wayne was staying for a few days to be close to his medical treatments. Wayne was in his pajamas watching a USC football game. Pat Wayne arrived with a couple of his children, and it was all very casual and comfortable.

There was a general air of illness about Wayne, so the only beverage was iced tea. Talk inevitably turned to the old days, of Ford and Hawks and Ward Bond. "Christ, everybody's gone," Wayne said. He asked Bogdanovich if he would be interested in directing a Batjac picture called *Beau John.* "It's kind of a half-western thing, it's not cowboys and Indians, you know, it's — oh, the humor and the wonderful relationship between this grandfather and the son and the son-in-law and the grandson. . . . I hope to hell I live to do it. Just a wonderful story." Bogdanovich said of course Wayne would be able to make it, and he'd be happy to direct it.

Beau John became the focus of his professional future, and Wayne proposed the project to Ron Howard. "I found a book," he told Howard. "I think it's a movie. It's you and me or it's nobody."

"It never got past the verbal stage," recalled Howard. "And at that point, he was showing signs of not being well. I was a little doubtful."

With more time on his hands, Wayne was able to look back at his career with equanimity. He was proud of his performance in *She Wore a Yellow Ribbon,* because it was a true character performance. He liked *Hondo, The Searchers, Red River,* and *True Grit.* He didn't talk much about *The Shootist* — his anger with Don Siegel had soured him on the picture.

Among his contemporaries, he loved Gary Cooper, didn't like Clark Gable. "You know why Gable's an actor?" he told his daughter Aissa. "It's the only thing he's smart enough to do." He had grown to like Clint Eastwood and he had a soft spot for Paul Newman: "Now *there's* an actor who's got it if he'd stop hurting himself playing those anti-hero roles. The man has real talent . . . when he isn't directing his own films." He also appreciated Robert Redford and George C. Scott.

And he had a personal favorite who habitually flew under the radar. "I think the best actor in the world today is James Garner. He can do anything — comedy, detective. Just his facial expressions alone are enough to crack you up. They rave about Brando and Scott, but they couldn't hold a candle to him." He had a blind spot about Gene Hackman, couldn't abide him, called him "the worst actor in town." On television his tastes mirrored

867

his audience's; he liked to watch Lucille Ball, Jackie Gleason, and *Barney Miller.*

If someone asked him about money, he would snort and give chapter and verse about his financial misadventures. "Wealth? Bob Hope has wealth. I've made money, but ill-timed investments cost me a fortune. I once lost $600,000 in a shrimp business in Panama. Three marriages were costly. I threw away a hell of a lot of money having a good time. I don't regret it. But after 25 years of hard work, I suddenly found myself starting all over again broke. . . . I'm not broke today by any means, but for a lifetime of work, I'm not rich, either. Bob Hope is rich."

William Wellman Jr. went to Palm Desert for a celebrity tennis tournament at Shadow Mountain. "I was coming out of my room and walking over to the courts walking over the grass next to the pool. And there was Duke sitting in a chair by a small table."

"Duke, how are you?" asked Wellman, who already knew the answer. Wayne looked tired and sick, and he was sitting by himself in Palm Desert playing a board game. "Bill, how are you?" Wayne cried with the old bonhomie. After the usual amount of small talk, he said, "God, I miss your dad. We should have made more pictures together."

Every goddamn day it was something different, something limiting.

Wayne began complaining of stomach pains. He said it felt like he had broken glass in his gut. He tried various over-the-counter stomach remedies, but nothing seemed to help except a bland diet of apples and watermelon. A biopsy was done that showed nothing amiss, but he knew. He'd been waiting, and he knew.

"I have it, Aissa," he told his daughter. "I feel it inside my body."

By December, the smell of food made him nauseated, and his diet consisted mostly of fruit. Pounds started vanishing, and he began to have trouble sleeping; he'd lie awake for hours, and pass the time by dictating business correspondence into his tape recorder. On Christmas Eve, he invited Joe de Franco and his wife and another couple to dinner, but he couldn't make it through — the smell of the food and liquor made him sick. He went to his room to lie down.

Without the acting fees that had once rolled in, the *Wild Goose* was becoming prohibitively expensive. Actually, it was eating him alive. "In the last few years, it was costing him $275,000 a year to keep it going," said Bert Minshall, the ship's captain. "The insurance was $30,000 a year alone."

"I hate to let her go," said Wayne. "I've had her a long time. Took her to Europe once, in the '60s. But with taxes what they are, what's the alternative? I obey the rules. I don't like them, but I obey them." Wayne began looking around for someone to take it off his hands — an open admission of his failing energy and health. But then his eternal restlessness would reassert itself: "I couldn't retire. That would kill me. What would I do? I'd go nuts. Work is the only thing I know. And as long as I can keep my dignity, I'm going to go on making movies. I like what I do. . . .

"As long as people want to see me in movies, I'm going to go on working. I even reckon they could re-release my movie *The Alamo*. Even the liberals aren't so blatantly against me anymore that they wouldn't recognize there was something to that picture besides my terrible conservative attitude."

His last public appearance of the year was on December 13, at the Beverly Hills Hotel, where he accepted a plaque from the Los Angeles Advertising Club for the Great Western Savings and Loan ads. Wayne had been advised by his doctor not to attend the lunch, but he showed up anyway. "The way my luck has been running lately, I'm surprised I didn't wind up making commercials for Ford Pintos . . . I've got a feeling the real reason you guys are gathered here today is to make an old actor happy — and if I meet an old actor on my way home, I'll tell him all about you."

To a journalist friend, he would say, "I gotta say it, I've had a helluva good life. There's no way anyone could have had more fun. I got no complaints. Even with all the things that have happened to me. There's a saying they have in Mexico. 'He was ugly, he was strong, and had dignity.' Yeah, that's the kinda thing I'd like them to say about me."

Shortly before Christmas, he was seized by a terrible mood. Usually, his bursts of temper were over quickly and followed by apologies, but he was picking at Pat Stacy about everything, and she began to keep her distance. On Christmas Day, he wore his robe because he didn't feel up to getting dressed. He didn't have the stamina to open all his presents and went back to bed.

In the second week of January 1979, Wayne taped an interview with Barbara Walters aboard the *Wild Goose* for a March airing. It may have only been

TV, but he was invigorated by the prospect of once again having a camera aimed at him.

"Are you romantic?" Walters asked him.

"Very much. Very much so. Easily hurt."

"Would you want to get married again?"

"If I were a young man of 50 or so, yes. But I think it's pretty ridiculous at 71 to start thinking about marriage."

"What's your idea of a very good day?"

"Well, getting up in the morning. Being still here. As far as I'm concerned, I've had enough experience to know that if I open my eyes and look outside, and it's a nice, foggy day, it's great. If it's a sunny day, it's beautiful."

"By the end of the two days we spent with him," said Walters, "there wasn't one of us who didn't feel affection and respect for the man. He was straightforward, honest and tough, in the best sense of the word. He never once tried to force his views upon us, and was enormously considerate." At the end of the second day, Walters asked Wayne to pose with her crew for a picture.

The day after the interview was completed, Wayne entered UCLA Medical Center for exploratory surgery. Mike and his son Chris came to visit. The TV was on, and the Steelers were playing the Cowboys. "Who are you pulling for?" Wayne asked his grandson. "The Steelers," said Chris.

"Well then, I'll pull for the Cowboys. Wanna wager?"

They settled on a dollar. Mike and Chris were home by the time the Cowboys won. "He won't remember [the bet]," said Chris. "He'll remember," said his father. The next time Chris went to visit his grandfather, he was met with a question:

"Where's my dollar?"

"You really want it?"

"Of course I want it. If you're not going to pay off, don't bet."

Chris handed over the dollar.

He knew what the doctors would find; he told Pat Stacy that if anything happened to him, she should keep an eye on Marisa — she was the only one of his children he was worried about. As they wheeled him off to the operating room, he smiled and said, "See you in the movies!"

As soon as Dr. William Longmire opened Wayne up, he knew the prognosis was bad. There was a malignancy in the stomach, a large one that was likely to have spread. Longmire quickly sent some tissue out to pathology and the verdict came back: malignant carcinoma. Longmire and the other doctors settled in for a long day as they performed a complete gastrectomy. The operation began at 9:45 A.M. and went until 7 P.M. During the nine and a half hours of surgery, Wayne's stomach and his gall bladder were removed, as well as some gastric lymph nodes. Longmire constructed two small pouches out of a portion of Wayne's small intestine to serve as a stomach.

Cancer cells were found in the lymph nodes. But the next day, a consultant to the medical team that carried out the grueling operation announced that "there was no clinical evidence" that the malignancy had spread and said that "without question," Wayne would be able to go back to making films.

When reporters pressed him about the possibility of the cancer having spread, the consultant said, "I did not categorically state that it hasn't [spread], I said there is no evidence." The implications of a cascading series of health emergencies for a man who had endured two major surgeries within a year were clear, but the hospital, and presumably the family, kept a stoic public facade. Wayne was moved to room 951 at the UCLA Medical Center.

Gastric carcinoma spreads fast and has a very low five-year survival rate. Because the cancer had been found in the lymph nodes, there was a 90 percent probability that it had spread. Medical professionals reading between the lines knew that Wayne's survival was measured in months, not years.

Each day, three thousand letters and one thousand phone calls arrived at the hospital. The flowers that arrived were parceled out to the very young and the very old after Wayne read the attached cards. He was sitting up in a chair and walking short distances.

Recovery was incremental; he and Pat Stacy would play cards, he would watch television, mostly news and game shows — *Wheel of Fortune, Password, Hollywood Squares,* playing along, answering the questions. Stacy was heartened when he began yelling at Walter Cronkite. His walks down the hall were accompanied by an IV pole, and he was usually supported by Stacy, Michael, or Patrick. He had drainage tubes on both sides of his body. On January 28, he reached a milestone: he walked the entire length of the hall and back without assistance.

On February 10, he left the hospital and returned to Newport Beach. He was optimistic at this point — there was no talk about dying, but much talk about what had to be done to adjust to life without a stomach. He ate very little, and much of what he did eat he couldn't keep down.

He was diminishing daily. Except for his eyes — as his body shrank, as his face hollowed out, his eyes became bigger. His daughter Aissa wrote that "they still shone clear and calm and resolute. Even when I was deeply depressed, I could still lose myself for a time in his incandescent blue eyes."

Six weeks after the surgery, Wayne began radiation treatments; the target began in his central abdomen from the navel to the sternum and then broadened out to the left side of his chest to the armpit. After a few weeks of treatment, his appetite disappeared, and he developed a bright red radiation burn on his chest. By the end of March, his weight dropped below 190 pounds. As his condition weakened, his mood darkened. He didn't complain about the pain, but he complained bitterly about his invalid status, his desire for real food. The children all visited regularly, but Pilar didn't, although she sent over food — spinach soufflés, light food he could digest. He didn't want her food, didn't want any food.

He made arrangements to donate some of his most prized possessions to the National Cowboy & Western Heritage Museum in Oklahoma City. He had begun giving them things years before — a saddle here, a gun there. When his donation was complete, it comprised more than two hundred items. There were forty-five guns and seventeen paintings — five by Olaf Wieghorst, two by Edward Borein, and a beautiful painting by Harold von Schmidt entitled *The Searchers.* There was a Chinese lacquer painting of two horses that had hung over the mantel in the Newport Beach house for years, and a terra-cotta horse from the T'ang dynasty. There were also forty-six bronzes, some by Charles Russell, more by Harry Jackson.

Some of his most valued books were included in the donation, including his complete set of Edward Curtis's *The North American Indian,* and twenty loose-leaf folios of Curtis's images. Also included were books by Winston Churchill and Douglas Southall Freeman and his collection of sixty-four Hopi kachina dolls collected over the years while making movies in Arizona and Utah.

Most of the time he was angry; sometimes he was furious. Now, he couldn't even shoot commercials for Great Western anymore — he'd lost too much weight — he was down to 180 pounds. After he was released from the hospital, he didn't even go to the Balboa Yacht Club, probably because he didn't want to see the looks on people's faces when they saw him. George Valenzuela, his favorite waiter, had noticed that he was shrinking, and that was before the surgery.

Luster Bayless called and he could hear a lot of clinking going on. Wayne explained that he had to eat every couple of hours — something to do with his stomach being gone. It was a long conversation, more about Bayless than about Wayne. Bayless remembered that it was as if Wayne didn't want to hang up and go back to his life.

Wayne's last time aboard the *Wild Goose* came on Easter weekend 1979. He issued orders to Bert Minshall: "I don't want any damn long faces on board here, and no tears. I'm doing fine, so no crying for me — you tell them all that."

The trip was a simple one, Newport to Catalina and back. He must have known he would never see Catalina again, and he seemed to enjoy just taking it all in. He played cards and backgammon, had quiet talks with Ethan and Marisa.

Anything but bland liquids came right back up, so his diet was limited to tapioca, food processed in a blender, protein drinks.

"He was breathless with pain, and he had lost so much weight because he couldn't eat," remembered Bert Minshall. "He and the kids would spend hours just sitting in the sun on the gray deck chairs. At one point, Ethan took the helm and his father looked proud. He went over and gave the boy a gentle hug, but he didn't say anything.

"He also seemed to enjoy standing on the forward deck alone, the salt spray splashing at him. I don't recall him ever spending so much time out there alone."

He also had fits of temper. "He was bitching at Pat Stacy, accusing her of going off with other guys," said Minshall. "Which wasn't true — she was a good companion. When would she have done it? At first, she had a trailer on the waterfront a few yards from the *Wild Goose,* then he rented her a house across the street from his house."

The *Wild Goose* anchored at its usual spot in White's Cove. He played some gin with Stacy and began reminiscing — hunting with Johnny Weissmuller; the buffalo roaming wild in the Catalina hills; times with Pappy, Ward, and the rest of the crew on the *Araner,* long weekends when nobody drew a sober breath. In the six years Pat Stacy had been with him, he'd never talked about Pappy as much as he did that day on the *Wild Goose.*

The next day he wanted to go ashore and do some shopping in Avalon. He slipped away and came back with his arms full of gifts to hand out on Easter morning. On Easter Sunday, he handed out the gifts — he gave Stacy a miniature of two rabbits locked in a hug. Then he announced it was time for a hike across the isthmus. He'd been making that jaunt for nearly sixty years, and wasn't about to stop now. Besides, he needed the exercise.

Wayne, Ethan, and Pat Stacy went ashore in the dinghy and began walking, but the trip was too ambitious. He made it one way, but was too exhausted to walk back. He and Ethan hitched a ride back to the dock.

After the boat returned to Newport, Wayne lingered on board longer than usual. Minshall asked him if there was anything he needed. "No, Bert there's nothing I need. Goodbye, my friend. Thanks, Bert. I had a nice time."

Minshall never saw him again.

And then, astonishingly, Wayne agreed to present the Best Picture Oscar at the Academy Awards. Nobody wanted him to appear in public with such a great weight loss, but he didn't want to talk about it. "I'm going to do it," he snapped. "That's all."

By the time of the telecast, on April 9, 1979, he needed a new tuxedo. He didn't want to go to Sy Devore's shop on Vine Street, so Devore said he'd come to the Batjac offices and do the fittings there. While they waited for the haberdasher to show up, Wayne and Tom Kane made small talk. Kane was having raccoon problems at his house, with the animals coming right into the kitchen through the cat door to eat the cat food.

"You've got to shoot the bastards," said Wayne, who went on to say that even if Kane closed off the cat door, it wouldn't help. "They'll tear the chimney out of your house. I know all about them."

For the week before the ceremony, Wayne underwent an exercise regimen, so that even if he didn't look like the John Wayne the audience knew, he would at least move and stand like the John Wayne the audience knew.

The morning of the Oscars, Wayne went to Hoag Hospital in Newport Beach for his daily radiation treatment, then made the hour-and-a-half journey to Los Angeles. He rested until it was time for his rehearsal. He had been invited to the Governor's Ball after the ceremony, but had to decline. What was the point? He couldn't eat anything, he couldn't drink anything, and he didn't have the strength to dance.

He had insisted that Pat Stacy and Marisa, who were both accompanying him, buy new dresses for the occasion. He explained that he wanted Marisa to feel special, that he had always promised to take her to the Oscars when she was older, but tonight was the night, because "who knows when I'll be able to take her again. I want her to look like a princess."

He got there forty-five minutes before the broadcast started — a pro to the last. Word quickly went out that Duke Wayne was in the house, and soon he was besieged. Laurence Olivier stopped by, and so did Cary Grant. They talked about their young children. Then it was Lauren Bacall, and Jane Fonda, who wanted to say hello to her father's old friend.

When Wayne finally walked backstage, producer Howard W. Koch was stunned. "He looked like death," said Koch. "I was really worried."

On cue, despite the pain, Wayne walked down a

large staircase and was greeted by a huge and heartfelt standing ovation from the audience. Despite the obvious fact that he was dying, the love seemed to energize him.

"That's just about the only medicine a fella'd ever really need. Believe me when I tell you I'm mighty pleased that I can amble down here tonight. Oscar and I have something in common. Oscar first came to the Hollywood scene in 1928. So did I. We're both a little weather-beaten, but we're here and plan to be around for a whole lot longer. My job here tonight is to identify your five choices for outstanding picture of the year, and to announce the winner. So, let's move 'em out!"

He read the names of the nominees — *Coming Home, Heaven Can Wait, Midnight Express, An Unmarried Woman,* and the winner: *The Deer Hunter.* It was not a choice that could have pleased him, but the Oscars were the centerpiece of the industry he loved and he would never have been intentionally rude and voiced displeasure with the picture. Besides, he had more important things to worry about.

After the show was over, he dropped into the press room to congratulate the winners and posed for a couple of shots. He stood there by himself, let the photographers take a few pictures, and then went home.

In so many ways, this last appearance was congruent with the image he embodied, with the legend he had created — a man alone, seeing his promises through to the end. As Molly Haskell wrote, "He allowed us to see, in his last appearance, a once-majestic frame withered away by the ravages of cancer, allowed us to hear a once-resonant voice that could hardly get out a few well-known names. . . . It was in retrospect, perhaps his most heroic performance. With this parting gesture, his legend, and the larger myth he represented, were ennobled rather than diminished by the shadow of mortality."

Like nearly everything else in his life, he did it and didn't regret it. For that matter, he admitted to regretting only one thing: "One time I caught a giant Mahi Mahi in the waters off Hawaii. I weighed the fish and then ate it. Later, when the boat docked, I discovered I had eaten the world's record catch for that species. I should have had that son of a bitch mounted."

He began pulling away from old friends. The last time Cecilia deMille Presley saw him he was clearly dying, but he didn't seem to feel sorry for himself. "To Duke, a body that didn't work was annoying," she said. On April 17, his cough was so violent he couldn't sleep, and there was blood in his phlegm. It was pneumonia, so he went on heavy antibiotics and more tapioca pudding. He avoided looking in the mirror.

In the last week in April, Maureen O'Hara arrived. She had had cancer surgery herself not long before, and Wayne had called to lend his support. When she arrived, Wayne was propped up in bed so his remaining lung wouldn't fill with fluid. The air in the room was stale. O'Hara must have seen the pictures of him at the Oscar ceremony, but she was still stunned by his appearance. He reached out his hand and she took it, then she put her head down on the bed and began to cry.

"Is that for Charlie?" he asked — Charlie Blair, a brigadier general in the Air Force. O'Hara had married him in 1968 and spent ten years with him until he was killed in an airplane crash.

"Yes," she lied.

At one point, he began to cry, saying, "Why you? Why me?" O'Hara started to cry again because it was the only time in their long relationship that she had ever known him to break down. "Maureen, why did you and I have such lousy luck?" he said.

They began to talk, and they kept talking for the next day and a half. They talked about chess and steaks and flying and John Ford. Always John Ford.

Wayne insisted she stay the night in the bedroom across from his. The next morning, Wayne and O'Hara sat on the deck with the kids around them. O'Hara told a story about Wayne getting drunk as a lord at John Ford's house one night in the 1940s, and Ford ordering her to get him home. She said she couldn't handle him alone, but Ford insisted it was her responsibility.

O'Hara decided to drive to Lakeside Golf Club, where she figured she could enlist reinforcements. Somewhere on Ventura Boulevard, Wayne suddenly decided he needed another drink and demanded that O'Hara pull over.

He chose a house at random and began pounding on the door. A middle-aged couple in pajamas came to the door to be met by John Wayne and Maureen O'Hara standing on their porch. "Good evening," said Wayne. "We need a drink." The couple invited them in and Wayne and O'Hara made small talk while Wayne had his drink. The kids loved the story and asked their father if it was actually true. "Well, if your Auntie Maureen says I did . . . I guess I did." She left later that day.

Shortly after O'Hara left, Claire Trevor and her husband, Milton Bren — who was dying of cancer himself — came by for a short visit. A day later, Yakima Canutt stopped by. They passed the time discussing ideas for Great Western commercials. Wayne called Olive Carey regularly, seemed to take strength from her indomitable spirit.

While the death watch went on inside the house, outside there was a series of impromptu celebrations. On weekends, the boating community in Newport Beach formed parades in the harbor. Wayne would sit on his porch and the boats would sail past, with the people on board waving hello. Wayne cheerily waved to every boat even if he didn't know them. "It was how people let him know they cared about him," said Tom Fuentes.

On May 2, three weeks after the Oscar ceremony, he collapsed in the kitchen. "Something is wrong with me, Aissa. Something is really wrong." First he was taken to Hoag Hospital in Newport, where X rays revealed an intestinal obstruction. The doctor at Hoag said that Wayne needed to be taken to UCLA for emergency surgery. He was in agony; he couldn't sit up, could only lie down, so the station wagon's backseat was folded down and he lay there on top of some blankets while Ethan drove him to UCLA.

In his bedroom, he had left his favorite dark suit out. "He knew," said Gretchen Wayne.

By the time they got to UCLA, the place was crawling with TV cameras — someone at Hoag had alerted them. The next morning, Dr. Longmire was operating again, but this time there was nothing to be done — the cancer was everywhere — "diffuse carcinomatosis" as the profession calls it. The radiation hadn't worked. Nothing had worked. Some thought was given to chemo-therapy, but the oncologists decided that Wayne was too weak, that the chemo would kill him before the cancer would. They decided to try interferon as a Hail Mary.

Wayne had entered that stage of terminal illness where nothing stabilizes, where one condition provokes another condition, and the treatment for the first condition only exacerbates the second or the third.

Old friends rallied. Ollie Carey called, and Wayne complained about what the doctors had done to his body. "They didn't leave me anything," he said. "Well," she replied, "you've still got your balls and your brain, don't you?" He laughed and had to admit that was true.

Sometimes Wayne was quiet, other times he'd unleash his temper; once, enraged by his inability to eat anything but bland foods, he threw a bowl of tapioca pudding on the floor. Pat Stacy called Mary St. John to help out, and she came as soon as she could. The first time she saw Wayne, St. John let out an involuntary gasp at his emaciation.

He thought about suicide, asking Patrick to fetch the .38 he kept by his bed. His son refused, as did Stacy. He raged at her until he fell back exhausted onto the pillow.

Michael stopped by the hospital every morning on the way to his office on Wilshire. One day his dad called early and asked him to bring him a USC cap. It seemed that the doctors had given him a UCLA cap, but "I just can't wear it next to my head." Michael brought him the cap and his father wore it underneath the UCLA cap. He enjoyed going down the hall in his wheelchair tipping his UCLA cap to everybody and showing off the USC cap beneath it.

George O'Brien called his son Darcy, who had become a novelist and professor. "You need to write the Duke," George said. "I think he's dying." Darcy's letter was about that long-ago idyllic vacation off Catalina, when Wayne had been so kind to a young boy and helped him dive for abalone. Wayne took the trouble to write "the nicest letter" back. O'Brien kept it framed over his desk until his own premature death.

Johnny Weissmuller, a fellow client of Bö Roos and an occasional drinking buddy of Wayne's, was having psychological difficulties that might have been Alzheimer's. He was being transferred to a mental institution, and Wayne got on the phone to try to help. He apologized to Weissmuller's wife for not being able to do more. "Maria, I'm dying myself . . . If I could, I'd go down there [to the hospital] and crack a few heads." Later on, before hanging up, he told her, "I'm on the way to the happy hunting grounds where old elephants go to die."

Some days he was acquiescent to the doctors and appreciative of whatever of life was on offer. "What a lovely morning," he would say on those days. Other days he raged. "Goddamn you," he would say before they gave him an injection, "every time I turn around you're trying to stick me with that thing. Why are you sons of bitches giving me this shit? Do you want me so drugged that I can't fight back? Jesus Christ!"

Visits were mostly limited to family and the inner circle. Dozens of people called continually — Ann-Margret, Lauren Bacall. And Stacy Keach called, which puzzled the family until he explained. "When I was a kid out there in the valley I was selling Christmas wreaths door to door one year. And I came to Wayne's house and he invited me in. He said, 'Come in, son, and warm up a bit.' I've never forgotten that gesture. Even though I've never had the pleasure of working with him on a film, I remember that and I'd just like his family and all the rest of you to know how highly I regard him."

On May 5, President Carter visited Wayne. Like everybody else, Carter was shocked at Wayne's appearance, but managed to conceal it. Wayne told Carter that he approved of the new left-hand part in his hair, that it improved his looks, and as a show business professional he knew what he was talking about. Pointing to an intravenous tube in his arm, Wayne told the president that he'd be happy to offer him some of his delicious meal, but he only had one straw.

Robert Parrish cabled: "Dear Duke," it read. "Among many others throughout the world, my heart is with you." Wayne dictated a reply: "Dear Bobby, Your thoughtfulness was very much appreciated. The farther out you go, the lonelier it gets. Affectionately, Duke."

On May 7, doctors told the family that the cancer had metastasized. The next day, Jimmy Stewart and Paul Keyes visited. Burt Kennedy came with Al Murphy, who had worked as an assistant director at Batjac for years and who had changed his name from Silverstein. As the two men were ushered into the room, Mike Wayne joked, "The reason Duke didn't want to see you was because Al is a Jew."

Wayne smiled and pointed to the ceiling. "It's the *other* Jew I don't want to see."

Michael Caine's wife, Shakira, was at the UCLA Medical Center for some minor surgery, and one day while Caine was visiting her he heard a familiar voice calling him. Wayne's room was two doors away from Shakira Caine's. Wayne was pleased to see Caine, and the two talked until a nurse threw Caine out.

From then on, Caine would pop in every time he visited his wife. Occasionally, he would join Wayne for a long, slow walk down the hospital corridor. Wayne wore pajamas, a robe, a baseball cap. One day Caine asked Wayne how long he expected to be in the hospital.

"It's got me this time, Mike," Wayne observed. "I won't be getting out of here." Caine was struck by the tone — no sadness or self-pity, just a statement of fact, as if Wayne had been in a fair fight and lost. Tears welled up in Caine's eyes, but Wayne didn't want to see it. "Get the hell out of here and go and enjoy yourself," he ordered.

One day, Wayne slowly made his way down to the hospital mail room on the first floor and apologized to the staff for all the extra work he was making for them. He told them that it wouldn't be too much longer.

On May 10, Frank Sinatra and his wife, Barbara, came. When they emerged from the room, they were both shaken, and Barbara Sinatra rushed over to Pat Stacy to apologize. She had been stunned by Wayne's deterioration and had told him she would pray to Saint Jude. Then she remembered that Saint Jude is the patron saint of lost causes. "I meant to say I'd pray to the saint of hope," she told Stacy. "Please tell him that." As an old woman herself, Barbara Sinatra's main memory was of how utterly devastated she had been by Wayne's condition.

Maureen O'Hara testified before Congress in order to get quick approval for the striking of a Congressional Gold Medal to honor Wayne, the eighty-fifth person in history to receive it. "To the people of the world, John Wayne is not just an actor," she said. "John Wayne is the United States of America. He is what they believe America to be." The medal, which had previously honored Jonas Salk, the Wright brothers, Charles Lindbergh, and Bob Hope, was unanimously approved with the support of President Carter on May 23 and the order was signed three days later, on Wayne's seventy-second birthday.

Old friends wrote letters to buck him up. Gregory Peck wrote, telling Wayne that he had to "get your conservative ass out of there" in order to pick up his Congressional Medal. James Cagney wrote, telling Wayne he was pulling for him and sending along the regards of Frank McHugh, who had worked with Wayne in *The Telegraph Trail* in 1933.

And Ronald Reagan wrote, telling Wayne "we'll keep on praying until they decide you can get into a saloon fight (on the studio back lot of course) or go fishing in Baja for real. . . . Nancy sends her love — I would too but there might be talk."

Mike Wayne finally completed a deal to sell the *Wild Goose* for $650,000, but Wayne ordered that $40,000 be spent overhauling the engines because he didn't want to take advantage of the man buying the boat. Bert Minshall got $6,000 as severance.

Wayne was no longer taking walks down the hospital corridor. He needed help to get from the bed to the bathroom. Sometimes there were tears of frustration. His seventy-second birthday was greeted by terrible pain that provoked a regimen of narcotics, and he slept through most of the day. The next morning he woke up, so everybody there sang "Happy Birthday" around the bed and passed around pieces of cake, but he was too weak to open presents. By this time, all but the oldest friends were turned away. Henry Hathaway came on May 28 and spent a half hour with his old friend. Wayne insisted on getting out of his bed and sitting in a chair for old Henry.

By May 29, the hospital began administering morphine as a regular part of Wayne's medication. Occasionally he would say, "I'm sorry," but he stopped complaining. He had lost nearly one hundred pounds. His chest and abdomen were a network of surgical scars and radiation burns, his arms and legs bruised and mottled from needles.

In the first week in June, he began to turn inward. When the nurses came in to give him Demerol or morphine, he rolled over and let them do what they wanted. He was just too tired.

"At the end, the cancer was everywhere," said Patrick Wayne. "He was in excruciating pain, and he never complained. He was so strong, so bulletproof all his life, and part of me believed he could beat the cancer back again. I don't think he did, though. He had a bedsore on his back the size of a grapefruit, an open wound that would not heal. He never complained. Underneath it all, he was a human being. Not superhuman, like he could play, but a human being. But an incredible human being."

Mike Wayne called Louis and Alice Johnson in Arizona and told them if they wanted to see their friend one last time, they had to come now. They came, and so did Mary St. John. Through his haze, Wayne asked what she thought about death, and she quoted the *Rubáiyát of Omar Khayyám:*

Strange, is it not? That of the myriads who
Before us pass'd the door of Darkness through
Not one returns to tell us of the Road,
Which to discover we must travel too.

He asked her to repeat it, then said, "You know, I never thought of it that way."

She took his hand and kissed it, and he said, "Well, Mary, I guess the Red Witch finally got me."

There was nothing to be done except suffer along with him. "You just prayed, saying, 'My God, don't let him suffer another day,' " said Gretchen Wayne.

Years before, Jane Fonda had told Gretchen Wayne it wasn't unusual for her to come down to the kitchen in the morning wiping the sleep from her eyes to find John Wayne having a cup of coffee with her father. Wayne's gregariousness had been one of the few things that could lift Henry Fonda out of his solitary nature, but that close friendship had ended with the McCarthy period.

Now, Henry Fonda told Michael that he'd like to see Duke, but he didn't want to cause any fuss. Michael said that his father would be very pleased that his old friend wanted to visit. Fonda went in the room to find Wayne sleeping. He just stood at the foot of the bed for a while, paying his respects, saying goodbye.

Josie called. Wayne had stopped taking calls, but that one he took. To Josie's own dying day in 2003 she never spoke of what they talked about. But later she told her grandchildren her verdict on the man who had been her first and only true love.

"We were married when we were young," she told Chris Wayne. "Duke was a good man. He was honest, he had a conscience, he had a good heart. He was a man of his word. He *tried*."

"The last week," said Pat Wayne, "he went into deeper and deeper sleeps, and he was awake less and less." On June 8, he began slipping in and out of a coma, and his breathing began to grow shallow.

And then, on June 10, at about 9 P.M. he suddenly woke up, and was amazingly alert and responsive. "For two hours, maybe three, he was totally alive and with us, talking to all of us," remembered Patrick Wayne. "Six of the seven children were there, and we all had a chance to have a last conversation with him. And he had all of his humor, all of his gregariousness. He was once again the whole man." Pat Stacy was there, and she agreed with Patrick that those few hours were a last flair of light. "His blue eyes were shining. He showed no pain. He seemed to be enjoying every moment of those three hours."

He knew he was in the hospital, but he also seemed to think that he was still working and making movies. No matter — for one last time, he was John Wayne — the Duke. Gretchen Wayne said that "He was lucid, he was funny, he felt good. At the end, he accepted it. He didn't fight it. He said, 'It's been great.'"

"Then he went back to sleep," said Patrick Wayne. "I treasure those two hours."

Late on June 10 or early on June 11, Father Robert Curtis was called to Wayne's bedside. He looked at Wayne and asked him, "Is it your wish that you become a Catholic?"

"Yes it is, Father," Wayne said. They went through the baptism ceremony together, ending with "I baptize you in the name of the Father, the Son and Holy Ghost." Then the priest gave him Extreme Unction, absolving him of all sins — the Last Rites.

The priest said that Wayne was lucid, and knew what he was doing. "I gave him the sacraments. But it was impossible to give him Holy Communion because of his condition — he couldn't swallow the water."

Patrick Wayne's memory of the event was slightly different. "On the morning of his death, the chaplain came by and said he'd like to see my dad. I told him he'd been in a coma, but I would ask. He was asleep, but I leaned over and said, 'Dad, the chaplain's here.' And he roused himself and murmured 'OK.' That's when the chaplain baptized him."

Aissa Wayne was there, and she said that at the time of the conversion her father was under the influence of industrial doses of morphine and was drifting in and out of consciousness. As the priest said the prayers in Latin, Aissa saw her father faintly nod his head, acknowledging that he knew the priest was there and that they were praying. "I knew firsthand how my father felt about Catholicism," she recalled. "I was raised a Catholic, and my father took no interest at all, never once attending church with me and my mom. Our entire lives, he showed no inclination toward organized religion of any type."

But Wayne's grandson Chris knew a priest at Loyola Marymount who used to see Wayne shopping for Christmas presents at Sears. "When you have as many kids as I do, you buy in bulk," he told the priest. The same priest would occasionally see Wayne at the 5 A.M. Mass. "It's me, father," Wayne would say after the priest did a double take.

Wayne's grandson Matthew Munoz was visiting him along with his mother, Melinda, and he came to believe that Wayne's conversion was inevitable. "My grandmother was very devout and so was my mother. In fact, my grandfather . . . was very true to God. He always believed in God, but he wasn't much of a church attendee. I really think my grandfather's admiration of my grandmother is what made him take that spiritual step and say yes. I also believe my grandmother's prayers were heard."

"My dad was not a churchgoing man," said Patrick Wayne, "although all of us kids were raised Catholic because of our mothers. He always said that he was a 'Presbygoddamnterian.' But as far as I know he was never baptized until that last day."

On the morning of June 11, the doctors told the family he was going to die that day. Supposedly he opened his eyes that morning and fixed on Pat Stacy. She asked him if he knew who she was. "Of course I know who you are," he said. "You're my girl. I love you." Wayne closed his eyes and went back to sleep, a deep sleep. Hours went by. The nurse called the children into the room. His breathing became shallow, more a series of gasps than anything else, and there was a longer time between each breath.

Aissa was holding his right hand and she noticed that the cancer had left his hands undiminished. They were still huge and all-encompassing. The man in the bed drew in his breath. There was a pause. He never exhaled.

The man the world knew as John Wayne but who always thought of himself as Duke Morrison died on Monday, June 11, 1979, at 5:23 in the afternoon. He was seventy-two years old. The cause of death was listed as respiratory arrest of five minutes, caused by gastric cancer of eight months. The attending physician might as well have listed the cause of death as "life."

As the news spread across the world, the reactions were close to unanimous. The controversy of his World War II nonservice, of his fierce conservatism and support of the blacklist, faded beside the loss of his passing. For decades, he had been America's great stone wall, impervious to fashion and time. Now, suddenly, the wall was gone.

The *Los Angeles Times* led the front page with his death, which continued onto six pages inside. The *Herald-Examiner* also led with his death. President Carter said that Wayne's "ruggedness, the tough independence, the sense of personal conviction and courage — on and off the screen — reflected the best of our national character." James Stewart said that "John Wayne was probably the most admired actor in the world. His passing marks a great loss for his family, for the film industry, and for the entire world."

Jack Valenti, president of the Motion Picture Association of America, always had a knack for flamboyant metaphor and said, "The Duke is dead, which means the tallest tree in the movie forest has just been felled. There won't ever be anyone like him. God, we will miss him."

In France, the three national TV networks

893

showed Wayne's best-known films in a tribute they called "John Wayne, Duke of the Wide Open Spaces."

William F. Buckley Jr. wrote a charming reminiscence regarding Wayne's appearance in an ad for *National Review* in 1969 — his picture with a quote: "*National Review* is my favorite magazine. Why don't you give it a try?" A year later, Wayne received a solicitation from the magazine illustrated with his own pitch. He sent it to Buckley with a scrawled note: "Bill, What do you need to be convinced? Duke."

"The miracle is the memory," wrote Buckley. "Of all those villainous men dispatched by John Wayne, surely the most widely viewed executive of good causes — frontier justice, battles against totalitarian forces, the defense of the weak — in human history. His memory keeps us cheerful."

But not everybody was overwhelmed with grief. The director — and World War II veteran — William Wyler wrote a letter to *Newsweek* referring to Wayne as "a great American hero fighting for God and country in all services and all wars. And it was all done before cameras in Hollywood and on safe locations. That's damn good acting!"

Four days after Wayne died, a funeral Mass was held at Our Lady Queen of Angels at Corona del Mar at four in the morning to avoid crowds and the usual celebrity circus. The Mass was conducted by the archbishop of Panama. John Wayne was buried shortly after the sun rose at Pacific View Memorial Park in Newport Beach. Seven children, twenty-one grandchildren, and his estranged wife, Pilar, were present.

The next day, a steady stream of cars entered the Pacific View Memorial Park. They weren't allowed to go to the gravesite, but circled a make-shift memorial the cemetery had erected by a flagpole. The largest of the arrangements was a four-foot-wide design that featured red and white roses forming an American flag.

For years, Wayne lay in an unmarked grave — Michael didn't want tourists making a pilgrimage to the site and wanted to follow his father's wishes that everything be quiet and dignified. Finally, he relented; the stone that marks John Wayne's resting place carries a quote from the man who lies beneath: "Tomorrow is the most important thing in life. Comes to us at midnight very clean. It's perfect when it arrives and puts itself in our hands. It hopes we've learned something from yesterday."

The tribute that might have meant the most to Wayne happened in Durango, Mexico, where Burt Lancaster was on location. When word came that John Wayne had died, the cast and crew paused for a minute of silence. They were making *Cattle Annie and Little Britches.*

They were making a western.

EPILOGUE

"I've had the most appealing of lives. I've been lucky enough to portray man against the elements at the same time as there was always someone there to bring me the orange juice."
— JOHN WAYNE

"I've played the kind of man I'd like to have been."
— JOHN WAYNE

Wayne's will was filed a week after he died. The thirty-page document, dated and signed October 5, 1978, denied any bequest to Pilar because she had earlier entered into a private settlement with Wayne. "I am married to Pilar Wayne," the will stated, "but she and I are separated and for this reason I intentionally make no provision in this will for her."

The will set up a trust for Josie, out of which she was to be paid $3,000 a month. Mike received all of his father's Class A preferred stock in Batjac Productions, which gave the oldest son ownership of the company and of the Batjac film library. Also receiving special attention was his daughter Toni, who was the beneficiary of a separate trust involving her proportionate share of the remainder of the estate. Pat Stacy received $30,000, Mary St.

John $10,000.

The remainder of the personal property was to be divided equally among the children, except for his collection of western art, which had been previously deeded over to the National Cowboy & Western Heritage Museum in Oklahoma City. The executors were Mike Wayne, Louis Johnson, and John S. Warren.

The estate was valued at $6.8 million, with real property valued at $1 million, personal property at $5.75 million, and annual income from personal property at $100,000. A careful reading of the will made it clear that most of the estate was in property — there was little cash.

Michael Wayne told Stacy that she could stay in the house Wayne had rented for her until the lease was up, and she would remain on the Batjac payroll for the rest of the year or until she got another job, whichever came first.

The house in Newport Beach was sold in March 1980 for $3.48 million. It was torn down in 2002, and replaced with something far larger and gaudier. Louis Johnson sold the 26 Bar Ranch, the Red River Land Company, and the Red River Feed Yard in January 1980 for $45 million, half of which went to the Wayne estate.

Honors quickly accrued to Wayne's memory and image. The house where Marion Morrison was born was turned into a museum. The Orange County airport was renamed the John Wayne Airport, with an impressive statue of Wayne outside the terminal. Two years after his death, the UCLA Medical School's Division of Surgical Oncology became the John Wayne Cancer Clinic.

At least four life-sized or larger bronze statues of him dot the American landscape, and there are other commemorations: the John Wayne Pioneer Trail in Washington state, and part of Arizona Highway 347 is called the John Wayne Parkway.

In 1991, the *Wild Goose* was purchased by the former owner of the Tropicana Hotel in Las Vegas. Today, the ship remains a floating shrine to the memory of John Wayne and is available for charter out of Newport Beach. Likewise, the bar at the Balboa Yacht Club in Newport Beach is called Duke's Place, where there is a floor-to-ceiling painting of Wayne at the helm of the *Wild Goose.*

Pilar would marry twice more, although her identity stayed that of Mrs. John Wayne, surrounded as she was by John Wayne memorabilia, including her own paintings that often featured a representation of her late husband somewhere in the composition. With her husband dead, Josie was free to remarry in the eyes of the Church, which she did in 1996. She died in 2003 at the age of 95.

In 2011, Ethan Wayne auctioned off a large batch of Wayne's personal effects, from his annotated script for *Stagecoach,* through costumes to personal possessions such as eyeglasses and prescription bottles. The auction brought more than $5.3 million from fans eager to possess something Wayne had once touched, once worn. His cap from *The Green Berets* brought $179,250 (a record price for a costume hat), his hat from *Big Jake* and *The Cowboys* brought $119,500, a holster and belt from *El Dorado* brought $77,675, his driver's license brought $89,625, and one of the eyepatches from *True Grit* brought $47,800.

Mike Wayne ran Batjac until his own death in 2003, after which it was taken over by his wife, Gretchen. Once, he was asked what his father would think of the large collection of John Wayne posters and memorabilia he had amassed. "He'd look at it and say, 'That's great,' " said Mike. "And then he'd never give it another thought."

Mike came to some realizations about his father's place in American folklore, and of how a man whose early life had been chaotic and insecure came to place such a high value on certainty — on- and offscreen.

> The thing that he required as an actor was a strong male role that had a philosophy. That runs consistently through the roles that he played. . . . He was a strong man with strong beliefs and he stuck to those beliefs. Now the beliefs [of the character] weren't always right . . . but the character stuck to those beliefs. He was a man that had conviction, that had integrity and so he was able to portray that and more [importantly] project it. . . .
>
> Because of his films, my father came to symbolize the American man throughout the world, whether he was wearing a soldier suit or a cowboy hat or a police uniform. The . . . values they presented — honesty, integrity, independence — were qualities he had on and off screen.
>
> He wasn't a cowboy or a rancher; he was a movie star. He wasn't a hero; he was a movie star. But for many people, he was a symbol of America.

The impact of most stars recedes after they die, for the movie business is one of temporal enthusiasms, and standards of masculinity change nearly as much as standards of beauty. But to a great extent Wayne remains, his films in constant rotation, his image immediately recognizable.

He was a rich character hiding in plain sight — deeply flawed, deeply moving, earthy and warm, a Scots-Irish brawler by blood and by temperament, full of love and rage and forgiveness. He was a freedom fighter whose best friends included flagrant anti-Semites and racists, a deeply conservative man who believed passionately in freedom of speech, an emotionally expansive man who was a little afraid of women, a man with a father he adored who spent years in search of a father substitute, a fierce patriot who didn't serve, an insecure young man who grew to be a secure husband and father. And a fine actor who only grudgingly stepped outside his comfort zone.

The people that knew him, and the people that worked with him, would spend the rest of their own lives happily talking about him. "The thing about Duke is he's like a big kid," said Howard Hawks. "I don't think, with all that's happened to him over the years, that he's ever really come to terms with it."

The word Hawks was searching for was "innocence," a quality that derived from a rare purity of being. Wayne was by turns enthusiastic, generous, excitable, easily moved to both anger and laughter, always apologizing for the former, never for the latter. To a great extent, he was the same man at seventy that he had been at thirty — there was never anything pretentious about him, and he always seemed surprised and pleased by praise, perhaps because he received so little of it for so long.

"He treated me square, he treated me with class and he was damn good," said stuntman Dean Smith. "When I met him, I didn't have a quarter, and now I'm eighty years old and I've got a thirteen-year-old son and two ranches. And I'm gonna be like Old Duke — I'm gonna milk that cow until she kicks me."

Underneath the surface certainty was an overwhelming sense of responsibility and a tendency to repress insecurity whenever it arose, which resulted in explosions of anger if he felt ignored or powerless. He needed approval far more than he wanted money, and at his best or worst he was always relentlessly honest.

"If he told you tomorrow's Christmas," said Ben Johnson, "you could get your stocking ready. He was that kind of person."

Near the end of Harry Carey Jr.'s life, an autographed picture of Wayne was prominently displayed in his bedroom. It was a shot from *Hondo,* of Wayne with his dog, with an inscription to Carey's mother: "Ollie Dear — If we could turn it back I'd like it to be about here, or Big Bear. Duke." Below that inscription was a smaller one, also in Wayne's hand: "Me too. Lassie." (Big Bear was a reference to *The Shepherd of the Hills,* and his co-star Harry Carey Sr.)

Pilar judged her husband to be someone who refused to rely on talent, and believed predominantly in effort. "He got up every morning determined to do his best. . . . Though the results varied, the effort never did. He believed that hard work, sweat rather than talent, was what it took to succeed."

"I think he was very aware of what he had to live up to," said Budd Boetticher, "but I don't know that Duke was ever happy. Obviously he was happier on the set or carousing than he was at home. He worked hard not to be lonely, which tells me that he must have been. Anybody who keeps that busy has got to be lonely."

Many actors have a way of becoming what they play, but, as with Cary Grant, John Wayne first had to devise a screen character. After that, he became what he wanted to be, and he played John Wayne so well that it gradually overlapped with — but never obliterated — Duke Morrison.

Although he enacted a great many scenes of violence, that's not what the audience remembered as much as a prevailing forthright attitude and, paradoxically, his grace — the way he could give a mythic rhythm to pure movement.

Perhaps the most appropriate definition of star acting as it was practiced by Wayne came from Charles Laughton. The great actor was asked about the difference between him and an actor like Gary Cooper. "We act in opposite ways," Laughton said. "His is presentational acting. Mine is representational acting. I get at a part from the outside. He gets at it from the inside, from his own clear way of looking at life. His is the right way, if you can do it. I could learn to do, but it would take me a year to do what he can do instinctively, and I haven't the time."

The genre that Wayne personified is more or less dead, except when a powerful director or star gets an urge to make a vanity western. Sometimes they're good — Clint Eastwood's *Unforgiven,* Kevin Costner's *Open Range.* Sometimes they're just okay — the Coen brothers' remake of *True Grit,* relentlessly bent toward their obsession with bleak Americana, with Jeff Bridges strenuously imitating Nick Nolte. And sometimes they're not so good — James Mangold's *3:10 to Yuma,* or Quentin Tarantino's fatuous *Django Unchained.*

"Westerns didn't die," said Andrew Fenady, "they were murdered. By Altman, by Peckinpah, by the revisionists. Around the time of Vietnam, suddenly there couldn't be heroes. The righteous revisionists took great delight in demeaning and defiling and perverting anybody that ever wore a badge, a uniform, or moved west.

"And something else happened: the western got absorbed. *Star Wars* was like a Borden Chase western, with two uneasy friends, except with rockets and spaceships instead of horses and wagons. Setting it in space worked. And today, kids don't know from westerns."

For years, the debate about Wayne centered around the ridiculous question of whether or not he could act, with liberals generally taking the negative position. But, as James Baldwin — a much better movie critic than most movie critics — pointed out, movie stars are primarily escape personalities for the audience: "No one, for example, will ever really know whether Katharine Hepburn or Bette Davis or Humphrey Bogart or Spencer Tracy or Clark Gable — or John Wayne — can, or could, really act, or not . . . acting is not what they are required to do. Their acting ability, so far from being what attracts their audience, can often be what drives their audience away. One does not go to see them act: one goes to watch them *be*."

But the truth is that Wayne could act, could take on any color demanded. For John Ford, he was a lonely romantic; for Raoul Walsh he was a brawler; for Howard Hawks, he could be either one mean SOB, eyes fixed firmly on the prize, or a quietly secure man, determined and unruffled.

"Wayne [could] be tough or tender . . . sociable

or cantankerous," wrote Jeanine Basinger, before wittily describing the ultimate non-movie lover: "The person who walks out of *Red River* talking about Montgomery Clift."

Whatever he played, the power of Wayne's personality shone through — clarity triumphant. Wayne played the kind of man he needed to believe in, the kind of man the audience needed to believe in, until "John Wayne" became a statement as much as a name. The actor became his own genre. Once he was asked what he thought he brought to American movies. His answer was simple: "vitality."

Politeness mattered to him; so did something that might be called gallantry. "He didn't suffer fools gladly," wrote a critic who knew him, "but he did suffer them occasionally, when he knew that his indifference would hurt like a slap to the face."

Movie stars often hide their true selves from their public, which can result in inadvertent and humiliating exposures. But Wayne never obscured his flaws, and often went far out of his way to expose them, because pretending otherwise would have been a breach in the binding contract he had with his audience: to tell the truth as he saw it. Unfortunately, his unified field theory of American society caused many to ignore the questioning, complicated humanity of his best performances.

As an actor, he could extract nuances of behavioral beauty out of primal emotion. Often, he embodied self-reliance, but he also embodied generosity of soul and spirit — not common qualities in the latter part of the twentieth century, let alone today.

His fellow conservatives appropriated convenient

snapshots of Wayne's career that emphasized his rugged individualism as a means of promoting their own philosophy, without ever seeming to notice that the self-sufficient men he played had a way of ending up hopelessly isolated or dead.

You pay your money and you take your choice — a heroic frontiersman embodying Manifest Destiny, or a displaced loner uncomfortable with the civilization he's helping to forge.

Or both — a human jigsaw encompassing the warring halves of American masculinity.

In one sense, time ultimately worked against Wayne, as it works against everybody. Nothing could have been more foreign to him than the Method technique of dredging up emotional memories to animate the inner life of his characters — the grinding difficulty and persistent financial humiliation of his childhood and young manhood was something he always sought to escape and relived only grudgingly.

Instead, he cultivated what Andrew Sarris referred to as "a . . . Jungian process" of developing an entirely new persona that gradually enveloped him like a suit of clothes. He consciously went outside of himself, personifying a myth of the past that helped define the present. First he invented the personality, then he projected it. In the process, Wayne became a populist movie star, someone to whom the critics came only late, and then, for the most part, reluctantly — a midwesterner who became a Man of the West.

When he died, the editorialists said that the last simple American hero was gone, but that indicated both that they hadn't seen a lot of John Wayne movies and that they thought times had changed. Neither his movies nor his politics went away.

Certainly, the political and social landscape of America of the early twenty-first century is one that Wayne would immediately recognize, because America is a perennial circular conversation — generally a loud one — between Jeffersonian and Jacksonian principles, and John Wayne incarnated the extremes of socialization and isolation more comprehensively than any leading man before or since.

Tracy had Hepburn, Wayne had O'Hara — the woman who understood him and could more than hold her own. In her memoirs she wrote, "He was smart but not shrewd, and was cheated out of a fortune more than once. . . . He loved ladies and liked women, but . . . was terribly unlucky in marriage and never understood why. . . . Duke was one of the most decent men I have ever known. . . . He felt forever a slave to his image."

In conversation, O'Hara elaborated on her beloved friend: "He came to work. He knew his lines. He worked like a dog. He tried to make each movie the best he possibly could. He wanted to satisfy the fans who were coming to his films."

And about John Ford, that great tortured — and torturing — genius, she gave vent to a profound monologue of rage and regret at the gaping holes that time leaves in our lives, as well as the debt we owe to the people who define our dreams. Wayne and O'Hara took what Ford dished out because

we respected his ability as a director. He was the best, by God. And Duke had made so many little westerns and each time he worked with Ford, he was thrilled to be making a great picture, with a great director.

If John Ford walked in the door right now, and

said "Let's go," I would say "Yes, sir." I'd jump and I'd be there. In spite of everything. *Because he was the best!* If you watched him direct, if you had a chair at the back of the set and kept quiet, if you just watched him work, you would be astounded. He told the cameraman what he wanted, but he didn't tell an actor how to do it — he just told us what he wanted. The rest was up to you. And then you'd do it, and he'd say, "Cut, print, next shot."

He didn't do too much talking. He hired you because he liked the way you worked. He liked what he knew he could get out of you. He didn't go into deep detail about the movement of your little finger. If an accident happened and you stopped and said, "I'm sorry," he'd say, "Just a minute. I am the director. I tell you when to stop. I am the only person that says 'Cut.' If you make a mistake, keep going and make it up." And we all knew that and we all would keep going and make it up. That was the freedom that was so wonderful, the freedom that he gave you, and the belief in you that he gave you.

And every night you went home saying, "By God, I did a good day's work today." You knew it was work you were going to be proud of.

Duke Morrison began as an awkward, insecure boy tormented by terror dreams, and became the emphatic representation of American masculinity. "I found myself in some of these parts," he would say, "found the things I want to believe in and I think other people have made similar discoveries for themselves. Ford never shot the story, he shot the myth. I sometimes think the myth is what makes belief possible."

Take him or leave him, he made the myth seem more authentic than it had been before, more authentic than it has been since. Wayne's characters had an obstinate bravery that derived from his own innate stubbornness. Stuck in a bad place, they would succeed simply because they refused to fail. As one writer noted, Wayne's spirit runs deep in the American grain — the spirit that makes firemen rush into a burning building, makes a bystander dive into a river to rescue a drowning stranger, makes a lawyer pound away for a decade over a wrongfully convicted man nobody else cares about. Just because it's the right thing to do.

Wayne's films with Ford and Hawks remain touchstones of film culture, and in the climax of *The Searchers* he performs what Molly Haskell correctly calls "one of the most beautiful scenes of Christian reconciliation in art." Ford's films manage something John Sacret Young calls "double visions of events. There's a vital immediacy, and also a sense of memory image — how we remember things on the horizon of our own and our country's history." In the foreground of the best of them was Wayne's ability to emphasize pain and endurance, out of which emerged bravery, which can be roughly defined as fear that has said its prayers.

Because of Ford, because of Hawks, because of his own driving intent, John Wayne has maintained his place as an American icon — *the* American icon. Thirty thousand people yearly make the pilgrimage to his birthplace in Winterset, Iowa, the heartland he escaped from geographically but belonged to emotionally. "People consider our site a shrine," says Brian Downes, the director of the birthplace museum. "A few actually cry."

"Do I miss him?" echoed Maureen O'Hara. "Oh, God, yes. There are so many times I'd like to call Duke, or the old boy [Ford] to ask their advice, ask them what they think. But I had a wonderful life with them. Sometimes I wondered what they liked about me, and then I realized I was the only female man left in their lives."

For Wayne, talking about the old days with Ford always stirred the spirit of reverie, as well as a sadness about the old days being dead and gone — at least until the movies were shown once again. Wayne could talk about his life with a rare sense of objectivity, as well as wonder and gratitude.

"Lucky career," he would say. "The type of pictures I've been in so many people can identify with, all around the world. They can immediately accept me into their social feelings. Old Duke, he was all right, they might say, and I'm not sure they'd say it to Olivier or about him, wonderful as he is.

"People say John Wayne isn't an actor. OK, I'm a personality. But what it is, for cryin' out loud, is that I don't want the butcher or the baker or the candlestick maker to *think* I'm an actor. I want them to know I'm one of them, and getting by."

So Duke Morrison transformed himself into John Wayne, a merging of great virtues and great flaws, all of which he acknowledged, all of which he played. There was a fair amount of overlap between Wayne's personality and his screen character — the humor, the gusto, the irascibility, the sheer emotional and physical size — but there was also a childlike quality far more apparent off-screen than on.

And there was also a knowledge of the world and the theater that verged on sophistication, although he would have avoided the word. Once, gazing at the Heisman trophies in a USC trophy case, probably with no small amount of envy, he began reciting Shakespeare. "What a piece of work is a man! how noble in reason, how infinite in faculties, in form and moving, how express and admirable! in action, how like an angel! in apprehension, how like a god! The beauty of the world! The paragon of animals!" He stopped, enjoying the incongruity. "Hamlet, act two, scene two. I could tell you the whole play right down to 'Goodnight, Sweet Prince.' "

Take him as an innocent man in primary colors, the incarnation of our remembered — or imagined — spirit: bold, defiant, ambitious, heedless of consequences, occasionally mistaken, primarily alone, implicitly nostalgic. At his best he was an American amalgam of Prince Hal *and* Falstaff, for our time, for all time — larger than life, transcending death.

Words written by Borden Chase about Tom Dunson stand well for the man who played him: "Everybody said, 'You can't make it. You'll never get there.' He was the only one believed he could. He had to believe it. So he started thinking one way, his way. He told men what to do and made 'em do it. Otherwise, we wouldn't have got as far as we did. . . .

"All he knew was, he had to get there."

ACKNOWLEDGMENTS

The other shoe finally dropped.

After I published *Print the Legend* in 1999, I was assailed by people who thought John Ford was all well and good, but what was really needed was a biography of John Wayne. After spending six years on Ford, the last thing I wanted to do was saddle up and head back to Monument Valley, either metaphorically or geographically. Ten years and two books later, it seemed like a much better idea.

Gretchen Wayne agreed with me that it was time for a comprehensive biography of the man she called Grandaddy. She put both her own memories and the archives of the Batjac company at my disposal, including a series of oral histories that her late husband, Michael, commissioned shortly after his father died. Gretchen never asked for approvals of any kind. I hope the result is worthy of her trust.

Dan Ford gave me the oral history he did with Tom Kane, the story editor at Batjac for thirty years. Dan was also there whenever I needed to clear up an abstruse point about his grandfather and John Wayne.

Brian Downes, director of the John Wayne Birthplace in Winterset, Iowa, funneled information about Winterset to me and was a never-ending source of encouragement. Tim Lilley published *The Big Trail,* a newsletter about John Wayne filled with interviews with dozens of people that have since gone ahead. He was happy to open his archives to me.

I owe a special debt to John Sacret Young for sharing the notes of his encounters with John Ford. Animation historian Mike Barrier helped fill in the historical record regarding the Wayne westerns produced by Leon Schlesinger, as did Jerry Beck. Frank Thompson has written extensively about *The Alamo,* and gave me his interviews with Al Ybarra and Happy Shahan.

Joe Musso shared his collection of Wayne memorabilia, undoubtedly the finest outside the Wayne family. Jeff Morey helped with matters relating to firearms and Wyatt Earp, his two great specialties.

Robert Osborne is well loved both for his duties as host on Turner Classic Movies and as a valued friend of the Eyman family. Bob used his influence to get me to people who have never spoken about Wayne for the record. Looking forward to our next dinner, pal. The same can be said for Leonard Maltin, a friend for more than forty years and counting, who gave me the benefit of his interview transcripts and good advice.

I haven't known James Curtis for quite that long, but sometimes it seems like it. Jim keeps me sane, keeps me laughing, and his own books give me something to aim for. He's always happy to point out the many ways in which I come up short. Kevin Brownlow, the doyen of all film historians, remembered his own meeting with John Wayne with total specificity and then supplied the transcript of the interview!

And a very special thank-you to Robert Wagner, my literary collaborator — one of Hollywood's great gentlemen, who can always be counted on to help out a friend. Thanks, RJ. Then there was unit publicist extraordinaire Rob Harris, who used his influence to enable one crucial interview.

Jeff Heise surpassed his own amazing efforts by serving as my researcher on the book, just as he has for twenty years. Every week, Jeff would find something I didn't know existed. The commitment he's demonstrated to the books we've worked on more than entitles him to this book's dedication.

To all of the following who spoke to me about John Ford and John Wayne, together or separately, my gratitude:

Julie Adams, John Agar, Eddie Albert, Peter Bogdanovich, Adrian Booth, Yakima Canutt, Harry Carey Jr., Marilyn Fix Carey, Larry Cohen, Andrew Fenady, Joe de Franco, Andre de Toth, Angie Dickinson, Ed Faulkner, Rudi Fehr, Tom Fuentes, James Garner, Kristin Glover, Colin Grant, Coleen Gray, William Harbach, Dennis Hopper, Robert Horton, Ron Howard, Marsha Hunt, Tab Hunter, Anne Jeffries, Burt Kennedy, George Kennedy, Howard W. Koch, P. F. Kluge, Karen Steele Kramer, Syd Kronenthal, Dorothy Lamour, Betty Lasky, Janet Leigh, Stephen Longstreet, James Lydon, Andrew V. McLaglen, Lee Meriwether, Bert Minshall, Walter Mirisch, Hal Needham, Jean (Mrs. Frank) Nugent, Hugh O'Brian, Darcy O'Brien, Maureen O'Hara, Carolyn Roos Olsen, Robert Parrish, Stephanie Powers, Cecilia deMille Presley, Robert Relyea, Mickey Rooney, Ann Rutherford, Mark Rydell,

William Self, Alan Shayne, Robert Shelton, Vincent Sherman, Barbara Sinatra, Dean Smith, Cass Warner Sperling, Robert Stack, Miles Hood Swarthout, Rod Taylor, Christopher Trumbo, Robert Walker Jr., Alicia Wayne McFarlane, Christopher Wayne, Gretchen Wayne, John Wayne, Michael Wayne, Patrick Wayne, William Wellman, William Wellman Jr., Haskell Wexler, Stuart Whitman.

At libraries, first and foremost comes Ned Comstock at the USC Cinema-Television Library, who always goes the extra mile — a true gentleman and a scholar. Also at USC Special Collections, thanks to Rachelle Smith.

Charles Silver at the Museum of Modern Art always has material that can't be found anywhere else. Besides that, nobody loves John Ford more than Charles, which means we're both members of the same band of brothers.

At the Margaret Herrick Library at the Motion Picture Academy: Marisa Duron. At Special Collections: Jenny Romero and Barbara Hall.

At the Warner Bros. Archive: Jonathan Auxier and Sandra Joy Lee Aguilar.

James V. D'Arc at Brigham Young has become a close friend, which makes my frequent appearances in the Special Collections department a pleasure for both of us. Among many other prizes, Jim has a huge collection relating to Republic Pictures, without which any understanding of Wayne's early career is incomprehensible.

At Janklow & Nesbit, I am represented by the founder of the firm, the amazing Mort Janklow, backed up by Judythe Cohen.

I've had the signal honor of being published by Simon & Schuster for twenty years, where Bob Bender edits my manuscripts with wit and forbearance, enlivened by the occasional sigh of justified dismay. Johanna Li puts up with both of us. And then there's Gypsy da Silva, associate director of the copyediting department, who has earned my devotion many times over. Once again I benefit from the gentle (sometimes) attentions of Fred Chase's excellent copyediting. Bill Molesky's amazing eyes and attention to detail kept the book trending toward the specific and the correct.

My wife, Lynn, is my advisor, my companion on our research travels, my best friend, my source of strength, my love.

Scott Eyman
January 2010–December 2013
West Palm Beach, Hollywood, Aspen,
Venice, Athens, Istanbul, Kanab, Moab,
Provo, Funchal, Tangier, Barcelona.

NOTES

SOURCE NOTES FOR JOHN WAYNE CAN BE FOUND IN THE ORIGINAL SIMON & SCHUSTER, INC. EDITION

BIBLIOGRAPHY

Autry, Gene, with Mickey Herskowitz. *Back in the Saddle Again.* Garden City: Doubleday, 1978.

Bach, Steven. *Marlene Dietrich: Life and Legend.* New York: William Morrow, 1992.

Bakewell, William. *Hollywood Be Thy Name.* Metuchen: Scarecrow, 1991.

Baldwin, James. *The Devil Finds Work.* New York: Dial, 1976.

Balio, Tino. *United Artists, Vol. 2, 1951-1978: The Company That Changed the Film Industry.* Madison: University of Wisconsin Press, 2009.

Bandy, Mary Lea, and Kevin Stoehr. *Ride, Boldly Ride: The Evolution of the American Western.* Berkeley: University of California Press, 2012.

Barrier, Michael. *Hollywood Cartoons.* New York: Oxford University Press, 1999.

Baxter, John. *Von Sternberg.* Lexington: University Press of Kentucky, 2010.

Behlmer, Rudy, ed. *Henry Hathaway: A Directors Guild of America Oral History.* Lanham: Scarecrow, 2001.

———. *Memo from Darryl F. Zanuck.* New York: Grove, 1993.

Berg, A. Scott. *Goldwyn.* New York: Alfred A. Knopf, 1989.

————. *Kate Remembered*. New York: Putnam, 2003.

Bernstein, Matthew. *Walter Wanger: Hollywood Independent*. Berkeley: University of California Press, 1994.

Bogdanovich, Peter. *Who the Hell's in It*. New York: Alfred A. Knopf, 2004.

Bosworth, Patricia. *Montgomery Clift*. New York: Harcourt Brace Jovanovich, 1978.

Bragg, Melvyn. *Richard Burton: A Life*. Boston: Little, Brown, 1988.

Branden, Barbara. *The Passion of Ayn Rand*. New York: Doubleday, 1986.

Brown, Peter Harry, and Pat Broeske. *Howard Hughes: The Untold Story*. New York: Da Capo, 2004.

Bruskin, David N. *Behind the Three Stooges: The White Brothers*. Los Angeles: Directors Guild of America, 1993.

Buford, Kate. *Burt Lancaster: An American Life*. New York: Alfred A. Knopf, 2000.

Caine, Michael. *The Elephant to Hollywood*. New York: Holt, 2010.

————. *What's It All About?* New York: Turtle Bay, 1992.

Canutt, Yakima, with Oliver Drake. *Stunt Man*. New York: Walker, 1979.

Capra, Frank. *The Name Above the Title*. New York: Macmillan, 1971.

Cardiff, Jack. *Magic Hour*. Boston: Faber & Faber, 1996.

Carter, Jimmy. *White House Diary*. New York: Farrar, Straus & Giroux, 2010.

Clark, Donald, and Christopher Andersen. *John Wayne's The Alamo*. New York: Citadel, 1994.

Davis, Ronald L. *Duke: The Life and Image of John*

Wayne. Norman: University of Oklahoma Press, 1998.

Dewey, Donald. *James Stewart.* Atlanta: Turner, 1996.

Dick, Bernard. *Hal Wallis: Producer to the Stars.* Lexington: University Press of Kentucky, 2004.

Didion, Joan. *Slouching Towards Bethlehem.* New York: Farrar, Straus & Giroux, 1968.

Dmytryk, Edward. *It's a Hell of a Life But Not a Bad Living.* New York: Times Books, 1978.

————. *Odd Man Out.* Carbondale: Southern Illinois University Press, 1996.

Douglas, Kirk. *The Ragman's Son.* New York: Simon & Schuster, 1988.

Eels, George. *Hedda and Louella.* New York: Warner, 1973.

Eisenschitz, Bernard. *Nicholas Ray: An American Journey.* London: Faber & Faber, 1993.

Evarts, Hal G. "Log of *The Big Trail*" (unpublished). USC Cinema Library, 20th Century Fox Collection, August 27, 1930.

Eyman, Scott. *Empire of Dreams: The Epic Life of Cecil B. DeMille.* New York: Simon & Schuster, 2010.

————. *Five American Cinematographers.* Metuchen: Scarecrow, 1987.

————. *Print the Legend: The Life and Times of John Ford.* New York: Simon & Schuster, 1999.

Fagen, Herb. *Duke, We're Glad We Knew You.* New York: Citadel, 1996.

Fernett, Gene. *Next Time Drive Off the Cliff!* Cocoa: Cinememories, 1968.

Fishgall, Gary. *Against Type: The Biography of Burt Lancaster.* New York: Scribner's, 1995.

Frankel, Glenn. *The Searchers: The Making of an*

921

American Legend. New York: Bloomsbury, 2013.

Fraser-Cavassoni, Natasha. *Sam Spiegel.* New York: Simon & Schuster, 2003.

Frost, Jennifer. *Hedda Hopper's Hollywood: Celebrity Gossip and American Conservatism.* New York: New York University Press, 2011.

Fujiwara, Chris. *The World and Its Double: The Life and Work of Otto Preminger.* New York: Faber & Faber, 2008.

Gabler, Neal. *Walt Disney: The Triumph of the American Imagination.* New York: Alfred A. Knopf, 2006.

————. *Winchell: Gossip, Power and the Culture of Celebrity.* New York: Alfred A. Knopf, 1994.

Garnett, Tay, with Fredda Dudley Balling. *Light Your Torches and Pull Up Your Tights.* New Rochelle: Arlington House, 1973.

Gassner, John, and Dudley Nichols. *Great Film Plays.* New York: Crown, 1959.

George-Warren, Holly. *Public Cowboy No. 1: The Life and Times of Gene Autry.* New York: Oxford University Press, 2007.

Graham, Sheilah. *Confessions of a Hollywood Columnist.* New York: Bantam, 1970.

Grobel, Lawrence. *The Hustons.* New York: Scribner's, 1989.

Guiles, Fred Lawrence. *Tyrone Power: The Last Idol.* Garden City: Doubleday, 1979.

Gussow, Mel. *Darryl F. Zanuck: Don't Say Yes Until I Finish Talking.* New York: Da Capo, 1980.

Higham, Charles. *In and Out of Hollywood.* Madison: Terrace, 2009.

Hillier, Jim, and Peter Wollen. *Howard Hawks: American Artist.* London: BFI, 1996.

Humphries, Reynold. *Hollywood's Blacklists: A Political and Cultural History.* Edinburgh: Edinburgh University Press, 2010.

Hunter, Tab, with Eddie Muller. *Tab Hunter Confidential.* Chapel Hill: Algonquin, 2005.

Hurst, Richard Maurice. *Republic Studios: Between Poverty Row and the Majors.* Metuchen: Scarecrow, 1979.

Huston, John. *An Open Book.* New York: Alfred A. Knopf, 1980.

Johnson, Nora. *Flashback.* Garden City: Doubleday, 1979.

Kazanjian, Howard, and Chris Enss. *The Young Duke.* Guilford: Globe Pequot, 2007.

Keel, Howard, with Joyce Spizer. *Only Make Believe: My Life in Show Business.* Fort Lee: Barricade, 2005.

Kennedy, Burt. *Hollywood Trail Boss.* New York: Boulevard, 1997.

Kennedy, George. *Trust Me.* Milwaukee: Applause, 2011.

Knox, Mickey. *The Good, the Bad, the Dolce Vita.* New York: Nation Books, 2004.

Kotsilibas-Davis, James, and Myrna Loy. *Myrna Loy: Being and Becoming.* New York: Donald I. Fine, 1988.

Lamour, Dorothy, with Dick McInnes. *My Side of the Road.* Englewood Cliffs: Prentice Hall, 1980.

Landesman, Fred. *The John Wayne Filmography.* Jefferson: McFarland, 2004.

Leaming, Barbara. *Katharine Hepburn.* New York: Crown, 1995.

———. *Orson Welles.* New York: Viking, 1985.

LeRoy, Mervyn, with Dick Kleiner. *Mervyn LeRoy:*

Take One. New York: Hawthorn, 1974.

Lewis, Jerry, with James Kaplan. *Dean and Me: A Love Story.* New York: Doubleday, 2005.

Lilley, Tim. *Campfire Conversations Complete.* Akron: Big Trail, 2010.

Lloyd, Norman, with Francine Parker. *Stages.* Metuchen: Scarecrow, 1990.

Madsen, Axel. *Stanwyck.* New York: Harper-Collins, 1994.

Mathis, Jack. *Republic Confidential — Volume 1: The Studio.* Barrington: Jack Mathis Advertising, 1999.

McBride, Joseph. *Hawks on Hawks.* Berkeley: University of California Press, 1982.

McCarthy, Todd. *Howard Hawks: The Grey Fox of Hollywood.* New York: Grove, 1997.

McCarthy, Todd, and Charles Flynn. *Kings of the Bs.* New York: Dutton, 1975.

McClelland, Doug. *Forties Film Talk.* Jefferson: McFarland, 1992.

McConnell, Scott. *100 Voices: An Oral History of Ayn Rand.* New York: New American Library, 2010.

McGilligan, Patrick. *Backstory.* Berkeley: University of California Press, 1986.

———. *Backstory 2.* Berkeley: University of California Press, 1991.

———. *Backstory 3.* Berkeley: University of California Press, 1997.

McGivern, Carolyn. *The Lost Films of John Wayne.* Nashville: Cumberland House, 2006.

McIntosh, Elizabeth P. *Sisterhood of Spies: Women of the OSS.* Annapolis: Naval Institute Press, 1998.

McMurtry, Larry. *Literary Life: A Second Memoir.*

New York: Simon & Schuster, 2009.

Mirisch, Walter. *I Thought We Were Making Movies, Not History.* Madison: University of Wisconsin Press, 2008.

Mosley, Leonard. *Zanuck.* Boston: Little, Brown, 1984.

Munn, Michael. *John Wayne: The Man Behind the Myth.* New York: New American Library, 2003.

Needham, Hal. *Stuntman!* New York: Little, Brown, 2011.

O'Hara, Maureen, with John Nicoletti. *'Tis Herself.* New York: Simon & Schuster, 2004.

Olsen, Carolyn Roos, with Marilyn Hudson. *Hollywood's Man Who Worried for the Stars: The Story of Bö Roos.* Bloomington: AuthorHouse, 2008.

Paris, Barry. *Louise Brooks.* New York: Alfred A. Knopf, 1989.

Parrish, Robert. *Growing Up in Hollywood.* New York: Harcourt Brace Jovanovich, 1976.

————. *Hollywood Doesn't Live Here Anymore.* Boston: Little, Brown, 1988.

Pattie, Jane. *John Wayne: There Rode a Legend.* Wilma Russell's Western Classics, 2000.

Pippin, Robert B. *Hollywood Westerns and American Myth.* New Haven: Yale University Press, 2010.

Preminger, Otto. *Preminger: An Autobiography.* Garden City: Doubleday, 1977.

Prouty, Howard, ed. *Variety Television Reviews,* Vol. 1, Vol. 2, Vol. 10. New York: Garland, 1989, 1991.

Ray, Nicholas. *I was Interrupted: Nicholas Ray on Making Movies.* Berkeley: University of California Press, 1995.

Read, Piers Paul. *Alec Guinness.* New York: Simon & Schuster, 2005.

Riva, Maria. *Marlene Dietrich.* New York: Alfred A. Knopf, 1992.

Roberts, Jerry, ed. *Mitchum in His Own Words.* New York: Limelight, 2000.

Roberts, Randy, and James S. Olson. *John Wayne: American.* New York: Free Press, 1995.

Rosenfeld, Seth. *Subversives: The FBI's War on Student Radicals and Reagan's Rise to Power.* New York: Farrar, Straus & Giroux, 2012.

Sanders, Coyne Steven, and Tom Gilbert. *Desilu: The Story of Lucille Ball and Desi Arnaz.* New York: It Books, 2011.

Sbardellati, John. *J. Edgar Hoover Goes to the Movies: The FBI and the Origins of Hollywood's Cold War.* Ithaca: Cornell University Press, 2012.

Schickel, Richard. *Clint Eastwood.* New York: Alfred A. Knopf, 1996.

Schwartz, Nancy Lynn. *The Hollywood Writer's War.* New York: Alfred A. Knopf, 1982.

Server, Lee. *Robert Mitchum: Baby, I Don't Care.* New York: St. Martin's, 2001.

Shavelson, Melville. *How to Make a Jewish Movie.* Englewood Cliffs: Prentice-Hall, 1971.

Shaw, Sam. *John Wayne: In the Camera Eye.* New York: Exeter, 1979.

Sherman, Vincent. *Studio Affairs: My Life as a Film Director.* Lexington: University Press of Kentucky, 1996.

Siegel, Don. *A Siegel Film.* Boston: Faber & Faber, 1993.

Silver, Alain, and James Ursini. *Whatever Happened to Robert Aldrich?* New York: Limelight, 1995.

Small, Edward, with Robert E. Kent. "You Don't Have to Be Crazy to Be in Show Business, but

It Helps!" (unpublished). USC Cinema Library.

Solomon, Aubrey. *The Fox Film Corporation, 1915-1935: A History and Filmography.* Jefferson: McFarland, 2011.

Stacy, Pat, with Beverly Linet. *Duke: A Love Story.* New York: Atheneum, 1983.

Suid, Lawrence. *Guts and Glory: The Making of the American Military Image in Film,* 2nd ed. Lexington: University Press of Kentucky, 2002.

Takei, George. *To the Stars: The Autobiography of George Takei.* New York: Pocket Books, 1994.

Thomas, Bob. *Clown Prince of Hollywood.* New York: McGraw-Hill, 1990.

Thompson, Frank. *Alamo Movies.* East Berlin, Penn. Old Mill, 1991.

Thomson, David. *Showman: The Life of David O. Selznick.* New York: Alfred A. Knopf, 1992.

Turk, Edward Baron. *Hollywood Diva: A Biography of Jeanette MacDonald.* Berkeley: University of California Press, 1998.

Turner, George E., with Orville Goldner. Expanded and revised by Michael H. Price and Douglas Turner. *Spawn of Skull Island: The Making of King Kong.* Baltimore: Luminary, 2002.

Tuska, Jon. *The Filming of the West.* Garden City: Doubleday, 1976.

———. *The Vanishing Legion: A History of Mascot Pictures, 1927-1935.* Jefferson: McFarland, 1982.

Vaughan, Robert. *A Fortunate Life.* New York: St. Martin's, 2008.

Vaz, Mark Cotta. *Living Dangerously: The Adven-*

tures of Merian C. Cooper. New York: Villard, 2005.

Wallis, Hal, with Charles Higham. *Starmaker.* New York: Macmillan, 1980.

Walsh, Raoul. *Each Man in His Time.* New York: Farrar, Straus & Giroux, 1974.

Wayne, Aissa, with Steve Delsohn. *John Wayne, My Father.* New York: Random House, 1991.

Wills, Garry. *John Wayne's America: The Politics of Celebrity.* New York: Simon & Schuster, 1997.

Worsley, Wallace, with Sue Dwiggins Worsley. *From Oz to E.T.* Lanham: Scarecrow, 1997.

ABOUT THE AUTHOR

Scott Eyman has written eleven books, including, with veteran actor Robert Wagner, the *New York Times* bestseller *Pieces of My Heart*. Among his other books are *Empire of Dreams: The Epic Life of Cecil B. DeMille,* winner of the 2011 Richard Wall Memorial Book Award; *Lion of Hollywood: The Life and Legend of Louis B. Mayer; Print the Legend: The Life and Times of John Ford; Ernst Lubitsch: Laughter in Paradise; The Speed of Sound*; and *John Ford: The Searcher*. He, his wife, Lynn, and Clementine and other assorted animals live in West Palm Beach.